Implementing Effective IT Governan

Other publications by Van Haren Publishing

Van Haren Publishing (VHP) specializes in titles on Best Practices, methods and standards within four domains:
- IT and IT Management
- Architecture (Enterprise and IT)
- Business Management and
- Project Management

Van Haren Publishing offers a wide collection of whitepapers, templates, free e-books, trainer materials etc. in the **Van Haren Publishing Knowledge Base**: www.vanharen.net for more details.

Van Haren Publishing is also publishing on behalf of leading organizations and companies: ASLBiSL Foundation, CA, Centre Henri Tudor, Gaming Works, IACCM, IAOP, IPMA-NL, ITSqc, NAF, Ngi, PMI-NL, PON, The Open Group, The SOX Institute.

Topics are (per domain):

IT and IT Management	Architecture (Enterprise and IT)	Project, Program and Risk Management
ABC of ICT	ArchiMate®	A4-Projectmanagement
ASL®	GEA®	DSDM/Atern
CATS CM®	Novius Architectuur Methode	ICB / NCB
CMMI®	TOGAF®	ISO 21500
COBIT®		MINCE®
e-CF	**Business Management**	M_o_R®
ISO 20000	BABOK® Guide	MSP™
ISO 27001/27002	BiSL®	P3O®
ISPL	EFQM	PMBOK® Guide
IT Service CMM	eSCM	PRINCE2®
ITIL®	IACCM	
MOF	ISA-95	
MSF	ISO 9000/9001	
SABSA	Novius B&IP	
	OPBOK	
	SAP	
	SixSigma	
	SOX	
	SqEME®	

For the latest information on VHP publications, visit our website: www.vanharen.net.

Implementing Effective IT Governance and IT Management

A Practical Guide to World Class Current and Emerging Best Practices

Expanding the IT Ruler on How to Align, Plan, Deploy and Govern Information Technology Resources for Improved Competitive Advantage, Integration with the Business, Profitability and Control in Global Enterprises

2nd Edition

Dr. Gad J. Selig, PMP, COP

Colofon

Title:	Implementing Effective IT Governance and IT Management
Subtitle:	A Practical Guide To World Class Current and Emerging Best Practices
Author:	Dr. Gad J Selig PMP, COP
Editor:	Steve Newton
Publisher:	Van Haren Publishing, Zaltbommel, www.vanharen.net
ISBN Hard copy:	978 94 018 0008 2
ISBN eBook:	978 94 018 0528 5
Edition:	First edition, first impression, March 2008
	Second edition, first impression, February 2015
DTP:	CO2 Premedia, Amersfoort - NL
Copyright:	© Van Haren Publishing 2008, 2015

For any further enquiries about Van Haren Publishing, please send an e-mail to: info@vanharen.net

Foreword One

Effective IT governance and management, that is closely aligned to the business needs and supported by a strong business partnership, is extremely vital to the success of the IT function within corporate enterprises and on a global basis. Dr. Selig's book on this very topic is a great resource for all IT practitioners, senior business professionals and brings together every critical aspect relating to IT governance.

The second edition lays out a roadmap to executing within a solid governance model. It looks at all aspects of establishing, planning, implementing, growing and sustaining an IT ecosystem. The combination of case studies and disciplined approaches to building well-structured processes, committed leaders and change agents will help the board, executive management and most of all, CIOs and IT professionals think through what has worked, what can work and how to deploy IT governance successfully.

Being a CIO for many years in a highly competitive industry, I have developed a respect for the process side of running IT like a business. There has always been a need to balance governance for IT with the demands and services needed to support the business. This requires effective implementation of guiding principles and controls to ensure corporate enterprises optimize their investments and, more importantly, ensures that all IT resources are well organized and utilized to help drive business value.

In my experience, Information Technology and its effective management is a fundamental cornerstone of any well-run business. Ensuring that the IT function is fully supporting the business strategy and goals of the company is all about ensuring that the IT organization, processes and performance are designed with a view to constantly providing and measuring business value. Successful CIOs recognize that IT has become far more than a means of increasing efficiency and reducing costs. Rather, they see IT as a prime stimulus for, and an enabler of, business innovation and transformation – and they themselves are viewed as key collaborators, facilitators and partners in a process that develops business and IT strategies in concert.

Ever since the recent economic recession, coupled with the growing reliance on social media and mobile - one thing we are sure of is that "Change is the New Norm"!

Therefore, never before has it been more critical to cultivate a holistic management model for the information technology function that is well aligned to the business needs. Business today is faced with far more rapidly changing and challenging market conditions, industry disruption, ever-changing regulations, the need for accessible analytics and more demanding and impatient customers. In parallel to this, new technology approaches such as cloud, digital, mobile, 'big data', Internet of Things, and visual analytics, all present new ways of doing things that, therefore, challenge the status quo. These external challenges, coupled with the new technology opportunities, along with the need to support normal business demands such as; to market and administer a new product quickly, scale and protect the core infrastructure and company data, drive company change, all taken together elevate the dependency that successful businesses today have on technology and hence highlights the need for a strong and comprehensive governance model between IT and the business. IT practitioners today have to work with an ever-changing business and IT landscape, where the pace of change is tremendous, business competition and demand for IT services is extremely high, budgets are challenged and talented technical resources are always scare – this book should help provide some innovative insights into IT governance in an era of change and complexities!

I have known Dr. Selig for more than five years and have enrolled members of my senior staff onto an IT governance seminar led by him. He is a seasoned IT veteran who has organized a set of proven, fundamental approaches for the IT professional and has a passion for sharing these approaches. In this book, Dr. Selig combines practical business experience and practices along with academic principles, which together provide a valuable and insightful contribution to help advance the role of IT and its value to the business. Whether you are a board member, a CEO, a practicing CIO, or a student of IT, this book will provide a reference and guide to ensure that your IT function is well aligned to your business needs and is well managed and governed to achieve maximum business value for your organization.

Ursuline Foley
Enterprise/Corporate CIO
Major Insurance/Reinsurance Company

Foreword Two

Dr. Selig's second edition of the book on IT governance is an excellent addition to the knowledge base focused on the business of information technology. It is an excellent compilation of practical and useful information on the governance of IT in business and government.

The book highlights many of the concepts I have endorsed and encouraged for years as well as new ideas and information. The book is comprehensive and written in a reader-friendly way.

I look forward to recommending this book to readers at all levels in my client organizations dealing with the issues, and looking for solutions, in the complex and fast-changing world of IT governance.

IT governance offers you the who, what, where, when, and how to properly organize, plan, align, manage, and measure the effectiveness of the IT function in any organization. Dr. Selig provides a good balance between the people, technology, and process challenges essential to optimizing IT as an expensive corporate asset.

The book reinforces the fact that IT is not an independent organization silo. It must be aligned and integrated effectively with the business, and in government the mission, throughout the organization. Dr. Selig shows the balance - that IT supports the business or organization mission, but also, when properly aligned, managed, and resourced, will enable the organization to prosper, innovate, and grow effectively.

I have known Dr. Selig more than 25 years as a client, Alliance Partner, and good friend. He is a seasoned educator and business, consulting and IT veteran. He has organized a set of fundamental approaches for the IT professional and business and government executives. In this book, Dr. Selig's practical experience as a leader provides a valuable contribution to advance the field. Whether you are a board member or CEO, a practicing

CIO, or a student of IT, this book will guide you through complex business, process and technological roadmaps that work.

Dr. Selig's book is an excellent reference source in a critical area with many fast-changing parts. It is a must-have for teachers, executives, and managers dealing with IT.

John A. McCreight
Founder & Chairman
McCreight & Company, Inc. ~ CIO Group, LLC ~ Board Effectiveness Partners, LLC ~ Second Opinion, LLC

Introduction

The issues, opportunities and challenges of aligning information technology more closely with an organization and effectively governing an organization's Information Technology (IT) investments, resources, major initiatives and superior uninterrupted service is becoming a major concern of the board and executive management in enterprises on a global basis. Information technology (IT) has become an integral part of many organizations and is fundamental to sustain growth, innovation and transformation and support continuing operations in most organizations. Therefore, an integrated and comprehensive approach to IT governance is required, which includes all the activities of business/IT alignment, global resource planning, execution and governance of IT as well as the leadership of those entrusted with the task. Effective 'management' includes the activities of planning, investment, integration, measurement, innovation and business transformation, deployment and services required to manage a complex strategic asset.

The author views IT governance as the focal point for more effective IT management around which there are many important issues such as alignment, leadership, planning, execution, accountability, metrics and related topics. In other words, superior IT governance represents the path to world class IT management practices.

None of this is easy, or obvious, and this pragmatic and actionable 'how to guide' is intended to pull together, from about 200 sources, current and emerging best practices and draw from over twenty IT governance best practice case studies. Some of these case studies are included in the book.

Effective IT governance represents a journey (not an end state in itself), which focuses on sustaining value and confidence across the business. Today, many companies start on a narrow path or shotgun approach and focus on the compliance component (e.g. Sarbanes-Oxley and others) of IT governance, without developing a more comprehensive framework with a prioritized roadmap based on the highest value delivered to the organization.

In reviewing the current literature, completing over twenty case studies and conducting numerous private and public IT governance workshops and consulting assignments both domestically and internationally over the past few years, attended by thousands of executives, managers and practitioners on IT/business alignment, planning, deployment (e.g. program/project management, IT service management, outsourcing, cloud computing, data management, etc.) and governance (e.g. performance management and control), much has been written and documented about the individual components of IT governance. However, much less has been written about a comprehensive and integrated IT/business alignment, planning, execution and governance approach that represents a balanced approach consisting both of a strategic top-down framework and roadmap together with bottom-up implementation principles and practices that address the broad range of IT issues, constraints and opportunities in a planned, coordinated, prioritized, cost effective and value delivery manner.

The purpose of the book is not to repeat in greater details what has been published previously, but to describe each of the major components in an overall comprehensive framework and roadmap in sufficient detail for executives, managers and professionals. It is hoped that the book can serve as a guideline for any organization in any industry to formulate and tailor an effective approach to IT governance for its environment and to help transition the IT organization to a higher level of maturity, effectiveness and responsiveness.

The second edition of the book contains a new chapter on cloud computing, data management and governance, updates to the case studies and new material. Throughout the entire book the text has been updated on leadership, transformation, AgilePM and Scrum, ITIL 2011 Edition, performance management, risk management, CGEIT (COBIT IT Governance), cloud sourcing, security, select ISO standards related to IT governance and other topics.

■ THE MARKET FOR THE BOOK

Many executives, managers and practitioners have expressed the need for a comprehensive, yet practical guide, based on real world experiences, on the subject of implementing IT successfully.

The book has been written by a former business and IT executive and practitioner who has managed businesses and IT organizations, managed strategic change and advised major public and private organizations on business and IT strategy and governance. He has also completed numerous consulting assignments, conducted private and public workshops and graduate business and engineering courses on the fundamentals of managing and implementing strategy, innovation, management, IT strategy formulation, governance and transformation of IT to integrate seamlessly with the business.

Our intended audiences include the following groups:

- **Directors of corporate boards** – who have overall fiduciary accountability to provide oversight for the business and key functions of the business.
- **Executives** – who are primarily responsible for developing and/or approving business/ IT strategy and then overseeing its implementation and governance (the 'C' suite of corporate officers).
- **Managers and professionals** – who are primarily responsible for implementing and governing IT in their organizations and institutions,
- **Consultants and other advisors** – who are involved in advising, planning, organizing, directing and governing IT initiatives to help transform businesses and organizations to compete more effectively around the world
- **Academicians, graduate and upper level undergraduate students** – who must teach and master a fundamental understanding of IT and how it impacts businesses, management, employees, the regulators and investors.

The demand for an updated comprehensive, pragmatic and actionable 'how to' guide to help mangers and practitioners plan, deploy and sustain an effective IT governance and management environment and culture has been expressed by many managers and professionals in the private, public and academic sectors.

ORGANIZATION OF THE BOOK

The book is divided into two parts and ten chapters, which cover the three critical pillars necessary to develop, execute and sustain a robust and effective IT governance and management environment - leadership, people and organization, flexible and scalable processes and enabling technologies.

Part I covers the overview, business/IT alignment, strategic planning, demand management, the integrated IT governance framework and leadership, teams and organization. Part II covers the process and technology topics including: execution and delivery management (includes program/project management, IT service management and delivery with IT Infrastructure Library {ITIL} and strategic sourcing and outsourcing); performance measurements, risk and contingency management (e.g. includes COBIT, the balanced scorecard and other metrics and controls), cloud computing, data management and enabling technologies.

Part I Business/IT Strategy, Alignment, Leadership, Teams and Organization

Part I of the book focuses on the chapters covering business/IT strategy, alignment, leadership, teams and organization required to develop and execute an effective IT governance environment. It focuses on the strategy formulation, people and organizational aspects.

Chapter 1 Introduction to IT/Business Alignment, Planning, Execution and Governance

Covers the key IT/business alignment, integration, planning, execution, governance issues, constraints and opportunities; discusses the roles of the board, executive management and practitioners; reviews the value propositions for IT governance, provides an overview of demand management, decision rights, balanced scorecard metrics and how much governance is required; reviews select regulations and their compliance requirements; identifies the steps in making IT governance real and provides an assessment technique to determine the current level of IT governance maturity in an organization and illustrates a blueprint of a future state of IT governance. It also covers functional and IT components related to governance such as platform, infrastructure, application development, operations, security and related topics.

Chapter 2 Overview of a Comprehensive IT Governance and Management Framework and Select Industry Current and Emerging Best Practice Frameworks, Standards and Guidelines

Describes and illustrates a comprehensive IT alignment, execution framework and its major components. References and brief descriptions of related current and emerging industry best practices, standards and guidelines, including maturity models are discussed such as COBIT, Strategic Planning, ISO 9001 (Quality), ISO 20000 (IT Service Management), ISO 27002 (IT Security), ISO 38500 (IT Governance) and ISO 31000 (Risk Management), PMI's PMBOK Guide v5, PMI's Standard for Program Management v3, PMI's Standard for Portfolio Management v3, Project and Portfolio Management, AgilePM (Project Management) and Scrum, CMMI, People-CMM, ITIL 2011 Edition, PRINCE2, PMMM, ITIM, VAL-IT, ISO 21500 (Guidance on Project Management), SDLC/IDLC, Lean & Six Sigma, eSCM, OPBOK, Baldrige, Lean IT, TOGAF, BABOK Guide, BISL, the balanced scorecard, related professional certifications and others and how, if followed, they can result in more effective IT governance and management.

Chapter 3 Business and IT Alignment, Strategic/Operating Planning and Portfolio Investment Management Excellence (Demand Management)

Covers the business and IT strategic planning cycle, executive steering groups, business/ IT integration maturity model, IT planning through execution management flow, IT investment portfolio selection and prioritization attributes and VOC engagement model.

Chapter 4 Principles for Managing Successful Organizational Change, Prerequisites for World Class Leadership and Developing High Performance Teams

Covers key leadership, talent, people and soft skills and competencies required for success. It also covers the attributes of successful traditional and virtual teams in a global environment. It discusses technologies used by virtual teams located anywhere. It also reviews a framework for managing successful change in helping to transition and transform organizations to higher levels of IT maturity and effectiveness. It also covers the shadow IT organization and structure and how to strength the partnership between more sophisticated IT technology users and the IT organization.

Part II IT Governance and Its Critical Processes and Enabling Technologies

Part II of the book focuses on the chapters covering project management, IT service management, outsourcing, cloud computing, big data management, analytics and metrics related to IT governance.

Chapter 5 Program and Project Management Excellence (Execution Management)

Program and project management is a major component of effective IT execution management. It discusses the right and pragmatic ways to manage programs and projects within a flexible and scalable process, accommodating both fast track and complex initiatives. It provides multiple checklists, templates and metrics to help deliver programs and projects on time, within scope, within budget, with high quality and to the customer's satisfaction and/or get them back on track. It references a self-assessment maturity model that can be used to assess the current and target the future maturity level of an organization and suggests a transition plan to get there. It also covers Agile project management and Scrum.

Chapter 6 IT Service Management (ITSM) Excellence (Execution Management)

Describes the principles and practices of IT service management and operations providing an overview of ITIL 2011 Edition (IT Infrastructure Library), its processes and components. Specific objectives, benefits, and key performance indicators are covered. It illustrates a self-assessment maturity model that can be used to assess the current and target the future maturity level of an organization and suggests a transition plan to get there.

Chapter 7 Strategic Sourcing, Outsourcing, Vendor Management and Excellence

Provides the fundamentals of strategic sourcing and outsourcing such as issues, concerns, opportunities, value propositions, outsourcing lifecycle, the outsourcing business case, risks, modes of outsourcing (e.g. on-shore, rural shore, near shore, off shore, best shore, etc.), vendor selection, due diligence, contract negotiations and ongoing management roles, including relationship management, metrics, escalation and disengagement considerations. It also covers key components of crowd sourcing.

Chapter 8 Performance Management, Metrics, Management Controls, COBIT®, Risk Management, Business Continuity and Enabling Technology Excellence

Covers the principles and practices of achieving IT performance excellence using balanced scorecard metrics and linking critical success factors to historic and predictive key performance indicators (KPIs). It reviews COBIT. It also covers risk management, assessment and mitigation strategies, and business and IT continuity planning and disaster recovery. Finally, it describes a suite of technology tools that support and enable the key IT alignment, execution and governance functions and processes.

Chapter 9 Cloud Computing, Data Management and Governance Issues, Opportunities, Considerations and Strategies
Cloud computing usually involves a large number of computers connected through a real-time communication network such as the Internet. The phrase is often used in reference to network-based services which appear to be provided by real server hardware, simulated by software running on one or more real machines. Cloud computing is a form of outsourcing with its own issues, opportunities, risks and metrics. Big data, analytics, business intelligence and decision support system are components of data management and require the use of databases, statistics and software tools and analytical skills to extract information to help make decisions to reduce costs, improve quality, reduce risks and assist in focusing on the most valuable customers. The data management and governance issues and strategies are addressed in this chapter.

Chapter 10 Summary, Lessons Learned, Critical Success Factors and Future Challenges
Summarizes the components required to anticipate and proactively implement IT governance and management effectively. It provides a summary checklist of all of the key components and critical success factors identified in each chapter to make IT governance real, effective and sustainable.

Acknowledgements

I gratefully acknowledge the help and support of a number of individuals, organizations and their members in the private, public and academic sectors in conducting the research, editing the book, participating in developing the case studies, allowing me to consult and/or teach for them and influencing, reinforcing and validating the findings, recommendations, critical success factors and lessons learned.

Select organizations include: The Industry Advisory Board members at the University of Bridgeport and its Board members, many of whom allowed me to conduct case studies or workshops at their facilities such as ADP, Avon, Crisply, GE, X.L. Financial, IAOP, ITSqc, IPC Corp., Oracle, Pitney Bowes, Unilever, Vodaphone and Xerox. In addition, many extraordinary managers and professionals helped me from the Project Management Institute (PMI), the Information Technology Governance Institute and its sister organization, ISACA, the International Association of Outsourcing Professionals, the CIO Group, The Advisory Council (TAC) and select members of the Society for Information Management (SIM).

I would also like to thank specific people for their help, contributions and insights: Christine Bullen formerly at Stevens Institute of Technology, Paul Bateman at AXA, Mark Richards at e-Richards, Rebecca Brunotti, formerly of the General Services Administration – Federal Technology Services, Joann Martin formerly at Pitney Bowes, Nicholas Willcox at Unilever, Tarek Sobh at the University of Bridgeport, Michael Corbett at IAOP, Dick Lefave formerly at Sprint-Nextel and one of my co-authors of our Strategic Sourcing and Outsourcing book, Peter Shay at TAC, Jim Shay at Cyber Defense, Urs Foley at X.L. Financial, Michael Fry and Beth Gollogly at Xerox, Greg Fell, formerly at Terex and now at Crisply, Art Parkos and Rajiv Arora at Pitney Bowes, Susan Certoma at Broadridge, Israel Hersh and Joe Smularski at IPC Systems, Robert Testa at ADP, Ketan Risbud at Avon, John McCreight at McCreight and Company, and others.

A special thanks goes to Nirmala Devi Jeyakumar and Manali Khaniwale Vispute, my graduate assistants at the University of Bridgeport who helped me with conducting research for the book and coordinating the many revisions to the manuscript. I also want to thank the many executives, managers and professionals who have attended my seminars and workshops over the years, as well as my students who have attended my graduate classes. All of them have contributed to my knowledge and challenged me to learn more and stay current in a rapidly changing field.

In addition, I would like to thank my publisher, Bart Verbrugge at Van Haren Publishing for his friendship, editorial suggestions and encouragement to complete this project, as well as my editor, Steve Newton.

I would like to dedicate this book to my wife, mate and life-long partner, Phyllis, for her love, dedication, understanding, and support that she has given me throughout our time together. Our children, Camy, Dan, Gabe, our children through marriage, Beth and Andy and our grandchildren, Jason, Jacob, Jesse, Samantha and Zachery who also inspired me to finish the project so that I could devote more time to them.

Dr. Gad J. Selig, PMP, COP
Fairfield, CT

Contents

PART I LEADERSHIP, PEOPLE, ORGANIZATION AND STRATEGY   1

1 INTRODUCTION TO IT/BUSINESS ALIGNMENT, PLANNING, EXECUTION AND GOVERNANCE 3

1.1 What is Covered in This Chapter? 3
1.2 Overview.. 3
1.3 Definition, Purpose and Scope of IT Governance 10
1.4 Linking the CEO Role to Achieving Business Growth, Improving Profitability and Creating an Effective Governance and Compliance Environment 16
1.5 Overview of the Integrated IT Governance Framework, Major Components and Prerequisites 18
1.6 Steps in Making IT Governance Real 26
1.7 Case Study – Global Consumer Goods Company 31
1.8 Summary and Key Take Aways... 34

2 OVERVIEW OF INTEGRATED IT GOVERNANCE AND MANAGEMENT FRAMEWORK AND SELECTION OF CURRENT AND EMERGING BEST PRACTICE FRAMEWORKS, STANDARDS AND GUIDELINES 37

2.1 What is Covered in This Chapter? 37
2.2 Overview 37
2.3 Integrated IT Governance Framework and Roadmap.................... 42
2.4 Select Examples of Current and Emerging Business/IT Alignment and Governance Reference Models, Frameworks and Standards 46
2.5 Case Study – Leading Business Services/Manufacturing Company 87
2.6 Summary, Implications and Key Take Aways 87

3 BUSINESS/IT ALIGNMENT, STRATEGIC PLANNING AND PORTFOLIO INVESTMENT MANAGEMENT EXCELLENCE (DEMAND MANAGEMENT) 97

3.1 What is Covered in This Chapter? 97
3.2 Overview.. 97
3.3 Principles of Aligning IT to the Business More Effectively 110
3.4 Setting a Direction for Improved Business/IT Alignment Through Planning Related Processes 113
3.5 Strategic IT Investment Portfolio Management Alternatives........ 124

3.6 IT Engagement and Relationship Model and Roles 125
3.7 Case Study – Regional Financial Services Organization 127
3.8 Summary and Key Take Aways 129

4 PRINCIPLES FOR MANAGING SUCCESSFUL ORGANIZATIONAL CHANGE, PREREQUISITES FOR WORLD CLASS LEADERSHIP AND DEVELOPING HIGH PERFORMANCE TEAMS 131

4.1 What is Covered in This Chapter? 131
4.2 Overview 131
4.3 Framework for managing accelerating change 135
4.4 Organizing for the IT governance initiative 137
4.5 World Class Leadership Principles and Practices 139
4.6 Principles for Creating and Sustaining High Performance Teams 145
4.7 Case Study – Global Business Outsourcing Services Company 150
4.8 Summary and Key Take Aways 152

Part II IT Governance, the Major Component Processes and Enabling Technologies   155

5 PROGRAM AND PROJECT MANAGEMENT EXCELLENCE (EXECUTION MANAGEMENT) 157

5.1 What is Covered in This Chapter? 157
5.2 Overview 157
5.3 Project Management is Complex but Has Significant Value 162
5.4 Principles for Achieving Excellence in Program/Project Management 166
5.5 Making the Choice – Program and Project Management Light or Complex 173
5.6 Program and Project Governance Excellence 180
5.7 Agile Project Management (AgilePM®) and Scrum 185
5.8 Case Study – U.S. Federal Government Agency 188
5.9 Summary and Key Take Aways 188

6 IT SERVICE MANAGEMENT (ITSM) EXCELLENCE (EXECUTION MANAGEMENT) 193

6.1 What Is Covered in This Chapter? 193
6.2 Overview 193
6.3 Principles for Achieving IT Service Management Excellence 194
6.4 What is ITIL and Why is It Different? 199
6.5 ITIL Frameworks, Certifications and Qualifications 202
6.6 Select ITIL® 2011 Edition Processes and Functions by Core Phases 207
6.7 Steps in Making ITIL Real and Effective 215
6.8 Case Study – Global Manufacturing Organization 216
6.9 Summary and Key Take Aways 218

7 STRATEGIC SOURCING, OUTSOURCING AND VENDOR MANAGEMENT EXCELLENCE 221

7.1 What is Covered in This Chapter? 221
7.2 Overview 221

7.3	Principles and Practices for Outsourcing Excellence from a Customer Perspective	233
7.4	Vendor Selection, Contract Negotiations and Risk Management	241
7.5	Crowdsourcing	252
7.6	Steps in Making Outsourcing Real	253
7.7	Case Study – Major Pharmaceutical Company	255
7.8	Summary Steps and Key Take Aways	257

8 PERFORMANCE MANAGEMENT, METRICS, MANAGEMENT CONTROLS, COBIT®, RISK MANAGEMENT, BUSINESS CONTINUITY AND ENABLING TECHNOLOGY EXCELLENCE ... **261**

8.1	What is Covered in This Chapter?	261
8.2	Overview	261
8.3	Principles for Achieving Performance Management and Control Excellence	266
8.4	COBIT® - Control Objectives for Information and Related Technologies	275
8.5	Risk Assessment, Management and Mitigation	276
8.6	Business and IT Continuity and Protection Plan Checklist	280
8.7	Enabling Technologies to Improve IT Governance	281
8.8	IBM Process Reference Model for IT (PRM-IT)	284
8.9	Case Study – Global Manufacturing and Managed Services Company	285
8.10	Summary and Key Take Aways	285

9 CLOUD COMPUTING, DATA MANAGEMENT AND GOVERNANCE ISSUES, OPPORTUNITIES, CONSIDERATIONS AND APPROACHES ... **289**

9.1	What is Covered in This Chapter?	289
9.2	Overview and Definitions	289
9.3	Cloud Computing	292
9.4	Data Management	304
9.5	Case Study – Major Insurance and Reinsurance Company	313
9.6	Summary and Key Take Aways	316

10 SUMMARY, LESSONS LEARNED, CRITICAL SUCCESS FACTORS & FUTURE CHALLENGES ... **319**

10.1	What Is Covered in This Chapter?	319
10.2	Migration Plan for Making IT Governance Real and Sustainable	319
10.3	Composite Checklist for Implementing and Sustaining Successful IT Governance in Organizations	320
10.4	Lessons Learned	337
10.5	Critical Success Factors	338
10.6	Implications for the Future and Personal Action Plan	339

Appendix A	Glossary	341
Appendix B	References, alphabetical	371
Appendix C	References - Topic List	395
Appendix D	Managing Accelerating Change and Transformation Framework	419

PART

I

LEADERSHIP, PEOPLE, ORGANIZATION AND STRATEGY

Part I of the book covers chapters 1 through 4. It focuses on an overview of IT governance, alignment and strategy, leadership teams, organization and managing change. It also references current and emerging best practice industry frameworks, guidelines and standards that are useful and applicable to IT management and governance and its major components.

1 Introduction to IT/Business Alignment, Planning, Execution and Governance

On Change and Innovation:
"Never be afraid to try something new.
Remember, amateurs built the Ark, professionals built the Titanic!"
Anonymous

1.1 WHAT IS COVERED IN THIS CHAPTER?

- Provide an overview and summary of the key business/IT planning, execution, governance issues, constraints, opportunities and processes;
- Discuss the roles of the board, and responsibilities of executive management and the CIO;
- Review the value propositions for IT governance;
- Provide an overview of IT demand management, decision rights, balanced scorecard metrics and how much governance is really required;
- Identify steps in making IT governance real and pragmatic;
- Discuss an assessment technique to determine the current level of IT governance maturity in an organization and illustrate a blueprint of an ideal, future target state of IT governance.

1.2 OVERVIEW

The issues, opportunities and challenges of aligning information technology more closely with an organization and effectively governing and managing an organization's Information Technology (IT) investments, resources, major initiatives and superior uninterrupted service are becoming a major concern of the board and executive management in enterprises on a global basis. IT has become a critical function in most organizations and is fundamental to support, and sustain innovation, growth and survival.

Therefore, a comprehensive top-down approach with bottom-up execution of IT governance, a key component of enterprise governance, which includes all the activities of business/IT alignment, planning, execution, management, control and governance of IT as well as the leadership of those entrusted with the task, is critical to achieve a cost effective solution and approach. Effective 'management' includes the activities of planning, investment, integration, measurement, deployment and providing the services required to manage a complex and valuable strategic asset. Enterprise governance represents the entire management accountability and control framework of an organization, including roles and responsibilities of the board, the CEO and other functional managers, to ensure that the organization meets its objectives and plans in an ethical manner. Enterprise governance and corporate governance are terms used interchangeably.

None of this is easy, or obvious, and this pragmatic and actionable 'how to guide' is intended to draw from over 500 current and emerging best practice sources and over twenty-five IT governance best practice case studies, some of which are included in the book.

The purpose of the book is not to repeat in greater detail, what has been published previously, but to describe each of the major IT governance components as part of an overall comprehensive framework and roadmap in sufficient detail for executives, managers and professionals to serve as a guideline and starting point for any size organization in any industry to develop and tailor a workable and realistic approach to its environment, strategies, priorities, capabilities and available resources, and to transition IT organizations to a higher level of maturity, effectiveness, responsiveness and management.

1.2.1 Today's business challenges and drivers

Our world is in a time of remarkable and sometimes overwhelming change. The pace of change is accelerating on a global basis. Pressures for reducing costs, increasing speed to market, continuous improvements, greater innovation and creativity, more compliance, more effective accountability, globalization and more demanding and sophisticated customers are some of the pressures facing business and IT executives.

Figure 1.1 illustrates select pressures and drivers that organizations must deal with in a rapidly and dynamically changing global environment.

1.2.2 Scope and definition of enterprise governance and its relationship to business and IT governance

The discipline of enterprise governance begins at the top. The critical questions here are: How is a corporation's board of directors structured? Does it operate in a way that ensures their ability to fulfill their obligation to safeguard the resources of the company and the interests of corporate stakeholders?

Figure 1.1 Today's business challenges

Effective corporate governance requires the board to focus on general oversight and stewardship of the corporation, and to refrain from involvement in the day-to-day operations of the company. In this way, the board is able to maintain an integrated and relatively objective perspective on the company's operations, which helps it to steer the firm in the direction that will most benefit not only shareholders, but also the corporation in its entirety (Lam, 2014).

According to the International Federation of Accountants (IFAC), "Enterprise governance constitutes the entire accountability framework of the organization." Enterprise governance is the set of responsibilities and practices exercised by the board and executive management with the goal of providing strategic direction, ensuring that plans and objectives are achieved, assessing that risks are proactively managed and assuring that the enterprise's resources are used responsibly.

In an increasingly information technology-dependent world, the impact of the extraordinary changes brought about by the nexus of mobile and cloud technologies, social media and big data is increasingly being felt in the board room. As leaders of enterprises of every type and size, board directors can no longer afford to ignore, delegate or avoid IT-related decisions. Competitive, financial and reputational risk is increased if boards fail to recognize their role in governing technology as an asset and in removing barriers to improving enterprise information technology governance. Directors' awareness of the need for IT governance is increasing.

Enterprise governance includes the leadership and governance oversight of enterprise architecture to align business strategy, structures, systems, policies, processes and relational mechanisms. This strategic oversight enables customers, shareholders, stakeholders, people in IT and from across the business (including HR, communications, finance, engineering operations, marketing and others) to cost effectively engage to create enterprise value from the use of data and information, services and technologies. In short, enterprise governance represents the highest level of organizational and managerial discipline.

Enterprise governance deals with the separation of ownership and control of an organization (e.g. board members represent the stockholders), while business governance focuses on the direction, control and execution of the business plan and strategies by the CEO and his/her team and IT governance focuses on the direction, control and execution of IT plans and strategies (e.g. CIO and his/her team). Figure 1.2 compares and differentiates the key characteristics of enterprise governance versus business governance versus IT governance.

Enterprise governance drives business and all functional governance (e.g. IT)

Enterprise Governance	Business Governance	IT Governance
Separation of Ownership & Control (Board)	Direction & Control of the Business (CEO and Executives)	Direction and Control of IT (CIO and Direct Reports)
• Roles of Board and Executives • Regulatory Compliance Oversight • Shareholder Rights • Business Operations & Control Oversight • Financial Accounting & Reporting Oversight • Risk Management Oversight	• Business Strategy, Plans & Objectives • Manage Execution • Performance Metrics, Controls and Incentives • Intellectual Capital and Management/Succession Planning • Manage Innovation, Proactive Change and Continuous Improvements	• IT Strategy, Plans & Objectives • Alignment with Business Plans and Objectives • IT Assets and Resources • Demand Management (Customer) • Value Delivery and Execution Management (PM, Service Management) • Risk, Change & Performance Management

Figure 1.2 Enterprise governance versus business governance versus IT governance

1.2.3 The board's role in IT governance

Historically, the board of directors of public companies has focused, through committees, on such issues as audit, executive compensation, executive succession planning and others.

With the growing importance of IT in an increasing number of organizations, the board is forming a committee that focuses on IT strategy, investments and IT governance as part of enterprise governance. Based on a report by the IT Governance Institute, "IT governance is the responsibility of the board of directors and executive management. It is an integral part of enterprise governance and consists of the leadership and organizational structures and processes that ensure that the organization's IT function sustains and extends the organization's strategies and objectives." (IT Governance Institute, 2003)

1.2.4 Major challenges and issues faced by IT

In our research, we compiled a list of IT challenges and issues identified by multiple independent sources. There appears to be a common thread running through these issues and therefore, we have summarized them into strategic, value enhancing and execution questions.

Board and executive questions for IT:
- Does the IT strategy align with the business strategy?
- Is the IT investment justified based on its contributions to the business?
- How likely will IT meet or exceed its plans, objectives and initiatives?
- Is IT being managed prudently, effectively? How is that measured?
- How is IT delivering value? Is there a consistent IT business case format used for justifying IT investments?
- Is IT developing and maintaining constructive relationships with customers, vendors and others?
- Is IT delivering projects and services on time, within scope, within budget and with high quality?
- Is IT staffed adequately, with the right skills and competencies?
- Is there a standard measurement for IT investment across the firm?
- How does IT management and operations compare to other best practice organizations?
- How is IT managing and planning for contingencies, disasters, security, back-up and privacy?
- How is IT measuring its performance? What are the key performance measures?
- How effectively is IT communicating its progress and problems to its constituents such as executive management, sponsors, user community and other constituents?
- What controls and documentation have been instituted in IT? Are they sufficient?
- Does the board review and approve the overall IT strategy? Major projects?
- Is a risk management policy, assessment and mitigation practice followed for IT?
- Is IT compliant to federal, state and country (for global organizations) regulations and internal policies and controls?
- Are IT audit policies, procedures and processes in place and followed?
- Is there a succession plan in place for the CIO and key direct reports?

Top issues identified and ranked by over 100 CIOs in a CIO article (Nash, 2012) included:
1. Coping with accelerating change (and become one of the key drivers of innovation change).
2. Aligning IT strategy with the business strategy and enterprise governance.
3. Meeting the business needs effectively.
4. Infrastructure and IT service management (reliability and scalability).
5. Dealing with senior management and the board (get a seat at the 'C' table).
6. Managing costs, budgets and resources (internal and external).
7. Security, privacy, compliance and mitigating risks.

8. Recruiting and retaining staff.
9. Strengthening governance policies and practices.
10. Maintaining exemplary skills and knowledge (continuous learning),

Select issues addressed by a panel of CIOs of global organizations such as Pepsi, GE, IBM, Ogilvy and Mather, Pitney Bowes and others at a recent Society for Information Management (SIM) Chapter meeting:

- How do you align the IT strategy with the business strategy? What processes and tools are used? Who is involved? What worked? What did not?
- How and in what areas is IT delivering value to your organizations? How is it measured?
- How do you ensure that IT delivers on its plans and commitments and executes effectively? Program/project management? IT service management? Security? Privacy? Business and IT continuity? IT performance metrics? Data management and analytics?
- How is IT developing/sustaining constructive and positive relationships with its customer community? Executive management? Vendors?
- What IT controls, governance and compliance frameworks, processes, tools and techniques are being used? What worked? What did not?
- Has your business aligned itself with technology, innovation, the customer and is it open to managing accelerating change?
- How is IT performance measured? What KPIs are used at CIO level? Above CIO Level? Below CIO level?
- How effective is IT in marketing and communicating its progress and performance results to its constituents? What tools and techniques are used? How often?
- How do you sustain continuous improvement initiatives to increase the level of IT maturity and effectiveness, staff development, constituent ownership and decision rights?
- How are you sustaining compliance in processes and reporting?
- Does the board/operating committee/senior business leadership review and approve the IT strategy, priorities and funding? Major changes to plan, programs and budgets?

Summary of key strategic, value enhancing and execution questions
Strategic questions - are we doing the right thing? Is the investment in IT:

- In line with our business vision, strategy and capital budgeting?
- Consistent with our business principles, plan and direction?
- Contributing to our strategic objectives, sustainable competitive differentiation and business continuity support?
- Providing optimum value at an acceptable level of risk?
- Representing a long term view (roadmap)?
- Including an architectural roadmap based on a detailed analysis of the current state or condition of IT?

Value questions – are we getting the benefits:
- From a clear and shared understanding and commitment to achieve the expected benefits?
- From clear accountability for achieving the benefits which should be linked to MBOs (Management by Objectives) and incentive compensation schemes for individuals and business units and/or functional areas?
- Based on relevant and meaningful metrics and linked to corporate performance measurement systems?
- Based on a consistent benefits realization process and sign-off?

Delivery and execution questions – are we deploying well and effectively? How do we measure our results:
- Scalable, disciplined and consistent management, governance, delivery of quality projects and operations;
- Appropriate and sufficient resources available with the right competencies, capabilities and attitudes;

Major IT challenges must be dealt with as part of an IT planning and governance process

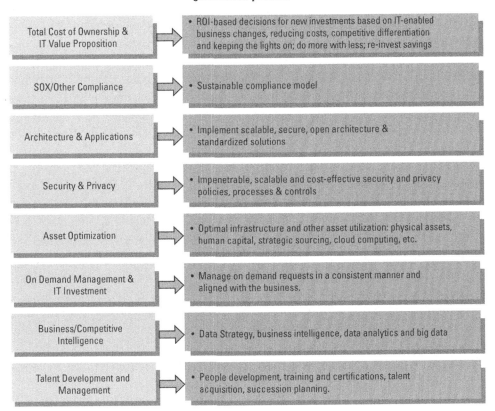

Figure 1.3 Major challenges for IT

- A consistent set of metrics linked to critical success factors and realistic key performance indicators (KPIs);
- Using succession planning.

Figure 1.3 summarizes the major IT challenges being addressed by a major global software organization as part of its IT planning and governance process.

At the end of the day, it comes down to a need for a plan and action program than can be executed. At the same time, the role of the CIO is also undergoing significant change. Successful CIOs recognize that IT has become far more than a means of increasing efficiency and reducing costs. Rather, they see IT as a prime stimulus for, and enabler of, business innovation and change – and themselves as key collaborators in a process that develops business and IT strategies in concert. Throughout the book we address many of the above challenges and issues.

■ 1.3   DEFINITION, PURPOSE AND SCOPE OF IT GOVERNANCE

Definition of IT governance
Governance formalizes and clarifies oversight, accountability and decision rights for a wide array of IT strategy, integration, resource and control activities. It is a collection of management, planning and performance review policies, practices and processes with associated decision rights, which establish authority, sponsorship, controls, a baseline and performance metrics over investments, plans, budgets, commitments, services, major changes, security, privacy, business continuity, risk assessment and compliance with laws and organizational policies. (Peter Weill, et al., 2004, and modified by the author.)

Purpose of IT governance:
- Align IT investments and priorities more closely with the business strategy and risk appetite;
- Manage, evaluate, prioritize, fund, measure and monitor requests for IT services and the resulting work and deliverables, in a more consistent and repeatable manner that optimizes returns to the business (e.g. portfolio investment management);
- Responsible utilization of resources and assets;
- Establish and clarify accountability and decision rights (clearly defines roles, responsibility and authority);
- Ensure that IT delivers on its plans, budgets and commitments;
- Manage major risks, threats, change and contingencies proactively;
- Improve IT organizational performance, compliance, maturity, staff development and outsourcing initiatives;
- Improve the voice of the customer (VOC), demand management and overall customer and constituent satisfaction and responsiveness;

■ Manage and think globally, but act locally;

■ Champion innovation and proactive change within the IT function and the business.

Scope of IT governance:

Key IT governance strategy and resource decisions must address the following topics (modified from Peter Weill, et al., 2004; Charles Popper, 2000; ISACA, 2013; ISO 38500:2008):

■ **IT principles** – high level statements about how IT is used in the business (e.g. scale, simplify and integrate; reduce TCO (Total Cost of Operations) and self-fund by re-investing savings; invest in customer-facing and other revenue generation systems; transform business and IT through business process transformation; strategic plan directions, PMO (Project Management Office), sustain innovation and assure regulatory compliance, etc.).

■ **IT architecture** – organizing logic for data analytics, applications and infrastructure captured in a set of policies, relationships, processes, standards and technical choices (e.g. cloud omputing) to achieve desired business and technical integration, standardization and cost optimization.

■ **SOA architecture** – service oriented architecture (SOA) is a business-centric IT architectural approach that supports the integration of the business as linked, repeatable business tasks or services. SOA helps users build composite applications that draw upon functionality from multiple sources within and beyond the enterprise to support business processes.

■ **IT (enterprise) infrastructure** – centrally coordinated, based on shared IT services that provide the foundation for the enterprise's IT capability and support, which may be insourced, outsourced or both. This should follow the TOGAF guideline for enterprise architecture defined in greater detail in Chapter 2. TOGAF guidelines may also be used for the IT and SOA architecture areas.

■ **Business application needs** – specifying the business need for purchased or internally developed IT applications.

■ **IT investment and prioritization** – decisions about how much and where to invest in IT (e.g. capital and expense), including development and maintenance projects, infrastructure, security, people, keeping the lights on, etc.

■ **People (human capital) development** – decisions about how to develop and maintain global IT leadership, management and technical skills and competencies (e.g. how much and where to spend on training and development, industry certifications, etc.).

■ **IT governance policies, processes, mechanisms, tools and metrics** – decisions on composition and roles of steering groups, advisory councils, technical and architecture working committees, project teams; key performance indicators (KPIs); chargeback alternatives; performance reporting, meaningful audit processes and the need to have a business owner for each project and investment. It is important to adopt an outcomes-based approach to IT governance. This will ensure that an organization is appropriately guided in its use of IT.

1.3.1 Who benefits from effective and sustainable IT governance?

Everyone in an organization benefits from effective IT governance. According to Charles Popper (Popper, 2003; Selig, 2008), the following audiences benefit:

■ What executives get:
  - Business improvements that result from knowledgeable participation in IT decision-making from an enterprise perspective;
  - Ensures that key IT investments support the business and provide optimum returns to the business;
  - Ensures compliance with laws and regulations.
■ What mid-level business managers get:
  - Convinces senior business managers that their combined business-IT resources are being managed effectively;
  - Helps to communicate with peers in IT to ensure that business services for which they are responsible will meet commitments.
■ What senior IT managers get:
  - Obtains sponsorship and support and a clear focus on important strategic and operational initiatives;
  - Improves customer relationships by delivering results in a more predictable and consistent manner, with the involvement of the customer.
■ What program/project and operations managers get:
  - Helps in resolving issues, review progress and enable faster decisions.
■ What everyone gets:
  - Facilitates communications about how IT contributes to the business;
  - Improves coordination, cooperation, communications and synergy across the organization;
  - Less stress.

1.3.2 Value propositions from best-in-class companies on business and/or IT governance

Based on primary and secondary market research, the author identified a number of benefits attributed to major organizations relating to improved governance business and/or IT structures and environments (Selig, 2008):

■ Lowers cost of operations by accomplishing more work consistently in less time and with fewer resources without sacrificing quality (General Motors);
■ Provides better control and more consistent approach to governance, prioritization, development funding and operations (Xerox);
■ Develops a better working relationship and communications with the customer (Sikorsky);
■ Provides for a consistent process for more effectively tracking progress, solving problems, escalating issues and gate reviews (Cigna);
■ Aligns initiatives and investments more directly with business strategy (GE);
■ Improves governance, communications, visibility and risk mitigation for all constituents (Robbins Gioia);

- Facilitates business and regulatory compliance with documentation and traceability as evidence (Purdue Pharma);
- Increases our customer satisfaction by listening proactively to the customers and validating requirements on an iterative and frequent basis (Johnson and Johnson);
- Reuse of consistent and repeatable processes helps to reduce time and costs and speeds up higher quality deliverables (IBM).

1.3.3 Successful IT governance is built on threecCritical pillars – leadership, organization and decision rights, scalable processes and enabling technologies

Effective IT governance is built on three critical pillars. These pillars include (Jerry Luftman, et al., 2010; Board Effectiveness Partners, 2004; Richard Melnicoff, et al., 2005; David Pultorak, et al., 2005; Ahmad and Shamsudin, 2013):

1. Leadership, organization and decision rights;
2. Flexible and scalable processes;
3. The use of enabling technology.

- **Leadership, organization and decision rights** - defines the organization structure, roles and responsibilities, decision rights (decision influencers and makers), a shared vision and interface/integration touch points and champions for proactive change:
  - Roles and responsibilities are well-defined with respect to each of the IT governance components and processes, including the steering and review hierarchies for investment authorizations, resolution of issues and formal periodic reviews;
  - Clear hand-off and interface agreements and contracts exist for internal and external work and deliverables;
  - Motivated leaders and change champions with the right talent, drive and competencies;
  - Meaningful metrics;
  - CIO is a change agent who links process to technology within the business, and provides the tools for enablement, innovation and transformation.

- **Flexible and scalable processes** - the IT governance model places heavy emphasis on the importance of process transformation and improvement: (e.g. planning, project management, portfolio investment management, risk management, IT service management, performance management, vendor management, controls, security and audits, etc.):
  - Processes are well-defined, documented, measured;
  - Processes define interfaces between organizations and ensure that workflow spans boundaries and silos including organization end-to-end view vendors, geography, technology and culture;
  - Processes should be flexible, scalable and consistently applied, with common sense.

■ **Enabling technology** - leverage leading tools and technologies that support the major IT governance components:
- Processes are supported by software tools that support the IT imperatives and components (e.g. planning and budgeting, portfolio investment management, project management, risk and change management, IT service management processes, financial, asset and performance management and scorecards, etc.);
- Tools provide governance, communications and effectiveness metrics to accelerate decisions, follow-up and management actions.

If anyone of the above pillars is missing or ineffective, the IT governance initiative will not be effective or sustainable. In addition, over-dependence on one dimension over the others will result in sub-optimal performance.

1.3.4 Results of ineffective IT governance can be devastating

A number of negative impacts may result from poor IT governance. These include the following (IT Governance Institute, 'The CEO's Guide to IT Value and Risk', 2006):

■ Business losses and disruptions, damaged reputations and weakened competitive positions (e.g. Nike lost an estimated $200 million, while running into difficulties installing a supply chain software system. Hershey attempted to install SAP several years ago and at that time, was not successful. It cost the company significant money and lots of embarrassment. Whirlpool ran into significant trouble in attempting to implement a supply chain management system, which did not provide accurate inventory counts at various inventory stages.).

■ Schedules not met, higher costs, poorer quality and unsatisfied customers.

■ Core business processes are negatively impacted (e.g. SAP and other enterprise resource planning systems impact many critical business processes) by poor quality of IT deliverables (an operational meltdown of the Southern Pacific-Union Pacific merger was traced largely to the inability to co-ordinate their IT systems).

■ Failure of IT to demonstrate its investment benefits or value propositions.

Poor regulatory compliance procedures, controls, audits and/or unethical executive business practices resulted in the demise of such companies as Enron, Andersen certified public accounting firm and the jailing of former heads of Tyco and WorldCom. Others like Parmalat and Global Crossing were also impacted by compliance issues.

The simple fact is that a poorly executed IT operation will result in the business not working. In addition, business and IT continuity and resumption plans have become critical.

1.3.5 The implications of Sarbanes Oxley Act (SOX) and other regulations on IT governance

In general, governance should be the responsibility of the board of directors and executive management in organizations. In order to develop an effective compliance program, executives must understand that compliance can and does involve more than just SOX. It can involve multiple national, international, local and industry specific regulations, as well as best practices, guidelines, frameworks and standards.

Compliance with a growing number of regulations and laws regarding financial disclosure, privacy, environmental conformance and others, developed by the SEC (Securities and Exchange Commission), FDA (Food and Drug Administration), EPA (Environmental Protection Agency), SOX (Sarbanes Oxley Act of 2002 and subsequent revisions), HIPPA (Health Insurance Portability and Accountability Act of 1996 and subsequent revisions), Basel III (regulation focused on strengthening EU banking capital liquidity requirements) and specific industry-focused regulations in banking, insurance, brokerage, healthcare, pharmaceutical and others are creating new and greater IT reporting and systems support requirements for organizations. Much like IT governance, in order to achieve sustainable compliance this complex and confusing mix can be approached most effectively as a single comprehensive compliance program that addresses people, process and technology (Howe, 2012).

Regulatory, audit and management requirements generally determine the level of management and administrative controls a company deploys. As an example, Section 302 of Sarbanes-Oxley requires CFOs and CEOs to personally certify and attest to the accuracy of their companies' financial results. Section 404 of Sarbanes-Oxley focuses on financial controls and requires IT to be able to document and trace a company's financials (e.g. Profit and Loss, Balance Sheet, etc.) back to the systems, software and operational processes and sources of the transactions that comprised the numbers. A company has to demonstrate a documented audit trail to be in compliance and to further demonstrate how an organization plans to sustain that compliance effort. Select implications of the Sarbanes-Oxley Act on IT include:

- Improves financial reporting/disclosures – new requirement to report on internal controls for financial statements – Section 404;
- Expands insider accountability – new requirements for code of ethics for executive management and protection for whistleblowers;
- The external auditors can insist that any gaps in IT controls must be addressed before an overall opinion is reached on the effectiveness of the internal company controls;
- Requires a backup for all "financially significant files, storage of those files and periodic restoration of backup files";
- Requires IT change management tracking and documentation for financial systems;
- Requires the maintenance of logs for user access to financial databases, security logs, administrative logs, problem and incident logs as well as an independent review of the logs to detect any activities that could adversely impact financials;
- Requires systems documentation and verification that data is properly handed off from one system to another;
- Companies are required to disclose on almost real-time basis any information concerning material changes in its financial condition or operations – Section 409;

- It is a crime for any person to corruptly alter, destroy, mutilate, or conceal any document with the intent to impair the object's integrity or availability for use in an official proceeding – Section 902;
- Section 906 addresses criminal penalties for certifying a misleading or fraudulent financial report. Under SOX 906, penalties can be upwards of $5 million in fines and 20 years in prison;
- Strengthen overall corporate governance.

In recent years, several amendments have been made to the legislation (e.g. Dodd-Frank Act of 2010; Jobs Act of 2012). These amendments attempt to ensure that the legislation is in step with the needs of economic activity and the fact that some companies may be unable to afford Sarbanes-Oxley provisions in exceptional circumstances (Mackaden, 2014).

In a growing number of companies subject to SOX, the CIO must internally certify the accuracy of the information audit trial each quarter to support the CEO/CFO SOX certifications.

There is a growing library of books, articles and documents that provide recommendations on how to deal with these regulatory and legal requirements (see Appendices B and C for references).

1.4 LINKING THE CEO ROLE TO ACHIEVING BUSINESS GROWTH, IMPROVING PROFITABILITY AND CREATING AN EFFECTIVE GOVERNANCE AND COMPLIANCE ENVIRONMENT

The role of the CEO and the executive management team is complex and requires a balance between sustaining growth and profitability while optimizing organizational effectiveness, managing proactive change and complying with the growing and confusing number of regulatory requirements.

Executing enterprise-wide strategic initiatives and managing effective business operations is a complex undertaking that requires effective corporate and IT governance to play a growing role in how the CEO and the executive team deploy the organization's strategy and measure their performance.

As Michael Cinema, President and CEO of Etienne Aligner Group stated, "The board of directors is well aware of its role to oversee the company's organizational strategies, structures, systems, staff, performance and standards. As president, it is my responsibility to ensure that they extend that oversight to the company's IT as well, and with our growing reliance on IT for competitive advantage, we simply cannot afford to apply to our IT anything less than the level of commitment we apply to overall governance." (IT Governance Institute, 2006.)

Figure 1.4 identifies the attributes that must be addressed for effective growth and profitability. Effective governance is a prominent component for both.

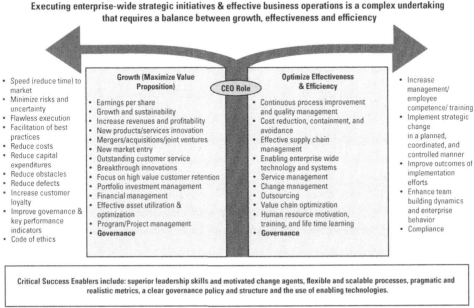

Figure 1.4 Linking the role of the CEO to the success of strategic enterprise initiatives and governance

1.4.1 How much governance is required and when is enough, enough?

There are few, if any, standards or guidelines developed that identify and clearly lay out in more detail what level of governance is required for either management or IT effectiveness by an organization. Generally, it is dependent on a number of factors such as:

- Investment $ (capital and expense) criticality to the organization (mission critical);
- Degree of business dependency on technology;
- Strategic corporate value proposition and alternatives for focus (e.g. growth centric, customer centric, process centric, cost centric, etc.);
- Management philosophy and policy (e.g. first mover versus follower);
- Program/project and/or operational importance;
- Complexity, scope, size and duration of initiative;
- Number of interfaces and integration requirements with the business;
- Degree of risk and potential impact (of doing or not doing);
- Number of organizations, departments, locations and resources involved;
- Customer or sponsor requirements;
- Regulatory, legal, control and compliance required;
- Degree of accountability desired and required;

- Level of security required or desired;
- Level of privacy desired;
- Audit, documentation and traceability requirements.

Chapter 2 discusses many of the current and emerging standards, guidelines and frameworks either developed or being developed, that help to improve the overall IT alignment, execution, governance, control, strategic sourcing and outsourcing management and performance management processes.

■ 1.5   OVERVIEW OF THE INTEGRATED IT GOVERNANCE FRAMEWORK, MAJOR COMPONENTS AND PREREQUISITES

Grounded in industry best practice research and required to plan, develop, deploy and sustain a cost effective approach to IT governance, the blended and integrated governance framework consists of five critical IT governance imperatives (which leverage best practice models and are 'must do's') and address the following work areas:

- **Business strategy, plan and objectives (demand management)** – this involves the development of the business strategy and plan which should drive the IT strategy and plan.
- **IT strategy, plan and objectives (demand management)** – this should be based on the business plan and objectives and will provide the direction and priorities of the IT functions and resources. This should also include portfolio management investments, a prioritization scheme and identify the decision rights (who influences decisions and who is authorized to make the decisions) on a wide variety of IT areas. In addition, the CIO is responsible for the infrastructure investments such as servers, networks, systems software and management.
- **IT plan execution (execution management)** – this encompasses the processes of program and project management, IT service management (including ITIL – IT Infrastructure Library), risk and threat management, change management, security, contingency plans, outsourcing, data management and others.
- **Performance management, risk management and management controls (execution management)** – this includes such areas as the balanced scorecard, key performance indicators, COBIT, and regulatory compliance areas. More details on these topics are provided in Chapters 2 and 8.
- **Vendor management and outsourcing management (execution management)** – since companies are increasing their outsourcing spending, selecting and managing the vendors and their deliverables has become critical.
- **People development, continuous process improvement and learning** - it is critical to invest in people, knowledge management and sustain continuous process improvement and innovation initiatives.

For each IT governance imperative, a description of the key components are provided and further detailed in subsequent chapters. Step one for a new CIO is to assess the current IT governance environment and what shape IT is in.

Figure 1.5 illustrates each of the major work areas or components of the IT governance framework including a short description of each component and provides select references (Gad Selig, 2008).

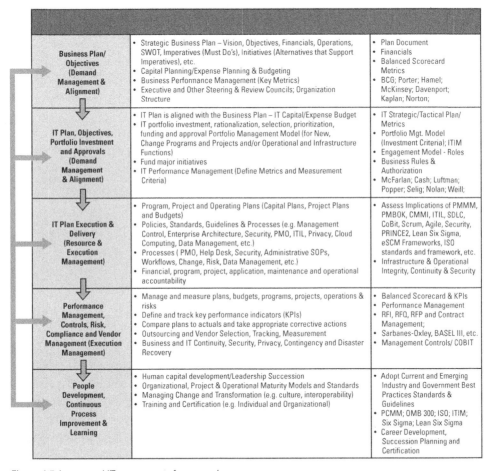

Identifies the major areas that must be addressed on the journey to a higher level of IT governance maturity and effectiveness

Business Plan/ Objectives (Demand Management & Alignment)	• Strategic Business Plan – Vision, Objectives, Financials, Operations, SWOT, Imperatives (Must Do's), Initiatives (Alternatives that Support Imperatives), etc. • Capital Planning/Expense Planning & Budgeting • Business Performance Management (Key Metrics) • Executive and Other Steering & Review Councils; Organization Structure	• Plan Document • Financials • Balanced Scorecard Metrics • BCG; Porter; Hamel; McKinsey; Davenport; Kaplan; Norton;
IT Plan, Objectives, Portfolio Investment and Approvals (Demand Management & Alignment)	• IT Plan is aligned with the Business Plan – IT Capital/Expense Budget • IT portfolio investment, rationalization, selection, prioritization, funding and approval Portfolio Management Model (for New, Change Programs and Projects and/or Operational and Infrastructure Functions) • Fund major initiatives • IT Performance Management (Define Metrics and Measurement Criteria)	• IT Strategic/Tactical Plan/ Metrics • Portfolio Mgt. Model (Investment Criteria); ITIM • Engagement Model - Roles • Business Rules & Authorization • McFarlan; Cash; Luftman; Popper; Selig; Nolan; Weill;
IT Plan Execution & Delivery (Resource & Execution Management)	• Program, Project and Operating Plans (Capital Plans, Project Plans and Budgets) • Policies, Standards, Guidelines & Processes (e.g. Management Control, Enterprise Architecture, Security, PMO, ITIL, Privacy, Cloud Computing, Data Management, etc.) • Processes (PMO, Help Desk, Security, Administrative SOPs, Workflows, Change, Risk, Data Management, etc.) • Financial, program, project, application, maintenance and operational accountability	• Assess Implications of PMMM, PMBOK, CMMI, ITIL, SDLC, CoBit, Scrum, Agile, Security, PRINCE2, Lean Six Sigma, eSCM Frameworks, ISO standards and framework, etc. • Infrastructure & Operational Integrity, Continuity & Security
Performance Management, Controls, Risk, Compliance and Vendor Management (Execution Management)	• Manage and measure plans, budgets, programs, projects, operations & risks • Define and track key performance indicators (KPIs) • Compare plans to actuals and take appropriate corrective actions • Outsourcing and Vendor Selection, Tracking, Measurement • Business and IT Continuity, Security, Privacy, Contingency and Disaster Recovery	• Balanced Scorecard & KPIs • Performance Management • RFI, RFQ, RFP and Contract Management; • Sarbanes-Oxley, BASEL III, etc. • Management Controls/ COBIT
People Development, Continuous Process Improvement & Learning	• Human capital development/Leadership Succession • Organizational, Project & Operational Maturity Models and Standards • Managing Change and Transformation (e.g. culture, interoperability) • Training and Certification (e.g. Individual and Organizational)	• Adopt Current and Emerging Industry and Government Best Practices Standards & Guidelines • PCMM; OMB 300; ISO; ITIM; Six Sigma; Lean Six Sigma • Career Development, Succession Planning and Certification

Figure 1.5 Integrated IT governance framework

1.5.1 Key work breakdown areas required to plan and manage an IT Governance initiative

Today, many companies start on a narrow path or shot gun approach without developing a more comprehensive framework with a prioritized roadmap based on the highest value delivery to the organization. A good place to start in the IT governance initiative is to decompose it into manageable and assignable work packages as in a work breakdown structure and assign these work packages to champions and owners responsible for them.

Figure 1.6 illustrates such a work breakdown for the major and key work areas of IT governance including planning, execution and performance management.

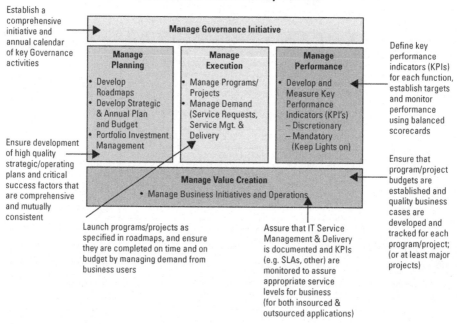

Figure 1.6 Key work breakdown areas for IT governance

1.5.2 IT governance – decision rights and authority

Peter Weill and Jeane Ross (Weill and Ross, 2004) identified the concept of IT decision rights as an important component of effective IT governance. The purpose of a decision rights matrix is to identify the IT decision influencers and decision makers in an organization in order to clarify the decision roles and authority levels for the major IT areas. It eliminates confusion, identifies accountability and clearly defines decision roles and scope. It is similar to a RACI (Responsible, Accountable, Consulted, Informed) chart used in project management to define roles in programs and projects

Figure 1.7 provides an illustrative example of a partial IT governance decision rights matrix for a financial services organization.

A Decisions Rights Matrix identifying Decision Influencers and Decision Makers is Necessary to Clarify Decision Roles and Authority Levels for the Major IT Governance Components

IT Governance Component	Input to Decision	Decision Authority	Comments/Examples (Varies by Organization)
IT Principles (High value statements about how IT will be used to create business value)	Business Units	IT Senior Leadership Group & CIO; Executive Officer Group	• Scale, simplify, integrate • Reduce cost of IT & self fund • Re-engineer/consistent processes • Invest in customer facing systems • Investment $ Threshold Approvals • KPIs/CSFs
IT Investment, Plan, Prioritization, Critical Success Factors and Key Performance Indicators (KPIs)	Business Units	IT Steering Committee (ITSC) (Business & IT Executives); Projects over $500K:	• ITSC recommends priority to CEO for any projects requiring over $500K • Identify, track and measure critical success factors and associated KPIs
Business Applications	Business Units and Corporate Functional Unit Heads	IT Steering Committee	Significant business application spend must be approved during the annual budget process, and if over $500K, approved by ITSC
IT Infrastructure and Architecture	IT Steering Committee	IT Architecture/ Technology Review Board (and Business Units (for related applications)	Significant infrastructure spend must be approved during the annual budget process, and if over $500K, approved by ITSC
Outsourcing & Vendor Management +++ Others	IT Steering Committee + Business Units	Senior leadership (Depends on scope)	Significant outsourcing initiative should be recommended by ITSC & approved by Executive officer Group

Figure 1.7 IT governance decision rights (illustrative example – financial service organization)

1.5.3 Business/IT steering and governance boards, working committees and roles

Many top performing companies have established multi-level and multi-disciplinary business/IT steering and governance boards and working committees with clear roles and responsibilities to ensure appropriate commitments, sponsorship, escalation, risk assessment, ownership, more effective communications and more formal visibility and commitment of the board, executive management and other constituents.

Why are they important?

■ Helps to ensure alignment across all of the parts of an organization. It is recognized that the demand for IT resources will exceed available resources/budget and establishing organization wide and business unit priorities is essential;

■ Provides a forum for investment decision making which is synchronized with the business;

- Builds an enterprise view and helps to eliminate stovepipe systems, equipment, processes, and duplication of efforts across the organization.

What (charter) should they focus on?
- To review and approve strategic plans, major programs/projects and establish priorities among competing requests for resources to ensure that everyone is aligned on those initiatives with highest 'value add' to the organization as a whole;
- To establish and support processes where needed to effectively fulfill the charge outlined;
- To conduct formal periodic reviews of major initiatives, and operational service performance.

Roles and responsibilities:
- Review and approve overall IT plans;
- Review, prioritize, approve major IT Investments;
- Conduct formal periodic project progress and performance reviews;
- Final escalation point for major business/IT issues resolution;
- Support and sponsor IT governance policy and process improvement programs impacting the executive steering board membership organizations and help deploy them in their organizations.

Other steering and working committees:
- Successful IT governance requires multi-level and multi-functional participation. Many organizations establish additional business/IT working committees at the business unit level as well as major functional areas such as supply chain management, global financials, marketing and sales, research and development and others as necessary;
- Program and projects working groups focus on specific initiatives.

Figure 1.8 illustrates an example of the business/IT steering and governance boards and roles at multiple levels for a large organization.

1.5.4 IT demand management - sources and classifications

Typically, requests for IT services should be identified and accommodated for in the strategic and tactical plans and budgets. If they are not, they would be classified as 'out-of-plan'. Each request should be evaluated on its own merits against consistent evaluation criteria discussed in more detail in Chapter 3.

Demand for IT services generally come in several flavors – mandatory (must do's such as addressing service interruptions, standard maintenance, keeping the lights on and/or regulatory compliance) and discretionary (could do's if aligned, feasible, cost justified, strategic and requested by executive management). Both mandatory and discretionary requests should be approved by the business/IT leadership in the IT strategic and

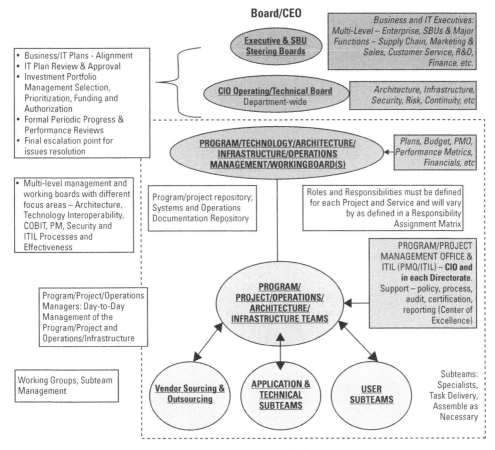

Figure 1.8 Business/IT steering and governance boards, committees and roles

operating plans or in accordance with an organization's decision rights and approval authority guidelines established for IT.

The following considerations will further help prioritize business needs with IT:

■ Clearly define and relate the value (e.g. cost reduction, containment and avoidance; increased revenues; faster access to information; shorter time to market, better customer service, etc.) that IT provides in support of the business;
■ Identify value adding activities (e.g. value chain and other business models/attributes) and strategies that would be enhanced through IT);
■ Focus on listening to the voice of the customer;
■ Ensure that all IT initiatives are evaluated using a consistent, but flexible set of investment selection, prioritization and review criteria to assure a strong link to the business plan, project implementation and ongoing operations;
■ Develop a strategic IT plan that identifies major initiatives, technical/architecture, operational, organizational, people development and financial objectives and measurements in support of the business.

Figure 1.9 illustrates a demand management chart for a major bank.

IT Demands Generally Come in Several Flavors – Mandatory or Core, Discretionary and Strategic – These should be identified and resourced in the IT Strategic and Operating Plan and Budgets - If they are not in the plan, each request should be evaluated on its own merits against consistent alignment, investment and service criteria. A steady state (normalized and repeatable) service could be included in a service catalogue.

Classification	Type of Request or Demand Mgt.	Comments/Description
Mandatory or Core (Business Enablement)	Service Interruption (Break & Fix)	A problem caused the disruption of IT service and must be fixed and restored as soon as possible
	Maintenance	Scheduled maintenance must be performed to keep applications and infrastructure operating efficiently
	Keep the Lights On and Legal/Regulatory	The costs and resources required to support the basic steady state operations of the business, including some components of infrastructure
Discretionary* (Require ROI)	Major New/Change (Complex) Initiatives (Full Risk Mitigation)	Complex new initiatives or major changes (major enhancements or modifications) to systems, processes or infrastructure and provide new or additional functionality or capacity
	Fast Track (New/Change) (Simple or Limited Scope) Standard (Repetitive) Request	Simple new initiatives and minor changes that do not required the rigor and discipline of a complex initiative and be fast tracked. Describe product/service (functions, features and price and place in a product/service catalogue)
Strategic	Major initiative – Realistic ROI may not be doable – too early	A strategic initiative may fall into several categories – first market mover (new product or service); R & D; competitive advantage, etc.

Figure 1.9 IT demand management – classifications

*Note: Criteria for differentiating between complex or fast track initiatives or service catalogue listings will vary for each organization.

1.5.5 Business/IT governance performance management and the balanced scorecard

A performance management plan must be developed for IT. The development of the performance management plan should be a collaborative effort between the business and IT. It should be based on a number of objectives such as strategic, financials, customer, quality, process innovation, operational and service effectiveness which, in turn, support an organization's business vision, mission, plans, objectives and financials.

It is important to measure the performance of IT in terms that can be understood by the business. It is equally important to have two types of reporting systems based on critical success factors and key performance indicators: those that are developed by IT for the external (out of IT) environment such as executive management, the board and the business managers/users and those developed for internal use by IT management.

The execution of these plans and objectives must be monitored and measured by a combination of balanced scorecard key performance indicators (KPIs) as well as formal and informal status review meetings and reports (e.g. report cards, dashboards). Figure 1.10 illustrates high level business and IT balanced scorecard categories and related metrics. The outcomes should link critical success factors to KPIs that are measurable, part of a standard reporting system and linked to a governance component. If one cannot measure the result, they do not count. Chapter 8 provides more details on performance management, controls, balanced scorecard and other metrics.

Link Critical Success Factors (CSFs) to Key Performance Indicators (KPI's) for business and IT (Illustrative Example)
Balanced Scorecard – Key Performance Measures – Business*
- **Financial (including compliance)** – revenue &, profit growth, budgets/expenses, ROA, ROI, NPV, cost reduction, laws and regulations, etc.
- **Strategic/Customer** – new product/service development, intellectual property, asset management, portfolio valuation, customer satisfaction, improvement in employee and organizational skills and maturity, etc.
- **Internal/External Processes** – process and/or technology innovation and transformation in sales and marketing, productivity, regulatory compliance, human resources, operations, engineering, manufacturing, customer service, IT, purchasing, vendor management, etc.
- **Learning and Growth** – people development, education, training, certification, job rotation, mentoring, etc.

Link Business to IT Metrics

Balanced Score Card – Key Performance Indicators - Information Technology**
- **Financials** – revenue and profit growth, cost reduction & self funding, budgets/actuals/variances, ROI, Payback, NPV, cost per IT customer, % of IT budget to revenue
- **Strategic** – competitive positioning, business value, alignment, differentiation through technology, growth, etc.
- **Customer (User) Satisfaction** – ownership, commitment, involvement, part of team, level of service
- **Employee Satisfaction/People Development** – training, certification, productivity, turnover
- **Program/Project Management Process*** – time/schedule, budget/cost, deliverables, scope, quality, resources, number of risks, number of changes, key issues, earned value, % of rework, etc.
- **Service (Operations) Process*** – service levels, uptime, service delivery, reliability, redundancy, availability, problem reporting and control, scalability, backup & disaster recovery plans, mean time to repair, response times, amount of errors and rework, etc.

* Modified from Kaplan and Norton, 2001
** (Note: For each category, more granular metrics are available, depending what needs to be measured)

Figure 1.10 Select balanced scorecard metrics for business and IT governance

■ 1.6   STEPS IN MAKING IT GOVERNANCE REAL

IT governance represents a journey towards continuous improvement and greater effectiveness. The journey is difficult, but can be facilitated by the following steps:

- Must have a corporate mandate from the top – the board and the executive team (including the CIO) are committed to implementing and sustaining a robust governance environment;
- Must have dedicated and available resources – identify executive champion and multi-disciplinary team (to focus on each IT governance component);
- Do your homework – educate yourself on past, current and emerging best practices;
- Market the IT governance value propositions and benefits to the organization – develop and conduct a communications, awareness and public relations campaign;
- Develop a tailored IT governance framework and roadmap for your organization based on current and emerging industry best practices;
- Assess the 'current state' of the level of IT governance maturity, or other frameworks that relate to specific IT governance components such as project management, maturity model (PMMM), vendor management (eSCM), performance management (balanced scorecard) and others, as a reference base (where are we today?), using a leading industry best practice framework such as CMMI or another framework that may apply to a specific component of IT governance;
- Develop a 'future state' IT governance blueprint (where you want to be) and keep it in focus;
- Decompose the IT governance components into well-defined work packages (assign an owner and champion to each process component);
- Develop an IT governance action plan, identify deliverables, establish priorities, milestones, allocate resources and measure progress;
- Sponsor organizational and individual certifications in the IT governance component areas, where they are available (e.g. PMP, ITIL, IT security, IT audit, BCP, outsourcing, eSCM, COP, etc.);
- Identify enabling technologies to support the IT governance initiative;
- Establish a 'web portal' to access IT governance policies, processes, information, communications and to provide support;
- Market and communicate the IT 'value proposition' and celebrate wins;
- Plan for and sustain IT Governance process improvements and link to a reward and incentive structure. Create a 'Continuous IT Governance Improvement' group to sustain the framework;
- Don't focus on specific ROI as a measure of success; use TCO (total cost of operations) and business innovation and transformation metrics as measures of improvement.

1.6.1 Avoiding IT governance implementation pitfalls

To avoid IT governance implementation pitfalls, key factors to remember include the following:

■ Treat the implementation initiative as a program or project with a series of phases with timetables and deliverables;
■ Remember that implementation requires cultural change and transformation, which requires:
  • Marketing of the value proposition and overcoming resistance to change;
  • Managing culture change and transformation;
  • Obtaining executive management buy-in and ownership;
  • Mobilizing commitment for change at multiple organization levels.
■ Manage expectations of all constituents – IT governance takes time and represents a series of continuous improvement and change processes.
■ Demonstrate measurable and incremental improvements in the environment and communicate them to the constituents.

1.6.2 A first step - assess current maturity levels of key IT governance components

As an organization develops its IT governance strategy, it is useful to assess the level of maturity of the IT governance. An industry standard methodology that is useful for this purpose is SEI's Capability Maturity Model Integrated (CMMI®) framework (Software Engineering Institute, 2002 and 2005). The model consists of five levels of maturity and can be used to analyze the current state of the major IT governance components as well as to establish a targeted future state maturity level for each major IT governance component.

The framework consists of five levels of maturity:
1. **Initial level**: the IT governance processes are characterized as ad hoc and occasionally even chaotic. Few processes are defined and success depends on individual efforts.
2. **Repeatable level**: basic IT governance processes are established. The necessary discipline is evolving to repeat earlier successes.
3. **Defined level**: the IT governance processes are documented, standardized and integrated into the management policies and procedures. All governance processes are implemented using approved versions as part of the IT governance policy and framework.
4. **Managed level**: define, collect and make decisions based on each IT governance component's measurements. IT governance processes and metrics are quantitatively understood, reported and controlled on an enterprise level.
5. **Optimizing level**: continuous process improvement is enabled by quantitative feedback from the process, from piloting innovative ideas and from adopting external industry best practices and standards.

Figure 1.11 provides an illustration of the CMMI® model levels and illustrates an insurance company's current state maturity level and its objective for a targeted future state maturity level.

Illustrates an Organization's Current and Future Targeted State of IT Governance Maturity. All Organizations Require a Roadmap and Plan to Move Up to Higher Levels of Maturity and Effectiveness

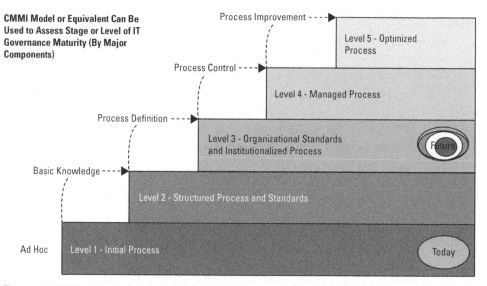

Figure 1.11 High level assessment of current state and targeted future state based on the CMMI® model (source: modified from Software Engineering Institute, Carnegie Mellon University)

Relates IT/Business alignment criteria to assist enterprises to evaluate their level of maturity and set a direction to improve, in six areas.

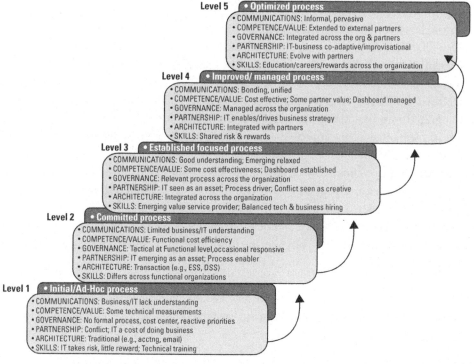

Figure 1.12 Business/IT Alignment Maturity Assessment Model (source: Jerry Luftman, et al., 2010)

Figure 1.12 was developed by Luftman suggesting an overlay framework to the CMMI model that focuses on assessing an organization's maturity based on the following six factors: communications, value, governance, partnership, architecture and skills (Jerry Luftman, 2004).

1.6.3 IT governance – current and future state transformation roadmap

In order to develop and/or improve the IT governance process, an organization must assess its current and future governance state and develop a transition roadmap for its IT transformation.

Figure 1.13 illustrates a roadmap for an organization to follow as IT transitions from its current state to its desired future state or environment.

IT Governance Process Improvement Flow - In order to develop and/or improve a governance process (business or IT), an organization must assess its current & future IT governance state and develop a plan to transform IT.

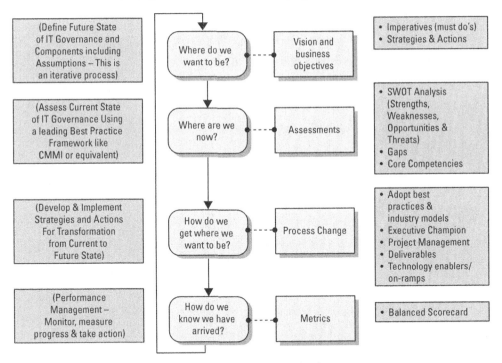

Figure 1.13 IT governance – current and future state transformation flow

1.6.4 Future state of IT governance – a blueprint concept

When all is said and done, most organizations would like to have an effective IT governance process and environment. Figure 1.14 identifies a blueprint of the 'ideal' future state and the key components that are necessary for effective governance deployment and strategic planning (business/IT alignment driven), application and infrastructure development (metrics driven) programs and projects and IT service

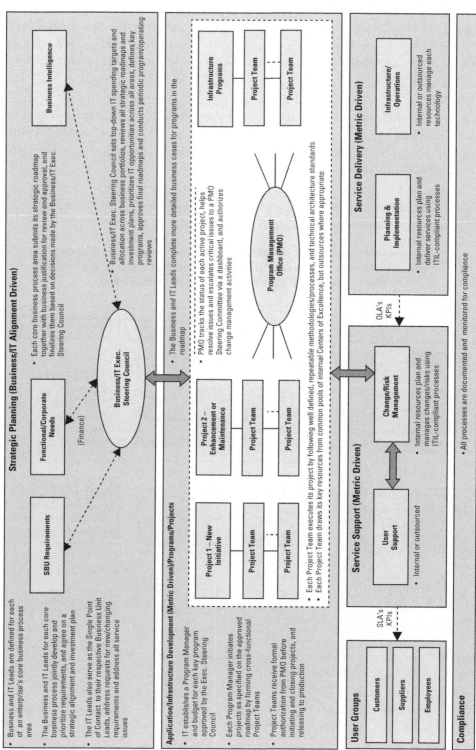

Figure 1.14 Future state IT governance – a blueprint concept

support and delivery (metrics driven). Other components that should be added include architecture, security, business continuity, back up and disaster recovery and related areas.

◾ 1.7 CASE STUDY – GLOBAL CONSUMER GOODS COMPANY

A number of IT governance case studies are included in the book representing mid-size to large global organizations in a variety of industries including consumer products, manufacturing, financial services, pharmaceuticals, entertainment and diversified industries. The identities of the organizations have been kept confidential. The data for each of the case studies was collected through interviews with CEOs, CIOs, direct reports to the CIOs and other executives and professionals, as well as a review of appropriate plans, budgets, metrics, controls and processes and has been disguised to protect the identity of the participating organizations.

The format of the case studies is consistent with Figure 1.15, which represents an IT governance case study for a global consumer goods organization.

Environment & Drivers	Approach
• Annual Revenue range – $6 - 10 billion • Number of Employees – 30,000 - 40,000 • Number of IT Employees – 1,200 - 2,000 • IT spend as a % of revenues – 2 - 3% • Very competitive industry with operations in 50 - 70 countries • Brand management driven with strong focus on marketing and sales • CIO reports to CEO and is a member of the Executive Management Team & sits at the "C" table • Company has transitioned from a decentralized environment to a more coordinated regional & global management environment to take advantage of operating synergies	• Company has been moving towards a more coordinated global and regional operating environment by establishing various steering committees that focus on the specific functional/process areas such as Supply Chain, Marketing and IT to assist in working and creating synergies across global regions • Senior IT management representatives are members of each of the key business councils • IT established a strategic planning process, which links to the portfolio investment process, capital and expense budget process and program/project execution process • IT established a global architecture group to coordinate consistent hardware and software (e.g. operating systems, major application packages, etc.)
Issues, Objectives, Constraints & Opportunities	Approach (continued)
• IT strategic plan process is linked to annual operating plan & budget (capital and expense) • IT has consolidated and streamlined disparate applications and operating systems. Global IT consistency is a challenge but is improving • Better alignment of business requirements with IT and evaluation of risk from a global and regional perspective • Standardize and simplify processes, tools and technologies to drive performance and accountability improvements • Implement a culture of continuous improvement across IT • Lack of consistency on IT performance metrics and SLAs	• Established a strong Project Management Office, which has developed a uniform and consistent process that has been rolled out globally across all regions in a coordinated and collaborative manner • Involve the business owner (Globally and Regionally) to assure closer alignment between the business and IT • The company has introduced IT Governance into various sub-process areas to help improve their IT Governance maturity. Sub areas include: – Lifecycle Management: Plan and Organize; Acquire and Implement; Deliver and Support; Monitor and Evaluate – Technology Services (Operations & Infrastructure): Service Strategy; Service Design; Service Operation (Includes end user computing, LAN/WAN, Service Desk, Servers, Mainframe, etc.)

Figure 1.15 Case Study – Global Consumer Good Company

Results – Alignment (Business/IT)	Results - IT Service Management (Includes ITIL)
• CIO sits on the Executive Management Operating Council and is an equal peer/partner with business & assures a closer alignment of IT support for business • A 3 year financial plan is developed for IT, about 50% is dedicated to supporting the business unit applications (charged back) and 50% to infrastructure and keeping the lights on • IT portfolio investment management is a rolling process & identifies IT capital spend by geography and functions. It is prioritized based on discretionary and mandatory criteria with top down and bottom up input • Balanced scorecard and report card metrics are linked to critical success factors of business and IT(financials, cost, performance, quality, etc.) • Established a customer/IT engagement (single point of contact) model to improve relationships, build trust and focus on priorities of major business functions	• A variety of metrics and tools are used to measure the efficiency, capacity and availability, utilization and service-ability of the operations and infrastructure assets and group • Elements of ITIL processes are implemented in the IT operations and infrastructure area • The IT infrastructure (Operations and Telecommunications) are centralized through the CIO organizations with strong dotted line coordination throughout the globe
Results - Program/Project/Portfolio Management	Results - Performance Management
• Established a PMO center of excellence • Developing a flexible and scalable PM process to handle agile and complex projects • Implementing a global Portfolio/Project Management tool • Company uses a systems development model (SDM) based on a waterfall sequential design model • Project Delivery has been the focus with not enough emphasis on post-implementation support • More workflow automation is desired in the PM process and phases	• Select IT metrics are included in the IT monthly status report (e.g. key line items designated as green, yellow and red) • An annual user satisfaction survey is conducted by IT measuring eight areas of IT delivery: communications, responsiveness, up-time, alignment, business process transformation, IT process transformation (streamline IT process), project, relationship mgt. and application support • A monthly Serbanes Oxley report is issued & tracks a number of required categories • A narrative IT annual report is issued reporting news, strategies, major project status, etc. • Elements of COBIT 5 have been implemented
Results – Cloud Computing	Results– Strategic Sourcing and Outsourcing
• VMware is used for all virtualization strategy • A Private Internal Cloud (VMware vCloud Suite) is used • Firewalls and External URLs are regularly scanned for vulnerabilities by the Security Team. 128-bit SSL encryption is used for all e-Commerce URLs • All Database servers with customer information (credit card numbers, address, phone numbers) are encrypted and require a Dual factor Authentication. Only the Database Administrators with highest privileges have access to them. All login attempts and other activities to these servers are logged for security reasons • Company uses Splunk for searching, monitoring and analyzing machine generated Big Data • A plan to have a passive site @ Sungard is in process. This will enable the migration of all Tier 1 applications from company to Sungard at a click of button in case of any failures. Please note this flexibility is only possible by Virtualization and hence company has taken the initiative towards "Drive to 95%" (95% application on virtual platform).	• Project Initiated - Business Analysts gather requirements • Infrastructure Architect specs the Hardware and Software Cost • If approved on a Physical platform, order placed with Vendor by the procurement team. If approved on a Virtual Platform, licensing orders are placed • Once the Hardware is on site, the Datacenter/Operations Team updates - ITSM (BMC Remedy) Database with - Configuration Items (CIs), Server build Incidents, Network requirements, etc • Once the OS is setup, the Application team works with the System Admins to install the application • 4 Environments are initiated in parallel - Development, QAF (Functional), QAP (Production) and Production. Development and QAF are initiated on Virtual Servers (using VMware); QAP is identical to Production • Vendor has a contract for Website Design and Development. Company has an onsite support team from vendor • Disaster Recovery contract with vendor.

Figure 1.15 Case Study – Global Consumer Good Company (continued)

Results - Data Management and Big Data	Critical Success Factors
• Company uses Splunk for searching, monitoring and analyzing machine generated Big Data. Splunk's pricing is based on the amount of data indexed per day • Company uses Splunk's Enterprise licensing which allows unlimited people to use the software, create unlimited searches, alerts, correlations, reports, dashboards and automated remedial actions • To circumvent external security risks, company decided to host the Big Data in-house. This reduces the cost of Cloud Hosting in terms of per/gigabit Data usage, Firewalls, Encryption tools and the risk of Cloud security breach • Because all the Data mining is done in-house, Network Bandwidth can be used efficiently. There is no need to create special security rules because all the existing internal security rules apply to Splunk's Software Cons • High storage requirement. Splunk captures every minute detail and event log in its database thus making it extremely expensive on the Storage front • A 5-year forecast helps determine the storage capacity required • To keep the storage utilization in check, the Database Administrators and Splunk's in-house Application Developers had to come up with scripts and scheduled tasks to compress and/or eliminated unwanted data. This is extremely time and resource consuming • Introduction to Implementing Automated remedial actions (one of Splunk's key feature) requires great amount of testing and scenario building. Company is still in testing stage to utilize this feature. Each remedial action requires rigorous testing before implemented in Production Environment thus making it extremely time consuming to come up with automated solutions to a problem	• Corporate, Regional and Business unit IT functions must work closely together to achieve more consistency and economies of scale • Flexible IT Governance processes are critical to success
Lessons Learned • IT governance is a journey towards continuous improvement • Cultural and organizational transformation is difficult, but necessary to survive • Involve local, regional and corporate management employees in direction setting and execution initiatives in a spirit of cooperation, communications, trust and partnership • Established global centers of excellence (located in multiple regions) for IT and let them lead by example: Web/e-business, Core center applications, Infra-structure, PMO/SDLC, Enterprise Data Architecture, Advanced Technology, etc.	

Figure 1.15 Case Study – Global Consumer Good Company (continued)

IT Mission & Key Management Principles – Consumer Goods Organization
(Illustrative Example)

IT Mission
• **Enable business growth**
• **Advance Business Transformation**
• **Increase the productivity of associates and Sales Representatives**
• **Support our global operating model**

Growth Enablers

Maintain a deep understanding of our business	Achieve business alignment	Deliver contemporary business solutions
• Anticipate business needs • Proactively identify how information and technology can drive the direct selling business model • Partner with the business to implement "hard to do" transformation • Leverage our cross-functional and cross-geography view	• IT strategy in step with business strategy • Forge strong relationships with business partners • Communicate early, frequently and simply • Ensure IT talent is aligned with growth strategies	• Champion integration and collaboration • Reduce the number of solutions while supporting business differences across markets • Provide information for business decision making • Affordable and suitable alternatives

Operational Levers

Lead through process discipline	Provide the best value	Maintain Service Excellence
• Comply fully with our project management and software development methodologies • Adhere to IT Governance policies and procedures • Ensure adequate controls and KPIs • Sponsor appropriate certifications	• Implement make vs. buy decisions that deliver speed, competitive advantage, affordability • Leverage worldwide IT resources • Effectively manage services and assets	• Systems are reliable and available to optimize revenue and representative service • The enterprise is secure, controlled and protected • Disciplined problem, change & risk management

Figure 1.15 Case Study – Global Consumer Good Company (continued)

■ 1.8 SUMMARY AND KEY TAKE AWAYS

1.8.1 Summary

IT governance is a broad and complex topic with many parts. IT governance represents a journey. It is not a one-time event and to achieve higher levels of IT maturity, IT governance should be persistently and relentlessly pursued both from a top-down and a bottom-up perspective. Creating and sustaining a more effective IT governance environment will take time and resources, and should be focused on achieving incremental IT governance successes in priority areas based on their value proposition or the reduction of major 'pain points' to the organization.

It is critical to break down or segment the IT governance initiative into manageable, assignable and measurable components or work packages with targeted deliverables. It is important to define clear roles for the board, executive management and the IT governance project team, including ownership and accountability for each component and the overall initiative.

IT governance requires all three critical pillars to succeed: leadership, organization and people, scalable and flexible processes and enabling technologies.

1.8.2 Key take aways

The approach to IT governance must be consistent, but yet scalable and tailored to each organization's environment and management style, key issues, opportunities, level of maturity, audit/legal requirements, available resources and cultural readiness. Remember, IT governance represents a journey, hopefully, towards higher levels of IT maturity and effectiveness and should be fully integrated with enterprise governance.

2

Overview of Integrated IT Governance and Management Framework and Selection of Current and Emerging Best Practice Frameworks, Standards and Guidelines

■ 2.1   WHAT IS COVERED IN THIS CHAPTER?

"A Chinese philosopher once said that a smart man learns from his own mistakes and a wise man from the mistakes of others, but a fool never learns. Most of us would rather be smart and wise than foolish. In order to avoid taking the fool's path to potential disaster, it is important for companies to develop organizational processes that allow them to learn from their mistakes. Ideally, the same processes would also allow them to learn from the mistakes and the best practices of other companies."   Anonymous

- Describes an integrated IT governance framework and the related industry standards, guidelines and frameworks;
- Provides an overview of select examples of current and emerging industry best practice frameworks, maturity models, guidelines and standards together with the appropriate references;
- Discusses the implications of these frameworks on an organization's approach to improving IT governance and management.

■ 2.2   OVERVIEW

There is a growing number of models, frameworks and standards that address one or more aspects of IT governance. There are few that integrate the components necessary to plan, develop and deploy a comprehensive IT governance framework and roadmap to help guide organizational process improvement initiatives in this area. An excellent reference book that helped the author with this chapter is, 'Global Standards and Publications', published by Van Haren Publishing (2014).

Usually, organizations begin an IT governance analysis and improvement project based on some kind of issue or pain point. Some organizations use the COBIT® 5.0 (Control Objectives for Information and Related Technologies, IT Governance Institute, 2012) as a checklist focused primarily on the control aspects of improving IT governance. Others approach the problem from a security perspective and use ISO 27000 (IT Security Management, which represent a series of more than 20 standards) as a framework. Still others approach it from a project management perspective and use PMBOK® (Project Management Body of Knowledge, Project Management Institute, 2013), PMMM® (Project Management Maturity Model, Crawford, 2002), PRINCE2 (AXELOS, 2009) or Agile or Scrum or a hybrid model, consisting of a combination of methods. Others have embraced the IT service management model based on the ITIL® 2011 Edition framework (IT Infrastructure Library) and ISO 2000:2011 (IT Service Management). Several organizations have embarked on the quality improvement route through the use of ISO 9001-2000 or (Lean) Six Sigma (LSS, is more popular in Europe than Six Sigma) or Lean. Still others use frameworks such as CMMI® (Capabilities Maturity Model Integrated, Software Engineering Institute, 2002, 2006) for systems and software development and eSCM® (eSourcing Capability Model) by the ITSqc {IT Services Qualification Center at Carnegie Mellon University – Hyder, 2006; Hefley, 2006}) to facilitate the outsourcing process. The University of Amsterdam developed the Amsterdam Information Management Model (AIM), a generic framework for information management which is being used in Europe (Rick Maes, et al., 2000). Efforts are being made by several groups to correlate COBIT with ITIL, applicable ISO standards, CMMI, PRINCE2, PMBOK Guide, eSCM, ISO 9001, ISO 27000 series and other frameworks to develop a more streamlined set of processes and guidelines to improve the IT governance environment in organizations.

Figure 2.1 provides a summary of the key IT governance frameworks, standards and models and their general use and source.

There are a variety of models for different uses and focus areas, many of them complement each other.

MODEL	GENERAL USE	SOURCE and/or Website(s)
COBIT®	IT Control Objectives	ISACA – www.isaca.org
ITIM	IT Investment Management	GSA – www.gsa.gov
ISO®/IEC 38500:2008	Corporate Governance of Information Technology	ISO (International Standards Organization) – www.iso.org
CMMI®	Systems and Software Development and Systems Integration	SEI (Software Engineering Institute) – www.sei.cmu.edu/cmmi
Balanced Scorecard	Corporation and IT Measurement (Scorecard) Scheme	Kaplan and Norton – www.balancedscorecard.org
e-Sourcing Capability Model	Sourcing (for both Service Providers and Customers/Clients)	ITSqc (IT Services Qualification Center) – www.itsqc.org
OPBOK®	Outsourcing and Sourcing	IAOP (International Association of Outsourcing) – www.iaop.org
People - CMM® (P-CMM)	Human Asset Management	SEI – www.sei.cmu.edu/cmmi

Figure 2.1 Summary of select current and emerging frameworks that enable IT governance and continuous improvement

MODEL	GENERAL USE	SOURCE and/or Website(s)
Six Sigma®	Quality Management and Process Improvement	Motorola – www.motorola.com ; ISSSP (International Society of Six Sigma Professionals) – www.isssp.com;
ISO® 9001:2000	Quality Management	ISO – www.iso.org
ISO®/IEC 27001	Information Security Management	ISO - www.iso.org
ISO®/IEC 20000:2011 and ITIL®	IT Infrastructure Library and IT Operations/Infrastructure Management	ISO – www.iso.org; www.axelos. com; ITSMP (IT Service Management Professionals) – www.itsm.org
PMBOK®/OPM3®/ PMMM/PRINCE2®/ISO 21500	Program, Project & Portfolio Management	PMI (Project Management Institute)/ Project Management Solutions, Inc./ AXELOS, Inc. - www.pmi.org; www.iso.org; www.axelos.org; www.pmsolutions.com
Amsterdam Information Management Model	IT Management	University of Amsterdam; www.primavera.fee.uva.nl (dutch only)
Lean IT	Lean IT, where waste is minimized for work that adds no value to a product or service.	www.lean.org
Agile	A set of "light" software development methods based on iterative and incremental development and are used also for product development design, engineering and other areas.	www.agilemanifesto.org
Scrum	Scrum is an agile method (an iterative and incremental approach for completing software development projects or complex projects).	www.scrum.org
ICB® (IPMA Competence Baseline)	IPMA (International Project Management Association) is a competence baseline for project management.	www.ipma.ch
ISO 31000	Standard for risk management – provides generic guidelines for the design, implementation and maintenance of risk management throughout an organization.	ISO – www.iso.org
e-CF (European e-Competence Framework)	e-CF is a competence framework applied to IT skills. Version 3 (2014) is being developed as a European standard.	www.ecompetences.eu
BABOK® Guide	Represents the Business Analysis Body of Knowledge (BABOK ® guide) and is a framework for business analysts.	www.iiba.org
ASL® 2; 2008 (Application Services Library)	It is a framework and collection of best practices for application development.	www.aslbislfoundation.org

Figure 2.1 Summary of select current and emerging frameworks that enable IT governance and continuous improvement (continued)

MODEL	GENERAL USE	SOURCE and/or Website(s)
BISL®:2012	BISL® - Business Information Services Library. It focuses on how business organizations can improve control over their information systems.	ASL BISL Foundation - www.aslbislfoundation.org
TOGAF®	It is an enterprise architecture standard used by organizations to improve business efficiency via enterprise architecture professionals.	Open Group Standard – www.opengroup.org/togaf
P3M3®	P3M3® is a portfolio, program and project management maturity model used to help assess an organization's performance and level of maturity in the PPPM areas and develop improvement plans.	www.axelos.com
ARCHIMATE®	It is an open and independent modeling language for enterprise architecture that is supported by variety of vendor tools.	www.opengroup.org/archimate
COSO	Committee of sponsoring organizations of the Treadway Commission. The COSO framework is focused on improving organizational performance and governance through effective internal control, enterprise risk management, and fraud deterrence.	www.coso.org

CMMI® and People-CMMI® are registered trademarks of Carnegie Mellon University. COBIT® is a registered trademark of the IT Governance Institute (ITGI). ISO® is a registered trademark of the International Organization for Standardization. ITIL® is a registered trademark of AXELOS. Six Sigma® is a trademark of Motorola, Inc.

Figure 2.1 Summary of select current and emerging frameworks that enable IT governance and continuous improvement (continued)

To establish and successfully deploy an IT governance initiative effectively, it must permeate the enterprise and can be characterized as a mix of formal systematic processes blended with behavioral science techniques and people skills. Nick Robinson suggested a generic IT governance model which consists of multiple layers split into categories broadly covering business drivers, internal environment and culture, entrustment network and accountability, decision models and authority, value realization and delivery, performance management and value management (Nick Robinson, 2007). Figure 2.2 illustrates this model.

While this model lays out a conceptual framework, it requires much more detailed policies, processes and tools for practical deployment.

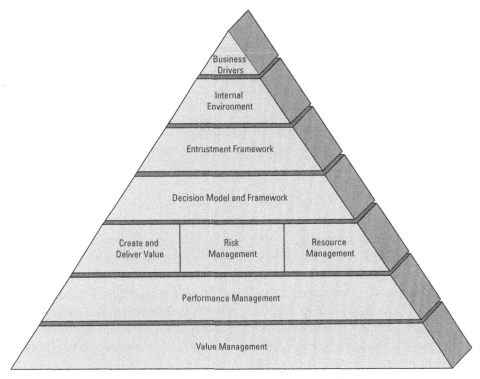

Figure 2.2 The Generic IT Governance Model (source: Nick Robinson, 2007)

2.2.1 Limitations of existing models, standards and frameworks

Most of the current models do not address the entire body of knowledge or lifecycle of IT governance. While some provide a checklist of processes such as COBIT, most fall short by not providing the 'how to' processes, templates, checklists and tools for effective deployment and continuous improvement. Another shortcoming of many current models, with some exceptions, is that they do not readily provide methods to appraise capabilities or provide guidance for the improvement of IT governance processes. Some of the frameworks have structures that are either too flexible or too rigid and are not easily scalable or adaptable to either small, medium or large organizations.

A practical approach to IT governance for many organizations is to select the best of all of the models and standards, develop a blend of the best attributes of each of the frameworks and tailor an approach that is realistic and sustainable for their respective environment driven by their pain points and significant improvement opportunities, or both.

2.2.2 Benefits of using a comprehensive IT governance framework leveraging best practice models

- Grounded in industry best practice research and experience;
- Improves credibility and confidence;
- Overcomes vertical silos and tends to focus on the enterprise as a whole (end-to-end);

- Faster and more ready acceptance;
- Better resource utilization (reduce, contain and/or avoid costs and/or revenue growth) based on consistent standards and/or more uniform use;
- Improves customer satisfaction and responsiveness;
- Common terminology and definitions;
- Clear accountability;
- Consistent, repeatable, end-to-end measurable processes;
- Accelerated deployment (do not have to re-invent the wheel).

2.3   INTEGRATED IT GOVERNANCE FRAMEWORK AND ROADMAP

Based on our findings, many organizations start or focus the IT governance initiative on their 'pain' points and expand from there. Given that most organizations are at different levels of maturity for each of the major components of IT governance, or IT governance as a whole, there appears to be no one best approach for all organizations. Rather, each organization should tailor its approach to its environment and consider such factors as the organization's operating and management philosophy, key issues and opportunities, its change tolerance, current state and level of maturity, desired future state of maturity, audit and legal compliance requirements, its cultural readiness and the degree of executive management sponsorship provided.

At the end of the day, every organization must address each of the following major components of IT governance:

- **Business strategy, plan and objectives (demand management)** - this involves the development of the business strategy and plan and must drive the IT strategy and plan.
- **IT strategy, plan and objectives (demand management)** – this should be based on the business plan and objectives and should provide the direction and investment priorities of the IT functions and resources. This should also include portfolio investment management and priorities, and identify the decision rights (who influences decisions on IT and who is authorized to make the decisions on a wide variety of areas) as well as the value propositions of IT in support of the business.
- **IT plan execution (execution management)** – this encompasses the tools, processes and metrics required to assist in the execution of systems and services such as program and project management, IT service management and delivery (including ITIL – IT Infrastructure Library), change management, security management, business and IT continuity, contingency, disaster recovery management, application development/ maintenance, outsourcing and others.
- **Performance management, management controls and compliance (execution management))** – this would include such areas as the balanced scorecard, key performance indicators, risk management, COBIT and regulatory compliance areas,

management controls and audits including Sarbanes-Oxley, HIPPA, Basel III and other general or industry-specific regulations.

■ **Vendor management and outsourcing management (execution management)** – since organizations are increasing their outsourcing spending as a percent of their budget, selecting and managing the service providers effectively has become more critical.

■ **People development, continuous IT governance process improvement and learning** – to stay at the top of one's game, it has also become critical to invest in learning and education, knowledge management, continuous process improvement and succession planning.

Most of today's IT models, frameworks and standards only address one or a limited number of the components that should be an integral part of a comprehensive IT

Identifies the major areas that must be addressed on the journey to a higher level of IT governance maturity and effectiveness

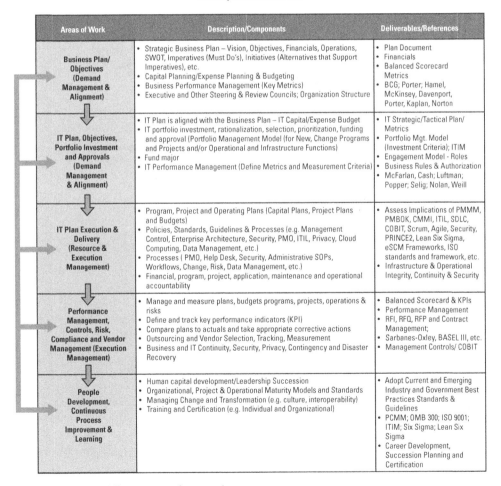

Areas of Work	Description/Components	Deliverables/References
Business Plan/ Objectives (Demand Management & Alignment)	• Strategic Business Plan – Vision, Objectives, Financials, Operations, SWOT, Imperatives (Must Do's), Initiatives (Alternatives that Support Imperatives), etc. • Capital Planning/Expense Planning & Budgeting • Business Performance Management (Key Metrics) • Executive and Other Steering & Review Councils; Organization Structure	• Plan Document • Financials • Balanced Scorecard Metrics • BCG; Porter; Hamel, McKinsey, Davenport, Porter, Kaplan, Norton
IT Plan, Objectives, Portfolio Investment and Approvals (Demand Management & Alignment)	• IT Plan is aligned with the Business Plan – IT Capital/Expense Budget • IT portfolio investment, rationalization, selection, prioritization, funding and approval (Portfolio Management Model (for New, Change Programs and Projects and/or Operational and Infrastructure Functions) • Fund major • IT Performance Management (Define Metrics and Measurement Criteria)	• IT Strategic/Tactical Plan/ Metrics • Portfolio Mgt. Model (Investment Criteria); ITIM • Engagement Model - Roles • Business Rules & Authorization • McFarlan, Cash; Luftman; Popper; Selig; Nolan, Weill
IT Plan Execution & Delivery (Resource & Execution Management)	• Program, Project and Operating Plans (Capital Plans, Project Plans and Budgets) • Policies, Standards, Guidelines & Processes (e.g. Management Control, Enterprise Architecture, Security, PMO, ITIL, Privacy, Cloud Computing, Data Management, etc.) • Processes (PMO, Help Desk, Security, Administrative SOPs, Workflows, Change, Risk, Data Management, etc.) • Financial, program, project, application, maintenance and operational accountability	• Assess Implications of PMMM, PMBOK, CMMI, ITIL, SDLC, COBIT, Scrum, Agile, Security, PRINCE2, Lean Six Sigma, eSCM Frameworks, ISO standards and framework, etc. • Infrastructure & Operational Integrity, Continuity & Security
Performance Management, Controls, Risk, Compliance and Vendor Management (Execution Management)	• Manage and measure plans, budgets programs, projects, operations & risks • Define and track key performance indicators (KPI) • Compare plans to actuals and take appropriate corrective actions • Outsourcing and Vendor Selection, Tracking, Measurement • Business and IT Continuity, Security, Privacy, Contingency and Disaster Recovery	• Balanced Scorecard & KPIs • Performance Management • RFI, RFQ, RFP and Contract Management; • Sarbanes-Oxley, BASEL III, etc. • Management Controls/ COBIT
People Development, Continuous Process Improvement & Learning	• Human capital development/Leadership Succession • Organizational, Project & Operational Maturity Models and Standards • Managing Change and Transformation (e.g. culture, interoperability) • Training and Certification (e.g. Individual and Organizational)	• Adopt Current and Emerging Industry and Government Best Practices Standards & Guidelines • PCMM; OMB 300; ISO 9001; ITIM; Six Sigma; Lean Six Sigma • Career Development, Succession Planning and Certification

Figure 2.3 Integrated IT governance framework

governance solution. Many of the current models are being used by industry and should be understood, leveraged, integrated and/or tailored. These should be used to develop an integrated approach to IT governance.

The proposed integrated IT governance framework described in this chapter references the previously cited industry frameworks, standards and guidelines as well as additional ones that are relevant for improving IT governance maturity and effectiveness in organizations.

Figure 2.3 provides an illustration of the integrated IT governance framework and its proposed major components listing select references as a pragmatic approach to improving the IT governance environment. This was briefly covered in Chapter 1.

Figure 2.4 illustrates the CMMI® model related to IT governance in general. It is difficult to assess IT governance as a whole in this way. Rather it must be broken down into as many components as an organization must deploy that are part of IT governance.

CMMI®* or An Equivalent Model can be used to self - assess the level of an enterprise's IT Governance maturity & develop a plan and strategy to achieve higher levels of maturity for each of the major and sub-components of IT Governance.

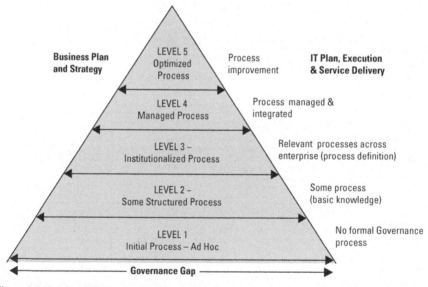

Figure 2.4 High level IT governance maturity levels

Figure 2.5 represents a template that integrates the major and key sub-components of IT governance (see Figure 2.3) with the CMMI® model levels to provide a self-assessment tool to help evaluate the current level of maturity for each component. The major components and sub-components can be tailored according the needs of a particular organization to help develop a roadmap for achieving a higher level of IT governance

The template can be used to assess the level of IT Governance and its major component, level of, maturity and effectiveness (1=low; 5=high). Additional IT Governance components from COBIT®, ISO® or others may be added across the horizontal axis as required.

Maturity	Attributes	Values								Major IT Governance Components	
Level 5	• Optimized process									Other	People Development and Learning (Chapter 4)
	• Metrics driven process improvements									Succession Planning	
Level 4	• Process managed and used by all									Education, Training and Learning	
Level 3	• Enterprise wide process and standards									Knowledge Management	
Level 2	• Basic Process									Continuous Process Improvement	
	• Basic Knowledge									Other	Performance Management and Controls (Chapter 8)
Level 1	• Ad hoc									Controls and Audit (COBIT)	
	• No established practices or processes									MBO's and incentives tied to CSFs	
										Key Performance Indicators	
										Critical Success Factors/CSFs	
										Other	Execution Management (Chapters 2, 5, 6, 7, 9)
										Data Management	
										Cloud Computing	
										Enterprise Architecture	
										Vendor Management	
										ITSM + ITIL	
										Risk Management	
										Resource Management	
										Program/Project Management	
										Other	Demand Management and Alignment (Chapter 3)
										Portfolio Investment Management	
										IT Plan	
										Business Plan	

Figure 2.5 IT governance maturity self-assessment framework

maturity and effectiveness. In addition, Figure 2.5 also identifies the chapters in the book that provide an overview of the 'how to's' for each of the essential components of IT governance.

■ 2.4 SELECT EXAMPLES OF CURRENT AND EMERGING BUSINESS/ IT ALIGNMENT AND GOVERNANCE REFERENCE MODELS, FRAMEWORKS AND STANDARDS

This section summarizes select current and emerging industry best practice models, frameworks and standards relating to IT governance and its major components.

2.4.1 COSO

COSO is an acronym for Committee of Sponsoring Organizations of the Treadway Commission. It is a U.S. private sector initiative, formed in 1985 to identify the factors that cause fraudulent financial reporting in corporations and make recommendations to reduce these incidents. COSO is sponsored and funded by several accounting and audit associations and institutions such as the American Institute of Certified Accountants, the American Accounting Association, Financial Executives International, the Institute of Internal Auditors and Institute of Management Accountants. In 2013, COSO released COSO 2913 of its 'International Control – Integrated Framework' (COSO, 2013).

The COSO framework defines internal control as a process, impacted by an organization's board of directors, management and other personnel, designed to provide reasonable assurance regarding the achievement of objectives in the following categories:
■ Effectiveness and efficiency of operations and Internal controls;
■ Reliability of financial reporting;
■ Compliance with the applicable laws and regulations (Including SOX 404 Compliance).

The COSO internal control framework consists of five components:
1. Control Environment – sets the tone of the organization by creating awareness of the importance of control and is the foundation for all of the other components.
2. Risk Assessment – sets the stage for assessing risks to achieve objectives and then managing those risks.
3. Control Activities – these are the policies, procedures and tools which help to ensure that management directives are deployed.
4. Information and Communications – information systems play a key role in internal control systems by producing financial, operational and compliance reports and information.
5. Monitoring – internal control systems need to be monitored for compliance and continuous improvement.

COSO has served as a blueprint for establishing internal controls that promote efficiency, minimize risks, and help to ensure the reliability of financial statements and comply with laws and regulations. Many organizations are using the COSO framework to improve their business and, to a lesser extent, their IT governance and control environments.

2.4.2 ITIM, IT Investment Management - stages of maturity and critical processes

The General Accounting Office (GAO), an agency of the U.S. Federal Government, developed the IT Investment Management (ITIM) framework. It represents a maturity assessment model composed of five progressive stages of maturity and provides a method for evaluating and assessing how well an agency is selecting its IT investments, aligning the IT investments to support the agency's mission and managing its IT resources and investments.

At the Stage 1 level of maturity, an agency is selecting investments in an unstructured, ad hoc manner. Project outcomes are unpredictable and successes are not repeatable as the agency is creating awareness of the investment process. Stage 2 processes lay the foundation for sound IT investment by helping the agency to attain successful, predictable, and repeatable investment control processes at the project level. Stage 3 represents a major step forward in maturity, in which the agency moves from project-centric processes to a portfolio approach, evaluating potential investments by how well they support the agency's missions, strategies, and goals. At Stage 4, an agency uses consistent evaluation techniques to improve its IT investment processes and its investment portfolio. It is able to plan and implement the 'de-selection' of obsolete, high-risk, or low-value IT investments. The most advanced organizations, operating at Stage 5 maturity, benchmark their IT investment processes relative to other 'best-in-class' organizations and look for breakthrough information technologies that will enable them to change and improve their business performance (General Accounting Office, 2004).

Figure 2.6 illustrates the ITIM Framework which can be used by both private and public organizations. More details on portfolio investment management are discussed in Chapter 3.

2.4.3 *PMBOK® Guide* - Project Management Body of Knowledge

The *PMBOK® Guide* was developed by the Project Management Institute (PMI) as a process-based framework for project management consisting of ten knowledge areas and five process areas (initiation, planning, execution, control and termination). It is the primary framework used in the Project Management Professional (PMP) certification examination, which certifies individuals as PMPs (Project Management Institute, 2004). The current version of the *PMBOK® Guide* is the fifth edition and was released in 2013 (PMI, 2013). The *PMBOK® Guide* is a subset of the Project Management Body of Knowledge.

ITIM identifies the IT investment stages, their characteristics and the levels of maturity. It also identifies criteria for IT investment oversight.

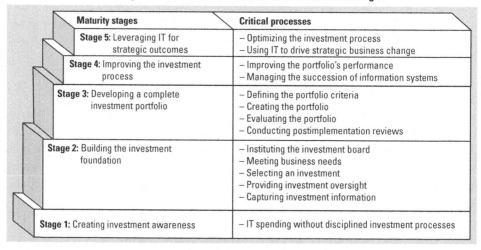

Maturity stages	Critical processes
Stage 5: Leveraging IT for strategic outcomes	– Optimizing the investment process – Using IT to drive strategic business change
Stage 4: Improving the investment process	– Improving the portfolio's performance – Managing the succession of information systems
Stage 3: Developing a complete investment portfolio	– Defining the portfolio criteria – Creating the portfolio – Evaluating the portfolio – Conducting postimplementation reviews
Stage 2: Building the investment foundation	– Instituting the investment board – Meeting business needs – Selecting an investment – Providing investment oversight – Capturing investment information
Stage 1: Creating investment awareness	– IT spending without disciplined investment processes

Figure 2.6 IT Investment Management (ITIM) Maturity Stages (source: General Accounting Office)

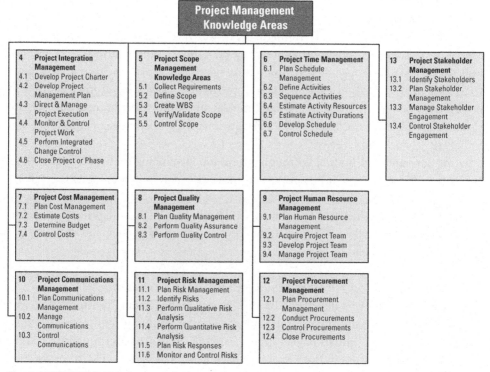

Project Management Knowledge Areas

4 Project Integration Management
4.1 Develop Project Charter
4.2 Develop Project Management Plan
4.3 Direct & Manage Project Execution
4.4 Monitor & Control Project Work
4.5 Perform Integrated Change Control
4.6 Close Project or Phase

5 Project Scope Management Knowledge Areas
5.1 Collect Requirements
5.2 Define Scope
5.3 Create WBS
5.4 Verify/Validate Scope
5.5 Control Scope

6 Project Time Management
6.1 Plan Schedule Management
6.2 Define Activities
6.3 Sequence Activities
6.4 Estimate Activity Resources
6.5 Estimate Activity Durations
6.6 Develop Schedule
6.7 Control Schedule

13 Project Stakeholder Management
13.1 Identify Stakeholders
13.2 Plan Stakeholder Management
13.3 Manage Stakeholder Engagement
13.4 Control Stakeholder Engagement

7 Project Cost Management
7.1 Plan Cost Management
7.2 Estimate Costs
7.3 Determine Budget
7.4 Control Costs

8 Project Quality Management
8.1 Plan Quality Management
8.2 Perform Quality Assurance
8.3 Perform Quality Control

9 Project Human Resource Management
9.1 Plan Human Resource Management
9.2 Acquire Project Team
9.3 Develop Project Team
9.4 Manage Project Team

10 Project Communications Management
10.1 Plan Communications Management
10.2 Manage Communications
10.3 Control Communications

11 Project Risk Management
11.1 Plan Risk Management
11.2 Identify Risks
11.3 Perform Qualitative Risk Analysis
11.4 Perform Quantitative Risk Analysis
11.5 Plan Risk Responses
11.6 Monitor and Control Risks

12 Project Procurement Management
12.1 Plan Procurement Management
12.2 Conduct Procurements
12.3 Control Procurements
12.4 Close Procurements

Figure 2.7 *PMBOK Guide*'s Process Groups and Knowledge Areas (Source: *PMBOK® Guide*, Fifth Edition)

Knowledge Areas	Project Management Process Groups				
	Initiating Process Group	Planning Process Group	Executing Process Group	Monitoring and Controlling Process Group	Closing Process Group
4. Project Integration Management	4.1 Develop Project Charter	4.2 Develop Project Management Plan	4.3 Direct and Manage Project Work	4.4 Monitor and Control Project Work 4.5 Perform Integrated Change Control	4.6 Close Project or Phase
5. Project Scope Management		5.1 Plan Scope Management 5.2 Collect Requirements 5.3 Define Scope 5.4 Create WBS		5.5 Validate Scope 5.6 Control Scope	
6. Project Time Management		6.1 Plan Schedule Management 6.2 Define Activities 6.3 Sequence Activities 6.4 Estimate Activity Resources 6.5 Estimate Activity Durations 6.6 Develop Schedule		6.7 Control Schedule	
7. Project Cost Management		7.1 Plan Cost Management 7.2 Estimate Costs 7.3 Determine Budget		7.4 Control Costs	
8. Project Quality Management		8.1 Plan Quality Management	8.2 Perform Quality Assurance	8.3 Control Quality	
9. Project Human Resource Management		9.1 Plan Human Resource Management	9.2 Acquire Project Team 9.3 Develop Project Team 9.4 Manage Project Team		
10. Project Communications Management		10.1 Plan Communications Management	10.3 Manage Communications	10.2 Control Communications	
11. Project Risk Management		11.1 Plan Risk Management 11.2 Identify Risks 11.3 Perform Qualititative Risk Analysis 11.4 Perform Quantitative Risk Analysis 11.5 Perform Risk Responses		11.6 Control Risks	
12. Project Procuremet Management		12.1 Plan Procurement Management	12.2 Conduct Procurement	12.3 Control Procurement	12.4 Close Procurement
13. Project Stakeholder Management	13.1 Identify Stakeholders	13.2 Plan Stakeholder Management	13.3 Manage Stakeholder Engagement	13.4 Control Stakeholder Engagement	

Figure 2.7 *PMBOK Guide's* Process Groups and Knowledge Areas (source: PMBOK® Guide, Fifth Edition) (continued)

The *PMBOK® Guide* approach is consistent with other management standards such as ISO 21500 for project management, ISO/IEC 9001:2008 for quality management and CMMI (Capability Maturity Model Integrated) from the Software Engineering Institute. The guide identifies 47 processes that fall into the five basic process groups previously mentioned. Each of the ten knowledge areas identifies the processes that are advised to be accomplished within its discipline in order to achieve effective management of a project. Each of these processes also falls into one of the five basic process groups, creating a matrix structure such that every process can be related to one knowledge area and one process group.

As more individuals are PMP certified, the overall project management effectiveness and maturity level should improve in any organization.

Figure 2.7 illustrates the ten knowledge areas of *PMBOK Guide*, their major components and how they relate to the five process areas.

2.4.4 OPM3® - Organizational Project Maturity Model

PMI's OPM3® is a guideline comprised of three key interlocking elements that are intended to improve the systematic management of projects, programs, and portfolios and closer align them with the strategic goals and objectives of an organization:

■ Knowledge Element – describes organization project management maturity, explains why it is important and how maturity can be recognized;
■ Assessment Element - identifies methods, processes and procedures that an organization can use to self-assess its PM maturity;
■ Improvement Element – provides a process for moving an organization from its current level of maturity to higher levels of maturity.

OPM3® was first developed in 1998. The second edition (2008) was recognized by the American National Standards Institute (ANSI) as an ANSI standard (ANSI/PMI 08-004-2008). The third edition was published in 2013.

OPM3 is not an organization certification framework, but represents a continuous improvement process. Figure 2.8 shows the OPM3 Framework and its elements.

2.4.5 PMMM® - Project Management Maturity Model

The PMMM® (Project Management Maturity Model) blends PMI's PMBOK® ten knowledge areas with the Software Engineering Institute's (SEI) CMMI®'s five (Capabilities Maturity Model Integrated) levels of maturity and enables organizations to self-asses their project management capabilities in the PMBOK areas at any given level. They can then focus on identified activities that would help to achieve continuous improvements up the PM maturity ladder.

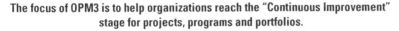

The focus of OPM3 is to help organizations reach the "Continuous Improvement" stage for projects, programs and portfolios.

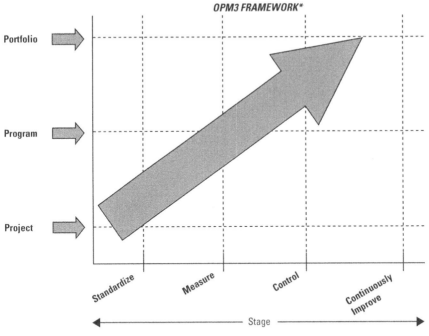

Figure 2.8 OPM3 Framework (source: PMI, 2013)

PMMM identifies a well-defined and easy to use roadmap to improve organizational PM maturity. PMMM enables an organization to assess its project management capabilities in the *PMBOK Guide* knowledge areas at any given level.

Figure 2.9 depicts the PMMM Framework. It can help organizations assess their current state of project management maturity and develop a roadmap for improvement.

2.4.6 CMMI® - Capability Maturity Model Integrated

CMM was developed by the Software Engineering Institute (at Carnegie Mellon University) based on a government grant and is a process improvement model, originally developed to manage software development efforts and provide a method for assessing the capability of contractors for the U.S. Government (Ahern, 2004).

CMMI, the successor to CMM, focuses on the disciplines of software, systems and hardware process improvements, providing a set of practices that address productivity, performance, costs, and overall customer satisfaction which is being applied to a broader range of initiatives (software development, systems engineering, product development, etc.). The current version 1.3 was released in 2010. An important change in the most recent version is the addition of Agile, recognizing the growth of fast track iterative development needs.

Maps PMI's 10 PMBOK Knowledge Areas with SEI's 5 Level Maturity Model*

Levels of Management Maturity	Level 1 Initial Process	Level 2 Structured Process and Standards	Level 3 Organizational Standards and Institutionalized Process	Level 4 Managed Process	Level 5 Optimized Process
Project Integration Management	No established practices standards, or Project Office. Work preformed in ad hoc fashion	Basic, documented processes for project planning and reporting. Management only involved on high-visibility projects.	Project integration efforts institutionalized with procedures and standards. Project Office beginning to integrate project data.	Processes/ standards utilized by all projects and integrated with other corporate processes/ systems. Decisions based on performance metrics.	Project integration improvement procedures utilized. Lessons learned regularly examined and used to improve documented processes.
Project Scope Management	General statement of business requirements. Little/no scope management or documentation. Management aware of key milestones only.	Basic scope management process in place. Scope management techniques regularly applied on larger, more visible projects.	Full project management process documented and utilized by most projects. Stakeholders actively participating in scope decisions.	Project management processes used on all projects. Projects managed and evaluated in light of other projects.	Effectiveness and efficiency metrics drive project scope decisions by appropriate levels of management. Focus on high utilization of value.
Project Time Management	No established planning or scheduling standards. Lack of documentation makes it difficult to achieve repeatable project success.	Basic processes exist but not required for planning and scheduling. Standard scheduling approaches utilized for large, visible projects.	Time management processes documented and utilized by most projects. Organization wide integration includes inter-project dependencies.	Time management utilizes historical data to forecast future performance. Management decisions based on efficiency and effectiveness metrics.	Improvement procedures utilized for time management processes. Lessons learned are examined and used to improve documented processes.
Project Cost Management	No established practices or standards. Cost process documentation is ad hoc and individual project teams follow informal practices.	Processes exist for cost estimating, reporting, and performance measurement. Cost management processes are used for large, visible projects.	Cost processes are organizational standard and utilized by most projects. Costs are fully integrated into project office resource library.	Cost planning and tracking integrated with Project Office, financial, and human resources systems. Standards tied to corporate processes.	Lessons learned improve documented processes. Management actively uses efficiency and effectiveness metrics for decision-making.
Project Quality Management	No established project quality practices or standards. Management is considering how they should define "quality".	Basic organizational project quality policy has been adopted. Management encourages quality policy application on large, visible projects.	Quality process is well documented and an organizational standard. Management involved in quality oversight for most projects.	All projects required to use quality planning standard processes. The Project Office coordinates quality standards and assurance.	The quality process includes guidelines for feeding improvements back into the process. Metrics are key to product quality decisions.

Figure 2.9 PM Solutions' Project Management Maturity Model (PMMM) (source: Ken Crawford, 2014 with modifications)

Levels of Management Maturity	Level 1 Initial Process	Level 2 Structured Process and Standards	Level 3 Organizational Standards and Institutionalized Process	Level 4 Managed Process	Level 5 Optimized Process
Project Human Resource Management	No repeatable process applied to planning and staffing projects. Project teams are ad hoc. Human resource time and cost is not measured.	Repeatable process in place that defines how to plan and manage the human resources. Resource tracking for highly visible projects only.	Most projects follow established resource management process. Professional development program establishes project management career path.	Resource forecasts used for project planning and prioritization. Project team performance measured and integrated with career development.	Process engages teams to document project lessons learned. Improvements are incorporated into human resources management process.
Project Communications Management	There is an ad hoc communications process in place whereby projects are expected to provide informal status to management.	Basic process is established. Large, highly visible projects follow the process and provide progress reporting for triple constraints.	Active involvement by management for project performance reviews. Most projects are executing a formal project communications plan.	Communications management plan is required for all projects. Com-munications plans are integrated into corporate communications structure.	An improvement process is in place to continuously improve project communications management. Lessons learned are captured and incorporated.
Project Risk Management	No established practices or standards in place. Documentation is minimal and results are not shared. Risk response is reactive.	Processes are documented and utilized for large projects. Management consistently involved with risks on large, visible projects.	Risk management processes are utilized for most projects. Metrics are used to support risk decisions at the project and the program levels.	Management is actively engaged in organization-wide risk management. Risk systems are fully integrated with time, cost, and resource systems.	Improvement processes are utilized to ensure projects are continually measured and managed against value-based performance metrics.
Project Procurement/ Vendor Management	No project procurement process in place. Methods are ad hoc. Contracts managed at a final delivery level.	Basic process documented for procurement of goods and services. Procurement process mostly utilized by large or highly visible projects.	Process an organizational standard and used by most projects. Project team and purchasing department integrated in the procurement process.	Make/buy decisions are made with an organizational perspective. Vendor is integrated into the organization's project management mechanisms	Procurement process reviewed periodically. On-going process improvements focus on procurement efficiency and effective metrics.
Project Stakeholder Management	No Stakeholder Involvement.	Basic stakeholder processes established.	Stakeholder Processes are standardized. Stakeholders and project team work closely together as a team.	Management sponsors a formal engagement model with roles, processes and metrics that are defined.	Managing stakeholders is a routine part of the business in a partnership environment

Figure 2.9 PM Solutions' Project Management Maturity Model (PMMM) (source: Ken Crawford, 2014 with modifications) (continued)

CMMI integrates traditionally separate organizational functions, sets process improvement goals and priorities, provides guidance for quality processes, and provides a point of reference for appraising current processes. The CMMI models are collections of best practices that help organizations to improve their processes:

- The CMMI for Acquisition (CMMI-ACQ) model provides guidance on managing the supply chain to meet the needs of the customer;
- The CMMI for Development (CMMI-DEV) model supports improvements in the effectiveness, efficiency, and quality of product and service development;
- The CMMI for Services (CMMI-SVC) model provides guidance on establishing, managing, and delivering services that meet the needs of customers and end users;
- The People CMM provides guidance on managing and developing the workforce.

The purpose of CMMI is to provide guidance for improving an organization's processes and its ability to manage the development, acquisition and maintenance of products and services. CMMI provides a structure that helps an organization to assess its organizational maturity and process area capability, establish priorities for improvement and guide the implementation of these improvements. CMMI process areas consist of five maturity levels as illustrated in Figure 2.10.

In addition, there are four process areas defined by CMMI, namely process management, project management, engineering and support. CMMI certification is performed by licensed third party independent organizations. The CMMI certification usually applies to an organization as a whole, or parts of an organization. Since obtaining the CMMI certification is not cheap, some organizations use the CMMI framework as a self-assessment tool for improving their processes, rather than apply for certification. Frequently, the companies that obtain certification are the service providers and outsourcing vendors in the IT space who use the certification for both continuous process improvement and market positioning purposes.

2.4.7 People Capability Maturity Model (P-CMM®)

The People Capability Maturity Model (P-CMM) framework maintained by the Carnegie Mellon's SEI helps organizations in developing their workforce maturity and in addressing their critical people issues. Based on the best practices in fields such as human resources, knowledge management and organizational development, P-CMM guides organizations in improving their processes for managing and developing their workforces. P-CMM helps organizations characterize the maturity of their workforce practices, establish a program of continuous workforce development, set priorities for improvement actions, integrate workforce development with process improvement, and establish a culture of excellence.

P-CMM provides a roadmap for implementing workforce practices that continuously improve the capability of an organization's workforce.

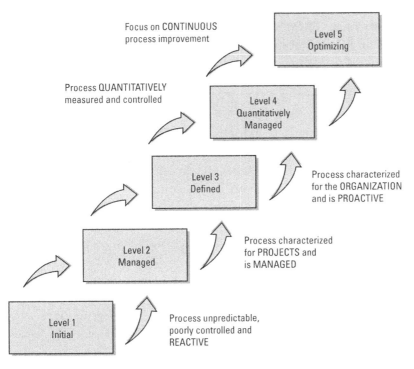

Figure 2.10 CMMI® process areas by maturity level

Level	Focus	Key Process Areas	Implications
5 Optimizing	Continuous Process Improvement	• Organizational Innovation and Deployment	Highest Quality / Lowest Risk
4 Quantitatively Managed	Quantitatively Managed and Measured	• Enterprise-Wide Process Adoption • Formalize and Measure Project Management and Lifecycle Management	Higher Quality / Lower Risk
3 Defined	Process Standardization	• Requirements Development • Technical Solution • Product/System/Software Processes and Lifecycle Documented • Verification • Validation • Organizational Process Focus	Medium Quality / Medium Risk
2 Managed	Basic Project Management Process Documentation	• Requirements Management • Project Planning • Project Monitoring and Control • Supplier Agreement Management	Low Quality / High Risk
1 Initial	Process is Informal and Adhoc	• None	Lowest Quality / Highest Risk

The philosophy underlying P-CMM is based on ten principles:
1. In mature organizations, workforce capability is directly related to business performance.
2. Workforce capability is a competitive issue and a source of strategic advantage.
3. Workforce capability must be defined in relation to the organization's strategic business objectives.
4. Knowledge-intense work shifts the focus from job elements to workforce competences.
5. Capability can be measured and improved at multiple levels, including individuals, workgroups (teams), workforce competences and the organization.
6. An organization should invest in improving the capability of those workforce competences that are critical to its core competence as a business.
7. Operational management is responsible for the capability of the workforce.
8. The improvement of workforce capability can be pursued as a process composed from proven practices and procedures.
9. The organization is responsible for providing improvement opportunities, while individuals are responsible for taking advantage of them.
10. Since technologies and organizational forms evolve rapidly, organizations must continually evolve their workforce practices and develop new workforce competences.

The P-CMM consists of five maturity levels that establish successive foundations for continuously improving individual competences, developing effective teams, motivating improved performance and shaping the workforce the organization needs to accomplish its future business plans. Each maturity level is a well-defined evolutionary plateau that institutionalizes new capabilities for developing the organization's workforce. By following the maturity framework, an organization can avoid introducing workforce practices that its employees are unprepared to implement effectively.

The five stages of the P-CMM framework are:
1. **P-CMM - Initial Level** – characteristics include; inconsistency in performing practices, unclear rules and responsibility, and emotionally detached workforce.
2. **P-CMM - Managed Level** – characteristics include: work overload, environmental distractions, unclear performance objectives or feedback, lack of relevant knowledge or skill, poor communication and low morale.
3. **P-CMM - Defined Level** – although basic workforce practices are performed, there is inconsistency in how these practices are performed across units and little synergy across the organization. The organization misses opportunities to standardize workforce practices because the common knowledge and skills needed for conducting its business activities have not been identified.
4. **P-CMM - Predictable Level** – the organization manages and exploits the capability created by its framework of workforce competences. The organization is now able to manage its capability and performance quantitatively. The organization is able to predict its capability for performing work because it can quantify the capability of

its workforce and of the competence-based processes they use in performing their assignments.

5. **P-CMM - Optimizing Level** – the entire organization is focused on continual improvement. These improvements are made to the capability of individuals and workgroups, to the performance of competence-based processes and to workforce practices and activities. Maturity Level 5 organizations treat change management as an ordinary business process to be performed in an orderly way on a regular basis.

The P-CMM includes practices in the areas of:
- Staffing (includes recruiting, selection and planning);
- Managing performance;
- Training;
- Compensation;
- Work environment;
- Career development;
- Organizational and individual competence;
- Mentoring and coaching;
- Team and culture development.

The ultimate motivation for the P-CMM is to improve the ability of organizations to attract, develop, motivate, organize and retain the talent needed to steadily improve systems and software and other organizational development capability (Curtis, Hefley and Miller, 2007).

2.4.8 PRINCE2® – Projects in Controlled Environments

PRINCE2, an enhancement to PRINCE, was developed by the CCTA (Central Computer Telecommunications Agency, part of the UK Government, now known as OGC – Office of Government Commerce). It has become a de facto standard used extensively by the UK Government and its vendors to manage IT projects and is widely utilized in the private and public sectors, both in the UK and internationally. Although PRINCE was originally developed for IT projects, the method has also been used on non-IT projects. (CCTA now OGC, 1998). PRINCE2 is now owned by AXELOS and the latest version was published in 2009 in two volumes:
- *Managing Successful Projects with PRINCE2;*
- *Directing Successful Projects with PRINCE2.*

Key features of PRINCE2:
- Focuses on business justification;
- Identifies a defined organization structure and processes for the project management team;
- Emphasis on dividing (work breakdown) the project into manageable and controllable stages;

- Flexibility to be applied at a level appropriate to the project;
- Utilizes a product-based planning approach;
- Used as a standard for UK government systems projects.

The set of PRINCE2 themes describes:
- How baselines for benefits, risks, scope, quality, cost and time are established (in the Business Case, Quality and Plans themes);
- How the project management team monitors and controls the work as the project progresses (in the Progress, Quality, Change and Risk themes).

PRINCE2 is a process-based approach for project management and provides a tailored and scalable method for the management of all types of projects. Each process is defined with its key inputs and outputs together with the specific objectives to be achieved and the activities to be implemented. Figure 2.11 illustrates the PRINCE2 process model.

PRINCE2 Process Model*

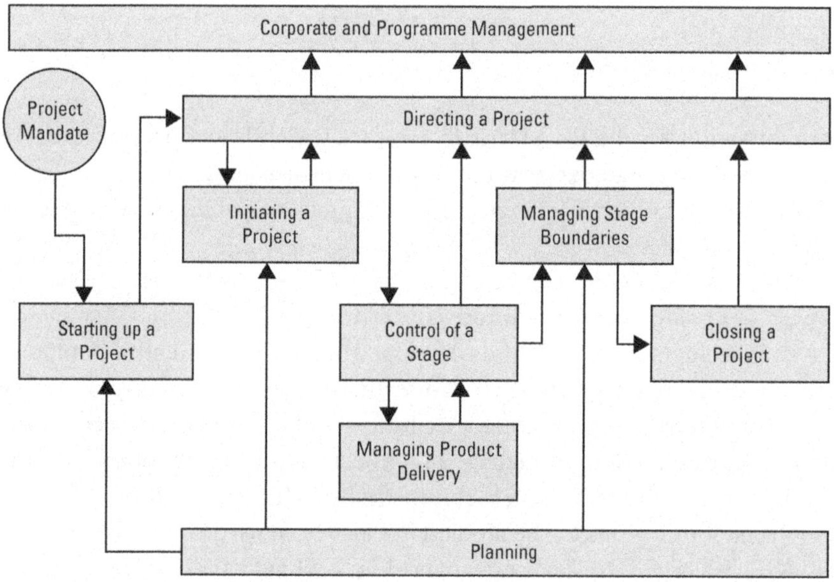

Figure 2.11 PRINCE2 process model

2.4.9 ISO 9000/9001:2008 – quality management system
ISO 9001 focuses on quality improvements and the reduction of defects and applies to an organization's overall operations. It strives to satisfy customers by continuing to improve the quality of an organization's process, operations and products.

ISO certification is performed by licensed independent third parties and is recognized globally. It usually applies to an entire organization for certification purposes, as opposed to certifications for individuals such as PMI's PMP, AXELOS' PRINCE2 and ITIL.

The ISO 9001 series is primarily concerned with 'quality management' and consists of four major generic business processes:
1. The management of resources.
2. The quality of the product.
3. The maintenance of quality records.
4. The requirement of continual improvement.

It also includes eight quality management principles: customer focus, leadership, involvement of people, process approach, system approach to management, continual improvement, a factual approach to decision-making and mutually beneficial supplier relationships. These principles can be used by senior management as a framework to guide their organizations towards improved performance.

ISO 9001 is under revision, with an updated version due by the end of 2015. The new version will follow a new, higher level structure to make it easier to use in conjunction with other management system standards, with increased importance given to risk.

2.4.10 Six Sigma®, Lean Six Sigma and Lean – quality, process and VOC (voice of the customer) improvement

Six Sigma has evolved from quality improvement practices (developed in Japan by Deming and others) and was popularized first by Motorola and then by GE in the United States. Six Sigma is an attitude and a frame of mind, not just a methodology. To be successful, the Six Sigma initiative and scope must be enterprise-wide.

Organizationally, Six Sigma represents a managerial methodology for continuous process and product improvement throughout an organization identified by process improvement techniques and measured quantitatively through process variance statistics. If performance is measured and graphically illustrated so that the most frequently occurring value is in the middle of the range and other probabilities tail off symmetrically in both directions, this is known as a normal distribution or a Bell Curve. The Sigma measure represents the standard deviation. Six Sigma means six times sigma, indicating 3.4 defects per million opportunities.

Six Sigma represents an individual versus an organizational certification. Individuals are certified as black belts (and other colored belts) in the public domain by the Association of Systems Quality (ASQ) and various corporations like Motorola and GE, who sponsor certification programs for their employees and in some cases, their vendors.

It is an organizational initiative or discipline that measures statistical variances and determines what pieces of a process must be improved by: measuring the inputs, efficiency and outputs; mapping them against requirements; identifying improvements areas and resetting benchmarks at higher levels. There are eight suggested steps required to achieve positive results (GE, 2002):

- Identify strategic business objectives;
- Identify core, key sub and enabling processes;
- Identify process owners;
- Identify key metrics and dashboards (KPIs, key performance indicators);
- Collect data from KPIs and analyze;
- Select process improvement criteria;
- Prioritize process improvement projects;
- Continual management of processes.

Some companies use either two to three processes as part of their Six Sigma process improvement methodology:

- Improved Control – *DMAIC*: Define, Measure, Analyze, Improve, Control. DMAIC is a structured problem solving roadmap and tools.
- Product & Process Redesign – *DMADV*: Define, Measure, Analyze, Re-Design, and Verify. DMADV is a data-driven quality strategy for designing product and process.
- DFFS (Design for Six Sigma) is an approach for the deployment of Six Sigma.

To be successful, Six Sigma requires a radical change in the way an organization works.

According to GE, customers and shareholders love it. It drives customer centricity or tends to optimize the voice of the customer (VOC), reduces costs and improves product, service and systems capability and performance.

Each Six Sigma project carried out within an organization follows a defined sequence of steps and has quantified project targets (such as cost reduction and/or profit increase).

An improvement over Six Sigma is Lean Six Sigma. Lean Six Sigma is a methodology that relies on a collaborative team effort to improve performance by systematically removing waste; combining Lean Manufacturing/Lean Enterprise and Six Sigma to eliminate eight kinds of waste: defects, overproduction, waiting, non-utilized talent, transportation, inventory, motion and downtime. The DMAIC toolkit for Lean Six Sigma comprises all the Lean and Six Sigma tools.

In recent years, the concept of Lean Manufacturing or Lean has become more popular. Lean is a management philosophy focused on reducing waste (e.g. overproduction, waiting time, transportation, processing, inventory, motion and scrap) initially in manufactured products and now spreading to other areas of a business. Lean is all about getting the right things, to the right place, at the right time, in the right quantity, while minimizing waste and being flexible and open to change. The seminal book *Lean Thinking* by James Womack and Daniel Jones, suggested five core concepts (Womack and Jones, 1996):

- Specify value in the eyes of the customer;
- Identify the value stream and eliminate waste;
- Make value flow at the pull of the customer;
- Involve and empower employees;
- Continuously improve in the pursuit of perfection.

2.4.11 Lean IT

Lean IT is associated with the development and management of Information Technology products and services. The central concern, applied in the context of IT, is the elimination of waste, where waste is work that adds no value to a product or service. Lean IT is not a well-defined framework. There is only one book so far that describes Lean IT in a formal manner: *Lean IT: Enabling and Sustaining Your Lean Transformation* by Steven Bell and Michael Orzen, published in 2011.

Lean IT focuses on maximizing customer value by minimizing waste. That means the focus is to achieve operational excellence through improved agility, service quality and process efficiency. It means building a customer and value-oriented culture in which employees engage in Lean IT processes. It also means involving all employees to continually improve services and preserve value with less effort, and optimizing IT operations and processes that support the most business critical applications and services.

There are many aspects of Lean IT within two primary dimensions:
- Outward-facing Lean IT: engaging information, information systems, and the IT organization in partnership with the business to continuously improve and innovate business processes and management systems.
- Inward-facing Lean IT: helping the IT organization achieve operational excellence, applying the principles and tools of continuous improvement to IT operations, services, software development, and projects.

These two dimensions are not separate but complementary. They serve the ultimate objective of Lean transformation: creating value for the enterprise and its customers. Lean IT is based on enterprise Lean principles, laying a solid foundation at the base. The following three foundation elements support a strong social structure; constancy of purpose, respect for people and pursuit of perfection.

The principal focus of Lean IT is problem solving for the primary purpose of delivering value to the customer, achieved by the systematic elimination of waste throughout the value stream. A five-step thought process for implementing Lean thinking refers to:
1. Specify value from the standpoint of the end customer.
2. Identify all the steps in the value stream, eliminating whenever possible those steps that do not create value.
3. Make the value-creating steps occur in tight sequence.

4. As flow is introduced, let customers pull value from the next upstream activity.
5. As value is specified, value streams are identified, wasted steps are removed, and flow and pull are introduced. Begin the process again and continue it until a state of perfection is reached in which perfect value is created with no waste.

2.4.12 ISO/IEC 20000 – ITSM (IT service management)

The standard was originally developed and published in 2000 as BS15000 by a committee of the British Standards Institute, which comprised IT service managers from vendor and user groups, including the itSMF-I, OGC and others. Version 2 of the standard was developed in 2002. Today, ISO/IEC 20000:2011 is a service management system (SMS) standard, which specifies requirements for the service provider to plan, establish, implement, operate, monitor, review, maintain and improve an SMS. This standard consists of several parts. ISO/IEC 20000 helps organizations benchmark how they deliver managed services, measure service levels and assess their performance. It is broadly aligned with, and draws strongly on, ITIL.

ISO/IEC 20000 applies to IT service management users and providers. The standard comprises two parts:
- Part 1 – Specification: this is the documented requirements that an organization must comply with in order to achieve formal certification for ISO/IEC 20000;
- Part 2 – Code of Practice: expansion and explanation of the requirements in Part 1.

Both parts share a common structure including the following parts:
- Scope;
- Terms and definitions;
- Requirements for a management system;
- Planning and implementing service management;
- Planning and implementing new or changed services;
- Service delivery processes;
- Relationship processes;
- Resolution processes;
- Control processes;
- Release processes.

There are five key process areas, these being: service delivery, relationship management, resolution management, control and release.

The service delivery process consists of: service level management, service reporting, service continuity and availability management, budgeting and accounting for IT services, capacity management and information security management. The relationship processes are: business relationship management and supplier management. The resolution processes are: incident management and problem management. The control processes are: configuration management and change management. The release process is defined as a standalone process.

The ISO/IEC 20000 standard is concerned with IT service management and primarily represents a measure of process conformance to be achieved by an organization. The relationship between ISO/IEC 20000 and ITIL is synergistic, where the standard addresses the questions relating to IT service management as to the 'why and what'. ITIL addresses the question of 'how' by providing the process definitions and additional details. Therefore, ITIL is aligned with ISO/IEC 20000. ISO 20000 uses the process-based approach of other management system standards such ISO 27001:2005, ISO 9001:2008 and ISO 14001:2004, including the Plan-Do-Check-Act (PDCA) cycle and requirements for continual improvement. More information on IT service management and ITIL is provided in Chapter 6.

2.4.13 ITIL® – IT Infrastructure Library

IT service management and delivery is about maximizing the ability of IT to provide services that are cost effective and meet or exceed the needs and expectations of the business to:
- Reduce the costs of operations;
- Improve service quality;
- Improve customer satisfaction;
- Improve compliance.

The ITIL framework provides an effective foundation for higher quality IT service management and delivery processes and disciplines. It aligns with ISO/IEC 20000. It was owned and maintained by OGC (Office of Government Commerce in the UK) and was developed in recognition of the increasing dependence of organizations on IT services to support organizational needs. ITIL has been owned by AXELOS since 2013.

ITIL v2 consisted of twelve repeatable, consistent documented processes for improving IT service management and delivery segmented into two main areas:
- Service Delivery Processes – focus on management control to improve the quality, stability and IT cost structure;
- Service Support Processes – focus on operational aspects of IT to detect and correct problems, and ensure appropriate change, configuration and release management, authorization and documentation.

ITIL primarily focuses on IT operations and infrastructure services. It represents a standardized approach that should be applied consistently, but flexibly with the use of common terminology:
- Focuses on IT services for business/IT alignment and value propositions;
- Standardization of processes and key performance indicators;
- Provides the quality assurance foundation for ISO 9001;
- Industry supported software and tools;
- Supports Sarbanes-Oxley;
- ITIL aligns with the ISO standard (ISO/IEC 20000).

Figure 2.12 provides an overview of the ITIL®.

The latest version of ITIL is ITIL 2011® Edition and is more strategic and IT governance oriented. It uses a lifecycle approach to ITIL. It also recognizes that the practice of IT has matured and shifts its emphasis from enhancing the performance of IT processes to serving the customer. The ITIL 2011® Edition best practices are described in five core guides that map the entire ITIL Service Lifecycle:

- Service Strategy – understanding who the IT customers are, the service offerings to meet their needs, and the IT capabilities and resource to deliver the services;
- Service Design – assures that new and changed services are designed effectively to meet customer expectations, including the technology, architecture and processes that will be required;
- Service Transition – the service design is built, tested and moved into production to assure that the business customer can achieve the desired value;
- Service Operation – delivers the service on an ongoing basis, including managing disruptions to service and supporting end-users;
- Continual Service Improvement – measures and improves the service levels, the technology and the efficiency and effectiveness or processes. It incorporates many of the same concepts articulated in the Deming Cycle of Plan-Do-Check-Act (PDCA).

More details on ITIL 2011® Edition are provided in Chapter 6. Figure 2.13 depicts ITIL® 2011 Edition - Lifecycle Phases and Processes.

2.4.14 COBIT® – Control Objectives for Information and Related Technology

COBIT® defines high level business control and audit objectives for the IT processes linked to business objectives, and supports these with detailed control objectives to provide management assurance and/or advice for improvement. The control objectives are further supported by audit guidelines which enable auditors and managers to review specific IT processes to help assure management where controls are sufficient or to recommend changes.

COBIT®5 is about linking business goals to IT objectives (note the linkage here from vision to mission to goals to objectives). COBIT 5 (launched April 2012) provides metrics and maturity models to measure whether or not the IT organization has achieved its objectives.

COBIT® is owned and supported by ISACA. It was released in 1996; the current Version 5.0 (April 2012) brings together COBIT 4.1, Val IT 2.0 and Risk IT frameworks.

The COBIT® 5 principles and enablers are generic and useful for enterprises of all sizes. COBIT® 5 provides a set of 36 governance and management processes within the

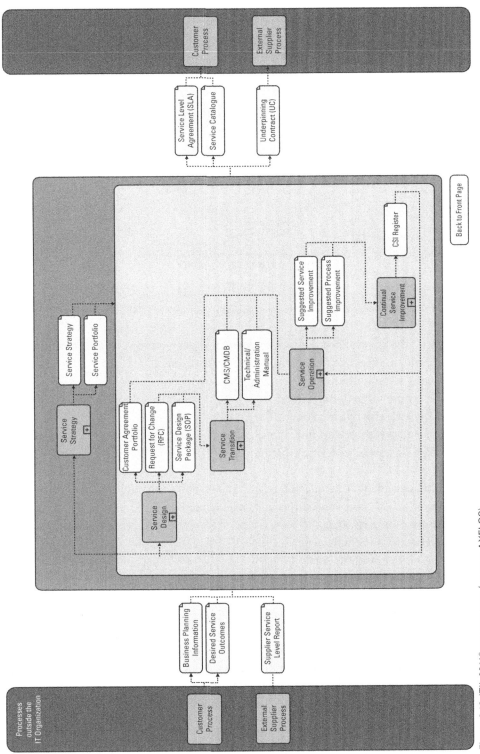

Figure 2.12 ITIL 2011® process map (source: AXELOS)

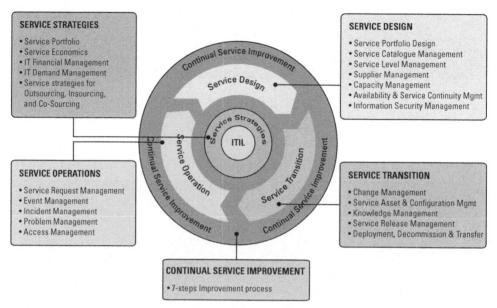

Figure 2.13 ITIL 2011® Edition lifecycle phases and processes (source: AXELOS)

framework. The governance domain contains five governance processes; within each process, evaluate, direct, and monitor practices are defined:

- EDM1: set and maintain the governance framework;
- EDM2: ensure value optimization;
- EDM3: ensure risk optimization;
- EDM4: ensure resource optimization;
- EDM5: ensure stakeholder transparency.

The four management domains, in line with the responsibility areas of plan, build, run, and monitor (PBRM) provide end-to-end coverage of IT:

- Align, plan, and organize;
- Build, acquire, and implement;
- Deliver, service, and support;
- Monitor, evaluate, and assess.

An analysis of the four management domains of COBIT 5 illustrates its direct relationship with ITIL:

1. The align, plan, and organize domain relates to the service strategy and design phases.
2. The build, acquire, and implement domain relates to the service transition phase.
3. The deliver, service, and support domain relates to the service operation phase.
4. And finally, the monitor, evaluate, and assess domain relates to the continual service improvement phase.

All aspects of COBIT 5 are in line with the responsibility areas of plan, build, run and monitor. In other words, COBIT 5 follows the PDCA cycle of Plan, Do, Check, and Act.

COBIT has been positioned at a high level, and has been aligned and harmonized with other, more detailed, IT standards and proven practices such as COSO, ITIL, ISO 27000, CMMI, TOGAF and *PMBOK Guide*. COBIT 5 acts as an integrator of these different guidance materials, summarizing key objectives under one umbrella framework that links the proven practice models with governance and business requirements.

COBIT does not provide detailed policies and procedures on how to develop the content or what content needs to be included in the processes on the checklist. That is the responsibility of each organization. Chapters 4 through 9 provide more details on the content of 'how to's' for each of the major components of IT governance based on a blend of best practices.

Figures 2.14 & 2.15 illustrate the key areas that the reference model provides of the four COBIT domains and their related IT processes.

COBIT® Management and Governance Areas

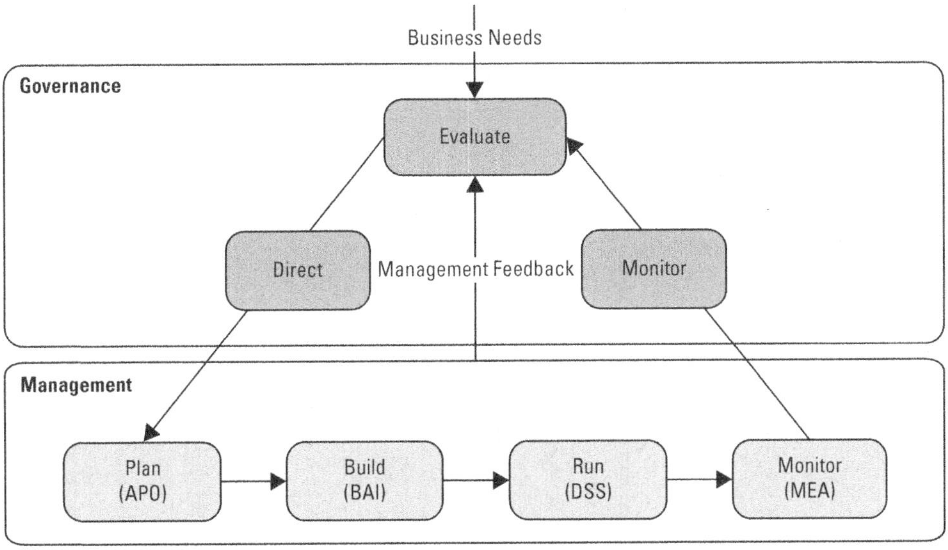

Figure 2.14 COBIT® 5 – governance and management of key areas (source: ISACA, 2012)

2.4.15 Val IT domains and processes

The Val IT framework is a comprehensive and pragmatic organizing framework that enables the creation of business value from IT-enabled investments. Val IT is integrated in CoBIT®5. It provides a set of practical governance principles, processes, practices and supporting guidelines that help boards, executive management teams and other enterprise leaders to optimize the value from IT investments.

Val IT takes the enterprise governance view. It helps executives focus on two of four fundamental IT governance-related questions. 'Are we doing the right things?' (the

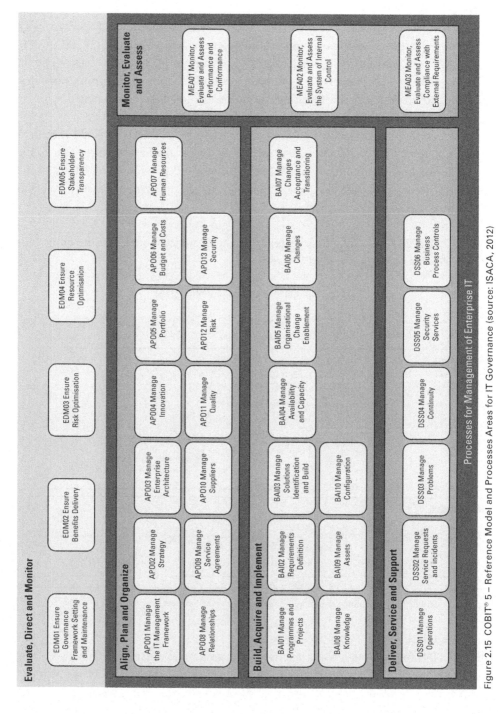

Figure 2.15 COBIT® 5 – Reference Model and Processes Areas for IT Governance (source: ISACA, 2012)

strategic question) and 'Are we getting the benefits?' (the value question). COBIT®, on the other hand, takes the IT view, helping executives focus on answering the questions 'Are we doing them the right way?' (the architecture question) and 'Are we getting them done well?' (the delivery question) (ITGI, 2008).

ITGI regards value delivery as one of the five focus areas of IT governance. In addition to value delivery, the other four areas are strategic alignment, risk management, resource management, and performance management. Value delivery depends on the other focus areas in that it requires strategic alignment, is enabled by risk management and resource management, and – together with the other areas – is monitored by performance measurement.

The relationship between the Val IT domains and their processes is illustrated in Figure 2.16.

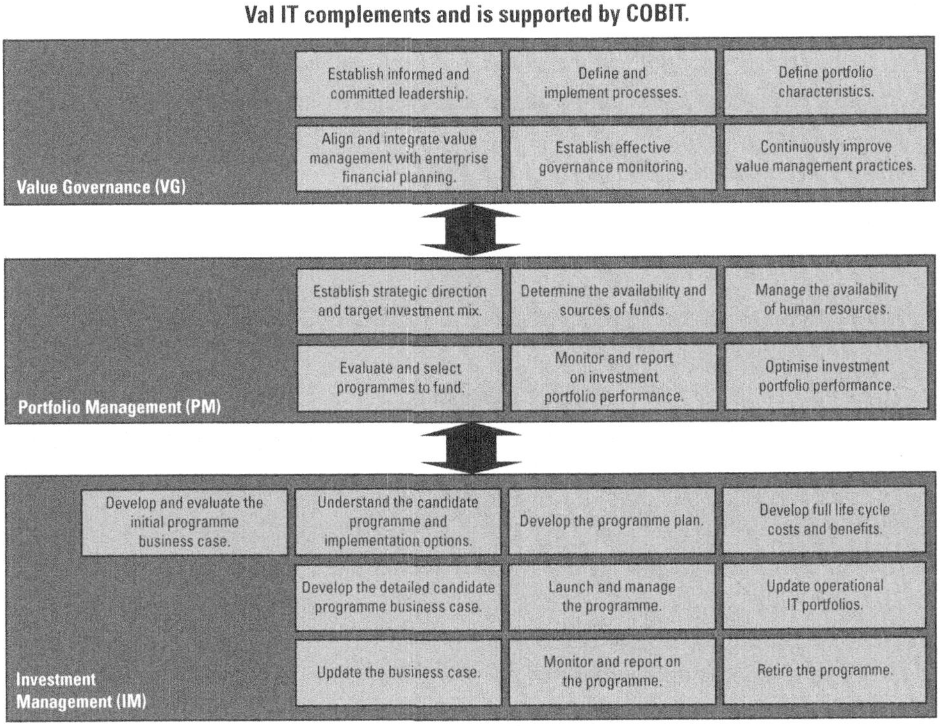

Figure 2.16 Val IT domains and processes (source: ISACA, 2008)

2.4.16 ISO/IEC 27000 - IT security management

ISO/IEC 27000 represents a series of information security management standards developed by ISO and IEC and published over the past few years. The family of ISO/IEC 27000 standards is broad in scope and is adaptable to any organization.

The purpose of ISO/IEC 27001 is to help organizations establish and maintain an information security management system (ISMS). It is designed to be used for certification purposes.

ISO 27001 is a specification that sets out specific requirements, all of which must be followed, and against which an organization's Information Security Management

System (ISMS) can be audited and certified. All the other standards in the ISO 27000 series are codes of practice; these provide non-mandatory best practice guidelines which organizations may follow, in whole or in part, at their own discretion. Key concepts that govern the standards are:

- Organizations are encouraged to assess their own information security risks;
- Organizations should implement appropriate information security controls according to their needs;
- Guidance should be taken from the relevant standards;
- Organizations should continually assess changes in the threats and risks to information security issues.

ISO/IEC 27001 suggests that an organization structures every process using the Plan-Do-Check-Act (PDCA) model. This means that every process should be:

- Planned (Plan);
- Implemented, operated, and maintained (Do);
- Monitored, measured, audited, and reviewed (Check);
- Improved (Act).

The PDCA model is woven into every aspect of the ISO/IEC 27001 standard.

2.4.17 ISO 38500 – corporate governance of Information technology

ISO/IEC 38500:2008 provides guiding principles for directors of organizations (including owners, board members, directors, partners, senior executives, or similar) on the effective, efficient, and acceptable use of IT within their organizations.

ISO/IEC 38500:2008 is owned by the International Standards Organization (ISO) and the International Electro-technical Commission (IEC). The standard helps to clarify IT governance from the top down by describing it as the means through which directors can demonstrate to all stakeholders and compliance bodies their effective stewardship over IT resources by ensuring that an appropriate governance and security framework exists for all IT activities as a result of covering the following principles:

- Responsibility – employees know their responsibilities both in terms of demand and supply of IT and have the authority to meet them;
- Strategy – business strategies should be aligned with IT possibilities, and all IT within an organization should support the business strategies;
- Acquisition – all IT investments must be made on the basis of a business case with regular monitoring in place to assess whether the assumptions still hold;
- Performance – the performance of IT systems should lead to business benefits and therefore it is necessary that IT supports the business effectively;
- Conformance – IT systems should help to ensure that business processes comply with legislation and regulations; IT itself must also comply with legal requirements and agreed internal rules;

■ Human behavior – IT policies, practices and decisions respect human behavior and acknowledge the needs of all the people in the process.

The standard consists of three parts: scope, framework and guidance, and helps to define accountability.

2.4.18 eSCM® – the eSourcing capability models for service providers and client organizations

The IT Services Qualification Center (ITSqc) (spin-off from Carnegie Mellon University) created two capability models and qualification methods to improve sourcing relationships in the Internet-enabled economy. ITSqc developed the eSourcing Capability Model for both service providers (eSCM-SP V2, 2009) and client organizations (eSCM-CL V1, 2010).

The eSCM-SP model represents an approach to certifying service provider organizations. The purpose of the service provider model (Hyder, 2002, 2014) is as follows:
■ To help IT-enabled sourcing service providers appraise and improve their ability to provide high quality sourcing services;
■ To give them a way to differentiate themselves from the competition;
■ To enable prospective clients to evaluate service providers based on their eSCM-SP level of certification and practice satisfaction profile.

The purpose of the eSCM-CL client organization model (Hefley, 2006, 2014) is:
■ To give client organizations guidance that will help them improve their capability across the sourcing lifecycle;
■ To provide client organizations with an objective means of evaluating their sourcing capability and maturity.

eSCM-SP – structure for service providers
The eSCM-SP model has three purposes: to give service providers guidance that will help them improve their capability across the sourcing lifecycle; to provide clients with an objective means of evaluating the capability of service providers; and to offer service providers a standard to use when differentiating themselves from competitors. It consists of 84 practices that address the capabilities needed by IT-enabled service providers. Each practice has three dimensions:
■ Sourcing Lifecycle:
  • Ongoing (spans entire lifecycle);
  • Initiation (negotiation, agreement, deployment);
  • Delivery (delivery of service);
  • Completion (transferring responsibility back to client).
■ Capability Area – there are ten ongoing capability areas (knowledge management, people management, performance management, relationship management, technology

management, threat management, service transfer, contracting, service design and development and service delivery).

■ Capability Level – the third dimension of the eSCM-SP is capability levels. The five capability levels (similar but not identical to the CMMI maturity levels) describe a continuous improvement path that clients should expect service providers to achieve and they are:

- Level 1 – Providing services;
- Level 2 – Consistently meeting requirements;
- Level 3 – Managing organizational performance;
- Level 4 – Proactively enhancing value;
- Level 5 – Sustaining excellence.

eSCM-CL - structure for client organizations

The eSCM-CL model has two purposes: to give client organizations guidance that will help them improve their capability across the sourcing lifecycle, and to provide these organizations with an objective means of evaluating their sourcing capability.

It consists of 95 practices that address the capabilities needed by IT service providers. Each practice has three dimensions: sourcing lifecycle (with five phases - ongoing, analysis, initiation, delivery and completion), capability areas (these include nine ongoing capability areas such as sourcing strategy management, governance management, relationship management, etc.) and eight are temporal and associated with a single phase of the sourcing lifecycle such as in the analysis phases.

There are two capability areas (sourcing opportunity and sourcing approach) and five capability levels (performing sourcing, consistently managing sourcing, managing organizational sourcing performance, proactively enhancing value and sustaining excellence).

Uses of eSCM:

The uses of the eSCM frameworks for customers and service providers include:

■ Customers of service providers:
- Use eSCM evaluations to determine provider capabilities;
- Evaluate multiple potential providers;
- Reduce risks in sourcing relationships.

■ Service providers:
- Systematically assess their existing capabilities and implement improvement efforts;
- Use results to set priorities for improvement efforts;
- Implement in conjunction with other quality initiatives;
- Improve their relationships with clients;
- Demonstrate their capability to clients through certification,

2.4.19 OPBOK® (Outsourcing Professional Body of Knowledge)

The International Association of Outsourcing Professionals (IAOP) is a global standard-setting organization and advocate for the outsourcing profession. The IAOP developed the Outsourcing Professional Body of Knowledge (OPBOK) as the generally accepted set of knowledge and best practices applicable to the successful design, implementation and management of outsourcing contracts. The current version is OPBOK version 10 (2014). It provides:

- A framework for understanding what outsourcing is and how it fits within contemporary business operations;
- The knowledge and practice areas generally accepted as critical to outsourcing success;
- A glossary of terms commonly used within the field.

There are ten knowledge areas and standards in OPBOK as follows:
1. Defining and communicating outsourcing as a management practice.
2. Developing and managing an organization's end-to-end process for outsourcing.
3. Integrating outsourcing into an organization's business strategy and operations.
4. Creating, leading and sustaining high performance outsourcing project teams.
5. Developing and communicating outsourcing business requirements.
6. Selecting outsourcing service providers.
7. Developing the outsourcing financial case and pricing.
8. Negotiating and contracting for outsourcing.
9. Managing the transition to an outsourced environment.
10. Outsourcing governance.

It reflects major updates from IAOP of the commonly accepted practices and skills required to ensure outsourcing success. It is the basis for IAOP's Certified Outsourcing Professional (COP)® qualification and certification programs.

2.4.20 ISO 21500 – guidance on project management

ISO 21500 provides a comprehensive and structured set of concepts and processes that are considered to form good practice in project management.

ISO 21500 provides guidance for project management and can be used by any type of organization and for any type of project. ISO 21500 was developed on the basis of inputs from hundreds of project management experts, standards development committees from more than thirty countries and project management associations like IPMA (International Project Management Association) and PMI (Project Management Institute). It was published in September 2012.

ISO 21500 is the first of a family of ISO standards for the portfolio, program and project management environment currently under development. This will be based on an overall framework that defines project, program and portfolio management (PPP), including the governance and terminology.

The guideline identifies 39 processes that fall into five basic process groups and ten subject groups that cover the typical managerial aspects for most projects. The five process groups are Initiating, Planning, Implementing, Controlling and Closing. The ten subject groups are Integration, Stakeholder, Scope, Resource, Time, Cost, Risk, Quality, Procurement and Communication.

Each of the ten subject groups contains the processes that need to be accomplished within its discipline in order to achieve effective management of a project. Each of these processes also falls into one of the five basic process groups, creating a matrix structure such that every process can be related to one subject group and one process group.

2.4.21 ISO 31000 – standard for risk management

ISO 31000:2009 comprises principles, a framework and a process for the management of risk that is applicable to any type of organization. ISO 31000:2009 provides guidance on the implementation of risk management. It was first published as a standard in November 2009 and is owned by the International Standards Organization (ISO). The ISO 31000 family includes:

- ISO 31000:2009 – Principles and Guidelines on Implementation;
- ISO/IEC 31010:2009 – Risk Management – Risk Assessment Techniques;
- ISO Guide 73:2009 – Risk Management – Vocabulary.

ISO 31000 provides generic guidelines for the design, implementation and maintenance of risk management processes throughout an organization. The scope of this approach to risk management is to enable all strategic, management and operational tasks of an organization throughout projects, functions, and processes to be aligned to a common set of risk management objectives.

It comprises three building blocks. The first of these building blocks, the Risk Management Infrastructure, states that risk management should contain the following principles:

- Creates value;
- Integral part of organizational processes;
- Part of decision-making;
- Explicitly addresses uncertainty;
- Systematic, structured and timely;
- Based on the best available information;
- Tailored to the organization;
- Takes human and cultural factors into account;
- Transparent and inclusive;
- Dynamic, iterative and responsive to change;
- Facilitates continual improvement of the organization.

The second building block, the Risk Management Framework, is about creating the right risk framework through management commitment. Once commitment is established, there is a cycle of actions that includes the following four steps:
1. Design.
2. Implementation.
3. Monitoring and review.
4. Continual improvement.

The third building block, the Risk Management Process, was originally adopted from the standard AS/NZS 4360:2004, which assures that communication and monitoring is done throughout the process.

2.4.22 Baldrige National Quality Award

This award is named after Malcolm Baldrige who was US Secretary of Commerce from 1981 until 1987. Baldrige was a proponent of quality management as a key to US prosperity and long-term strength. In recognition of his contributions, Congress named the award in his honor. The Baldrige Award is given by the President of the United States to businesses - manufacturing and service, small and large - and to education, health care and nonprofit organizations that apply and are judged to be outstanding in seven areas: leadership; strategic planning; customer and market focus; measurement, analysis, and knowledge management; human resource focus; process management; and results.

The US Congress established the award program in 1987 to recognize U.S. organizations for their achievements in quality and performance and to raise awareness about the importance of quality and performance excellence as a competitive edge. Three awards may be given annually in each of these categories: manufacturing, service, small business, education, health care and nonprofit. The U.S. Commerce Department's National Institute of Standards and Technology (NIST) manages the Baldrige National Quality Program in close cooperation with the private sector.

The Baldrige performance excellence criteria are applicable to any organization. Seven categories make up the award criteria:
1. Leadership - examines how senior executives guide the organization and how the organization addresses its responsibilities to the public and practices good citizenship.
2. Strategic planning - examines how the organization sets strategic directions and how it determines key action plans.
3. Customer and market focus - examines how the organization determines requirements and expectations of customers and markets; builds relationships with customers; and acquires, satisfies, and retains customers.
4. Measurement, analysis, and knowledge management - examines the management, effective use, analysis, and improvement of data and information to support key organization processes and the organization's performance management system.

5. Human resource focus - examines how the organization enables its workforce to develop its full potential and how the workforce is aligned with the organization's objectives.
6. Process management - examines aspects of how key production/delivery and support processes are designed, managed, and improved.
7. Business results - examines the organization's performance and improvement in its key business areas: customer satisfaction, financial and marketplace performance, human resources, supplier and partner performance, operational performance, governance and social responsibility. The category also examines how the organization performs relative to competitors.

For many organizations, using the criteria resulted in better employee relations, higher productivity, greater customer satisfaction, increased market share and improved profitability. According to a report by the Conference Board, a business membership organization, "A majority of large U.S. firms have used the criteria of the Malcolm Baldrige National Quality Award for self-improvement, and the evidence suggests a long-term link between use of the Baldrige criteria and improved business performance."

2.4.23 AIM – Amsterdam Information Management Model

The Amsterdam Information management Model (AIM) is a reinterpretation of the Strategic Alignment Model originally developed by John Henderson and N. (Venkat) Venkatraman and applied to IT by A. Abcouwer, et al. AIM is a model for interrelating the different components of information management. It is used in the area of business-IT alignment and sourcing. It can be useful to consider IT governance issues as well. It is a high-level view of the entire field of information management; its main application is in the analysis of organizational and responsibility issues.

The framework is used to support strategic discussions in the three different ways:
1. **Descriptive, orientation** – the framework offers a map of the entire information management domain, to be used for positioning specific information management issues that are being discussed in the organization.
2. **Specification, design** – the framework is used to re-organize the information management organization, e.g. specifying the role of the Chief Information Officer (CIO), or determining the responsibility of an outsourcing service provider.
3. **Prescriptive, normative** – the map is used as a diagnostic instrument to find gaps in an organization's information management, specifically aimed at identifying missing interrelationships between the various components of the framework.

The framework primarily provides a reference base for the positioning of information management issues at organization and/or business unit levels. From a normative point of view, the framework states that each of the nine areas and their mutual relations should be addressed. The central axes of the framework are core to information management.

The strength of the AIM is that it is very helpful in discussing information management at an enterprise level, illustrating how different aspects of an organization interrelate.

The weakness of the AIM is that it is too conceptual and does not provide specific solutions and requires more detailed frameworks, to support any implementation. Figure 2.17 represents the framework.

The framework extends the Strategic Alignment Model developed by Henderson and Venkatraman from a 2×2 matrix to a 3×3 matrix focusing on interactions and relations of strategy, structure and operations represented by the business, information/communications and technology components.

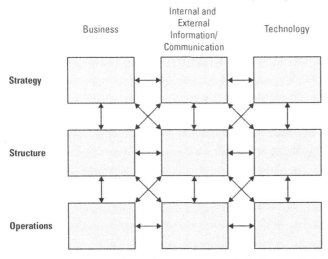

Figure 2.17 The Amsterdam Information Management Model (source: University of Amsterdam)

2.4.24 The balanced scorecard
The balanced scorecard system, developed by Robert Kaplan and David Norton in 1992, is a management system that provides a clear prescription as to what companies should 'measure' to clarify their vision and strategy and translate these into actions with respect to four areas:
1. Financial – to succeed financially, how should we appear to our customer and what should we measure? These are primarily historic performance measures.
2. Customer – this area focuses on customer satisfaction, loyalty, retention and exceptional customer service. These metrics can be used as future predictors of success by monitoring the level of customer satisfaction.
3. Business process – this area focuses on business processes and how they can be improved. The original balanced scorecard concentrated on internal processes. This has since been modified to include both internal and external processes based on the growing network of interdependent suppliers, providers and customers. This area can also be used as part of a corporate report card for future success based on the improvements in quality, lower defect rates, increasing process cycle times, deployment of new technology and systems and others.

4. Learning and growth – addresses the issues and actions regarding the managing change, growth, innovation and organizational learning. This area can also be used as an indicator of future success by comparing such areas as research and development and people development against best practice organizations.

To translate their vision and plans into actions for each of the above areas, organizations should identify the following elements: objectives, measures, targets, initiatives and accountability. It is important to note that all of the balanced scorecard areas must be used to evaluate the current performance and to project the future performance of organization. More information on the balanced scorecard is provided in Chapter 8.

2.4.25 Enterprise technology architecture domains

As identified in Chapter 1, enterprise technology architecture (ETA) is a vital complement of IT governance. Figure 2.18 identifies twelve ETA domains ranging from application development architecture and tools, network architecture, web architecture, data architecture, hardware architecture and other domains.

Client Platform	ETA Strategy and Standards	Application Development
Server Platforms	Network Infrastructure	Business Components
System Management	Middleware	Collaboration
Security	Information Management	Web Management

Figure 2.18 Enterprise technology architecture

The architecture domains are used to help define a consistent approach to developing each of the domains and their respective approval processes, tools, acceptable or preferred vendors and related areas.

2.4.26 ArchiMate®

ArchiMate® is an open and independent modeling language for enterprise architecture that is supported by different tool vendors and consulting firms.

Developed by the members of The Open Group, ArchiMate® 2.1 was released in December 2013 and is aligned with TOGAF®, see Section 2.4.27. As a result, enterprise architects using the language can improve the way key business and IT stakeholders collaborate and adapt to change.

The standard contains the formal definition of ArchiMate as a visual design language, together with concepts for specifying inter-related architectures, and specific viewpoints for typical stakeholders. The standard also includes a chapter addressing considerations regarding language extensions.

The contents of the standard include the following:
- The overall modeling framework that ArchiMate uses;
- The structure of the modeling language;
- A detailed breakdown of the constituent elements of the modeling framework covering the three layers (business/application/technology), cross-layer dependencies and alignment, and relationships within the framework;
- Architectural viewpoints, including a set of standard viewpoints;
- Optional extensions to the framework;
- Commentary around future direction of the specification;
- Notation overviews and summaries.

ArchiMate 2.1 improves collaboration through clearer understanding across multiple functions, including business executives, enterprise architects, systems analysts, software engineers, business process consultants, and infrastructure engineers. The standard enables the creation of fully integrated models of an organization's enterprise architecture, the motivation behind it, and the projects and migration paths to implement it. ArchiMate already follows terms defined in the TOGAF framework, and Version 2.1 of the specification enables modeling throughout the TOGAF Architecture Development Method (ADM) cycle.

2.4.27 TOGAF®

TOGAF® is an enterprise architecture method and framework used by organizations to improve business efficiency. It is a reliable enterprise architecture standard, ensuring consistent standards, methods, and communication among enterprise architecture professionals.

TOGAF has continuously evolved and improved by the members of The Open Group since it was first published by them in 1995. The Open Group is a global consortium that enables the achievement of business objectives through IT standards. With more than 400 member organizations, the diverse membership spans all sectors of the IT community – customers, systems and solutions suppliers, tool vendors, integrators and consultants, as well as academics and researchers. Version 9.1 (2009) is the current version.

The standard is divided into seven parts:
- Part I (Introduction): this part provides a high-level introduction to the key concepts of enterprise architecture and in particular the TOGAF approach. It contains the definitions of terms used throughout TOGAF and release notes detailing the changes between this version and the previous version of TOGAF.
- Part II (Architecture Development Method): this is the core of TOGAF. It describes the TOGAF Architecture Development Method (ADM), a step-by-step approach to developing an enterprise architecture.

- Part III (ADM Guidelines & Techniques): this part contains a collection of guidelines and techniques available for use in applying TOGAF and the TOGAF ADM.
- Part IV (Architecture Content Framework): this part describes the TOGAF content framework, including a structured meta-model for architectural artifacts, the use of reusable architecture building blocks, and an overview of typical architecture deliverables.
- Part V (Enterprise Continuum & Tools): this part discusses appropriate taxonomies and tools to categorize and store the outputs of architecture activity within an enterprise.
- Part VI (TOGAF Reference Models): this part provides a selection of architectural reference models, which includes the TOGAF Foundation Architecture and the Integrated Information Infrastructure Reference Model (III-RM).
- Part VII (Architecture Capability Framework): this part discusses the organization, processes, skills, roles, and responsibilities required to establish and operate an architecture function within an enterprise.

TOGAF can be used for developing a broad range of different enterprise architectures. TOGAF covers the development of four related types of architecture. These four types of architecture which are commonly accepted as subsets of an overall enterprise architecture are: business, data, application and technology.

2.4.28 *BABOK® Guide* – Business Analysis Body of Knowledge

The Business Analysis Body of Knowledge (*BABOK® Guide*) developed by the International Institute of Business Analysis (IIBA) is a framework that describes what business analysis is, what tasks are performed as part of business analysis, and which techniques and competences are relevant to performing these tasks.

Version 2 of the *BABOK® Guide* defines business analysis as "the set of tasks and techniques used to work as a liaison among stakeholders in order to understand the structure, policies and operations of an organization, and recommend solutions that enable the organization to achieve its goals". Business analysis helps organizations define their problems and opportunities, assess and validate potential solutions, and verify that implemented solutions actually deliver the benefits they were designed to.

The *BABOK® Guide* describes six knowledge areas:
1. Business Analysis Planning and Monitoring: governs how all other business analysis tasks are performed.
2. Elicitation: how to identify and understand requirements.
3. Requirements Management and Communication: describes how to structure, organize and communicate requirements to stakeholders.
4. Enterprise Analysis: explains how to define business needs and assess whether a particular problem is worthy of further effort in order to solve it.

5. Requirements Analysis: discusses how to assess requirements in order to understand what is needed to solve a problem or capitalize on an opportunity.
6. Solution Assessment and Validation: describes how to assess current and potential solutions and address any shortcomings, and to facilitate the transition to a new solution.

2.4.29 BiSL®

BiSL (Business Information Services Library) is a framework and collection of best practices for business information management. BiSL (Business Information Services Library) was developed by a Dutch IT service provider, Pink Roccade and made public in 2005. BiSL was then transferred into the public domain and adopted by the ASL BiSL Foundation. The current version is the 2nd Edition, published in 2012.

BiSL focuses on how business organizations can improve control over their information systems: demand for business support, use of information systems, and contracts and other arrangements with IT suppliers. BiSL offers guidance in business information management: support for the use of information systems in the business processes, operational IT control and information management.

The library consists of a framework, best practices, standard templates and a self-assessment. The BiSL framework gives a description of all the processes that enable the control of information systems from a business perspective. The framework distinguishes seven process clusters, which are positioned at the operational, managing and strategic levels:

The *use management* cluster provides optimum, ongoing support for the relevant business processes. The *functionality management* cluster structures and effects changes in information provision. The *connecting processes* cluster focuses on decision-making related to which changes need to be made to the information provision, and how they are implemented within the user organization. The *management processes* cluster ensures that all the activities within the business information management domain are managed in an integrated way. There are three further clusters at the strategic level, which are concerned with the formulation of policies for information provision and the organizations involved in this activity.

2.4.30 ASL®

ASL (Application Services Library) was developed by a Dutch IT service provider, Pink Roccade, in the 1990s and was made public in 2001. Since 2002 the framework and the accompanying best practices have been maintained by the ASL BiSL Foundation. The current version is ASL2, published in 2009.

ASL is concerned with managing the support, maintenance, renewal and strategy of applications in an economically sound manner. The library consists of a framework, best practices, standard templates and a self-assessment. The ASL framework provides descriptions of all the processes that are needed for application management.

The framework distinguishes six process clusters, which are viewed at operational, managing and strategic levels. The *application support cluster* at the operational level aims to ensure that the current applications are used in the most effective way to support the business processes, using a minimum of resources and leading to a minimum of operational disruptions.

The *application maintenance and renewal cluster* ensures that the applications are modified in line with changing requirements, usually as a result of changes in the business processes, keeping the applications up-to-date. The connecting processes form the bridge between the *service organization cluster* and the *development and maintenance cluster.*

The management processes ensure that the operational clusters are managed in an integrated way.

Finally, there are two clusters at the strategic level. The aim of the *application strategy cluster* is to address the long-term strategy for the application(s). The processes needed for the long-term strategy for the application management organization are described in the *application management organization strategy cluster.*

2.4.31 P3M3® (Portfolio, Program and Project Management)

P3M3® provides a framework with which organizations can assess their current performance and put improvement plans in place. P3M3® was released in June 2008, with a further update, Version 2.1, being released in February 2010. P3M3® is now owned by AXELOS.

P3M3® consists of a hierarchical collection of elements describing the characteristics of effective processes. It uses a five-level maturity framework:
- Level 1 – Awareness of process;
- Level 2 – Repeatable process;
- Level 3 – Defined process;
- Level 4 – Managed process;
- Level 5 – Optimized process.

P3M3® focuses on seven process perspectives, which exist in all three models (Portfolio Program and Project Management) and can be assessed at all five maturity levels:
1. Management control.
2. Benefits management.
3. Financial management.
4. Stakeholder engagement.

5. Risk management.
6. Organizational governance.
7. Resource management.

2.4.32 Agile, Agile Manifesto and Agile project management

Agile refers to a set of software development methods based on iterative and incremental development, where requirements and solutions evolve through collaboration between self-organizing, cross-functional teams. The principles of the Agile approach are also used in other disciplines, for example design and engineering, product development, manufacturing and Agile project management.

The Agile Manifesto was written in February 2001, at a summit of independent-minded practitioners of several programming methods. The Agile Manifesto has twelve underlying principles:

1. Customer satisfaction through the rapid delivery of useful software.
2. Welcome changing requirements, even late in development.
3. Working software is delivered frequently (weeks rather than months).
4. Working software is the principal measure of progress.
5. Sustainable development, able to maintain a constant pace.
6. Close, daily co-operation between business people and developers.
7. Face-to-face conversation is the best form of communication (co-location).8. Projects are built around motivated individuals, who should be trusted.
9. Continuous attention to technical excellence and good design.
10. Simplicity.
11. Self-organizing teams.
12. Regular adaptation to changing circumstances.

Agile project management is an iterative and incremental method of managing a variety of projects in a highly flexible and interactive manner (e.g. Agile software development). Agile techniques may also be called extreme project management. It is a variation of the iterative lifecycle where deliverables are submitted in stages.

Agile methods are mentioned in the *Guide to the Project Management Body of Knowledge (PMBOK® Guide)* under the project lifecycle definition: "Adaptive project lifecycle, a project lifecycle, also known as change-driven or Agile methods, that is intended to facilitate change and require a high degree of ongoing stakeholder involvement. Adaptive lifecycles are also iterative and incremental, but differ in that iterations are very rapid (usually 2-4 weeks in length) and are fixed in time and resources."

Incremental software development methods have been traced back to 1957. 'Lightweight' software development methods evolved in the mid-1990s as a reaction against 'heavyweight' methods, which were characterized by their critics as a heavily regulated, regimented, micromanaged and represented by the waterfall model of development. Supporters of lightweight methods (and now Agile methods) contend that they are a return to earlier practices in software development. Early implementations of lightweight methods include Scrum (1993), Crystal Clear, Extreme Programming (XP, 1996), Adaptive Software Development, Feature Driven Development, DSDM (1995, called DSDM-Atern since 2008), and the Rational Unified Process (RUP, 1998). These are now typically referred to as Agile methods, after the Agile Manifesto.

2.4.33 Scrum

Scrum is an Agile method (an iterative and incremental approach) for completing complex projects. Scrum was originally formalized for software development projects, but works well for any complex, innovative scope of work.

The Scrum Guide is the official Scrum framework developed by Ken Schwaber and Jeff Sutherland, co-creators of Scrum. The current version is Scrum Guide Version 2013. Chapter 5 contains more details on Scrum.

2.4.34 e-CF (European e-Competence Framework for IT)

The development of the e-CF started in 2005 after recommendations from the European e-Skills Forum that national IT framework stakeholders and IT experts should consider developing a European e-competence framework. With the introduction of Version 3.0 in 2014, the CEN started the process to make the e-CF a European standard.

A competence is defined in the e-CF as a 'demonstrated ability to apply knowledge, skills and attitudes to achieving observable results'. Each of the 40 competences in e-CF 3.0 is described in four so called 'dimensions':
1. The e-Competence area taken from a simple IT process model: plan – build – run – enable – manage.
2. A generic description in terms of the behavior showing the competence and the expected contribution at the workplace.
3. Proficiency levels based on a mix of:
   - Autonomy (from 'being instructed' to 'making choices');
   - Context complexity (from 'structured/predictable' to 'unstructured/unpredictable');
   - Behavior (from 'able to apply' to 'able to conceive').
4. Knowledge and skills examples that may be relevant for competence performance as described in dimensions 2 and 3.

For most competences in the e-CF only two or three levels are defined. The e-CF is published by the CEN IT Skills Workshop as a CEN Workshop Agreement (CWA) and consists of four parts:
- Part 1 is the standard itself;
- Part 2 contains guidance on the use of the standard;
- Part 3 documents how the e-CF was developed;
- Part 4 illustrates the application of e-CF in practice by providing 15 case studies.

2.4.35 ICB® (IPMA Competence Baseline)

The International Project Management Association (IPMA) is a worldwide not-for-profit project management association with 55 member associations (2014). IPMA published the first official version of the ICB (Version 2.0) in 1999, with a small modification in 2001. Version 3 was published in 2007.

A central concept represents the integration of all competences of project management as seen through the eyes of the project manager when evaluating a specific situation. After processing the information received, the competent and responsible professional in project management takes appropriate action.

The ICB Version 3 defines 46 competence elements covering the technical competences for project management (twenty elements), the professional behavior of project management personnel (fifteen elements) and the relationships with the context of the projects, programs and portfolios (eleven elements). Each competence element consists of a title, a description of the content, a list of possible process steps and the experience criteria required for each IPMA level.

The ICB does not recommend or include specific methodologies, methods or tools. The subject areas are described together with methods for determining tasks and, where they illustrate the latter well, some examples of methods. Methods and tools may be defined by the organization. The project manager should choose appropriate methods and tools for a practical project situation.

IPMA offers a four level certification program based on the IPMA Competence Baseline (ICB):
- IPMA Level-A® (Certified Projects Director);
- IPMA Level-B® (Certified Program Manager or Certified Senior Project Manager);
- IPMA Level-C® (Certified Project Manager);
- IPMA Level-D® (Certified Project Management).

2.4.36 Representative examples of popular industry certifications related to IT governance and its major components

A growing number of companies are sponsoring and requiring industry recognized professional certifications. The certification provides a certain amount of credibility to either an individual or an organization depending on the type of certification it is. Figure 2.19 identifies representative examples of individual or organizational (or both) professional certifications. It is not intended to list all organizations who provide certifications. Some provide few while others provide many types or certifications, usually within a focused area such as project management, IT governance, IT security, IT service management and ITIL and so forth.

Model/ Certification	General Use	Sources	Type of Certification I = Individual O = Organization	Approximate Number of Certifications
Agile Project Management	Agile Project Management	Project Management Institute APMI International – www.apmi-international.com	I	Many
CISM/CGEIT/ CISA/CRISC/ COBIT	IT Governance, Control, Security, Risk Management and Audit	ISACA www.isaca.org	I	Many
CMMI	Software Development	SEI (Software Engineering Institute) at CMU (Carnegie Mellon University) www.sei.cmu.edu	O	Few
CPP, CPPM, CPPC	Purchasing	American Purchasing Society www.american-purchasing.com	I	3
COP	Outsourcing, Outsource Governance	IAOP (International Association of Outsourcing Professionals) www.outsourcingprofessional.org	I	3
E-Sourcing Capability eSCM-SP and eSCM-CL	IT Sourcing Capability Models for Service Providers (SP) and Clients (CL)	ITSqc (IT Services Qualification Center) www.itsqc.org	O	Few
ISO - ALL	Quality Management and IT Security Management	ISO (International Standards Org.) www.iso.org	O	Many
ISO 20000/ ITIL/IT Service Management	IT Infrastructure, Services and Operations Management	ISO/British Standards Organization/itSMF International www.iso.org, www.itsmfi.org, www.axelos.com, www.apmg.org	O/I	Many
People - CMM	Human Asset Management	SEI (Software Engineering Institute) at CMU (Carnegie Mellon University) www.sei.cmu.edu	O	Few
PMBOK/ OPM3/ PRINCE2	Program and Project Management, Portfolio and Investment Management	PMI (Project Management Institute)/Project Management www.pmi.org, www.axelos.com	I	Many
Scrum	Iterative Methodology	www.scrum.org	I	Few

Figure 2.19 Representative examples of popular industry certifications related to IT governance and its major components

Model/ Certification	General Use	Sources	Type of Certification I = Individual O = Organization	Approximate Number of Certifications
Six Sigma	Quality Management and Process Improvement	Motorola, www.iienet.org, www.ASQ.org, www.sixsigmaonline.org/index.html	O/I	Few
SPSM	Supply Management	Senior Professional in Supply Management Program www.nextlevelpurchasing.com	I	Few

Figure 2.19 Representative examples of popular industry certifications related to IT governance and its major components (continued)

■ 2.5   CASE STUDY – LEADING BUSINESS SERVICES/ MANUFACTURING COMPANY

Figure 2.20 illustrates an IT governance case study of a business services/manufacturing company.

■ 2.6   SUMMARY, IMPLICATIONS AND KEY TAKE AWAYS

2.6.1 Summary and implications

The growing number of current and emerging best practice frameworks, guidelines and/or standards covering some aspects of IT governance imply that there is still no one best way for all organizations to improve the effectiveness and efficiency of their IT assets.

- ■ There are a growing number of continuous improvement frameworks and models that apply to IT governance and one or more of its major components;
- ■ All of them focus on helping either individuals and/or organizations improve their effectiveness, competences and maturity levels in one or more areas of IT governance;
- ■ Most of the current practices do not provide the details of 'how to do' IT governance from a strategic top-down and pragmatic bottom-up perspective;
- ■ An organization should leverage, adopt and tailor those models, frameworks and/or standards that address those issues, opportunities, pain points and threats most critical to the organization and create an IT governance roadmap with clearly defined the roles and responsibilities for IT governance development, process ownership and continuous improvement.

Environment & Drivers	Approach
• Revenue Range – $3.0 - $4.0 billion • Number of Employees – Range – 10,000 - 15,000 • Industry Classification – Business Services and Products • Management Philosophy – Conservative • Number of Countries with Operations – 50 - 60 • Number of Full Time IT Professionals & Consultants/ Range – 500 - 800 • IT Organization – Centralized with distributed customer facing business support • CIO reports to CFO (direct line) CEO (dotted line) and has direct reports responsible for: Planning and Program Office, Infrastructure & Sourcing Office, Enterprise Business Applications (ERP and other enterprise applications), IT Support for Products, Customer Facing Applications (CRM) and Web Technologies and Enterprise Information Management • Company periodically conducts SCAMPI (Standard CMMI Appraisal Method for Process Improvement) reviews for such IT processes such as: Requirements Development, Project Planning and Control, Supplier Agreement Management, Product Quality Assurance and others to continuously improve the processes	• Describe general steps/phases/actions to improve IT Governance: Senior Executive Sponsorship (CEO, CFO and CIO). We Require very clear capital improvement requests – Capital Investment Proposal (CIP) process for investment across all of IT beyond certain thresholds. We will be changing our chargeback and allocation process so that IT costs are borne by Business unit who gets benefits. Establishment of the Business Relationship Management capability and formalization of Business and Functional IT plans aligned to Business goals. Execution of change control boards within each of those. Establishment an execution of IT enterprise wide IT Investment Council • Sponsorship – CEO, CFO, CIO • Methods for Improvement – Steering Committee, Tiger Team, Use of Industry or tailored standards or guidelines (e.g. PM, ITIL, ISO, Security, COBIT 5, CMM, others) – Mix – partial elements of ITIL in some IT areas, some methods through external providers (hosting/ outsourcing) • Priority –Business & IT Transformation, IT Governance, Optimized Sourcing (Applications, Infrastructure), Improved Planning and Program Management, IT Service Management, Security
Issues, Objectives, Constraints & Opportunities	**Results – Alignment (Business/ IT)**

• Identify key issues, constraints, objectives and opportunities relating to IT Governance and Management
  – Issues: Operational – Supplier performance impacting service levels., balancing large transformation programs with legacy system retirements; Financial- High IT Costs compared to industry benchmarks
  – Objectives: Delivering Business Transformation via common processes, IT Cost Optimization – To be in first quartile of cost efficiency metrics, Delivering value add services to internal and external customers, Enable Business Transformation through ERP, CRM, other Customer and Product related IT capabilities, Applications Portfolio Optimization, Analytics and Data Management
  – Constraints: Timelines – Communicated plan to shareholders that will constrain flexibility from schedule perspective, Financial (Cost Optimization Targets), Operational (existing suboptimal contracts and their execution in terms of outsourcing providers, older platforms with limited capabilities will need to exist for few years before being retired./replaced), People – Organization's ability to align it's operating model / change in-time & effectively to keep pace with Business and IT Transformation initiatives
  – Opportunities: - Leverage Transformation program to align ourselves better with core processes, Business Relationship Management, deploy improved Governance – e.g. Change Control Boards / Councils, Improved Outsourcing Models, Optimized IT Cost, Simplified Technology Landscape, Improve Security and Compliance
	• Describe methods/processes for aligning and integrating IT more effectively into the business
	• Business leadership actively facilitates and participates in Technology Steering Committee for key IT Investment Decisions, IT Operating Plans well defined and shared with CEO/CFO level Business Leadership on a Quarterly Basis, Operational Leadership Teams have routine meetings on Service Level Metrics and Root Cause Analysis
	• How successful is (or has been) the process and how do you know? – This is still in progress with many of the capabilities being established within last 12-18 months under the new CIO. Metrics and data have started to demonstrate that positive outcomes are resulting from better awareness of weaknesses and improved focus on overcoming them

Figure 2.20 Case study – leading business services/manufacturing company

Results - Program/Project/Portfolio Management/SDM	Results - Performance Management
• A corporate planning office owns the capital budgeting process for major (high dollar value) projects but there is no overall portfolio management function. Projects or programs are typically approved within business units and associated functions. Business units are responsible for the execution and oversight of their own IT projects. The central IT organization conducts a monthly project review where major projects report on planned vs. actual spend, resource utilization, estimated cost at completion, and estimated project completion date. Projects also report on quality and progress using metrics of their own choosing, and work with their sponsor to define critical success drivers that represent project outcomes from a business perspective that can be measured. A customized SharePoint team site serves as the data repository and report generator for this information, as well as risks, issues and milestones • Company uses a single standard PM process for initiating projects, reporting status during their execution, and closing out projects • Within the execution phase of projects, project managers choose from a standard waterfall or a standard Scrum methodology. PMs are allowed to tailor the SDM or utilize a non-standard SDM to address the unique needs of their project. For example, aligning with the SDM of a supplier or implementation partner	• Monthly reviews and reports on major IT projects and all projects over $100k in development and key infrastructure metrics • Monthly reports initiated for reporting on major non-project efforts (e.g. business relationship management, project scoping/origination etc.) • Daily operational review meetings within IT focus on key problems • Use a balanced scorecard system to track key IT activities and commitments (including outsourcing contracts)
Results - IT Service Management (Includes ITIL)	Results – Cloud Computing and Data Management
• Limited components of ITIL have been implemented (e.g. Incident and Problem Management; Security; Disaster Recovery, etc.) in the IT Operations Infrastructure area	• Describe governance structure, metrics, processes, tools used, security, privacy, access and other issues: cloud computing is usually considered as a potential option while evaluating IT investments. Routine vendor discussions take place to explore opportunities where cloud-based platforms (HW/SW) align with our IT and business strategy and objectives. Some key enterprise applications are cloud-based, especially in the CRM/Go • Company already have an private cloud today and have IAAS from suppliers (30% of servers are IAAS based). Public/private cloud options are also being evaluated on an ongoing basis for our future state infrastructure capabilities. Voice services are based on cloud • Data management: revamping tools and policies to make data management more streamlined, efficient, secure and private. CIO direct report responsible for information management on enterprise scale. We are revamping data governance as part of a global transformation program. We are ensuring that Personal Identifiable Information (PII) is encrypted • Company is also engaging in a private cloud- based data warehouse/analytics platform

Figure 2.20 Case study – leading business services/manufacturing company (continued)

Results – Strategic Sourcing and Outsourcing	Lessons Learned

• A formal sourcing process has been implemented. The IT infrastructure organization owns IT sourcing program office, while Corporate Indirect Procurement is heavily involved on an ongoing basis on IT procurement, negotiations and IT spend analytics aspects
• Focus of outsourcing is repetitive / transactional type of work and processes (e.g. applications and infrastructure maintenance), some internal organization areas need more design/architecture type of skills and competencies
• Maintain internal control over strategy and engineering (design) in most IT areas
• Use Tier 1 and 2 outsourcing vendors
• Improving outsourcing metrics is an on-going objective. Outcome-based outsourcing contracts are in place for infrastructure and applications - focused on meeting/ exceeding service levels
• 2/3rd of resources and all of ADM/AMS towers are outsourced
• Data centers are all co-located (cloud)/outsourced
• We have longstanding outsourcing contracts – sole sourced, vendor has not provided optimal services. Outcome-based contracts. We recently changed outsourcing leadership and management resources
	• Describe lessons learned in your IT governance improvement efforts:
	  – What worked? Metrics, reporting, increased transparency, empowerment of middle management, consistent leadership communications on strategic intent, priorities, objectives
	  – What did not work? Outsourcing – complacency resulted in a multi-year of outsourcing. Unclear ownership and inconsistencies in IT spend on infrastructure, applications etc. Execution of outsourcing contracts in the past not fully optimal – impacted service levels, affected IT's perception in the organization to some extent

Critical Success Factors • Strong C-level executive sponsorship • Having right skills from IT perspective – resources that understand the business and can close the business–IT alignment gaps, establish strong working relationships with and respect the business • IT organization's ability to operate in constrained environment, culture that helps focus on the right investments by maximizing value from limited people, process and technology resources • IT and business strategy alignment - balancing cost, value and risk • Operational, financial metrics and reporting • Well-defined roles, responsibilities and PM decision criteria • Ongoing communications and change managemen.t • Agile, scalable and adaptable technology & process landscape • Standards, policies, procedures and associated measures and incentives • Talent management and leadership development • Business architecture-driven IT operating model	

Figure 2.20 Case study – leading business services/manufacturing company (continued)

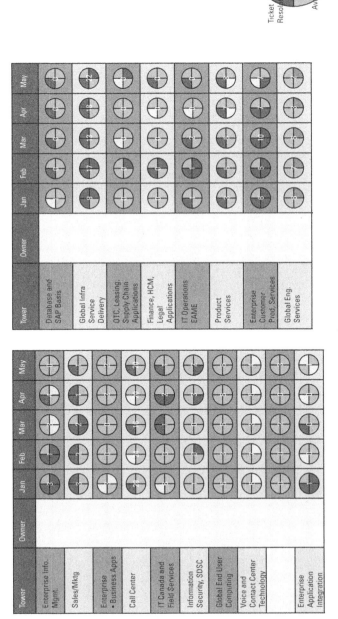

Figure 2.20 Case Study -IT Op Excellence –Accountability –Leading Business Services/Manufacturing Company

Key Measure	Target	Feb	Mar	Apr	May	Trend	Comments
Clients							
NPS / Client Sat Scores							
Support Desk Overall Sat % Excellent / % poor	none/2.28	91.56/1.14	90.78/1.58	89.89/1.95	91.08/2.08	↖	Focus on causes of poor surveys, convert more tickets to excellent
Engineering Sat % Excellent / % Poor	none/3	91/2	87/2	91/0	88/2	↗	
NPS - Completed Products (Avg)	TBD	100%	-33%	n/a	n/a	↑	Only completed project (European Sales Commission was under 100K and didn't fill out NPS)
# Client Products with SLAs Missed	0/89	6	14	9	5	↗	Tier3 Malaysia, India, Call Center Harlow, C+ Accounting, E2 MyBills
Products & Clients - # Customer Impacting Outages							
Product 1	0	0	0	4	0	↗	
Product 2	0	5	10	4	6	↖	India (2 outages), Brazil, Malaysia, North America (2 outages)
Product 3	0	0	1	0	0	↗	
Product 4	0	0	0	0	0		
Product 5 (Saas)	0	0	0	0	0		
Product 6	0	0	0	4	4	↑	Issue in XYZ cloud, Provider (ABC) issue subsequently identified as XYZ software bug.
<....>.Com	0	2	0	3	2	↗	Middleware upgrade resulted in queue backlogs, Provider (XYZ) performance issue
All Others including client impact in Call Center	0	17	9	12	7	↗	
Internal Applications - # User Impacting Outages							
Enterprise Communication Apps	0	2	5	3	0	↗	

Figure 2.20 Case study – leading business services/manufacturing company

Key Measure	Target	Feb	Mar	Apr	May	Trend	Comments
Core Internal Business Apps	0	8	3	5	3	↗	Remedy (2)
Security							
# Severe IDS Alerts	0	3	1	3	1	↗	
% Devices w/ AV (Workstations / Servers)	98%	90%	91%	90%	90%	↖	Servers SCCM : 97%; Servers Non SCCM : 91%; Workstations: 85%
Audits							
# Audits Conducted (YTD)	36	0	2	4	5	↖	
Critical Outstanding Items - # late / Total	0/0	6/14	1/8	4/12	2 of 8	↖	
Disaster Recovery							
# Conducted / # Planned (YTD)	9	0/9	0/9	0/9	0/13	↑	DR plans being developed for 2014
Project Delivery							
Business Value Delivered							
# Client Facing Projects Completed		0	1	0	0	↑	
# Internal Projects Completed		1	2	0	1	↖	
$ Revenue Impact Delivered		5.6	0	0	1.571	↖	
$ SG&A Impact + $ COGS impact		6.6	6.47	0	2.026	↖	
$ Incr/Decr IT Total Spend Impact		-0.05	1.35	0	0.388	↖	
$ Incr/Decr TC Budget Impact		0	0.742	0	0	↑	
In-Flight Project Status							
# Green		13	11	13	16	↖	
# Yellow		7	7	5	4	↗	
# Red		3	3	3	1	↗	**XYZ Storage Optimization and Enterprise Backup Implementation:** storage migration of ABC, XYZ and DEF servers delayed due to year end freeze.

Figure 2.20 Case study – leading business services/manufacturing company (continued)

Key Measure	Target	Feb	Mar	Apr	May	Trend	Comments
Financials							
Op Ex (YTD)	$XYZ M	$XYZ M	$XYZM	$XYZM	$XYZM		
Cap Ex (YTD)		$XK	$YK	$XYZK	$XYZK		
Headcount	X	X	X	X	X		
Capital Investment Proposals							
# Requiring IT Approved		0	1	2	1		SVoC Data Quality
$ Incr/Decr IT Total Spend Impact (Millions)	$	-$	0.045	0.323	0.229		SVoC Data Quality
$ Incr/Decr TC Budget Impact (Millions)	$	-$	-	0.063	0.063		SVoC Data Quality
$ Business Value of CIP (Millions)	$	-$	3.977	-0.323	-0.229		BV = TBD from IT summary, hence just using costs
Operational							
Help Desk # Contacts		14286	15708	14084	12993	↗	
# / % Self Service	Future					↗	
% FCR		65%	75%	73%	70%	↗	Trending at/above 70% mark for three consecutive months.
ADM							
#Incidents Opened/Closed/Remaining		766/757/152	856/796/175	769/785/113	703/671/124	↗	While the count went down, we closed fewer incidents than we opened
Avg Age/Median of Open Incidents	28/7	14/5	15/6	15/6	14/6	↗	
# SR tickets Opened/Closed/Remaining		1825/1894/407	1988/1977/437	1862/2003/361	1900/1896/363	↑	
Avg Age/Median of Open SR Tickets	28/7	19/8	17/8	15/7	14/7	↗	
#Project Tickets Opened/Closed/ Remaining		23/29/108	22/40/110	24/47/103	15/44/85	↗	Fewer projects being opened, focus on closing out open projects
Supplier 1 CSLs - Missed / Total	0/56	3/56	1/56	3/56	0/56	↗	

Figure 2.20 Case study – leading business services/manufacturing company (continued)

Key Measure	Target	Feb	Mar	Apr	May	Trend	Comments
Supplier 1 Key Measures - Missed / Total	0/138	4/138	1/138	4/138	0/138	↗	
ISS							
#Incidents Opened/Close/Remaining		2604/3589/95	4449/4426/67	4135/4099/96	3840/3847/87	↗	Continuing to trend down
Avg Age/Median of Open Incidents	7/7	5/3	6/4	5/4	5/2	↗	
# SR tickets Opened/Closed/Remaining		2824/2700/350	2994/3040/233	3067/2980/295	2993/3037/334	↗	Fewer opened, higher remaining at end of month. Need to focus on closure
Avg Age/Median of Open SR Tickets	7/3	7/4	6/4	4/4	6/3	↖	
#Project Tickets Opened/Closed/Remaining		2/1/2	5/9/2	5/12/0	5/4/1	↑	
Supplier 1 CSLs - Missed / Total	0/46	0/46	3/46	0/46	2/46	↗	North America – 24x7 availability of data network connections from the switches inward, EMEA – Responsiveness on Sev 1 enterprise outage
Supplier 1 Key Measures - Missed / Total	0/51	6/51	6/51	3/51	6/51	↖	North America - Timliness of cross-functional incident resolution, EAME - Wireless, file, & printer availability, responsiveness of cross-functional service requests
Employee							
Turn-Over		2	2	3	0		
Diverse Hires	.	0/1	1/1	0/0	1/3		X, Y, Z

Figure 2.20 Case study – leading business services/manufacturing company (continued)

2.6.2 Key take aways

The selection of a particular framework or combination of frameworks is largely dependent on the strategic objectives, available resources of an organization and their desired outcomes. All of the frameworks require the management of change, cultural transformation, education and training.

The integrated IT governance framework model provides a comprehensive framework, based on a minimum set of required components that should provide an appropriate baseline to develop a roadmap to steer a more effective journey towards a higher level of IT maturity for an organization. However, each organization must tailor its approach to address its environment, current level of maturity, pain points and/or opportunities and other factors.

Business/IT Alignment, Strategic Planning and Portfolio Investment Management Excellence (Demand Management)

"IT alignment and planning is a journey, not a destination. It takes many small things to make it a success and not one big thing."

Selig & Waterhouse, 2006

■ 3.1   WHAT IS COVERED IN THIS CHAPTER?

- ■ Identifies the principles for effectively aligning IT to the business;
- ■ Illustrates business and IT strategy and plan development frameworks;
- ■ Provides a high level process flow of business/IT planning through execution;
- ■ Describes the enablers and inhibitors of business/IT alignment;
- ■ Discusses investment portfolio management and consistent criteria for analysis, selection, prioritization and funding of IT initiatives;
- ■ Describes the business and IT engagement and relationship model to establish and sustain solid relationships, communications, trust and collaboration.

■ 3.2   OVERVIEW

According to Craig Symons at Forrester Research, "aligning IT strategy with business strategy has been one of the top issues confronting IT and business executives for more than 20 years. Why is alignment so elusive, and when can enterprises ever expect to attain it?" He goes on to state, "IT and business alignment begins and ends with good IT governance. Alignment of IT strategy and business strategy is the byproduct of strong IT governance structures and processes that have matured to the point of being part of an organization's culture. IT governance is about optimizing investments in information technology, and optimization implies that these investments are aligned with overall business unit strategies. More importantly, strategy alignment must be monitored and measured, and management must be held accountable for results." (Symons, 2005)

Enterprise engineering has recently emerged as a new discipline to address the intensified complexity and dynamics of the evolving enterprise by designing, aligning, and governing its development. Enterprise designers employ various approaches, frameworks, and methodologies to design and align various components in the enterprise, including the business and IT components of an enterprise (De Vries, 2013).

As business and technology have become increasingly intertwined, the strategic alignment of the two has emerged as a major corporate issue. Cooperation and collaboration are becoming increasingly important in the modern business environment. The resulting emergence of new forms of relationships is challenging managers to understand fundamental dynamics of cooperation in order to evaluate and restructure their relationships.

Alignment focuses on activities that business and IT executives at an organization should do to work jointly to meet the business goals and to make the organization more effective. "CIO's who achieve alignment typically do so by establishing a set of well-planned process improvement programs that systematically address obstacles and go beyond executive level conversation to permeate the entire IT organization and its culture." (Clemons, Rowe and Redi, 1992).

Successful business/IT alignment means developing and sustaining a mutually symbiotic relationship between business and IT – a relationship that benefits both parties. This requires that IT executives be recognized as essential to the development of credible business strategies and operations, and business executives be considered equally essential to the development of credible IT strategies and operations.

Key questions to address in improving business/IT alignment include:
- How can organizations align their businesses more effectively?
- How can organizations assess and measure alignment?
- How can organizations improve their alignment?
- How can organizations achieve higher levels of alignment maturity?
- Do your processes and related measurements recognize and take into account the strong co-dependencies between the business and IT people, processes and technology?
- What information is critical to support the strategic business plan initiatives and objectives?
- What changes in business direction (and priorities) are planned or anticipated for the plan period?
- What are the current/projected major business/functional opportunities, issues, risks, threats and constraints?
- What strategic or tactical value does IT provide to your business or function?

- How can IT add more strategic value to the business (e.g. revenue growth, cost reduction/containment/avoidance, reduce speed to market, business process transformation, business/competitive intelligence, etc.)?
- Is IT developing and maintaining superior and constructive relationships with customers, vendors and others? How can they be improved?
- How effectively is IT communicating its progress and problems to its constituents? Is a relationship and engagement model used?
- What governance processes and controls have been instituted in IT?
- Does the board/operating committee/senior business leadership review and approve the IT strategy, priorities and funding?

Forrester Research developed a template for helping organizations assess the level of business/IT alignment maturity. Figure 3.1 represents the alignment maturity assessment template that can be used by organizations to assess where they are today and as a baseline to develop a plan for achieving a higher level of alignment maturity in the future.

Level	Phase	Description
5	Optimized Process	There is advanced understanding of IT and business strategy alignment. Processes have been refined to a level of external best practices, based on results of continuous improvement and maturity modeling with other organizations. External experts are leveraged, and benchmarks are used for guidance. Monitoring, self-assessment, and communication about alignment expectations are pervasive.
4	Defined and Managed Process	The need for IT and business strategy alignment is understood and accepted. A baseline set of processes is defined, documented, and integrated into strategic and operational planning. Measurement criteria are developed, and activity is monitored. Overall accountability is clear, and management is rewarded based on results.
3	Repeatable Processes	There is awareness of alignment issues across the enterprise. Alignment activities are under development, which include processes, structures, and educational activities. Some strategy alignment takes place in some business units but not across the entire enterprise. Some attempts are made to measure and quantify the benefits.
2	Initial Processes	There is evidence that the organization recognizes the need to align IT and business strategy. However, there are no standard processes. There are fragmented attempts, often on a case-by-case basis within individual business units.
1	Ad hoc	There is a complete lack of any effort to align IT and business strategy. IT functions in a purely support role.

Figure 3.1 Business/IT Alignment Maturity Assessment Template (source: Jeff Hammond, "Development Landscape," Forrester Research, 2013)

3.2.1 Strategic change and strategy implementation framework

In today's business environment, the complexities and challenges in implementing strategic change are greater, 'time to change' has become a competitive differentiator, and the risks and stakes are higher. According to John McCreight, "Strategic success involves making painful decisions to stop or refocus established initiatives, in order to reallocate resources, including leaders, to a higher priority initiative. We believe the following framework provides the tools to evaluate, refine, implement, and track initiatives to achieve strategic change and long-term, sustainable success." (McCreight & Company, 2006)

A strategy implementation framework encompasses:
- Clear and quantifiable strategic goals and objectives;
- Enabling strategic initiatives;
- Enabling strategic assets;
- Enabling change management competencies and tools with frequent progress milestones.

Strategic change is difficult, complex and expensive to implement. There are barriers and resistance to change in every organization. Creating a dynamic strategic vision, supported from the top to the bottom, requires a holistic perspective and integrated participation at all levels. The board and senior management must define strategic goals in concrete terms that can be understood and supported across the enterprise. Key questions to answer include: what good will come from it, in what time frame, and how will success be measured quantitatively?

Strategic goals should be designed by the CEO and senior leadership team and then approved in the boardroom. At the highest level, strategic goals are developed to create significant, sustainable, and scalable increases in shareholder value. These goals are then cascaded down into the business units and departments (e.g. Information Technology) to define supporting initiatives at every level and the execution and governance processes, controls and key performance indicators.

Organizations must inventory assets available to support strategic initiatives. Enabling assets may be distributed across an enterprise. Organizations with superior agility to share and integrate assets across departments and business units will be capable of meeting strategic goals more efficiently and effectively than their less agile competitors.

Outlining and resourcing enabling assets across the enterprise, such as those highlighted in Figure 3.2, provides a tool to communicate to the enterprise. Using this tool has enabled companies to recognize gaps between their assets and actions that they would need to implement their strategic initiatives. In these cases, companies can invest in building enabling strategic assets key attributes as a prerequisite to launching and executing strategic initiatives.

The following is an outline the senior leadership team could create to describe the competencies, tools, portfolio investment priorities and resources necessary for

Senior management must set the tone and operating environment in order to motivate organizations to enable strategic assets and key attributes.

Agility	Board and Director Effectiveness	Brands	Competence	Confidence
Courage	Creativity	Culture	Distribution Networks	Financial Resources
Governance	Image	Intellectual Property	Leadership	Location
Partners	Passion	Processes	Products	Services
Talent	Information Technology	Time	Will	Others

Figure 3.2 Enabling strategic assets (source: modified from McCreight & Company, 2008)

sustainable strategic change. This outline can serve as a reminder of what is important for the successful implementation of strategic initiatives:

- Program and portfolio investment management disciplines;
- Rewards that encourage prudent risk taking (no pain, no gain);
- Finance and leadership resources, including sponsorship (at multiple levels in the enterprise);
- Information, technology and process resources with the passion and 'can do' attitude

3.2.2 The role of the board and executive management

The board and executive management must play an increasingly important role in facilitating the alignment of the business and IT. This should include the following activities:

- Assess that the IT strategy and plan are aligned with the organization's strategy, goals and plan;
- Evaluate whether IT is delivering against the strategy through clear objectives, expectations and key performance indicators (KPIs);
- Direct the IT strategy by determining the level of IT investments, balancing the investments between growing the enterprise and supporting the ongoing operations of the enterprise as well as viewing the needs of the enterprise as a whole and each business unit alone and mitigating priority and fund allocations which will occur;
- Ensure an open and collaborative culture between IT and the business.

3.2.3 The changing role of the CIO

In the past, many organizations have practiced a reactive agenda for IT by defining the CIO's priorities by what had to be done – taking cost out, ensuring the continuity of the business, maintaining the integrity, security and privacy of data, and so forth – as well as keeping pace with the changing demands of the business.

World class enterprises have recognized the enormous impact that IT can make – not only on growth and responsiveness, but also on innovation and business transformation. In these organizations, IT is a business enabler. These organizations recognize that information technology can provide business leverage and be a driver of top-line growth. They look to their CIO for the ability to drive this growth. They are using technology to render more efficiency across the business and to enable the business to integrate and exploit new requirements more readily. They are also using technology to provide new distribution channels, understand different ways to segment markets and develop profound new customer and market insights. Superior alignment of the business with IT represents a key success factor and represents a 'win-win' environment for both the business and IT.

3.2.4 Components of effective alignment
John Henderson and N. (Venkat) Venkatraman first developed a strategic alignment model in 1990 which was modified by Jerry Luftman, et al. in 1999 based on a study of over 500 firms representing 15 industries. The model consists of twelve components and it is the relationship and the processes linking each of the components that define business/IT alignment. (Henderson and Venkatraman, 1990; Luftman, Papp and Brier, 1999).

According to Jerry Luftman, Raymond Papp and Tom Brier, "Achieving alignment is evolutionary and dynamic. It requires strong support from senior management, good working relationships, strong leadership, appropriate prioritization, trust, and effective communications, as well as thorough understanding of the business environment." (Luftman, Papp and Brier, 1999).

The components of the model, which have been further modified by the author, are:

Business strategy:
- **Business scope** – includes the industry, markets, products, services, customers, regulations and locations where an enterprise competes as well as the competitors, suppliers and other constituents that affect the competitive business environment.
- **Distinctive competencies** – the critical success factors and core competencies that provide a firm with a potential competitive edge. This includes brand and marketing, research and development, manufacturing and/or operations and new product development, innovation (e.g. product, process and/or technology), cost and pricing structure, and sales and distribution channels, logistics and supply chain management and culture.
- **Business governance** – this involves how companies set the relationship among management, stockholders and the board of directors. Also included are how the companies are affected by government regulations, and how the firm manages its relationships and alliances with strategic partners. Finally, the performance management, measurements and controls are included.

Organization processes and infrastructure
- **Administration structure** – the way the firm organizes and structures its business and defines the decision rights, authority and accountability. Examples include

centralized, decentralized, matrix, horizontal, vertical, geographic, federated and functional organizations.

- **Processes** - how the firm's business activities (the work performed by employees) operate or flow. Major issues include value added activities, process improvement and integration and interface points between functions, departments or business units and external forces.
- **Skills** – people considerations such as how to hire/fire, motivate, train/educate, incentivize, manage change and culture.

IT strategy

- **Technology scope** – the important information applications, data management and technologies.
- **Systematic competencies** – those capabilities (e.g. access to relevant information that is important to the creation/achievement of a company's strategies) that distinguish the IT services.
- **IT governance** – how the authority for resources, risk, and responsibility for IT is shared between business partners, IT management and service providers. Program and project selection, prioritization and approval issues are included here.

IT processes and infrastructure

- **IT architecture** – the technology priorities, policies, and choices that allow applications, software, networks, hardware, and data management to be integrated into a cohesive platform.
- **Processes** – those practices and activities carried out to develop synergistic plans with business, develop and maintain applications, manage IT infrastructure and institutionalize consistent IT governance processes.
- **Skills** – IT human resource considerations such as how to hire/fire, motivate, train/educate, compensate, incentivize, change and manage succession.

3.2.5 Enablers of business/IT alignment

According to a study by IBM's Advanced Business Institute, the key enablers to business/IT alignment include:

- Senior executive support for IT;
- IT involved in business strategy development;
- IT understands the business;
- Business – IT partnership;
- Well-prioritized IT projects;
- IT demonstrates leadership and accountability.

Both the business and IT executives and professionals should cooperate to build up a comprehensive strategy that will lead to formulating a process of continuous improvement for more effective alignment. For example, one firm that successfully used cross-functional teams for strategy development is Bristol-Myers Squibb. At

Bristol-Myers Squibb, an IT review board composed of business and IT executives leads the strategy and planning processes, identifies opportunities, and defines priorities for IT. It also tracks projects and uses the concept of an IT–business liaison to maintain and ensure closer collaboration.

3.2.6 Inhibitors of business/IT alignment

The business/IT alignment inhibitors are:
- IT and the business lack close relationships and may not have common goals;
- IT does not prioritize projects well and in a timely manner;
- IT fails to meet its commitments;
- IT does not understand the core business or mission of the organization;
- Senior executives do not understand the value of IT and therefore are not committed;
- IT management lacks dynamic business-oriented leadership.

The inhibitors of alignment are the reverse of the enablers. The first inhibitor is the lack of close relationship between the business and the IT function. In some organizations, IT executives do not participate in any strategy formulation meeting nor have a seat at the 'C' suite. One other indicator is where the CIO reports to CFO. This represents a constraint and handicap to more effective alignment. If these initiatives are not well-defined and prioritized, then the IT department could be spending time and resources on projects that are not as important to the business. Only business executives (as sponsors or champions or owners) can drive and validate the realization of value from IT-related projects. It is critical to have a strong partnership to ensure better collaboration and bonding. The vehicles for this governance process include collaborative steering committees, business and IT liaisons, budget and human resource allocation processes, value assessments and a seat for the IT executive at the executive ('C') table.

3.2.7 Overcoming business/IT alignment obstacles and constraints

There are a number of obstacles and constraints that must be overcome if an organization is to improve its business/IT alignment. In a study of over 100 organizations, Giga Research identified and compared characteristics of aligned and unaligned IT organizations. It seems that while IT management may have fallen short in some areas of alignment, there are conditions out of IT's control that make alignment difficult in some cases. In table 3.1 are the Giga Research results (Leganza, 2003).

Others reasons why business and IT do not achieve good alignment include:
- Political reasons – traditionally, business executives and leaders have been from non-IT fields. However, that trend is changing in more progressive organizations;
- Absence of a clear business strategy and plan;
- Conflicting organizational entities.

Table 3.1 Attributes of Aligned and Unaligned Organizations

Attributes	Not Aligned	Aligned
Reporting structure	IT reports into the CFO or an operational executive with significant non-IT responsibilities.	IT reports into an executive that understands the strategic potential of IT and the various IT-related units report into an executive whose sole responsibility is IT. CIO also has a seat at the 'C' table.
Cultural attitude towards IT	IT is treated as a utility or commodity.	IT is perceived as having contributed significantly to strategic business success.
Perception of IT service	IT has a recent history of unsatisfactory service, at least the perception of disorder, and/or high cost.	IT has previously worked long and hard to overcome perceptions of poor service and is proactive in monitoring dashboards that monitor service levels.
IT access to business goals and strategy	IT leadership is not aware of business goals or the business strategy at a meaningful level of detail.	IT leadership is in the loop regarding business planning at a detailed level and keeps pace with frequent changes. In many cases, the IT organization includes relationship managers that keep in close contact with internal business partners.
IT planning and project prioritization	There is no process for prioritizing projects or tasks within IT based on business priorities.	The IT organization has dynamic and pragmatic planning processes that parallel the business partners.
Business project prioritization	There is no enterprise-wide or cross-silo prioritization process for business initiatives.	There are structures and processes for setting enterprise-wide priorities across business units.
Communication regarding the role of IT	The business is unaware of the role of IT in any strategic endeavors.	IT leadership has actively communicated the successes of IT with business executives and business partners.
Communication style	IT leadership and middle management communicate more effectively with technical staff than business people.	IT leadership and middle management speak in business terms and communicate effectively with business people.
Strategic role of IT	IT is not 'at the table'.	IT is 'at the table' or 'C suite'.

3.2.8 Select business/IT alignment metrics

The business and the IT department need to collaborate and develop accurate metrics that are linked to the business objectives, priorities and performance. Below are some examples of business/IT alignment metrics:

- Revenue growth;
- Return on investment;
- Decrease in total cost of ownership (TCO);
- Increase in employee productivity;
- Business process cost and time reduction;
- Speed to market;
- Customer satisfaction;
- Increased quality of products and services;

- Number of business and IT strategic planning and operational review meetings;
- Development and use of a business and IT engagement and relationship partnership model.

3.2.9 Business/IT alignment and demand management

Demands for IT services are either planned or unplanned and generally come in several flavors – mandatory or core (must do's such as service interruptions, standard maintenance, keeping the lights on and/or regulatory compliance) and discretionary (could do's if aligned, feasible, cost justified and/or strategic). In an ideal world, both mandatory and discretionary requests should be approved by the business/IT leadership if they have been identified in the IT strategic and operating plans in accordance with the organization's decision rights and approval authority guidelines. The following considerations will further help align business needs with IT:

- Clearly define and relate the value (e.g. cost reduction, containment and avoidance; increased revenues; faster access to information; shorter time to market etc.) that IT provides in support of the business. Identify value-adding activities (e.g. value chain and other business models/attributes) and strategies that would enhance them through IT.
- Focus on listening to the voice of the customer and develop a business/IT engagement and relationship building model to improve cooperation, build trust and improve communications.
- Ensure that all IT initiatives are evaluated using a consistent but flexible set of investment selection, prioritization and approval criteria to assure a strong link to the business plan, deployment and integration into the ongoing operations (see Figure 3.3). The figure identifies key selection criteria such as new/incremental revenues, strategic fit, ROI, intellectual capital, cost reduction and business transformation.
- Develop a strategic IT plan that identifies major initiatives, technical/architecture, operational, organizational, people development and financial objectives and measurements in support of the business. This is discussed in more detail in Sections 3.3 and 3.4 of this chapter.

Figure 3.4 illustrates an example of IT investment spend alternatives and the percentage of investments in each category for a technology organization. These should be driven by business needs and priorities and will vary by organization and from year to year based on the organization's business strategy, objectives and priorities. It is interesting to note that for this particular organization, the projected spend is segmented into three major 'buckets' or investment portfolios:

- **Portfolio 1: Revenue growth projects** – focus IT projects on such areas as new product development, customer relationship management, customer interface systems, distribution systems, marketing, e-commerce, social media and other factors.
- **Portfolio 2: Cost reduction, avoidance and containment projects** – focus on business transformation, innovation, quality, supply chain, ERP systems, etc.

Business Plan/Portfolio/Project/SDLC/IDLC/PDLC - Imperatives must be identified in the business plan, compete for funding (Portfolio Management), must be decomposed into programs/projects and with the application of life cycle methodologies, facilitate quality deployment and on-going IT service management and delivery

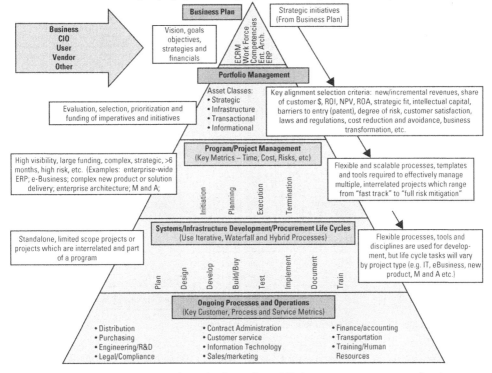

Figure 3.3 Business/IT alignment, project selection and portfolio investment management triangle

■ **Portfolio 3: Business enablement projects** – this contains several areas such as infrastructure, service delivery, compliance, employee development and governance. Others can be added as well.

Based on the business strategy and plan of an organization, the percent spend will change from year to year and will also vary by organization and industry.

3.2.10 A global insurance company example of a world class business/IT alignment process

AXA Equitable is a New York-based, wholly owned subsidiary of the giant financial services firm AXA, which is headquartered in Paris. AXA Equitable has about 10,000 employees in the U.S., with about 700 in the IT organization. AXA US decided to increase its investment in IT significantly. As a result, there was a proliferation of projects that seemed to be chosen based on qualitative analysis alone.

Since business/IT alignment represented the front-end of the IT governance framework and it was a 'big pain point' for the company that had to be corrected, the company's IT governance improvement initiative started there. The VP of AXA-Technology Services Strategic Management Office, was tasked with establishing a fair and accepted means

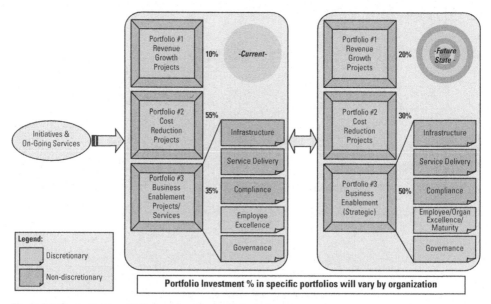

IT Investment Management Portfolio Alternatives Consist of Discretionary (Optional), Strategic and Mandatory (Keep the Lights ON) Requirements and the Amount of Investment % in Each Portfolio Should be Driven by Business Needs and Will Change from Year to Year and Organization to Organization

Figure 3.4 Strategic IT portfolio investment spend alternatives

of choosing between a large array of prospective IT investments – that is, develop a governance process – based on business analysis and a sound economic model that aligned IT investments much more objectively and closely with the business.

The business /IT alignment and governance component was designed with the following elements:

- **Executive top-down governance direction** – a business/IT governance committee was formed consisting of the CEO and his direct reports, which included the CIO and business unit heads, to determine IT spend levels on IT initiatives for the company. Each initiative had to undergo two filters, one focused on the alignment of business objectives with IT initiatives first, and the second focused on cost/benefit analysis.
- **Filter 1: Business and IT strategy alignment** – the first filter involved the identification and weighting of key business strategy objectives (e.g. increase revenue by 25%; reduce expense base by 30%; improve customer satisfaction by 15%, etc.) These objectives were plotted on an X-Y chart with corresponding IT projects, which were ranked by five levels of potential impact (e.g. extreme, strong, moderate, low and none). To help focus on the most important business objectives, all projects classified by the executive governance committee as having extreme, strong or medium impact on the business were identified in a Strategic Alignment Master List', which represented preliminary approval for further consideration and provided the input document for Filter 2. Concurrently, a 'total pool of money' was allocated for IT projects for the coming plan year, which was further segmented into two parts,

the business-as-usual part (funds to keep the operation going and the lights on) and the discretionary portion (where the investment choices had to be made). In addition, separate 'buckets' of budget allocations were established for corporate and business unit projects.

- **Filter 2: IT project business case** – for the top ranked projects identified in Filter 1, IT with the business developed a business case to determine the costs and benefits (e.g. ROI, NPV, payback, risks, etc.). Based on a combination of Filters 1 and 2 ranking, a priority list of projects was developed. The 'pool of IT project money' was allocated to the priority project list until allfunds were fully allocated. The remaining unfunded projects were either postponed, recycled or cancelled.
- **PMO handoff** – those projects that were approved at the Executive Governance Committee meeting were assigned to the Project Management Office for assignments to the appropriate department for development and deployment through the project management lifecycle process.

The results of the AXA IT investment governance process were very positive. There was a strong sense of direction and rationality regarding how the business is using IT to advance its position. The methodology has been applied outside of IT but within other AXA organizations. The benefits realized are attractive:

- Executive-awareness of the importance of a well-defined, repeatable project evaluation, prioritization, approval and governance system;
- Organizational commitment for the deployment of an enterprise investment management framework;
- Increased knowledge and understanding of the business/IT alignment process and how it improves organizational performance and buy-in;
- Identification and prioritization of key business objectives that provided an explicit rationale for investment decisions;
- Creation of a common and consistent way to assess project value across the enterprise;
- A prioritized list of proposed projects for each business area approved and owned by that business area.

This model has been implemented as a continuous improvement process that links strategy, governance and budget. Enterprises must determine the strategic direction they want to take, decide on the best investments for maximizing progress in that direction, and then allocate the budget and time for implementation. As projects proceed and the environment changes, it is necessary to track and modify the program in a seamless fashion. In essence, the insurance company used a two-tier weighted scoring model to align IT projects more closely with the business and it is working for them.

Table 3.2 illustrates a generic IT project screening matrix originally developed by Clifford Gray and Erik Larson and modified by the author (Gray and Larson, 2008). By multiplying the weights of the project criteria by the values assigned to each project, a weighted score is calculated for each project and those with the highest scores are selected, until the funding is exhausted.

Table 3.2 IT Project Screening Matrix

Project Filter Criteria	Strong Champion	Aligned to Business Strategy/Objective	Priority	Cost Benefit	Competitive Advantage	Regulatory Requirement	Weight Total
Weight	3.0	5.0	3.0	4.0	2.0	4.0	
Project 1 Value	5	5	2	0	1	4	
Project 2 Value	2	3	3	1	5	1	
Project 3 Value	4	4	2	3	3	3	

In summary, for IT investments to be aligned with the business more closely, they must be prioritized both by their impact on helping the business achieve its objectives and by the result of a business case analysis. It is critical that this 'approved master list of aligned projects' are allocated the right and sufficient resources to complete the projects.

It should also be remembered that in multi-divisional companies it is critical to develop a consistent and equitable investment prioritization methodology to evaluate enterprise-wide IT initiatives versus individual business unit IT initiatives.

■ 3.3 PRINCIPLES OF ALIGNING IT TO THE BUSINESS MORE EFFECTIVELY

Based on the research, including a review of best practice organizations such as GE, IBM, Starwood Hotels, Unilever, Avon, United Technologies, Xerox, Pitney Bowes and others, there are several strategic planning, management control and supplementary principles and practices that, when deployed well, will improve the business/IT alignment environment. They include, but are not limited to the following:

3.3.1 Strategic planning practices
This process should be a formal process developed as a partnership and contract (in the loose definition of the word) between the business and IT. It should clearly focus on defining and relating the value that IT provides in support of the business. Specific planning principles and practices should be deployed such as (Selig, 1983, 2008):

■ **Strategic planning program and processes** – develop a strategic IT plan that is an integral part of the strategic business plan. The plan framework, format and process should be consistent, repeatable and similar, allowing for functional differences between the business units and functions and IT, to facilitate business/IT alignment and integration.

- **Executive steering committee(s)** – involves top management in the business/IT planning process to establish overall IT direction, investment levels and approval of major initiatives across the enterprise. Each business unit and corporate staff function should have an equivalent body to focus on their respective areas to establish priorities and formalize periodic reviews.
- **Investment portfolio management, capital and expense planning & budgeting** – ensures that all IT investments are evaluated, prioritized, funded, approved and monitored using a consistent, but flexible process and a common set of evaluation criteria that are linked to the strategic and annual operating plans and budgets, both capital and expense, at multiple organizational levels.
- **Performance management and measurement** – monitors strategic plan outcomes based on specific balanced scorecard and service level measurement categories and metrics, and establishes organizational and functional accountability linked to MBO (management by objectives) performance criteria and reviews.
- **Planning guidelines and requisites** – a set of general instructions describing the format, content and timing of the business and IT plans. These are general in nature as opposed to specific standards and should provide the business units with some latitude and flexibility to accommodate local conditions.

3.3.2 Management control practices

These management control practices focus on the tactical and operating plans and programs, with the emphasis on the day-to-day operational environment:

- **Formalize multi-level business/IT functional/operations/technology steering and governance boards** - with specific roles and decision rights in the day-to-day implementation and service management of the tactical IT plans, programs and services.
- **Tactical/operating plans and resource allocation** – establishes annual and near term IT objectives, programs, projects and the resources to accomplish the objectives (e.g. application development plan, infrastructure refresh plan, etc.).
- **Budget/accounting/charge-back** – establishes budgets and monitors expenditures; charges IT costs back to the business or functional users to assure more effective involvement and ownership by the business.
- **Performance management and measurement** – collects, analyzes and reports on performance of results against objectives at a more detailed and operational level than at the strategic plan level (see Chapter 8 - Performance Management). In addition, formal periodic monthly and quarterly review meetings should be held to review the status of major initiatives and the ongoing performance of IT.

3.3.3 Supplementary practices

These programs will vary by organization and can result in improving business/IT alignment:

- **IT/customer engagement and relationship model** – establishes a customer focused relationship model to facilitate interfaces, decisions, resolution of issues, collaborative plan development, better communications and build trust between IT and the business. Several case study companies developed for this book confirmed the use of multi-level business/IT relationship models at the enterprise business unit and project levels.

- **Program Management Office (PMO)** – establishes the processes, tools and business/IT unit roles and responsibilities for program and project management. Initially, PMOs were established by IT to help manage IT programs and projects. As organizations recognize the increased benefits that a PMO brings to an environment, PMOs are being established at the executive level by a growing number of organizations to assure that major corporate business initiatives utilize the same discipline and structure as IT initiatives to implement them within scope, on-time, within budget and to the customer's satisfaction.

- **Marketing, public relations and communications program for IT** – most IT departments are terrible in promoting and marketing their accomplishments and value. This function creates awareness and promotes executive, management and employee education and commitment to the value of IT in support of the business through newsletters, websites, press releases, testimonials and other marketing and public relation events.

- **IT charter** – promotes effective and definitive interaction and links between IT and the business/functional groups they support. A charter can provide information on scope, roles and responsibilities, and provides specific program or project authority and limits to that authority.

- **Standards and guidelines** – adopt and maintain best practice standards and flexible guidelines to describe and document business/IT alignment, investment and planning processes, policies and procedures for IT governance and other areas within IT. A financial services organization developed a simple guideline for its customers entitled, 'How to request IT services and get them approved', which was a major success.

- **Organizational and people development, skills and competencies** – develop a proactive learning environment by encouraging and rewarding education, training and certification (where appropriate).

- **Annual/semi-annual IT management meeting** – conduct periodic business/IT management meetings to share best practices, develop stronger relationships and address organizational-wide issues and opportunities.

■ 3.4 SETTING A DIRECTION FOR IMPROVED BUSINESS/IT ALIGNMENT THROUGH PLANNING RELATED PROCESSES

"Few of the things we want most are attainable by means that appear possible. It is the function of planning to make the impossible possible."

Russell Ackoff

The strategic, annual and project plans of an organization must be linked to corresponding business plans for effective alignment. To ensure that the IT organization is focusing on the appropriate investments and providing the level of service necessary in support of business operations and transformation, each significant IT objective must be linked to a specific business objective with a business owner, who is accountable for evaluating the performance towards that objective. In a large U.S. manufacturing company, individual IT units submit lists of proposed projects and budgets. A corporate group assembles these lists and helps business executives evaluate and approve the investments. In a survey conducted by CIO Magazine, "plan reviews and project prioritization was rated as the most effective practice to establish business/IT alignment."

The importance of business and IT planning has been identified by many individual and corporate researchers over the years such as McLean, Soden, Porter, Hamel, Luftman, Wetherbe, Selig, Kaplan, T. Henderson, Hitt, McFarlan, Prahalahad, Treacy, Rockart, Nolan, and many others. The importance of planning is suggested by the following factors:

- Identify and focus on critical issues, opportunities, objectives, scope and deliverables in a phased and structured manner;
- Minimize risks, obstacles and constraints;
- Provide a roadmap and process for action;
- Obtain a better understanding of the alternatives;
- Provide a baseline for monitoring and controlling work and progress;
- Establish a foundation for more effective communications, commitment, buy-in and consensus building;
- Better anticipate and plan for change;
- Better manage expectations of all constituents.

Many businesses and IT planning processes and techniques have been documented in previous research such as IBM's Business Systems Planning, Richard Nolan's Stages of Growth, John Rockart's Critical Success Factors, John Porter's Value Chain Analysis and Competitive Forces Model and many others. Some of these are very complex and detailed, while others are more streamlined.

3.4.1 Key principles for effective business/IT strategic plan alignment

IT plans should be developed iteratively with the business and updated as necessary. Additional principles to strengthen plan alignment include:

- Ownership – CIO with involvement of IT leadership and of the executive officers and business unit leadership.
- Frequency – IT strategic plan is written/revised/refreshed annually, although major changes may cause the plan to be updated more frequently.
- Time horizon – IT strategic plan usually covers a two to three year period with annual operating plans identifying capital and expense budget levels for the first year of the plan cycle.
- Plan process – IT reviews the business strategic plan major objectives, themes and priorities with the business units and corporate services.
- IT interviews the business units to align and map IT objectives, initiatives and priorities with the business, using the key plan questions and discussion topics.
- IT identifies major new or enhancement business application or service support initiatives as well as significant technology refresh requirements (e.g. replace obsolete technology; support anticipated growth and new infrastructure requirements) using the business/IT strategic plan initiative alignment template adopted by a case study manufacturing company (see Figure 3.15).
- Both the business-driven initiatives and the infrastructure initiatives are combined in the IT strategic plan (which includes a rough estimate of capital funding needs) and presented to the executive operating committee and SBU heads for approval.
- Communication of the IT strategic plan – a short version (highlights) of the approved plan is posted on the IT web intranet and reviewed with the IT department and appropriate business constituents.
- Link to annual operating plan and budget plan – the annual capital and expense budget are approved by the executive team for the initiatives identified in the plan. Often, new or break-fix initiatives come up during the year (not in original plan) that require prioritization, funding and resources. A formal portfolio investment management approval process is followed for that purpose.
- Link to portfolio of projects for annual operating plan – once the annual operating plan and budget have been approved, a project list and related business cases are prepared, prioritized and reviewed. Projects charters are developed for approved projects and the appropriate implementation resources are allocated and/or committed.
- Link to annual MBOs (management by objectives), performance measurements, KPIs and rewards/incentives – both the strategic plan and annual operating plan must be driven by measurable outcomes (e.g. cost, time, profit, volume, customer satisfaction, strategic competitive value, etc.) and appropriate management actions taken according to positive or negative results.

Another good example of a well-publicized business/IT alignment turnaround case is Toyota Motor, USA. In 2002, the Toyota business units and IT were not aligned and the IT organization lost their credibility with the business due to late projects, high costs, poor perceived business value and the physical isolation of key IT liaison managers from the business.

Recognizing this fact, the CIO took the following steps to regain IT's credibility and improve its alignment with the business (Wailgum, April 15, 2005):

- **Established the Toyota Value Action Program** – a team of eight staff were established and responsible for translating the CIO's vision into actionable items. The team identified 18 business driven initiatives including increasing employee training and development, gaining cost savings, making process improvements, resolving inefficiencies and implementing a metrics program. Each initiative was assigned a project owner and a team. The CIO insisted that each initiative have one or more metrics to check its success.
- **Established the Office of the CIO** – this most significant initiative called for improved alignment with the business side. At the heart of this new effort would be a revamped Office of the CIO structure with new roles, reporting lines and responsibilities for business and IT executives.
- **Implemented a business/IT engagement model** - as part of the overhaul, the CIO took top-flight personnel out of the IT building and embedded them as divisional information officers, or DIOs, in all of the business unit locations. These DIOs were accountable for IT strategy, development and services, and they sat on the management committees headed by top business executives. The DIOs' goal is to forge relationships with tier-one and tier-two execs (VP and senior director levels). "I still believe in managing IT centrally, but it was incumbent on us to physically distribute IT into the businesses," commented the CIO. "They could provide more local attention while keeping the enterprise vision alive." The difference between the previous relationship managers and the new DIOs is that DIOs have complete accountability and responsibility for the business area they serve, together with their business counterparts.
- **'Town Hall' meeting** – similarly, IT senior management held 'Town Hall' meetings to announce the changes and deal with questions.
- **Pay for performance** – for the first time, the CIO also tied part of the senior IT managers' bonuses to their success in meeting the goals of each of their annual plans. These managers are judged on 10 areas and on how well they meet the objectives in those areas - for example, meeting project-based goals (whether the project was done on time, and on budget) and operational goals (implementing new governance and portfolio management processes).
- **Executive steering committee** – to further strengthen the IT-business bond, the CIO chartered the executive steering committee, or ESC, to approve all major IT projects. The executive steering committee controls all of the project funds in one pool of cash, and it releases funds for each project as each phase of the project's goals are achieved. Everyone in the company can look at which dollars were (and were not) going to be spent. The pool's administrators can sweep unused funds out, and other projects can go after those funds.

The CIO said that the organizational structure today is "almost unrecognizable" to the IT employees she inherited. One key element of success was rotating IT people into other parts of the company and bringing business people into IT.

3.4.2 High level flow – business/IT planning, investment approval, execution and evaluation

Figure 3.5 illustrates a high level flow linking the business plan to the IT plan and the subsequent selection of initiatives and deployment and evaluation of those initiatives. It includes setting priorities, identifying project selection and approval criteria (discussed in more detail in Chapter 5), managing and controlling initiatives and evaluating their results.

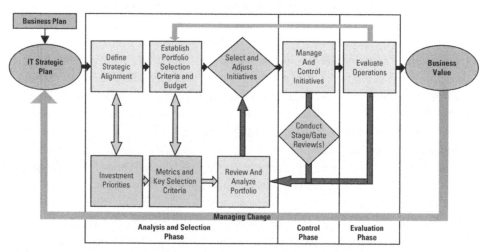

Figure 3.5 High level flow – business/IT planning, investment approval and execution

3.4.3 Business and IT strategy and plan development frameworks

As mentioned previously, a pragmatic business and IT planning process that has been used successfully in industry is called, 'pressure point analysis' and this can be used to develop both business and IT plans. It is primarily based on analyzing internal and external pressures and trends and addressing the following six basic questions:

■ **Where are we?** This question establishes the baseline or current state reference base for either the business or IT plans. It considers internal factors, such the strengths, weaknesses, opportunities and threats. It also identifies core competencies and any gaps in the strategy. External trends and pressures such as industry, competition, globalization, lifestyle, regulations, technology, economics and environmental factors are evaluated, as well as customer and prospect input.

■ **Why change?** Since change is inevitable and rapid, the assumptions on which the current baseline, plan and strategy are based will also change. As Gary Hamel stated, "If organizations are to survive and prosper, they must continuously reinvent themselves" (Hamel, 2000). This question identifies the reasons and motivations for change and examines high level alternatives for the business or IT to consider.

■ **What could we do?** If there were no constraints (e.g. financial, time, regulatory, resources, etc.) placed on an organization, this question helps them dream of what could be done.

■ **What should we do?** This question narrows the strategic choices based on a company's vision, objectives, direction and any constraints such as capital, people resources, time, intellectual property, existing knowledge and experience and the risk of the initiative. It addresses the question of why that vision and its related goals, objectives and strategies are achievable and what should be done.

■ **How do we get there?** Any business or IT plan should have 'mandatory' strategies if an organization is to grow and prosper. These mandatory strategy classifications are called imperatives. For a business plan, select imperatives can include achieving continual growth, maximizing customer intimacy, maximizing shareholder value, achieving operational excellence and integrating technology into the organization seamlessly. How this is done will vary by organization and Figure 3.6 suggests some choices. On the IT front, the imperatives can include such factors as enterprise and information architecture, maximizing customer intimacy, new applications in support of the business, effective IT service and infrastructure management and finally, people and process development and improvement. For each business or IT imperative, multiple actions can be pursued. Examples of select alternative strategies are provided in the Figure 3.6 and Figure 3.7, which illustrate the business and IT strategy and plan development frameworks respectively.

■ **Did we get there?** This question deals with performance metrics and management controls designed to ensure that the plan goals and objectives are met.

Figure 3.8 illustrates an IT plan presentation template that can be used to present a high level summary of key plan elements and maps them to the six plan questions previously described.

3.4.4 Business and IT plan outlines

Business and IT plan outlines and contents vary widely from company to company. However, to put a stake in the ground, a generic business plan outline for a manufacturing company is outlined in Figure 3.9. By applying the six questions previously described to the outline, a plan can be generated.

Figures 3.10, 3.11 and 3.12 provide sample IT plan outlines for a financial services company, a major university and a generic format which can be tailored to any organization.

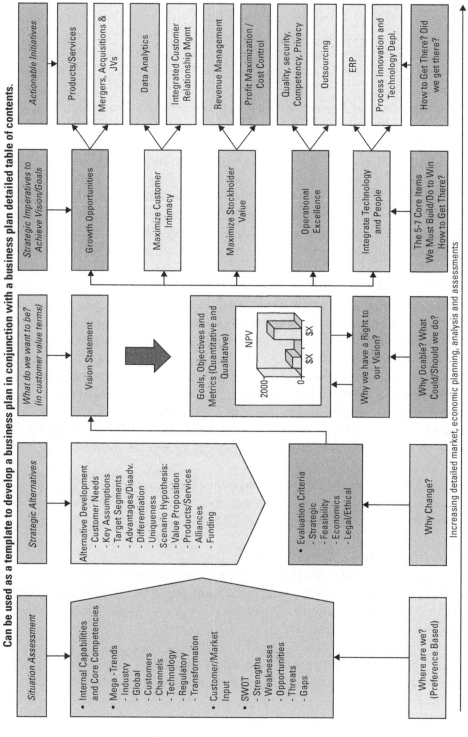

Figure 3.6 Business strategy and plan development Framework

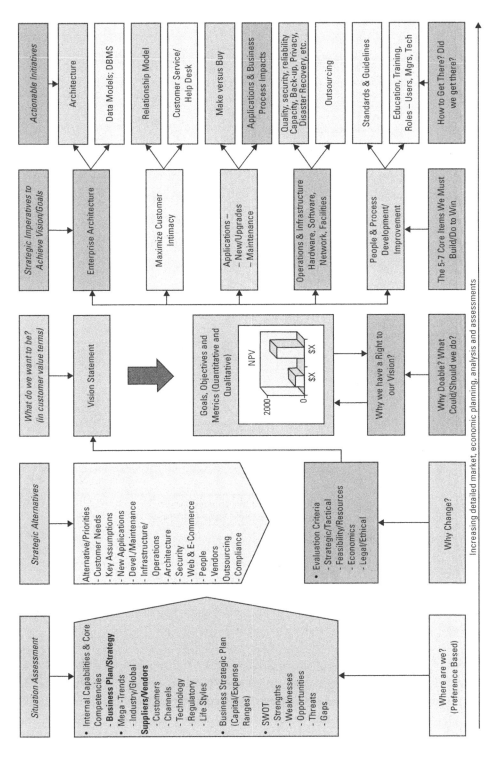

Figure 3.7 IT strategy and plan Development Framework

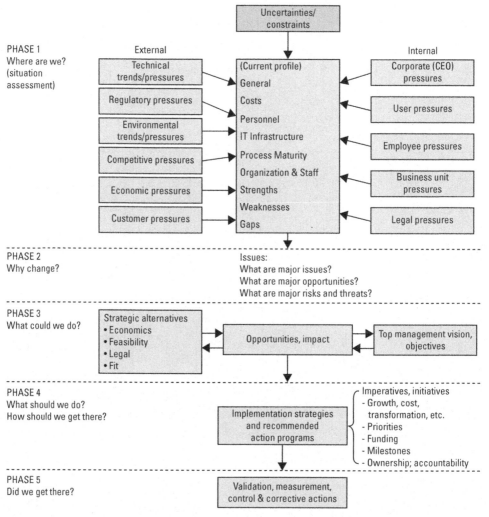

Figure 3.8 IT plan presentation template

3.4.5 Business and IT strategic planning cycle and alignment

The IT planning cycle should closely parallel the business planning cycle. IT plans should be developed iteratively with the business. Figure 3.13 describes the phases and steps involved in developing a strategic IT plan.

Figure 3.14 illustrates a manufacturing company's strategic planning process and timetable. It identifies the roles of the business and IT leaders starting in the first quarter of the plan year and culminating in approved projects and initiatives in the final quarter of the plan year which becomes the tactical or operating master project plan for the following year.

Figure 3.15 illustrates a business/IT alignment template used by the same organization for two of its business units, corporate service functions and IT. Representatives of each

Section	Section

1. Executive Summary
  • Business Proposition
  • Current status of Enterprise
  • Market Need being met
  • Enterprise's Product/Service Competitive Advantage(s)/Differentiators
  • Management Expertise
  • Financials
	4. Operations or Manufacturing and/or Procurement Plan
	  • Facilities
	  • Make versus Buy Decisions/Procurement
	  • Capital Items
	  • Product Support
	  • Quality Control and Assurance
	  • Logistics and Control
	  • Supply Chain Management
	  • Capacity Planning/Production Planning/Shopfloor Control
	  • Inventory Control

2. Vision and Mission Statement	

3. Marketing Plan
  • Market/Industry Analysis
  • Product/Service Offerings and Development
  • Competitive Situation/Differentiation
  • Pricing
  • Channels of Distribution
  • Promotional Plan and Positioning
  • Customer Service
  • Positioning Strategy
  • Social Media/Internet
	5. Human Resources Plan
	  • Management Team Background & Requirements
	  • Positions/Employee skills
	  • Training and special people issues
	  • Succession Planning
	  • Benefits/Compensation
	
	6. Risk Analysis
	  • Business /Operational Risks
	  • Economic/Political Risks
	  • Business Continuity Risks
	  • Technology Risks
	  • Other Risks
	
	7. Financial Plan
	  • Income Statements (Actual and Pro Forma)
	  • Balance Sheet (Actual and Pro Forma)
	  • Cash Flow Statement (Actual and Pro Forma)
	  • Capital Budget (Actual and Pro Forma)
	  • Sources and Uses of Funds

Figure 3.9 Business plan organizational elements (source: modified from Connecticut Innovations Inc.)

1. Objectives of Document
2. Executive Summary
3. Previous IT Plan Strategies, Accomplishments and Status (including a SWOT and Gap Analysis)
4. Corporate Strategy Map and Major Business Initiatives
5. Business Unit Strategies (all include Current and Target State) (New and Revisions to IT Applications are Identified)
  – Retail Banking
  – Commercial Banking
  – Real Estate
  – Shared Services
    Human Resource
    Finance
    Legal
    M & A and Planning
    Bank Operations
    Information Technology
6. IT Infrastructure Strategies (Technology Refresh and New Requirements; Cloud Computing & Data Management)
7. Principles of IT
8. IT Financials (mostly capital requirements as well as multi-year project budgets)

Figure 3.10 IT plan outline – financial services company

1. Executive Summary
2. Business Vision, Goals & Mission
3. IT Vision and Mission
4. Where we are today: The Scope of the Challenge
5. Competitive Challenge (Comparison to Other Best Practice Organizations on Multiple Levels)
6. Aligning IT with University's Strategic Goals
7. Strategic Goals and Initiatives
   Strategic Programs – Schools, Institutes, Degrees
   IT Applications, Infrastructure and Governance
   Customer Relationship Management (for different constituents – students (& student parents), faculty, administration, alumni, other)
   Courseware – Traditional and On-line Delivery
   Marketing and Promotion
   Process Excellence
8. Financials (High Level) – (These are linked to first year of the annual operating plan and budget)
9. Appendices
   Competitive Analysis
   SWOT Analysis
   Major Risks and Risk Mitigation
   Business and IT Governance – Roles, Responsibilities and Ownership
   IT Guiding Principles
   Decision Rights (e.g. Recommenders, Influencers and Decision Makers)

Figure 3.11 IT Plan outline - major university

1. **Executive Summary**
2. **Introduction and Background**
   - Purpose & Objectives
   - Plan Methodology and Team
   - Business Vision, Objectives and Strategies
   - IT Vision, Objectives and Strategies
3. **Situation Assessment (Where are we? – Reference Base)**
   - External Trends – Technology, Environment, Economic, Life-Style, Markets & Customers, Regulatory, Competition, etc.
   - Internal Pressures – CEO, Business Units, Functional Departments, Employees, Unions, etc.
   - IT Organization Profile – Organization, Staffing and skills; User Needs and Satisfaction; Level of Maturity; Revenue/expense profile; Infrastructure profile; application profile; Core Competencies; Strengths & Weaknesses
4. **Major Business/IT Gaps, Needs, Opportunities and Alternatives (Why Change? What Could We Do?)**
   - **Macro Assessment of Needs** (Discretionary and non-Discretionary) and Opportunities by Company, Business Units and Key Functional Areas
   - **Macro Assessment of Costs, Benefits, Value, Risk (of doing and not doing) and Priorities** (by Company, SBUs and Key Functions)
   - Infrastructure Alternatives
   - Architecture Alternatives
   - Application Alternatives
   - Organization/Control/Administration
   - People Development
   - Business IT Continuity, Security and Backup

(4.Continued)
   - Build versus buy (Outsourcing)
   - Funding levels and prioritization
   - Standards and Compliance
   - Governance policy and process
   - Data Management
   - Security
   - Privacy
5. **Strategies and Actions (What Should We Do? How Do We Get There?)**
   - New/ Enhancement Applications
   - Maintenance
   - Discretionary projects
   - Non-Discretionary support activities
   - Architecture Direction
   - Infrastructure Direction
   - Resource requirements
   - Contingency, Security, Risk, Disaster Recovery and Privacy
   - Governance & Compliance
6. **Financials**
   - Capital and Expense
   - Headcount – Fulltime and Contractors
7. **Plan Execution (Did We Get There?)**
   - Critical Success Factors
   - Key Performance Indicators and Report Cards

Figure 3.12 IT Plan outline – generic

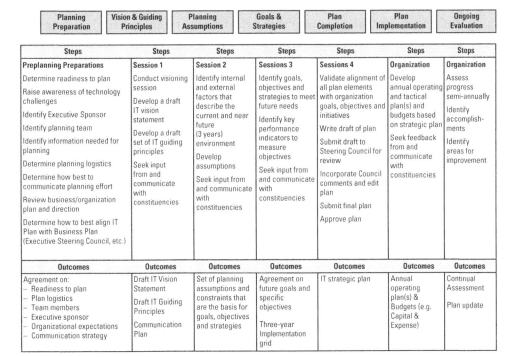

Planning Preparation	Vision & Guiding Principles	Planning Assumptions	Goals & Strategies	Plan Completion	Plan Implementation	Ongoing Evaluation
Steps	**Steps**	**Steps**	**Steps**	**Steps**	**Steps**	**Steps**
Preplanning Preparations	Session 1	Session 2	Sessions 3	Sessions 4	Organization	Organization
Determine readiness to plan	Conduct visioning session	Identify internal and external factors that describe the current and near future (3 years) environment	Identify goals, objectives and strategies to meet future needs	Validate alignment of all plan elements with organization goals, objectives and initiatives	Develop annual operating and tactical plan(s) and budgets based on strategic plan	Assess progress semi-annually
Raise awareness of technology challenges	Develop a draft IT vision statement		Identify key performance indicators to measure objectives	Write draft of plan	Seek feedback from and communicate with constituencies	Identify accomplishments
Identify Executive Sponsor				Submit draft to Steering Council for review		Identify areas for improvement
Identify planning team	Develop a draft set of IT guiding principles	Develop assumptions				
Identify information needed for planning		Seek input from and communicate with constituencies	Seek input from and communicate with constituencies	Incorporate Council comments and edit plan		
Determine planning logistics	Seek input from and communicate with constituencies			Submit final plan		
Determine how best to communicate planning effort				Approve plan		
Review business/organization plan and direction						
Determine how to best align IT Plan with Business Plan (Executive Steering Council, etc.)						
Outcomes	**Outcomes**	**Outcomes**	**Outcomes**	**Outcomes**	**Outcomes**	**Outcomes**
Agreement on: – Readiness to plan – Plan logistics – Team members – Executive sponsor – Organizational expectations – Communication strategy	Draft IT Vision Statement Draft IT Guiding Principles Communication Plan	Set of planning assumptions and constraints that are the basis for goals, objectives and strategies	Agreement on future goals and specific objectives Three-year Implementation grid	IT strategic plan	Annual operating plan(s) & Budgets (e.g. Capital & Expense)	Continual Assessment Plan update

Figure 3.13 IT strategic planning cycle – steps and outcomes

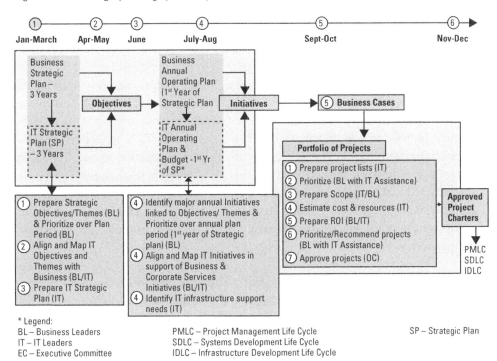

* Legend:
BL – Business Leaders   PMLC – Project Management Life Cycle   SP – Strategic Plan
IT – IT Leaders   SDLC – Systems Development Life Cycle
EC – Executive Committee   IDLC – Infrastructure Development Life Cycle

Figure 3.14 Strategic planning process and timetable – manufacturing company

unit identify an IT initiative (project) with its attributes in support of the business unit or corporate function for funding, approval and priority decisions made by the senior managers involved in each initiative

Category	Business Unit "A"	Business Unit "B"	Corporate Service/ Function	Information Technology
Business Initiative				
Business Owner				
Business Lead				
Critical Success Factors, Metrics and KPIs				
High Level Benefits/Measures				
High Level Requirements				
IT Issue/Opportunity				
High Level Deliverables				
Phases/Milestones				
Priority				

Figure 3:15 Business/IT plan initiatives alignment template – manufacturing Company

■ 3.5 STRATEGIC IT INVESTMENT PORTFOLIO MANAGEMENT ALTERNATIVES

There are several objectives in portfolio management: maximizing the value of the portfolio, seeking the right balance of projects, and ensuring that the portfolio is strategically aligned. There are many tools – some quantitative, others graphical, some strategic – designed to help a company choose the right portfolio of projects. A portfolio management system should consist of a macro-decision process designed to allocate resources across strategic buckets (enterprise-wide; strategic business units; corporate staff functions) and a micro process designed to select and prioritize specific projects. A uniform stage-gate process, along with effective portfolio reviews, is an integral part of the portfolio management process (see AXA Equitable example case previously described in this chapter).

Figure 3.3 identified a number of IT investment and prioritization evaluation criteria to help filter the IT investment choices and make the appropriate decisions based on the strategic question: are we doing the right thing and are we getting the appropriate value delivered:

- In line with our business vision?
- Consistent with our business principles, plan and direction?
- Contributing to our strategic objectives and sustainable competitive differentiation?
- Providing optimum value at an acceptable level of risk?

In addition, the following prerequisites should precede any investments decisions:

Portfolio investment management:
- Define investment criteria to evaluate, prioritize and authorize investments;
- Manage, monitor and govern the overall portfolio performance;
- Analyze the alternatives and use consistent metrics (e.g. ROI, NPV, payback);
- Assign clear accountability, ownership and decision rights.

Business case development:
- Opportunity or problem drivers (pain points);
- Objectives and scope;
- Assumptions and constraints;
- Costs/benefits;
- Deliverables;
- Risk, financial returns, strategic fit, compliance and other factors.

3.5.1 The five stages of IT investment management maturity

As previously described in Figure 2.5, the IT Investment Management (ITIM) developed by the General Accounting Office of the US Federal Government describes the IT investment maturity stages and related processes. This can be used to develop a plan to improve this component of IT governance for an organization.

3.6 IT ENGAGEMENT AND RELATIONSHIP MODEL AND ROLES

IT must become more customer-centric and marketing oriented to develop closer and more collaborative relationships with the business. A growing number of enterprises have instituted a business and IT engagement and relationship model. The goals of the model are to develop a strong and sustainable partnership between the business and IT.

Key elements of the model include:
- Single point or limited points of contact – establish a single point or limited points of contact between IT and the business to build a better partnership, collaboration and trust between IT and the business;
- Rules of engagement – define standard, enterprise-wide rules of engagement for acquiring IT services;
- Accountability – clarify roles, responsibilities and accountabilities for plans, budgets, work requests and issues resolution, escalation and performance reviews within IT and between business and IT;
- Consistent process – improve service delivery through a consistent process for engaging the right people at the right time using a consistent set of people, process and technology.

Figure 3.16 illustrates a business and IT engagement and relationship model, which can be tailored for an organization and should established at multiple levels (e.g. enterprise; business unit; project).

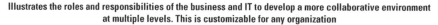

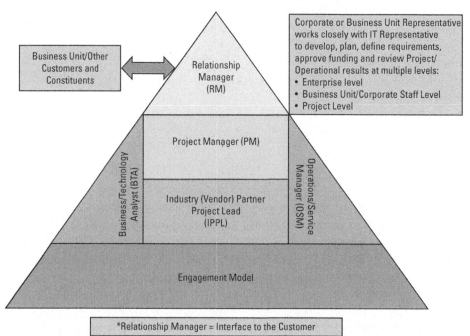

Role	Responsibilities
Customer	• Initiates request/project with Relationship Manager • Develops and approves business case • Approves statement of work and requirements • Approves deliverables from a business perspective • Participates in governance, business issue(s) resolution and user training • Conducts and approves user acceptance testing and operational service levels • Participates in post-implementation review/assessment
Relationship Manager (RM)	• Serves as the primary POC (Point of Contact) between the customer/process owner and IT • Develops Service Level Agreements (SLAs) and other KPIs with the customer/process owner • Ensures that appropriate authorizations and funds are obtained and available for all requests • Ensures projects follow the Change and Release Management process

Figure 3.16 Business/IT engagements and relationship model

Role	Responsibilities
Business and Technology Analyst (BTA)	• Collaborates with Relationship Manager and customer/process owners to identify opportunities for exploiting technology to achieve strategic business advantage • Has responsibility for the overall technology design of a given system: – Oversight and direction for architectural decisions – Consultative support during infrastructure deployment • Ensures that technology decisions conform with enterprise architecture guidelines • BTA coordinates status, activities and deliverables with the Lead PM
Operations/ Service Manager (OM)	• Coordinates and provides operational oversight for technical infrastructure components and projects in support of the Relationship Manager or the business • Provides accurate reporting of progress for all technical components of projects • Conducts and approves operational acceptance testing prior to steady-state implementation • Tracks configuration, release controls, help desk services and operational continuity
Project Manager (PM)	• May be the Relationship Manager • Project Manager is responsible for the deliverables, and coordinates project activities, status and deliverables with the Project Team and provides status reports
Industry (Vendor) Partner Project Lead (IPPL)	• Project Lead coordinates project activities, status and deliverables with the Project Team and provides status reports to Project Manager • Manages day-to-day project activities • Along with the Project Manager, is responsible for managing deliverables

Figure 3.16 Business/IT engagements and relationship model (continued)

◼ 3.7   CASE STUDY – REGIONAL FINANCIAL SERVICES ORGANIZATION

Figure 3.17 illustrates an IT governance case study for a regional financial services organization.

Environment	Approach
• Asset range – $25 - 40 billion • Business Units – Commercial Banking, Retail Banking and Wealth Management • Number of employees – 4,000 - 6,000 • Number of IT employees – 200 - 400 • Very competitive industry with many mergers and consolidations • Conservative management (risk averse) • High use of technology for product delivery and business unit support • CIO reports into President and CEO and is a member of the Executive Management Team	• Adopted COBIT as the general framework to guide IT process improvements for development and operations • Reviewing ISO 38500 (IT governance) for potential applicability • Adopted ISO 27000 framework for IT security • Executive Capital Committee approves major investment funding in IT • IT Steering Committee (business and IT relationship model) establishes IT priorities, reviews progress and approves major changes

Figure 3.17 Case study – regional financial services organization

Issues and Challenges	Approach (continued)
• Align IT more closely with the business • Increase profitability and growth • Make IT more customer facing and focused • Facilitate and sustain compliance requirements • Integrate new acquisitions as seamlessly as possible	• Revised general IT principles which guide how IT is managed (e.g. trust, flexibility, security, speed, transparency [IT is transparent to business]) • Established decision authority over major IT decisions with definitive parameters, roles and responsibilities for such items as funding approvals, architecture, security, projects • Established a strong Project Management Office with certification requirements
Results - Alignment	**Results - IT Service Management**
• Capital budgeting process is linked to strategic and annual operating plan for IT and business • IT/Business Steering Committee assures a closer alignment of IT support for business • Balanced scorecard and report card metrics are linked to critical success factors of business and IT (speed, financials, cost, performance, quality, etc.) • Established a customer/IT engagement (single point of contact) model to improve relationships, build trust and focus on priorities • Closer alignment is being improved continuously	• A variety of metrics and tools are used to measure the efficiency, capacity and availability, utilization and service-ability of the operations and infrastructure assets and group • Adopted select ITIL processes
Results - Program/Project Management	**Results - Performance Management & Management Controls**
• Established a PMO center of excellence staffed with certified PMPs • Developed a flexible and scalable PM process to handle Agile and complex projects • Educated and trained both IT and user community on PM best practices • Created a booklet on, "How to Get Your IT Projects Approved" • Significant improvement in delivering projects on time and within budget (20-30%)	• COBIT, ISO 27000 and select ITIL processes are used as the frameworks to define, develop and deploy the IT management and security controls • Select IT metrics are included in the company's balanced scorecard: financial (e.g. keep lights on spend, IT spend versus company revenues, IT spend per employee); non-financial (e.g. turnover. Quality, risk mitigation index, etc.) • Quarterly IT report card (financial; projects; production/operations, etc.
Cloud Computing and Data Management	**Critical Success Factors**
• Private cloud computing is being deployed at the company for select applications • The issues of "data" privacy, access, security, sharing and data element dictionary are being addressed in the development of the data management policy, procedures and technology	• Executive sponsorship is critical, along with the support of CEO • CIO and executive team must be proactive and provide oversight • IT governance must be decomposed and assigned to process owners with schedules, budgets, deliverables and metrics • Metrics should be linked to business and IT critical success factors
Strategic Sourcing and Outsourcing	**Lessons Learned**
• A centralized procurement function manages all contracts • It works closely with the procurement department on all IT vendor agreements	• IT governance is a journey towards continuous improvement • It is harder than you think and takes longer than you estimated • The improvements in time, speed, flexible discipline, cost reduction, alignment and compliance are beneficial • Integrating IT governance principles and practices is not simple with new acquisitions. It takes lots of work

Figure 3.17 Case study – regional financial services organization (continued)

■ 3.8   SUMMARY AND KEY TAKE AWAYS

3.8.1 Summary

Business/IT alignment is complex, multi-dimensional and never complete. However, there are business/IT alignment principles (e.g. planning, investment portfolio management, relationship/partnering models, steering and governance boards, etc.) that if implemented, will help to achieve a more effective and collaborative alignment.

Therefore, it is important not only to focus on measurements based on value realization (e.g. quantitative), but also to take into account the enterprise's performance and process improvements in creating the value.

Improving business/IT alignment can be achieved by implementing formal IT governance processes and mechanisms. Improving alignment maturity, like governance, is a journey based on a dynamic process that should be continuously improved. For organizations that are at the high end of the maturity model (level 4 or 5), business and IT strategy and operational alignment are an integral part of their culture. They constantly monitor alignment through key performance metrics and other techniques on a continuous basis.

Business/IT alignment will remain a major issue in some organizations, until they realize that they both need each other to sustain the growth and prosperity of the enterprise. Business and IT executives should:
- Improve the relationship between the business and IT functional areas;
- Work hard towards mutual cooperation, respect, understanding and participation in strategy development;
- Communicate more frequently and honestly;
- Work towards minimizing activities that inhibit alignment.

3.8.2 Key take aways
- Ensure that IT supports the strategies of the business by developing a strategic and operating IT plan as a full partner with the business, based on similar processes;
- Establish a practical and realistic framework for measurement and reporting the results;
- Identify value-adding business activities (e.g. value chain and other models/attributes) and strategies that would enhance these through IT, deploy incremental deliverables and communicate the benefits achieved;
- Ensure the appropriate commitment and participation of both executive management and the senior management team through steering boards and formal reviews, and link alignment objectives to performance objectives, performance evaluations and rewards;

- Establish a public relations/marketing function in IT to create awareness of the value and benefits created by IT for the organization and to improve communications;
- A successful allocation of IT resources occurs only if multiple perspectives are evaluated and the decision is not based solely on the passion of the advocate. Enterprises need to evaluate the financial perspective, the risk level and – most importantly – whether the project contributes to the achievement of the business objectives.

4 Principles for Managing Successful Organizational Change, Prerequisites for World Class Leadership and Developing High Performance Teams

"It is no use saying we are doing our best. You have got to succeed in doing what is necessary."

Winston Churchill, former British Prime Minister

■ 4.1 WHAT IS COVERED IN THIS CHAPTER?

- Describes a framework for managing successful change in helping to transition organizations to higher levels of IT governance maturity:
- Reviews key leadership, people and soft skills and competencies required for success:
- Identifies the attributes of high performance teams.

■ 4.2 OVERVIEW

"You miss 100% of the shots you never take."

Wayne Gretsky, hockey great

As previously discussed, effective IT governance is built on three critical pillars. One of these pillars focuses on effective and motivated leadership and change agents, building high performance teams and managing organizational change successfully.

Based on the large amount of research completed in these areas by individuals and institutions such as Peter Drucker, Beth Cohen, Peter Senge, David McClellan, John Kotter, Gary Hamel, Michael Treacy and many others, the author has adopted and modified several principles and practices in each of the areas covered in this chapter to make them pragmatic and actionable in helping organizations transform themselves to higher levels of IT governance maturity.

4.2.1 Coping with the realities of change
"When you win, nothing hurts,"

Joe Namath, football great

Formalizing and institutionalizing IT governance may require significant change in an organization depending on its current level of maturity, culture, management philosophy, available funding and resources, time constraints, business strategy, pain points, priorities and other factors. There are a number of realities of change that organizations must take into consideration when embarking on new or major change initiatives, such as IT governance. They include:

- Change has no conscience, plays no favorites, takes no prisoners and ruthlessly destroys organizations with non-adaptive or non-innovative cultures.
- A common response to change is caution. It is wrong today. Picking up speed protects you better in today's world to cope with constant and accelerating change. One major global organization, which uses 'Lean' processes, focuses its change efforts on 'cycle time reduction'.
- Success comes from cool headed thinking, clear focus and well-aimed action. So create a culture that is steady under fire.
- Initiative must always come from individuals and not just the companies, so create a shared vision and mobilize commitment.
- Inertia is more crippling than mistakes (you should learn from mistakes). Inaction is the most costly error.
- Innovate, bust out of old routines and be willing to make radical changes to improve.
- Be willing to bend and learn because in a rapidly changing world, new competencies are required.

4.2.2 Major impediments to successful change
According to Norman Augustine, former Chairman and CEO of Lockheed Martin Corp., "It is better to be 70% correct and take advantage of an opportunity, rather than 100% correct after the opportunity has passed." The following constraints to implementing successful change must be overcome to improve IT governance:

- No champion;
- Low risk tolerance;
- Inflexible processes;
- Procrastination and uncertainty;
- Unclear objectives, fuzzy scope and ambiguous accountability;
- No reward, recognition or celebration mechanisms;
- Poor execution;
- Weak leader and change agents;
- Lack of decisiveness.

4.2.3 The nature of organizational change and key components of managing large scale enterprise change successfully

Large scale organizational change is represented by any substantive modification to some part of the organization (e.g. mergers and acquisitions, new leadership, new technology, major process transformation, formalized governance, etc.). The forces for change come from either external forces influencing the organization's environment that force the organization to alter the way in which it competes, such as competitors, regulators, globalization, technology, economy, life styles and customers, and/or internal forces inside the organization that cause it to change its strategy and structure.

Generally there are two types of change:
- **Planned (proactive) change** – change that is designed and implemented in an orderly and timely fashion in anticipation of future events and projected results. IT governance should be a planned, proactive initiative if it is to be accomplished in a cost effective and least disruptive manner.
- **Reactive change** – change that is piecemeal or an unanticipated response to events and circumstances as they develop, or are forced on organizations, due to regulatory, customer, competitive and other conditions.

Change should be thought about as a continuous process, not an event that utilizes a wide range of tools, processes and technologies. One has to consider how to deal with and accommodate resistance to change and the psychological and social aspects of change.

As organizations transition to a more mature and effective governance environment, a 'sea change' has to occur, either through incremental and/or radical change that could involve large scale change, depending on an organization's level of maturity, management philosophy and cultural readiness.

4.2.4 A process for generating commitment

IT governance provides a natural antidote to fear and resistance to change. IT governance is also a good business practice that yields positive results. The difference between successful IT projects and unsuccessful IT projects usually boils down to business commitment. IT governance is the best way for generating the kind of business commitment required for guiding IT projects from conception through successful completion.

Today, all business leaders are required to make critical decisions about the role and value of new technologies. Despite the accelerated pace of business, people resist the urge to make rushed or injudicious decisions about IT investments. Poor decisions can be expensive to fix and often result in lost time, which cannot be recovered.

It is helpful to think of IT governance as a process for making absolutely certain that the company's key executives and managers meet together and say, "This is what we are going to do – are we in agreement?" In business, almost everything depends on some kind of process. Why should IT governance be the exception to the rule? (Fell, 2013)

John Kotter, a Harvard University professor, is a recognized expert on leadership and managing change successful. According to Kotter (with some modification by the author), the four key principles for managing large scale change successfully include (Kotter, 1996):

- **Engage the top and lead the change:**
  - Create the 'value proposition' and market the case for change;
  - Committed leadership;
  - Develop a plan and ensure consequence management.
- **Cascade down and across the organization and break down barriers including silos:**
  - Create cross-functional and global teams (where appropriate);
  - Compete on 'speed';
  - Ensure a performance-driven approach.
- **Mobilize the organization and create ownership:**
  - Roll out the change initiative;
  - Measure results of change (pre-change versus post-change baselines);
  - Embrace continuous learning, knowledge and best practice sharing.
- **Attributes of effective change teams and agents:**
  - Strong and focused leader;
  - Credibility and authority (charter) to lead the initiative;
  - 'Chutzpa', persistent and change zealots;
  - Ability to demonstrate and communicate 'early wins' to build the momentum;
  - Create a sense of urgency and avoid stagnation;
  - Knock obstacles out of the way, diplomatically or otherwise.

By applying Kotter's principles to facilitating the transition to a successful IT governance culture and environment, the following steps can be followed:

- **Proactively design and manage the IT governance program** – requires executive management sponsorship, an executive champion and creating a shared vision that is pragmatic, achievable, marketable, beneficial and measurable. Link goals, objectives and strategies to the vision and performance evaluations.
- **Mobilize commitment and provide the right incentives** – there is a strong commitment to the change from key senior managers, professionals and other relevant constituents. They are committed to make it happen, make it work and invest their attention and energy for the benefit of the enterprise as a whole. Create a multi-disciplinary empowered 'tiger team' representing all key constituents to collaborate, develop, market and coordinate execution in their respective areas of influence and responsibility.

- **Make tradeoffs and choices and clarify escalation and exception decisions** – IT governance is complex, and requires tradeoffs and choices, which impact resources, costs, priorities, level of detail required, who approves choices, to whom are issues escalated etc. At the end of the day, a key question that must be answered is, "When is enough, enough?"
- **Make change last, assign ownership and accountability** – change is reinforced, supported, rewarded, communicated (the results are through the Web and Intranet) and recognized and championed by owners who are accountable to facilitate the change so that it endures and flourishes throughout the organization.
- **Monitor progress, common processes, technology and learning** – develop/ adapt common policies, practices, processes and technologies which are consistent across the IT governance landscape and enable (not hinder) progress, learning and best practice benchmarking. Make IT governance an objective in the periodic performance evaluation system of key employees and reward significant progress.

4.3   FRAMEWORK FOR MANAGING ACCELERATING CHANGE

A framework for change should be a practical and useable roadmap for managing the change that assures the conditions of the change are met well, accepted by the organization in general and integrated into the operations and culture of the organization.

According to John Kotter, there are two necessary conditions for accelerating change successfully:
1. Leadership for change and changing systems, processes, structures and technologies.
2. Capabilities that are weaved into the fabric of the organization.

Kotter goes on to suggest that there are five essential elements of change:
1. Creating a shared need.
2. Shaping a vision.
3. Mobilizing commitment.
4. Making change last.
5. Monitoring progress and continuous learning.

Successful change requires strong committed leadership and a respected champion throughout the entire initiative and also to sustain a continuous improvement effort that should be reinforced by specific actions such as:
- Let people know that the change is not an option;
- Communicate clearly that performance measures and rewards are linked to measurable improvements as a result of the change initiative;
- Make space for 'grieving' based on the old environment, but encourage 'moving on' to the new environment;

■ Ensure that the change process 'conditions' and 'elements' are fulfilled:
  • Must lead by example with passion, energy and the right attitude;
  • Leadership cannot do it alone and in isolation - other motivated change agents must be enlisted at all levels of the organization.
■ Change requires work and attention – planning, management and governance;
■ Change requires supporting systems, structures, tools and training.

Figure 4.1 illustrates a framework and the respective phases necessary for managing major change used by a large financial service and insurance organization. It can be adopted and tailored for IT governance and its components, either individually or as a whole. Furthermore, Figure 4.1 also identifies specific questions that should be addressed for key change elements.

Appendix D provides an example of a change framework segmented into people and organization elements, process elements and technology elements.

Used to Help Organization Transition from the Current Environment to a Future Environment

Leading Change:
– Is there a strong change leadership team (CLT) and champion? Knowledgeable in the model and tools?
– Is the CLT actively involved in leading and driving the change process and initiatives?
– Are CLT members monitoring all "essential elements" and "necessary conditions"?

-------------------------------- **A Framework for Managing Change** --------------------------------

Creating Shared Need:	Shaping Vision:	Making Commitment:	Making Change Endure:	Monitoring Progress & Learning:
– Is the reason to change, whether driven by threat or opportunity, instilled within organization? – Is it widely shared through data, demonstration, demand or diagnosis? – Does the need for change exceed its resistance?	– Is the desired outcome of change clear, and legitimate? – Is the outcome expressed in simple terms? – Is it widely understood and shared?	– Is there a strong commitment from all key constituents to invest in the change, make it work, and demand and receive management attention?	– Once the change is started, can we implement it on a sustained basis? – Are the results transferred throughout the organization?	– Do we know our real progress? – Have benchmarks and metrics been set to guarantee accountability? – Has organization feedback and learning been captured?

Changing Systems, Structures & Capabilities:
– Is change woven into the very fabric of the organization?
– Are management practices used to complement and reinforce change?
– How have we addressed issues of: staffing & development, measurements & rewards?
– Is there a communication strategy?
– Do we know how the organizational structure must be changed?

Figure 4.1 Framework for managing change and related questions

■ 4.4   ORGANIZING FOR THE IT GOVERNANCE INITIATIVE

An effective IT governance environment represented by level 3 or higher on the CMMI maturity model is difficult to achieve. It takes time, resources and the right skills and attitudes. The journey can be less arduous by following a modified version of Kotter's eight stage process for leading change:

- **Establish a sense of urgency** – motivated by a threat or an opportunity;
- **Create the guiding coalition** – identify the group and individuals that lead the change, encourage change agents to solicit broad based support and facilitate the execution through empowerment;
- **Develop a vision and strategy** – develop a realistic vision and supporting strategies;
- **Communicate the vision and strategy** – over-communicating is good;
- **Empower broad based actions** – encourage risk-taking and overcome and/or neutralize obstacles;
- **Generate short-term wins** – complete short-term wins that are communicated to the constituents and are very effective for gaining support and sustaining the change direction;
- **Consolidate gains and produce more change** – leverage increased credibility from successes, which facilitates and stimulates the introduction of more change;
- **Anchor new approaches in the culture** – institutionalize the process, adapt enabling technology and tools, and link progress to performance.

A growing number of organizations have recognized the benefits of improving the IT governance environment in their organizations and have established IT governance functions in their IT organizations. Figures 4.2 and 4.3 represent two examples of IT organization structures of companies in the food and manufacturing industries respectively. Clearly, these structures will vary from organization to organization based on size, management orientation (e.g. centralized, de-centralized, federated, etc.), geographic presence, home country versus global orientation, credibility and influence of the CIO and other factors.

In either case, the following activities will further help to organize a successful IT governance initiative:

- Identify executive champion and multi-disciplinary team (to focus on each major IT governance component);
- Do homework – get up-to-date on current and emerging best practices;
- Market and communicate the IT governance value proposition;
- Develop a tailored IT governance framework and roadmap for your organization based on current and emerging industry best practices;
- Decompose the IT governance components into well-defined work packages (assign an owner and champion to each process component);
- Assess the 'current state' of the level of IT governance maturity;

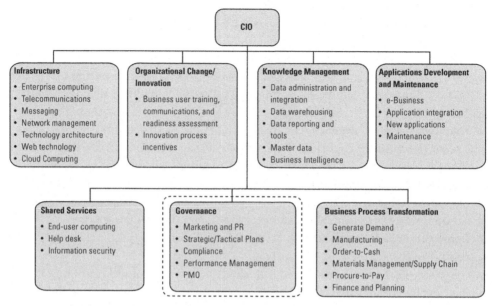

Figure 4.2 IT Organization structure for a food company

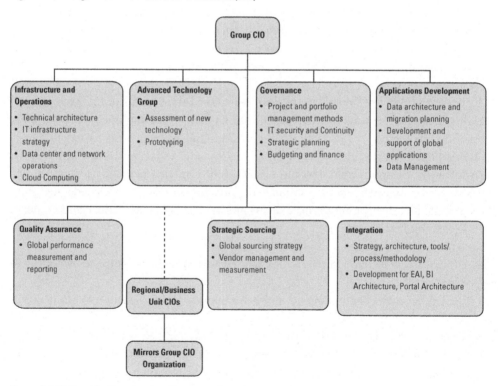

Figure 4.3 IT Organization structure for a manufacturing company

- Develop a 'future state' IT governance blueprint (where you want to be) and keep it in focus;
- Develop an IT governance action plan, identify deliverables, establish priorities, milestones and allocate resources;
- Identify enabling technologies to support the IT governance initiative.

4.5   WORLD CLASS LEADERSHIP PRINCIPLES AND PRACTICES

According to the Chinese philosopher Lao Tzu (6th century b. Chr.), a great leader has the following attributes:
- To lead people, walk beside them;
- As for the best leaders, the people do not notice their existence;
- The next best, the people honor and praise;
- The next, the people fear; and the next, the people hate;
- When the best leader's work is done, the people say, "We did it ourselves!"

4.5.1 Key leadership and people skills and competencies required for success

The success of major enterprise initiative like IT governance is more often determined by people using soft skills such as leadership communications, integrity, persistence, judgment, managing expectations, inter-personal skills, team building and managing change and innovation rather than by 'hard' skills such as plans, procedures, processes and technologies.

Figure 4.4 identifies select people and hard skills required to execute IT governance and other initiatives effectively. Most of the soft skills are below the water line, and are invisible and less obvious than the visible tip of the iceberg, which is represented by the hard skills. Both are necessary to achieve success.

Most world class organizations develop leadership and management succession plans that are based on a specific set of skills and competencies. Figure 4.5 represents a blend of the major skills and competencies required for leadership positions in these companies. They are broken into five areas: leadership, marketing and customer focus, critical thinking, achieving results and effective execution and functional expertise. These can apply to IT governance as well as many other enterprise initiatives.

4.5.2 Leadership profiles for winning

David McCleland, the former Harvard University psychologist, developed the concept of leadership profiles for winning (McCleland, 1995). The key actions of outstanding

**The success and advancement of professionals up the organizational ladder
is more often determined by leadership, people, team building and managing change and
innovation skills well than by hard skills such as developing and/or applying policies,
procedures, processes and technologies**

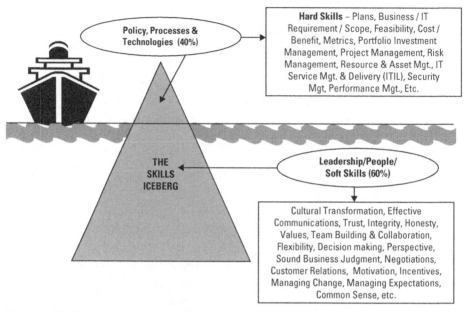

Figure 4.4 The IT governance skills iceberg

**The Leadership Competency Model represents a blend of models
developed by select leading edge organizations such as Verizon, Motorola,
Proctor and Gamble, GE and Others**

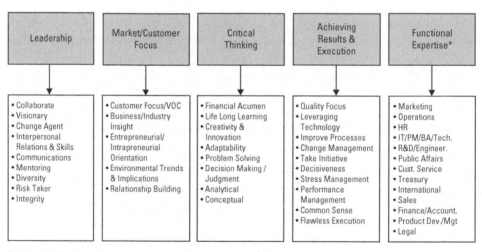

Figure 4.5 The Leadership Competency Model

leaders identified in his research can be applied to developing and sustaining an organizational-wide IT governance initiative:

- **Passion for winning** – asks big questions about what is possible and takes major entrepreneurial action over time to deliver sustainable profitable business.
- **Breakthrough thinking** – uses their insights into complex situations to break existing business paradigms and create major new opportunities by reinventing the organization.
- **Political acumen** – understands the influence (decision-making and power structures, climate, culture and politics) which shapes how organizations work. They adapt their approach to optimize results.
- **Seizing the future** – gets to the future first by taking decisive action today (requires speed and being a first mover) to create new markets for tomorrow.
- **Change catalyst** – energizes others towards new, better ways of operating and generating success, communicates a vision and knocks obstacles out of the way.
- **Developing others** – invests time, money and energy in developing others to build the organization's capability for the future as well as coaching and mentoring future leaders.
- **Holding people accountable** – holds people and teams accountable for delivering agreed objectives and consistently measures and rewards results or changes performance for the better.
- **Empowering others** – creates commitment by empowering others to act and streamlining organizational decision making and approval processes (e.g. decision rights).
- **Strategic influencing** – builds commitment by influencing others positively without using hierarchical power to adopt a specific course of action to orchestrate change.
- **TeamcCommitment** – works co-operatively with others across the organization to achieve shared goals, places high value on being part of a team and acts to further the interests of the team above their own.
- **Team leadership** – adjusts their leadership styles to optimize team outputs and inspires others to higher standards of performance by setting examples and energizing the team.

4.5.3 One CIO's rules for IT service and governance

Many CIOs today have created their own set of leadership and management rules, written them down, distributed them to their organization and integrated them into the daily life of the organization. Some lists are very specific covering such areas as governance, alignment, compliance and capital expenditures, while others relate to actionable principles.

Bill Godfrey, former CIO of Dow Jones, developed a set of rules that, "… in one form or another are there to sustain, protect and foster alignment." (Wailgum, 2005). Godfrey's fourteen big rules for IT service and governance are:

Rule 1 – Strategic planning
- All technology divisions will have a documented technology plan;
- All technology divisions will have published goals and objectives.

Rule 2 – Production prioritization
- Production problems classified as 'severity one' production problems take resource precedent over all else. Management and staff will work on 'severity one' problems immediately and continually until resolved.

Rule 3 – Enterprise architecture
- All technology divisions will have a documented high level architecture;
- All technology divisions will adhere to infrastructure standards or seek exception approval;
- All technology projects costing more than $250,000 in total must be approved through an 'early look' screening process prior to capital approval submission.

Rule 4 – Project management
- There will be 100% adherence to the project management process for all non-trivial development projects (projects estimated to take more than two weeks of staff time);
- All development projects will have a specifically identified business sponsor and a specifically identified IT project leader prior to initiation;
- All development projects requiring infrastructure support will directly involve infrastructure support staff during project initiation, giving the infrastructure staff an opportunity to directly participate in the design of systems solutions.

Rule 5 – Time management
- All staff time will be appropriately entered into the IT time reporting system on a weekly basis.

Rule 6 – Technology business management
- As represented in approved budgets, technology costs will not exceed plan unless explicit approval is granted by the CIO;
- Technology contracts will be managed and approved through business management services or purchasing;
- All third-party contractors and consultants will sign non-disclosure agreements, managed under the non-employee security policy, and managed through the company's preferred vendor program.

Rule 7 – Capital approval management

- All projects will adhere to corporate expenditure authorization processes;
- All projects are required to have appropriate IT senior leadership team sign-offs prior to business line submission;
- For all projects requiring CIO approval, all staff work and IT senior leadership team approvals will be complete prior to seeking CIO approval;
- Any project with a total cost of more than $250,000 will be submitted to finance for formal business case review.

Rule 8 – Requesting proposals from third parties

- All requests for proposals from third parties will be reviewed and approved by the CIO prior to execution;
- All requests for proposals from third parties which could have infrastructure implications will be reviewed and approved by IT infrastructure services prior to execution.

Rule 9 – Relationship management

- Business technology directors are 100% accountable for all technology, direct and indirect, in support of their assigned business lines;
- Business technology directors 'own' all business application vendor relationships;
- Enterprises technology directors 'own' all infrastructure vendor relationships.

Rule 10 – Infrastructure management

- Enterprise infrastructure services is 100% accountable for the global infrastructure;
- Enterprise infrastructure services is the only organization that makes infrastructure decisions;
- Enterprise infrastructure services owns and manages all infrastructure capital.

Rule 11 – Compliance with audit, regulatory and legal requirements

- Information technology services will comply with all audit, regulatory and legal requirements;
- The IT senior leadership team is accountable for compliance.

Rule 12 – Operations procedural compliance

- There will be 100% compliance with [the] enterprise change control policy and procedure;
- All production applications will be supported by a service level agreement between IT and the business.

Rule 13 – Information security

- All technology staff will comply with the company's information security policy;
- Information security approval must be secured prior to implementing new technology or making major enhancements to existing technology. This review and approval is to

take place before any informal or formal obligations are made between the company and a supplier;
- All access to a financially significant application will be managed and controlled through information security.

Rule 14 – Sarbanes-Oxley compliance
- There will be 100% compliance to all Sarbanes-Oxley controls;
- All IT leaders will be thoroughly familiar with the IT general control policies regarding governance, project management, operations, access control and data management;
- All IT leaders, supervisor and above, are responsible and accountable for Sarbanes-Oxley compliance across their respective areas of control.

4.5.4 SMART (Specific, Measurable, Assignable, Realistic and Time related)

George T. Doran developed a simple paradigm called 'SMART' to help leaders and organizations formulate objectives based on easily remembered attributes. Table 4.1 represents an adoption of Doran's attributes to IT governance (Doran, 1981).

Table 4.1 Doran's Attributes Adopted for IT Governance (illustrative example)

Attribute	Description	IT Governance Example
S = Specific	Be specific in targeting an objective.	Achieve CMMI level 3 maturity for three major IT governance components.
M = Measurable	Establish a measurable indicator(s) of progress.	Improve customer satisfaction; reduce costs; etc.
A = Assignable	Make the objective assignable to one person for completion.	Assign an IT manager as owner.
R = Realistic	State what can realistically be done with available resources.	Improve one (1) level of maturity per year across the organization.
T = Time related	State when the objective can be achieved.	Achieve specific objective (see above) within two years on an enterprise-wide scale.

4.5.5 What management expects from an IT governance project manager

The following attributes are essential attributes of a successful project manager:
- Develop a realistic and pragmatic IT governance plan and program;
- Focus on deliverables and results (as opposed to stringent process adherence – use common sense and good judgment);
- Work with customers/constituents to define requirements and scope;
- Effective status reporting (Theory of No Surprises);
- Good motivator, mentor and coach;
- Ability to handle inter-personal problems;
- Self-starter, committed, driven, persistent and able to lead by example;
- Trustworthy, loyal and credible;
- Listens well and is open minded;

- Tolerant of diversity;
- Confident;
- Ethical and honest;
- Possesses good negotiations skills;
- Professional behavior;
- Great communicator.

4.5.6 Non-trainable skills (ones where you can't go off to class and learn them)

These are the personal skills that one can enhance and encourage but not train into someone without them – they are the skills that will make one successful in a job, desirable as an employee and essential in a leader who is responsible for change:
- Creativity;
- Priority assessment – what's most important when there is too little time/resources;
- Resourcefulness – the ability to get around obstacles;
- Adaptability – the ability to deal with ambiguity and non-closed items and changes;
- Emotional control;
- Rapport-building;
- Drive;
- Self-insight;
- Initiative (stepping outside what's required, going the extra mile);
- Judgment – coming to an appropriate conclusion based on the data available;
- Professional commitment – do what it takes to get the job done;
- Independence (versus constant following);
- Risk taking.

■ 4.6 PRINCIPLES FOR CREATING AND SUSTAINING HIGH PERFORMANCE TEAMS

"Always tell people the truth, because they know it already."

Jack Welsh, Former Chairman and CEO, GE

"Always do the right thing, you will gratify some people and astonish the rest,"

Mark Twain, American author

Many companies, such as Haliburton, Quaker Oates, TRW and General Mills, who have established effective team environments and culture, reported a 20-40% gain in productivity after 12–18 months (Johnson, 2002).

Organizations are developing increasingly complex team based organizational structures (Snyder, 2003; Katzenback and Smith, 2001; Lohr, 2007; DeGraff & Quinn, 2007; Aasi, et al., 2014) with the purpose to:

■ Address constantly changing business needs that compel organizational structures to be fluid and where team members can be moved to where their expertise is required.
■ Build a successful organization of the future (which is now), the following principles should guide that effort:
  • Organize for continuous change – stability is out and 'organizational whitewater' is in;
  • Develop and support knowledge workers – the person(s) whose intellectual capital will fuel future innovation;
  • Harvest global brains – national boundaries are no longer barriers to innovation. Global 'centers of excellence', focusing on different IT competencies, have and are being set up companies such as IBM, Intel, Google, Toyota, Cisco and others;
  • Enable networks of cross-specialization experts – silos and smokestacks are dying. Future success will depend on how efficiently a company links its 'centers of excellence' to create value and share learnings, independent of location.

According to Bill Snyder, the characteristics of world class team members include (Snyder, 2003):
■ Represent inter-disciplinary and cross-functional business units;
■ Either serve in a full-time assignment reporting directly to a team leader, or report part-time to team leaders and part-time to their functional bosses, as in a matrix organization;
■ Can be co-located or work at different locations, virtually;
■ Are knowledge workers.

For enterprise governance to improve the bottom line, well-lead multi-disciplinary and cross-functional teams must be established with wide representation from the business and IT. A team represents a collection of people who rely on group collaboration such that each of the team members experiences an optimum level of success, achieving both personal and team-based goals and objectives.

A team chartered to develop an IT governance initiative and plan should include the CIO (as the champion), his or her direct reports, and have representation from both key business units and corporate staff functions such as finance, audit, operations, legal and the executive office. The composition of the various working committee(s) should reflect the responsibility for developing and deploying the key IT governance components such as alignment, planning, program and project management, IT service management, strategic sourcing and performance management and controls.

4.6.1 Problems and issues With teams

The traditional problems and issues with teams should be identified, prioritized and overcome. They include such things as:

- Insufficient commitment to the team;
- Tolerance of mediocre participation and contribution;
- Groupthink – tends to minimize individual creativity and motivation;
- Conflicting personal agendas of team members and the resultant mistrust;
- Poor or inappropriate team leadership;
- Unclear scope and objectives;
- Lack of role clarity, communication and rules of operation;
- Lack of ability to work through differences of opinions;
- A closed climate that prevents members from expressing honestly how they feel about issues;
- Emphasis on process versus results;
- Poor management of constituent expectations;
- Performance appraisals and compensation systems that are more aligned to individual versus team performance;
- Individual 'star' contributors who value their independence and don't really want to play the interdependent 'team game'.

If teams are to be successful, the organization's culture needs to be supportive of them. To change the culture, requires a change in behaviors and rewards, which will provide people with a new set of experiences (hopefully positive).

4.6.2 A win-win team attitude

If a company wants to receive the maximum benefits from its teams, it must develop a positive win-win attitude using the following tips suggested by Linda McDermott et al. and supplemented by the author (McDermott, Brawley, Nolan and Waite, 1998; Bossidy and Charan, 2002; Brammer and Pavelin, 2013):

- Focus on the benefits of working in a team;
- Seek the good in people around you;
- Seek the good in your workplace;
- Learn to forgive (everyone learns from mistakes);
- Find humor in everyday occurrences;
- Let your positive attitude in one area spill over into another;
- Talk positively with yourself and others;
- Avoid attitude downers – you are in control of your attitude, not others;
- Take responsibility and be accountable;
- Stand up and speak up for what you believe in;
- Be flexible and willing to compromise;
- Creating team charters and boundaries to clarify missions, roles and responsibilities;
- Create ownership at every organizational level where teams operate;
- A formal team governance process with meaningful metrics and actions is necessary;

- Deliver short term incremental deliverables that work (decompose complex programs or projects) to establish team credibility and visibility;
- Recognize and reward exceptional team performance.

4.6.3 Building blocks for team development and effectiveness

Teams represent a form of organization. Most organizations function with some form of structure, rules and processes. Effective world class teams also require building blocks and guidelines to work smartly. These include some of the following:

- Goals – are clear to all, challenging yet realistic. Each individual's work relates to overall team goals and objectives;
- Roles – mutually understood; everyone knows why they are on the team. Authority and responsibilities are consistent;
- Boundaries – describes the scope and parameters of what the team is empowered to do and what is off-limits;
- Processes – key processes are in place to support the work of the team:
  - Problem solving and issue identification;
  - Planning, decision making and authority;
  - Handling conflict, resolution or escalation;
  - Managing expectations of constituents;
  - Contents, format and frequent of communications;
  - Meeting management – agendas, minutes, follow-up actions;
  - Resource management and allocation;
  - Team training and new team memberaAbsorption;
  - Evaluation of team effectiveness and performance;
  - Team dissolution and reassignment of team members;
  - Interactions with other teams and organizations.
- Relationships – team members communicate openly and demonstrate trust for one another. The team establishes relationships beyond itself (external touch points), as needed in the organization.

The first critical step in developing high performance teams is to 'set them up for success'. Senior management and other key stakeholders (or the team itself, if it a self-directed team) should hold planning discussions to reach consensus on such issues as:

- The team's purpose, charter, boundaries, scope and expected outcomes;
- The team's structure, team leader (individual or shared or self-directed) and team members;
- Strategies for management commitment, support, resource allocation and issues escalation;
- The team's measures of success, key performance indicators and their links to MBO (management by objectives), compensation and incentives;
- The team's rules and processes for communications, progress reporting, meetings, conflict-resolution, problem and issues workouts, self-assessment, managing expectations of stakeholders, etc.

Figure 4.6 summarizes a list of operating characteristics generally present in effective high performance teams.

Clear Purpose	The vision, mission, goal or task of the team has been defined and is now accepted by everyone. There is an action plan.
Informality	The climate tends to be informal, comfortable, and relaxed. There are no obvious tensions or signs of boredom.
Participation	There is much discussion and everyone is encouraged to participate.
Listening	The members use effective listening techniques such as questioning, paraphrasing and summarizing to get ideas out.
Civilized Disagreement	There is disagreement, but the team is comfortable with this and shows no signs of avoiding, smoothing over, or suppressing conflict.
Consensus and Fast Decisions	For important decisions, the goal is substantial but not necessarily unanimous agreement through open discussion of everyone's ideas, avoidance of formal voting, or easy compromises. It is also important to avoid or minimize "groupthink" which often limits individual creativity and may sub-optimize the team's actions.
Open communication	Team members feel free to express their feelings on the tasks as well as on the group's operation. There are few hidden agendas. Communication takes place outside of meetings.
Clear Roles and Work Assignments	There are clear expectations about roles played by each team member. When action is taken, clear assignments are made, accepted and carried out. Work is fairly distributed among members.
Shared Leadership	While the team has a formal leader, leadership functions shift from time to time depending upon the circumstances, the needs of the group, and the skills of the members. The former leader models the appropriate behavior and helps establish positive norms.
External Relations	The team spends time developing key outside relationships, mobilizing resources, and building credibility with important players in other parts of the organization.
Style and Cultural Diversity	The team has a broad spectrum of team-player types representing different cultures including members who emphasize attention to task, goal setting, focus on process and questions about how the team is functioning.
Self-Assessment	Periodically, the team steps back to examine how well it is functioning, examines what may be interfering with its effectiveness and takes corrective actions.
Use of Technology	Organizations are creating "global centers of excellence" to take advantage of global brains. This has accelerated the use of technology to save time, costs and facilitate collaboration amongst multi-location team members.

Figure 4.6 Summary of operating characteristics present in world class teams

4.6.4 Select technologies for teams

As organizations become more global, they are establishing 'centers of excellence' in many parts of the world to take advantage of global brains, reduced labor rates, unique and specialized skills, rare resources and, perhaps, more lax regulatory environments than exist in their home base.

Technologies used by teams generally improve communications and collaboration, increase decision making speed and time to market, reduce costs and take advantage of a twenty-four hour work day. In addition, as organizations increase their outsourcing expenditures, technology is playing a growing and increasingly important role in connecting the customers with their service providers and suppliers. Figure 4.7 provides examples of select technologies used by traditional and virtual teams based in the same or different geographic locations and/or time zones.

Technologies used by teams generally improve communications and collaboration, increase decision making speed and reduce costs.

Technologies for Teams:

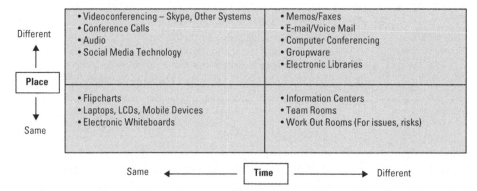

Figure 4.7 Select technologies for teams

■ 4.7   CASE STUDY – GLOBAL BUSINESS OUTSOURCING SERVICES COMPANY

Figure 4.8 illustrates an IT governance case study of a global business outsourcing service company. This company is the only one of the case study companies that requires all direct reports to the CIO to be TOM (Target Operating Model) certified. TOM is a description of the state of the operations of a business and a roadmap to enable a company to achieve it. It defines the people, process and technology required to deliver a strategy or implement a plan.

Environment & Drivers	Approach
• Revenue range – $10.0 - $14.0 billion	• Describe general steps/phases/actions to improve IT governance
• Number of employees – range – 50,000 - 70,000	
• Industry classification – Business, Accounting & HR Services	• All service managers responsible for business units (which are IT intensive) work closely with IT to develop project priorities
• Management philosophy – conservative/risk takers/ others	• Every manager in CIO organization must become ITIL certified
• Number of countries with operations – 100+	
• Number of full time IT professionals/range – 6,000 - 8,000	• All senior directors reporting to CIO must be TOM (Target Operating Model)* certified
• IT organization – centralized	* *Note*: Target Operating Model is a description of the state of the operations of a business and a roadmap to enable a company to achieve it. It defines the people, process and technology required to deliver a strategy or implement a plan.
• CIO is a member of the executive committee and reports directly to the CEO	
• Chief security officer (CSO) reports to CEO	

Figure 4.8 Case Study – global business outsourcing service company

Issues, Objectives, Constraints & Opportunities	Approach (continued)
• Identify key issues, constraints, objectives and opportunities relating to IT governance and management – Key issues identified include: • IT security – maintain high security standards based on ISO 27001:2013 - IT security guidelines • Stability of electronic power grids (business is very dependent on electric power in USA) • Managing the effective flow – prioritizing and processing requests for IT services • Revising and maintaining reliable IT metrics for internal management and customers	• TOM, ITIL and related project management disciplines are tailored to the needs of the company • ISO 27001:2013 is used as a guideline for the IT security policy and procedures.
Results – Alignment (Business/IT) Describe methods/processes for aligning and integrating IT more effectively into the business • Company uses "Business/IT Relationship Management Teams" comprised of both business and IT managers to integrate business and IT plans, evaluate new project priorities, make go/no-go decisions on projects and conduct post-mortems of problems to reduce and/or eliminate them	**Results - IT Service Management (Includes ITIL)** Describe IT infrastructure and operations • Company has multiple data centers used for processing their customer services and back-up • ITIL 2011 is widely used in the environment

Results - Program/Project/Portfolio Management/SDM
Describe the program/project/portfolio management organization, roles, processes, tools, metrics, etc
• Company uses Planview as their PM Tool (enterprise-wide PM) for:
  – Portfolio investment management
  – Managing projects
  – Generating PM metrics
• See "Business/IT Relationship Teams" above
• Company supports PM certifications
	Results - Performance Management
	Describe performance management/metrics
	• PM metrics used - costs, schedule, customer satisfaction, deliverables, etc.
	• Infrastructure and operations:
	  – SLAs (service level agreements) are used between customers (users) and IT (e.g. number of incidents and fix time, etc.)
	  – OLAs (operational level agreements) are used within IT (e.g. operations and software engineering) and include resolution of problem vs response times

Results – Cloud Computing and Data Management Cloud computing: a Cisco-based private cloud is used for revenue generating applications. A public cloud supplied by "Connected Backup Company" provides backup and recovery capability and is also used to provide extranets for customers Data management: a Sybell system is used for select data management applications that are customer driven A chief security officer reporting to the CEO establishes security and privacy policy, processes and procedures for the company and IT	**Critical Success Factors** Describe CSFs to improve IT governance and management • Systems (data center) availability is very high (consistently 99.9+2.) and backed-up twice (in tandem) • Company sponsors certification of key employees and managers on TOM, ITIL and PM
Results– Strategic Sourcing and Outsourcing Describe organization, process, tools, key vendors, metrics and issues • Limited outsourcing is used due to the high security requirements and the perceived risks and potential liabilities	**Lessons Learned** Describe the lessons learned in your IT governance improvement efforts: • Company is big on "post-mortem" reviews of problems that occurred to learn from the mistakes and prevent the same mistakes from recurring • ITIL was implemented in a phased approach that caused unnecessary confusion according to company; ITIL should have been implemented in all locations at the same time throughout the company and may have been more efficient

Figure 4.8 Case Study – global business outsourcing service company (continued)

■ 4.8 SUMMARY AND KEY TAKE AWAYS

4.8.1 Summary – checklist for managing accelerating change
■ Define the change – create a common understanding of the change;
■ Build company capacity – change management skills, resources and roles (champion, sponsors, agents, targets);
■ Assess the climate – implementation history and stress levels;
■ Generate sponsorship – construct, cascade and sponsor role;
■ Get the right talent – with the right skills and attitudes;
■ Determine change approach – commitment or compliance;
■ Develop target readiness – identify and manage resistance to change at all levels and determine how to overcome it;
■ Develop the communications plan – communicate in terms of frame of reference;
■ Develop reinforcement strategy – align rewards and efforts required to achieve IT governance objectives and measure results;
■ Create cultural fit – identify conflicts and unwritten rules;
■ Prioritize action – a project plan;
■ Evaluate the change process;
■ Reward significant progress – link incentive pay and other rewards to quantifiable objectives.

4.8.2 Summary – checklist for leadership and effective teams
■ Clear purpose, common vision and accountability;
■ Obsession with external customer;
■ Participation and well-defined roles;
■ Civilized disagreement and style diversity – allow for workout meetings and discussions;
■ Encourage open communications – silence is consent – voice your ideas;
■ Encourage flexible discipline and even expulsion of non-productive team members;
■ Blend of informality and formality;
■ Focus both on process and end results. However, remember that results are more important than process;
■ Acknowledgement of the need for change;
■ Strong respect and trust between members and leaders;
■ Single point of contact for official team progress and communications (do not feed rumor-mill);
■ Self-assessment of team members and adjustment;
■ No ideas are bad ideas; encourage no blame game;
■ Use automated tools to increase speed and communications.

4.8.3 Key take aways

Steven Covey identified the seven habits of highly effective people. These not only impact how well individuals perform, but also how well organizations and teams perform. These habits represent superior take aways from this chapter (Covey, 1989):

- **Be proactive** – take the initiative; act or be acted upon;
- **Begin with the end in mind** – vision, mission, scope, deliverables and boundaries;
- **Put first things first** – time bounds; time management (A,B,C); prioritize;
- **Think and act win/win** – everyone wins if team wins – individuals, team members, leaders and organization;
- **Seek first to understand, then to be understood** – active listening; diagnose before you prescribe;
- **Synergize** – creative collaboration and innovation; value differences;
- **Sharpen the saw** – continuous learning and renewal; adopt best practices; create a knowledge management database of lessons learned (good and bad) – enable easy access to them.

"As a general rule, leaders have become leaders because they have done more, been better, worked harder and somehow differentiated themselves in some ways. They've accomplished this more or less on their own all along the way."

Gregg Miller, President, RACOM Corporation

PART

IT GOVERNANCE, THE MAJOR COMPONENT PROCESSES AND ENABLING TECHNOLOGIES

Part II of the book covers Chapters 5 through 10. This includes an overview of the critical process components of IT governance such as program and project management, IT service management, strategic sourcing and outsourcing, performance management and controls, risk management, cloud computing and data management, select enabling technologies, critical success factors, lessons learned and a composite checklist of required IT governance activities.

Well documented processes that are consistent, repeatable, flexible and technology-enabled are one of the single biggest contributors to improved reliability and therefore quality in both product and service delivery. The following identifies and groups the benefits that can be achieved through the use of consistent, but flexible process implementation and improvement:

- Cost – reduction, avoidance and containment;
- Efficiency – automation, reliability, consistency, speed and easier to train personnel;
- Governance – compliance, auditable, alignment, measurable, quality and effectiveness.

5 Program and Project Management Excellence (Execution Management)

"But in science, the credit goes to the man who convinces the world, not the man to whom the idea first occurs."

Sir Francis Darwin, 1914

"Almost all IT projects require teamwork and collaboration across multiple functional areas of the company. The success of an IT project depends less on technology than it does on managing a smooth transition from an old business process to a new business process."

Greg Fell, former CIO, Terex

5.1   WHAT IS COVERED IN THIS CHAPTER?

- Provides an overview of the key principles, issues, concepts and processes for effectively managing enterprise-wide and limited scope programs and projects;
- Identifies the driving forces, value propositions and key principles and practices for achieving excellence in program and project management as part of IT governance;
- Reviews the self-assessment project management (PM) maturity level assessment technique;
- Links the IT plan to programs and projects that support the business;
- Learn how to use the program/project type-scale matrix to determine which PM methodology – light (fast track or Agile) or complex to use as part of a scalable and flexible framework;
- Understand the mandatory and discretionary key performance indicators and metrics necessary to manage programs and projects effectively;
- Reviews the principles and practices of AgilePM and Scrum.

5.2   OVERVIEW

Program management represents large complex initiatives with at least two or more interrelated projects as part of the program (e.g. SAP implementation). Project management usually represents one discrete project with multiple activities and tasks. The key metrics in programs and projects are scope, time, cost, quality and customer satisfaction. Portfolio investment management is the process for evaluating the feasibility and priorities of either programs or projects. Program management, project management and portfolio investment management are major components of effective IT governance that focus on execution management. Significant research has been conducted in the area of program and project management resulting in many publications as is evidenced by the references provided in the book.

It is not the intention of this chapter to rehash what has already been published, but rather to provide a blend of practical and useable frameworks, checklists, tools, templates, techniques and metrics to help deliver programs and projects on time, within scope, within budget, with high quality and to the customer's satisfaction, get them back on track and/or cancel disasters about to happen. It references several self-assessment maturity models that can be used to assess the current maturity level of an organization and suggests a transition plan to improve PM practices. It also suggests a scalable and flexible PM lifecycle framework based on a blend of best practices that are tailorable to handle different project types (e.g. simple, moderate and complex), and that can be institutionalized in many organizational environments (e.g. small, medium and large).

5.2.1 Key definitions

So that the reader is on the same map as the author, Figure 5.1 provides a working definition of key terms such as programs, projects, tasks and processes. In addition, the extensive glossary provided includes many more project management and other IT governance terms and definitions.

Term	Definition	Examples
Program	Consists of multiple inter-related projects that are inter-related and is usually large, complex and with high visibility, high $ value & high risk.	An Enterprise Resource Planning System like SAP or Oracle
Project	A discrete, one-time event that consists of such attributes as time, cost, resources, risk, deliverables, quality, customers, etc.	Sap Module - Purchasing
Portfolio	A collection of projects that require evaluation, selection, funding and prioritization to become an approved project.	Upgrade to a system, Design a new system or product, Replacement of an operating system.
Task	A discrete element of work	Order equipment
Process	A continuous work effort to support a business or IT function	Service Management; Service Desk; Sales Order Process

Figure 5.1 Key program/project management and portfolio investment management definitions

5.2.2 Trends in program and project management

According to the Project Management Institute (PMI), the International Project Management Association (IPMA) and others, the profession of project management has undergone tremendous growth in the past few years. With this growth, significant changes to the field of project management have evolved in the use of more sophisticated processes, tools, knowledge management, technologies and certifications. Table 5.1 identifies the past, present and future trends in project management.

Table 5.1 Trends in Project Management

PAST	FUTURE
Few Projects	Many Projects
Authoritarian Management Style	Participative Management
Simple Projects	Complex Projects
Employees Easy to Manage	Employees More Difficult to Manage
Few Opportunities	More Opportunities
Few Tools Available	More Tools Available
No User Involvement	Increasing User Involvement
Unique Mgt./Project	Std. Mgt. for All Projects
Manual PM Processes	Automated PM Processes
Individual Project Status Reporting	Multi-Project Status Reporting
Little Mgt. Support/Understanding	More Mgt. Sponsorship and Commitment
Limited Project Integration	More Complex and Integrated Enterprise-Wide Systems
Waterfall (Synchronous Development)	More Iterative and Agile Development

5.2.3 Project management skills

As the complexity of projects increase, the project manager and team must have or attain a broad range of skills in order to be effective. Figure 5.2 identifies the skills required in the complex and fast paced project environments of the future.

5.2.4 How much program and project management is required?

Many organizations have been challenged by the question of, "How much program and project management is required in our organizational and project environment?" There is no simple or straight forward answer to this question. The answer depends on many factors relating to the organizational philosophy and policies and specifics program or project variables such as:

- Degree of visibility and strategic value of the initiative;
- Financial value (one time and recurring costs);
- Strategic value and visibility to organization;
- Complexity, scope and size;
- Duration;
- Number of interfaces and integration requirements with other systems;
- Degree of risk;
- Speed of required implementation;

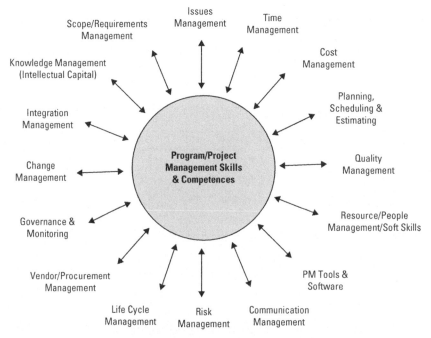

Figure 5.2 Project management is complex and requires multiple skills

■ Senior management and PM's management style, philosophy and level of organizational PM maturity;
■ Number of organizations, departments, locations and resources involved;
■ Executive management and/or customer requirements and sponsorship;
■ Degree of outsourcing; on-shore and off-shore sourcing;
■ Regulatory and compliance requirements.

For a growing number of organizations, a light or fast track project management process which addresses, at a minimum, the project's sponsor and owner, requirements, objectives, scope, risks and contingencies, constraints, schedule, budget, and deliverables is often sufficient. This is covered in greater detail in Section 5.5.

5.2.5 Why is program/project management important?

The objective of project management is to make the most effective use of multiple resources by delivering projects on time, on budget, within scope, with high quality, to the customer's satisfaction, with minimum, or no, rework and the mitigation of the major risks. The resources include personnel, equipment, facilities, materials, capital, technology, external resources (e.g. suppliers and service providers), intellectual property and other assets.

As all kinds of programs and projects become more pervasive in organizations in order to manage a wide range of initiatives such as new product development, mergers and acquisitions, new enterprise-wide information systems, new building and facilities construction and others, both private and public sector leaders have recognized that project management is a strategic imperative. Project management provides organizations and people with a powerful set of processes, tools and technologies that improve their ability to plan, implement, integrate and manage activities to meet business objectives in an effective (if done correctly) and disciplined manner. Project management is a results-oriented management discipline that places a high value on building collaborative relationships among a diverse set of people located anywhere to complete specific deliverables.

5.2.6 The five 'W's' and two 'H's' of project management

It is important at an early stage to establish the basic questions that will help to define the parameters of a program or project. The fundamental questions that help to scope a project include:

- **Why**... are we doing this? Are we solving a newly discovered problem, fixing an existing problem, pursuing an opportunity, cutting costs, increasing revenues, eliminating waste or increasing productivity? Everyone, from top to bottom, must know the answer, and the answer must be on this list.
- **Who**... wants this done? Is it an executive sponsor, project task force/project manager and team, owner(s) of deliverables, customers, or outside stakeholders? Has that person/team sold the 'why' and assumed responsibility and commitment from key people (e.g. resources, capital, etc.)?
- **What**... are the details? Is the project feasible? Is it linked to the organization's vision and plan? Are all the resources (human, financial, material, facilities, etc.) available and committed? Have the project's scope and objectives been approved and sold to all? Have risks been evaluated and contingencies planned for? Have interface and integration concerns been addressed?
- **How**... will we do this? How much will be built? How much bought? How much will be outsourced? How will we audit outsourced progress/quality? How will issues/problems be addressed and escalated?
- **When**... are deliverables required? Are deadlines, schedules, milestones, and critical path tasks identified and are all involved aware of them? What status reporting processes, metrics and performance reporting mechanisms are needed or in place?
- **Where**... will this be done and where are the affected stakeholders? Where are the departments, functions, locations, countries and people?
- **How much**... is the budget? How much has been budgeted, committed, allocated and spent? How will we measure the performance and key metrics? How will any variances between budgets, actuals and baselines be addressed? If major changes to the requirements, scope and environment are necessary, how will they be reviewed, approved and funded?

■ 5.3 PROJECT MANAGEMENT IS COMPLEX BUT HAS SIGNIFICANT VALUE

According to Bruce Barkley, "Projects must be internally and externally integrated; internal integration means that project work packages, deliverables and systems are connected; external integration means that the project interfaces with customer systems and produces value for the customer and the market and industry as a whole." (Barkley, 2006). In addition to customers, select projects are also linked with supplier systems, government systems (e.g. financial reporting, taxes, etc.) and outsourcing service providers. Therefore, as programs and projects become more integrated, their complexity rises.

5.3.1 Major causes of program/project failures and challenges
There are many reasons for program and project failures and challenges. Select reasons include:
- Lack of, or poor business case;
- Lack of executive commitment, visibility and accountability;
- Poorly or insufficiently defined requirements, scope, objectives and deliverables;
- Poor communications amongst constituents;
- Failure to treat a project as a start-up initiative;
- Unrealistic expectations;
- Limited constituent involvement and ownership;
- Lack of, or insufficient (and the right kind of) resources;
- Lack of, or poor integration within the organization and to other systems;
- No plan, no risk assessment and mitigation, no contingency plan alternatives;
- Lack of meaningful measurable controls and metrics;
- Ineffective implementation strategy;
- Underestimation of project complexity, costs and time;
- Poor or unreliable vendor deliverables;
- Lack of training for either the project team or those constituents who are impacted by the project;
- Inflexible, limited or no project management process;
- Poor use or over-reliance on the use of PM tools and software;
- Vendor failure.

5.3.2 The cost of program and project management failure
The Standish Group, Gartner and IDG have conducted periodic annual surveys on the state of project management in the USA. These surveys divide programs and projects into three classifications – failed, challenged and successful. The first class represents failed projects that have been started, but never finished for a variety of reasons – the sponsor resigned, the need went away, poor requirements definition, avoiding a disaster about to happen and scope creep. The second class represents challenged projects, which have been implemented, but with one or more significant challenges such as over-budget,

over-schedule, under-scoped and reworked due to changing requirements. The third class represents successful projects that have been implemented, generally on time, within budget, within scope, with reasonable quality and to the customer's satisfaction.

According to a blend of surveys, the estimated annual cost range of failed and challenged projects in the USA approximates to $150 to 200 billion. Figure 5.3 illustrates these numbers for small, medium and large organizations.

Nearly $^3/_4$ of all projects fail or run into trouble

An estimated **$150 – 200+ billion per year is spent on failed and challenged projects in USA** (out of a total estimated spend of $500 billion)

Successful (S) = completed on-time, on-budget and within scope

Challenged (C) = completed, but with time and/or budget overruns and fewer features than originally specified

Failed (F) = cancelled before completion

Company Size	S	C	F
Large	9%	62%	29%
Medium	16%	47%	37%
Small	28%	50%	22%

Source: Blend of surveys by the Standish Group, Gartner & IDC

Figure 5.3 The cost of project failure

Several questions that the author asked senior executives of companies regarding their project environments are: "How much of these costs is contributed by your organization? Do you really have a good grasp of this kind of information? How effective are your organization's project management governance policies, frameworks, standards, processes, tools, disciplines, training programs and PM metrics?" More often than not, senior executives do not have readily available answers to these questions. That is part of the problem and can also become part of the solution. This information, or lack thereof, can be used to ignite specific actions in organizations by creating greater awareness of the impact on lower profitability due to poor project management practices and rallying the troops to a call-to-action to improve the effectiveness of the project and organization environment.

5.3.3 Actions to overcome project management obstacles
For every obstacle found in project management, there is an action that will help to eliminate, neutralize and avoid the obstacle. Figure 5.4 describes key obstacles and suggested actions to minimize the impact of the obstacles.

5.3.4 Value propositions of PM from leading organizations
Based on primary and secondary research and consulting assignment observations conducted by the author, the following leading organizations summarized the

Obstacles	Actions
Resistance to PM due to time investment	Create flexible and scalable PM processes with mandatory and discretionary components (e.g. "fast track" vs. "full risk mitigation or complex projects")
Lack of PM value proposition awareness	• Quantify PM benefits (time savings, quality improvements, cost reductions, customer satisfaction and create/maintain a scorecard) • Create PM advocacy groups that share information, follow uniform process and document PM value lessons learned • Market and communicate value of PM to multiple constituencies
Limited support from the top	• Identify proactive PM executive champions and use them to persuade others • Demonstrate benefits of PM by using key metrics (e.g. improved customer satisfaction, reduced cycle time) to gain supports
Insufficient dedicated qualified PM resources	• Continuous training of relevant constituencies • Reward and recognition of relevant certification • Career path options – professionalize PM • Funding and support of "PM Centers of Excellence"

Figure 5.4 Select actions to overcome major PM obstacles

value of applying best practice project management principles and practices in their environments (Selig, September 2004 & 2014):

■ Provided better control of scope changes and ensured efficient use of project dollars (Cisco);

■ Use of consistent and repeatable PM processes on a global basis reduced project time, and costs, sped up project deliverables, facilitated training and improved the effectiveness of global project teams (IBM);

■ Developed a better working relationship and communications with the customer and other project constituents (Pitney Bowes);

■ Aligned project initiatives and investments more effectively with the business and customer needs, reduced rework and cycle time and helped to improve the voice of the customer (GE);

■ Improved IT project accountability and documentation (Purdue Pharma);

■ Increased our customer satisfaction by demonstrating our commitment to on-time product delivery schedules (Alcatel - Lucent);

■ Project management education and certification resulted in more cost effective and timely program/project performance and vendor (outsourcing) management (US Federal Government Agency).

Several companies such as AT&T, IBM, Cisco, a major pharmaceutical company and a global telecommunications company provided similar key drivers as reasons for supporting formalized project management in their environments:

■ Improved customer satisfaction and service;

■ Reduced costs and improved our investment portfolio management prioritization and alignment;

■ Reduced cycle time for new product development and commercialization and new systems implementation;

- ▥ Improved quality;
- ▥ Improved business process efficiencies and increased speed to market;
- ▥ Increased our ability to manage and mitigate risks more prudently.

A telecom company used its expertise in project management as a marketing and sales tool for its customers to illustrate how they control and meet promised customer delivery dates for products. It developed a series of project management brochures and booklets prepared for both internal company constituents such as executives, project management professionals, employees and customers. Figure 5.5 identifies the purpose of each of the documentation guides and brochures.

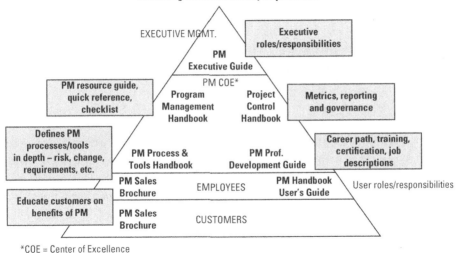

A Telecom company strongly supported project management disciplines and developed a series of PM documentation for different constituents. A PM sales brochure was developed for its customers that promoted the idea that by implementing a PM best practices, the customer's benefited in many ways, including on time delivery of products.

*COE = Center of Excellence

Figure 5.5 Project management expertise used as a marketing tool with customers

5.3.5 Assessing the level of project management maturity in organizations

There are several self-assessment techniques available for organizations to evaluate the current state of their project management policy, process, environment and capabilities, determine their maturity level and develop a plan to improve the PM environment as part of an overall plan to improve the IT governance environment.

A selection of these techniques was described in Chapter 2. They include the Project Management Maturity Assessment Model (PMMM®), which plots SEI's Five Level Capability Maturity Model Integrated (CMMI®) with PMI's ten knowledge areas and describes fifty (50) separate cells with their attributes. This is illustrated in Figure 2.9 and can be used as a tool for the self-assessment. Another technique for self-assessment is PMI's Organizational Project Maturity Model (OPM3®), which utilizes three elements in the organizational maturity assessment process – knowledge, assessment and improvement. It is described in Section 2.4.4 and illustrated in Figure 2.8.

Another tool is represented by Figure 2.5, which provides for an overall, IT governance – self assessment framework. With this tool, the program/project management box can be expanded to review each project management phase (e.g. initiation, planning, executing, controlling [in all phases] and termination) and its details by each of the five CMMI® levels.

Still another technique is usually administered by an external and objective PM expert and is based on a series of interviews, which use a common set of questions to analyze and evaluate all aspects of the project management environment, culture, processes, tools, capabilities and attitudes and help to develop an action plan for improvement. Obviously, the outcome of any of the assessments should be an actionable improvement plan.

■ 5.4   PRINCIPLES FOR ACHIEVING EXCELLENCE IN PROGRAM/ PROJECT MANAGEMENT

5.4.1 Key attributes of successful program- and project-based organizational cultures and environments

Based on many of the case studies analyzed, a review of the literature and numerous consulting assignments, it is clear that organizations continue to struggle with establishing and enforcing a formal program/project management policy and process that is sustainable. In addition, a number of key project management principles and practices were identified and consistently applied, for the most part, by leading edge successful organizations. (Selig, 2008)

These principles and practices can represent a checklist for helping companies achieve improvements and higher levels of project management maturity and effectiveness in their environments. They have been organized into logical categories to facilitate their use.

Program/project management excellence and visibility:
Top management must prioritize projects based on consistent and repeatable evaluation and selection processes:
■ Customers must approve and set priorities among projects;
■ Implement projects successfully (e.g. on-time, on-budget, within scope, with high quality and to the customers satisfaction);
■ The CEO (e.g. with the buy-in of the CIO; CFO; CMO; COO; etc.) is committed to implementing PM as a core competence to manage all types of projects;
■ Conduct formal periodic PM assessments and reviews with senior management;

- Projects must be limited to a size that can be fully understood by the project manager;
- Successful project management must be a joint effort between customers and the project teams. But the final responsibility for success or failure lies with the customer;
- Market and communicate the benefits and positive results of good fundamental project management disciplines through newsletters, websites, word of mouth, customer testimonials and other promotional vehicles;
- Develop a business case for major, complex and moderate projects (defined later in the chapter);
- An essential element of every project is a project plan based on a work breakdown structure, with assignable work packages, task identification, estimating, budgeting and scheduling;
- Planning is everything and ongoing – detailed, systematic and team-involved;
- What is not documented has not been said or does not exist;
- The more ridiculous the deadline, the more it costs to try to meet it;
- Project sponsors and constituents must be active participants – builds relationships, communications and commitment;
- Use industry standards and guidelines to guide your PM direction - CMMI, PMI, PMMM, ISO 21500, PRINCE2, Six Sigma and others.

Sponsorship, accountability and leadership:
- All programs/projects must have a sponsor and/or owner and an overall program/project manager;Key roles and responsibilities must be formally agreed upfront and communicated to all of the constituencies where individuals are assigned specific actions in the form of a **RACI** matrix (**R**esponsible, **A**ccountable, **C**onsulted, **I**nformed) which becomes part of the project documentation;
- Program/project scope, requirements and deliverables should be approved upfront by the sponsor;
- Program/project costs and benefits (including non-financial benefits) should be quantified and approved by the sponsor and charged back to the sponsor or owner;
- Fast projects have strong leaders who create a sense of urgency and speed;
- Professionalize PM, reward certification and celebrate successes;
- Program/project scope, requirements and deliverables (as in a charter) should be approved upfront by the sponsor and monitored throughout the lifecycle phases;
- Create a Program Management Office (PMO) as a center of excellence to develop and maintain PM processes, coordinate training and certification, manage or consult on select large projects or those projects in trouble and facilitate project planning, status reporting and periodic formal reviews;
- Project managers must focus on five dimensions of project success – on time, within budget, within scope, with acceptable quality and to the customer's satisfaction;
- Project lifecycle with go/no-go gates allows for phase-gate project reviews and adjustments and/or cancellations;
- A project manager's most valuable and least used word is 'No';

- The same work under the same conditions will be estimated differently by five different estimators or by one estimator five different times;
- A project manager's responsibility must be matched by equivalent authority;
- Project management must be sold and resold via the value propositions;
- Project team members deserve a clear, written charter and guidelines as to the tasks they must perform and the time available to perform them;
- Questions generated by the project team deserve direct answers from the customer;
- Great project managers do not encourage burnout;
- Establish project review panels consisting of key constituents and conduct formal reviews with follow-up actions, dates and assigned responsibility;
- Use external subject matter PM experts as needed.

Program/project management (PM) governance policy, change control and escalation
Key practices for successful and sustainable superior project management best practices include the following:
- A formal PM governance policy should be established, defining the components of the policy and identifying what is mandatory and discretionary and who has decision authority for approval, resource allocation, escalation and change authorization;
- A formal governance calendar should be published which identifies formal project reviews, status reports (e.g. weekly, bi-weekly, monthly, quarterly), funding reviews, etc.;
- A flexible and scalable PM process should be established and continuously improved to accommodate different project types;
- A PM center of excellence (PMO) should be established to develop criteria for PM competences, encourage PM training and certification, provide expert PM help, act as PM advocates and conduct periodic health checks on select programs/projects;
- Establish a reward and recognition system to recognize PM excellence and encourage certification;
- Deliver short term incremental project deliverables that work to establish credibility and visibility (decompose complex programs and projects into no more than 80 hour work packages with targeted deliverables, formal project reviews, etc.);
- Incorporate PM objectives into annual performance reviews;
- Consistent program and project metrics should be instituted based on time, cost, resources, quality and customer satisfaction (including earned value, where applicable). There are a number of tools that can help with estimating, resource allocation, level loading and resource utilization;
- The ability to compare planned to actual results or baselines is essential for effective project management;
- Management must be provided with meaningful visibility into projects if suspicion and distrust are to be minimized;
- The key to good project management is effective and honest communications;
- A formal escalation process, with clear accountability and roles should be established to resolve key program/project issues, risks and to approve changes;

- A consistent methodology must be developed and applied to report the **RAG** (e.g. **R**ed, **A**mber or **G**reen status of programs, projects or other major tasks. Red = big trouble; Amber = emerging trouble; Green = everything is on target);
- Reporting must be produced on a consistent basis (e.g. weekly, bi-weekly, monthly, other) using a consistent format (e.g. with allowances made for the audience of the report);
- A formal time tracking system should be in place to record how time is spent on projects;
- A formal link including rework to the change management process must be established to manage and monitor significant changes to budgets, schedules, versions and/or documentation.

Resource optimization, availability and commitment:
- Sponsors and program/project managers should have access to the right resources based on the project phase and task requirements and competences needed;
- The availability and commitment of the resources should be guaranteed by senior management once the program/project is approved and resourced.

Program/project repository and lessons learned:
- Lessons learned should be developed and made available to all constituencies who require them, with consideration given to security and access policies;
- Current and evolving best practice benchmarking should be tracked and adopted;
- Maintain a PM knowledge management system of lessons learned and lessons to be changed;
- Desirable work must be rewarded; undesirable work must be changed.

5.4.2 Project management lifecycle phases and key components

Programs and projects by definition are onetime events with a start and end date. Therefore, all projects have a lifecycle. Lifecycles may vary by project. For example, the lifecycle of a new product development project is somewhat different than a project lifecycle for an information system or merger and acquisition. In addition, PMI's *PMBOK® Guide* identifies five project phases – initiation, planning, execution, control and termination or closure. Other project lifecycle phases may have more or less phases. As a practical matter, the actual number of lifecycle phases that a company uses is less important as long as there is agreement that a project lifecycle process with specific phases, components, metrics and templates is used on a consistent, but scalable basis.

To keep things simple, Figure 5.6 represents a project management lifecycle based on four phases – initiation, planning, execution and termination. The author, as well as many project management professionals, believes that 'control' is not really a separate phase in the lifecycle, but rather, an integral part of all of the lifecycle phases. The actual number of phases is not as important as long as a project lifecycle is adopted and consistently applied and that the value of the lifecycle itself is recognized in an organization. The benefits of a project lifecycle include:

- Creates visibility and a roadmap through phase-gate approvals;
- Establishes uniform and consistent phases;
- Disciplines and structures the process;
- Forces incremental go/no-go decisions at gate reviews;
- Forces early attention to details and potential corrections;
- Has a beginning and an end;
- Establishes project planning and control mechanisms;
- Accommodates change and risk;
- Creates a framework for improved communications, commitment, buy-in and visibility;
- Facilitates the integration of the program/project results and deliverables into the organization's core businesses, related systems, infrastructure and culture.

Figure 5.6 also identifies the key components of each of the phases. Not every component must or should be used for every project, but it provides a checklist that can be applied to either light or complex projects, which are discussed in more detail in Section 5.5. The author believes that a number of the above elements are critical to help organizations develop superior project management environments and therefore, deserve more in-depth coverage.

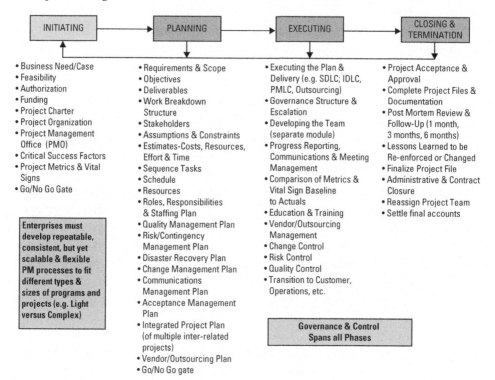

Figure 5.6 Project management lifecycle phases and key components

5.4.3 Basic project management mechanics

Most projects, with a few exceptions, should include certain basic fundamental mechanics. These include:

- **Project definition and charter** – objectives, organization, scope and boundaries, funding and assumptions. This may also include a business case, depending on the project.
- **Planning** – work breakdown, tasks and/or activities including dependencies, durations, assignable work packages, estimated (elapsed time and effort to perform work), baseline budgets and costs and a quality management plan.
- **Scheduling** – allocation of resources, milestones, critical path, logic dependencies and networks, and float/slack tasks and activities.
- **Governance, control and progress reporting** – schedule, cost, resources, deliverables, scope, communications and status reporting, and other metrics such as cost performance index and schedule performance index, managing expectations, variance analysis, quality control, risk analysis and contingencies, escalation, change authorization, and disaster planning and recovery.
- **Final review, acceptance and operationalization** – customer approval and acceptance, final documentation, lessons learned, transition into operations and post-mortem reviews.

The business case

Not all projects require a business case. There are many factors that should determine if a potential program or project requires a business case. Key criteria can include such elements as: size and complexity, investment amount required, degree of risk, degree of impact on the organization, competitive advantage or survival, organizational scope and geographic coverage, degree of visibility and others.

Figure 5.7 provides a composite project business case outline used by several organizations.

5.4.4 Project management plan (PMP)

A project management plan is unique to each project. It provides all stakeholders engaged in project activities with a uniform baseline of project understanding within its operating and performance environment, including requirements, schedule, resources, risks, constraints and outcomes. It also serves as a communications tool, a roadmap, and commitment to stakeholders across the project phases. It needs to be thorough, justifiable, flexible, public and realistic.

In developing a realistic and pragmatic plan, it is important to recognize that every project has a customer and, often, IT has to help the customer to define what they want and what their role is in a project by getting the right people involved in each phase.

1. **Executive Summary (Synopsis of Business Case Assessment):**	4. **Proposed Solutions**
Purpose, Objectives, Strategy and Scope	Proposed Requirements, Processes, Functions and
Description of Opportunity, Value and Alignment	Technology
Dependencies, Assumptions, Constraints	Proposed Cost/Benefit Analysis
Sponsor and Management Team	Major Issues, Constraints and Sensitivities
Costs/Benefits/Risks	Impact on the Organization, Resources, People,
2. **Assessment of Current Environment (Reference Base –Where are we today?):**	Technology
	Pros/Cons of each solution
Current Processes, Functions and Technology	5. **Recommended Approach**
Current Costs, Resources, Volumes, Locations	Macro Plan, Milestones and Schedule
Major Issues, Constraints and Sensitivities	Critical Success Factors
3. **Change Analysis (Why Change?)**	Macro Plan, Milestones and Schedule
Value Proposition Analysis	Conversion, Transition Plan and Team
Financial Analysis (description and quantification;	Quality and Test Plan
full economic life cycle; best case, worse case,	Key Performance Indicators
most likely case; cash flow (cash in and cash out);	6. **Appendices**
costs/savings)	Detailed Project Plan
Non-Financial benefits	Detailed Cost Benefit Analysis
Risk Analysis & Mitigation	Detailed Risk Management Plan
	Detailed Contingency and Backup Plan
	Detailed Communications Plan
	Critical Success Factors

Figure 5.7 Generic project business case outline

Contents of a PMP

Project management plans should be prepared for projects in accordance with the organization's project management policies and guidelines. Each PMP can include the following components:

- Requirements and objectives;
- Work scope and deliverables;
- Work breakdown structure and tasks;
- Project organization;
- Roles and responsibility assignment matrix – who does what;
- Schedule – including start date, end date, major milestones and deliverables;
- Budgets, funding and resource requirements and allocation;
- Integration and interface plan;
- Quality plan;
- Security plan;
- Risk, contingency and disaster recovery plan;
- Monitoring, communications, control and reporting plan;
- Escalation policy;
- Operation and maintenance plan;
- Change management and authorization plan;
- Training, testing and documentation;
- Key contacts;
- Glossary of terms;
- Appendix.

■ 5.5 MAKING THE CHOICE – PROGRAM AND PROJECT MANAGEMENT LIGHT OR COMPLEX

5.5.1 IT request and demand management gate review

Chapter 3 discussed the business/IT alignment, strategic planning, and project and portfolio investment management processes. Once a program or project is approved as part of a plan, or sometimes even outside of a plan, it should undergo a business case review before it receives final approval and funding to further validate that the project is aligned with the business and contributes its share of benefits to the organization. Figure 5.8 illustrates an IT project request gate review and approval process flow. Each project must pass each go/no-go gate to be approved and resourced. Once a project is approved, then it is commissioned, resources assigned and the project management lifecycle begins. In some organizations, a number of these activities are conducted in parallel and not always sequentially.

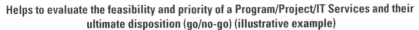

Helps to evaluate the feasibility and priority of a Program/Project/IT Services and their ultimate disposition (go/no-go) (illustrative example)

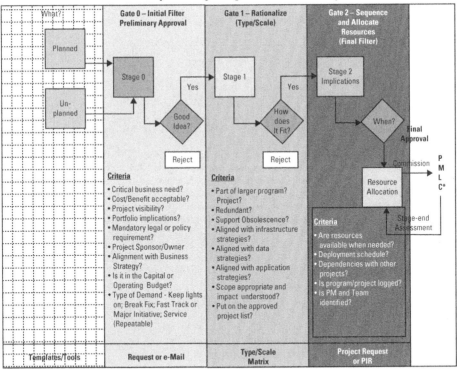

*PMLC = Project Management Life Cycle

Figure 5.8 IT project request gate approval process flow

Figure 5.9 provides a checklist of business, technical, financial and other business case factors that are part of the project review and approval process.

Select Criteria used to Help Evaluate an IT Request and/or Business Case

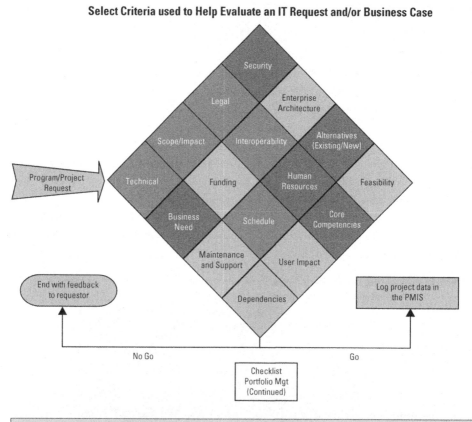

No Go   Go

Checklist
Portfolio Mgt
(Continued)

(To be used as a guideline to assist in evaluating New or Changes in Scope Requests for IT Services)

Scope, Impact, Business Need and Feasibility
What is the scope and impact of the request? Enterprise wide? Geography? Number of People?
Is it solution technically feasible? Economically feasible? Legally feasible?
Is the request identified in the strategic and/or operating plan and budget?
What is the impact of the proposed solution on the user community? High? Medium? Low?
What business need will be satisfied by approving this request? High Impact? Low Impact? Mandatory?
Strategic? Discretionary?

Technical/Interoperability/Enterprise Architecture
Is this a new technology? Has it been tested?
Is it an extension or replacement of an existing technology?
Does the proposed solution impact the approved enterprise architecture and approved infrastructure
components?
Does the solution represent a standard solution? A proprietary solution?
Is the proposed solution independent or is it dependent on other infrastructure components?
Does it comply with the interoperability standards and guidelines?
Does the solution require back-up, redundancy and contingency plans?
What degree of risk does the proposed solution pose? High? Medium? Low?
Is the capacity of the proposed solution expandable to accommodate growth in volume? Locations?
Employees? Etc.?

Figure 5.9 Business/technical/financial business case checklist

> **Legal, Regulatory and Security**
> Is the request legal?
> Is this request ethical?
> Does this request comply with current regulatory policies and guidelines?
> Does the request comply with published security regulations and guidelines?
> As a result of this request, are new or modifications required to security regulations and guidelines?
>
> **Core Competencies and Human Resources**
> Do we have the core competencies to design and implement the proposed solution?
> Do we have sufficient and the right kind of human resources to implement the solution?
> Do we have to outsource the solution to an industry partner? Other?
>
> **Alternatives Considered**
> What alternative solutions have been analyzed?
> Why was the recommended alternative selected?
>
> **Funding and Financials**
> Is this request a funded (budgeted) requirement defined as part of the annual budget process?
>   – Defined/explicit?
>   – Realignment/reallocation?
> Is this an unplanned and unfunded request?
> Does this request impact the enterprise architecture and/or infrastructure integrity?
> Does the request require a reallocation of previously approved funding?
> Is the requested completion date acceptable? Doable?
>
> **Schedule and Time Frame**
> Is the requested schedule doable with the resources available?
> Can the request completion date be met, given other priorities?

Figure 5.9 Business/technical/financial business case checklist (continued)

5.5.2 Program/project type/scale matrix

Once a program or project is approved, a favorite question asked by many is, "How much project management process and documentation is required for this project and what project management path should be used?" Best practice companies like IBM, GE, Boeing, Bechtel and others have developed very detailed, robust and scalable project management methodologies, these are repeatable and can be consistently applied to a wide variety of projects on a global basis. The key word is 'scalable' for different types of projects (e.g. small, medium and large).

Since all programs and projects are not equal, organizations are increasingly implementing a flexible and scalable program and project management lifecycle consisting of multiple paths such as fast track or light versus complex process with the associated checklists and supporting tools. A growing number of organizations have developed the equivalent of a Chinese menu (choose from either column A and/or B), to provide more choices within a broad framework of project management best practices, where the project manager and the team either get to pick the project management process and/or templates, within an overall framework established by the organization, or are required to adhere to a particular path because of contractual or compliance requirements. This is how the term 'fast track or light' versus complex project management evolved and it also helped to overcome the often heard complaint that project management requires substantial documentation.

One method that provides a consistent way to help select the appropriate project management process path for organizations to follow in managing their projects is to create a project type-scale matrix. Figure 5.10 illustrates the project type-scale matrix. It provides a structured approach to determine the appropriate project management templates (and documentation) to use in order to plan, manage, monitor and control a program or project throughout its lifecycle phases. In essence, the project-type-scale matrix identifies the level of project management documentation required for three types of projects – simple, moderate and complex. It has been designed as a guideline to help organizations provide flexibility and choice, but within a consistent and repeatable framework. If necessary, more project types can be defined by an organization but for many the three types previously mentioned are sufficient.

Figure 5.10 identifies eleven complexity factors on the vertical axis and accommodates three value ratings ranging from a low of 1 to a high of 5. Each of the eleven elements is ranked and the total numeric value is summarized. At the bottom of the matrix, there is a point guide as to which projects are classified as simple, moderate or complex. It suggests the templates that should be used for each of the project types and the appropriate approval levels required based on the numeric value of each project. The matrix can be tailored to different environments by changing the complexity factors, their values and respective weights.

5.5.3 Project management lifecycle phases and select templates
The project type-scale matrix must be used in conjunction with Figure 5.11 which illustrates the project management lifecycle phases and defines the associated templates that represent the documentation required for different types of projects. The matrix identifies the recommended templates that should be used by project type. The templates are all web-based and vary in size from one page to over ten pages. Each template also contains mandatory and discretionary information that needs to be completed for each project. In this way, the 'light' (or low risk) project management process can be used for 'simple' and 'some moderate projects' and only requires the use of two templates while 'complex' (or high risk) projects such as a SAP installation would require the use of all or most of the project templates.

Figure 5.12 identifies the program/project management lifecycle phases, key phase components and the related templates that could be used in each phase (color coded) depending on the type of project (e.g. simple, moderate and complex).

A key question that organizations need to ask is: "Where do we start? Should we apply these templates to all active projects or just some projects?" The most practical answer is to conduct a ranking of currently active programs or projects in a company by using

[Insert PROJECT # - NAME]

The Project Type/Scale Matrix provides a structured and consistent approach to determine the appropriate PM Template (s) for managing/monitoring/controlling a program/project.

PROJECT TYPE/SCALE ASSESSMENT

Directions: Calculate the matrix score by subjectively using the guidelines below to assign a number between 1 and 5 to each of the 11 factors.

	COMPLEXITY FACTOR	LOW=1	MED = 3	HIGH = 5	NOTES
1	Project Type	UPGRADE Involves a change in capacity of existing technology or service. Usually additional capacity or additional location.	NEW ADDITION Involves the addition of a new technology or service with no replacement of existing technology or service.	REPLACEMENT Involves the replacement of old technology or service with a new technology or service	Degree of difficulty influenced by new technology and whether it replaces older technology or is simply added to the environment
2	Technology	Established company standard	A standard in the industry, but new to company	A new technology, not necessarily a standard, no internal expertise.	Open standards should be encouraged
3	Scope	Involves only one location and one function	Involves only one region and up to four functions	Involves all regions (locations) and cross-functional	The wider the geographic scope the more complex the project
4	End User Impact	Completely transparent to end users	Minimal amount of communication necessary to inform end users of planned changes. No training required	Changes require frequent communication and some degree of end user training	
5	Implementation technique	Can be implemented without disturbing existing service, users can migrate to new environment	New technology/service is installed in parallel and users are migrated in segments.	"Flash cut" requires new technology/service to replace old with no overlap.	
6	Capital Required (Life Cycle)	Relatively small capital (<$50k)	Medium capital required ($50k - $2.5 million)	Large capital required (>$2.5 mil)	
7	Operating Costs (Annual)	Small operating costs (< $100k/yr)	Medium operating cost ($101k-$999k/yr)	Large operating cost ($>1.0 mil/yr)	Includes depreciation, equipment lease, maintenance, etc.
8	Vendor relationship	No new vendors involved, upgrade using existing vendor product	No new vendor involved, using a new product from existing vendor.	New vendor with no prior business relationship	Established vendors are easier to do business with
9	Resource Requirements	Can be completed with use of only internal FTS resources (and industry partners)	Requires minimal resource dependency outside company (e.g. Phone Bridge)	Requires significant resource requirement from outside FTS and/or vendor (e.g. Enterprise Architecture, participation on project)	
10	Project Duration	<3 months	3-12 months	>12 months	
11	Other			Legal requirement and/or critical to business	
	TOTAL POINTS RANGE	11 to 55 Points			TOTAL PROJECT Type/Scale SCORE

DEFINITIONS

TYPE	Key Attributes	# of points	Recommended Template	Approvals
Simple	Low Complexity	Less than 20 Pts	Template - PR, PCR*	Director or Delegate
Moderate	Medium complexity	Between 20 and 35 Points	Template - PR, PIR, DTD, PCR (Others Optional)	CIO or Delegate
Complex	High visibility: AC directed: Multiple organizations affected	Greater than 35 Points	Template - All for tech. projects, otherwise TAD, IITOR, RFI opt.	ITRB or Delegate

*Assumes informal planning (additional templates are optional)

Figure 5.10 Program/project type-scale matrix (for systems, hardware, software and/or networks)

PM Phases

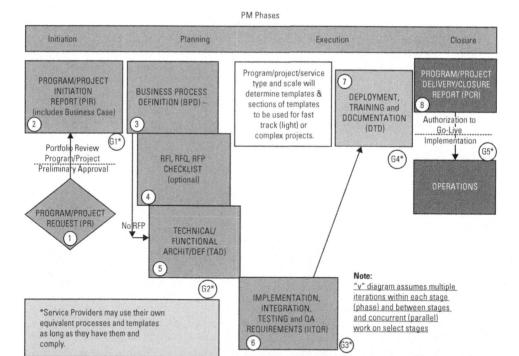

* G1-5: Go/No Go Gate Reviews

Phase(s)	Template(s)	Purpose/Description
Initiation	0. Program/Project Request (PR)	Obtains customer or other constituent authorization to request IT services
	1. Program/Project Initiation Report (PIR)	Provides sufficient high-level information on a program or project to either approve or reject the request (e.g. scope, requirements, etc.)
Planning	2. Business Project Definition (BPD)	Describes the major business objectives that the system, component or deliverable will satisfy and/or impact
	3. RFI, RFQ, RFP Checklists	Identifies the contents of a solicitation to vendors in the form of: Request for Information, Request for Quote and/or Request for Proposal
	4. Technical/Functional Architecture Definition (TAD)	Describes the complete system and/or component from a functional, technical and operational aspect
Execution**	5. Implementation, Integration, Testing and QA Requirements (IITQR)	Describes how the system and/or components is to be implemented integrated, tested and transitioned to the customer, operations and other environments
	6. Deployment, Training and Documentation (DTD)	Describes the actual installation and cutover of the system or components and identifies the training and documentation requirements
Closure	7. Program/Project Delivery/ Closure Report (PCR)	Verifies and evaluates that the program/project objectives, costs, benefits and deliverables have been satisfactorily implemented and documents lessons learned

Figure 5.11 Project management lifecycle phases and related templates

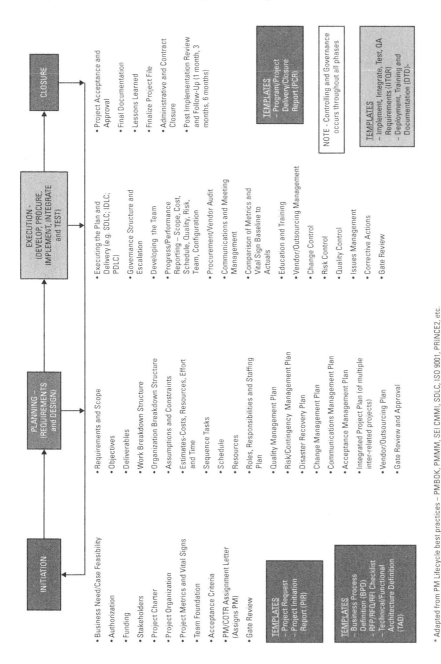

* Adapted from PM Lifecycle best practices – PMBOK, PMMM, SEI CMMI, SDLC, ISO 9001, PRINCE2, etc.

Figure 5.12 Program/project management lifecycle phases, key components and related templates

the project type-scale matrix. Figure 5.13 illustrates the results of such an evaluation for a service organization in terms of the 80/20 rule, where a small number of projects consume a majority of the IT project resources. Therefore, in this particular organization, the starting point should be complex projects, followed by moderate projects.

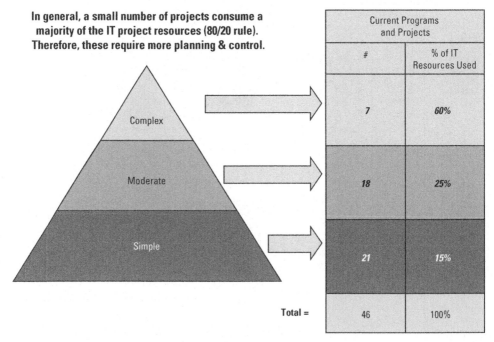

In general, a small number of projects consume a majority of the IT project resources (80/20 rule). Therefore, these require more planning & control.

Current Programs and Projects	
#	% of IT Resources Used
7	60%
18	25%
21	15%
Total = 46	100%

Figure 5.13 Project type-scale matrix ranking of IT projects

■ 5.6   PROGRAM AND PROJECT GOVERNANCE EXCELLENCE

5.6.1 Prerequisites for effective project management execution and governance

For each project phase or activity, the project manager should:

■ Review the project plan as a reminder of the desired results of that phase or activity;

■ Conduct a kick-off meeting to clarify the phase deliverables, reinforce roles and responsibilities of project team members, create a shared sense of responsibility, gain commitment from the project team members, and ensure that all project team members have whatever they need to be successful in their roles;

■ Provide authorization to project team members to start work on their activities;

■ Conduct regular status meetings and/or provide regular status reports based on a maximum time reporting period of 80 hours (or less);

■ If needed, provide training or other interventions to team members;

■ Distribute progress reports according to a communications plan;

■ Develop a governance and control policy and communicate it to all project constituents.

The project manager has the responsibility during the execution phase to compare and analyze a project's implementation progress against the baseline and take actions to correct all significant issues and variances. This includes:

■ Schedule;

■ Cost, benefits and budgets;

- Quality;
- Key deliverables;
- Human resources;
- Resource and asset allocation;
- Technology;
- Vendor deliverables.

In the implementation phase, the project manager must constantly balance the monitoring, control and governance process that provides a disciplined framework to administer, monitor and control work, including:
- Resources (budget);
- Time (start and completion dates, critical path);
- Product (deliverables);
- Quality;
- Managing expectations;
- What, when and to whom to communicate.

From time to time, the project manager needs help in resolving issues with difficult customers, non-supportive constituents or troublesome service providers. A formal project governance and escalation hierarchy with clear roles and handoffs is required. Figure 5.14 depicts such an organization.

A formal program/project review process should be established and followed with clearly defined roles and responsibilities

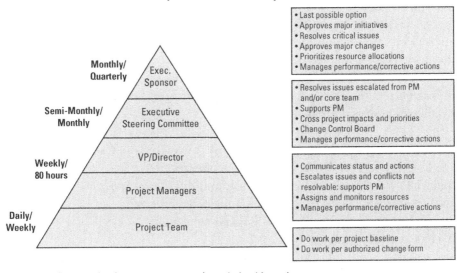

Figure 5.14 Program/project governance and escalation hierarchy

5.6.2 Program Management Office (PMO) – roles and areas of focus
The role of the PMO is to champion PM benefit awareness, help develop project management expertise and provide administrative support (processes, tools, techniques,

training, and help desks) to sustain a vibrant and effective project environment in organizations. Specific PMO roles and responsibilities will vary from company to company, but can include the following:

- Act as a center of excellence and focal point for project management skills, competences, methodologies, benefits and advocacy;
- Develop, maintain and administer all PM processes, techniques, templates and tools to ensure effective project management implementation;
- Coordinate project management education and training;
- Establish a 'project database repository' to enable project managers, sponsors and other constituents to plan and track the progress of all projects;
- Define common project management metrics and vital signs and ensure that they are applied;
- Assist project managers, team members and other project constituencies to resolve project management issues, concerns and questions;
- Conduct select project assessment reviews;
- Assist with 'troubled' projects.

Figure 5.15 depicts a typical Project Management Office with many of its suggested functional roles. It represents a composite of several organizations' PMOs.

5.6.3 The discipline of the 80 hour rule

The '80 hour' rule facilitates project planning, scheduling, monitoring, reporting and project governance. It eliminates elastic yardsticks and subjective criteria in relation to monitoring project progress or lack of positive progress. There is no activity, task or event in any project which cannot be broken down into '80 hours' or less vis-à-vis incremental deliverables, formalized project reviews and meetings, and formal status reports. There is no magic to the rule. It requires discipline, planning, thought and the ability to think in terms of decomposing projects into manageable and assignable work packages. It should be applied in the planning phase when the work breakdown structure, schedule, budget and deliverables are developed.

The advantages of the 80 hour rule forces the project manager and team to:
- Focus fast, thereby reducing or eliminating scope creep;
- Get down to details early, so facilitating planning, budgeting and scheduling;
- Identify incremental deliverables (think product, not process);
- Facilitate status reviews, communications and reporting;
- Overcome project drifting;
- Identify roles, responsibility and ownership at an early stage.

5.6.4 Mandatory and discretionary project management key performance indicators

Project management metrics and key performance indicators (KPIs) should be easily captured as normal outputs of transaction-based systems in an organization, such

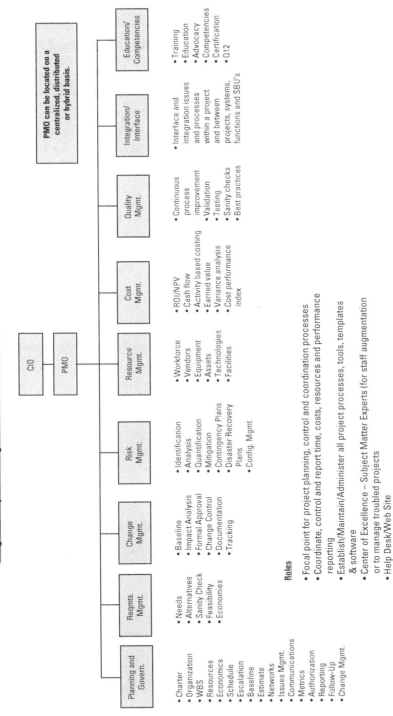

Program/Project Management Office – Roles and Areas of Focus (Illustrative example)

PMO can be located on a centralized, distributed or hybrid basis.

CIO

PMO

Planning and Govern.
- Charter
- Organization
- WBS
- Resources
- Economics
- Schedule
- Escalation
- Baseline
- Estimate
- Networks
- Issues Mgmt.
- Communications
- Metrics
- Authorization
- Reporting
- Follow-Up
- Change Mgmt.

Reqmts. Mgmt.
- Needs
- Alternatives
- Sanity Check
- Feasibility
- Economies

Change Mgmt.
- Baseline
- Impact Analysis
- Formal Approval
- Change Control
- Documentation
- Tracking

Risk Mgmt.
- Identification
- Analysis
- Quantification
- Mitigation
- Contingency Plans
- Disaster Recovery Plans
- Config. Mgmt.

Resource Mgmt.
- Workforce
- Vendors
- Equipment
- Assets
- Technologies
- Facilities

Cost Mgmt.
- ROI/NPV
- Cash flow
- Activity based costing
- Earned value
- Variance analysis
- Cost performance index

Quality Mgmt.
- Continuous process improvement
- Validation
- Testing
- Sanity checks
- Best practices

Integration/Interface
- Interface and integration issues and processes within a project and between projects, systems, functions and SBU's

Education/Competencies
- Training
- Education
- Advocacy
- Competencies
- Certification
- Q12

Roles
- Focal point for project planning, control and coordination processes
- Coordinate, control and report time, costs, resources and performance reporting
- Establish/Maintain/Administer all project processes, tools, templates & software
- Center of Excellence – Subject Matter Experts (for staff augmentation or to manage troubled projects
- Help Desk/Web Site

Figure 5.15 Project Management Office (PMO)

as accounting and/or project management time reporting tracking and purchasing systems. The KPIs should communicate the health of a program or project, a task, phase and/or deliverable and should be determined by each organization in terms of whether it is mandatory or discretionary. The KPIs should also link business objectives to projects as part of IT governance and should measure progress against a baseline for possible corrective actions. Most organizations will not support, or have difficulties supporting, multiple unsynchronized project data collection and reporting systems that are not an integral part of their operational or financial performance reporting and review processes.

The characteristics of KPIs should be quantifiable, trackable, measurable, comparable and actionable. Each organization must decide which project KPIs are mandatory and which are discretionary. Some suggestions follow for each category:

Suggested mandatory metrics:
- Time and schedule;
- Costs - actual versus budgeted costs;
- Status of critical path - are we on target based on date;
- Deliverable hit ratio – number of planned versus completed deliverables (schedule);
- Top issues – number of open issues should be a minimized;
- Top risks of the project (should always be in focus) – with contingency plans;
- Customer satisfaction.

Suggested discretionary metrics:
- Milestone hit ratio – number of planned versus actual milestones achieved on targeted period;
- Actual versus budgeted resources (number of people);
- Number of program/project changes;
- Percent of rework and number of changes requested (including costs of change and rework);
- Cost performance index (CPI);
- Schedule performance index (SPI);
- Earned value – requires a time reporting system in place.

5.6.5 Sample PM center of excellence Organization and roles – major multinational organization

Organizations are setting up project management centers of excellence. Some make the PMO the center of excellence. Others establish separate organizations to be the PM center of excellence and the PMO with specific and non-overlapping roles. Figure 5.16 depicts a PM center of excellence organization for a large global product and service organization.

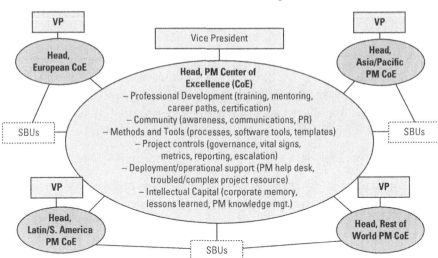

PM CoE's are regionalized, work closely together and support the geographic regions and business units in those regions.

Figure 5.16 Project management center of excellence organizational roles (major multinational corporation)

∎ 5.7   AGILE PROJECT MANAGEMENT (AGILEPM®) AND SCRUM

Agile is a family of methods and best practices, (e.g. ASD, DSDM Atern, RUP (Rational Unified Process) and Scrum). The Manifesto for Agile Software Development (Agile Manifesto, see Section 2.4.32) is an overview of the Agile principles.

For a given Agile project, the choice of which of the Agile PMLC model types provides a better fit is subjective (Wysocki, 2014). Some more details are provided for two popular methods – Agile Project Management and Scrum.

5.7.1 Agile Project Management (AgilePM®)
Richard Pharro, President of APMG International suggested that, "Agile Project Management enables organizations to gain the benefits of an agile approach without introducing unnecessary risks. This ensures 'going agile' becomes a measured and balanced change, keeping what is good in the current organization and retaining existing good practices around project management and delivery, whilst gaining the benefits of a more agile way of working." (Pharro, 2014).

Agile Project Management (AgilePM) combines the effective use of people's knowledge together with techniques such as iterative development and modeling to achieve tight project delivery timescales. It offers flexibility while still recognizing the processes that give project managers confidence to run their projects effectively.

DSDM (Dynamic Systems Development Method) is the longest-established Agile method, launched in 1995. The method has evolved over the years and DSDM Atern is the latest version.

AgilePM is very similar to DSDM Atern. Both require the creation of a high level plan, based on outline requirements and a high level view of the solution to be created. From that point onwards, the end project is created iteratively and incrementally, with each increment building on the output of increments preceding it. Unlike a traditional project, the detailed plans for each step are created by the team members themselves and not the project manager.

Within each stage of the project, the team works in an iterative and incremental style in close collaboration with a representative of the business/customer in order to understand the detail of the next step and to create and validate an evolving solution.

Organizations seeking to adopt an AgilePM approach are sometimes concerned about some of the messages and myths of Agile, and it can be very difficult to separate rumor from fact. This has led some to an incorrect perception that Agile is only applicable for small, simple pieces of work, and that organizations would need to choose either Agile or formal project management and corporate processes. However, this perception is incorrect.

One advantage of AgilePM for the organization is that they can adopt an Agile approach that has a track record of successful management and delivery in the corporate environment, and an approach that complements and works with existing corporate PM processes, such as PMI or PRINCE2, quality and audit processes.

Another benefit for the organization is that AgilePM, and its parent method DSDM Atern, has a formal recognized certification process for individuals. Within the organization, this can be used to develop professionalism in employees, and as part of staff professional development.

5.7.2 Scrum

Scrum is an iterative and incremental Agile software development framework for managing software and other initiatives. Its focus is on "a flexible, holistic product development strategy where a development team works as a unit to reach a common goal" as opposed to a "traditional sequential approach". Scrum communication is among all team members and disciplines in the project.

A key principle of Scrum is its recognition that during a project, the customers can change their minds about what they want and need (often called requirements churn), and that unpredicted challenges cannot be easily addressed in a traditional predictive or planned manner.

Scrum is a process framework that has been used to manage complex product development since the early 1990s. The Scrum framework consists of Scrum Teams and their associated roles, events, artifacts and rules. Each component within the framework serves a specific purpose and is essential to Scrum's success and usage. It is lightweight, simple to understand and sometimes, difficult to master.

Scrum employs an iterative, incremental approach to optimize predictability and control risk. Three pillars uphold every implementation of empirical process control: transparency, inspection and adaptation (Schwaber and Sutherland, July 2013).

Transparency
Significant aspects of the process must be visible to those responsible for the outcome. Transparency requires those aspects be defined by a common standard or language so observers share a common understanding of what is being worked on and agree when the work is done.

Inspection
Scrum users must frequently inspect Scrum artifacts and progress toward a goal to detect undesirable variances. Their inspection should not be so frequent that inspection gets in the way of the work. Inspections are most beneficial when diligently performed by skilled inspectors at the point of work.

Adaptation
If an inspector determines that one or more aspects of a process deviate outside acceptable limits, and that the resulting product will be unacceptable, the process or the material being processed must be adjusted. An adjustment must be made as soon as possible to minimize further deviation.

The Scrum Team
The Scrum Team consists of a Product Owner, the Development Team, and a Scrum Master. Scrum Teams are self-organizing and cross-functional. Self-organizing teams choose how best to accomplish their work, rather than being directed by others outside the team. Cross-functional teams have all the competences needed to accomplish the work without depending on others who are not part of the team. The team model in Scrum is designed to optimize flexibility, creativity, and productivity (Schwaber & Sutherland, July 2013).

The Scrum Master
The Scrum Master is responsible for ensuring Scrum is understood and enacted. Scrum Masters do this by ensuring that the Scrum Team adheres to Scrum theory, practices, and rules.

The Scrum Master is a servant-leader for the Scrum Team. The Scrum Master helps those outside the Scrum Team understand which of their interactions with the Scrum Team are helpful and which are not. The Scrum Master helps everyone change these interactions to maximize the value created by the Scrum Team.

Sprint
The heart of Scrum is a Sprint, a time-box of one month or less during which a 'Done', useable and potentially releasable product increment is created. Sprints have consistent durations throughout a development effort. A new Sprint starts immediately after the conclusion of the previous Sprint.

Sprints contain and consist of the Sprint Planning Meeting, Daily Scrums, the development work, the Sprint Review, and the Sprint Retrospective.

Sprints are limited to one calendar month. When a Sprint's horizon is too long the definition of what is being built may change, complexity may rise, and risk may increase. Sprints enable predictability by ensuring inspection and adaptation of progress toward a goal at least every calendar month. Sprints also limit risk to one calendar month of cost.

In Scrum, there are at least three certification bodies (Scrum.org, Scrum Alliance, AgileScrum, etc).

■ 5.8   CASE STUDY – U.S. FEDERAL GOVERNMENT AGENCY

Figure 5.17 describes a US Federal Government Agency case study. It illustrates how a high level work breakdown structure of the four separate phases of the initiative, starting with one PMO in one IT function, grew into an overall PMO for the entire IT organization and evolved into an IT governance improvement project.

■ 5.9   SUMMARY AND KEY TAKE AWAYS

5.9.1 Summary
Critical success factors for achieving program and project management excellence include:
■ **Create the right environment and culture**:
  - Establish the appropriate organizational mindset, culture and environment;
  - Obtain executive sponsorship, commitment and multi-level management buy-in;
  - Obtain customer/other stakeholder/project team commitments and ownership;
  - Success depends on creating a sustainable foundation (e.g. policy, process, metrics) for managing programs and projects, and integrating results and methodologies into the culture of the organization;

Environment & Drivers	Approach

• Federal government is focusing on reducing costs and becoming more efficient through automation performance management
• This agency provides IT systems and infrastructure support for several other agencies
• Key areas of focus on government professionals and executives are greater accountability and improving their IT organizational and individual skills, competencies and maturity levels
	• Completed assessment of one function within the IT organization and identified gaps and a plan to fill gaps
	• Sponsored by CIO
	• Three levels of steering were established:
	  – Business/IT Steering Committee – senior managers who focused on prioritizing initiatives and funding
	  – IT Technology Steering Committee –concerned with architecture, interoperability standards and compatibility issues
	  – IT PMO – established to develop consistent and scalable PM policies and processes

Issues and/or Opportunities	**Approach (continued)**

• Improve CMMI level of maturity from the low end of Level 1 to Level 3 within a three year period, initially in the PM area and then in other IT governance areas
• Due to significant outsourcing, government employees had to be trained in more formal PM techniques
• Ad hoc and inconsistent PM and operational policies and processes which must be improved throughout IT organization
	• Formed an IT Governance Tiger Team, with representation of all IT departments and facilities by an external consultant to develop, review and deploy the IT governance framework and phased plan (see next slide) with the following priorities:
	  – Program/Project Management and PMO
	  – IT work Flows, Decision Rules and Authority Levels
	  – IT Operations and Infrastructure
	  – Performance Management & Management Controls

Results – Alignment	**Results - IT Service Management & Delivery**
• Business/IT Steering Group focused on alignment and major investment priorities • Capital budgeting is part of but precedes the IT Strategic Plan • IT Annual Operating plan represents the budget authority and authorized spend levels	• Implementing the ITIL processes in the IT Operations and Infrastructure area • Improved the compliance reporting and documentation process and facilitated adherence to government regulations
Results - Program/Project Management	**Results - Performance Management**
• All agency government employees had to attend mandatory PM training • A consistent, but scalable PM policy and process was deployed and resulted in significant reduction in rework and improved productivity through flexible discipline based on three types of projects (e.g. simple, moderate and complex) utilizing consistent templates as required	• Project Management metrics for critical projects were more tightly controlled than for smaller projects • IT Operations and Infrastructure used daily, weekly, monthly and quarterly metrics to measure customer satisfaction and service level performance, which has improved consistently
Cloud Computing and Data Management	**Critical Success Factors**
• Cloud Computing is an outsourcing choice being evaluated by this organization • Data Management is receiving more attention and funding due to its growing importance. A task force has been established to develop an overall plan and approach	• CIO must sponsor and support • All functions must be represented in the initiative to develop trust, better communications and more effective alignment
Sourcing and Outsourcing	**Lessons Learned**
• The Federal Government is a mature outsourcing and contract management organization which utilized many SLA's and other vendor metrics	• It always takes longer to implement process changes that anticipated • Must constantly market the value proposition of IT governance and process disciplines • Celebrate and communicate wins

Figure 5.17 Case Study - U.S. Federal Government Agency

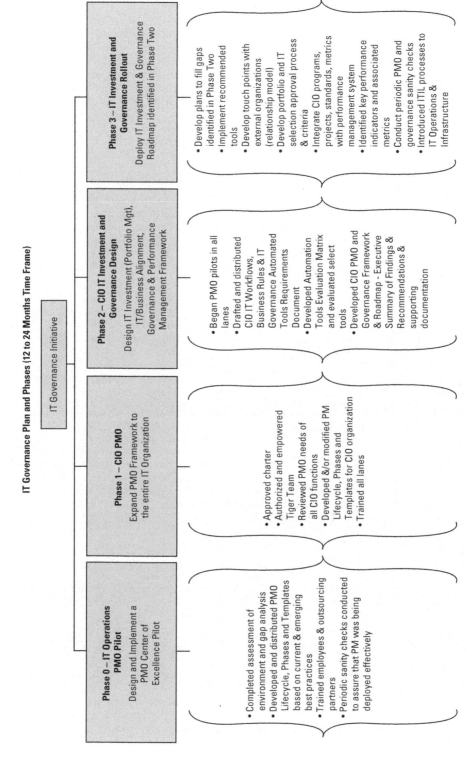

IT Governance Plan and Phases (12 to 24 Months Time Frame)

IT Governance Initiative

Phase 0 – IT Operations PMO Pilot

Design and Implement a PMO Center of Excellence Pilot

- Completed assessment of environment and gap analysis
- Developed and distributed PMO Lifecycle, Phases and Templates based on current & emerging best practices
- Trained employees & outsourcing partners
- Periodic sanity checks conducted to assure that PM was being deployed effectively

Phase 1 – CIO PMO

Expand PMO Framework to the entire IT Organization

- Approved charter
- Authorized and empowered Tiger Team
- Reviewed PMO needs of all CIO functions
- Developed &/or modified PM Lifecycle, Phases and Templates for CIO organization
- Trained all lanes

Phase 2 – CIO IT Investment and Governance Design

Design IT Investment (Portfolio Mgt), IT/Business Alignment, Governance & Performance Management Framework

- Began PMO pilots in all lanes
- Drafted and distributed CIO IT Workflows, Business Rules & IT Governance Automated Tools Requirements Document
- Developed Automation Tools Evaluation Matrix and evaluated select tools
- Developed CIO PMO and Governance Framework & Roadmap - Executive Summary of Findings & Recommendations & supporting documentation

Phase 3 – IT Investment and Governance Rollout

Deploy IT Investment & Governance Roadmap identified in Phase Two

- Develop plans to fill gaps identified in Phase Two
- Implement recommended tools
- Develop touch points with external organizations (relationship model)
- Develop portfolio and IT selection approval process & criteria
- Integrate CIO programs, projects, standards, metrics with performance management system
- Identified key performance indicators and associated metrics
- Conduct periodic PMO and governance sanity checks
- Introduced ITIL processes to IT Operations & Infrastructure

Figure 5.17 Case Study - U.S. Federal Government Agency (continued)

- Define roles and get the right people involved in every program/project phase;
- Market and re-enforce (e.g. training, rewards, mentors, tools, flexible processes) the value and benefits of good PM practices;
- Adopt a flexible and scalable PM process (phases, templates, repository, tools and tailor when required) to accommodate different program and project types based on current and emerging industry best practices;
- Time is the one resource you cannot replace. It is gone forever once it has passed. Delays are a major killer of IT projects. Do not allow internal politics, department or business unit 'silos' to delay an IT project.

■ **Develop program/project plans(based on a flexible and scalable process):**
- Define the project's scope, objectives, requirements and deliverables;
- Establish well-defined phases/tasks, go/no-go gates and milestones (break the job down into manageable work packages – 80 hour rule) with realistic baselines (costs, time, resources and contingencies) based on short term incremental and visible deliverables;
- Define a responsibility assignment matrix – Responsible, Accountable, Consulted, and/or Informed (RACI);
- Establish formal change management and risk management processes;
- Utilize the 80 hour rule in plans to identify specific deliverables every 80 hours (Scrum uses 80 to 160 hours).

■ **Ensure governance and excellent communications:**
- Establish a governance, control, reporting and escalation policy and process;
- Manage the expectations of all stakeholders proactively;
- Identify, measure and track mandatory and discretionary vital signs, metrics, key issues and take necessary actions quickly – knock obstacles out of the way;
- Establish frequent and open communications with stakeholders (both formal and informal review meetings) on a daily, weekly, monthly and quarterly basis depending on the project's importance and closeness to being implemented;
- Ensure accurate, timely and meaningful monitoring and progress reporting.

■ **Institutionalize a PM policy with flexible and scalable processes:**
- Create PM centers of excellence (e.g. advocacy center, help desk, education, training, subject matter expert help, process development, project tracking, certification requirements, etc.);
- Create a reward and/or recognition policy to re-enforce and sustain;
- Conduct formal program/project reviews;
- Develop and use consistent, flexible and scalable PM processes (e.g. fast track or light versus complex projects) and automate processes and tools (web-based). Use iterative methods where appropriate;
- Capture and apply lessons learned and focus on continuous improvement.

5.9.2 Key take aways

Project management is a key component of IT governance. Key take aways for effective project management include:

- Executive sponsorship, management buy-in and customer ownership is critical;
- Planning is vital – scope, requirements, schedule and iterative reviews with stakeholders;
- Project leadership and team building is essential – the team must be empowered to make decisions;
- A flexible and scalable process is crucial (e.g. light versus complex PM methods);
- A formal governance and escalation process with meaningful metrics (measurable, traceable, comparable and accurate) with consequential actions is essential;
- Effective, frequent, honest and open communications is essential;
- Risk management and change management are imperative;
- The focus should be on frequent delivery of products;
- Decomposing complex projects via work breakdown structure (WBS) techniques into manageable work packages (80 hour rule) is essential;
- Get the right people involved and committed during each phase;
- Establish project acceptance criteria between customer and project manager;
- Competing on speed is doable and sustainable;
- Establish clear and unambiguous accountability (roles and responsibilities);
- Let the business and project dictate the level of PM detail required; however, establish a minimum set of PM processes;
- Do PM well and fast (automate as much as possible);
- Make PM an integral part of the corporate and IT governance policy, process and culture;
- Provide and mandate PM education and training for all levels of the organization;
- Know where you are going and know when you have gotten there.

Remember, the keys to success are managing the expectations of all constituents, delivering what you promise in order to maintain credibility, execute as flawlessly as possible and create value for the customer and organization through **flexible discipline**.

6 IT Service Management (ITSM) Excellence (Execution Management)

To quote from one of Bob Dylan's Songs titled "The times are a changing".

This quote is very appropriate for this chapter, since the explosion of IT services means that organizations will have to be as flexible as possible to be successful in the rapidly changing world of technologies, markets and processes.

6.1   WHAT IS COVERED IN THIS CHAPTER?

- Understand and review the best practice principles and practices for achieving and sustaining IT service management (ITSM) excellence;
- Describe the benefits and drawbacks of ITIL (IT Infrastructure Library);
- Review the IT Infrastructure Library (ITIL 2011);
- Define how to deploy an ITIL framework in an organization;
- Review a case study of a large manufacturing organization.

6.2   OVERVIEW

IT service management (ITSM) frameworks have helped IT functions and vendors change from a product (hardware/application) focus to a service focus. Since the 1980s, and with increased enthusiasm in the last ten years, we have witnessed major changes in ITSM business models, standards, collaborations, and work practices. In addition, ITSM frameworks represent processes that transform the focus and work practices in service provisioning. ITSM frameworks can provide organizations with a means to exploit their capabilities and resources and transform business processes. ITSM is a process-oriented service improvement framework similar to total quality management (TQM), business process management (BPM), and business process re-engineering (BPR), (APMG International, 2011; Maronne, et al., 2014).

This chapter describes the principles and practices of IT service management. It provides an overview of ITIL® (IT Infrastructure Library) 2011 Edition. Specific objectives, benefits, and key performance indicators are covered. It illustrates a self-assessment maturity model that can be used to both assess the current, and target the future desired maturity level of an organization and suggests a transition plan to get there.

ITIL offers a systematic approach to the delivery of quality IT services. It provides a detailed description of most of the important processes of an IT organization, and includes information and procedures, tasks, roles and responsibilities. These can be used as a basis for tailoring the framework to the needs of individual organizations. IT service management is about maximizing the ability of IT to provide services that are cost effective and meet or exceed the needs and expectations of the business to:

- Reduce the costs of operations;
- Improve service quality;
- Improve customer satisfaction;
- Improve compliance.

Figure 6.1 illustrates the benefits of a well-executed IT service management strategy.

Well executed IT Service Management is about optimizing the ability of IT to provide services that are cost-effective and meet the needs of the business.

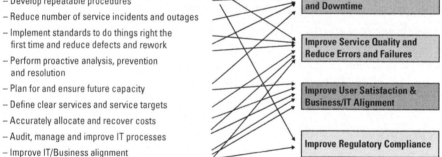

Figure 6.1 Benefits map of IT service management

■ 6.3 PRINCIPLES FOR ACHIEVING IT SERVICE MANAGEMENT EXCELLENCE

A service is a means of delivering value to customers by facilitating outcomes customers want to achieve without the ownership of specific resources and risks. To increase the probability of the desired outcomes, services enhance the performance of associated tasks and reduce the effect of various constraints.

To achieve economies of scales as well as increasing cost effectiveness, services are often 'bundled' or 'grouped' together. The service provider thus offers various service packages. A service package is a collection of two or more services (that can consist of a combination of core services, enabling services and enhancing services) which have been combined to help deliver specific business outcomes.

In order to offer and provide services, the service provider must effectively and efficiently manage the entire lifecycle of the services. This can be accomplished by using an approach called service management. Service management is a set of specialized organizational capabilities for providing value to customers in the form of services. Transforming the service provider's capabilities and resources into valuable services is the core of service management. Service management is also a professional practice supported by an extensive body of knowledge, experience and skills.

There are three main types of service providers. Although almost all aspects of service management apply equally to all types of service provider, there are certain aspects that take on different meanings depending on the type of provider. These aspects include terms like customers, contracts, competition, market spaces, revenue and strategy:
- Internal service provider – an internal service provider that is embedded within a business unit. There may be several of this type of service providers within an organization.
- Shared services unit – an internal service provider that provides shared IT services to more than one business unit.
- External service provider – a service provider that provides IT services to external customers.

Processes define actions, dependencies, and sequence. Process characteristics include:
- Measurability – we are able to measure the process in a relevant manner. It is performance-driven. Managers want to measure cost, quality and other variables while practitioners are concerned with duration and productivity.
- Specific results – the reason a process exists is to deliver a specific result. This result must be individually identifiable and countable.
- Customers – every process delivers its primary results to a customer or stakeholder. Customers may be internal or external to the organization, but the process must meet their expectations.
- Responsiveness to specific triggers – while a process may be ongoing or iterative, it should be traceable to a specific trigger.

There is no single best way to organize service management, and best practices described in ITIL need to be tailored to suit individual organizations and situations. A function is a team or group of people and the tools or other resources they use to carry out one or more processes or activities (Bernard, April 2012).

ITIL defines four functions as follows:

- Service desk – this function acts as the single point of contact and communication to the users and a point of coordination for several IT groups and processes.IT operations management – this function executes the daily operational activities needed to manage IT services and the supporting IT infrastructure. IT operations management has two sub-functions; IT operations controls and facilities management.
- Technical management – this function provides detailed technical skills and resources needed to support the ongoing operation of IT services and the management of the IT infrastructure. Technical management also plays an important role in the design, testing, release and improvement of IT services.
- Application management – is responsible for managing applications throughout their lifecycle. The application management function supports and maintains operational applications. Application management also plays an important role in the design, testing, release and improvement of IT services.

6.3.1 Top concerns of CIOs

A recent CIO Magazine survey, identified the infrastructure and IT service management as one of the top ten issues CIOs are dealing with (www.cio.com/state):

1. Aligning IT strategy with business strategy & governance.
2. Meeting business and user needs.
3. Infrastructure and IT service management.
4. Coping with accelerating change.
5. Dealing with senior management.
6. Managing costs, budgets and resources.
7. Keeping up with technology.
8. Recruiting and retaining staff.
9. Executing projects effectively (time and resource management).
10. Maintaining skills and knowledge.

6.3.2 Select best practices for achieving superior IT service management

Based on a review of best practice companies, a number of consistent practices seem to be prevalent in these organizations regarding superior IT service management. They include:

- All steady-state operations (e.g. data center, help desk, network control center, etc.) must have a primary owner and secondary (backup) owner.
- The overall ITSM budget should be divided into a set of defined products and services so that all IT costs can be mapped to supportable business and/or IT processes either directly or indirectly.
- All IT services should consistently achieve the desired level of efficiency, productivity, reliability and availability as measured by the appropriate key performance indicators (e.g. service level agreements, customer satisfaction, costs, risk factors, etc.).

- Most IT services should be described as processes that are well documented, consistently performed and repeatable to maximize their efficiency and facilitate training and measurement (e.g. key performance indicators).
- Most ITSM services should be charged back to the user or customer organization to achieve a greater level of accountability. This requires an established asset management system, a service level management process and a service catalog.
- The use of an IT service catalog that can define, price and provide estimated installation times for repetitive productized IT services (e.g. install a new computer or network connection) is growing in use and can benefit the customer by providing an easy way to select, order and communicate to IT the required services desired by the customer. The service catalog is only partially applied to complex, one time initiatives that are not repetitive (i.e. it can be used to quantity associated maintenance costs).
- A formal ITSM governance, reporting and escalation process should be established to resolve key operational issues, risks, and conduct periodic reviews All steady-state operations have business continuity, backup (including one or more off-site locations), disaster recovery and security policies and procedures.
- All ITSM related processes should be documented in a consistent, repeatable and standard framework, consisting of lifecycles, processes and metrics such as ITIL (IT Infrastructure Library) or ISO/IEC 20000 and continuously improved.
- Optimizing the utilization of IT assets and resources is critical.

6.3.3 ISO/IEC 20000 – Standard for IT Service Management

The current version of ISO/IEC 20000-1:2011 is aimed at a broad range of IT professionals who are looking for guidance and direction to improve IT service quality.

The core of the ISO/IEC 20000 (further in this book: ISO 20000) standard consists of several documents:

- ISO/IEC 20000-1:2011 – Service Management System Requirements – this is the formal specification of the standard. It describes the required activities, documents and records defined in 256 'shall' statements.
- ISO/IEC 20000-2:2012 – Code of Practice – describes the best practices in detail and provides guidance to auditors and recommendations for service providers planning for service improvements defined in 'should' statements.
- ISO/IEC Technical Report (TR) 20000-3:2012 – Guidance on Scope Definition and Applicability of ISO/IEC 20000-1 – provides guidance on determining the scope of certification and applicability of the standard.
- ISO/IEC TR 20000-4:2010 – Process Reference Model – facilitates the development of a process assessment model that will be described in ISO/IEC TR 15504-8 Information Technology - Process Assessment.
- ISO/IEC TR 20000-5:2013 – Exemplar Implementation Plan for ISO/IEC 20000-1 – provides guidance on the implementation of the standard's requirements.

Other parts of the standard are currently being planned.

ISO 20000 promotes the "adoption of an integrated process approach to effectively deliver managed services to meet the business and customer requirements".

ISO 20000 does not prescribe that its requirements must be met by following the ITIL recommendations, so there are many possible ways to achieve compliance. Introducing ITIL, however, is the most widely used approach for obtaining an ISO 20000 certification.

One reason for creating ITIL V3 was to achieve better alignment with the ISO 20000 standard. The principle of continual improvement has found its way into the ITIL books. The processes of ITIL 2011 Edition and ISO 20000 are very much in line (for example, there is an Information Security management process in ITIL, as required by ISO 20000).

As a result, ITIL offers a broad range of best practice recommendations which are the perfect basis for developing ISO 20000 compliant processes for an organization – the implementation of ITIL seems to be the best current available route towards ISO 20000 certification.

How much does the implementation in an organization of ISO 20000 cost? Unfortunately, this question is hard to answer. The formal ISO 20000 audit itself is usually a very small proportion of the total cost that an organization will incur. In most cases, closing the gaps to become ISO compliant is by far the biggest part of a certification project.

As a result, the total cost heavily depends on:
- The number of ITIL processes that are already implemented;
- Existing certifications, e.g. ISO 9000;
- The size of the IT organization;
- The complexity of the services.

Most service providers meeting the ISO 20000 requirements have experienced higher customer satisfaction, an improved service quality, an increase in process efficiency and greater IT professionalism. There are many benefits of being certified or simply using the standard even when not seeking certification. Below are a few examples:
- To qualify for new customers: more and more companies and organizations consider ISO 20000 certification an essential requirement for conducting business with a new vendor or supplier;
- To enter global markets: the ISO 20000 standards are widely recognized;
- To objectively measure compliance with an international quality standard for ITSM;
- To streamline various process improvements that may go on simultaneously in the service provider's organization;
- To provide guidance on prioritizing the best practices to be implemented;
- To give a service provider a competitive edge.

The ISO 20000 standard is concerned with IT service management and primarily represents a measure of process conformance to be achieved by an organization. In other words, ISO 20000 is a corporate standard and its certification applies to organizations, while ITIL focuses on individual certifications.

The relationship between ISO 20000 and ITIL is synergistic. The standard addresses the questions relating to IT service management as the 'why and what?'. ITIL, on the other hand, complements the standard by addressing the question of 'how'? and providing the process definitions and other details.

Figure 6.2 illustrates a schematic that identifies the ISO 20000 processes.

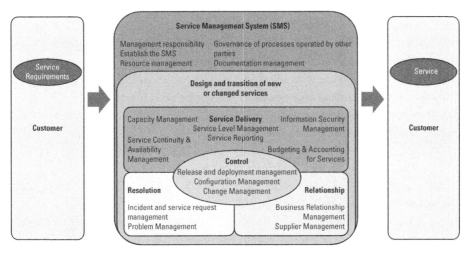

Figure 6.2 ISO 20000 process schematic

■ 6.4   WHAT IS ITIL AND WHY IS IT DIFFERENT?

6.4.1 History and key elements of ITIL (IT Infrastructure Library)

Initiated by CCTA (UK government's Central Computing and Telecommunications Agency – now the OGC – Office of Government Commerce) in the 1980s, ITIL represents a systematic approach to the management and delivery of quality IT services. ITIL is vendor neutral, flexible and scalable and focuses on best practices that can be utilized in different ways, depending on the needs and maturity level of organizations. Major elements of ITIL include:

- The ITIL framework provides an effective foundation for higher quality IT service management.
- ITIL consists of repeatable, documented best practice lifecycle phases and key processes based on common terminology essential for more effectively managing and improving IT service management. It includes checklists, tasks, procedures and responsibilities.

- ITIL aligns with an ISO standard (ISO 20000).
- Since 2013, ITIL is owned by AXELOS and the current version is ITIL 2011 Edition, which updated ITIL V3. There are four qualification (certification) levels relating the ITIL framework. They are:
  - Foundation Level;
  - Intermediate Levels (Lifecycle Stream and Capability Stream);
  - ITIL Expert;
  - ITIL Master.
- itSMF (Information Technology Service Management Forum) – was originally established in the UK and the Netherlands in the early 1990s and has since expanded into over forty-five country chapters, loosely coordinated under the umbrella organization, itSMF International (itSMF-I). The organization promotes the IT service management profession and shares information amongst the chapters. itSMF-I promotes the use of ITIL, ISO 20000 and other relevant frameworks.
- ITIL provides a standardized approach and terminology:
  - Standardization of processes and key performance indicators;
  - Provides the quality assurance foundation for ISO 9001;
  - Industry supported software and tools;
  - Supports Sarbanes-Oxley and other regulations.

6.4.2 ITIL value propositions – leading company examples

A growing number of global organizations claimed to have achieved significant benefits with the use of ITIL (Shaw, 2001; Gartner, 2005; Bernard, 2012):

- **Proctor & Gamble** – started using ITIL about three years ago and realized a 6 to 8% reduction in IT total cost of operations (TCO).
- **Ontario Justice Enterprise** – embraced ITIL two and a half years ago and created a virtual help desk that cut support costs by 40%.
- **Caterpillar** – embarked on an ITIL initiative 18 months ago. After applying ITIL principles, the rate of reaching the target response time for incident management on web-related services jumped from 60% to more than 90%.
- **Large global manufacturing company** – due to lengthy problem resolution times and costs and extended service outages, this organization established an ITSM initiative with an owner who was given the power to enforce. The result was a savings of $30 Million over a three year period.
- **Petro Canada** – outsourced its IT infrastructure to multiple outsourcing vendors using ITIL process definitions and terminology. Vendors were required to perform the work on-site and integrate into the in-house process flows (ITIL-based). Petro-Canada was better able to manage inter-vendor relationships, cooperation and measurement of service levels and other key performance indicators.
- **Major global consumer goods company** – conducted an external assessment of ITSM maturity and decided to deploy ITIL on a global basis to clarify roles and accountability, standardize the use of processes and tools and improve compliance.

- **Major beverage company and a major home products company** – ITIL was used as a precursor to get their IT organizations in order to facilitate the outsourcing of selective IT processes.

6.4.3 Advantages of ITIL to customers, constituents and the IT organization

Using ITIL as part of ITSM provides advantages to the customer, the business and the IT organization.

Advantages of ITIL to customer and business

- Provision of IT services becomes more customer-focused and agreements about service quality and adherence to SLAs improve the relationship;
- The services are described better, in customer language, and in more appropriate detail (as in an IT service catalog);
- The quality and cost of the services are managed better and more effectively;
- Communication with the IT organization is improved by agreeing to limited points of contact;
- Provides 'cost' visibility to the customer and a better understanding of TCO (total cost of operations).

Advantages of ITIL to the IT organization

- The IT organization develops a clearer structure, improves accountability and documentation. It provides a standardized approach to managing and controlling IT;
- Change, problem and release management are all formalized, authorized and traceable. It facilitates the control of increased scale and complexity of the modern IT organization;
- Facilitates decisions to outsource select services;
- Encourages the cultural change and migration towards a more effective and more mature organization;
- Facilitates SOX and other compliance regulations;
- Universally accepted as a good practice guidance for IT service management, with process and service focus;
- Supported by a vast community of ITIL practitioners, gathered around itSMF (IT Service Management Forum).

6.4.4 Potential issues and constraints with ITIL

As with all things, where there are advantages, there are also issues or limitations. These include the following:

- Introduction of ITIL is lengthy and represents a significant cost and resource commitment. IT requires prioritization and agreement on key processes, checklists and accountability for implementation and continuous process improvement;
- Improvement in the provision of services and cost reductions are insufficiently visible and poorly communicated to the customer and the business. Immediate ROI cannot always be demonstrated;

- A successful implementation requires the involvement and commitment of personnel at all levels in the organization;
- Failing to do an assessment before implementing ITIL practices (identifying how the current organization structure compares to the ITIL framework and the changes that will be needed to the organization and its culture);
- Short term expectations (it is not a quick fix, achieved with just a handful of personnel trained and the purchase of some ITIL tools). It requires investment, training, change management and process discipline.

6.5   ITIL FRAMEWORKS, CERTIFICATIONS AND QUALIFICATIONS

6.5.1 Background

ITIL 2011 Edition approaches IT service management from a life-cycle perspective and the way the various phases and processes are linked and interrelated. In ITIL, there are 26 processes and four functions. ITIL offers a systematic approach to the delivery of quality of IT services. It provides a detailed description of most of the important processes for an IT organization, and includes information about procedures, tasks, roles, and responsibilities. These can be used as a basis for tailoring the framework to the needs of individual organizations. The main difference between ITIL Version 2 and 3 lies in the service lifecycle, introduced in Version 3. Where the foundation scope of Version 2 focused on single practices, clustered in delivery, support and security management, the scope in Version 3 takes the entire service lifecycle into account. ITIL 2011 Edition is a significant improvement over previous versions of ITIL.

6.5.2 Summary of ITIL® 2011 Edition service lifecycle, core guides, processes, objectives and related activities

The latest version of ITIL (2011 Edition) is more strategic and IT governance oriented. It uses a lifecycle approach to ITIL. It recognizes that the practice of IT has matured and shifts its emphasis from enhancing the performance of IT processes to serving the customer. The ITIL best practices are described in five core guides that map the entire ITIL service lifecycle.

This part briefly defines the purpose, objectives and processes in each of the five core guides that map the entire ITIL service lifecycle.

Service Strategy (SS) – understanding who the IT customers are, the service offerings to meet their needs and the capabilities and resource to deliver the services.

The objectives of service strategy include, but are not limited to: Develop a service plan for IT operations and infrastructure in alignment with the overall IT plan;
- Identify the portfolio selection criteria for new IT service (demand management);
- Develop a financial budget for the service organization (including a charge-back system to the customers).

To ensure that the services are planned and funded, the following actions should be taken:
- Involve all constituents in the service planning process;
- Ensure that adequate resources are allocated to implement the plan;
- Establish key metrics to measure progress against plan.

Service Design (SD) – assures that new and changed services are designed effectively to meet customer expectations, including the technology, architecture and processes that will be required.

The objectives of Service Design include, but are not limited to:
- To design new or modified services into the IT production environment;
- To contribute to the business objectives;
- To minimize or prevent risks;
- To contribute to satisfying the current and future market needs;
- To support the development of policies and standards regarding IT services;
- To contribute to the quality of IT services;
- To assess and improve the effectiveness and efficiency of IT services;
- To contribute, where possible, to saving time and money.

In order to ensure that the services that are developed meet the customer's expectations, the following actions should be taken:
- The new service must be documented from the concept phase of the service portfolio and it must be kept-to date throughout the process;
- The service level requirements (SLR) must be clearly defined, documented, signed off and understood by all stakeholders before the service is actually designed;
- Based on the SLRs, the capacity management team can model these requirements within the existing infrastructure to assist in supporting the outputs from the demand management process;
- If it appears that a new infrastructure is needed or more support is desired, then financial management must be involved;
- Before the implementation phase begins, a business impact analysis (BIA) and a risk assessment must be performed. This will provide valuable information for IT service continuity management (ITSCM), availability management and capacity management;
- The service desk must be brought up to speed regarding the new service delivery before the new services are delivered;
- Service transition can develop a plan for the implementation of the service;
- Supplier management must be involved if there are purchases to be made.

Service Transition (ST) – includes the management and coordination of the processes, systems and functions required for the packaging, building, testing, and deployment of a release into production, and establish the service specified in the customer and stakeholder requirements.

The objectives of Service Transition include:
- The necessary means to realize, plan and manage the new service;
- Ensuring the minimum impact for the services which are already in production;
- Improving customer satisfaction;
- Supporting the change process of the business (client) with training, education and pilots;
- Reducing variations in the performance and known errors of the new/changed service;
- Ensuring the service meets the requirements of the service specifications, once the deployment is completed.

To ensure a smooth transition, the following actions should be taken:
- Complete documentation on the service must be available (e.g. inputs, outputs, metrics, controls, responsibilities);
- Complete training and education of customers, IT and other constituents impacted by the service;
- Conduct a post-transition review to assure that service objectives have been met;

Service Operation (SO) – the objectives of Service Operations include:
- Coordinating and fulfilling the activities and processes required to provide and manage services for business users and customers;
- Managing the technology, facilities and people required to provide and support the services.

To ensure that IT operations are working well, the following actions should be taken:
- Develop daily, weekly and other periodic performance dashboards and reports;
- Hold a daily meeting to review key problems and outages;
- Coordinate with the help desk to ensure that all incidents and problems are resourced in a timely manner;
- Continual service improvement – measures and improves the service levels, the technology and the effectiveness of processes. It incorporates many of the same concepts articulated in the Deming Cycle of Plan-Do-Check-Act;
- Deliver the service on an ongoing basis, including managing disruptions to service and supporting end-users.

Continual Service improvement (CSI) – the main objectives of Continual Service Improvement (CSI) are:
- To measure and analyze service level achievements by comparing them to the requirements in the service level agreement (SLA);
- To recommend improvements in all phases of the lifecycle;

- To introduce activities which will increase the quality, efficiency, effectiveness and customer satisfaction of the services and the IT service management processes;
- To operate more cost effective IT services without sacrificing customer satisfaction;
- To use suitable quality management methods for improvement activities.

To ensure continuous improvement, the following actions should be taken:
- Establish resources required to perform the function;
- Maintain a current state baseline of services so one can measure any changes (hopefully improvements).

Figure 6.3 shows the ITIL service lifecycle. Figure 6.4 maps the relevant ITIL processes and related activities to each of the lifecycle phases. Many of the processes are defined in greater detail in this chapter.

ITIL® 2011 consists of five phases – Service Strategy, Service Design, Service Transition, Service Operation and Continual Service Improvement. Each phase consists of numerous processes, functions and related activities.

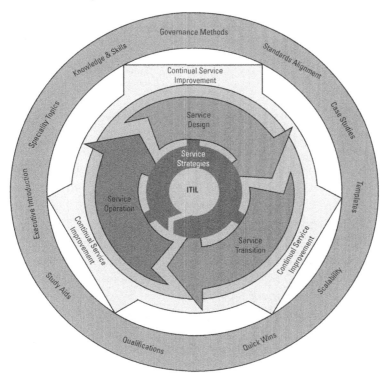

Figure 6.3 IT Service Management lifecycle (ITIL® 2011 Edition. Source: AXELOS)

6.5.3 ITIL® 2011 Edition certifications and qualifications

For ITIL 2011 Edition, there are four qualification levels:
- **Foundation level** (pastel green badge) – this level is aimed at basic knowledge of, and insight into, the core principles and processes of ITIL.

Service Strategy (SS)	Service Design (SD)	Service Transition (ST)	Service Operation (SO)	Continual Service Improvement (CSI)

• Defining the market
  – Understand customers
  – Understand opportunity
• Develop Business Case/Strategy/ Value Proposition
• Develop the IT Service Plan
• Service Portfolio Management
• Financial Management
• Demand Management
• Service Strategies (outsourcing, insourcing, hybrid)
	• Service Catalogue Management
	• Service Level Management
	• Capacity Management
	• Availability Management
	• IT Service Continuity Management (ITSCM)
	• Information Security Management
	• Supplier Management
		• Transition Planning and Support
		• Change Management
		• Change Evaluation
		• Release and Deployment Management
		• Service Validation and Testing Evaluation
		• Service Knowledge Management (includes Configuration Management)
			• Event Management
			• Incident Management
			• Problem Management (Root Cause Analysis)
			• Request Fulfillment (Service Desk)
			• Monitoring and Control IT Operations
			• IT Operations (Function)
			  – Design and Planning
			  – Deployment
			  – Operations
			  – Technical Support
			• Identity Management
			• Application Management (Function)
				• Defining Cycle: (Deming)
				  – Plan
				  – Do
				  – Check
				  – Act
				• Control and Measurement (Metrics)

Figure 6.4 ITIL® 2011 Edition service lifecycle, related processes and selected activities

- ■ **Intermediate levels**:
  - • **Intermediate Level 1** (Capability – burgundy badge) – the first intermediate level is aimed at the service lifecycle and is built up around the five core books of ITIL: Service Strategy, Service Design, Service Transition, Service Operation and Continual Service Improvement.
  - • **Intermediate Level 2** (Lifecycle – teal badge) – the second intermediate level is aimed at capabilities and is built up around four clusters: service portfolio and relationship management, service design & optimization, service monitoring & control and service operation & support.

  The two middle levels are aimed at an insight into, and application of, the knowledge of ITIL.
- ■ **ITIL Expert Certification** (lilac badge) – obtaining the ITIL Expert certification demonstrates an advanced understanding of ITIL. To become an ITIL Expert, one must have an ITIL Foundation Certificate (V3 or newer), 15 credits from the ITIL Intermediate level, and five credits from Managing across the Lifecycle.
- ■ **ITIL Master Qualification** (purple badge) – senior-level IT service managers, executive and consultants who have worked in IT service management for at least five years and have earned the ITIL Expert certification are eligible to earn the ITIL Master Qualification. Instead of taking an exam, ITIL Master Qualification

applicants must be able to explain and justify how they selected and applied a wide range of knowledge, principles, methods and techniques from ITIL to achieve desired business outcomes.

For every element in the scheme, a number of credits can be obtained. Figure 6.4 presents a schematic of the certification framework and its components. The numbers of credits for each component are shown.

This diagram represents the ITIL qualification scheme for certifications, and indicates the number of credits assigned to each qualification. It also shows the route to Expert Level. The ITIL Master point schema is being developed

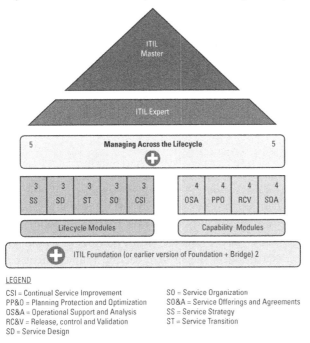

Figure 6.5 ITIL® 2011 Edition qualifications and certification schema diagram (Source: AXELOS)

■ 6.6   SELECT ITIL® 2011 EDITION PROCESSES AND FUNCTIONS BY CORE PHASES

Select ITIL® 2011 Edition processes and functions are defined in more detail in the following section under each respective core phase:

6.6.1 Service Strategy (SS)

Select functions and processes in Service Strategy include:
- Defining the market, customers and opportunity;
- Develop the IT service plan, business case strategy and value proposition;
- Develop service portfolio management and identify the services that are offered;

- Demand management – develop how demands and requests for IT services will be evaluated, prioritized, selected and authorized;
- IT financial – provide cost-effective oversight of the IT assets and resources used in providing IT services, including budgeting, accounting and charging of services.

  - Key benefits:
    - Provides accurate cost information to support IT investments;
    - Provides a budget of expected IT costs;
    - Collects and defines the true cost of providing IT services and allows for accurate accounting of these cost by IT customers;
    - Allows for the recovery of costs via charge-back of IT services to customers and helps in focusing on IT/client priorities.
  - Key implication: IT organizations are being driven to operate as internal service providers. This demands that they have mature financial management capabilities and can accurately convey and recover costs for IT services.
  - Select KPIs: cost tracking; budgeting; charge backs; asset tracking, value, utilization and retirement.

6.6.2 Service Design (SD)

Select functions and processes in Service Design include:

- **Service level management** – improves and maintains IT service quality and performance through a continuous cycle of a monitoring and reporting on IT service key performance indicators and results. Institutes corrective actions to eliminate poor service and supports business continuity and operating improvements. In ITIL 2011 Edition, the process supports the service catalog management by providing information and trends regarding customer satisfaction.

  - Key benefits:
    - Ensures customer requirements are known and that services are designed to meet these requirements;
    - Sets forth defined service targets that all IT groups can work towards;
    - Places a focus on service monitoring and improvement to identify and resolve issues;
    - Ensures that IT is focused on the most important areas.
  - Key implication: service level management should manage through a defined service level agreement or contract that describes what services and corresponding SLAs are available to IT customers, with corresponding rewards and penalties if they are met or missed respectively. Service catalogs list all services and summarize each service and its key attributes.
  - Select KPIs: SLAs (depends on what is critical to measure that should be related to CSFs of organization); customer satisfaction surveys; etc.

■ **Capacity management** – ensures that all of the current and future infrastructure and operational capacity (e.g. storage, bandwidth, hardware, etc.) aspects needed to satisfy the business requirements are scalable, backed-up and provided in a cost effective manner. It deals with service capacity management in general and the component capacity management.

- Key benefits:
  - Ensures that the existing infrastructure is optimized in terms of capacity when compared to the agreed service targets;
  - Understands the way in which the infrastructure is currently being used and will be used in the future;
  - Works to ensure that future capacity exists to meet business requirements and that it is provided in a cost effective basis.
- Key implication: capacity management is concerned with both optimizing the current environment and planning for future business requirements.
- Select KPIs: capacity, volume and speed metrics.

■ **Availability management** – optimizes the capability of the IT Infrastructure, services and supporting organization to deliver a cost effective and sustained level of availability that enables the business to achieve its business objectives.

- Key benefits:
  - Services can be designed to meet target service levels instead of defining the target and then hoping it is possible;
  - Provides a formal way to measure availability of IT services from a user perspective;
  - Over time, can reduce the number and impact of incidents by increasing resilience and reliability.
- Key implication: it is a proactive process that strives to ensure that availability targets are reasonable and achievable and that IT services are designed with this number in mind.
- Select KPIs: rate of availability; overall uptime and downtime; number of faults; mean time to repair; reasons, duration and impact on business of downtime due to unavailability of appropriate resources.

■ **IT service continuity (ITSCM) management** – supports the overall business continuity management process by ensuring that the required IT technical and service facilities (e.g. computer systems, networks, applications, technical support and service desk) can be recovered within the required and approved timeframes. This also requires the development and maintenance of a backup, contingency and disaster recovery plan and facilities.

- Key benefits:
  - Decrease the cost and impact to the business when a crisis occurs;
  - Improves the relationship between IT and the business;
  - Potentially lower insurance premiums;
  - Ability to adhere to regulatory requirements;
  - Competitive advantage when securing business partners.
- Key implication: the IT service continuity plan is a part of the overall business continuity plan and is focused on the continuity of business critical IT services. ITSCM is focused on technical and operational aspects and interacts with other ITIL processes (e.g. service level, availability, configuration, capacity and change management).
- Select KPIs: lower insurance premiums; impact and costs of major disruptions and discontinuity.

■ **Information security management** – ensures a high (whatever is necessary) level of security so that the IT infrastructure and services, as well as the business functions they support, are not compromised. ISO 27000 provides a series of information security standards as part of a framework for best practices.

- Key benefits:
  - Provides secure policies and procedures to protect infrastructure components;
  - Creates awareness to protect and secure IT resources throughout the organization.
- Key implication: IT organizations are being driven to become more secure and protect the information, infrastructure and people resources working in their environments. Security is not really a step in the lifecycle, it is a continual process and is an integral component of all of the services.
- Select KPIs: number of security breaches; impact/cost of security violations.

■ **Service catalog management** – includes description details and the status of all existing services and business processes they support, as well as those in development. There are two components of the Service Catalog: 1) The Business Service Catalog contains the details delivered to the customer. It represents the customer's view and 2) The Technical Service Catalog expand the Business Service Catalog with relationships to the supporting services, shared services, components and CIs (configuration items) necessary to support the provision of the service to business (it is not viewable by the customer).

- Key benefits:
  - Simplifies the ordering of IT services from a customer's viewpoint;
  - Provides a consistent description of IT services that can simplify pricing, scheduling and service fulfillment;
  - Sustains a more proactive service level management process and function.

- Key implication: it helps customers to interface and request well-defined services from IT in a consistent and effective manner.
- Select KPIs: number of services included in the service catalog; number of repetitive services ordered by customers from the catalog, etc.

■ **Supplier management** – involves the selection, contract management and ongoing management of third party service providers.

- Key benefits:
  - Provides a consistent process for dealing with service providers and outsourcing vendors.
- Key implication: this is a relatively new process within the ITIL suite. Other organizations such as the International Association of Outsourcing Professionals and Carnegie Mellon's IT Services Qualification Center have developed lifecycle phases, processes and certification programs for individuals and organizations, respectively.
- Select KPIs: SLAs, balance scorecard metrics.

6.6.3 Service Transition (ST)

Select functions and processes in Service Transition include:

■ **Service knowledge management systems (SKMS) [includes configuration management]** – knowledge management is important in presenting and using a wealth of knowledge stored and shared in a database of IT service management. Knowledge management addresses planning the knowledge management strategy, transferring and sharing knowledge throughout the organization, managing information and using knowledge management in a service environment. SKMS is supported by configuration management systems and CMDB(s) integrated with asset management.

■ **Configuration management** – accounts for all of the IT assets (infrastructure) and configuration items (CIs) within the organization and its services by maintaining, documenting and verifying the configurations and their versions. It provides a sound basis for enabling incident management, problem management, change management and release management to be managed effectively.

- Key benefits:
  - Identifies and records the information required to manage IT services;
  - Ensures that a central repository of configuration information is up-to-date, and accurately reflects the actual infrastructure;
  - Documents relationships of IT components to IT services;
  - Improves the economic and effective delivery of IT services.
- Key Implication: most IT organizations do not have a good understanding of how their infrastructure devices/components are interrelated or how they support key business processes and functions.

- Select KPIs: incidents/problems traced back to improperly made changes; cycle time to approve and implement changes; unauthorized IT components in Infrastructure; number of planned versus of unplanned changes; average cost or time to make change by type (e.g. mandatory, discretionary, etc.)

■ **Change management** – the process of controlling changes to improve infrastructure and service with minimum disruption. Ensures that a consistent and repeatable process with the appropriate decision criteria is used to review, fund, prioritize, document and authorize all changes in order to minimize the impact of change-related incidences on service quality and consequently improve the operational and infrastructure aspects in support of the business.

- Key benefits:
  - Provides governance as to how IT changes are requested, funded, prioritized, assessed, authorized, documented and implemented;
  - Minimizes the number of unauthorized changes and allows for introduction of change based on business needs;
  - Minimizes risk and disruption caused by failed changes via performance of impact assessments, development of back-out plans, etc.
- Key implication: An effective change management process is critical for minimizing IT service disruptions and service level violations caused by unauthorized, uncoordinated changes to the IT production environment. Scope includes hardware, network, systems, software and 'live' application software.
- Select KPIs: number of requested changes; number of successful changes; number of pending changes; time or cost of changes per change type.

■ **Release and deployment management** – ensures that all technical and non-technical aspects of an authorized release (e.g. hardware, software, network, application rollouts) and rollouts are managed in a coordinated manner with the appropriate checklists and signoffs between the appropriate constituents (e.g. development, architecture, operations, maintenance, vendors, etc.). Release types include: major, minor and emergency fixes.

- Key benefits:
  - Provides a consistent, customer-focused approach to deploying large releases into production;
  - Bundles similar changes together to decrease impact on the business and the workload on IT;
  - Better control on installed hardware and software leading to reduced costs in licensing and maintenance.
- Key implication: release management works to bridge the gap between development and operations by ensuring that new/updated services are not just 'thrown over the fence' and formalizes the transfer process from development to production.

- Select KPIs: number of major, minor and emergency releases; problems attributed to type of release – new, changed or deleted objects.

■ **Transition planning and support** – this process focuses on plans and coordinates the resources to move a new or changed service into production within the projected cost, quality and time estimates. This is not really a new process, since both release and change management incorporated sections of these activities in their scope. However, the renaming of the process to transition planning and support brings more visibility to an area that has suffered from poor or inadequate management and coordination for a long time in IT, namely transitioning either internally or vendor-developed systems into IT operations, without the appropriate tests, pilots, documentation, training and acceptance processes.

■ **Service validation and testing evaluation** – service validation and testing represents quality assurance, addressed. The process describes the progression of testing and quality control in terms of incremental contributions to business value. It also defines how to plan, guide and execute the evaluation process, including such assessment factors as service provider capability, organizational philosophy and management style, resources, modeling, metrics, purpose and use.

6.6.4 Service Operation (SO)

Select functions and processes in Service Operation include:

■ **Request fulfillment (service desk)** – the service desk represents a function and acts as the single point of contact for the management of incidents and problem resolution and restoration coordination to normal operational services with minimal business impact on the customer (inside or outside of the company) within agreed or contracted service levels and business priorities.

- Key benefits:
  - Provides a single point of contact for customer service requests;
  - Focuses on service support and reporting of incidents;
  - Provides a single point to manage and coordinate incident and problem resolution, coordination and communications;
  - Maintains a log and record of reported incidents, problems and their resolution in a database;
  - Can produce cost reduction through efficient use of resources;
  - Promotes customer retention and satisfaction.
- Key implication: The ITIL-based service desk becomes the primary source of communication to the end users for service, operational and infrastructure related issues.
- Select KPIs: number of incidents reported by type; number of calls handled per worker or workstation; average time to resolve incidents; number of priority incidents and response time; number of incidents or problems routed to first,

second or third level of support; speed to respond to customer and keep customer current on status of problem and its resolution; etc.

- **Incident management** – defines process for logging, recording and resolving incidents. Restores normal service operation as quickly as possible and minimizes the adverse impact on business operations, thus ensuring that the best possible levels of service quality and availability are maintained.

  - Key benefits:
    - Ensures that incidents are detected and that their impact on the business is known;
    - Ensures the best use of resources to support the business during service failures or disruptions;
    - Works to minimize the time to restore service and the negative effect on business operations.
  - Key implication: incident management is about doing whatever is necessary to restore service to users when a disruption occurs in order to minimize business impact.
  - Select KPIs: total number of incidents reported and resolved by type and/or priority; average time to incident resolution; average cost per incident; percent of closed incidents.

- **Problem management** – a problem is either an unknown underlying cause of one or more incidents, or a known error and for which a work-around has been identified. Problem management supports incident management by providing work-arounds and quick fixes, but does not have the responsibility for resolving the incidents.

  - Key benefits:
    - Places primary focus on root cause analysis and error prevention; not just on service restoration;
    - Ensures better utilization of technical subject matter experts by enabling them to avoid routine event handling and resolution activities;
    - Supports fault management and service desk via population of knowledge base and development of fault/incident work-around procedures.
  - Key implication: problem Management should be proactive and focused on prevention, rather than fire-fighting.
  - Select KPIs: number of problems reported and resolved by time and/or type; amount of time/cost spent to fix; percent of recurring problems; number of closed problems by type of fix – permanent, work-around or quick fix; etc.

- **Event management** – this process includes providing support for managing events.
- **Access management** – access data is now incorporated into the CMDB at the information integration layer of the service knowledge management process. This

incorporates some of the security considerations from ITIL V2 and expands the security guidelines regarding access to specific information and databases.

■ **Monitoring and control of IT operations** – this new process focuses on the day-to-day management of IT services, including plans, policies, procedures, processes, metrics and status reporting.

■ **Application management** – it encompasses a set of best practices proposed to improve the overall quality of IT software development and support through the lifecycle of software development projects, with particular attention to gathering and defining requirements that meet business objectives.

■ **Identity management** – less commonly called access and identity management, as a process it focuses on granting authorized users the right to use a service, while preventing access to non-authorized users. Certain identity management processes executes policies defined in the information security management system.

6.6.5 Continual Service Improvement (CSI)

■ Define cycle for continuous improvement using the steps of: Plan, Do, Check, Act;
■ Control and measurement (metrics) of IT services.

Overall, ITIL® 2011 Edition represents a substantive improvement over ITIL V2 and V3 by filling significant gaps with useful and pragmatic content and much improved emphasis on services (Bernard, April, 2012). It will be up to each organization to tailor ITIL into a best practice for its environment, level of maturity, pain points, opportunities and other factors.

■ 6.7   STEPS IN MAKING ITIL REAL AND EFFECTIVE

As with other IT governance improvement initiatives, making ITIL real and sustainable requires a number of steps:

■ Must have corporate mandate from the top;
■ Must have dedicated and available resources;
■ Identify executive champion and multi-disciplinary team;
■ Do homework and educate yourself on current and emerging best practices and trends;
■ Conduct an IT service management maturity assessment using a leading best practice process such as CMMI to assess and define current and target-state baselines for each ITIL process and function. Use these baselines to gauge progress and eventually to support implementation success through process improvement;
■ Analyze assessment results and establish a roadmap to achieve a higher level of ITIL maturity;
■ Must recognize that 90% of an ITSM initiative is a 'culture change' and prepare accordingly for a lengthy and involved period of adjustment;

- Develop and prioritize a program roadmap – process refinement sequence, benefits realization, timetable, and priorities, etc.;
- Assign an owner to one or more process areas;
- Encourage and sponsor ITIL certification for key individuals;
- Develop and conduct a communication and awareness campaign;
- Establish a 'web portal' to communicate progress and disseminate information;
- Plan for, and sustain, process improvements and link to a reward and incentive structure. Create a 'Continuous Service Improvement' group to sustain the framework;
- Don't focus on specific ROI as a gauge of success… Use TCO (Total Cost of Operations) as a measure of improvement.

6.7.1 ITIL process area maturity level ranking matrix

Figure 2.5 (in Chapter 2) provides an illustration of an IT governance self-assessment maturity ranking matrix. It can be used as part of a self- assessment by organizations to determine their level of maturity and expertise in each of the respective ITIL guides and process areas (it must be adapted to include more ITIL processes). Once completed, this could suggest where organizations should start, or focus on their quest for providing more effective IT services to an organization.

To design and help implement each of the process areas or function, the following documents should be completed by each organization implementing ITIL:

- Process roles, responsibilities and ownership;
- Policies;
- Process workflow;
- Process activities and work instructions;
- Templates and report design;
- Prioritization and escalation attributes and procedures;
- Closure procedures;
- Monitoring and control procedures;
- Verification strategy and audit schedule;
- Key metrics;
- Communications plan and notifications.

■ 6.8   CASE STUDY – GLOBAL MANUFACTURING ORGANIZATION

Figure 6.7 depicts a case study of a large global manufacturing organization with headquarters outside the United States. They have achieved significant success by deploying ITIL globally based on a self- assessment study.

Environment & Drivers	Approach

• Annual revenue range – $45 to 55 billion
• Number of Employees – 200,000+
• Number of IT employees – 3,500 - 5,000
• IT spend as a % of revenue – 1.1 to 2.5%
• Conservative management, very financially focused
• Brand management driven
• Decentralized on a regional (geographic) basis
• Think globally, act locally
• Technology used primarily to increase efficiency, reduce costs with limited focus on growth
• Company has primarily grown through acquisitions
• CIOs (corporate and regional) report to CFOs and are not part of the Senior Executive Management Team
• Industry is consolidating both on markets (fewer and larger customers/channels) and manufacturing
	• External assessment of IT maturity was completed with mixed results for each IT governance component (range from beginning of Level 1 to Level 3 in some regions)
	• Regional Business/IT Executive Steering Group – Approves major IT investments across all companies (e.g. >$1.0 million) in region to optimize strategy and alignment
	• Each major program/project is steered and monitored by a Program/Project Steering Committee, comprised of Business/IT folks with decision making rights
	• Corporate and regional CIOs is developing three IT policies for adoption and deployment by regional teams to improve effectiveness, efficiency and better control of compliance:
	  – Project Management Policy & process (using PMI's PMBOK and PRINCE2). Global training is required., but regional have enforcement flexibility
	  – ITIL policies and processes are being developed and deployed in IT Operations on a consistent basis globally, with an initial focus on 6 process areas
	  – IT architecture and security is consistent applied global
	  – People skills, competence & career choices model in-process

Issues and/or Problems	**Results – Alignment**
• Consolidate data centers by region to further reduce costs • Balance investments to support growth while integrating and streamlining the back office IT operational resources • Two levels of steering (regional and business unit) is being simplified to one to simplify one face to customer • Lack of consistent IT policies, practices and standards • Limited compliance documentation and limited sustainability	• IT/Business Investment Steering Committee significantly improved closer alignment • Established Single Point of Contact between IT and Business Units for Requirements and Priorities • Alignment has improved significantly, but requirements seem to be always greater than available resources (resource management allocation is being addressed organizationally and being enables with technology)
Results - Program/Project Management	**Results – Performance Management**

• PM training for all IT folks was mandated by the Corporate CIO
• While a consistent and uniform PM policy and process was developed based on industry standards, each region is empowered to implement based on their environment and culture – some regions are more disciplined than others
• Major project metrics monitored include schedule, cost, quality, number of open issues and customer satisfaction
	• Key performance indicators for IT are:
	  – Costs and headcount for IT budget (pressure to constantly reduce is continuous)
	  – Major projects, which represent 50-70% of the IT resources are tracked closely based on cost, schedule, resources and high risks. Minor projects are much less rigorously managed
	  – IT Service Management and Delivery uses several tools to track and report a variety of dashboard & key performance indicators (e.g. SLAs, asset utilization, men time to repair incidents, etc.)

Results - IT Service Management & Delivery	**Cloud Computing and Data Management**
• ITIL is being adopted as the process standard for IT operations and infrastructure • Six ITIL processes have been identified as priorities (e.g. change mgt., configuration mgt., service level mgt., release mgt., incident mgt. & problem mgt.) • Corporate and regional Centers of Excellence have been formed to develop, adopt, train and deploy ITIL within their region • The initiative was launched in 2005-2006 – too early to assess results	• Cloud Computing - Developing cloud computing policy, procedures and metrics • Data Management - Key issues are data privacy, data access and security • Using ISO 27000 Components for IT Security guidelines

Figure 6.6 Case study - global manufacturing organization

Strategic Sourcing and Outsourcing	Lessons Learned
• Mature sourcing and contract organization • IT works with a central procurement and contract organization	• Management style in each region will determine the level and degree of IT governance enforcement • Conduct an assessment of IT maturity levels, based on industry best practices, for each governance area, identify gaps and develop a plan to fill gaps • Large, complex and highly visible programs and projects are tightly controlled, while others are controlled based on the discretion of the Project Board and project Manager for the project • Conduct a detailed post-mortem on completed or challenged projects and record lesson learned
Critical Success Factors • Global CIO sponsorship of consistent global processes and term definitions for Project Management, ITIL and Security, which are deployed with regional and local flexibility • Clearly defined roles and responsibilities for global and regional IT organizations • Mandated education and training in these areas • Sponsor and reward applicable industry certifications • Use outside consultants to fill gaps and get started	

Figure 6.6 Case study - global manufacturing organization (continued)

■ 6.9   SUMMARY AND KEY TAKE AWAYS

6.9.1 Summary

IT service management is complex, and requires dedicated resources and leadership to implement effectively. It helps to transition an organization from chaos to order, from a reactive to a proactive environment, from firefighting (most of the time) to a planned environment (with firefighting some of the time), and from random service efforts to predictable and more cost effective service quality. An IT service management initiative does not end after the framework has been implemented. It must be continually monitored, maintained and improved. ITIL consists of a repository of five books of best practices that can guide an organization's people, processes and technology towards a common objective of delivering IT service excellence.

ITIL, much like other IT governance frameworks, represents a journey that is based on a combination of formal lifecycle phases, processes and checklists combined with common sense and managing change proactively. Each organization can tailor ITIL to fit its environment, culture, resources and level of maturity.

6.9.2 Key take aways
- ■ IT service management puts a heavy emphasis on the importance of the service lifecycle and the implementation and improvement of key process areas;
- ■ Identify priorities and critical success factors;
- ■ Processes should be well-defined and documented, define organizational interfaces, scalable, flexible and measurable;

- Roles and responsibilities should be well-defined with respect to each ITSM function and process;
- Leverage tools to support and enable the efficient management of ITSM processes;
- Measure and communicate lifecycle and process refinement progress as well as financial and service improvement benefits;
- An IT organization should not lose itself in a process culture. At the end of the day, an organization must deliver timely services to the customer on an end-to-end management cycle, following the processes, where appropriate.

7 Strategic Sourcing, Outsourcing and Vendor Management Excellence

"It is not the strongest among the species that survive nor is it the most intelligent. It's those that are most adaptive to change."

Charles Darwin

7.1 WHAT IS COVERED IN THIS CHAPTER?

- Discuss major strategic sourcing and outsourcing definitions, trends, opportunities, issues and challenges;
- Review the strategic sourcing business case process and contents, and identify build versus buy criteria;
- Describe the outsourcing end-to-end lifecycle process, stages, key deliverables and go/no-go criteria and identify why and what organization's outsource;
- Describe the vendor selection, evaluation, contract negotiations and award process;
- Discuss how to manage the outsourcing relationship, governance process, key metrics, escalation model and manage outsourcing risks;
- Identify steps in making outsourcing real;
- Review an outsourcing case study of a pharmaceutical company.

7.2 OVERVIEW

According to James Brian Quinn of Dartmouth College, "Outsourcing is one of the greatest organizational and industry structure shifts of the 21st century." (Quinn, 2000). Strategic IT sourcing, outsourcing and vendor management is part of execution management and due to its growth has become a critical component of IT governance. John Halvey and Barbara Melby, stated in their book on IT outsourcing, "Virtually every Fortune 500 company in this country, and an increasing number of companies throughout the world, outsource some significant portion of their IT services." (Halvey and Melby, 2005). According to a blend of International Data Corporation, AMR and Gartner estimates, the IT outsourcing business will exceed $1.0 trillion by 2015 - 2016.

This does not include other outsourcing services such as business process outsourcing, legal, accounting, manufacturing, customer services, medical, administrative services and many others.

Again, it is not the intention of this chapter to rehash what has already been published, but rather to provide a blend of pragmatic and actionable checklists, techniques, lessons learned and critical success factors based on current and emerging outsourcing best practices to help organizations plan, negotiate, deploy and manage successful outsourcing deals and relationships.

7.2.1 Strategic sourcing and outsourcing definitions

According to the International Association of Outsourcing Professionals (IAOP) outsourcing is a long-term, results-oriented business relationship with a specialized third party services provider that can be strategic and transformational, or tactical, or both (IAOP, 2014):

- **Strategic or transformational sourcing** – assets and processes are transferred to service providers and/or core competencies are supplemented by service providers' centers of excellence (e.g. R & D, product design/development, etc.). This represents a business focus and is all about creating value, aligning with the business processes that change in line with strategic business goals and objectives, and is based on the creation of a win-win partnership between the customer and the service provider.
- **Tactical outsourcing** – can include staff supplementation and easily scalable IT services such as additional web server or application services provider (ASP) capacity, where there are no asset transfers. These are often linked to specific problems or opportunities in a company with an operational focus and are all about adding resources or capacity for a limited time period.

Other terms that are associated with outsourcing include:
- Onshore (home country) outsourcing – obtaining services from an external source in your home country;
- Rural outsourcing – variation of home country outsourcing where an organization obtains the services of an external source in a rural area of the home country, where the service is usually less expensive than in an urban part of the country;
- Near - shore outsourcing – refers to a service provider located in a nearby country to your home country, often one that shares a border. Canada or Mexico are near-shore countries for United States-based customers;
- Offshore outsourcing – refers to contracting with a company that is geographically distant, like India, Ireland, China, Philippines, Israel and Rumania, where an ocean separates the countries;
- Best – shore outsourcing – a recently coined term that describes the 'shore' that offers the best 'deal' for the customer;
- In-sourcing – internal capabilities are used to conduct the services;

- Co-sourcing or multi-sourcing – represents a combination of insourcing and outsourcing;
- Application service provider (ASP) – outsourced services are offered to the customer over a network;
- Cloud – obtain pre-defined outsourcing services from a vendor through the Internet;
- Multi-vendor sourcing – obtain services from multiple vendors;
- Partnership – involves two or more organizations working together on strategic initiatives that leverage expertise from each organization.

Figure 7.1 summarizes the above sourcing alternatives, their characteristics, advantages and disadvantages.

Sourcing Strategy	Characteristics	Advantages	Disadvantages
In-sourcing	Internal capacities are used for the design, development, maintenance, execution and/or offer of support for the service. Another form of in-sourcing is known as "Captive" division where a company sets up and manages an outsourcing entity off-shore.	– Direct control (competitive advantage) – Freedom of choice – Rapid prototyping of leading-edge services – Familiar policies and processes – Company-specific knowledge	– Scale limitations – Cost/time to market for services readily available outside – Dependant on internal resources, skills/ competencies
Outsourcing	Engaging an external organization for the design, development, maintenance, execution and/or offering of support of the service.	– Economies of scale – Purchased expertise – Focus on company core competencies – Test drive/trial of new services – Access to innovative resources	– Less direct control – Exit barriers – Solvency risk of suppliers – Unknown supplier skills and competencies – More challenging business process integration – Increased governance required
Co-sourcing or multi-sourcing	Often a combination of insourcing and outsourcing, using a number of organizations. Generally involves external organizations working together in designing, developing, transitioning, maintaining, operating and/ or supporting a portion of a service.	– Time to market – Leveraged expertise – Control – Use of specialized providers	– Project complexity – Intellectual property and copyright protection – Culture clash between companies

Figure 7.1 Summary of sourcing delivery alternatives

Sourcing Strategy	Characteristics	Advantages	Disadvantages
The Cloud	Cloud service providers offer specific pre-defined services, usually on-demand. These services can be offered internally, but generally refer to outsourced service provisioning. Clouds can be private or public.	– Services are easily defined – Sourcing is straightforward – Mapping between the service and business outcome is relatively straightforward – Greater customer control of the service	– Internal clouds are still complex – Focus could mask the relationship between IT activities and business outcomes – Difficulty coordinating insourced offerings with external cloud services – Security and privacy of information and business continuity management
Application service provider	Computer-based services are offered to the customer over a network.	– Access to expensive and complex solutions – Low-cost location and pay on-demand – Support and upgrades included – Security and ITSM operations included	– Culture clash between companies – Access to facilities only, not knowledge – Often usage-based charging models
Multi-vendor sourcing	This category involves sourcing different services from different vendors, often representing different sourcing options from the above.	– Less risk as the organization is not tied to single vendor (do not put all your eggs in one basket). – Leverage if specialized skills in different organizations ensures a more complete support model	– Difficulty in coordinating activities and services from different vendors; governance – more difficult – Requires a very clear understanding of the overall value chain and each vendor's role
Partnership	Formal arrangements between two or more organizations to work together on strategic initiatives that leverage critical expertise or market opportunities.	– Time to market – Market expansion/entrance – Competitive response – Leveraged expertise – Trust, alignment and mutual benefit – "Risk and reward" agreements	– Project complexity – Intellectual property and copyright protection – Culture clash between companies
Crowd sourcing	Obtain service ideas and problem solving by outsourcing the problem through social networks and the internet to an unidentified entity or the "crowd". This may also be considered as a new form of collaborative alliance.	– Provides innovative solutions (open model) from a diverse crowd outside an organization – Can be a source of competitive advantage – Can be enabled by contacts collaborative communities	– Difficult to protect new potential intellectual property and research ideas – Quality of ideas may be suspect – The value and impact of ideas may be limited due to insufficient financial incentives

Figure 7.1 Summary of sourcing delivery alternatives (continued)

In addition to the IAOP, another excellent reference for client and service provider outsourcing best practice frameworks, processes and tools was developed by a consortium led by Carnegie Mellon University's Information Technology Services Qualification Center (ITSqc). ITSqc published two documents, one of which is the eSourcing Capability Model for Service Providers and the other is the eSourcing Capability Model for Client Organizations. Both are referenced in more detail in Section 2.4.18.

7.2.2 Major outsourcing drivers and challenges

Global sourcing is a significant market and deserves clear understanding and careful consideration in every business environment. The information technology (IT) and business process outsourcing (BPO) markets are a significant aspect of global sourcing and garner huge amounts of reviews, research and reporting. However, historically, the areas of supply chain, logistics and procurement, and manufacturing (e.g.: everything from textiles to electronics) have accounted for the largest sectors in global spending – each of these is twice the size of IT sourcing. Part of the explanation here is that the manufacturing and other areas have been engaged in global sourcing for a much longer period of time.

The service-based sourcing has expanded beyond Information Technology Outsourcing (ITO) to general Business Process Outsourcing (BPO) and many specialized segments such as Human Resource Outsourcing (HRO), Financial Systems Outsourcing (FSO), and Legal Resource Outsourcing (LRO). These service-based offerings have joined with the increasing sourcing activity in manufacturing, supply chain management, research and development, etc., resulting in a fast-growing global market in outsourcing of all kinds.

The following list is an overview of the seven primary drivers of global sourcing:

- **Economics** – this driver focuses on the fundamental question of how to bring together the best mix of resources to produce the quality product or service for the marketplace. The pressure from top management to reduce costs is a fundamental factor in this driver. This focus on lowering costs fuels the interest in global sourcing because of the labor arbitrage benefits of using resources housed in a lower-wage location. Therefore economics is a fundamental issue in the 'shoring' question: is work performed in an on-shore, near-shore or off-shore location? The answer to this question raises both issues and opportunities which will be discussed later in this book. Another aspect of the economic question is the structure of the relationship. This can range from a simple contract for work performed to a much more complex arrangement involving, for example, the investment of capital from a client organization into a provider organization, or the transfer of assets from one to the other. In some instances, client organizations are required to carry out part of their business in a location to be able to market to the population.
- **Resource management** – this driver addresses the strategy adopted to access the best resources to achieve the product and service goals of the organization. 'Best' is

defined in a variety of ways, for example, least costly, specialized, those enhancing or supplementing existing capabilities, the provision of unique or scarce capabilities, the use of specialized resources for a finite period of time, and access to innovative approaches.

- **Decreasing time to market** – while related to resource management, this driver is important and should be viewed independently. In the current global, fast-paced marketplace, an organization's ability to get its product or service to the customer, in a timely manner, is critical to its competitive success. The resources – human, technological, capacity - required to decrease the time to market can be obtained through sourcing.

- **Flexible and scalable operations and technology** – flexibility and scalability allow organizations to move and change with the demands of the marketplace. For example, if an organization needs specialized resources such as people or manufacturing capacity on a short-term basis, it can acquire the resources on a temporary, as-needed basis, without committing the organization to long-term expenditures on these resources. This allows scaling up when needed and down when the opportunity is no longer present. This driver also allows an organization to experiment with new products or services without significant investment.

- **Transformation and innovation** – seeking innovation outside the organization through outsourcing has been used as a transformation technique. This driver can be operationalized in a variety of ways: bring in innovative ideas by using external resources working with internal staff, use specialized external resources with new and different skills, processes or technology to carry out innovation for the organization, and use the concepts of 'open innovation' to make the organizational boundary porous.

- **Regulatory and legal Issues** – the regulatory and legal landscape of a location can become important factors in the sourcing decision. This is not restricted to off-shore considerations. Within a specific country, there can be differing regulations that may affect sourcing engagements in both positive and negative ways. Some of the regulatory issues are related to economics; for example, there may be incentives provided by the local government to encourage the establishment of sourcing businesses in their area. Others may be logistical issues such as problems associated with trans-border data flow. Legal issues run the range of contracting provisions to intellectual property protection. When an organization is engaged with a multiplicity of providers, there may be an increasing level of complexity associated with this driver.

- **Enabling mechanisms** – the availability of reliable, world-wide communications and software tools has provided an enabling mechanism that supports global sourcing. In addition we have seen the development of advisory firms, consultants and specialized legal services to assist any organization in getting started with global sourcing as well as organizations and websites evaluating sourcing providers (Bullen, Lefave, Selig, 2010).

Figure 7.2 identifies additional key sourcing drivers.

Factors Impacting the Desire to Outsource and/or Offshore

Financial Savings – (cost reduction, containment and/or avoidance)	• Wage Arbitrage – utilizing off-shore resources with materially identical skill sets and a lower wage base • CAPEX Conversion – reducing investment and converting previous and planned capital expenses into operating expenses through an outsourcing contract • Tax Optimization – taking advantage of tax regulations (such as those that favor foreign direct investment or, in some cases, local investment in certain industries or types of activities) • Bench Optimization – utilizing a service provider organization's excess work force to deal with potential peaks and valleys in demand for highly cyclical resource roles (short term flexibility).
Operating Model Flexibility and Innovation	• Modular Reconfiguration /Scalability– enabling rapid reconfiguration of resource deployments to deal with changing market conditions and specialty resource requirements (long-term flexibility) • Innovation Enablement – exposure to new incremental/radical innovative processes, technology and talent from vendor.
Talent Management	• Talent Acquisition – seeking skilled, qualified resources in sourcing locations to fulfill immediate requirements through a contractual sourcing or captive arrangement • Talent Focus – freeing up human resources and executive management to focus on core competencies.
Process Transformation	• Leading Best Practice Adoption – adopting vendor developed processes, products or technology leading practices • Technology Transformation – adopting a vendor platform to further advance available technologies for use in either intra-company processes or new product development or inter-company initiatives (supply chain) • Quality Assurance ("QA") – implementing more rigorous QA processes and standards as a result of entering into a contractual services arrangement, often lead by the vendor project team • Cultural Proficiency – leveraging a vendor's local knowledge to gain competitive access to new markets.
Regulatory Advantages and Compliance	• Documentation Quality – especially in government-regulated industries, high quality documentation is essential to passing regular inspections and facilitating compliance with regulation – often vendors perform this activity at an enterprise level • Regulatory Knowledge – leveraging vendor knowledge of specific regulatory requirements (e.g. customs, tax incentives, Sarbanes-Oxley).

Figure 7.2 Key strategic sourcing and outsourcing drivers (Source: Deloitte Consulting, 2013)

7.2.3 Why do organizations outsource?

There are many reasons why organizations choose to outsource or in-source or deploy a combination of both strategies. Figure 7.3 provides a list of outsourcing (or buy) and in-sourcing (or build) motivations.

BUY (OUTSOURCING) CRITERIA	BUILD (IN-SOURCING) CRITERIA
Cost reduction, containment and/or avoidance	Competitive advantage (proprietary requirements)
Speed up time-to-market	Expertise available in-house
Assist a rapid growth situation or overflow situations	May be less expensive than buying
Aggressive schedule	Can be completed on time
Politically correct	Opportunity costs trade-offs
Share risk	No suitable vendors available
Improve flexibility & scalability	Core competences (fundamental business of the firm)
Leverage new skills/resources/management/ process/technologies	Security, privacy and control are critical
Avoid major capital investments	Strategic initiative or function or process
Improve performance	Threat to intellectual property theft
Enable innovation and transformation	Lower risk

Figure 7.3 Outsourcing motivations – build versus buy

7.2.4 What do organizations outsource?

Today, virtually any IT function can be outsourced such as:

- **IT architecture** – includes database management, data architecture, etc.;
- **IT infrastructure** – elements of the IT infrastructure include computer center, network management and operations, help desk operations, data entry, hardware maintenance and service, cloud applications, servers, etc.;
- **Systems and software applications development and maintenance** – coding, testing, integration, maintenance, analytics, social media, etc.;
- **Web development and hosting** – e-commerce front-end, middleware and back-end systems;
- **Training, education and certification** – IT, customer and management personnel.

Examples of IT and other outsourcing deals demonstrate the extent to which select companies outsource both core functions and non-core functions or processes:

- Brokerage firm – outsourced data center and network operations;
- Computer manufacturer – outsourced assembly of its PCs and call center;
- Medical office – outsourced transcription of doctor's voice recording notes on a patient off-shore;
- Bank – outsourced customer service center and IT help desk;
- Pharmaceutical company – outsourced manufacture of product;
- University – hired a service provider to manage its entire IT function and transferred all IT assets to the service provider;
- Architecture firm – outsourced design and blueprints of buildings to Eastern Europe;
- Airplane manufacturer – outsourced the manufacture of different components to strategic partner vendors in different countries with large market potential;
- Retail firm – outsourced their payroll and select accounting functions;

- Consulting firm – outsourced the design, development and maintenance of their website;
- Law firm – experimenting with outsourcing legal research off-shore for US clients.

The above indicates that we operate in a global economy and doing business in developing and emerging countries is part of the model. It is always useful to start with a business model evaluation of the outsourcing opportunity and then an assessment of what is core and non-core to IT and what can be supplemented by global service provider resources. As an example, a large telecommunications company uses offshore locations in India and Brazil to promote a follow the sun model for IT testing and production support.

7.2.5 Benefits of outsourcing from a customer and service provider perspective

There are many benefits to outsourcing from a customer's perspective. They include:
- Enables business to focus on strategic functions;
- Lowers annual operating costs and capital investments;
- Frees up time and resources (opportunity costs) to focus on core strengths;
- Increases speed to market;
- Provides access to scarce or supplementary resources;
- Capital infusion (depending on what is outsourced) for assets that are transferred;
- More politically acceptable in certain situations, if the in-house function does not have a good reputation;
- Provides scalable resources and bench strength;
- Enables greater innovation;
- Improves productivity and quality through individual or company certifications.

There are also benefits and market realities from a service provider perspective such as:
- Substantial revenue stream potential and growing global market;
- Long term customer relationships with opportunities for cross-selling and up-selling other products and services;
- Customers are increasingly going with a limited number strategic sourcing specialists to develop longer term relationships and negotiate better deals.

7.2.6 Outsourcing – barriers and risks

While there are many good reasons to outsource, there are also barriers and risks that need to be overcome or mitigated especially in dealing with off-shore deals. Examples of such obstacles and risks include:
- Loss of control of confidential information;
- Function or process is too critical to outsource;
- Loss of flexibility due to inflexible contracts;
- Negative customer reaction;
- Employee resistance due to job loss or transfer;
- Poor outsourcing process or management;

- Service provider failure;
- Lack of intellectual property protection;
- Differences in culture and time zones relating to offshore deals;
- Regulatory and legal country differences;
- Lack of security and data protection;
- Legal and arbitration adjudication and dispute settlement;
- Off-shore bribery or bakshish.

7.2.7 Avoiding the major pitfalls of outsourcing

As in all things, sourcing also has pitfalls. These include the following:
- Lack of executive management commitment;
- Lack of a sourcing plan;
- Not having a plan to mitigate through a sourcing evaluation;
- Lack of a sourcing communications plan;
- Lack of knowledge of outsourcing processes and techniques;
- Failure to recognize outsourcing risks;
- Failure to obtain assistance from external outsourcing experts and professionals;
- Not dedicating the best and brightest internal resources;
- Rushing through the outsourcing requirements, scope, RFP and vendor selection and contract phases;
- Being unrealistic about benefits;
- Not recognizing the impact of cultural differences (true whether onshore, near-shore or off-shore);
- Underestimating what it will take to get the provider to become productive;
- Having no formal outsourcing governance program;
- Putting all the sourcing eggs in one basket. Split the work with at least two or a limited number of providers, or designate a primary and secondary service provider for back-up purposes;
- De-skilling by outsourcing all of an organization's knowledge and experience in particular areas, thus creating a dangerous dependence on the service provider;
- Hiring of unprepared or inadequate outsourcing consultants and/or vendors.

7.2.8 Key questions and considerations that can help to make the sourcing decision

Sourcing represents both opportunities and risks. However, in recent years, the growth and size of the global outsourcing market and the growing number of countries that are providing incentives to attract new or existing outsourcing providers (e.g. India, China, Malaysia, Philippines, Egypt, South Africa, Romania, etc.) to locate in their countries suggest that client companies, in general, are pursuing outsourcing opportunities and developing a sourcing strategy of some kind.

Typically, companies may decide to outsource based on one or more of the drivers. The decision will often depend not only on the drivers, but also on the underlying causes, issues, pain points, opportunities and potential risks associated with the decision. The decision to source or not to source can be facilitated by obtaining answers to a series of strategic, value and operational questions.

Table 7.1 provides a sample of key questions and considerations that will assist an organization in making the sourcing decision. The questions are categorized by the following segments: Strategic, Value and Delivery & Execution.

Table 7.1 Key Strategic, Value, Delivery and Execution Questions for Sourcing

Strategic Questions:
- Is the sourcing strategy in line with our business vision and strategy and competitive differentiation?
- Do we understand the risks?
    - Financial, operational, security, privacy, intellectual property, other?
    - Do we have adequate provisions in place for disaster prevention, recovery and contingencies?
    - Do we understand regulatory compliance requirements that apply to the outsourcing work and subsequently to the provider?
- Can outsourcing add strategic value?
    - Can this sourcing opportunity be created as a revenue source for the company alone or through a joint venture?
    - Revenue growth; cost reduction/containment/ avoidance; reduce speed to market; business process transformation; etc.?
- How can we measure the value of global sourcing?
    - Key performance measures.
    - Impact on the business/function/department/process
- What organizational resources are required to support global sourcing?
    - Skills.
    - Budget.
    - Competencies.
    - Certifications
- What governance, controls and consistent process should be institutionalized for effective sourcing?
- What experienced/qualified teams can we put in place?
    - For example: functional head, executive sponsor, auditor, accountant, lawyer, project manager and procurement
- Are there known providers for this service?
    - Do we understand their capabilities, capacity and scale to provide this service?

Value Questions:
- Will we reap benefits?
    - Clear accountability for achieving the benefits.
    - Linking benefits to MBOs and incentive compensation schemes.
    - An effective benefits realization process and sign-off within the company
- Do we have a clear current 'as is' profile?
    - Covering affected assets, people and processes.
    - Understanding licenses, costs, equipment, facilities etc
- Do we have the capability of effectively working with outsourcing providers?
    - What industry frameworks, standards and models should we use?
- Should we hire a consultant?
    - To assist in developing, reviewing and/or validating our sourcing strategy and approach?
    - As an advisory firm to help choose the provider(s)?

- Is this process or operation scalable?
  - Can it be leveraged with more volume, more customers, etc.?
- Is the cost of the operation competitive with what could be obtained in the market?
- Would de-skilling (loss of in-house expertise) have a negative impact?

Delivery & Execution Questions:
- Have we done in-house benchmarking to determine:
  - Are we deploying well and effectively: scalable, disciplined and consistent management, governance and delivery processes capabilities and attitudes?
  - Are appropriate and sufficient resources available with the right competencies, capabilities and attitudes at the right time?
- Would loss of data or content of this service/product hurt the firm?
  - How? What would be the impact? Financial? Business disruption?
- Overview of provider questions:
  - Is the provider certified vis-à-vis an industry standard (e.g. ISO 9000, CMMI, PMI, ITSqc, etc.)?
  - Does the provider have local and international presence and capability?
  - Has the firm had previous experience with the provider?
  - Does the provider have a superior reputation for delivering quality services at a reasonable cost? Is the provider financially stable?
  - What processes (e.g. transition management, project management, quality management, performance management, etc.) are being used by the vendor? Are they acceptable?
  - Is the provider undertaking sustainable practices?
- What is the 'optimum' relationship management model to be established between the company and the service provider?

Source: Bullen, Lefave & Selig, 2010

7.2.9 The information technology balancing dilemma

In most companies, IT needs to balance its resources between minimizing the total cost of operations while maximizing its use to help the company achieve solid growth, innovation and competitive advantage. Outsourcing can facilitate this balancing act. Figure 7.4 illustrates that outsourcing can contribute both to the cost reduction, containment and avoidance side as well as to increasing the value of an organization by allowing the organization to focus on core competencies innovations and other revenue generating functions.

Outsourcing Can Help to Reduce Total Cost of Operations (TCO) While Maximizing its Use to Achieve Growth and Competitive Advantage

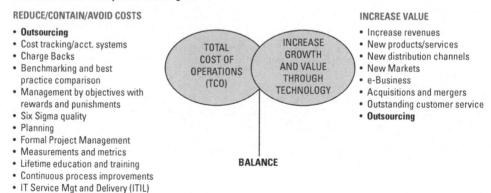

REDUCE/CONTAIN/AVOID COSTS

- **Outsourcing**
- Cost tracking/acct. systems
- Charge Backs
- Benchmarking and best practice comparison
- Management by objectives with rewards and punishments
- Six Sigma quality
- Planning
- Formal Project Management
- Measurements and metrics
- Lifetime education and training
- Continuous process improvements
- IT Service Mgt and Delivery (ITIL)

INCREASE VALUE

- Increase revenues
- New products/services
- New distribution channels
- New Markets
- e-Business
- Acquisitions and mergers
- Outstanding customer service
- **Outsourcing**

Figure 7.4 The information technology balancing dilemma

■ 7.3   PRINCIPLES AND PRACTICES FOR OUTSOURCING EXCELLENCE FROM A CUSTOMER PERSPECTIVE

Even with the increased outsourcing initiatives in customer organizations, it appears that organizations continue to struggle with establishing and enforcing a more formal, consistent and repeatable outsourcing policy, process and methodology. According to the ITSqc at Carnegie Mellon University, "Managing and meeting client expectations is a major challenge for service providers in these business relationships, and examples of failures abound." (Hefley and Locsche, 2006). They go on to summarize the key issues faced by customer organizations, which are also re-enforced and supplemented by the IAOP in their Outsourcing Body of Knowledge (OPBOK, IAOP, 2013):

- ■ Establishing an appropriate outsourcing strategy, business case and plan;
- ■ Identifying the appropriate outsourcing opportunities;
- ■ Developing appropriate approaches and techniques for outsourcing activities;
- ■ Identifying, selecting and negotiating a win-win deal with service providers;
- ■ Managing service provider governance and performance management;
- ■ Managing the transition from the customer to the service provider as a project;
- ■ Managing the ongoing relationship.

7.3.1 Key principles and practices for outsourcing excellence

Based on an extensive review of the literature, select case studies and numerous sourcing consulting engagements completed by the author, there are a number of best practice principles and practices that can represent a checklist for helping companies achieve improvements and higher levels of outsourcing maturity and effectiveness in their environment. Even with the increased outsourcing initiatives in customer organizations, it appears that organizations continue to struggle with establishing and enforcing a formal, consistent and repeatable outsourcing policy, process and methodology. The principles and practices listed below will help to develop a successful outsourcing environment for an organization.

General:

- ■ Have a clear strategy and plan that supports the business:
  - • What are you expecting to achieve and what would success look like?
  - • At what cost?
- ■ Ensure there is clarity of purpose for both sides with defined roles and responsibilities;
- ■ Establish key performance measures that are realistic and meaningful;
- ■ Empowerment - let people do what they are supposed to do – hold them accountable, both on the service provider and customer side;
- ■ Have an escalation policy and process with clear roles and responsibilities for both sides;
- ■ Undertake periodic formal progress reviews and reports based on specific metrics relating to the type of outsourcing service or project;

- For large initiatives, establish a high level peer outsourcing governance board for joint reviews;
- Assign a service provider account relationship manager as a single point of contact/ interface with the customer and establish a customer/service provider relationship model;
- Keep closer tabs on the relationship during first 90 days of a contract and make any necessary adjustments fast.

Customer do's:
Key customer to-do's should include:
- Seek executive alignment and commitment to outsourcing that creates a favorable outsourcing culture within the organization;
- Create a well-defined and realistic business case process and case;
- Establish a consistent and formal process for service provider selection and contract negotiations;
- Develop an outsourcing transition plan from pilot to full implementation provision for either re-deployment or termination of displaced resources;
- Build key performance indicators into the contract performance evaluation system with both rewards for extra-ordinary performance and penalties for poor performance;
- Make KPIs relevant, simple, comparable, easy to report and focused on measurable outcomes;
- Develop an outsourcing communication plan, risk management and mitigation plan, policy and process;
- Balance stakeholder needs – companies that successfully outsource continuously 'take the pulse' of all stakeholder groups to adjust their needs over time;
- Pursue stakeholder involvement on major outsourcing deals through governance boards, steering committees and working committees;
- Manage the expectations of all stakeholders well – deliver what you promise; don't over-promise things you or the outsourcing service provider cannot deliver – credibility is a fleeting attribute that if lost, is extremely difficult or almost impossible to regain;
- Recognise that experience matters – governance groups can rapidly fill their experience deficit through subject matter expert coaching or external consulting support;
- Understand that SLAs are not enough – service level agreements are extremely important and should be continuously refined and improved over the life of the contract. However, they must be augmented by other methods to ensure customer satisfaction (e.g. formal and/or informal surveys, listening to the voice of the customer, etc.);
- Develop disengagement options and conditions as part of the contract that includes renegotiations options;
- Make sure that a disaster prevention and recovery plan with contingencies is in place.

7.3.2 Strategic sourcing lifecycle roadmap

Outsourcing initiatives, like projects have lifecycles with phases or stages, or both. The process leading to successful management of global sourcing with a phased approach will be outlined here and will help guide a manager through the process in a logical and useful manner. The practices discussed here are relevant to both the client and provider organizations. The following is a brief description of the phases:

Figure 7.5 illustrates the strategic sourcing lifecycle roadmap including each phase with its tasks, deliverables and select checklists and templates (Bullen, Lefave & Selig, 2010).

- **Strategy formulation (Phase 0):**
  - Establishing a clear outsourcing strategy, business case and plan that aligns with the business;
  - Identifying the appropriate outsourcing opportunities;
  - Creating executive alignment and commitment to outsourcing that creates a favorable outsourcing culture within the organization;
  - Ensuring the experience base – organizations can rapidly fill their experience deficit through subject matter expert coaching or outside consulting support. Experience has been shown to be an important factor in creating successful engagements.
- **Feasibility (Phase 1):**
  - Creating a well-defined process and consistent format for developing a business case.
  - Obtaining executive approval and appropriate resources.
- **Provider selection (Phases 2 and 3):**
  - Identifying, selecting and negotiating a win-win deal with service providers.
  - Establishing a consistent and formal process for service provider selection and contract negotiations.
- **Commitment (Phase 4):**
  - Establishing well-defined roles and responsibilities for both the organization and the provider.
  - Assigning a service provider account relationship manager as a single point of contact/interface with the organization and establishing a relationship model that clearly defines roles for both organizational and provider personnel.
  - Building key performance indicators into the contract performance evaluation system with both rewards for extra-ordinary performance and penalties for poor performance.
  - Making KPIs relevant, simple, comparable, easy to report and focused on measurable outcomes. Be sure that the provider is not being measured on factors over which the provider has no control.
  - Developing disengagement options and conditions as part of the contract that includes renegotiations options.
  - Making sure that a disaster prevention and recovery plan with contingencies is in place.

	Phase 0: Strategy Formulation	Phase 1: Feasibility	Phase 2: Preparation	Phase 3: Evaluation	Phase 4: Commitment	Phase 5: Transition	Phase 6: On-going Management & Governance
			Provider Selection				
Objectives	• Determine business need • Align with business strategy • Develop sourcing strategy and identify areas of opportunity • Identify key drivers	• Develop business case • Develop base case (as is state before sourcing) and future scenarios (future state after sourcing) • Decompose into discrete components • Perform risk assessment: – Function – Country – Culture – Security – Etc	• Develop detailed requirements/scope • Finalize/issue RFP • Formulate provider selection criteria and weights	• Evaluate contract & provider pricing • Evaluate providers • Internal audit review for controls	• Select and negotiate provider proposals • Develop transition program • Finalize organization plan • Sign contract • External and internal communications • Manage organizational change	• Implement phased transition plan • 30/60/90 day phases • Establish relationship management strategy	• Manage to contract • Manage scope and changes • Monitor business value of engagement via business case • Issues management • Reorient retained organization
Deliverables & Decisions	• High level sourcing strategy • Validate strategy – Internal – External • Secure sponsor and management team • Inform executive team • Identify sourcing areas of opportunities and priorities • Examine sourcing geographic alternatives - on, off, best shore	• Business case • Identify PM and macro plan • Outsourcing market overview • Determine core vs. non-core functions, processes, technologies, etc • Risk assessment and mitigation plan • Consulting contract (optional) • External counsel agreement (optional) • Review and approve at appropriate levels: – Functional head / Business unit – CEO – Board of directors	• RFP • Identify resource requirements • Form pre-transition team • Identify providers (could use RFI to eliminate unqualified providers)	• Score vendors • Conduct due diligence – benchmark – site visits – references • Short list providers • Draft Master Service Agreement (MSA) and Statement of Work (SOW) • Approve budget • Change management process and authorization	• Finalize and sign contract – MSA and SOWs (Statement of Work) • Transition plan – pre and post checklist • Form post transition team • Risk mitigation, backup and contingency plan • Develop human resources and asset transfer and retention plan • Finalize governance plan, processes, metrics and roles • Finalize training plan • Finalize pilot testing and/or validation plan	• Execution of transition plan • Implement relationship management plan • Assess results of initial transition and fix issues • Knowledge transfer and finalize documentation • Clear hand-offs – who, what, when, how, where and finalize documentation	• Governance - schedule of activities and process • Change control process • Escalation process and roles • Management and performance reporting • Updated business case • Renew, expand or disengage contract • Build client/provider high performance teams • Institutionalize: – Sourcing process and continuously improve – Improve governance process – Lessons learned – Critical success factors
	go/no go	go/no go	go/no go	go/no go	go/no go	go/no go	
Enabling Checklists, Tools and Technologies	• Template – Business plan – Sourcing plan – Sourcing business case	• Business case template • Risk assessment template and framework	• Vendor evaluation scorecard and criteria • RFI/RFQ/RFP table of contents	• Criteria for vendor due diligence template • Master Service Agreement (MSA)	• Transition plan template • Communication and governance plan – Metrics – Framework – Escalation	• Transition checklists – Pre-transition – Post-transition • Relationship management practices	• Governance framework • The end game checklist

Figure 7.5 Strategic sourcing lifecycle roadmap (source: Christine Bullen, Dick Lefave & Gad Selig, 2010)

■ **Transition (Phase 5):**
- Managing the transition from the organization to the service provider as a project (see Chapter 8 for more details).
- Developing an outsourcing communication plan, risk management process and mitigation plan.
- Keeping close tabs on the relationship during first 90 days of a contract and making any necessary adjustments fast.

■ **Ongoing management and governance (Phase 6):**
- Implementing a governance plan for the provider and carrying out performance management.
- Creating an atmosphere of empowerment – letting people do what they are supposed to do – holding them accountable, both on the service provider and customer side.
- Having an escalation policy and process in place with clear roles and responsibilities for both sides to avoid losing time in correcting any issues.
- Conducting periodic formal progress reviews and reports based on specific metrics relating to the type of outsourcing service or project.
- For large initiatives, establishing a high level peer outsourcing governance board for joint reviews.
- Balancing stakeholder needs – companies that successfully outsource continuously 'take the pulse' of all stakeholder groups to adjust their needs over time.
- Managing the expectations of all stakeholders well – deliver what is promised; don't over-promise things that cannot be delivered by either the organization or the outsourcing service provider – credibility is a fleeting attribute that if lost, is extremely difficult or almost impossible to regain.
- Not relying solely on SLAs – service level agreements are extremely important and should be continuously refined and improved over the life of the contract. However, when parties in a relationship resort to the SLA, it implies very poor management of the relationship. The overall governance plan should be the primary way of managing the sourcing engagement. Satisfaction that the sourcing relationship is achieving its goals should be determined through a good relationship using both formal and informal communication and governance processes.

"The buyer needs a hundred eyes, the seller not one."

Jacula Prudentum, Circa 1500

7.3.3 Customer's outsourcing planning checklist

It is always useful to have a checklist as a reminder of the activities that should be considered. The following provides such a checklist for outsourcing:

■ Executive sponsor(s);
■ Charter define boundaries;
■ Appoint an outsourcing project team and manager – pre–outsourcing stage and post-outsourcing stage (if outsourcing is pursued);

- Project scope and requirements;
- Assumptions, obstacles and constraints;
- Core and non-core competencies;
- Critical success factors;
- Business case (cost/benefit analysis, including impact on current employees and unions, where applicable);
- Communications plan;
- Work breakdown structure;
- Roles and responsibilities – customer and service provider;
- Resource plan;
- Risk management and contingency plan;
- Procurement and contracting plan;
- Service provider selection and evaluation criteria with a consistent weighting scheme;
- Quality plan;
- Governance plan, escalation and key metrics;
- Project or service schedule and deliverables;
- Change management plan;
- Implementation, conversion and transition plan;
- Disengagement plan;
- Develop a list of qualified service providers for consideration.

7.3.4 Business and outsourcing performance management and the balanced scorecard

A performance management plan with metrics must be developed for outsourcing. The development of the performance management plan should be a collaborative effort within the client organization and between the client and the provider. It should be based on a number of objectives:

- Consistent with strategic objectives;
- Provide a financial benefit;
- Improve customer relationship;
- Increase customers and markets;
- Improve product or service quality;
- Improve process and product innovation;
- Make operations more effective or efficient, or both.

It is important to measure the performance of outsourcing initiatives and services in realistic and practical terms that can be understood by the business. It is equally important that the measurements be fair to the provider and that the performance is within the control of the provider. For example, it is inappropriate to penalize the provider for poor performance when the client's own processes created the poor performance situation.

A critical question that should be answered is: what key performance indicators (KPIs) should be tracked? The answer will depend on the objectives of the specific outsourcing service that is provided, and may include the following components:

- Costs (reduction/avoidance/containment);
- Revenues (new or incremental);
- Customer satisfaction;
- Reliability, availability and scalability of the service;
- Speed to market;
- Business transformation through process, product and technology innovation;
- Program/project management outcomes (e.g. time, cost, quality, service levels, etc.);
- Service management outcomes;
- Business and sourcing relationship & engagement management – level of executive and business interactions within client's organization and between client and vendor organizations.

The execution of these plans and objectives must be monitored and measured by a combination of balanced scorecard (as defined by Kaplan and Norton), key performance indicators (KPIs) as well as formal and informal status review meetings and reports (e.g. report cards, dashboards) (Kaplan and Norton, 1996). Figure 7.7 illustrates high level business and sourcing expanded balanced scorecard categories and related metrics. The outcomes should link critical success factors (CSFs) to KPIs that are measurable, part of a standard reporting system and linked to a governance and performance management process. If one cannot measure the results, they do not count. Remember, you get what you measure, so it is critical to measure the right things.

Key Performance Measures link Critical Success Factors (CSFs) to Key Performance Indicators (KPIs) for Sourcing (Illustrative Example)

Business* - Critical Success Factors + Key Performance Indicators
- Financial (including compliance) – revenue, profit growth, cost management, ROA, ROI, NPV, asset management, strategic/customer.
- Strategic/customer – new product/services development, intellectual property, asset management, customer satisfaction, share of customer dollar; % of repeat customer
- Internal/external processes – process transformation, process optimization, process automation
- Learning/growth – people development, education, training, certification, mentoring, R&D, new product/ services development.

Sourcing Engagement - Critical Success Factors + Key Performance Indicators
- Financial – ROI, NPV, cost management, value delivery, TCO
- Strategic - competitive positioning, new market opportunities, differentiation, innovation, growth
- Customer (user) satisfaction – ownership, commitment, product delivery, level of service, share of customer wallet
- Employee satisfaction – people development, training, certification, productivity
- Program/project management – time/schedule, governance, budget/cost, deliverables, scope, monitoring, risk
- Service/operations process – service levels, availability, timeliness, controls, scalability, reliability, security, privacy.

Figure 7.6 Select key performance measures – business and sourcing

7.3.5 Outsourcing governance and escalation roles – customer and vendor

Many top performing companies have established multi-level and multi-disciplinary business/sourcing steering and governance boards and working committees. These have clear roles and responsibilities to ensure appropriate commitments, sponsorship, escalation, ownership, more effective communications, and more formal visibility and commitment of the board, executive management and other constituents.

Why are they important?

■ Help to ensure alignment across all of the parts of an organization. It is recognized that the demand for sourcing resources will generally increase and consequently establishing organization-wide and business unit priorities and consistent processes and metrics is essential.

■ Provide a forum for investment decision making which is synchronized with the business.

■ Build an enterprise view that helps to eliminate or reduce the inefficiencies of stovepipe sourcing initiatives, systems, processes and duplication of efforts across an organization.

Primary focus:

■ To review and approve strategic plans, major programs/projects and establish priorities among competing requests for outsourcing resources to ensure that everyone is aligned on those initiatives with highest 'value add' to the organization as a whole.

■ To establish and support processes, where necessary, to effectively fulfill the charge outlined in a consistent, repeatable, yet flexible manner.

■ To conduct formal periodic reviews of major outsourcing initiatives, and operational service performance.

Roles and responsibilities:

■ Review and approve overall sourcing strategy plans and initiatives.

■ Review, prioritize and approve major sourcing projects by value to be delivered.

■ Conduct formal periodic project progress and performance reviews.

■ Final escalation point for major sourcing issues resolution.

■ Support and sponsor sourcing policy and process improvement programs.

Other steering and working committees:

■ Successful sourcing requires multi-level and multi-functional participation. Many organizations establish additional business/sourcing working committees at the business unit level as well as major functional areas such as supply chain management, financials, research and development, manufacturing, IT and others as necessary.

■ Program and project management working groups focus on specific initiatives.

Figure 7.7 illustrates an example of the business/sourcing steering and governance boards and roles at multiple levels for a large federal government agency, starting with an executive board and ending with project or operations working groups. At each level, it identifies select responsibilities of each of the groups. While this represents an approach used by a particular organization, others may not require such a complex structure and can certainly simplify or tailor it for their particular needs and environment.

A formal outsourcing governance and review process should be established and followed with clearly defined roles, responsibilities and actions.

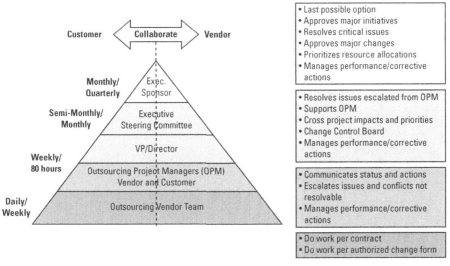

Figure 7.7 Outsourcing governance and escalation roles – customer and vendor

■ 7.4 VENDOR SELECTION, CONTRACT NEGOTIATIONS AND RISK MANAGEMENT

"The buyer needs a hundred eyes, the seller not one".

Jacula Prudentum, German verse, circa 1500

7.4.1 Steps in vendor selection and RFIs, RFQs and RFPs
There are a number of steps that, if followed will facilitate the vendor selection and negotiation process. These assume that an outsourcing business case has been completed and approved:
- Convene the project manager and vendor selection team;
- Identify appropriate and qualified vendors;
- Set a realistic schedule;
- Define vendor evaluation criteria and weights before issuing bid requests (to maintain objectivity);
- Prepare requests for proposal (RFPs); if necessary or desired, an RFI and an RFQ;

■ Evaluate the bids;

■ Conduct a due diligence investigation on the most likely service provider(s) to be selected. Visit the vendor locations and interview the people who will be doing the work;

■ Negotiate the deal;

■ Select a vendor;

■ Sign the contract.

Figure 7.8 identifies the vendor selection, evaluation, contract negotiations and award process flow.

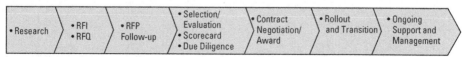

- Internal/external vendor research (assumes that business case has been approved) and requirements definition
- Evaluation criteria and Selection of Team

  - RFI/RFQ/RFP focused on services, infrastructure, technology skills, processes, HR policies, governance and metrics

    - Vendor presentations; reference checks; site visits; due diligence investigation

      - Debriefing sessions; Bidder's Conference
      - Weighted scorecard & Vendor Selection

        - Contract strategy, type & negotiations
        - Transition planning

          - Governance and metrics
          - Operating and relationship model/roles
          - Disengagement Considerations
          - Contractual triggers

Figure 7.8 Vendor selection, evaluation, contract negotiations and award process flow

Figure 7.9 defines the purpose and lists the major content categories for the request for information (RFI), request for quote (RFQ) and request for proposal (RFP).

7.4.2 Vendor evaluation criteria and weights

While companies may use different criteria and assign different weights for selection criteria, it is nevertheless important that within a given organization, the criteria and weights are consistently applied as objectively as possible. Figure 7.10 lists a number of vendor evaluation criteria organized by four major weighted categories: demonstrated competencies, total capabilities, fit and competitiveness of solution and relationship fit and dynamics.

7.4.3 Key contract negotiation pointers

The customer's negotiation team should include:

■ Procurement staff expert in dealing with technology vendors;

■ Legal staff with contract expertise;

■ Outsourcing project manager and relationship manager (if not the same);

Provide formal request for information, quotation and proposals from customer to service provider.

Request for Information (RFI)
The RFI is used to collect information (business, financial, product, service, other etc.) about companies.

Desired information:
- Company profile
- Products and services – current and future research and development focus and funding:
- Financial stability (growing or shrinking):
- Plans and direction
- Customer base and references
- Key players in organization
- Number of locations and strategic alliances
- Service, support and training facilities and resources
- Pre-installation and post-installation support, maintenance and service
+++

Provide formal request for information, quotation and proposals from customer to service provider.

Request for Quote (RFQ)
The RFQ is primarily used to solicit pricing and/or cost information from vendors.

Desired information:
- Requirements and deliverables (from RFP or high level prior to RFP)
- Contract type, terms and special conditions
- Pricing and discounts
- Change criteria and their impact on pricing
- Payment terms
+++

RFPs provide formal request for information, quotation and proposals from customer to service provider.

Request for Proposal (RFP)
The RFP is used to define the buyer's requirements, scope, objectives and deliverables in order for the vendor to provide a proposal to supply the product or service for evaluation by the buyer.

Desired information:
- Background
- Objectives and scope
- General/detailed requirements
- Functions, features and performance criteria
- Standards and regulatory compliance
- Constraints – time, business, technical, other
- Governance, reporting and dispute escalation
- Customer/vendor contacts
- Backup, recovery and contingency plans
- Vendor's quality assurance and risk mitigation plans
- Detailed schedule of deliverables
- Insurance
- Contract information and type
- Contract clauses – discretionary or mandatory clauses
- Recourse, remedies and warranty
- Pricing
- Change management
- Acceptance criteria
- Disengagement conditions and responsibilities
+++

Figure 7.9 RFIs, RFQs and RFPs

Relationship Management 20%	Breadth of Services 10%
- Partnership, trust - Single point of contact - Local presence/executive liaison - Cultural fit - Performance experience	- Type and scope of services - Ability to scale - Backup, redundancy & security - No single choke point - Change management
Vendor Capability 10%	**Experience** 20%
- Skills and competencies - Certifications - Bench strength - Financial strength - Local presence - Single point of contact	- Functional/industry knowledge - Application, service and technology - Training and currency of employees - Benchmarking - Certifications
Service Delivery 20%	**Economics & Contract Terms** 20%
- Quality of processes, tools and resources - Level of performance & management depth and capabilities - Governance and reporting	- Pricing, volume considerations and financial structure - Knowledge transfer and switching costs vs. value - Change flexibility and parameters - Disputes and adjudication

Figure 7.10 Scoring and evaluating potential vendors

- Senior management representative;
- Subject area experts brought in to advise the core team as needed (financial staff, technical staff, end users).

There are many legal terms and conditions that are omitted from the following negotiations list. Key outsourcing contract negotiation pointers should be able to validate in writing:

- Scope, requirements, deliverables and schedule;
- Create a mutual understanding of 'in scope'. Define a process for 'out-of-scope' requests and formal charge request;
- Financial and legal arrangements – payments, discounts, rewards and penalties, pricing formulas and changes; insurance, taxes, foreign exchange, indemnities, liability limitations, escrow, ownership and consequential damages;
- Acceptance criteria – quantitative and qualitative criteria;
- Metrics and service criteria – volume, capacity, speed, performance, quality documentation, training, mean time to repair, schedule, budget, program/project, etc. Consider metrics in three different areas:
  - Outcome and performance-based metrics (e.g. volume, speed, scalability, etc.);
  - Metrics for quality assurance (e.g. consistency, accuracy, satisfaction, etc.);
  - Key indicator project or operational metrics (e.g. schedule, reliability index, help desk problem resolution time, etc.).
- Governance, disputes, recourse, remedies, escalation and issues resolution;
- Support services – training, documentation, maintenance, service and transition;
- Updates, new releases, upgrades;
- Performance warrantees and service levels – OLAs (operational level agreements), SLAs (service level agreements) with incentives and penalties;

- Status reports, meetings, format and contents – What? When? To whom? How often?;
- Disengagement options – termination triggers, conditions, responsibilities, transition plan (who is responsible for what?);
- Define roles and responsibilities of both parties;
- Ownership of hardware, software, network, data contents, software licenses, etc.;
- Change management triggers, process and approvals;
- Confidentiality, non-disclosure and security (physical, logical) considerations;
- Intellectual property and content protection;
- Contingency, back-up and disaster recovery plans, processes and resources;
- Identify single point of contact(s) for coordination and follow-up;
- Pen an agreement that contains detailed service descriptions with adequate metrics for each activity;
- Make the supplier fully accountable for delivering services and subject to penalties when it misses service levels. Remove ambiguity from service descriptions.

Equally important is a breakdown of fees, types of contract (i.e. fixed priced, cost plus fixed fee, time and material, gain or risk sharing, volume or transaction based, etc.) as well as clearly outlining both the penalty and incentive provisions:

- Amounts period by period;
- Volume of work covered;
- Quality of work to be provided;
- Provision for over- and under-performance;
- Guidelines for selecting specific outsourcing metrics, including aligning metrics with the business objectives of the service;
- Selecting metrics that enhance the ability to diagnose problems, escalate attention and remedy performance issues;
- Limiting the metrics for each service to one or two encompassing measurements;
- Bundling outsourcing services to leverage resources and lower costs.

7.4.4 Select types of sourcing agreements

Generally, there are several popular approaches to creating an outsourcing agreement based on pricing, incentives, risk and need:

1. Cost plus – this form of a contract is used when the provider is paid for actual costs, plus a pre-determined profit based either on a fixed amount or on a percentage. The primary benefit of this type of agreement is that the client has direct visibility into the actual costs and details of the cost factors. It also allows the client to fix the profit level of the provider. The provider has low risk since the deliverables are clear and agreed upon as part of the contract. The downside of this agreement is that it offers very little incentive to the provider to improve the way the service is performed and no incentive to reduce actual costs. Within this category of agreements, there are variations such as:

2. Unit pricing – unit pricing agreements are used when the provider is delivering discrete units of service or product. The unit is sold to the client in fixed amounts at a price that includes all costs and profit margin. The client pays based on the actual number of units delivered. There may be rate changes based on the provider's ability to deliver a high number of units in a shorter period of time (higher payment as incentive). On the down side, failure to deliver the contracted number of units in a time period may result in lower payment per unit or a discount applied to the entire time period. The client views this kind of contract as providing at least the agreed upon amount of product in a time period for an anticipated price. The provider is driven to fulfilling the agreement while trying to lower its own internal unit costs.

3. Fixed price – a fixed-price contract is one where the amount of payment by a client does not vary with the amount of resources or time invested by a provider. Clients view this type of contract as protecting them from cost overruns and putting the responsibility for managing costs and risks on the provider. A fixed-price contract works best in situations where the costs are well-known in advance, that is, there is history and experience to determine the price of the work. However, in innovative work or where there are untested technologies involved in the process, this type of agreement can fail to deliver a result if costs begin to escalate. Because the provider is motivated to achieve its desired profit level by restricting investment in the work, this agreement works against a cooperative relationship focused on innovation.

4. Incentive-based pricing (or performance-based pricing) – this agreement is used to connect client payments with the achievement of specified performance on the part of the provider. This performance may be measured in terms of service levels, such as system availability rates in a data center support contract, units of service delivered or other measures of performance. A typical attachment to this sort of agreement is a standardized service level agreement (SLA), which typically contains objectives and measurable criteria for key aspects of performance that are tailored to the specific industry/activity that is the subject matter of the agreement. It is generally believed that incentive-based contracts are win-win for the client and provider and promote three important outcomes:

- Improved productivity for providers;
- Better relationships between clients and providers;
- Higher value outcomes for clients.

Incentive-based pricing provides risk sharing between the client and provider: if the provider performs well, they earn more and the client benefits from a better service or product. The provider is given the opportunity to manage the value they deliver to their customers and the opportunity to be directly involved with generating improved profits for both themselves and their customers.

5. Gain sharing – in a gain-sharing agreement, the provider receives a portion of any benefits that its work has generated for the customer. Typically the client benefits may be derived from a variety of areas: reducing the costs of raw materials, implementing and applying new technologies and process improvements suggested by the provider. These agreements are often tied into programs to develop a cycle of continuous organizational improvement. Gain-sharing benefits are usually stated in terms of a split of the value of the benefit and can range from 50/50 in generous agreements to 75/25 favoring the client.

6. Achievement bonuses – as the name implies, achievement bonuses are one-time payments for achieving a project milestone. The milestones are defined in the overall agreement between a client and provider and may be tied to several different kinds of criteria, for example:

- Early completion;
- High service levels;
- Improved throughput;
- Process time and quality improvements.

Achievement bonuses can be employed to encourage competition among providers in a multi-provider engagement where rankings are used to determine the top-performing providers and bonuses are determined by position in the ranking.

7. Risk/reward sharing – this is an agreement where both the client and provider have explicit investment in the outcome of the engagement and are mutually dependent on a positive outcome. The investment of funds on the part of the provider differentiates this type of contract from the others. Successful outcomes that add value to both parties are the goal. For example, if the provider invests resources in creating an innovative solution for the client and that solution creates value through increased revenue for the client, then both share in the revenues. The downside is, of course, that both will lose if revenues decrease. In this regard, risk/reward sharing is similar to a joint venture agreement, partnership or alliance. Clients and providers tend to work through integrated teams in these agreements with increased communication and partnering.

8. Partner marketing – partner marketing is an appropriate approach to a sourcing agreement when the provider agrees to promote the product or service of the client as part of the contract. An example of this is when a telecomm service client contracts with a provider and then the provider promotes the client's service to their customers. This is to be differentiated from 'reciprocity' where two organizations enter into a deal to purchase each other's products or services. Most organizations frown on reciprocity and it is often precluded by company policy.

Another example of partner marketing is when client organizations seek provider partners in locations where they also want to market their own products or services.

Working with a local provider can enhance the opportunity to introduce the client to the local marketplace. Some countries require a company to have business interests in the country before being able to sell their own products/services in that country. These business interests range from investing in manufacturing in the country to working with a partner in the country. A partner marketing agreement is created when the provider's responsibility for promoting the client's products or services is incorporated into the global sourcing agreement.

Figure 7.11 summarizes each of the contract and agreement types, scope, risk and value.

Type	Structure	Relationship	Scope	Risk	Value
Cost plus	Actual cost plus profit	Neutral	Variable	Carried by client	Direct visibility into actual costs
Unit pricing	Based on discrete units of service	Incentive for provider to reduce its unit costs	Variable	Carried by client	Minimum value guaranteed to client
Fixed price	Payment will never vary, not ideal for innovation	Works against cooperation	Fixed	Carried by provider	Client protected from cost overruns
Incentive-based pricing/ performance-based pricing	Payment tied directly with achievement	Win-win, encourages cooperation	Variable	Shared	Provider has opportunity to manage value
Gain sharing	Share benefits with provider	Encourages cooperation	Variable	Shared	Can provide continuous improvement to client
Achievement bonuses	One-time payments to provider as incentive	Encourages cooperation between client and provider, but can be used to create competition among providers	Variable	Carried by client	Can provide early completion, high service levels, improved throughput
Risk/reward sharing	Client and provider have explicit investment like a joint venture	Depends on cooperation	Highly variable	Shared	Can provide highly successful outcomes
Partner marketing	Provider helps to promote client products/services	Encourages cooperation	Fixed	Shared	Mutually beneficial

Figure 7.11 Sourcing contract/agreement types

7.4.5 Sourcing risks

Risks are a fact of business life and it only requires a review of the daily news to see the impact they have on an organization. The consequences of a business or process disruption affects corporate revenues, drives higher costs, poor asset utilization, excess inventory, shareholder lawsuits, and personnel turnover as well as the implication of negative publicity. Managing risk is a corporate-level effort and sourcing represents only one of many potential exposures that a company needs to plan for and handle carefully. Anticipating 'what could happen if' involves the development of multiple scenarios describing possible business outcomes affecting the company.

Before the catastrophic event of 9/11, New York City and its Mayor Giuliani used a multiple scenario approach to prepare the city for catastrophic events. As we all know, 9/11 represented the worst possible outcome but, despite this, the earlier risk management exercises using planned scenarios assisted the city in an orderly recovery. Anticipating a sourcing event requires similar scenario building and related risk analysis and mitigation. It should also be noted that some clients use sourcing to mitigate risks such as diverse suppliers or redundant data processing facilities. Sourcing could also involve exposure to secondary or tertiary risks from a supplier that is sub-contracted for work without the knowledge of the client. If the prime contractor does not agree to share information about its sub-contracting arrangements with the client, then it is impossible to plan for a failure of one of the secondary providers. An enterprise sourcing operating environment from a provider, customer and shared risk perspective is shown in Figure 7.12.

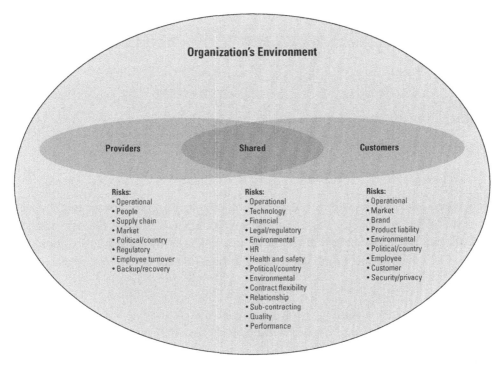

Figure 7.12 Potential sourcing risks for customers and providers

Risks affect not only the customer but also the provider. In Figure 7.12, risks can overlap and drive risk exposure requiring multiple mitigation plans. It is important for both parties to be aware of these exposures and how jointly they can reduce their mutually shared risks.

7.4.6 Risk management, assessment and mitigation

Sourcing engagements do not shield enterprises from the impacts of risks. The risks come in the form of failed contracts, business continuity disruptions, budget and scope creep, failed business and system processes and related areas. Sourcing can provide a means to further mitigate risk by contracting with a third party insurer to indemnify the client if the provider fails to deliver on specific commitments for any of variety of reasons. This provides a means to ensure continuity of business when a company is analyzing and quantifying the potential impact of specific risks.

The risk management process flow is shown in Figure 7.13

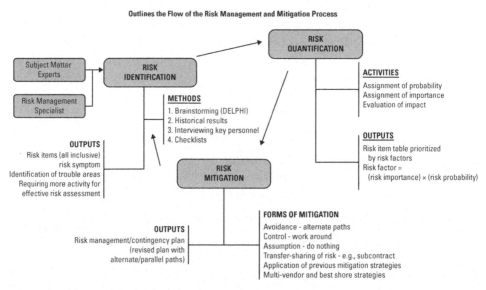

Figure 7.13 Risk management process flow for sourcing

This process flow begins with the identification of risks using various techniques such as brainstorming, historical trends and interviews. Once identified, the risks need to be evaluated and quantified. This will result in a risk ranking and a prioritization. For those events that represent significant risk, a mitigation plan needs to be prepared and executed.

Figure 7.14 presents a sourcing risk assessment matrix used to quantify risks and suggests risks that are high require a mitigation plan. The risk matrix is focused on scoring risks and provides a quantified way to indicate where mitigation plans are needed by quantifying two factors – the probability of the risk occurring versus the impact of the risk event. For example, all risks that have 15 or more points could have significant impact on disrupting the business or parts of it and, therefore, should have a mitigation and contingency plan.

Used to quantify risks and suggest areas that should have contingency plans (High risk areas are shaded)

Criteria — Risk Impact [R_I]

Criteria	Catastrophic (4)	Critical (3)	Marginal (2)	Negligible (1)
Operational	Unrecoverable impact to environment, business, function, process, system *and/or*	Major damage impact to environment, business, function, process, system *and/or*	Minor impact to environment, business, function, process, system *and/or*	Negligible impact to environment business, function, process, system *and/or*
Financial/Value	Unachievable *and/or* **ROI, Budget, Innovation**	Serious delay (>30% late) *and/or*	Moderate delay (10%-30% late) *and/or*	Will meet schedule but use all "slack time" *and/or*
PM & QM	Non-existent *and/or*	Poor *and/or*	Fair *and/or*	Good *and/or*
Relationship Management	None *and/or*	Limited – Multi-tier *and/or*	Adequate *and/or*	Partnering *and/or*
Vendor Performance	Non-achievement of business/technical performance	Significant degradation of technical/other performance	Some reduction in technical/other performance	Minimal to small reduction in technical performance, at the detailed level

Risk Probability [R_P] — Value (R_I) ▲

▼ Value (R_I) ▲	Catastrophic (4)	Critical (3)	Marginal (2)	Negligible (1)
Near Certain (5)	20	15	10	5
Probable (4)	16	12	8	4
Possible (3)	12	9	6	3
Marginal (2)	8	6	4	2

Criteria	
81%-99% Probability of Happening	Near Certain (5)
61%-80% Probability of Happening	Probable (4)
41%-60% Probability of Happening	Possible (3)
0%-40% Probability of Happening	Marginal (2)

Risk Exposure Key

Highest (R_E = 15-20) Contingency Plan Required	
High (R_E = 9-12) Contingency Plan Highly Recommended	
Medium (R_E = 4-8) Contingency Plan Discretionary	
Low (R_E = 1-3) Contingency Plan Not Required	

Risk Exposure $(R_E) = R_I \times R_P$

Figure 7.14 Sourcing risk assessment matrix

A risk management and mitigation process is shown in Figure 7.15. It guides the user through the structuring of a plan to include risk identification, probability of occurrence and impact; it also identifies what risk mitigation is required and provides suggested contingency actions.

- For each contingency plan, specify the circumstances that would trigger that plan into action.

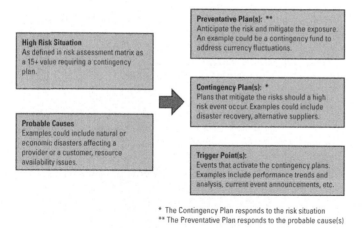

* The Contingency Plan responds to the risk situation
** The Preventative Plan responds to the probable cause(s)

Figure 7.15 Risk management and mitigation/contingency template

■ 7.5   CROWDSOURCING

7.5.1 Definition and process

Crowdsourcing is the practice of obtaining needed services, ideas, or content by soliciting contributions from a large group of people, and especially from an online community, rather than from traditional employees or suppliers.

This process is often used to subdivide work. Amongst numerous self-identified volunteers or part-time workers, each contributor at their own initiative will add a small portion to the greater result. It is distinguished from outsourcing in that the work comes from an undefined public rather than being commissioned from a specific, named vendor.

The term 'crowdsourcing' was coined in 2006 and can apply to a wide range of activities (Bruno, April, 2014). Crowdsourcing can involve division of labor for tedious tasks split to use crowd-based outsourcing, but it can also apply to specific requests.

Crowdsourcing has increasingly become a recognized sourcing mechanism for problem-solving in organizations by outsourcing the problem to an unidentified entity or the 'crowd'. While crowdsourcing provides several benefits for the participants involved, it also poses several challenges to effectively manage the crowd (Jain, August 2010).

7.5.2 Applications

Crowdsourcing can include anything from gathering feedback on a new idea, asking for assistance to solve a product problem, or looking for contractors, investors or new employees interested in participating in a project.

Crowdsourcing can provide organizations with richer content and perspectives from a more diverse crowd than what may be possible within an organizational unit or function, while allowing organizations a creative and cost-effective way to access innovative resources outside the boundaries of their unit, function or even outside their organization (Howe, 2008). This model of opening up the boundaries of an organization to tap the knowledge of external entities is increasingly becoming a source of advantage for organizations seeking to identify innovative ideas. For example, in the case of a new product development, crowdsourcing can provide organizations with a better sense of their customers needs while projecting a favorable image to the customers that the business is listening to them.

7.5.3 Concerns

There are various concerns about crowdsourcing, including:
- The value and impact of the work received from the crowd;
- The ethical implications of low wages paid to crowd workers.

Most of these criticisms are directed towards crowdsourcing systems that provide extrinsic monetary rewards to contributors, though some apply more generally to all crowdsourcing systems.

There is susceptibility to faulty results caused by targeted, malicious work efforts. Since crowd workers completing micro tasks may be paid per task, there is often a financial incentive to complete tasks quickly rather than well. Verifying responses is time-consuming, and so requesters often depend on having multiple workers complete the same task to correct errors. However, having each task completed multiple times increases the time and sometimes the monetary costs. (Wang, 2010).

One of the problems of crowdsourcing products is the lack of interaction between the crowd and the client. Usually there is little information about the final desired product, and there is often very limited interaction with the final client. This can decrease the quality of product because client interaction is a vital part of the design process.

■ 7.6   STEPS IN MAKING OUTSOURCING REAL

Outsourcing represents a journey towards continuous improvement and greater effectiveness. The journey is difficult, but can be facilitated by the following steps:
- Gather support and resources:
  - Must have a corporate mandate from the top – the board and the executive team are committed to implementing and sustaining a robust outsourcing environment.
  - Must have dedicated and available resources – identify executive champion and multi-disciplinary team (to focus on each outsourcing opportunity).

- Have realistic expectations as to savings and performance improvements. Build in the risk side as well. Do not over-sell – sourcing is not holy water.
- Market and communicate the sourcing 'value proposition' and celebrate wins.

■ Do homework:
- Educate yourself on past, current and emerging sourcing best practices.
- Make sure the issues within the scope of sourcing engagement are clear to the leadership team. Sometimes the truth hurts. If the environment is a mess and that fact is not clear, sourcing will in many cases make it very clear – very fast.
- Market the outsourcing value propositions and benefits to the organization - develop and conduct a communications, awareness and public relations campaign.

■ Follow a plan:
- Develop a tailored outsourcing framework and roadmap for your organization based on current and emerging industry best practices.
- Assess the 'current state' of the level of outsourcing maturity, or other frameworks that relate to specific outsourcing components such as project management, vendor management, performance management (balanced scorecard) and others as a reference base (where are we today?), using a leading industry best practice framework such as CMMI or ITSqc or another framework that may apply to a specific component of outsourcing.
- Develop a 'future state' outsourcing blueprint (where you want to be) and keep it in focus.
- Decompose the outsourcing components into well-defined work packages (assign an owner and champion to each process component).

■ Make the process visible:
- Develop an outsourcing action plan, identify deliverables, establish priorities and milestones, allocate resources and measure progress.
- Sponsor organizational and individual certifications in the outsourcing component areas, where they are available (e.g. PMP, COP, ITSqc, PRINCE2, etc.).
- Identify enabling technologies to support the outsourcing initiative.
- Establish a 'web portal' to access outsourcing policies, processes, information, communications and provide support.
- Market and communicate the sourcing 'value proposition' and celebrate wins.
- Plan for and sustain outsourcing process improvements and link to a reward and incentive structure. Create a 'Continuous Outsourcing Improvement' group to sustain the framework.

■ 7.7   CASE STUDY – MAJOR PHARMACEUTICAL COMPANY

Figure 7.16 describes an outsourcing case of a major pharmaceutical organization.

Environment	Areas of Outsourcing Opportunities

• Annual revenue range – $15.0 - $30.0 billion
• Number of employees range – 35,000 - 50,000
• Number of major locations – 10+
• Over 30 compounds in development
• Sourcing organization:
  – Federated structure
  – Number of employees - 200+
  – Outsourcing categories (BPO, IT, manufacturing, R&D, legal, real estate, etc.
  – Head of Sourcing (CPO) reports to: Head, Global Shared Services
• Major sourcing country locations – India, China, Philippines, Brazil, USA, Poland
• Management philosophy – conservative and risk averse
	• 35% of all R&D and 50% of all manufacturing will be outsourced by 2015 -2016
	• Other significant outsourcing opportunities being pursued and/or analyzed include:
	  – Logistics
	  – Finance and accounting
	  – Legal
	  – IT and call centers
	  – HR

Issues and Challenges	**Approach**

• Issues
  – Loss of institutional knowledge
  – Perceived lack of flexibility of outsourcing
  – Lack of support from functional leaders (initially)
• Challenges/obstacles
  – General resistance to change for outsourcing
  – Poor project management discipline to support sourcing
  – Scope creep and poor change management
• Drivers
  – Cost reduction, containment and avoidance
  – R&D for new compound development
  – Reduce time to market
  – Fund transformation
	• Formal sourcing process is standardized (see diagram at the end of the case)
	• A structural vendor selection process is used
	• In a mature space, forego the RFI/RFP and go right to the RFP and be very detailed
	• Hire good consulting help – external legal counsel and global expertise in outsourcing proved essential to the success of the RFP and vendor selection process for complex outsourcing deals

Vendor Characteristics and Contracts	**Results – Sourcing Project Management Timelines, Risk and Controls**

• Number of vendors - multiple
• Types of contracts - multiple
• Key vendor selection and sourcing criteria include:
  – Previous success rate within company
  – Trust in ability of service provider to deliver
  – Business case, cost and ROI (average 25%)
  – Regulatory experience
  – Geographic reach
  – Can supplier help us gain competitive advantage?
  – TBO: total benefits of ownership – offers best "value added" services –
    > Investment in technology and educational refreshment
    > Access to vendor key executives and subject matter experts
  – Offers least risk – financial stability; political and economic stability of country location, back up and recovery, etc.
  – Deal flow and establishing appropriate metrics
	• Timelines – time to resolve issues within the project depended on the buy-in of the owners to the process
	• Risk:
	  – risk was managed through discussions with the leadership team at regular staff meetings and with the head of Global Shared Services semi-weekly
	  – mitigation actions were implemented on high risk activities
	• Controls:
	  – frequent debriefings were generally very helpful and kept the project transition of BPO on track. However there was too much emphasis on cost control, which lead to slipped timelines, and in the long run, required even greater expenditures

Figure 7.16 Case ctudy – major pharmaceutical organization

Results – Vendor Characteristics and Contracts (continued)

- Company uses a "Master Service Agreement" (MSA) framework, including common terms and conditions and an overall structure for agreement
- Service Stream Attachments (SSA's) and their schedules define individual work streams
- The MSA framework is designed to be flexible, scalable and fast to execute, and contains a number of key areas:
  - Measurement and reporting of performance data
  - Compliance with regulations and audits
  - Assurance of quality and customer satisfaction
  - Definitions of charges, invoicing and payments
  - Protection of intellectual property rights
  - Requirements for data security and confidentiality
  - Definitions of representations and warranties
  - Definitions of indemnification
  - Management of the contract changes and authorizations
  - Management of governance, dispute resolution and escalation
  - Rights to termination (for convenience or cause)

Results – Governance, Performance and Key Metrics

- The MSA included a three tiered governance structure that retained control within the impacted company operations area, while providing for escalation:
  - Strategic committee – managed relationship
    - company/vendor executive sponsor and leadership committee
  - Management operating committee - executive management
    - company/vendor responsible executives, compliance officer, contract management, transition leads
  - Service Management Streams (per SSA) – project management
    - company/vendor service stream leads
- SSAs define the scope of services, service level agreements, and price for a given work-stream including: scope, responsibility matrix, transition plan, reports, service levels, pricing, service locations, business continuity, quality systems manual and other factors

Results – Future of Sourcing

- Sourcing has become strategic and transformational for the organization in many areas with trusted vendor partners and will continue to be so in future

Lessons Learned

- For a complex sourcing project use subject matter experts (SMEs), both inside and external, to deal with the large volume of issues that usually arise
- Orchestrate very direct, active, and continuous senior-level sponsorship
- Have a strong Project Management Office
- Be explicit in defining the links between each phase of a complex sourcing project
- Remember to emphasize the "softer" side of the project - leadership styles, team building, cultural diversity skills, etc.

Critical Success Factors

- As you communicate and negotiate with your chosen service providers, remember that you are entering into a long-term relationship with that organization
- Engage corporate communications early in order to understand that group's approach to communications concerning the project
- Provide the necessary project management resources with the right skills, when needed
- Do not underestimate the time needed for due diligence or the project as a whole. It usually will takes longer than you think
- Foster better synergy and communications among legal counsel, the consulting organizations, and the company business units
- Document meetings to confirm the understanding of issues, decisions and action follow-up
- Templates are useful in the sourcing process. They save time (and costs) and assure a consistent checklist to help with: RFPs, due diligence, vendor selection, transition activities and on-going governance and controls

Figure 7.16 Case ctudy – major pharmaceutical organization (continued)

Company sourcing process includes the following components: (illustrative example)

Identify Need and Feasibility	Solution Evaluation	Sourcing and Contracting	Change and Transition Management	Governance and Relationship Management
• Document baseline and scope • Identify sourcing model • Evaluate high level costs/risks to achieve – internal vs. external • Obtain sponsorship	• Define future state • Benchmark process, technology and organization innovation • Scan vendor environment • Determine benefits • Develop business case	• Competitive or comparative process – RFP • Collaborative solution and vendor evaluation • Market-based terms and conditions • Leverage 3rd party advisory services • Solid project management	• Active executive sponsorship • Clear decision process and roles • Aligned and understood objectives with business • Robust program and change management • Pre-post transition checklists	• Emphasis on relationship (i.e. long-term value) • Robust customer and service provider-facing model • Reorient retained organization • Use meaningful metrics and define governance roles

Figure 7.16 Case ctudy – major pharmaceutical organization (continued)

7.8   SUMMARY STEPS AND KEY TAKE AWAYS

7.8.1 Summary

Figure 7.17 provides a summary checklist for developing and managing successful outsourcing deals.

- **Develop a Plan and Build a Business Case**
  - Baseline model
  - Requirements & scope
  - Costs (realistic)/savings
  - Contingency Plan
  - Assumptions/Constraint
  - Obstacles
  - Metrics – OLAs, SLAs, Cost, Schedule, Other

- **Go/No-Go**
  - Communicate decision to stakeholders

- **RFP**
  - Preparation
  - Narrow the field - RFI, RFQ
  - Invitation to Vendors
    - Vendor briefings
    - Site visits
    - Vendor proposals

- **Evaluation & Selection**
  - Multidisciplinary team
  - Qualitative & quantitative evaluation criteria
  - Cultural match/bench strength
  - Due Diligence
  - Final selection

- **Contract Negotiation/Signing**
  - It takes two to tango
  - Contract types
    - Fixed price (well defined)
    - Time & material (not well defined)
    - Cost & fixed fee
    - Cost & variable fee
    - Unit price contract
  - Terms & Conditions
  - Change and Risk Management
  - Governance, Metrics and Escalation
  - Contingency and Disaster Recovery Options
  - Disengagement Options & Responsibilities
    - Triggers and Conditions
    - Ownership
    - Transition Roles/Responsibilities

- **Transition Management, Contract Management & Performance Monitoring**
  - Transition Planning, Roles, Pilot, Training & Readiness Validation
  - Assure compliance with project or service objectives, scope, schedule, & deliverables
  - Measure and evaluate delivered work
  - Vendor governance and reporting
  - Integrate vendor tasks and deliverables into Project Plan
  - Assign Senior Manager/Director/VP to manage vendor relationship with "clout"

Figure 7.17 Summary checklist for managing successful outsourcing deals

As an example, the CIO of a major global telecommunications company suggested the following simple and pragmatic model that works:

- Keep it simple: limit the number of vendors off-shore;
- Know who is off-shoring and to what other sub–off shoring countries;
- Train all levels of the IT organization – managers need to manage globally, not just locally (in-sourced and outsourced functions);
- Expect to spend time in the air. Visit, visit and visit at multiple levels;
- Put your IT managers in India, Brazil and China (get on the ground);
- Plan for turn-over (not just cheap labor anymore);
- Constantly revisit business cases and keep contracts alive;
- Grow beyond vendors (look at having your own presence in the countries – maximize effectiveness such as with captive subsidiaries).

7.8.2 Key take aways

- Executive sponsorship is critical;
- Get the right people involved in each stage;
- Know your current baseline and costs;
- Issue an RFP – contract with a primary and secondary vendor (do not put all of your eggs in one basket);
- Strong relationship management – create a customer/vendor team and engagement model with clearly defined roles and responsibilities;
- Communicate, communicate, communicate;
- Identify and measure meaningful performance metrics;
- Short versus long term contracts, with more frequent renewable periods;
- Vendor certification is better than no certification;
- Manage the vendor – do not let the vendor manage you;
- The secret to managing global sourcing well is to make it part of a strategic plan for resource utilization;
- Client managers require a comprehensive guide for developing a strategy for the use of global sourcing;
- Provider managers require an understanding of the motivation and goals of clients;
- An historical perspective helps to place global sourcing into a logical context;
- Many resources are available to understand the sourcing marketplace, but these must be used in the context of each organization's concerns and requirements;
- There are seven primary drivers of global sourcing;
- Terminology is evolving and therefore words and phrases must be defined within a context to ensure all parties are communicating effectively.

"Make your peace with outsourcing now. Either get on the outsourcing train or get in front of it."

"Customers are now adapting more disciplined approaches to the evaluation, selection, management and governance of outsourcing opportunities. The better the vendor can understand the customer's process, the more successful the vendor will be."

The Advisory Council, 2014

There is no magic: outsourcing is hard work!

8 Performance Management, Metrics, Management Controls, COBIT®, Risk Management, Business Continuity and Enabling Technology Excellence

"Those that keep score, know they are winning and have the necessary information to maintain the lead. Those that keep score, know they are losing but have the information they need to change direction. Those that don't keep score truly don't know their position and may be beyond help."

Unknown author

■ 8.1 WHAT IS COVERED IN THIS CHAPTER?

- Understand the issues, constraints and opportunities involved in improving IT performance management and measurement, management controls, risk management, compliance and business/IT continuity planning as components of IT governance;
- Understand the principles and practices of achieving IT performance management excellence using balanced scorecard and other metrics, and linking critical success factors to leading and lagging indicators;
- Discuss how COBIT and other frameworks can be used to establish the foundation for better IT management and governance controls;
- Describe the key attributes and functions that should be an integral part of any enabling technologies selected to support one or more components of IT governance.

■ 8.2 OVERVIEW

Over the past decade, the global IT industry has undergone a significant transformation. From the proliferation of digital tools and the rise of social media, to the growth in mobile networking and big data analytics of everyday life, technological advancements have fundamentally altered traditional patterns of work, life and connectivity. And yet, as IT has become increasingly pervasive, IT departments have faced their own sets of challenges.

In response, IT governance frameworks emerged to facilitate the proper alignment between the IT department and the enterprise, as well as to maintain optimal levels of IT investment and performance. However, to ensure that the proper foundation is in place for IT to not only support and improve business performance, but also become a source of innovation, organizations cannot put their faith in the adoption of abstract metrics. Instead, companies need to thoughtfully design, develop and adapt metrics that are aligned with and support organizational strategy and goals. How can an organization leverage metrics for successful business innovation and ongoing operations?

The advancement of data-driven decision-making across just about every industry has made metrics integral to demonstrating the value and performance of business programs and their supporting IT processes, within organizational boundaries and through supplier and customer ecosystems. Moreover, an emphasis on metrics and analytics has allowed business and IT to better adapt and refine strategic initiatives, as well as optimize resources with an eye toward sustaining and growing competitive advantages.

There are a number of ways in which metrics play a crucial role in maintaining a robust IT governance framework:

- Tracking metrics is fundamental to developing predictive models and assessing the key factors for future IT success;
- Metrics are the building blocks of larger analytics;
- Metrics are needed to ensure sufficient allocation of resources that focus on IT innovations;
- Metrics help in making specific processes visible, thus enabling organizations to isolate specific aspect of IT operations for tracking, measurement and assessment (Yo Delmar, 2014).

At the core, metrics play an important role in making specific processes visible. By establishing a particular set of metrics, organizations can focus on specific aspects of IT operations for tracking, measurement and assessment. The flipside, of course, is that because metrics highlight certain aspects of the process, while rendering others invisible, focusing on an incomplete or irrelevant set of metrics can actually prove to be detrimental.

8.2.1 Developing effective IT governance metrics

Metrics, like the organizations that use and rely on them are not one-size-fits-all. In light of the need to adapt IT governance frameworks to meet specific enterprise objectives, a key question remains: How can organizations ensure the development and adoption of effective IT performance metrics?

According to Yo Delmare, there are several things to consider when developing effective metrics:

- **Enterprise strategy, goals and key performance goals set the tone.** The aim of IT governance is to establish synchronicity among IT, business and third parties, as well as to measure the performance of IT in relation to business objectives. As a result, it is essential to develop performance metrics that are defined by enterprise goals and not the other way around. Key performance indicators (KPIs) can play a critical role in helping meet this demand because they are specifically designed to measure performance against organizational objectives and more specifically IT objectives.

- **Develop metrics that are responsive to a dynamic environment.** Today's business environment is anything but static. Companies find themselves engaged in a continuous cycle of change, innovation, renewal and reassessment. Given the pace at which technological changes have disrupted traditional workflows, this dynamism is inherent to the situation IT departments face on an ongoing basis. Against this backdrop, performance metrics need to be able to adapt to both organizational and technological change to generate valuable insights and business intelligence. This will empower organizations to make IT decisions that improve efficiency and have the potential to transform core business functions.

- **Design key metrics that provide value across multiple initiatives.** In recent years shrinking technology budgets and economic uncertainty have forced enterprises to do more with less. In response, organizations should develop metrics that can be deployed in a number of contexts to yield the greatest possible results. To maximize operational resources, metrics should enable organizations to become more efficient by helping identify aspects of legacy infrastructure in the IT ecosystem that have become obsolete or redundant. The true value lies in developing metrics that act as a foundation for larger analytics, which provide insights with the power to inform these types of business decisions.

- **Emphasize ease of implementation.** Strong analytics are only as good as the foundations on which they are built. As previously mentioned, metrics are the building blocks of analytics, which means that it is necessary to adopt metrics that can be easily implemented and understood. Ultimately, metrics will only be effective if employees know what is being measured, how it is calculated, what the targets are, how incentives work and, more important, what they can do to affect the outcome in a positive direction.

- **Remain open to change.** As important as metrics are, it is crucial to avoid becoming locked into a static set of metrics that no longer measure what really matters. Organizations should never discount the importance of continued analysis and appraisal of performance metrics. Constant reevaluation of metrics and their relevance to changing business goals is ultimately what will ensure the long-term success of a governance program.

8.2.2 Measuring IT performance

An effective governance program with the right metrics actually facilitates business innovation and growth. Peter Weill and Jeanne Ross, for example, note that all top performing organizations share one aspect in common when it comes to their IT governance programs. That is, "their governance made transparent the tensions around IT decisions given as standardized versus innovation." This suggests that a sound metrics program properly assesses and lays bare strategic, practical and operational considerations, which can empower organizations to invest in and support IT-related projects with transformative power (Weill & Ross, 2004).

As IT investments grow and become a larger share of an enterprise's capital expenditures, IT executives are being required by business executives to demonstrate the business value and alignment of their investments, as well as the reliability, availability, security, continuity and integrity of the information and supporting services. The IT performance management, control and reporting challenge is:

1. to communicate from IT outwardly to management and the user community at multiple levels (e.g. strategic, management, knowledge and operational) and to multiple audiences (e.g. board and/ or executive management, middle management) and
2. inwardly to direct and manage the IT organization.

Figure 8.1 represents a modification of a framework originally developed by Robert Anthony that illustrates the multiple levels and audiences that must be accommodated in any IT performance management reporting and control system (Anthony, 1965).

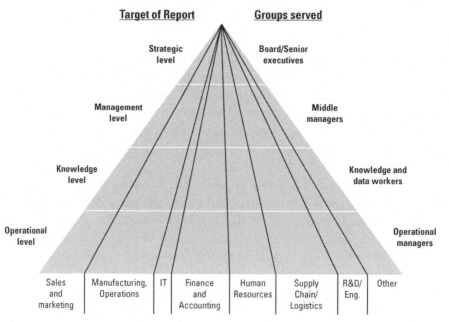

Figure 8.1 A framework for IT performance management, analysis, control and reporting – organizational levels and groups served (source: Robert Anthony, 1965)

Gartner's research suggests that IT must master the art of managing measures that matter to the business such as business process measures, product/service innovation and the value of money, as well as IT performance measures from multiple perspectives including alignment, contribution to the bottom line, innovation and transformation, project management and service levels (Gartner, 2012).

A performance management, control, continuity and compliance plan must be developed for IT as part of a governance initiative. The development of the plan should be a collaborative effort between the business and IT. It should be based on a number of objectives such as strategic, financials, quality, operational and service effectiveness which support an organization's business vision, mission, plans, objectives and financials.

There are many issues involved in measuring, monitoring and controlling IT that need to be addressed in a comprehensive manner:
- What industry frameworks would be helpful in this area?
- Who should own measurement? Control? Continuity of service? Compliance?
- What key performance indicators should be measured?
  - Business impact – revenues, costs, profits;
  - Workload, availability, capacity, reliability, scalability;
  - Agility and speed;
  - Alignment;
  - Rate of technology absorption;
  - Organization fluidity and synergy;
  - Process innovation (internal and external);
  - Program/project management effectiveness;
  - Service levels;
  - Integration;
  - Quality;
  - Investment impact;
  - Customer relationship;
  - Value chain impact;
  - Historic or predictive, or a hybrid of both factors.
- What to do with the measurements?
  - Establish a report card for performance;
  - Link each measure to a critical success factor either for the business, or for IT, or for both;
  - Create meaningful, understandable, relevant benchmarks;
  - Create a set of metrics outwardly bound from IT to the organization;
  - Create a set of metrics that are inwardly bound to help manage the IT organization.
- When should measurements be done? Continuously? Daily? Weekly? Monthly? Quarterly? Semi-annually? Annually?
- What level of measurement detail should be reported and in what reporting format? To whom?

■ 8.3 PRINCIPLES FOR ACHIEVING PERFORMANCE MANAGEMENT AND CONTROL EXCELLENCE

As part of improving IT governance, it is critical for an organization to establish an overall framework that includes amongst other things, an IT enterprise strategy (which includes business capability roadmaps and balanced scorecard metrics), performance management, management controls and compliance components. Figure 8.2 represents such a framework for a major communications company. It is interesting to note the highlighted areas since they specifically focus on IT strategy, compliance, lifecycle, business intelligence, data management and reporting.

**Key Components for Performance Management, Compliance and Reporting Include:
IT Enterprise Strategy, Enterprise Compliance, Lifecycle and Quality and Organizational Reporting**

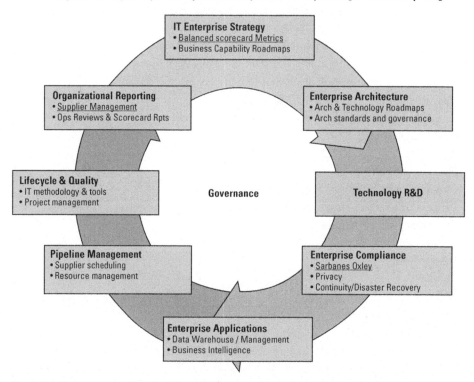

Figure 8.2 IT governance – how it works: major communications company

In addition, by using industry best practice frameworks or guidelines, and their components, such as domains and checklists including COSO®, COBIT®, Val IT® which were previously described in Chapter 2, a company can develop a more consistent and sustainable approach to making IT performance management and management controls more effective and sustainable. Of course, one needs to assign decision authority, ownership and link deliverables and performance to a reward structure to make individuals and teams more accountable. Figure 8.3 illustrates a high level framework linking COSO® and COBIT® with SOX (described in Chapter 1) and the balanced scorecard. Organizations that are not impacted by SOX can substitute whatever compliance regulations impact their environments.

A well-designed sustainable framework based on industry standards and guidelines can help create more consistency for performance and compliance management and controls.

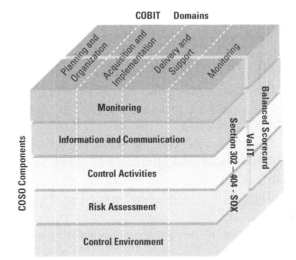

- Establish a baseline framework for measurement, reporting and control
- Optimize controls and related processes
- Integrate financial and KPI reporting and internal control processes
- Redirect efforts from risk aversion to risk intelligence
- Enhance market competitiveness
- Reduce the cost of compliance & certification
- Appoint owners to each component and link results with reward system

Figure 8.3 A framework for making IT performance management, management controls and compliance more consistent

Other principles for achieving performance management and management control excellence include:

- Identify critical success factors for the business and IT, and identify the key performance indicators (KPIs) linked to these factors;
- Build key performance indicators into your performance evaluation system, starting at the top and permeating to all positions that can influence those KPIs;
- Make KPIs relevant, simple, comparable, easy-to-report and focused on goals and objectives;
- Define and issue a management control policy and related procedures, which identify all of the areas requiring management controls, using COBIT as a checklist;
- Monitor, audit and assure that IT operates in accordance with the approved controls;
- Develop a risk management and mitigation plan, policy and process;
- Develop a business/IT continuity and disaster recovery plan and policy;
- Develop a clear performance review, escalation and issues resolution policy and process with clear accountability and responsibilities.

8.3.1 What critical success factors and key performance indicators should be tracked?

According to a Corporate Executive Board report, "...best practice IT organizations are increasingly adopting the balanced scorecard as a management tool incorporating financial, operational, talent management, project management and user satisfaction perspectives into assessments of the performance of the IT function" (Corporate Executive Board, 2003).

IT performance measures have evolved over time. Gartner and others have identified a number of limitations to current IT measurement systems and metrics such as:

- Output measures do not tell one how to improve;
- Historic metrics do not identify issues driving current or future performance;
- There is usually a lack of balance between leading or predictive metrics and lagging or historic metrics. There are usually many more lagging than leading indicators;
- Many systems reflect a lack of external comparison against best practice organizations;
- It is often difficult to measure strategic or added value;
- Too many metrics – a surplus of metrics overwhelms the scorecard reader (e.g. includes balanced scorecard and other metrics) and leads to suboptimal use of senior decision-makers' limited time;
- No individual impact – the absence of incentives linking individual behavior to IT balanced scorecard use hampers scorecard application and achievement of targets.

The execution of these plans and objectives must be monitored and measured by a combination of balanced scorecard key performance indicators (KPIs) as well as formal and informal status review meetings and reports (e.g. report cards, dashboards). The outcomes should link critical success factors to KPIs that are measurable, part of a standard reporting system and linked to a governance component. If one cannot measure it, it does not count. Remember, one gets what one measures, so it is critical to measure and control the right things.

The balanced scorecard system, developed by Robert Kaplan and David Norton, is a management system that provides a clear prescription as to what companies should 'measure' to clarify their vision and strategy and translate them into actions with respect to four areas: financial, customers, internal business processes and learning and growth.

Figure 8.4 illustrates the original balanced scorecard concept. Figure 8.5 identifies critical success factors, based on expanded balanced scorecard categories and relates them to key performance indicators as well as describing key historic and predictive performance metric attributes that are useful for IT.

Another example of an IT governance scorecard framework (e.g. includes the balanced scorecard and other metrics such as project management, service levels, quality measures, etc.) was developed by the IT Governance Institute in 2007. The IT Governance Balanced Scorecard Framework has four dimensions: corporate contribution, stakeholders, operational excellence and future orientation. Figure 8.6 illustrates the framework.

A number of the metrics related to the framework are integrated into Figure 8.8.

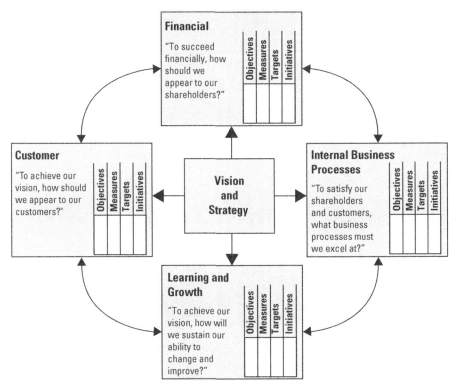

Identifies what companies should measure to translate their vision and strategy into actions.

Figure 8.4 The business balanced scorecard

8.3.2 Select examples of additional KPIs in support of IT governance components

Each company must tailor the CSFs and KPIs of the balanced scorecard to its business strategies, plans and objectives. Each company must also construct a performance report card that should have two audiences – business and IT. One part should focus on key KPIs that are business-centric and are used to communicate from IT outwardly to management and the user community. These include the need for IT to link IT strategy with the business strategy, to monitor service levels, while reducing the TCO (total cost of operations), and to better illustrate the business value of IT. The second part should be IT-centric and should be used by the CIO inwardly to direct, manage and control the performance of the IT organization in terms of customer satisfaction, human capital management, outsourcing vendor management, resource allocations, project management and service management and delivery.

For one global communications organization, the IT balanced scorecard:

- Supports the enterprise balanced scorecard;
- Aligns with IT customers' balanced scorecards;
- Cascades down to IT VP level balanced scorecards;
- Is directly tied to individual performance objectives.

What Key Performance Indicators Should Be Tracked for IT?
The CSFs and KPIs are best determined by the current environment, objectives and strategies of an organization. They must be measurable, comparable & reportable.

- **Critical Success Factor (CSFs) Categories:**
  - Financial
  - Customer
  - Employee
  - Process & Product Innovation
  - Program/Project Innovation
  - Service Level Innovation
  - Learning and Growth

- **Key Performance Indicators (KPIs):**
  - Financial
  - Customer – Internal & External
  - Performance – Team & Individual
  - Program/Project Mgt.
  - Skills/Competencies
  - Service availability & readiness

- **Attributes:**
  - Performance (Historic)
    - Time
    - Cost – Reduction, Containment & Avoidance
    - Profitability – Direct or Indirect
    - Responsiveness
    - Quality
    - Availability
    - Capacity
    - Reliability
  - Predictive (Future)
    - Maturity Level
    - Capability/Skills
    - Alignment
    - Key Issues
    - Major Risks
    - Customer Satisfaction

Reality Check – Do the CSFs and KPIs...
- Translate into specific actions?
- Help align business and IT?
- Provide leverage to institute change?
- Manage end-to-end results across silos?
- Drive performance and process improvements?
- Allow for benchmarking to compare best practice performance?
- Enhance your ability to compete in the future?
- Drive learning and innovation?
- Predictors of Future Poor Performance?

Figure 8.5 CSFs, KPIs and their key attributes related to IT

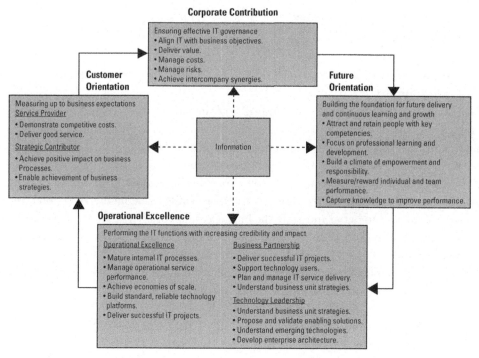

Figure 8.6 IT governance balanced scorecard framework (source: IT Governance Institute, 2007)

The same organization monitors performance against strategy for each major objective that is identified in the IT plan, and for each objective it also identifies the owner, the metrics used to measure results, specific targets, reports the status of each objective on a monthly basis and identifies any actions required. On a quarterly basis, an overall IT performance report card is issued to management. The focus includes alignment, major program/project investment management, key IT service management and delivery metrics, financial analysis of contributions and expenses, and asset utilization.

Figure 8.7 identifies an example of an outwardly focused report card for a financial service organization that includes both business centric and IT centric metrics.

Financial:
- IT Spending/Company FTE (Full Time Employees)
- IT Spending/Company Revenue
- Keep-the-Lights On Spending/Company FTE
- Some aspects of Innovation (as measured by volume increase, speed to market increase, defect reduction, process improvement)
- Total IT Budget versus Actuals and Key IT Components (Capital, Expense, People, Hardware, Software, Network, etc.)

Non-Financial:
- IT Employee Turnover
- Quality of Management Index (Measures IT worker satisfaction with IT management)
- Engaged Employee Index (Measures IT worker motivation)
- Risk Mitigation Index (Measures degree of risk mitigation actions)
*Note: Numerous intra-IT project and service level metrics are used as well.

Figure 8.7 High level IT balanced scorecard metrics used as part of a monthly executive operations review for a financial services organization

Figure 8.8 provides a series of composite balanced scorecard metrics, collected from both case study organizations and secondary research, and decomposed into performance metrics covering financial, project management, IT service management vendor performance, IT human resources, customers, strategic alignment, value delivery, risk management, operations excellence and risk management.

Based on a review of best practice case study companies using some form of balanced scorecard for IT, several critical success factors are necessary to successfully institutionalize IT balanced scorecards in organizations:
- Make key performance indicators simple, intuitively obvious and focused on goals;
- Develop key performance indicators with balance and the big picture in mind – outward from IT to the business and inward to manage IT;
- Integrate key performance indicators into individual and team performance evaluation systems;
- Broad executive commitment – use a mix of business and IT leadership in the design, selection, review and continuous improvement of metrics;
- Develop standard metrics definition based on consensus;

Financial Performance	
Most Common Metrics Total IT expenditures as a % of sales IT cost per employee Total IT spending by geography Percentage of IT expenditures new versus maintenance systems Percentage of "lights on" operating costs (including break/fix, depreciation) versus total IT spend	**IT Departmental Cost** IT cost per employee Total IT spending by geography Total IT spending by business unit Expenses compared to revenue per quarter Spend per portfolio category (e.g. new revenue generation, cost reduction, business transformation) Performance against IT spending performance Central IT spend as percentage of total IT spend Net present value delivered during payback period IT costs charged back to the business
Project and Investment Cost Performance Percentage of R&D investment resulting in operational applications Total value creation from IT enabled projects IT Project ROI, NPV, IRR Percentage of key projects completed on time within budget	
IT Service Management and Delivery Costs Dollar value of technology assets still in use beyond depreciation schedule Share of discretionary spending shared by IT Percentage reduction in maintenance cost of all systems Average network circuit cost reduction per quarter PC/laptop software maintenance cost per month per user Workstation software maintenance cost per month per workstation E-mail service: cost per month per user Infrastructure spending as a % of total IT spending Total maintenance cost Percentage of year-over-year cost reduction per service Total cost of ownership of IT services versus external benchmarks Service unit cost	

Project Management Performance	
Most Common Metrics Percentage of projects on time, on budget, within scope Percentage of projects compliant with architectural standards Customer Satisfaction Index	**Project Alignment with IT Strategy** Percent of projects directly linked to business objectives Percentage of applications deployed on a global basis Percentage of infrastructure standardization projects of total project pool Percentage of projects using common project methodology Percentage of application failures within first 90 days of deployment Percentage of "at-risk" projects that adopt quality, security, and compliance standards Increase in project management maturity Project quality index
Project Spending and Costs Actual versus planned ROI for implementation of key initiatives Percentage of projects with completed business case Percentage of budget allocated to unplanned projects Earned value (for Federal Government Projects) Cost Performance Index	
Project Timeliness and Delivery Percent and cost of project rework due to changed scope, poor requirements definition, etc. Average project duration Percentage of projects with detailed project plan Dollars saved through productivity improvement and reusable code Schedule performance index Percentage of project milestones delivered	

IT Service Management and Vendor Performance	
Most Common Metrics Key applications and systems availability Help-desk first-call resolution rate	**IT Vendor Management** IT contract cost ($) IT contract cost as a % of IT spend IT project completion (on time, within budget) SLA performance (%) Customer satisfaction index (%)
User-Centric Operational Performance Average number of incidents per user per month (average number of times end user experiences global desktop availability outages per month) Consistently available and reliable IT services to users Rate of failure incidents impacting business	**Help-Desk Performance** Mean time to repair for all network and desktop outages Mean time to repair for all application systems outages less than four hours Percentage of infrastructure service requests closed within service level agreements

Figure 8.8 Select IT balanced scorecard metrics – a composite of case study companies and research findings

Network and Systems Performance	**Operational Strategy Adoption**
Print server availability	Completion of service transformation with minimum
All critical systems and infrastructure have viable business continuity plans	business disruption
System/application database maintained with more than 95 percent	All announced changes completed within
accuracy	advertised downtime window
E-mail transmit less than 20 seconds (all regions)	Percentage of IT architectural plans approved,
Monthly average of network availability consistently more than 99.5 percent	reviewed, and accepted by business
Monthly average of critical systems availability consistently above 99.5	Number of applications used by more than one line
percent	of business
Mean time to repair for all client outages less than two hours	Percentage of desktop PC standardized
Network uptime	End-to-end availability for customer service
PC/laptop hardware fix or replacement within 48 hours	IT effectiveness in resource allocation supporting
Total cost of ownership of identified products and services compared to	business objectives
industry standards	Identify and manage strategic alliances with IT
	partners
Information Security	Decrease average development cost by 10 percent
Percent of systems compliant with IT security standards	
Number and type of security incidents time to respond and resolve security	
incidents	

IT HR Skills Management

Most Common Metrics	**Training and Personal Development**
Employee morale/satisfaction	Percentage of performance assessment and
Overall IT staff retention and attrition rate	development plans delivered to employees
	Percentage of employees with mentors
	Percentage of employees with individual
	development plans
	Percentage of individual training objectives met
	Employee "business knowledge" survey
	performance
	Percentage of managers trained in employee
	motivation
	Percentage of staff with appropriate measures for
	their personal goals
	Share of IT training spent in business units
	Number of IT person-hours spent at industry events
	Number of training hours per employee per quarter
Staffing	**Marketing/ PR - Related Metrics**
Percentage of non-entry-level position filled internally	Number of awards won by company for use of IT
Average tenure of solid performers (in years)	Competitiveness of current employment offer
Percentage of projects assignments that are cross-functional	versus industry
Ratio of skills sets needed to skills set represented	Citation of IT organization in press
Performance against staff diversity goals	
Number of candidates interviewed per open position	
IT headcount (number of full-time IT staff)	
Contractor headcount	
Percentage of planned staffing levels	
Average years of IT experience	
Percent of IT staff who are certified (number of industry recognized	
certifications)	

Customer Satisfaction

Most Common Metrics
Customer satisfaction survey – quarterly or semi-annually

Surveys
Overall business executive satisfaction rating

Survey Questions
Perceived versus actual price competitiveness of IT services
Perceived ability to deliver technical/business solutions and services
Quality of communication about available services and new technologies
Help-desk client satisfaction—percentage dissatisfied
Contribution to business process improvement and innovation
Contribution to business value creation
Contribution to corporate business strategy

Figure 8.8 Select IT balanced scorecard metrics – a composite of case study companies and research findings (continued)

Corporate Contribution (Strategic Alignment, Value Delivery and Risk Management)	Operational Excellence (Ensure and Sustain IT Governance)
• Percentage of IT funds allocated to strategic business projects • Percentage of IT development resources working on strategic business projects • Percentage of business objectives supported by IT objectives • Percentage of IT costs charged back to business • Development and updating of disaster recovery plan and risk assessment and mitigation plan (frequency of updates and test trials)	• Business and IT steering committees (number of meetings, membership, decision authority, etc.) • CIO sits on executive committee of organization • Number of business and IT alignment processes (e.g. plan, portfolio investment mgmt., project mgmt.) • Alignment of business and IT balanced scorecards • Maturity level of IT processes (e.g. CMMI or equivalent) • Number of IT processes covered by select standards (e.g. ISO, PMI, ITIL, outsourcing, etc.)
Stakeholders (Measuring Stakeholders Expectations)	**Future Orientation (Building IT Governance Capability)**
• Number of stakeholder surveys (and actions taken) • Ranking of stakeholder surveys (excellent, good, poor) • Clear communications in place between IT and stakeholders (frequency, website, level of detail) • IT compliance with regulations (privacy, SOX, Basel II, etc.)	• Existence of IT governance organization • Number of IT governance training sessions • Support and sponsorship of IT governance and related certifications (e.g. individual, organization) • Number of employees/vendors certified in some aspect of IT governance and related areas

Figure 8.8 Select IT balanced scorecard metrics – a composite of case study companies and research findings (continued)

8.3.3 Governance calendar

To establish more consistency in tracking performance, many organizations are issuing annual governance calendars. These calendars list key IT components and their periodic governance reporting, meeting and review periods, activities and events. Figure 8.9 illustrates one such governance calendar. This can also be developed on a more detailed and granular basis.

A Governance Schedule should be issued annually Identifying the Key Deliverables, Reports, Review Meetings, etc.

JAN	MARCH	MAY	JULY	AUGUST	OCT	DEC

Strategic & Operational Plans & Budgets (Capital & Expense) PROGRAMS, PROJECTS and INFRASTRUCTURE OPERATIONS PLANS/BUDGETS/REPORTS*

- **Strategic Plan**
  - Annual Operating Plan
  - Investment Approvals
  - Program/Project Reports, Metrics and Reviews
  - IT Service Management & Delivery (Operations and Infrastructure Reports, Metrics and Reviews

- **Program/Project Plans**
  - Charter
  - Schedule
  - Budget/Actuals
  - Deliverables

Weekly
  - Projects Status Report (milestones/issues)
  - Operations Status Project
  - Technical Exchange Group
  - Staff Meetings
  - Weekly Activity/Status Report to Management

Bi-Weekly/Monthly
  - Project Status Reviews (Financials, Schedule)
  - Monthly Management Report
  - Multiple Dashboards (Top 10 Projects + Key Service SLA's) – Green, Amber, Red Report

Bi-Monthly/Quarterly
  - Executive Steering/Governance Board Reviews

Semi-Annual/Annual
  - State of IT Report Card
  - Performance Reviews

Figure 8.9 Governance calendar

■ 8.4   COBIT® - CONTROL OBJECTIVES FOR INFORMATION AND RELATED TECHNOLOGIES

COBIT® is a model for control of the IT environment. COBIT® stands for Control Objectives for Information and related Technology. COBIT® is a model designed to control and help audit the IT function. COBIT®5 is about linking business goals to IT objectives (note the linkage here from vision to mission to goals to objectives). COBIT® 5 (launched April 2012) provides metrics and maturity models to measure whether or not the IT organization has achieved its objectives.

COBIT® is owned and supported by ISACA. The first version was released in 1996; the current Version 5.0 brings together COBIT 4.1, Val IT 2.0 and Risk IT frameworks.

The COBIT® 5 principles and enablers are generic and useful for enterprises of all sizes. COBIT® 5 provides a set of 36 governance and management processes within the framework. The governance domain contains five governance processes; within each process, evaluate, direct, and monitor practices are defined:
■ EDM1: Set and maintain the governance framework;
■ EDM2: Ensure value optimization;
■ EDM3: Ensure risk optimization;
■ EDM4: Ensure resource optimization;
■ EDM5: Ensure stakeholder transparency.

The four management domains, in line with the responsibility areas of plan, build, run, and monitor (PBRM) provide end-to-end coverage of IT and include:
■ Align, plan and organize;
■ Build, acquire and implement;
■ Deliver, service and support;
■ Monitor, evaluate and assess.

COBIT® 5 acts as an integrator for many IT governance-related guidelines.

COBIT® does not provide detailed policies and procedures for how to develop the content or what content needs to be included in the processes on the checklist. That is the responsibility of each organization. Chapters 4 through 9 provide more details on the content of 'how to's' for each of the major components of IT governance based on a blend of best practices.

Figure 2.15 illustrates the COBIT® reference model and process areas for IT governance.

More information on COBIT® is covered in Section 2.4.14.

8.4.1 IT Performance, control and compliance framework

A growing number of organizations are using the COSO®, COBIT® and other frameworks as a checklist to develop more effective IT controls. Critical success steps used by several best practice companies to improve controls include:

- Establish an IT governance and control framework, and organization;
- Establish a management compliance forum;
- Determine Sarbanes-Oxley and/or other regulatory compliance requirements;
- Determine IT owners for applications and general controls;
- Manage performance, control and compliance issues;
- VP appointed compliance steward;
- VP appointed applications and controls SMEs (subject matter experts);
- Design of IT control documentation;
- Review and audit of IT controls.

■ 8.5   RISK ASSESSMENT, MANAGEMENT AND MITIGATION

Risk management and mitigation should be an integral part of any IT governance strategy and action program. This section identifies several components of risk management that can be applied to each of the major elements of IT governance.

8.5.1 Risk management objectives and definition

Risk analysis is the systematic identification of potential areas of project uncertainty or concern. There are three primary aspects of risk management to be considered:

- Risk identification and analysis;
- Risk quantification;
- Risk response, mitigation and contingency plan development.

Risk management objectives include:

- To understand the concept of risk and the importance of risk management in the business, functional and IT environments;
- To understand the risk management methodology and framework, identify the various causes of risk and review the activities and tasks essential to minimize, avoid or address the consequences of the risk;
- To review the tools and techniques utilized in risk management in order to identify, analyze, quantify, prioritize and mitigate high risk areas;
- To develop risk mitigation and contingency strategies and plans.

8.5.2 Classification of risks

In order to address threats and their risk impact, each of the potential threats and risks should be identified in terms of:

Causes of risks:
- Man-made (e.g. terrorism; espionage; poor project management and poor service management);
- Natural (e.g. hurricanes, tornadoes, etc.);
- Industrial accidents (e.g. fire, flooding, etc.).

Business and IT continuity:
- Disruption of business processes and/or IT services;
- Loss of physical locations;
- Lack of, or inadequate, disaster prevention/recovery plans;
- Discontinuity of business services;
- Discontinuity of IT services;
- Loss of vital assets – physical, human, intellectual property, facilities, other;
- Loss of software, hardware, networks, data centers, network control centers, etc.

Security breaches:
- Physical;
- Logical;
- Information technology.

Theft
- Physical property;
- Intellectual property;
- Assets.

For each potential threat or risk, ask these questions, and then assign a value of high, medium, or low:
- What are the possible triggers for these risks?
- What is the probability that this risk will occur?
- What would be the impact on the organization if this risk should occur?
- What can be done to mitigate the risk (e.g.: avoid, mitigate, contingency)?

Figure 8.10 illustrates a risk analysis process flow. Figure 8.11 provides an example of a risk assessment and impact template. It helps to quantify the risk impact (e.g. catastrophic, critical, marginal and negligible) versus its probability of occurrence (e.g.: near certainty versus improbable). The template can be easily tailored by organizations to fit their requirements and environments.

Figure 8.12 provides a risk/threat assessment template that can facilitate the analysis of risks and their potential impact, and probability of occurrence on the organization. A contingency plan should be developed for all threats that appear in the high impact, high probability quadrant and may be developed for those threats that appear in the high impact, but low probability quadrant. This again is a function of the management philosophy and style of an organization.

Outlines the Flow of the Risk Management and Mitigation Process

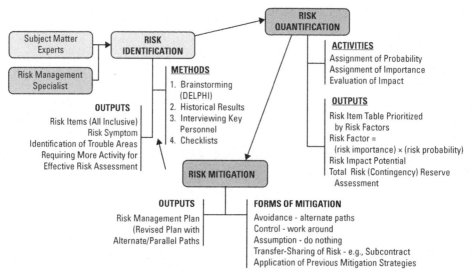

Figure 8.10 Risk analysis process flow schematic

8.5.3 Risk management mitigation options

Responses to risks and threats generally fit into one of the following categories:

- **Avoidance** – eliminate the risk by eliminating the cause;
- **Mitigation** – reduce the monetary value of the risk by reducing the probability, impact or both;
- **Acceptance** – simply accept the consequences;
- **Transfer** – to a third party.

There are several responses to potential risks:

- **Outsourcing** – get additional products/services from outside;
- **Create centers of excellence** on a global basis (don't put all of your eggs in one basket);
- **Contingency planning** – define action steps that will be taken in the event the risk event occurs, and estimate the costs associated with that action;
- **Alternative strategies** – consider changing the approach;
- **Insurance** – may protect against financial losses associated with certain types of risk.

In summary, a risk assessment matrix can be developed for each major component of IT governance.

Risk Exposure Key

- **Highest (R$_E$ = 15-20)** Contingency Plan Required
- **High (R$_E$ = 9-12)** Contingency Plan Highly Recommended
- **Medium (R$_E$ = 4-8)** Contingency Plan Discretionary
- **Low (R$_E$ = 1-3)** Contingency Plan Not Required

Risk Impact [R$_I$]

Criteria	Catastrophic (4)	Critical (3)	Marginal (2)	Negligible (1)
Hazard	Unrecoverable impact to environment, system, and/or personnel health *and/or*	Major damage impact to environment, system, and/or personnel health *and/or*	Minor impact to environment, system, and/or personnel health *and/or*	Negligible impact to environment, system, and/or personnel health *and/or*
Schedule	Unachievable *and/or*	Serious delay (>30% late) *and/or*	Moderate delay (10%-30% late) *and/or*	Will meet schedule but use all "slack time" *and/or*
Cost	Major budget overrun (>50%) *and/or*	Serious budget overrun (30%-50%) *and/or*	Budget overrun (10%-30%) *and/or*	Consumption of all management financial reserves *and/or*
Support	Unsupportable systems *and/or*	Major delays in systems modifications *and/or*	Minor delays in systems modifications *and/or*	Irritating and awkward maintenance *and/or*
Performance	Non-achievement of technical performance	Significant degradation of technical performance	Some reduction in technical performance	Minimal to small reduction in technical performance, at the detailed level

Risk Probability [R$_p$]

Criteria	Value (R$_E$) ▲	Catastrophic (4)	Critical (3)	Marginal (2)	Negligible (1)
81%-99% Probability of Happening	**Near Certain (5)**	20	15	10	5
61%-80% Probability of Happening	**Probable (4)**	16	12	8	4
41%-60% Probability of Happening	**Possible (3)**	12	9	6	3
21%-40% Probability of Happening	**Marginal (2)**	8	6	4	2
1%-20% Probability of Happening	**Improbable (1)**	4	3	2	1

Risk Exposure (R$_E$) = R$_I$ × R$_P$

Figure 8.11 Risk assessment matrix

• For each contingency plan, specify the circumstances that would trigger that plan into action.

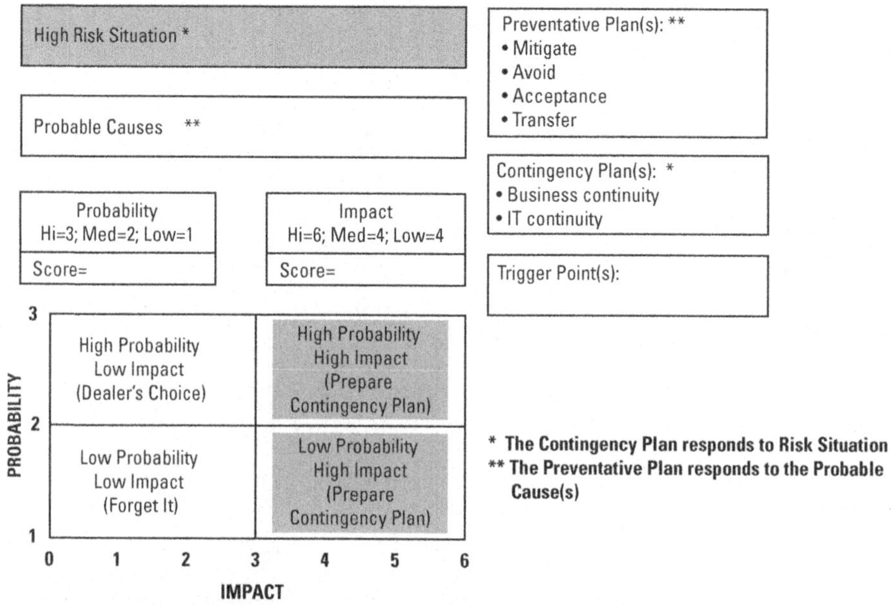

Figure 8.12 Risk management and mitigation template

■ 8.6 BUSINESS AND IT CONTINUITY AND PROTECTION PLAN CHECKLIST

In the review of literature, there is general consensus that there are a number of corporate governance principles and practices which, if followed, can better prepare organizations to detect, analyze and proactively mitigate and manage threats and their associated risks. These principles and practices can speed up the recovery process and minimize disruptions and losses. They include, but are not limited to:

■ Identify and classify potential threats and their risks using intelligence systems, processes (e.g. data collection and analysis; threat and/or impact assessment and evaluation; information dissemination to the right individuals; triggering events for potential action, and enabling technologies).

■ Institute a risk management and mitigation policy and process to assess the impact and probability of the occurrence of potential catastrophes and disasters on the organization and develop a mitigation and contingency plan.

■ Develop a business continuity plan and a disaster recovery plan.

■ Develop a corporate and information security plan and policy.

■ Identify roles and responsibilities for each component of the plan.

The above can serve as a guideline for organizations to select and customize the appropriate approach applicable to their environment, prioritize actions and ensure that the right resources are available. With some astute planning and a solid understanding of business and IT vulnerabilities and risk tolerance, it is possible to develop a pragmatic and effective business protection plan that will minimize disruptions and financial losses.

A business continuity and protection policy, plan, process and related templates should be developed, disseminated (to select constituents in the organizations) and updated periodically for all critical business units and functions. A business continuity and protection plan must contain a number of components: business impact analysis, risk assessment, mitigation and management, preparing for emergencies and business recovery processes.

A detailed business and IT continuity and plan outline and checklist are provided in Figure 8.13.

8.7   ENABLING TECHNOLOGIES TO IMPROVE IT GOVERNANCE

There are numerous software tools that enable enterprises to collect, record, analyze, track and report KPIs relating to each IT governance areas, but none thus far that address all of the areas. Several vendors are working on tools that address the enterprise governance processes.

Select technology software solution attributes necessary to support IT governance and its major components:
The following attributes, functions and features, at a minimum, should be included in software packages that support IT governance and its major components:
- **Demand and customer relationship management** – process IT requests, workflow, authorization, accommodate multiple designations (discretionary, mandatory and/or strategic, planned or unplanned, new, enhancements, maintenance and/or keep the lights on), etc.
- **Portfolio management** – investment and alignment evaluation criteria, rankings vis-à-vis alternatives, priorities, approval, etc.
- **Workflow, process management, tracking and authorization** – processes, phases and templates (imbedded and/or custom designed), go/no-go gates, etc.
- **Planning**
  - Link initiatives and track to strategic/tactical/capital/budget plans and initiatives:
  - 'What if' alternative analysis:
  - Work breakdown structure; work package management;
  - Task list;
  - Organization breakdown structure;
  - Estimating and budgeting;
  - Resource loading;
  - Scheduling – multiple techniques.

1.0	**Preparing the Plan**	4.2.4	Manpower Recovery Strategy
2.0	**Initiating the BCPP Project**	4.2.5	Establish the Disaster Recovery Team
2.1	Project Initiation Tasks	4.2.6	Establish the Business Recovery Team
2.1.1	Review of Existing BCPP	**4.3**	**Emergency Response Linkage to Business**
2.1.2	Benefits of Developing a BCPP (Value		**Recovery**
	Proposition and Marketing)	4.3.1	Alternative Business Process Strategy
2.1.3	BCPP Policy Statement	4.3.2	IT Systems, Networks and Data Backup and
2.1.4	Decision Authority and Approvals		Recovery Strategy
2.1.5	Communications Plan	4.3.3	Premises and Critical Equipment and Asset
2.2	Project Organization		Backup
2.2.1	Charter – Objectives, Timetable, Budget,	4.3.4	Customer Service and Call Center Backup
	Deliverables, Scope, Authorization	4.3.4	Administration and Operations Backup
2.2.2	Appoint Project Manager and Team	4.3.5	Insurance Coverage
2.2.3	Reporting Requirements and Metrics	4.4	Key Documents and Procedures
3.0	**Assessing Business Risk and Impact of**	4.4.1	Documents and Records Vital to the
	Potential Threats and Emergencies		Business
3.1	Threat Assessment	4.4.2	Off– Site Storage and Backup
3.1.1.	Environmental Disasters	4.4.3	Emergency Office Supplies
3.1.2	Terrorist or Other Deliberate Disruptions	**5.0**	**Disaster Recovery**
3.1.3	Loss of External Services – Supplies,	5.1.	Mobilizing the Disaster Recovery Team,
	Utilities, Raw Material		Roles, Responsibilities and Authority
3.1.4	Equipment or System or Information	5.2	Disaster Recovery Plan
	Technology Failures	5.2.1	Identification of Potential Disaster Status
3.1.5	Serious Security Breaches		and Assess Extent of Damage and Business
3.1.6	Other Emergencies		Impact
3.2	Business Risk Assessment	5.2.2	Notification and Reporting During Disaster
3.2.1	Major Business Processes and Locations		Recovery Phase
3.2.2	Assess Financial and Operational Impact	5.2.3	Prepare Specific Recovery Plans – Detailed
3.2.3	Determine Time Outage Impacts		Resumption, Recovery and Restoration
3.2.4	Key Business Executives/Personnel and	5.2.4	Communicate Status of Recovery
	Contact Information	5.2.5	Business Recovery Tasks
3.3	Information Technology	5.2.5.1	Power and Other Utilities
3.3.1	Determine Business and IT Dependencies	5.2.5.2	Premises, Fixtures, Furniture (Facilities
3.3.2	Major IT Systems, Networks and Data		Recovery Management)
3.3.3	Key IT Personnel and Contact Information	5.2.5.3	IT and Communications Systems and
3.3.4	Key IT Vendors and Facilities		Facilities
3.3.5	IT Recovery Policies and Procedures	5.2.5.4	Production Facilities and Equipment
3.4	Current Emergency Policies and	5.2.5.5	Operations
	Procedures	5.2.5.6	Distribution, Warehousing, Logistics and
3.4.1	Summary of Current Policies, Procedures		Supply Chain Management
	and Responsibilities for Handling	5.2.5.7	Sales, Marketing and Customer Service
	Emergencies	5.2.5.8	Engineering and Research and Development
3.4.2	Key Personnel and Contact Information for	5.2.5.9	Finance, Administration and Security
	Business Recovery Organization (BRO),	5.2.5. 10	Other +++
	Escalation and Delegation of Authority	**6.0**	**Testing the Business Recover Plan and**
3.4.3	External Emergency Services and Contact		**Process**
	Information	6.1	Planning the Tests
3.4.4	Building, Power, Information, Vital	6.1.1	Test Multiple Scenarios based on Different
	Records Backup		Threats
4.0	**Preparing for a Possible Emergency**	6.1.2	Evaluate Results, Identify Gaps and Improve
4.1.	Emergency Response Procedures	**7.0**	**Education, Training and Plan Updating**
4.2	Command, Control and Emergency	7.1.	Develop organizational awareness and
	Operations Center (Crisis Management)		training programs
4.2.1	Organization Chart	7.2	Develop Vehicles for Dissemination
4.2.2	Key Personnel and Emergency Contact		Information
	Information	7.3	Develop budget and schedule for plan
4.2.3	Key Vendors and Suppliers and Emergency		updates
	Contact Information	7.4	Plan Distribution, Audits and Security

Figure 8.13 Business/IT continuity plan and checklist outline

- **Program and project lifecycle support** – phases, templates, reviews, authorization, progress tracking and reporting, required to be updated and accessible at multiple levels, ability to link tasks to related tasks and/or projects and/or programs and record and/or report on multiple key performance indicators – budget, schedule and actuals with variance reporting, status of deliverables, current period, prior period, next period projections, year to date, inception to date, base lining and re-base lining comparisons, etc.
- **Asset management** – inventory of assets, $ value, utilization, aging, depreciation, asset refresh planning, asset retirement and disposal tracking, etc.
- **Configuration management** - asset description, features, costs, location, protocols supported, version and release control, etc.
- **Resource management** – skills inventory, labor rates, labor hours, facilities, inventory, forecasting, level loading, etc.
- **Cost management** – labor rates, procurement rates, committed costs, overhead rates, budget versus actual by labor or procurement category for this period, last period, year to date, inception to date, cost at completion, by product/service, etc.
- **Time management** – from lowest level (activity or tasks) to highest level (project or program), time reporting, budget versus actual comparison by labor or procurement category, etc.
- **Product/service catalog** – list of standard repetitive IT product and service solutions offered by IT with pricing and estimated deployment time, etc.
- **Financial management** – support capital and expense budgets, cost management, budget and forecasts, accommodate multiple baselines and changes, chargebacks, etc.
- **Performance management** – support and reporting of multiple balanced scorecard metrics - planning, project, operational and service performance dashboards, etc.
- **Service level management and support** – incident and problem reporting, tracking and resolution, help desk support, capacity and availability planning and forecasting, usage based tracking, cost allocation, quality control, security, etc.
- **Procurement, vendor, outsourcing management** – link to vendor governance and reporting, contract management, license tracking, metrics, escalation, etc.
- **Compliance management** – documentation, traceability, secure third party access, audit support, etc.
- **Communications management** – manage expectations of customers and constituents - types and frequency of reports, graphs, comparisons, method and frequency of communications supported (e-mail, web-casts, formal reviews, other).
- **Change management** – templates, process, recording, reporting, authorization, original baseline and re-baseline tracking, version control, etc.
- **Release management** – ensure that all aspects of a new or revised release (e.g. hardware, software, documentation, checklists and rollouts) are coordinated and approved by the impacted constituents (e.g. development, operations, client, sponsor, etc.).
- **Issues and problem management** – tracking, reporting and resolution status.

- **Security** – access control and authorization database, authentication, encryption, virus protection, etc.
- **Best practice knowledge management** – maintain a database of internal and external IT governance best practices and continuous improvement ideas and innovations, enable access for select constituents, etc.

■ 8.8   IBM PROCESS REFERENCE MODEL FOR IT (PRM-IT)

A number of IT management and governance models have also been developed by companies such as IBM, HP, CA and others. Some of these models are used to help market products and services related to IT products, services and processes. Others are generic and can be used as additional checklists and tools to help manage, control and govern IT more effectively, such as the IBM Process Reference Model for IT (PRM-IT).

Model purpose
The IBM Process Reference Model for IT (PRM-IT) is an integrated collection of the processes involved in using information technology (IT) to assist businesses in carrying out many or all of their fundamental purposes. It describes, at a generic level, the activities that are performed in order that IT provides value to the stakeholding business or businesses.

For most of these businesses, this use of IT has been a means to improve the business processes that underpin their value propositions to the industry segments they serve. For others, IT services have been major value propositions in their own right. As the reach and range of IT-based solutions and services has extended and become, to all intents and purposes, pervasive, these two uses of IT have converged.

So, as IT exploitation becomes synonymous with business success, the basis of this model is to describe an IT undertaking as if it is a business in its own right, and to apply the same business process description techniques to it as for any other business (IBM, 2008).

Viewpoint of the model
The focal point for all activities, and the executive accountable for IT value, is the CIO. Accordingly, PRM-IT considers the work done within IT from this perspective.

There are two main perspectives from the CIO's viewpoint:
- Control over IT activities:
  - Such control can be direct, in that the activities are performed by the in-house IT department;
  - Some activities can be performed within parts of the business, but under the guidance of IT-developed or owned standards – a typical example is that of

users within a business division developing applications, using technology and techniques established by IT;

- Many activities can be assigned to one or more third parties, covering the range from complete outsourcing through limited IT service out-tasking.
- Representing the IT endeavor to its stakeholders and to the wider operating environment.

The PRM-IT Framework uses eight major process categories:
- Governance and Management System – how IT ensures it is able to function effectively – IT control system;
- Customer Relationships – representing IT to its customers and meeting their needs;
- Direction – strategic decision making of IT in support of business;
- Realization – design, development and maintenance of all classes of IT solutions;
- Transition – control, deployment and reporting of all changes and technology resources;
- Operations – fulfillment and support of IT services and users;
- Resilience – continued readiness and integrity of the IT services;
- Administration – underpinning back office management of the IT function.

The eight major process categories contain a total of forty-six (46) processes across all eight categories. Figure 8.14 illustrates the categories and processes within each category.

PRM-IT version 3 contains a further level of decomposition of these processes into 307 activities. Like COBIT, this framework also complements select industry guidelines.

■ 8.9 CASE STUDY – GLOBAL MANUFACTURING AND MANAGED SERVICES COMPANY

Figure 8.15 represents a case study of a global manufacturing and service company.

■ 8.10 SUMMARY AND KEY TAKE AWAYS

8.10.1 Summary
Each organization should adopt those current and emerging industry performance management and control frameworks and models, and tailor them to fit its specific environment. Key points to remember include:
- IT should partner with finance, business and the internal auditors.
- Align IT objectives, strategies and initiatives with the customer and develop a set of critical success factors required to meet those objectives – then build key performance indicators to measure performance and monitor improvement and progress or issues toward those objectives.

PRM – IT version 3 – Represents a Framework for more Effective IT Management, Control and Governance

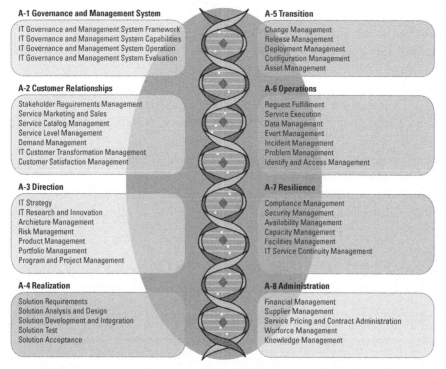

A-1 Governance and Management System

IT Governance and Management System Framework
IT Governance and Management System Capabilities
IT Governance and Management System Operation
IT Governance and Management System Evaluation

A-2 Customer Relationships

Stakeholder Requirements Management
Service Marketing and Sales
Service Catalog Management
Service Level Management
Demand Management
IT Customer Transformation Management
Customer Satisfaction Management

A-3 Direction

IT Strategy
IT Research and Innovation
Archieture Management
Risk Management
Product Management
Portfolio Management
Program and Project Management

A-4 Realization

Solution Requirements
Solution Analysis and Design
Solution Development and Integration
Solution Test
Solution Acceptance

A-5 Transition

Change Management
Release Management
Deployment Management
Configuration Management
Asset Management

A-6 Operations

Request Fulfillment
Service Execution
Data Management
Evert Management
Incident Management
Problem Management
Identify and Access Management

A-7 Resilience

Compliance Management
Security Management
Availability Management
Capacity Management
Facilities Management
IT Service Continuity Management

A-8 Administration

Financial Management
Supplier Management
Service Pricing and Contract Administration
Worforce Management
Knowledge Management

Figure 8.14 IBM's Process Reference Model for IT, its categories and processes

Environment & Drivers	Approach
• Revenue range – $20.0 billion - $22.0 billion • Number of employees range – 140,000 - 160,000 • Industry classification – manufacturing and services • Products/services - copiers, services, printers, outsourcing • Management philosophy – balanced risk taking • Number of countries with operations – 120 - 180 • Number of full time IT professionals/range – 1,000 - 1,200* • IT organization – centralized & global for manufacturing division and corporate; IT is primarily embedded in the managed services business • IT expense as a % of revenue approximates 3 - 4% • CIO reports to COO * Does not include IT professionals in the managed services business which is fee-based	• Enterprise risk (& threat) management committee reports to chief information security officer – (CISO reports to CIO) across and within business units • IT strategy is created by CIO in partnership with business units and corporate • Formal process where business & IT leaders are aligned for each business/IT area based on a relationship model. They work together to develop IT strategy for each business/corporate function, presented by CIO to management committee (CEO and direct reports) • Formal IT investment committees (business & IT members) decide on IT investments at three levels: Level 1 – enterprise governance (align business/IT at highest level) Level 2 – three boards (for each business unit and corporate) Level 3 – steering committee to watch over programs/projects that have been approved at higher levels

Figure 8.15 Case study – global manufacturing and managed services company

Issues	Results – Alignment (Business/ IT)

• Identify key issues, constraints, objectives and opportunities relating to IT governance and management
  – Issues/objectives in priority sequence: IT security, IT strategy and portfolio investment prioritization, financial governance (IT spend and cost for a specific line of business and benchmark investment governance), portfolio/ project management – measure ROI of projects and how best to ensure project management effectiveness, data management and architecture
	• Developing a process to:
	  – Clearly articulate total spend regarding supporting the SBUs and corporate functions (by line of business)
	• Technology Business Management (TBM)
	  – Where is money being spent (infrastructure, cost by application, cost by business unit, etc.)
	• Determine spend and assessment value on strategic or tactical initiatives and examine trade-offs (cost versus ROI)
	(Also see "Approach" quadrant above)

Results - Program/Project/Portfolio Management/ SDM
• One portfolio investment process (starts in IT strategy/plan phase)
• A gate approach for the time to market phase has been adopted for IT projects using a product development lifecycle framework
• Includes broad phases of development, business case and implementation
• Company uses both Waterfall (ERP projects) and Agile processes (iterative) for systems development methodology
• Working on implementing PM techniques and processes in a uniform manner across the enterprise using a combination of industry standards and company best practices
	Results - Performance Management
	• Continuous communications memo (monthly) from CIO to senior management committee highlighting:
	  – Critical events
	  – Status of major projects
	  – Major issues and risks
	• Report PM and operations scorecard using green, yellow and red indicated on key qualitative and quantitative measures

Results - IT Service Management (Includes ITIL) • ITIL has been deployed as a framework (incident, problem and change management, etc.) in the infrastructure and operational areas for several years	**Results – Cloud Computing and Data Management** • Architectural governance – cloud computing is viewed as a design choice managed through the formal architecture strategy • Company is initiating a plan to review its data management strategy and action programs relative to master data and governance, toolsets (for analytics etc.) as well as security, access and privacy
Results– Strategic Sourcing and Outsourcing • Very mature sourcing strategy, process and organization in place • Sourcing is shared between global procurement and IT (for IT sourcing opportunities)	**Lessons Learned** • Ensure messages are communicated on IT progress to create better awareness (did not do enough marketing of IT governance) • More training and awareness of IT governance benefits is critical
Critical Success Factors • Business and IT must be proactive partners • Business and IT must have sponsorship (CEO, management committee and/or CIO) • Enablers are underlying tools, processes and consistent data models, etc.	

Figure 8.15 Case study – global manufacturing and managed services company (continued)

■ Identify and prioritize the IT performance management and control policies and procedures to facilitate compliance, traceability, auditability, honesty, security, privacy and control.
■ Make sure that the reward and compensation structure is linked to continuous improvement performance management programs for individuals and teams:
  • Provide a link between outcomes and organizational objectives;
  • Communicate the impact of improvements to all of the stakeholders.

8.10.2 Key take aways

The bottom line for each organization is to define, track and enforce those KPIs that measure the CSFs and objectives and are relevant to the performance management practices and compensation incentives of their enterprises.

IT organizations that gain significant and sustainable improvement in their effectiveness have done so by balancing their focus between the management of IT and the application of IT in the business.

IT managers that want to build and sustain higher levels of business impact and effectiveness will implement 'continuous improvement programs' and report 'understandable' results through a robust performance management and control system.

With the right set of metrics, closely aligned to organization strategy and performance objectives, IT departments can become hubs of innovation that not only support sustained operational effectiveness, but lead the process of creating competitive advantage.

9 Cloud Computing, Data Management and Governance Issues, Opportunities, Considerations and Approaches

"This is what our customers are asking for to take them to the next level and free them from the bondage of mainframe and client-server software."

Marc Benioff, CEO, Salesforce.com

■ 9.1 WHAT IS COVERED IN THIS CHAPTER?

- Discuss cloud computing and data management, definitions, trends, issues, opportunities, risks and strategies;
- Describe cloud service and deployment models;
- Identify key performance indicators for the cloud and data management;
- Review data management services;
- Review cloud and data management security, privacy, back-up, recovery and quality;
- Identify steps in making cloud computing and data management real;
- Review a case study of an insurance/reinsurance company.

■ 9.2 OVERVIEW AND DEFINITIONS

Both cloud computing and data management have emerged as important growth areas in information technology and related areas. Due to the wide coverage in the literature, as identified in the reference section of this book, it is beyond the scope of this book to provide detailed coverage of both topics. However, since the topics have become critical components of IT governance, selectedpoints in both areas are covered to give the reader a better understanding of the issues, opportunities and risks they represent and how they relate to IT governance.

9.2.1 Cloud computing

Cloud-based services are on the rise. For example, Capgemini's latest World Quality Report estimates that cloud-based software testing will account for 32% of all testing by 2015 (Capgemini, 2013). A Gartner study estimates that the market for cloud computing will reach US \$160 billion by 2015 (Gartner, 2013). Cloud services allow companies to reduce, contain and avoid costs, and to operate more flexibly than with a traditional IT infrastructure and thus can enable them to pursue new opportunities. However, the promising opportunities of this technology go hand-in-hand with certain risks arising from migrating to and operating in a cloud service. These risks will be explored in more detail later in this chapter.

According to Michael Kravis, author of *Architecting the Cloud*, cloud computing combines the best of the mainframe era with the best of the PC-enabled client-server era along with the Internet, cloud and big data era. Many of the concepts of cloud computing have been around for years. What is new is that many of those lessons learned and techniques in computer science that have been perfected over the past few decades are now able to be simplified, automated, made available as on-demand services and offered at price points that are hard for the traditional on-premises organizations to compete against (Kravis, 2014).

The definition of cloud computing from the National Institute of Standards and Technology (NIST) has been adopted widely by other governing bodies and professional organizations, such as the European Network and Information Security Agency (ENISA), the British Standards Institution (BSI) and the Cloud Security Alliance (CSA), and, thus, will be used here: "Cloud computing is a model for enabling ubiquitous, convenient, on-demand network access to a shared pool of configurable computing resources (e.g., networks, servers, storage, applications, and services) that can be rapidly provisioned and released with minimal management effort or service provider interaction." The NIST definition characterizes important aspects of cloud computing and is intended to serve as a means for broad comparisons of cloud services and deployment strategies, and to provide a baseline for discussion from what is cloud computing to how to best to use cloud computing (NIST, 2011).

9.2.2 Data management

According to a recent IDG research study of over 180 IT professionals, organizations that deploy effective data management solutions, these can successfully support the operational, analytical and decision support systems that drive businesses (IDG, November, 2012). New technologies are collecting more data than ever before, yet many organizations are still looking for better ways to obtain more value from their data and compete more effectively in the market place.

Today's computing technology is capable of processing through huge datasets that were considered impossible a few years back. Data management vendors, such as Oracle, IBM, Microsoft and Taradata, have been responding with more powerful software and hardware. Some definitions follow:

- **Databases** store data generated by business apps, sensors, and transaction processing systems (TPS).

- **Data warehouses** integrate data from multiple database and data silos and organize them for complex analysis, knowledge discovery, and to support decision making.
- **Data marts** are small-scale data warehouses that support a single function or department.
- **Business intelligence (BI)** is a term which represent tools and techniques that process data and do statistical analysis for decision support in many business and technology functions - that is, discovering meaningful relationships in the data, gaining an insight, detecting trends, and identifying opportunities and risks.
- **Big data** is a broad term for any collection of data sets that are larger and complex and are difficult to process using traditional data processing applications. It requires a knowledge of databases, quantitative analysis, and software languages and tools to utilize effectively.
- **Decision support system** is typically a computer-based system that supports business and organizational decision making. An increasing amount of data for DSS uses databases, big data and business intelligence tools and techniques.
- **Metadata** describes other data and provides information about a specific item's content. As an example, a text document's metadata may contain information about how long a document is, who the author is, when it was created, and a short summary of the document.

As data becomes more complex and the volumes explode, database performance degrades. One solution is the use of master data and master data management (MDM), defined below (Efraim Turbin, et al., 2013).

- **Master data management (MDM)** is a set of processes to integrate data from various sources or enterprise applications in order to create and maintain a more unified view of a customer, product, or other core data entity that is shared across systems. Another term that is increasingly used for MDM is **unified data management (UDM),** which also addresses the organizational component of data management (e.g. policies, procedures, responsibilities, governance and controls).
- **Master reference file and data entities.** Realistically, MDM consolidates data from various data sources into a master reference file, which then feeds data back to the applications, thereby creating accurate and consistent data across the enterprise and developing a master reference file to obtain a more unified version of the data. A master data reference file is based on data entities.

A data entity is anything real or abstract about which a company wants to collect and store data. Master data entities are the main entities of a company, such as customers, products, suppliers, employees and assets. Data management issues, opportunities, risks and strategies are covered more in depth in this chapter.

■ 9.3   CLOUD COMPUTING

In this section we define the essential cloud characteristics, service models and development models.

According to NIST, the cloud model is composed of five essential characteristics, three service models and four deployment models (Mell, Peter, et al., 2011).

9.3.1 Essential characteristics of the cloud service models and cloud development models

The essential characteristics of the cloud are:

1. **On-demand self-service** – a customer can unilaterally provision computing capabilities, such as server time and network storage, as needed, automatically without requiring human interaction with each service provider.
2. **Broad network access** – capabilities are available over a network and accessed through standard mechanisms that promote use by heterogeneous thin or thick client platforms (e.g., mobile phones, tablets, laptops, and workstations).
3. **Resources pooling** – the providers' computing resources are pooled to serve multiple customers using a multi-tenant model, with different physical and virtual resources dynamically assigned and reassigned according to customer demand. There is a sense of location independence in that the customer generally has no control or knowledge over the exact location of the provided resources but may be able to specify location at a higher level of abstraction (e.g., country, state, or data center). Examples of resources include storage, processing, memory, and network bandwidth.
4. **Rapid elasticity** – capabilities can be elastically provisioned and released, in some cases automatically, to scale rapidly outward and inward commensurate with demand. To the customers, the capabilities available for provisioning often appear to be unlimited and can be appropriated in any quantity, at any time.
5. **Measured services** – cloud systems automatically control and optimize the use of resources by leveraging a pay-per-use capability at some level appropriate to the type of service (e.g., storage, processing, bandwidth, and active user accounts). Resource usage can be monitored, controlled, and reported, providing transparency for both the provider and customer of the utilized service.

There are three types of cloud service model:

1. **Software as a Service (SaaS)** – the capability provided to the customers is to use the provider's applications running on a cloud infrastructure (the collection of hardware and software that enables the five essential characteristics of cloud computing). The applications are accessible from various client devices through either a thin client interface, such as a web browser (e.g., web-based email), or a program interface. The customer does not manage or control the underlying cloud infrastructure including network, servers, operating systems, storage, or even individual application

capabilities, with the possible exception of limited user-specific application configuration settings.

2. **Platform as a Service (PaaS)** – the capabilities provided to the customers are to deploy onto the cloud infrastructure customer-created or acquired applications that are developed using programming languages, libraries, services and tools supported by the provider. The customer does not manage or control the underlying cloud infrastructure including network, servers, operating systems, or storage, but has control over the deployment applications and possibly configuration settings for the application-hosting environment.

3. **Infrastructure as a Service (IaaS)** – the capabilities provided to the customers are to provision processing, storage, networks, and other fundamental computing resources where the customer is able to deploy and run arbitrary software, which can include operating systems applications. The customer does not manage or control the underlying cloud infrastructure but has control over operating systems, storage, and developed applications; and possibly limited control of select networking components (e.g., host firewalls).

There four types of deployment model:

1. **Private cloud** – the cloud infrastructure is provided for exclusive use by a single organization comprising multiple customers (e.g., business units). It may be owned, managed and operated by the organization, a third party, or some combination of them, and it may exist on or off premises.

2. **Community cloud** – the cloud infrastructure is provisioned for exclusive use by a specific community of constituents from organizations that have shared concerns (e.g., mission, security requirements, policy and compliance considerations). It may be owned, managed, and operated by one or more organizations in the community, a third party, or some combination of them, and it may exist on or off premises.

3. **Public cloud** – the cloud infrastructure is provisioned for open use by the general public. It may be owned, managed, and operated by a business, academic, or governmental organization, or combination of them. It exists on the premises of the cloud provider.

4. **Hybrid cloud** – the infrastructure is a composition of two or more distinct cloud infrastructures (private, community, or public) that remain unique entities, but are bound together by standardized or proprietary technology that enables data and application portability.

A number of publications exist that cover the economic aspects of cloud computing and their migration (Jothy Rosenberg, et al., 2010). In additional, the pros and cons of potential technical architectures and operating models, such as Software as a Service (SaaS), Platform as a Service (PaaS) or Infrastructure as a Service (IaaS), are available (Barrie Sosinsky, 2011). Yet, from an information security, privacy and risk perspective, as well as the type of information being processed as a part of the respective cloud service, these must be evaluated with respect to such categories as mission critical, proprietary and /or routine (not essential). A systematic approach to the information being evaluated for migration and their risks and contingencies is important.

9.3.2 Cloud management strategies and systems

According to Kravis, a key question that must be addressed in deciding on whether to pursue a cloud strategy is, "What problem are we trying to solve and what are the business drivers?". The answer is different for every company, every culture, and every architecture. For example, for start-ups, building new in the cloud is relatively easy. Understanding how to best leverage cloud services is a much more complicated decision to make in large enterprises. If one of the business drivers is to "reduce IT infrastructure costs," an established enterprise will have to evaluate every component of the existing enterprise separately to determine what should be migrated to the cloud and which deployment model (public, private, hybrid) to use for each component (Michael J. Kravis, 2014).

9.3.3 Cloud management systems

A cloud management system is a combination of software and technologies designed to manage cloud environments. The industry has responded to the management challenges of cloud computing with cloud management systems. Citrix, Eucalyptus, HP Novell, OpenNebula and others are among the vendors that have developed management systems specifically for managing cloud environments.

At a minimum, a cloud management solution should be able to manage a pool of heterogeneous computer and network resources, provide access to end users, monitor security, manage resource allocation and manage select metrics (e.g. availability, etc.) (Tom Henderson, et al., 2010).

Enterprises with large scale cloud implementations may require more robust cloud management tools that include specific characteristics, such as the ability to manage multiple platforms from a single point of reference, including intelligent analytics to automated processes like application lifecycle management. Select cloud management tools should be able to handle systems failures automatically with capabilities such as self-monitoring, an incident notification mechanism, and include self-healing capabilities. As an example, Cisco recently launched its InterCloud solution to provide flexibility to dynamically manage workloads across public and private cloud environments.

9.3.4 Cloud management strategies

Public clouds are managed by public cloud service providers, which include the public cloud environment's servers, storage, networking and data center operations. Users of public cloud services can generally select from three basic categories:
1. User self-provisioning: customers purchase cloud services directly from the provider, typically through a web form or console interface. The customer pays on a per-transaction basis.

2. Advance provisioning: customers contract in advance a predetermined amount of resources, which are prepared in advance of service. The customer pays a flat fee or a monthly fee.
3. Dynamic provisioning: the provider allocates resources when the customer needs them, then decommissions them when they are no longer needed. The customer is charged on a pay-per-use basis.

Managing a private cloud requires software tools to help create a virtualized pool of compute resources, provide a self-service portal for end user and handle security, resource allocation, tracking and billing. Management tools for private clouds tend to be service driven, as opposed to resource driven, because cloud environments are typically highly virtualized and organized in terms of portable workloads.

In hybrid cloud environments, compute, network and storage resources must be managed across multiple domains, so a good management strategy should start by defining what needs to be managed, and where and how to do it. Policies to help govern these domains should include the configuration and installation of images, access control, and budgeting and reporting (Kelly Kevin, 2010).

9.3.5 Key factors to consider when choosing a cloud service model and selecting a cloud vvendor

In this section we define the factors to consider when choosing a cloud service model.

There are many factors that must be considered in choosing the right cloud service model. One should consider the feasibility and practicability based on the following factors:

- Technical – performance, scalability, regulations, business continuity, disaster recovery, etc.
- Financial – focus on one-time migration cost, the total cost of ownership (compare non-cloud and cloud cost environments) or the monthly operating costs.
- Strategic – does the cloud provide a competitive advantage? Will the cloud reduce the time-to-market for product or systems launches?
- Organizational – do the skills reside in-house to deploy to the cloud or not? What about the areas of web development, distributed computing and service oriented architectures?
- Risk – what is the risk tolerance of the organization? How important is vendor reliability and sustainability? What about security and reliability of the cloud?
- Quality – what is the reliability of the service? What is the duration of outages and how often they occur? How quickly are they fixed on the average?

Factors to consider when selecting a cloud vendor
Key factors to consider when selecting a cloud vendor are similar to selecting sourcing vendors described in Chapter 7 of the book and include the following:

Vendor capability:
- Skills and competences;
- Certifications;
- Bench strengths;
- Financial strengths, stability and references;
- Local presence;
- Single point of contact;
- Industry/application experience.

Service delivery:
- Quality of processes, tools, resources;
- Level of performance and management depth and capabilities;
- Governance and reporting;
- Backup and recovery.

Breadth of service:
- Type and scope of services;
- Ability to scale;
- Backup, redundancy and security;
- No signal choke point;
- Change management.

Relationship management:
- Partnership, trust;
- Single point of contact;
- Local presence/executive liaison;
- Cultural fit;
- Performance track record.

Economics and contract terms:
- Pricing, volume considerations and financial structure;
- Knowledge transfer and switching costs vs. value;
- Change flexibility and parameters;
- Disputes and adjudication;
- Disengagement and divorce options.

Experience:
- Functional/industry/technical knowledge (infrastructure, data center, network, etc.);
- Application, service and technology;
- Training and currency of employees, including certifications;
- Benchmarking.

Table 9.1 provides a cloud computing plan template with key areas and questions.

Table 9.1 Cloud Computing Plan Template, Key Areas and Questions

The following is a brief list of key topics and questions to consider before migrating a service to a cloud provider. This basic framework should help an organization plan a successful migration to the cloud (Bill Williams, 2012, with modifications by the author).

1.0 Architecture
1.1 What are the critical applications that drive your business on a daily basis? What are the applications that truly create competitive advantage in the marketplace? What applications could your business not function without?
   a. Where do these applications reside?
   b. How are they tied to upstream and downstream processes?
   c. Do these applications have business continuity/impacts?
   d. How many concurrent users?
   e. How many users at peak?
1.2 Is there a virtualization program in place?
1.3 If yes, what is the current status of the migration from physical to virtual machines?
1.4 If yes, is there a disaster recovery/business continuity plan in place for virtual machines?
1.5 If no virtualization program exists today, will there be one in six months? Twelve months? Longer?

2.0 Costs
2.1 What is the IT organization's total cost of operations (TCO)?
   a. Can the TCO be broken down by service?
     – Is the storage TCO a known quantity?
     – Is the server TCO a known quantity?
     – Is the network cost a known quantity?
     – Are there other services to consider?
   b. Can the TCO be broken down by department or application?
     – Human Resources?
     – Finance?
     – Operations?
     – Others?
2.2 What is the IT headcount by function? What is the full-time equivalent (FTE) cost of each individual by service? By application?
2.3 What are the facilities costs associated with power and cooling in the data center?
2.4 Regarding the services provided by your IT organization, what are the biggest cost centers?
2.5 What software programs are currently licensed?
   a. How are these licenses provisioned?
   b. Is usage tracked and monitored?
   c. Does ample capacity exist to match current and anticipated growth rates?
   d. When do these licenses expire? When are they up for renewal?
2.6 What are the maintenance charges related to each underlying service?
   a. Storage maintenance?
   b. Server maintenance?
   c. Software maintenance?
   d. Network maintenance?
2.7 For each of the above maintenance contracts, when do they expire? When are they up for renewal?
2.8 What is the overall growth rate for each underlying service?
   a. What is the storage growth rate?
   b. What is the server growth rate?
   c. What is your data growth rate?

3.0 Growth and sustainability

1. Are growth and sustainability initiatives (for example, new product development, process innovation, R&D, etc.) underway in your organization? Are growth and sustainability initiatives an area of focus for your company?
2. If so, who are the stakeholders? How will the success of these initiatives be measured? Who is accountable?
3. Given the costs for each of the services listed previously, along with projected growth rates, is there enough data to calculate the total offsets achievable by a move to the cloud?

4.0 Quality management and process innovation

4.1 Are there quality and/or process innovation initiatives — such as Kaizen, Six Sigma, Total Quality Management (TQM) or enterprise resource management system (ERP) — currently underway inside the organization? Planned?

4.2 If so, what services are being analyzed? (List all services.)
   a. What baseline key performance indicators (KPI) are being used to measure these services?
      - Total cost of ownership (TCO)?
      - Cost per user?
      - Availability?
      - Productivity? Performance?
      - Total time to market (TTM)?
      - Quality?
      - Other?
   b. Could a move to the cloud be tied to one or more of these ongoing quality and process innovation initiatives? If so, would the same metrics be used to measure success? Are there other metrics that should be considered? If so, list them here.

4.3 If there are no quality or process innovation initiatives currently under way, what are the primary metrics and KPIs used to benchmark, measure and improve the performance of departmental services?
   a. Total cost of ownership (TCO)?
   b. Availability?
   c. Productivity?
   d. Time to market (TTM)?
   e. Capacity?
   f. Quality?
   g. Other?

4.4 What services do these KPIs measure? (List all possible services.)

4.5 What (if any) service level agreements (SLA) exist for these services?

4.6 Given the available data regarding service delivery and availability, are there obvious areas of improvement that could be addressed by moving one or more of these services to the cloud? (List all possible services and corresponding benefits.)

4.7 Are these services intimately tied to other internal upstream or downstream processes? If so, could these processes be updated to support a cloud-based architecture without major architectural overhauls?

4.8 Who are the stakeholders that would need to support moving the selected services to the cloud? How are these individuals measured? How are their goals set? Who has responsibility for setting their goals and initiatives? (List all stakeholders and their primary concerns, goals, and vested interests.)

4.9 What level of risk is each organization willing to tolerate as a team? Who has the most to gain from a move to the cloud? Who has the most to lose?

5.0 Finance

5.1. What metrics does finance use to measure project/portfolio performance?
   a. Return on investment (ROI)?
   b. Payback method?
   c. Net present value (NPV)/internal rate of return (IRR)?
   d. Are there other metrics in use? (If so, list all additional metrics.)

5.2 If one or more of the services listed previously is moved to the cloud, how will the success of the migration(s) be measured?

5.3 Will each migration be reviewed by finance after completion? If so, plan to track savings as granularly as possible and at regular intervals to demonstrate returns over time (using the above metrics).

6.0	Cloud computing
6.1	Are the services selected good candidates for migrating to a public cloud platform? Private cloud? Hybrid cloud?
6.2	Have you evaluated offerings from multiple vendors? Have you compared pricing, basic and advanced features, and service level agreements (SLA)?
6.3	Are the providers' SLAs compatible with your current business priorities? Are there other upstream or downstream processes that would be impacted by a cloud service outage?
6.4	Will the new SLAs meet or exceed current SLAs for availability, performance and so on?
6.5	Factoring in for growth, will the providers' SLAs still be acceptable one year from now? Two? If growth rates exceed your projections, will the SLAs still be sufficient, or will increases in service levels be prohibitively expensive?
6.6	What disengagement options have you considered if the cloud vendor fails?

9.3.6 Issues, threats and opportunities of cloud computing

With cloud computing, the need for a pragmatic approach is critical because the issues, risks and vulnerabilities are greater as more control and dependence is shifted from the customer to the cloud service provider. Kravis suggests that organizations should develop answers to the following questions (Kravis, 2014):

1. **Why?** What problem are we trying to solve? What are the business goals and drivers?
2. **Who?** Who needs this problem solved? Who are all the actors involved (internal/external)?
3. **What?** What are the business and technical requirements? What legal and/or regulatory constrains apply? What are the risks?
4. **Where?** Where will these services be consumed? Are there any location-specific requirements (regulations, taxes, usability concerns, language/locale issues, etc.)?
5. **When?** When are these services needed? What is the budget? Are there dependencies on other projects/initiatives?
6. **How?** How can the organization deliver these services? What is the readiness of the organization, the architecture, the customer?

After collecting the information for these questions, organizations should be in a better position to select the best service model(s) and deployment model(s) for their company. Aside from the above questions, organizations must also address threats to, and vulnerabilities of, cloud computing. Select threats are listed below:

1. Security and privacy

As cloud computing is achieving increased popularity, concerns are being voiced about the security issues introduced through adoption of this new model. Cloud computing offers many benefits, but is vulnerable to threats. As cloud computing use increases, it is likely that more criminals will find new ways to exploit system vulnerabilities. Many underlying challenges and risks in cloud computing increase the threat of data compromise. To mitigate the threats, cloud computing stakeholders should heavily invest in risk assessment to ensure that the system is protected, secured, private and redundant. The U.S. now requires cloud providers to notify customers of breaches.

2. Vendor lock-in

Many cloud platforms and services are proprietary, meaning that they are built on the specific standards, tools and protocols developed by a particular vendor for its particular cloud offering. This can make migration from a proprietary cloud platform prohibitively complicated and expensive.

Three types of lock-ins can occur with cloud computing (Mark Hinkle, 2010):

- Platform lock-in: cloud services tend to be built on one of several possible virtualization platforms, for example VMware. Migrating from a cloud provider using one platform to a cloud provider using a different platform can be very complicated.
- Data lock-in: since the cloud is still new, standards of ownership, i.e. who actually owns the data once it lives on a cloud platform, are not yet developed, which could make it complicated if cloud computing users ever decide to move data off a cloud vendor's platform.
- Tools lock-in: if tools built to manage a cloud environment are not compatible with different kinds of both virtual and physical infrastructure, those tools will only be able to manage data or apps that live in the vendor's particular cloud environment. That becomes a customer problem when disengagement options are considered.

3. IT governance

Cloud computing requires an appropriate IT governance model to ensure a secured computing environment and compliance with all relevant organizational as well as information technology policies and procedures including regulations. As such, organizations need a set of capabilities that are essential when efficiently implementing and managing cloud services, including such tasks as demand management, relationship management, data security management, risk and compliance management, incident management, appropriate metrics, back-up, recovery and others.

4. Performance interference

Due to its multi-tenant nature and resource sharing, cloud computing must also deal with the 'noisy neighbor' effect. This effect, in essence, indicates that in a shared infrastructure the activity of a virtual machine on a neighboring core on the same physical host may lead to performance degradation of the virtual cloud machine in the same physical host.

5. Legal issues

One important but not often mentioned problem with cloud computing is that of who is in 'possession' of the data. If a cloud company is the processor of the data, the processor has certain legal rights. If the cloud company is the 'custodian' of the data, then a different set of rights would apply. The next problem in the legalities of cloud computing is the problem of legal ownership of the data. Many terms of service agreements are silent on the question of ownership. The legal issues are not confined to the time period in which the cloud-based application is actively being used. There must also be considerations for what happens when the provider-customer relationship ends. In most cases, this event will be addressed before an application is developed to the cloud. However, in the case of provider insolvencies or bankruptcy, the state of the data may become blurred.

6. Privacy

The increased use of cloud computing services such as Gmail and Google Docs has highlighted the issue of privacy concerns of cloud computing services. The providers of such services are in a position such that the greater use of cloud computing services has given access to a plethora of data. This access poses the immense risk of data being disclosed either accidently or deliberately. Solutions to privacy in cloud computing include policy and legislation as well as end users choices for how data is stored and protected. The cloud service provider needs to establish clear and relevant policies that describe how the data of each cloud user will be accessed, protected, secured and backed-up.

7. Compliance

A multitude of laws and regulations have forced specific compliance requirements on many companies that collect, generate or store data. These policies may require a wide array of data storage policies, such as how long information must be retained, the process used for deleting data and even certain recovery plans. Below are some examples of compliance laws and regulations.

- In the United States, the Health Insurance Portability and Accountability (HIPPA) Act requires a contingency plan that includes data backup plans, data recovery, and data access during emergencies;
- The privacy laws of Switzerland demand that private data, including emails, be physically stored in Switzerland;
- In the United Kingdom, the Civil Contingencies Act of 2004 sets forth guidance for a business contingency plan that includes policies for data storage.

In a virtualized cloud computing environment, customers may never know exactly where their data is stored. In fact, data may be stored across multiple data centers in an effort to improve reliability, increase performance, and provide redundancies. This geographic dispersion may make it more difficult to ascertain legal jurisdiction if disputes arise (Don Chambers, 2010).

8. Disaster recovery planning

All cloud vendors should demonstrate to their customers how they would recover from natural or man-made disaster and the policies, procedures and organization responsible for the plan and corrective actions.

9.3.7 Key performance indicators and metrics for the cloud

Key performance indicators used in the cloud environment are typically service level agreements (SLAs). A service level agreement is an agreement between the cloud service provider and the cloud service customer. Depending on the service model used by the vendor (e.g. SaaS, PaaS or IaaS), the SLAs may vary. SLAs are a pledge from a service provider that specific performance metrics will be met, and a certain level of security and privacy will be upheld. The more mission-critical the service being provided, the more SLAs the cloud service provider will be required to deliver to the customers. Cloud service vendors targeting enterprise customers will usually have tight SLA requirements.

Figure 8.8 lists a wide range of metrics used to measure the major components of IT governance. The following list shows the type of metrics-based SLAs that are common in contracts between cloud providers and enterprise cloud customers as examples:
- Overall uptime of application/service/networks/servers;
- Page-load times;
- Transaction processing times;
- Reporting response times;
- Incident notification and resolution times.

From a regulatory, security, and privacy perspective, the following list shows common requirements that enterprise cloud service customer should require in contracts:
- Security and privacy safeguards;
- Published incidence response plan;
- Web vulnerability scans and reports;
- Published disaster recovery plans;
- Safe harbor agreement (e.g. regulations that protect personal data in the U.S.A. and European Union);
- Data ownership declarations (e.g. who own the data?);
- Backup and recovery processes document;
- Source code escrow;
- Penalty clauses (e.g. for poor or non-performance as well as an incident retainer [resulting from too many incidents caused by the vendor]).

Enterprise customers expect periodic (e.g. it depends on the customer's requirement) reporting of metrics-based SLAs and often request the right to perform their own annual audit to track security, regulatory, and other SLAs. A best practice is to create a document that summarizes all of the security, privacy, and regulatory controls that are in place and provide that document to customers on request. Included in that document is a list of all certifications from the various past audits, such as SSAE16 (Statement on Standard for Attestation Engagements No. 16 which applies to service organizations, replaces SAS 70 and is published by the American Institute of Certified Public Accountants), HIPAA (Health Insurance and Portability Accountability Act), and so on.

9.3.8 IT governance and monitoring considerations for cloud computing
In the book, *IT Control Objectives for Cloud Computing: Controls and Assurance in the Cloud*, released by ISACA, the authors indicate that, in order to get benefit from cloud computing initiatives, companies need to develop a clear governance strategy and

management plan that sets the direction and objectives for cloud computing (ISACA, 2011).

As discussed in Chapter 1 of this book, enterprise governance has attracted much attention worldwide and has taken center-stage across boardrooms around the world. Given the fact that cloud computing is expected to play a key role in helping organizations achieve their business objectives, it is essential to address the role of enterprise governance over cloud computing. Since cloud computing is a component of IT, effective enterprise and IT governance principles and practices must be developed and followed in a cloud computing framework.

For cloud computing, Wen-Hsi Lydia Hsu suggested an IT governance model environment to include the following elements (Wen-Hsi Lydia Hsu, 2014):

■ Appoint a board member responsible for IT and cloud computing governance to work closely with the CEO and CIO.
■ Establish a four step process to establish an effective cloud computing environment:

Step 1: Set up cloud computing policies and standards
Good standards and practices will assist cloud governance to establish cloud business objectives and risk considerations. Therefore, it is important that companies establish their cloud computing standards and policies at the very first stage. The whole procedure is a continuing process and is performed based on the framework of cloud computing standards and policies.

Step 2: Evaluating risks associated with cloud computing
To establish appropriate governance mechanisms for cloud computing, an organization should set up cloud computing policies to evaluate the risks and opportunities that cloud computing presents to their company. Organizations should ask the following questions before implementing cloud computing services:
• What level of availability does the organization expect from the cloud service?
• How are identity and access managed in the cloud?
• Where will the organization's data be located?
• What are the service provider's disaster recovery capabilities? Have they been tested? Updated?
• How is the security of the organization's data managed?
• How is the whole system protected from internet threats?
• How are activities monitored and audited?
• What type of certification or assurance can the enterprise expect from the provider?

Step 3: Involve senior management in the process of implementing the cloud computing governance model
To establish appropriate governance of cloud computing, the chief information officer (CIO) must play a significant role in supporting boards, audit committees and management to understand and implement good governance over cloud computing.

CIOs need to exercise their responsibilities of due diligence to ensure that all the criteria are met. As part of implementing cloud computing services, enterprises need to evaluate their vulnerabilities, establish threat prevention policies and technologies periodically.

Step 4: Evaluate performance

It is important to evaluate the performance of the cloud computing governance model to align with its strategic priorities. A well-designed cloud computing governance model ensures that these policies and standards are consistent with the strategy of the organization. Both performance dashboards and balanced scorecards (BSCs) can be instrumental in helping organizations communicate their strategic objectives to meet their goals or their key performance indicators (KPIs). Monitoring is a critical component of any IT governance cloud-based system. A monitoring strategy and dual responsibilities (vendor and client) should be put in place early on and continuously improved over time. There is no single monitoring tool that will meet all the needs of a cloud solution. Managing a cloud solution without a monitoring strategy is like driving down the highway at night with the lights off. One might make it home safe, but one might not!

■ 9.4   DATA MANAGEMENT

According to Efraim Turbin, et al., the data lifecycle is a model that illustrates the way data travels through an organization, as shown in Figure 9.1. The data lifecycle begins with storage in a database, to being loaded into a data warehouse for analysis, then reported to knowledge workers or used in business applications. Supply chain management (SCM), customer relationship management (CRM), engineering or product decisions

The Data Management Lifecycle uses databases, data warehouses, data mining and data analytics to provide business and technical/medical/scientific intelligence for decision support that requires IT governance policies, procedures and metrics at multiple levels.

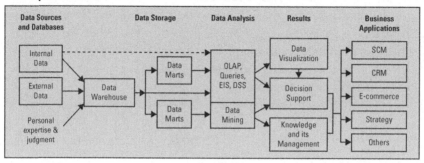

* Assumes the use of quantitative (statistical tools, modeling), tools (e.g. SAS, etc.), software skills and business intelligence (business function) knowledge.

Figure 9.1 Data management lifecycle (source: Efraim Turban, et al., 2013)

and e-commerce are enterprise applications that require up-to-date readily accessible data to function properly. Due to the many moving parts of the lifecycle, IT governance policies, procedures, processes and metrics are required to assure data accuracy, redundancy, security back-up, consistency, availability and key performance metrics.

9.4.1 Data management framework

The Data Management Association (DAMA) updated the DAMA International's Guide to the Data Management Body of Knowledge (DAMA DM-BOK Guide) in 2014. It is a collection of processes and knowledge areas that are generally accepted as best practices within the data management discipline. According to DAMA, data management is a broad term that describes the processes used to plan, specify, enable, create, acquire, maintain, use, archive, retrieve, control, and purge data. These processes overlap and interact within each data management knowledge area.

Figure 9.2 represents the DAMA DM-BOK2 Guide to the data management knowledge area. It is interesting to note that all of the eleven (11) knowledge areas include and connect to the data governance knowledge area.

Data Management Knowledge Areas: 2013 – all knowledge areas connect to data governance

Figure 9.2 The DAMA DM-BOK2 Guide - Knowledge Wheel (source: DAMA International, 2013)

The DAMA DM-BOK Guide provides guidelines and capability maturity models for the standardization of:
- Activities, processes, and best practices;
- Roles and responsibilities;

- Deliverables and metrics;
- A maturity model.

The DAMA DM-BOK Guide knowledge areas include:

- Data Governance – planning, oversight and control over management of data, and the use of data and data-related resources policies, processes and responsibilities;
- Data Architecture – the overall structure of data and data-related resources as an integral part of the enterprise architecture;
- Data Model and Design – analysis, design, building, testing and maintenance;
- Data Storage and Operations – structure physical data storage deployment and management;
- Data Security – ensuring privacy, confidentiality and appropriate access;
- Data Integration and Interoperability – acquisition, extraction, transformation, movement, delivery, replication, federation, virtualization and support;
- Documents and Contents – sorting, protecting, indexing, and enabling to data found in unstructured sources (electronic files and physical records), and making this data available for integration and interoperability with structured (database) data;
- Reference and Master Data – managing shared data to reduce redundancy and ensure better data quality through standardized definition and use of data values;
- Data Warehousing and Business Intelligence – managing analytical data processing and enabling access to decision support data for reporting and analysis;
- Metadata – collecting, categorizing, integrating, controlling, managing, and delivering metadata;
- Data Quality – defining, monitoring, maintaining data integrity and improving data quality.

Since data governance, as a part of IT governance, is our focus, the following data governance knowledge area topics are planned to be covered in detail in the second edition of the DAMA DM-BOK2 Guide, scheduled for release in 2015 by DAMA:

Section 1 – Data Governance
- Data governance – provides oversight for all data management, moving towards a unified theory of data management strategy and control;
- Stewardship and ownership – (Who owns the data? Who manages the data? Who is responsible for data accuracy, security, privacy, access, etc.?);
- Data valuation return on investment;
- Data governance and governance sector;
- Institutionalizing data governance;
- Governance repository.

Section 2 – Overall Data Management Maturity Model
- Maturity benchmarking;
- Maturity development (targets and activities);
- Data audits.

Section 3 – Business Cultural Development
- Explaining relationships between business process, data models, and databases;
- SDLC incorporated in various methodologies such as Waterfall and Agile;
- Change management;
- Communication challenges.

Section 4 – Data in Cloud
- Data protection;
- Data models.

Section 5 – Ethics
- Integrity;
- Privacy protection.

In 2011, the National Oceanic and Atmospheric Administration, part of the U.S. Department of Commerce, developed a template to assist data manager planners to develop a data management plan for any organization identifying key areas and related questions. Table 9.2 represents this template.

Table 9.2 Data Management Plan Template, Key Areas and Questions

This template is provided as an example to assist data management plan developers. It was developed by the U.S. Department of Commerce National Oceanic and Atmospheric Administration in 2011.

1.0 General description of data to be managed
1.1 Name of the dataset or data collection project.
1.2 Keywords that could be used to characterize the data, and vocabulary from which those keywords were obtained.
1.3 Summary description of the data to be generated.
1.4 What data types will you be creating or capturing? (e.g., digital numeric data, photographs, video, database tables, spreadsheets, paper records, physical samples, etc.).
1.5 How will you capture or create the data? (e.g., satellite, airplane, manual surveys, database, etc.).
1.6 Where will this data be stored electronically, in what repository?
1.7 What volume of the data is anticipated to be collected in the project time frame?
1.8 Will the data contain personally identifiable information or any information whose distribution may be restricted by law, company policy, privacy, or national security?

2.0 Points of contact
2.1 Who can, or could, represent this data collection project on an organization's data management integration team (DMIT)?
2.2 Who is the overall point of contact for the data collection?
2.3 Who is responsible for verifying the quality of the data?
2.4 Who is responsible for answering questions about the data collection?
2.5 Who is responsible for data documentation and metadata activities?

2.6 Who is responsible for the data storage and data disaster recovery activities?
2.7 Who is responsible for ensuring adherence to this data management plan, including ensuring that appropriate resources are available to implement the data management plan?
2.8 Who is responsible for establishing and enforcing the data access and privacy policy and procedures?

3.0 Data stewardship
3.1 Have data stewards been appointed across the organization to approve data formats, data dictionaries and access rules (who can access what data)?
3.2 What quality control procedure will be employed?
3.3 What is the overall lifecycle of the data from collection or acquisition to making it available to customers and finally, to retire the data or archive the data?
3.4 Who has final authority on resolving data management issues?

4.0 Data documentation
4.1 Which metadata repository will be used to document this data collection?
4.2 In addition to discovery-level metadata, what additional metadata or other documentation is necessary to fully describe the data and ensure its long-term usefulness? How will that metadata be collected and updated? Is there a requirement to document this data collection in other metadata repositories?
4.3 What standards will be used to represent data and metadata elements in this data collection? (e.g. ISO 19115-1:2014 (Metadata for geographic information) and related standards for data documentation).

5.0 Data sharing
5.1 Will the data be made available to the customer? If so, what is the expected date of first availability? Is this a one-time data collection, or an ongoing series?
5.2 Will users be subject to any access conditions or restrictions, such as submission of non-disclosure statements, special authorization or acceptance of a licensing agreement?
5.3 What data access protocols will be used to enable data sharing?
5.4 In what catalogs will these services or data be registered to enable discovery by users?

6.0 Initial data storage and protection
6.1 Where and how will the data be stored initially (i.e., prior to being sent to a long-term archive facility)?
6.2 How will the data be protected from accidental or malicious modification or deletion? Discuss data security back-up, disaster recovery/contingency planning, and off-site storage relevant to the data collection.
6.3 If there is to be any limitation to data access, how will this data be protected from unauthorized access? How will access permission be managed? What process is to be followed in the event of unauthorized access?

7.0 Long-term archiving and Preservation
7.1 In what data center will the data be archived and preserved? Have you begun discussions with that data center regarding your intended submission?
7.2 If you have not identified a data center, what is your long-term strategy for maintaining and archiving the data?
7.3 How will the costs of long-term data archiving be provided and maintained?
7.4 What transformations or procedures will be necessary to prepare data for preservation or sharing (e.g., quality control, format conversion, etc.)? What related information will be submitted to the archive to enable the future use and understanding of the data (e.g., metadata, references, reports, research papers, algorithms, special character sets or fonts, etc.)?

9.4.2 Unified data management and IT governance

According to Philip Russom, in many organizations today data and other information are managed in isolated silos by independent teams using various data management tools for data quality, data integration, data governance and stewardship, metadata and master data management, content management, database administration and architecture, and so on. In response to this situation, some organizations are adopting unified data management (UDM), a practice that holistically coordinates teams and integrates tools. Other common names for this practice include enterprise data management, enterprise information management and master data management. Regardless of what you call it, the 'big picture' that results from bringing diverse data disciplines together yields several benefits, such as cross-system data standards, cross-tool architectures, cross-team design and development synergies, leveraging data as an organizational asset, and assuring data's integrity and lineage as it travels across multiple organizations and technology platforms (Russom, 2010). UDM helps to create greater interoperability of data management within an organization and facilitates more effective data and IT governance.

9.4.3 Big data and analytics

The term big data refers to a deluge of information that is generated every second through a myriad of digital devices that record and practically dictate the patterns of one's personal or professional lives. The amount of data generated each day is so huge that an exact quantification is difficult. What is known is that is very 'big' and the sharing of information created by computers and then used by another set of computers continues to grow at an unprecedented and unimagined pace. The real challenge lies not in the availability of data, but in extracting useful knowledge effectively.

Businesses are interested in big data because they can reveal more patterns and interesting trends than smaller data sets, with the potential to provide new insights into customer behavior, weather patterns, financial market activity, or other phenomena. However, to derive business value from this data, organizations need new technologies and tools capable of managing and analyzing non-traditional data along with their traditional enterprise data. That is called information analytics which is part of business intelligence and decision support systems. A contemporary infrastructure for business intelligence has an array of tools for obtaining useful information from all the different types of data. These capabilities include data warehouses and data marts, analytical platforms, statistic and quantitative methods, software tools like SQL, SAS, Cognos, JavaScript, DBMS and others. Analytics using big data is just another way of looking at data and it should be treated as such. The urgency to implement a big data program should not trump the rationality for initiating the program in the first place. The business problem/enhancement on hand, the suitability and practically of solving the problem with a big data initiative and the expected return on investment (ROI) should be explicitly documented, agreed upon and approved. At a minimum, the following questions should be answered factually:

- What is the problem/objective of the big data and analytics project?
- Why does one think it can be solved using big data and analytics?
- When will the anticipated ROI be realized?
- Who are the team members? The individuals involved in the big data and analytics should have characteristics of embracing change, being receptive to emerging technologies and have a fondness for data manipulation.

- How will the different organizational units (e.g., IT, business, research) collaborate on the project and how will one know that one has reached the goal?
- What metrics will be used?
- How will IT be managed? Controlled? Monitored? Secured?

9.4.4 Challenges of data management

Often, enterprises tend to overlook the importance of having the right management and specialized skills required to get the most out of the data, such as a chief data executive, information architects and data scientists. Without a collaborative, well-thought-out approach, enterprises rush to deploy technology without fully understanding the goals, or requirements, or scope. As a result, they end up limiting the value of data management solutions and diminishing the impact that data-driven decisions can have on the business. Other obstacles faced when developing a unified data management strategy, as highlighted by an IDG survey, include (IDG, 2012):

- Complex and numerous data sources;
- Lack of an enterprise-wide, unified view of data;
- No formal data governance in place;
- Unclear roles/responsibilities for data management;
- Overlapping or competing data management processes;
- Lack of data integration or interoperability strategy;
- Inability to perform searches across multiple data silos.

When survey respondents attempted to address data management issues by implementing a solution, they have encountered the following stumbling blocks:

- Internal politics and ownership of data;
- No available budget to invest in a solution;
- Value of data management is unclear to executive and/or line of business decision makers;
- Insufficient infrastructure or tools in place to integrate a data management solution;
- No demand for a solution from the business;
- No overarching data management strategy exists to guide technology decisions;
- Concerns regarding user adoption and training needs;
- Limited data governance considerations;
- Insufficient people skills trained in the field.

Another important challenge in data management is to assure that the quality of the data is complete, reliable, validated, timely, accurate and not duplicated. Data quality management is a constant challenge and requires the highest business and IT collaboration. IT must work with the business to clear these hurdles and gain executive-level support and funding. Enterprises benefit most when they develop a comprehensive roadmap for their data management strategy that aligns with the business.

9.4.5 Data stewardship and data consistency across an enterprise

According to Robert Seiner, one of the critical success factors for improved information-based capabilities is the standardization and consistent use of data across the enterprise. This long-term value of the consistency in enterprise data will only be achieved through incremental improvements in data standardization, a process that must be guided by individuals who know the business and the data – namely the data stewards (Robert Seiner, 2004). Data steward roles are strongly aligned with the development of enterprise data standards that will lead to improved information-based capabilities. Data stewards role vary depending on their focus as follows:

- Data definition stewards (data definers) play a critical role in defining the data that is required to operate their business and to maintain the values and consistency of this data across the enterprise. Data definers are also responsible for identifying and leveraging existing data resources prior to creating new data and documenting the business definitions/descriptions of the data they need and their related values.
- Data production stewards (data producers) are accountable for making certain that all data is created in – or passed into – information systems, and complies with the standards set forth by the data definers.
- Data usage stewards (data users) are responsibly for understanding the data and the values of the data, and using the data for its intended purposes.

The responsibility to accept, propagate and comply with enterprise data standards is the primary responsibility of all data stewards.

Enterprise data management functions often measure the performance of the data stewardship program using two primary methods:
1. Business value measures (long-term) and
2. Acceptability and compliance measures (immediately measurable).

Business value measures directly attribute business values to the implementation of the data stewardship program, data standardization and improved data management discipline. In the private sector, business value is most often measured by increasing revenue and profitability, along with reductions in cost and improvements in productivity. In the public sector, only some of these types of business value measures are relevant, while others may require customization for not-for-profit businesses.

The business value measures are only examples of how the standardization of data through the implementation of the data administration discipline and the data stewardship program can result in new business capability and value. The ability to quantify these types of business measures will depend on the enterprise's ability to associate improved business decision making with increases in revenue/income, reduction in costs and improvements in productivity.

The second type of data stewardship performance measurements are called acceptability and compliance measures, which are ways to directly evaluate and measure the level of adoption of enterprise data standards and the data stewardship program. Sample measures in terms of quantifiable acceptability and compliance include:

■ Percentage/number of departments where a data standard (for a specific piece of data or data element) is accepted;
■ Percentage/number of information systems data elements that share a data standard;
■ Percentage/number of business processes that utilize a data standard;
■ Percentage/number of production reports (output) that utilize a data standard;
■ Percentage/number of people that use data standard elements;
■ Percentage/number of integrated business processes.

A strong commitment to enterprise standardization of data and recognition of the impact that standards have on improved information-based capabilities will allow the enterprise to successfully measure the business value of data stewardship stated earlier in this book.

9.4.6 Data governance and its relationship to IT governance

As previously discussed, high quality data is a key source of business value, but data quality issues in organizations are often addressed inadequately and inappropriately. Data governance policies, procedures and process are essential.

Data governance is the process of creating oversight, accountability and stewardship for your data assets. A multi-disciplinary framework that brings together multiple stakeholders (e.g. users of information, managers of information and executives) are important elements of creating an enterprise-wide approach.

Strong data governance addresses data quality, creation, maintenance, policies, procedures, compliance, validation, and risk management – and requires a true culture change to create enterprise-level information strategies. A data governance strategy must also be flexible since information needs are evolving rapidly. The skills needed to convert growing data sets into useable information continue to evolve as organizations migrate from data silos to shared actionable information environments.

In his book on *Enterprise Data Governance*, Pierre Bonnet identified the following enterprise data functions that should be part of any enterprise data governance strategy:

■ Ergonomics – unified interface for all data repositories.
■ Version management and control – creation of a version of that data, for example the description of a product. Automatic detection of the difference between versions and the possibility of merging the data from one version to another, once the versions are validated.

- The initialization and update of data depending on use context – different enrichment of data depending on the context in which it is used as, for example, multi-language, multi-channel, geographical sectors, etc. The use contexts are created by the business users of the data system who have the appropriate rights, without modification of the data model.
- Management of concepts related to time – the management of data history, definition of period of validity applied to data, data purging cycle etc.
- Validation rules – checking that any update on data is in line with validation rules. This function of governance is very important as it ensures the integrity and quality of the reference and master data.
- Data approval – co-ordination between users involved in the update of data. This relates to a workflow with a task list by user and often includes a data steward.
- Permission management – definitions of read only and update rights on data. These rights relate to a subset of data, data elements and use cases. A function allows the delegation of these rights to the user in a collaborative way of working, for example between head office and subsidiaries.
- Data hierarchy – automatic examination of the data model to compute the links dependencies between the business objects and data hierarchy management.

Data governance is a critical component of IT governance and enterprise governance, and should follow a flexible, but disciplined framework including policies, procedures, processes and metrics unique to data management but include the IT governance best practices described throughout this book.

9.5   CASE STUDY – MAJOR INSURANCE AND REINSURANCE COMPANY

Figure 9.3 illustrates a case of a major insurance/reinsurance company. The case highlights the importance of data governance, IT security and the growing use of cloud computing.

Environment & Drivers	Approach
• Revenue range (operating net income) range – $900 million - $1.1 billion • Number of employees – range – 3,000 - 5,000 • Industry classification - midsize insurance company • Products/services – property and casualty insurance • Management philosophy – conservative but innovative • Number of countries with operations/sales offices – 130 - 150 • Number of full time IT professionals/range – 500 - 800 • IT organization – decentralized with corporate CIO, shared services CIO and business unit CIOs • Corporate CIO reports to CFO	– Due to a decentralized organization, all CIO's (corporate, business units and shared services (infrastructure such as networks, email, server farms, etc.) meet weekly to discuss any enterprise-wide issues, technologies and common processes – The CIOs follow the 'Principles of IT', which focus on aligning business and IT (e.g. buy before build, internal sharing of best practices, etc.) – Technical standards committee coordinated by architecture group focus on recommending common systems and tools across business (e.g. Microsoft e-mail; Oracle, reporting tools, documentation) – An IT unit, aligned to a business risk management unit, together assess operating risks and develop contingency plans. – An internal audit committee conducts high impact business/IT project reviews, and ensures compliance to standards, controls and regulations

Figure 9.3 Case study – major insurance/reinsurance company

Issues	Results – Alignment (Business/ IT)
– Issues: data governance is a key issue which is in-process of being institutionalized across the enterprise via the establishment of a new business data management organization (responsible for enterprise data mastering, data conformance across multiple source systems, change control, etc.) – Security: IT security, creating awareness and establishing an IT security policy, procedures and guidelines which have been implemented (updated yearly and rolled out with yearly awareness training) and are being improved based upon ISO 27001:2013 - Information Technology Security Guidelines – To finalize "data penetration and protection" testing processes and controls. All enterprise systems and especially those that are either (a) externally-facing or (b) hosted externally to company's data center have to comply with security standards which include external penetration tests that are conducted by a third party on the company's behalf. Data protection, both confidential data and private data, is held to high standards such that certain contractual terms are built into external service provider agreements to ensure data protection and minimize the company's liability (penalty clauses with x times contract costs applied to vendors)	• Annually, IT strategic plans are developed in parallel with each business unit and corporate staff functions from June to October focusing on: – Existing and installed base (keeping lights ON) – Budget – capital and expense – Company-wide (enterprise- wide) and business unit projects • A uniform portfolio investment management system is used to prioritize and approve IT projects and budgets. The enterprise infrastructure projects have to be agreed by all CIOs as their budgets get charged back to the business and CIOs need to be in agreement on them. There is a degree of autonomy provided to each business segment such that the insurance business decide how they want to spend their discretionary budget alone with input from reinsurance and vice versa since each business will be charged directly for their discretionary projects. Guidance is provided overall as to what the company believes it can afford in terms of its last year's performance
Results - Program/Project/Portfolio Management	**Results - Performance Management**
• PMO Office develops standards, processes all PM training requirements and tracks key projects, Company has found it more beneficial to have a PMO operation per business and corporate function, which then sometimes needs to be summarized for CEO review at periods throughout the year • Use a blend of industry and tailored PM processes, technologies, metrics and tools. Company focuses hard on providing (a) a business perspective to project management (success criteria, benefits provided by milestone, business sponsor and governance, budget to actual) and also a risk management approach to project management (track key risks & issues from the start with mitigation plans for each) • Use traditional SDLC and PM processes including charter, business case, etc • Implementing a quasi-AgilePM methodology that includes iterative design and build phases (to fast track select projects). Company's preference is incremental implementation in order to show progress and gain early benefits	• From IT to executive management and users: – Monthly summary (two lines) developed for each major project that includes: deliverables, budget/actual/variances, major issues, risks and recommended resolutions – the key to write this in business language! – Monthly status reports distributed to CIO and users on major projects measuring progress to date and budget/actual to date and it also includes a risk management current status assessment. These reports use a RAG (Red, Amber and Green color code) to report on the status of a project • Company also have a business sponsor, business owner and governance structure for large projects which requires formal project status (milestones, budget tracking, resources, risks/ issues, etc.) • Within the IT function: – One-on-one meetings held between CIO and each direct report at bi-weekly meetings to review progress, issues, risks and budgets

Figure 9.3 Case study – major insurance/reinsurance company (continued)

Results - IT Service Management (Includes ITIL)	Results – Cloud Computing and Data Management

• Shared (infrastructure) services use ITIL processes and metrics in the IT operations
• ITIL does not provide an end-to-end view of the service delivery process (a deficiency in the ITIL framework according to the company) as it seems to organize infrastructure skill-sets and processes into silo's by their technology domain (network, operating system, maintenance, etc.)
	• Cloud computing:
	   – CIO steering committee – completed education on cloud computing for IT group education (Gartner and Chief Enterprise Architecture) covering topics such as: privacy, security, liability (3rd party), backup and disaster recovery, vendor availability of data (24/7), penalty of breach with vendor, metrics – SLAs (24/7 availability; outage delays, other)
	   – Select cloud applications are being implemented – note some external vendors are pushing clients towards the cloud (Oracle's new HR Fusion system is an example)
	• Data management:
	   – Company has a standardized chart of accounts, implemented on a single general ledger system
	   – Where possible, company has standardized from many of the same types system (from acquisitions!) to a single version of the same system
	   – Company's insurance business has multiple insurance source systems (very expensive to rationalize them) hence the strategy is to conform the data to support a single set of backend processes for finance, actuarial, enterprise risk management, etc. (example of conformance is to standardize all legal entity names centrally and then push this list as changes occur to those systems that need to use it)
	   – Data stewards (work together) across businesses –to approve data formats, data dictionaries and access rules (who can access what data)

Results– Strategic Sourcing and Outsourcing	**Lessons Learned**

• Use a centralized procurement function (centralized to achieve economies of scale across all of IT)
• A formal sourcing process is implemented
• Two levels of outsourcing partners are contracted:
   – Two to three vendors (off-shore) are contracted to provide commodity services such as development services and managed services (e.g. Sequel Server, maintenance, etc.). Vendors in this space might be TCS, Infosys, Cognizant, HCL
   – Strategic professional services vendors are used for strategy, architectural initiatives or researching new technology trends (e.g. IBM, Ernst and Young, Deloitte, etc.)
   – The Gartner Quadrant is used to help identify vendors
	• IT governance cannot be bureaucratic, it must provide business value. It is a means to an end, not the end itself
	• IT governance must be reevaluated periodically to make sure it is not rigid, remains flexible and is continuously improved…..and to ensure that it is aligned to the business organization (sometimes IT governance can go stale and fall behind how the business is operating and then IT fails!). There is no right or wrong on how IT governance is setup, but what is important is that it fits with the business organization and culture
	• The business needs to understand something about IT governance in order to be able to work with it. So, ensure that it is explained and expressed in such a way that they will embrace it and help to make it successful and part of their team

Critical Success Factors	
• Business/IT alignment – a strong relationship between the business and IT is necessary and is characterized by active, frequent, real and meaningful discussions and exchange of information. In many industries where IT is not the business product of the company, but more of an enabler of the business, then it is incumbent upon IT technicians and professionals to learn as much about the business as possible….to help bridge the IT/business relationship gap • IT should always seek to offer options to the business when trying to provide solutions, let the business weigh in heavily on the decision but give them full visibility to the benefits, costs, or risks that they might be willing to take in order to get a product to market sooner! • Right team and culture that encourages team work across IT – it's all about the business! Even when IT solves a major issue, give credit to the business as much and as often as possible, things like that convey to business that IT understands business importance • Flexible and agile processes are important (e.g. PM, ITIL, security, privacy, etc.) • Well-defined and uniform metrics for reporting progress help with full visibility to the business and in words & actions that they understand	

Figure 9.4 Case study – major insurance/reinsurance company (continued)

■ 9.6   SUMMARY AND KEY TAKE AWAYS

9.6.1 Summary

Both cloud computing and data management have become growing and important components of IT governance.

Cloud computing

The cloud computing model is composed of five essential characteristics, three service models and four deployment models. There are many factors that must be considered in choosing the right cloud service model. One should consider the feasibility and practicability based on the following factors:

- ■ Technical – performance, scalability, regulations, business continuity, disaster recovery, etc.
- ■ Financial – focus on one-time migration cost, the total cost of ownership (compare non-cloud and cloud cost environments) or the monthly operating costs.
- ■ Strategic – does the cloud provide a competitive advantage? Will the cloud reduce the time-to-market for product or systems launches?
- ■ Organizational – do the skills reside in-house to deploy to the cloud or not? What about the areas of web development, distributed computing and service oriented architectures?
- ■ Risk – what is the risk tolerance of the organization? How important is vendor reliability and sustainability? What about security and reliability of the cloud?
- ■ Quality – what is the reliability of the service? What is the duration of outages and how often they occur? How quickly are they fixed on the average?

Data management

There are eleven knowledge areas in data management as follows:

1. Data governance – planning, oversight, and control over the management of data and the use of data and data-related resources policies, processes and responsibilities.
2. Data architecture – the overall structure of data and data-related resources as an integral part of the enterprise architecture.
3. Data model and design – analysis, design, building and testing.
4. Data storage and operations – structure of the physical data storage deployment and associated management.
5. Data security – ensuring privacy, confidentiality and appropriate access.
6. Data integration and interoperability – acquisition, extraction, transformation, movement, delivery, replication, federation, virtualization and support.
7. Documents and contents – sorting, protecting, indexing, and enabling data to be found in unstructured sources (electronic files and physical records), and making this data available for integration and interoperability with structured (database) data.
8. Reference and master data – managing shared data to reduce redundancy and ensure better data quality through standardized definitions and use of data values.

9. Data warehousing and business intelligence – managing analytical data processing and enabling access to decision support data for reporting and analysis.
10. Metadata – collecting, categorizing, integrating, controlling, managing and delivering metadata.
11. Data quality – defining, monitoring, maintaining data integrity and improving data quality.

9.6.2 Key take aways

Key take aways for cloud computing and data management are:

- There must be dedicated and available resources for each component;
- Organization must develop action plans and strategies for cloud computing and data management governance, identify deliverables, establish priorities, justify returns on investments, allocate resources and measure progress;
- Issues of security, privacy, access, back-up and recovery, ownership of data and related topics must be addressed;
- Data stewards are important for enterprise data management inter-operability, consistency and accuracy;
- Cloud computing is a form of strategic sourcing and outsourcing, and should be managed accordingly with current and emerging best practices of vendor management, control and measurement.

10 Summary, Lessons Learned, Critical Success Factors & Future Challenges

"For to win one hundred victories in one hundred battles is not the Acme of skill. To subdue the enemy without fighting is the Acme of skill."

Sun Tzu (Chinese general, c. 500 b.Chr.), The Art of War

10.1 WHAT IS COVERED IN THIS CHAPTER?

- Identifies the steps necessary to make IT governance real and sustainable;
- Provides a composite master checklist (selected from all of the chapters) of the activities and tasks required to implement and sustain successful IT governance and its major components;
- Covers the lessons learned and critical success factors from current and emerging best practice organizations;
- Raises future challenges to IT governance.

10.2 MIGRATION PLAN FOR MAKING IT GOVERNANCE REAL AND SUSTAINABLE

IT is an integral part of the business, therefore IT governance must be an integral part of enterprise governance. The following actions are required to achieve a migration to higher levels of IT governance effectiveness and maturity:

- There must be a corporate mandate from the top – the board and the executive team (including the CEO and CIO) are committed to implementing and sustaining a robust governance environment.
- There must be dedicated and available resources – identify executive champion and multi-disciplinary team (to focus on each IT governance component).
- Executives must do homework – educate on past, current and emerging best practices.
- Executives must market the IT governance value propositions and benefits to the organization – develop and conduct a communications, awareness and public relations campaign.

■ An assessment of the 'current state' of the level of IT governance maturity, or other frameworks that relate to specific IT governance components such as business/IT alignment and planning, project management, maturity model (e.g. CMMI), IT governance for vendor management (eSCM), performance management (balanced scorecard), data management, IT service management and others, as a reference base (where are we today?), using a leading industry best practice framework such as CMMI or COBIT®, or a combination of frameworks that may apply to a specific component of IT governance.

■ There must be a 'future state' IT governance blueprint (where you want to be) developed and kept in focus.

■ There should be an activity to decompose the IT governance components into well-defined work packages (assign an owner and champion to each process component).

■ A tailored IT governance framework and roadmap must be developed for the organization based on current and emerging industry best practices.

■ Executives must develop an IT governance action plan, identify deliverables, establish priorities and milestones, allocate resources and measure progress.

■ The organization should sponsor organizational and individual certifications in the IT governance component areas, where they are available.

■ There must be activities to identify enabling technologies to support the IT governance initiative.

■ There should be a 'web portal' established to access IT governance policies, processes, information, communications and provide support.

■ Celebrate wins.

■ Plan for, and sustain, IT governance process improvements and link to a reward and incentive structure. Create a 'Continuous IT Governance Improvement' group to sustain the framework.

■ Don't focus on specific ROI as a measure of success - use TCO (total cost of operations) and business innovation and transformation metrics as measures of improvement.

■ 10.3 COMPOSITE CHECKLIST FOR IMPLEMENTING AND SUSTAINING SUCCESSFUL IT GOVERNANCE IN ORGANIZATIONS

This section provides a composite checklist of select best practices identified in the chapters of the book by chapter. It is intended to remind practitioners of the 'must do's' and brings together every critical aspect relating to IT governance in one convenient checklist to help the board, executive management and most of all, CIO's and IT professionals, think through what has worked, what can work and how to deploy IT governance successfully.

Chapter 1 – Introduction and Executive Overview

Summary of key strategic, value enhancing and execution questions:

The strategic questions are: Is the right thing being done? Is the investment in IT:
- In line with business vision and strategy?
- Consistent with business principles, plan and direction?
- Contributing to strategic objectives, sustainable competitive differentiation and business continuity support?
- Providing optimum value at an acceptable level of risk?
- Representing a long term view (roadmap)?
- Including an architectural roadmap based on a detailed analysis of the current state or condition of IT?
- Addressing the value questions – are the benefits being realized?
- Delivering a clear and shared understanding and commitment to achieve the expected benefits?
- Achieving clear accountability for achieving the benefits which should be linked to MBOs and incentive compensation schemes for individuals and business units or functional areas?
- Based on relevant and meaningful metrics?
- Based on a consistent benefits realization process and sign-off?
- Considering the execution questions – is the deployment successful and effective? How are results measured?
- Scalable, disciplined and with consistent management, governance and delivery processes together with validation steps?
- Utilizing appropriate and sufficient resources available with the right competencies?
- Using a consistent set of metrics linked to critical success factors and realistic key performance indicators (KPIs)?
- Addressing succession planning?

Purpose and Scope of IT Governance

Purpose of IT governance
The purpose of IT governance is to:
- Align IT investments and priorities more closely with the business.
- Manage, evaluate, prioritize, fund, measure and monitor requests for IT services and the resulting work and deliverables, in a more consistent and repeatable manner that optimize returns to the business.
- Ensure the eresponsible utilization of resources and assets.
- Establish and clarify accountability and decision rights (clearly defines roles and authority).
- Ensure that IT delivers on its plans, budgets and commitments.
- Manage major risks, threats, change and contingencies proactively.

- Improve IT organizational performance, compliance, maturity, staff development and outsourcing initiatives.
- Improve the response to the voice of the customer (VOC), demand management and overall customer and constituent satisfaction and responsiveness.
- Manage and think globally, but act locally.
- Champion innovation within the IT function and business.

Scope of IT Governance

Key IT governance strategy and resource decisions must address the following topics:

- **IT principles** – high level statements about how IT is used in the business (e.g. scale, simplify and integrate; reduce TCO (Total Cost of Operations) and self-fund by re-investing savings; invest in customer facing systems; transform business and IT through business process transformation; strategic plan directions, PMO (Project Management Office), sustain compliance and other regulatory compliance, etc.).
- **IT architecture** – organizing logic for data, including data management, applications and infrastructure (including cloud computing) captured in a set of policies, relationships, processes, standards and technical choices to achieve desired business and technical integration and to facilitate inter-operability.
- **SOA architecture** – service oriented architecture (SOA) is a business-centric IT architectural approach that supports the integration of the business as linked, repeatable business tasks or services. SOA helps users build composite applications that draw upon functionality from multiple sources within and beyond the enterprise to support business processes.
- **IT infrastructure, security and privacy** – centrally coordinated, based on shared IT services that provide the foundation for the enterprise's IT capability, support and security.
- **Business application needs** – specifying the business need for purchased or internally developed IT applications.
- **IT investment and prioritization** – decisions about how much and where to invest in IT (e.g. capital and expense), including development and maintenance projects, infrastructure, security, people, etc.
- **People (human capital) development** – decisions about how to develop and maintain global IT leadership, management and technical competences (e.g. how much and where to spend on training and development, industry certifications, etc.).
- **IT governance policies, processes, mechanisms, tools and metrics** – decisions on the composition and roles of steering groups, advisory councils, technical and architecture working committees, project teams; key performance indicators (KPIs); chargeback alternatives; performance reporting, meaningful audit process and the need to have a business owner for each project and investment.

We have defined three critical pillars of effective IT governance:

- **Leadership, organization and decision rights** – defines the organization structure, roles and responsibilities, decision rights (decision influencers and makers), a shared vision and interface/integration touch points and champions for proactive change.
- **Flexible and scalable processes** – the IT governance framework places a heavy emphasis on the importance of process transformation and improvement (e.g. planning, project management, portfolio investment management, risk management, IT service management and delivery, performance management, vendor management, controls and audits, etc.).
- **Enabling technology** – leverage leading tools and technologies that support the major IT governance components.

If any one of the above pillars is missing or ineffective, the IT governance initiative will not be effective or sustainable. In addition, over-dependence on one dimension at the expense of the others will result in sub-optimal performance.

Chapter 2 – Blended IT Governance Framework

Grounded in industry best practice research and required to plan, develop, deploy and sustain a cost effective approach to IT governance, the blended and integrated governance framework consists of five (5) critical IT governance imperatives (which leverage best practice models described in the chapter and are 'must do's') addressing the following work areas:

- **Business strategy, plan and objectives (demand management)** – this involves the development of the business strategy and plan which should drive the IT strategy and plan.
- **IT strategy, plan and objectives (demand management)** – this should be based on the business plan and objectives and will provide the direction and priorities of the IT functions and resources. This should also include portfolio investment management investments and a prioritization scheme, and identify the decision rights (who influences decisions and who is authorized to make the decisions) on a wide variety of IT areas. In addition, the CIO is responsible for the infrastructure investment for such items as capacity planning availability management, security management and related areas.
- **IT plan execution (execution management)** – this encompasses the processes of program and project management, IT service management and delivery (including ITIL – IT Infrastructure Library), risk and threat management, change management, security, privacy, contingency and back-up plans and others.
- **Performance management and management controls (execution management)** – this includes such areas as the balanced scorecard, key performance indicators, COBIT and regulatory compliance areas.
- **Vendor management and outsourcing management (execution management)** – since companies are increasing their outsourcing spending, selecting and managing the vendors and their deliverables has become critical.

▣ **People development, continuous process improvement and learning** – it is vital to invest in people and knowledge management, and sustain continuous process improvement and innovation initiatives, as well as developing and updating leadership, management and key technical personnel succession plans.

An organization should leverage, adopt and tailor those models, frameworks and/or standards that address the issues, opportunities, pain points and threats most critical to the organization and create an IT governance roadmap with clearly defined roles and responsibilities for IT governance development, process ownership and continuous improvement. The selection of a particular framework or combination of frameworks is largely dependent on the strategic objectives, the available resources of an organization and their desired outcomes. All of the frameworks require varying degrees of managing change and cultural transformation.

Chapter 3 – Business/IT Alignment, Strategic/Operational Planning and Portfolio Investment Management

There are several strategic planning, management control and supplementary principles and practices that, when deployed well, will improve the business and IT alignment environment. They include, but are not limited to, the following:

Strategic planning practices:

This process should be a formal process developed as a partnership and contract (in the loose definition of the word) between the business and IT. It should clearly focus on defining and relating the value that IT provides in support of the business. Specific planning principles and practices should be deployed such as (Selig, 1983):

▣ **Strategic planning program and processes** – develop a strategic IT plan that is an integral part of the strategic business plan. The plan framework, format and process should be consistent, repeatable and similar, allowing for functional differences between the business units and functions and IT, to facilitate alignment and integration.

▣ **Executive steering committee(s)** – involves top management in the IT/business planning process to establish overall IT direction, investment levels and approval of major initiatives across the enterprise. Each business unit and corporate staff function should have an equivalent body to focus on their respective areas in order to establish priorities and formalize periodic reviews.

▣ **Investment portfolio management, capital and expense planning & budgeting** – ensures that all IT investments are evaluated, prioritized, funded, approved and monitored using a consistent, but flexible process and a common set of evaluation criteria that are linked to the strategic and annual operating plans and budgets, both capital and expense, at multiple organizational levels.

▣ **Performance management and measurement** – monitors strategic plan outcomes based on specific balanced scorecard and service level measurement categories and metrics, and establishes organizational and functional accountability linked to MBO (management by objectives) performance criteria and reviews.

- **Planning guidelines and requisites** – a set of general instructions describing the format, content and timing of the business and IT plans. These are general in nature as opposed to specific standards, and should provide the business units some latitude and flexibility to accommodate local conditions.

Management control practices:

These management control practices focus on the tactical and operating plans and programs, and focus on the day-to-day operational environment:

- **Formalize multi-level IT/business functional/operations/technology steering and governance boards** with specific roles and decision rights in the day-to-day implementation and service management of the tactical IT plans, programs and services.
- **Tactical/operating plans and resource allocation** – establishes annual and near-term IT objectives, programs, projects and the resources to accomplish the objectives (e.g. application development plan, infrastructure refresh plan, etc.).
- **Budget/accounting/charge-back** – establishes budgets and monitors expenditures; charges IT costs back to the business or functional users to assure more effective involvement and ownership by the business.
- **Performance management and measurement** – collects, analyzes and reports on performance of results against objectives at a more detailed and operational level than at the strategic plan level (see Chapter 8 – Performance Management). In addition, formal periodic monthly and quarterly review meetings should be held to review the status of major initiatives and the ongoing performance of IT.

Supplementary practices:

These programs, which will vary by organization, can result in improving alignment:

- **IT/customer engagement and relationship model** – establishes a customer focused relationship model to facilitate interfaces, decisions, resolution of issues, collaborative plan development, better communications and build trust between IT and the business.
- **Program Management Office (PMO)** – establishes the processes, tools and IT/Business unit roles and responsibilities for program and project management. Initially, PMOs were established by IT to help manage IT programs and projects. As organizations recognized the increased benefits that a PMO brings to an environment, PMOs are now being established at the executive level by a growing number of organizations to assure that major corporate business initiatives utilize the same discipline and structure as IT initiatives to implement them within scope, on-time, within budget and to the customer's satisfaction.
- **Marketing, public relations and communications program for IT** – most IT departments are terrible in promoting and marketing their accomplishments and value. Developing this function to its full potential creates awareness and promotes

executive, management and employee education and commitment to the value of IT in support of the business through newsletters, websites, press releases, testimonials and other marketing and public relation events.

- **IT charter** – promotes effective and definitive interaction and links between IT and the business/functional groups they support. A charter can provide information on scope, roles and responsibilities, and provide specific program or project authority and limits to that authority.
- **Standards and guidelines** – adopt and maintain best practice standards and flexible guidelines to describe and document IT alignment, investment and planning processes, policies and procedures for IT governance and other areas within IT. For example, a financial services organization developed a simple guideline for its customers entitled, 'How to Request IT Services and Get Them Approved', which was a major success.
- **Organizational and people development, competences** – develop a proactive learning environment by encouraging and rewarding education, training and certification (where appropriate).
- **Annual/semi-annual IT management meeting** – conduct periodic IT/business management meetings to share best practices, develop stronger relationships, address organizational-wide issues and opportunities.

Key principles for effective business/IT strategic plan alignment

IT plans should be developed iteratively with the business and updated as necessary. Additional principles to strengthen plan alignment include:

- **Ownership** – CIO with involvement of IT leadership and of the executive officers & business unit leadership and relationship managers.
- **Frequency** – IT strategic plan is written/revised/refreshed annually, although major changes may cause the plan to be updated more frequently, or on an iterative basis.
- **Time horizon** – IT strategic plan usually covers a one to three year period with annual operating plans identifying capital and expense budget levels for the first year of the plan cycle.
- **Plan process** – IT reviews the business strategic plan major objectives, themes and priorities with the business units and corporate services.
- **IT interviews** – IT interviews the business units to align and map IT objectives, initiatives and priorities with the business, using the key plan questions and discussion topics.
- **New applications and services** - IT identifies major new or enhancement business application or service support initiatives as well as significant technology refresh requirements (e.g. replace obsolete technology, support anticipated growth and new infrastructure requirements) using the business/IT strategic plan initiative alignment template (see Figure 3.14).
- **Business and infrastructure initiatives** – both the business-driven initiatives and the infrastructure initiatives are combined in the IT strategic plan (which includes

a rough estimate of capital funding needs) and presented to the executive operating committee and SBU heads for approval.

- **Communication of the IT strategic plan** – a short version (highlights) of the approved plan is posted on the IT intranet and reviewed with the IT department and appropriate business constituents.
- **Link to annual operating plan and budget plan** – the annual capital and expense budget are approved by the executive team for the initiatives identified in the plan. Often, new or break-fix initiatives come up during the year (not included in the original plan) that require prioritization, funding and resources. A formal portfolio investment management approval process is followed for that purpose.
- **Link to portfolio of projects for annual operating plan** – once the annual operating plan and budget have been approved, a project list and related business cases are prepared, prioritized and reviewed. Projects charters are developed for approved projects and the appropriate implementation resources are allocated and/or committed.
- **Link to annual MBOs (management by objectives), performance measurements, KPIs and rewards/incentives** – both the strategic plan and annual operating plan must be driven by measurable outcomes (e.g. cost, time, profit, volume, customer satisfaction, strategic competitive value, etc.) and appropriate management actions taken according to positive or negative results.

Business and IT alignment will remain a major issue in some organizations until they realize that they both need each other to sustain the growth and prosperity of the enterprise.

Chapter 4 – Leadership, Teams and Managing Change

Key components of managing large scale enterprise change successfully
As organizations transition to a more mature and effective governance environment, a 'sea change' has to occur, either through incremental and/or radical change that could involve large scale change, depending on an organization's level of maturity, management philosophy and cultural readiness. The four key principles for managing large scale change successfully are (Kotter, 1996):
- **Engage the top and lead the change:**
  - Create the 'value proposition' and market the case for change;
  - Committed leadership;
  - Develop a plan and ensure consequence management.
- **Cascade down and across the organization and break down barriers including silos:**
  - Create cross-functional and global teams (where appropriate);
  - Compete on 'speed';
  - Ensure a performance-driven approach.

- ■ **Mobilize the organization and create ownership:**
  - Roll out the change initiative;
  - Measure results of change (pre-change versus post-change baselines);
  - Embrace continuous learning, knowledge and best practice sharing.
- ■ **Attributes of effective change teams and agents:**
  - Strong and focused leader;
  - Credibility and authority (charter) to lead the initiative;
  - 'Chutzpa', persistent and change zealots;
  - Ability to demonstrate and communicate 'early wins' to build the momentum;
  - Create a sense of urgency and avoid stagnation;
  - Knock obstacles out of the way, diplomatically or otherwise.

By applying the above principles to facilitate the transition to a successful IT governance culture and environment, the following steps can be followed:

- ■ **Proactively design and manage the IT governance program** – requires executive management sponsorship, an executive champion and creating a shared vision that is pragmatic, achievable, marketable, beneficial and measurable. Link goals, objectives and strategies to the vision and performance evaluations.
- ■ **Mobilize commitment, create the guiding coalition and provide the right incentives** – there is a strong commitment to the change from key senior managers, professionals and other relevant constituents. They are committed to make it happen, make it work and invest their attention and energy for the benefit of the enterprise as a whole. Create a multi-disciplinary empowered 'tiger team' representing all key constituents to collaborate, develop, market and facilitate execution in their respective areas of influence and responsibility.
- ■ **Make tradeoffs and choices, and clarify escalation and exception decisions** – IT governance is complex, and requires trade-offs and choices, which impact resources, costs, priorities, level of detail required, who approves choices, to whom are issues escalated etc. At the end of the day, a key question that must be answered is, "When is enough, enough?"
- ■ **Make change last, assign ownership and accountability** – change is reinforced, supported, rewarded, communicated (the results are through the web and intranet) and recognized and championed by owners who are accountable to facilitate the change so that it endures and flourishes throughout the organization.
- ■ **Monitor progress, common processes, technology and learning** – develop/adapt common policies, practices, processes and technologies which are consistent across the IT governance landscape and enable (not hinder) progress, learning and best practice benchmarking. Make IT governance an objective in the periodic performance evaluation system of key employees and reward significant progress.
- ■ **Establish a sense of urgency** – time is money.
- ■ **Generate short term wins** – complete short-term wins that are communicated to the constituents and are very effective for gaining support and sustaining the change of direction.

- **Consolidate gains and produce more change** – leverage increased credibility from successes, which facilitates and stimulates the introduction of more change.
- **Anchor new approaches in the culture** – institutionalize the process, adapt enabling technology and tools, and link progress to performance.

Leadership and teams:
- Clear purpose, common vision and accountability;
- Obsession with external customer;
- Participation and well-defined roles;
- Civilized disagreement and style diversity – allow for workout meetings and discussions;
- Encourage open communications – silence is consent – voice your ideas;
- Encourage flexible discipline and even expulsion of non-productive team members;
- Blend of informality and formality;
- Focus both on process and end results. However, remember that results are more important than process;
- Acknowledgement of the need for change;
- Strong respect and trust between members and leaders;
- Single point of contact for official team progress and communications (do not feed rumor-mill);
- Self-assessment of team members and adjustment;
- No ideas are bad ideas; encourage no blame game;
- Use automated tools to increase speed and communications;
- Encourage lifetime learning of IT talent at all levels of an organization to stay current in one of the fastest changing skill-sets in all fields.

Chapter 5 – Program and Project Management Excellence

Key attributes of a successful program and project-based environment
The following principles represent a checklist for helping companies achieve improvements in their program and project management practices and processes:

Program/project management excellence and visibility
The CEO, CIO and the executive team are committed to implementing PM as a core competence to manage all types of projects:
- Top management must prioritize projects based on a consistent set of evaluation attributes and investment prioritization processes.
- Customers must approve and set priorities among projects.
- Implement projects successfully (e.g. on-time, on-budget, within scope, with high quality and to the customer's satisfaction).
- Successful project management must be a joint effort between customers and the project teams. But the final responsibility for success or failure lies with the customer in terms of ownership of the results.

- Market and communicate the benefits and positive results of good fundamental project management disciplines through newsletters, websites, word of mouth, customer testimonials and other promotional vehicles.
- Develop a business case for major, complex and moderate projects.
- An essential element of every project is a complete project plan based on a work breakdown structure, with assignable work packages, task identification, estimating, budgeting and scheduling.
- Planning is everything and ongoing – detailed, systematic and team-involved.
- What is not documented, has not been said or does not exist.
- The more ridiculous the deadline, the more it costs to try to meet it.
- Project sponsors and constituents must be active participants – this builds relationships, communications and commitment.
- Use industry standards and guidelines to guide your PM direction - CMMI, PMBOK Guide, PRINCE2 and others.

Sponsorship and accountability

- All programs/projects must have a sponsor and/or owner and an overall program/project manager.
- Key roles and responsibilities must be formally agreed-to upfront and communicated to all of the constituencies where individuals are assigned specific actions in the form of a **RACI** matrix (**R**esponsible, **A**ccountable, **C**onsulted, **I**nformed) which becomes part of the project documentation.
- Program/project scope, requirements and deliverables should be approved upfront by the sponsor.
- Program/project costs and benefits (including non-financial benefits) should be quantified and approved by the sponsor and charged back to the sponsor or owner.
- Fast projects have strong leaders who create a sense of urgency and speed.
- Professionalize PM, reward certification and celebrate successes.
- Project managers must focus on five dimensions of project success – on time, within budget, within scope, with acceptable quality and to the customer's satisfaction.
- Project lifecycle with go/no-go gates allows for mid-course project reviews and adjustments and/or cancellations.
- A project manager's most valuable and least used word is 'No'.
- Project team members deserve a clear, written charter and guidelines as to the tasks they must perform and the time available to perform them.
- Establish project review panels consisting of key constituents and conduct formal reviews with follow-up actions, dates and assigned responsibility.
- Use external subject matter PM experts as needed.

Program/project management (PM) governance

Key practices for successful and sustainable project management best practices include the following:

- A formal PM governance policy should be established defining the components of the policy and identifying what is mandatory and discretionary, and who has decision authority for approval, resource allocation, escalation and change authorization.
- A formal governance calendar should be published which identifies formal project reviews, status reports (e.g. weekly, bi-weekly, monthly, quarterly), funding reviews, etc.
- A flexible and scalable PM process should be established and continuously improved to accommodate different project types such as light, moderate and complex.
- A PM center of excellence (PMO) should be established to develop criteria for PM competences, encourage PM training and certification, provide expert PM help, act as PM advocates and conduct periodic health checks on select programs/projects.
- Establish a reward and recognition system to recognize PM excellence and encourage certification.
- Deliver short term incremental project deliverables that work to establish credibility and visibility (decompose complex programs and projects into no more than 80 hour work packages with targeted deliverables, formal project reviews, etc.).
- Incorporate PM objectives into annual performance reviews.
- Consistent program and project metrics should be instituted based on time, cost, resources, quality and customer satisfaction (including earned value, where applicable). There are a number of tools that can help with estimating, resource allocation, level loading and resource utilization.
- Management must be provided with meaningful visibility into projects if suspicion and distrust are to be minimized. The ability to compare planned to actual results or baselines is essential for effective project management.
- The key to good project management is effective and honest communications.
- A formal escalation process, with clear accountability and roles should be established to resolve key program/project issues, risks and to approve changes.
- A consistent methodology must be developed and applied to report the **RAG** (e.g. **R**ed, **A**mber or **G**reen status of programs, projects or other major tasks. Red = big trouble; Amber = emerging trouble; Green = everything is on target).
- Reporting must be produced on a consistent basis (e.g. weekly, bi-weekly, monthly, other) using a consistent format (e.g. with allowances made for the audience of the report).
- A formal time tracking system should be in place to record how time is spent on projects.

Resource optimization, availability and commitment:

- Sponsors and program/project managers should have access to the right resources based on the project phase, task requirements and competences needed.

- The availability and commitment of the resources should be guaranteed by senior management once the program/project is approved and resourced.

Program/project management lessons learned:
- Lessons learned should be developed and made available to all constituencies who require them with consideration given to security and access policies.
- Current and evolving best practice benchmarking should be tracked, adopted and continuously improved.
- Maintain a PM knowledge management system of lessons learned and lessons to be changed.
- Desirable work must be rewarded; undesirable work must be changed.

Chapter 6 – IT Service Management
Based on a review of best practice companies, a number of consistent practices seem to be prevalent in these organizations regarding superior IT service management. They include:
- All steady-state server farms operations (e.g. data center, help desk, DBMS, network management) must have a primary owner and a secondary (backup) owner.
- The overall ITSM budget should be divided into a set of defined products and services so that all IT costs can be mapped to supportable business processes, either directly or indirectly.
- All IT services should consistently achieve the desired level of efficiency, productivity, reliability and availability as measured by the appropriate key performance indicators (e.g. service level agreements, customer satisfaction, costs, etc.).
- Most IT services should be described as processes that are well documented, consistently performed and repeatable to maximize their efficiency.
- Most ITSM services should be charged back to the user or customer organization to achieve a greater level of accountability.
- The use of an IT service catalog that can define, price and provide estimated installation time for repetitive productized IT services (install a new computer or network connection) is growing in use. It can benefit the customer by providing an easy way to select, order and communicate to IT the required services desired by the customer. The service catalog does not work for complex, one time initiatives that are not repetitive.
- A formal ITSM governance, reporting and escalation process should be established to resolve key operational issues and risks, and to conduct periodic reviews. All steady-state operations should have business continuity, backup (including one or more off-site locations), disaster recovery, and security policies and procedures.
- All ITSM-related processes should be documented in a consistent, repeatable and standard framework, consisting of lifecycles, processes and metrics such as ITIL (IT Infrastructure Library) and continuously improved.
- Optimizing the utilization of IT assets and resources is critical.

IT service management is complex, requires dedicated resources and leadership to implement effectively. It helps to transition an organization from chaos to order, from a reactive to a proactive environment, from firefighting (most of the time) to a planned environment (with firefighting some of the time), and from random service efforts to predictable and more cost effective service quality. ITIL, much like other IT governance frameworks, represents a journey that is based on a combination of formal lifecycle phases, processes and checklists combined with common sense and managing change proactively.

An IT service management initiative does not end after the framework has been implemented. It must be continually monitored, maintained and improved.

Chapter 7 – Strategic Sourcing, Outsourcing and Vendor Management
Even with the increased outsourcing initiatives in customer organizations, it appears that organizations continue to struggle with establishing and enforcing a more formal, consistent and repeatable outsourcing policy, process and method. There are a number of best practice principles and practices that can represent a checklist for helping companies achieve sourcing and outsourcing improvements:
- Establish an appropriate outsourcing strategy, business case and plan.
- Identify and prioritize the outsourcing opportunities.
- Develop appropriate approaches and techniques for outsourcing activities.
- Identify, select and negotiate a win-win deal with service providers.
- Manage service provider governance and performance management.
- Manage the transition from the customer to the service provider as a project.
- Manage the ongoing relationship.
- Conduct periodic formal progress reviews and reports based on specific metrics relating to the type of outsourcing service or project.
- For large initiatives, establish a high level peer outsourcing governance board for joint reviews.
- Assign a service provider account relationship manager as a single point of contact/ interface with the customer and establish a customer/service provider relationship model.

Customer to do's:
- Ensure there is executive alignment and commitment to outsourcing that creates a favorable outsourcing culture within the organization.
- Create a well-defined and realistic business case process and case with alternatives.
- Establish a consistent and formal process for service provider selection and contract negotiations.
- Develop an outsourcing transition plan from pilot to full implementation with either re-deployment or termination of displaced resources.

- Build key performance indicators into the contract performance evaluation system with both rewards for extra-ordinary performance and penalties for poor performance.
- Make KPIs relevant, simple, comparable, easy to report and focused on measurable outcomes.
- Develop an outsourcing communication plan, risk management and mitigation plan, policy and process.
- Balance stakeholder needs – companies that successfully outsource continuously 'take the pulse' of all stakeholder groups to adjust their needs over time.
- Pursue stakeholder involvement on major outsourcing deals through governance boards, steering committees and working committees.
- Manage the expectations of all stakeholders well – deliver what you promise; don't over-promise things you or the outsourcing service provider cannot deliver – credibility is a fleeting attribute that, if lost, is extremely difficult or almost impossible to regain.
- Recognize that experience matters – governance groups can rapidly fill their experience deficit through subject matter expert coaching or external consulting support.
- Understand that SLAs are not enough – service level agreements are extremely important and should be continuously refined and improved over the life of the contract. However, they must be augmented by other methods to ensure customer satisfaction (e.g. formal and/or informal surveys, listening to the voice of the customer, etc.).
- Develop disengagement options and conditions as part of the contract that includes renegotiations options. Don't put all of your eggs in one basket.
- Make sure that a disaster prevention and recovery plan with contingencies is in place.

Service provider to do's:
- Understand the expectations of the customer.
- Communicate your expectations of the customer to the customer.
- Recognize that industry and application knowledge, insight and skills are key.
- Ensure you are able to scale for volume, capacity, people resources, etc.
- A proven methodology, meaningful metrics and performance management reporting should be used.
- Outline processes and behaviors.
- Communicate critical information to avoid cultural misunderstandings.
- Build cross-cultural relationships that are vital to team success.
- Use a relationship model with escalation considerations.
- Have backup and recovery plans and facilities in place.

Chapter 8 – Performance Management, Management Controls and Enabling technologies

As part of improving IT governance, it is critical for an organization to establish an overall framework that includes, amongst other things, an IT enterprise strategy (which includes business capability roadmaps and balanced scorecard metrics), performance management, management controls and compliance components. By using industry best practice frameworks or guidelines, and their components, such as COSO® and COBIT®, a company can develop a more consistent and sustainable approach to making IT performance management and management controls more effective and sustainable. One needs to assign decision authority, ownership and link deliverables and performance to a reward structure to make individuals and teams more accountable.

Principles for achieving performance management and management control excellence include:
- Identify critical success factors for the business and IT, and identify the key performance indicators (KPIs) linked to these factors.
- Build key performance indicators into your performance evaluation system, starting at the top and permeating to all positions that can influence those KPIs.
- Make KPIs relevant, simple, comparable, easy-to-report and focused on goals and objectives.
- Define and issue a management control policy and related procedures, which identify all of the areas requiring management controls, using COBIT as a checklist.
- Monitor, audit and assure that IT operates in accordance with the approved controls.
- Develop a risk management and mitigation plan, policy and process.
- Develop a business/IT continuity and disaster recovery plan and policy.
- Develop a clear performance review, escalation and issues resolution policy, and process with clear accountability and responsibilities.
- Develop key performance indicators with balance and the big picture in mind (outward from IT to the business and inward to manage IT).
- Integrate key performance indicators into individual and team performance evaluation systems.
- Establish broad executive commitment – use a mix of business and IT leadership in the design, selection, review and continuous improvement of metrics.
- Develop a standard metrics definition based on consensus.
- Establish an IT governance and control framework.
- Establish a management compliance forum.
- Determine Sarbanes-Oxley and/or other regulatory compliance requirements.
- Determine the IT owners for applications and general controls.
- Manage performance, control and compliance issues.

The execution of these plans and objectives must be monitored and measured by a combination of balanced scorecard key performance indicators (KPIs) as well as formal and informal status review meetings and reports (e.g. report cards, dashboards). The outcomes should link critical success factors to KPIs that are measurable, part of a standard reporting system and associated with a governance component. If one cannot measure it, it does not count. Remember, one gets what one measures, so it is critical to measure and control the right things.

Chapter 9 – Cloud Computing, Data Management and Governance

Cloud computing

The cloud computing model is composed of five essential characteristics, three service models and four deployment models. There are many factors that must be considered in choosing the right cloud service model. One should consider the feasibility and practicability based on the following factors:

- Technical – performance, scalability, regulations, business continuity, disaster recovery, etc.
- Financial – focus on one-time migration cost, the total cost of ownership (compare non-cloud and cloud cost environments) or the monthly operating costs.
- Strategic – does the cloud provide a competitive advantage? Will the cloud reduce the time-to-market for product or systems launches?
- Organizational – do the skills reside in-house to deploy to the cloud or not? What about the areas of web development, distributed computing and service oriented architectures?
- Risk – what is the risk tolerance of the organization? How important is vendor reliability and sustainability? What about security and reliability of the cloud?
- Quality – what is the reliability of the service? What is the duration of outages and how often they occur? How quickly are they fixed on the average?
- Vendor reliability and sustainability.

Cloud computing is a form of strategic sourcing and outsourcing, and should be managed accordingly using current and emerging best practices and vendor management, control and measurement.

Data management

There are eleven knowledge areas in data management, as follows:

1. Data governance – planning, oversight, and control over the management of data and the use of data and data-related resources policies, processes and responsibilities.
2. Data architecture – the overall structure of data and data-related resources as an integral part of the enterprise architecture.
3. Data model and design – analysis, design, building, testing, and maintenance.
4. Data storage and operations – structure of the physical data storage deployment and associated management.
5. Data security – ensuring privacy, confidentiality and appropriate access.
6. Data integration and interoperability – acquisition, extraction, transformation, movement, delivery, replication, federation, virtualization and support.

7. Documents and contents – sorting, protecting, indexing, and enabling to data found in unstructured sources (electronic files and physical records), and making this data available for integration and interoperability with structured (database) data.
8. Reference and master data – managing shared data to reduce redundancy and ensure better data quality through standardized definition and use of data values.
9. Data warehousing and business intelligence – managing analytical data processing and enabling access to decision support data for reporting and analysis.
10. Metadata – collecting, categorizing, integrating, controlling, managing, and delivering metadata.
11. Data quality – defining, monitoring, maintaining data integrity and improving data quality.

Organization must develop cloud computing and data management governance action plans, identify deliverables, establish priorities, justify return on investments, allocate resources and measure progress. Issues of security, privacy, access, back-up and recovery, ownership of data and related topics must be addressed. Data stewards are important for enterprise data management interoperability and consistency.

10.4 LESSONS LEARNED

IT governance is a broad and complex topic with many moving parts. IT governance represents a journey. It is not a onetime event and to achieve higher levels of IT maturity, IT governance should be persistently and relentlessly pursued both from a top-down and a bottom-up perspective. Creating and sustaining a more effective IT governance environment will take time and resources and should be focused on achieving incremental IT governance successes in priority areas based on their value proposition or the reduction of major 'pain points' to the organization.

It is critical to break down or segment the IT governance initiative into manageable, assignable and measurable components or work packages with targeted deliverables. It is important to define clear roles for the board, executive management and the IT governance project team, including ownership and accountability for each component and the overall initiative.

Based on the extensive research and case studies, the major lessons learned clearly indicate that in order to be successful an IT governance initiative must:
- Have corporate mandate from the top;
- Have dedicated and available resources;
- Recognize that 80 to 90% of an IT governance initiative represents a 'cultural change' and organizations must prepare for a lengthy and involved period of adjustment;
- Use a phased approach to implement new processes and enabling technologies;

- ▪ Develop and conduct a marketing, communications and awareness campaign to focus on value propositions;
- ▪ Create a 'Continuous IT Governance Improvement Group' to sustain the momentum, be advocates, act as change agents and sustain the framework and components;
- ▪ Use 'total cost of operations' as a measure of improvement from the current state baseline to the future state baseline.

▪ 10.5 CRITICAL SUCCESS FACTORS

Critical success factors for achieving IT governance excellence include:
- ▪ **Create the right environment and culture**:
  - • Establish the appropriate organizational mindset, culture and environment;
  - • Obtain executive sponsorship, commitment and multi-level management buy-in and ownership;
  - • Establish an IT executive governance steering committee and working committee with clearly defined roles and responsibilities;
  - • Success depends on creating a sustainable foundation (e.g. policy, process, metrics) for managing programs and projects, and integrating results and methods into the culture of the organization;
  - • Define roles and get the right people involved in a phase;
  - • Market and re-enforce (e.g. training, rewards, mentors, tools, flexible processes) the value and benefits of good IT governance practices;
  - • Understand the risks, constraints and obstacles, and develop contingency plans and actions;
  - • Adopt a flexible and scalable IT governance process (phases, templates, repository, tools and tailor when required) to accommodate different levels of maturity and organizational styles.

- ▪ **Develop an IT governance implementation plan**:
  - • Define the project's charter and boundaries, including scope, objectives, requirements and deliverables;
  - • Establish well-defined phases/tasks, go/no-go gates and milestones (break the job down into manageable work packages – 80 hour rule) with realistic baselines (costs, time, resources and contingencies) based on short term incremental and visible deliverables;
  - • Define a responsibility assignment matrix – Responsible, Inform, Consult and/or Approve;
  - • Establish formal change management and risk management processes;
  - • Establish and assess the current baseline in terms of costs, resources, competences, documentation and levels of maturity and identify any gaps;
  - • Define the future desired or targeted baseline.

■ **Ensure governance and excellent communications**:
  - Establish a governance, control, reporting and escalation policy and process;
  - Manage the expectations of all stakeholders proactively;
  - Identify, measure and track mandatory and discretionary vital signs, metrics, key issues and take necessary actions quickly – knock obstacles out of the way;
  - Establish frequent and open communications with stakeholders (both formal and informal review meetings) on a daily, weekly, monthly and quarterly basis depending on the project's importance and closeness to being implemented;
  - Ensure accurate, timely and meaningful monitoring and progress reporting.

■ **Institutionalize and operationalize IT governance**
  - Create IT governance centers of excellence (e.g. advocacy center, help desk, education, training, subject matter expert help, process, project tracking, certification, website, etc.);
  - Create a reward and/or recognition policy to re-enforce and sustain;
  - Conduct formal program/project reviews;
  - Develop and use consistent, flexible and scalable processes (e.g. fast track or light versus complex projects) and automate processes and tools (web-based);
  - Capture and apply positive lessons learned, and focus on continuous improvement;
  - Conduct 'post-mortem' reviews of problems that occurred during implementation to learn from mistakes and prevent the same mistakes from recurring.

■ 10.6   IMPLICATIONS FOR THE FUTURE AND PERSONAL ACTION PLAN

Implications for the future

The approach to IT governance must be consistent, but yet scalable and tailored to each organization's environment and management style, issues, opportunities, level of maturity, audit/legal requirements, available resources and cultural readiness. Remember, IT governance represents a journey towards higher levels of IT maturity and effectiveness.

There are numerous alternative models and standards to help companies plan, deploy and manage an IT governance initiative which focuses on achieving these higher levels of IT maturity and effectiveness.

While there is no single right or best way for organizations to approach improvements in IT governance, this book proposes a comprehensive and blended IT governance framework and roadmap which identifies the appropriate current and emerging best practice methods for each of the major IT governance components that must be addressed in any approach and is critical for companies intending to achieve more effective alignment and management of IT. The framework can serve as a guideline for organizations to select and customize the appropriate approach applicable to their environment, priorities, capabilities and available resources. A balanced approach consisting of both a top-down framework and roadmap together with bottom-up implementation is essential for success.

Personal action plan

Based on the lessons learned and the critical success factors identified in this book and your own experience regarding IT governance:

- Identify your own and your organization's strengths, limitations and gaps.
- List and prioritize the gaps in the processes, skills, techniques and tools you and your organization wants and needs to develop and/or update.
- Define your and your organization's action plan for next steps:
  - Create awareness and commitment to action;
  - Develop a plan with ownership, milestones and metrics;
  - Use, as appropriate, internal/external subject matter experts to fill the gaps and facilitate organizational change and transformation;
  - Institute continuous learning and education – improve your competences and knowledge of the relevant standards, processes, tools, techniques, etc.;
  - Institute continuous process improvement based on current and emerging best practices.

"Now this is not the end. It is not even the beginning of the end. But it is, perhaps, the end of the beginning."

Sir Winston Churchill,
Former British Prime Minister, 1942

Appendix A Glossary

A:

Absorption Costing: A principle whereby fixed as well as variable costs are allotted to cost units and total overheads are absorbed according to activity level.

Acceptance: The agreement by the customer that the deliverable meets contractual requirements.

Accomplishment: The value of work completed in accordance with the predetermined baseline value for that work. The terms 'accomplishment', 'earned value', and 'baseline cost for work performed' are all synonymous.

Account Manager: The customer interface.

Accountability Matrix: See Responsibility Assignment Matrix.

Accounting Period: The period into which time is sectioned for cost accumulation, accounting, and performance measurement purposed.

Accrual: The recognition of events and conditions as they occur, rather than in the period of their incurrence, receipt, or payment.

Action Lists: Defined actions, allocated to recovery teams and individuals, within a phase of a plan. These are supported by reference data.

Activity: An element of work performed. An activity normally has an expected duration, an expected cost, and expected resource requirement. Activities are often synonymous with tasks.

Activity-Based Costing: Looks at aspects of an organization's operations and attempts to answer the very simple, but sometimes hard to answer question, "How much does it cost to do that?" For example, how much does a company spend processing a receivable or taking a customer call? How much does it cost a city to fill a pothole? The term relates to outsourcing in that once an organization can answer the cost question at the activity level, it can more objectively compare the cost of internal versus external sourcing for performing it.

Activity Definition: A narrative depiction of the detailed steps required to complete an activity, often including inputs and outputs (handoffs and deliverables) and responsibility assignment.

Activity Description (AD): A short phrase or label used in a project network diagram. The activity description normally describes the scope of work of the activity.

Activity Duration Estimating: Estimating the number of work periods, which will be needed to complete individual activities or tasks.

Activity-On-Arrow (AOA): See Arrow-Diagramming Method.

Activity-On-Node (AON): See Precedence Diagramming Method.

Actual Baseline Chart: A Bar (Gantt) Chart that compares the current schedule with the baseline schedule.

Actual Cost of Work Performed (ACWP): Total costs incurred (direct and indirect) in accomplishing work during a given time period. See also Earned Value.

Actual Finish Date (AF): The point in time that work actually ended on an activity or tasks. (Note in some application areas, the activity is considered 'finished' when work is 'substantially complete'.)

Actual Progress: All activities or portions thereof occurring prior to the status date on an updated schedule or progress report. Any one of a number of methods (milestone, percent complete, remaining duration, etc.) is used to evaluate or portray status to date on in-process activities; some measure accomplishments, others only assess time.

Actual Start Date (AS): The point in time that work actually started on an activity.

ACWP: Actual Cost of Work Performed.

Administrative Closure: Generating, gathering and disseminating information to formalize project completion.

Agreement: The written agreement (contract or statement of work) between the customer and the contractor covering the work to be performed.

Alert Phase: The first phase of a business continuity plan in which initial emergency procedures and damage assessments are activated.

Alignment: Process to ensure that IT supports the objectives and direction of the business.

Allocated Cost: A cost that can be directly identified with a business unit.

ANSI: American National Standards Institute, responsible for creating and managing US standards. See ISO.

AOA: Activity-On-Arrow

AON: Activity-On-Node

Application Area: Usually defined in terms of either the product of the project (i.e., by similar technologies or industry sectors), the type of customer (e.g., internal vs. external, government vs. commercial) or the function it supports (finance, manufacturing, etc...).

Apportioned Cost: A cost that is shared by a number of business units (an indirect cost). This cost must be shared out between these units on an equitable basis.

Arrow: The graphic presentation of an activity in ADM. See Arrow Diagramming Method.

Arrow Diagramming Method (ADM): A network diagramming technique in which activities are represented by arrows. The tail of the arrow represents the start and the head represents the finish of the activity (the length of the arrow does not represent the expected duration of the activity). Activities are connected at points called nodes (usually drawn as small circles) to illustrate the sequence in which the activities are expected to be performed. See also Precedence Diagramming Method.

ASPs: Application Service Providers are companies that remotely host software applications and provide access to, and the use of, the applications over the Internet or a private network. Typically, the service fee is usage-based, for example, per user per month.

Assessment: Analyze or evaluate or check whether a standard or guideline is being followed and/ or that efficiency, effectiveness or maturity targets are being met.

Asset: Component of a business process. Assets can include people, accommodation, computer systems, networks, paper records, fax machines, facilities etc.

Audit: (1) An independent review for the purpose of assessing compliance with scope, requirements, specifications, baselines, standards, procedures, instructions, codes, and contractual and licensing requirements. (2) An activity to determine through investigation the adequacy of, and adherence to, established procedures, instructions, specifications, codes, standards or regulations, and the effectiveness of implementation.

Authentication: The act of verifying the identity of a user and the user's eligibility to access computerized information. Authentication is designed to protect against fraudulent logon activity.

Authorized Work: That effort which has been defined and is on contract (original negotiated contract and all negotiated change orders).

Availability: Ability of a component or service to perform its required function at a stated instant or over a stated period of time. It is usually expressed as the availability ratio, i.e. the proportion of time that the service is actually available for use by the customers within the agreed service hours.

Availability Management: Availability Management is the process of ensuring the appropriate deployment of resources, methods and techniques, to support the availability of IT services agreed-to with a customer. Availability Management addresses issues such as optimizing maintenance, design measures to minimize the number of incidents.

B:

BAC: Baseline at Completion

Backup: Provisions made for backup and recovery of facilities, equipment, systems, people and other resources and/or assets.

Backward Pass: The calculation of late finish dates and late start dates for the uncompleted portions of all the network activities. Determined by working backwards through the network logic from the project's end date. The end date may be calculated in a forward pass or set by the customer or sponsor. See also Network Analysis.

Balanced Scorecard: Performance management tool that helps to breakdown key performance indicators into financial targets, internal processes, customer satisfaction and the learning and growth metrics used to measure an organization's effectiveness. Developed by Drs. Robert Kaplan and David Norton in 1992.

Bar Chart: A graphic display of schedule-related information. In the typical bar chart, activities or tasks & other project elements are listed down the left side of the chart, dates are shown across the top, and activity durations are shown as date-placed horizontal bars. Also called a Gantt chart.

Baseline: The original plan (for a project, a work package, an activity or task), plus or minus approved changes. Usually used with a modifier (e.g., cost baseline, schedule baseline, performance measurement baseline, people baseline). Also called a reference base.

Baseline Authorization (BA): A document which identifies the scope of work, baseline, and schedule. Once approved, the BA is a 'contract' between the customer (sponsor) and project management.

Baseline Maintenance: The term used to describe the control of revisions to the budgets. Baseline revisions are made as a result of contract or SOW changes, regulatory changes, or internal re-planning.

Baseline Rates: Established for all labor and other expense categories consistent with the methods employed to record actual costs.

BCWP: Budgeted (baseline) Cost for Work Performed.

BCWS: Budgeted (baseline) Cost for Work Scheduled.

Benchmark: An objective measure of performance that can be used to compare performance across organizations against best practice organizations. One can benchmark a variety of metrics such as cost, time, quality, speed, profit etc.

Best Practice: Proven activities, methodologies, processes and/or frameworks that have been successfully used by multiple organizations.

Bid: To submit a price for products or services; a proposal either verbal or written, for doing work and for supplying materials, equipment, people, systems and other resources.

Bid & Proposal (B&P): Effort associated with the preparation and submittal of pricing in the proposals.

Big Data: A broad term for any collection of data sets that are large and complex and are difficult to process using traditional data processing applications. It requires a knowledge of databases, quantitative analysis, and software languages and tools to utilize effectively.

Bottom-Up: Data collection starting at the lowest (usually the work package) level and, through the WBS, summarized to the contract, or SOW, or product, or systems level.

BPO: Business Process Outsourcing puts together two powerful business tools - business process management and outsourcing. Business process management uses technology to break down barriers between traditional functional silos, such as those found in finance, order processing, and call centers. Outsourcing uses the skills and resources of specialized external service providers to perform many of these critical, yet non-core activities. BPO means examining the processes that make up the business and its functional units, and streamlining them.

Brand: The identity of a product in the eyes of the buyer in terms of such attributes such as quality, value, durability, high technology, safety, etc.

Brand Management: The management of a brand from its inception to its maturity and decline.

British Standards Institute (BSI): The UK National Standards body, responsible for creating and maintaining British standards.

BS7799: The British standard for Information Security Management. This standard provides a comprehensive set of controls comprising best practices in information security.

Budget: The resources (measured in dollars, people-hours, or other definitive units) which are formally assigned for the accomplishment of a specified task or group of tasks.

Budget Allocation: An allocation of resources to the functional departments, measured in terms of people-hours, dollars, or other designated units, for accomplishing specific tasks.

Budget At Completion (BAC): The estimate total budgeted cost of the project when completed.

Budgeted Cost of Work Performed (BCWP): The value of work completed (including any overhead allocation) for activities (or portions of activities) during a given period (usually project-to-date). See also Earned Value.

Budgeted Cost of Work Scheduled (BCWS): The sum of the approved cost estimates (including any overhead allocation) for activities (or portions of activities) completed during a given period (usually project-to-date). See also Earned Value.

Business Case: The business, economic, technology and regulatory motivations for pursuing an initiative stated in terms of business, requirements, costs and benefits, resources and risk.

Business Design Phase: The period during the Systems Development Lifecycle when the development team performs system design activities requiring active customer participation and approval.

Business Function: A business unit within an organization, e.g. a department, division, branch.

Business Intelligence (BI): Represents tools and techniques that process data and do statistical analysis for decision support in many business and technology functions - that is discovery of meaningful relationships in the data, gain insight, detect trends, and identify opportunities and risks.

Business Planning: Planning that addresses such topics as the vision of the organization, the target markets, the products and services the organization will offer, how the organization will achieve and maintain a competitive advantage and financials. The process of producing a business plan.

Business Process (BP): A group of business activities undertaken by an organization in pursuit of a common goal. Typical business processes include receiving orders, marketing services, selling products, delivering services, distributing products, invoicing for services, accounting for money received. A business process usually depends upon several business functions for support, e.g. IT, personnel, operations. A business process rarely operates in isolation, i.e. other business processes will depend on it and it will depend on other processes.

Business Recovery Objective: The desired time within which business processes should be recovered, and the minimum staff, assets and services required within this time.

Business Recovery Plans: Documents describing the roles, responsibilities and actions necessary to resume business processes following a business disruption.

Business Requirements: Criteria that define a business need, opportunity and/or solution.

Business Unit: A segment of the business entity by which both revenues are received and expenditures are caused or controlled, such revenue and expenditure being used to evaluate segmental performance.

C:

Calendar Unit: The smallest unit of time used in scheduling the project. Calendar units are generally in hours, days, or weeks, but can also be in shifts or even in minutes.

Capability Maturity Model (CMM): The Capability Maturity Model for Software (CMM), developed the Software Engineering Institute (SEI), is a model used by many organizations to identify best practices useful in helping them assess and increase the maturity of their software development processes. CMMI (Capability Maturity Model Integrated) is an advanced form of CMM.

Capacity Management: The process of optimizing the cost, timing of acquisition, and deployment of IT resources, to support the agreements made with the customer. Capacity management addresses resource management, performance management, demand management, modeling, capacity planning, load management and application sizing. It emphasizes planning to ensure that the agreed to service levels can be fulfilled.

Capital Costs: Typically those costs apply to the physical (substantial) assets of the organization. Traditionally this was equipment necessary to produce the enterprise's product. Capital costs are the purchase or major enhancement of fixed assets, for example computer equipment, building and plant and are often also referred to as 'one-off' costs.

Capital Investment Proposal: The process of evaluating the proposed investment in initiatives or assets and the benefits to be obtained from their acquisition. The techniques used in the evaluation can be summarized as return on capital and payback period, and discounted cash flow methods.

Capitalization: The process of identifying major expenditure as capital, whether there is a substantial asset or not, to reduce the impact on the current financial year of such expenditure. The most common item for this to be applied to is software, whether developed in-house or purchased.

Captive Center: A company-owned offshore operation. The activities are performed offshore, but they are not outsourced to another company.

Cash Flow: The net flow of dollars into or out of a project. The algebraic sum, in any time period, of all cash receipts, expenses, and investments. Also called cash proceeds or cash generated. The stream of monetary (dollar) values - costs and benefits - resulting from a project investment.

CCB: Change Control Board.

Change Control: The process by which a change is proposed, evaluated, approved or rejected, scheduled, implemented, tested and tracked.

Change Control Board (CCB): A formally constituted group of stakeholders responsible for approving or rejecting changes to the project baselines.

Change in Scope: See Scope Change.

Change Log: A log of requests for change raised during the project, showing information on each change, its evaluation, what decisions have been made and its current status, e.g. Initiated, Reviewed, Approved, Implemented, Closed.

Change Management: See Change Control.

Change Order: A formal authorization by the customer, sponsor and/or project manager for a change or variance to an existing contract.

Chart of Accounts: Any numbering system used to monitor project costs by category (e.g., labor, supplies, and materials). The project chart of accounts is usually based upon the corporate chart of accounts of the primary performing organization.

Charter: See Project Charter.

Claim: A written statement requesting additional time and/or money for acts or omissions during the performance of the contract. The contract must provide for collecting the facts and identifying the circumstances for which the customer is responsible in order to be entitled to additional compensation and/or time.

Classification: Process of formally grouping configuration items by type e.g. software, hardware, documentation, environment, application.

Client: The customer who has contracted for services.

Cloud Computing: A model for enabling ubiquitous, convenient, on-demand network access to a shared pool of configurable computing resources (e.g., networks, servers, storage, applications, and services) that can be rapidly provisioned and released with minimal management effort or service provider interaction.

CMMI®: Capability Maturity Model Integrated- developed by the Software Engineering Institute (SEI) as a phased approach to develop software or systems with a focus on quality. CMMI® is an organizational certification.

Command, Control and Communications: The processes by which an organization retains overall co-ordination of its recovery effort during deployment of business recovery plans.

Committed Costs: Costs, which have been contractually committed, but not yet used on a project (should be considered when calculating earned value).

Communications Planning: Determining the information and communications needs of the project stakeholders.

Community Cloud: One of four cloud deployment models. In a community cloud model, more than one group with common and specific needs shares the cloud infrastructure.

Concurrent Engineering: An approach to project staffing that, in its most general form, calls for implementers to be involved in the design phase.

Configuration: (1) The requirements, design, and implementation that define a particular version of a product or system. (2) The functional and/or physical characteristics of a product or system.

Configuration Baseline: Configuration of a product or system established at a specific point in time, which captures both the structure and details of the product or system, and enables that product or system to be rebuilt at a later date.

Configuration Control: The process of evaluating, approving or disapproving, and coordinating changes to configuration items after final establishment of their configuration identification.

Configuration Documentation: Documents that define requirements, system design, build, production, and verification for a configuration item.

Configuration Identification: Activities that determine the product structure, the selection of configuration items, and the documentation of the configuration item's physical and functional characteristics including interfaces and subsequent changes. It includes the allocation of identification characters or numbers to the configuration items and their documents. It also includes the unique numbering of configuration control forms associated with changes and problems.

Configuration Item (CI): Component of an infrastructure - or an item, such as a request for change, associated with an infrastructure - which is (or is to be) under the control of configuration management. CIs may vary widely in complexity, size and type - from an entire system (including all hardware, software, network and documentation) to a single module or a minor hardware component.

Configuration Management Database: A database which contains all relevant details of each CI and details of the important relationships between CIs.

Configuration Management Tool (CM Tool): A software product providing automatic support for change, configuration or version control.

Configuration Management: The process of identifying and defining the elements in a system, controlling the release and change of these items throughout the lifecycle, recording and reporting the status of configuration items and change requests, and verifying the completeness and correctness of configuration items.

Constraint: The logical relationship between the start and/or finish of one activity and the start and/or finish of another activity. Also, conditions that define or restrict how project objectives are met (constraints may include policies, environment, staff, technology, budgets, regulations and schedules).

Context Diagram: The top-level diagram of a leveled set of data-flow diagrams that portrays all the net inputs and outputs of a system; also called the system interface model.

Contingencies: See Reserve and Contingency Planning.

Contingency Allowance: See Reserve.

Contingency Planning: The development of a management plan that identifies alternative strategies and plans to be used to ensure success if specified risk events occur.

Contingency Reserve: A separately planned cushion is used to allow for future situations, which may be planned for only in part (sometimes called 'known unknowns'). For example, rework is certain; the amount of rework is not. Contingency reserves may involve cost, schedule, people, etc. Contingency reserves are intended to reduce the impact of missing cost or schedule objectives. Contingency reserves are normally included in the project's cost and schedule baselines.

Continuity: Preventing, mitigating and recovering from disruption. The terms 'business resumption planning', 'disaster recovery planning' and 'contingency planning' may also be used in this context; they all concentrate on the recovery aspects of continuity.

Contract: A contract is a mutually binding agreement, which obligates the seller to provide the specified product, and obligates the buyer to pay for it. Contracts generally fall into one of three broad categories: (1) Fixed price or lump sum contracts—this category of contract involves a fixed total price for a well-defined product. Fixed price contracts may also include incentives for meeting or exceeding selected project objectives such as schedule targets. (2) Cost reimbursable contracts—this category of contract involves payment (reimbursement) to the contractor for its actual costs. Costs are usually classed as direct costs (costs incurred directly by the project, such as wages for members of the project team) and indirect costs (costs allocated to the project by the performing organization as a cost of doing business, such as salaries for corporate executives). Indirect costs are usually calculated as a percentage of direct costs. Cost reimbursable contracts often include incentives for meeting or exceeding selected project objectives such as schedule targets or total cost. (3) Unit price contracts—the contractor is paid a preset amount per unit of service (e.g., $100 per hour for professional services or $2.00 per cubic yard of earth removed) and the total value of the contract is a function of the quantities needed to complete the work.

Contract Administration: Managing the relationship with the seller.

Contract Change (Contract Directed Change): A revision approved by the customer in writing directing a change to the contract. Contract changes authorize a change in scope of work or schedule and normally result in a dollar change to the total contract baseline.

Contract Close-out: Completion and settlement of the contract, including resolution of all outstanding items.

Contract Cost: The contract target cost (excluding profit or fee) negotiated for all authorized work defined in the statement of work when the contract is defined.

Contract Date: Any date specified in the contract or imposed on any project activity or event that impacts the activity/project schedule.

Contract Price/Contract Target Price: The total value, including fee, for the contract.

Control: The process of comparing actual performance with planned performance, analyzing variances, evaluating possible alternatives, analyzing issues and taking appropriate corrective action as needed.

Control Charts: A graphic display of the results, over time and against established control limits, of a process. They are used to determine if the process is 'in control' or in need of adjustment.

Control Framework: A tool for business process owners that facilitates the discharge of their responsibilities through the provision of a supporting control model.

COP: Certified Outsourcing Professional. This is an individual certification issued by the international association of outsourcing professionals.

Core Competencies: The unique internal skills and knowledge sets that define an organization's competitive advantage and strengths.

Corporate Governance: See Enterprise Governance

Corrective Action: Changes made to bring expected future performance of the project into line with the plan.

Corrective Action Log: A log established to monitor action items and corrective actions.

COSO: Committee of Sponsoring Organizations of the Treadway Commission. Internationally accepted standard for corporate governance. See www.coso.org.

Cost: A measurement, in monetary terms, of the amount of resources used for some purpose.

Cost Benefit Analysis: Evaluation of the estimated cost to achieve project objectives against the value (benefits) of the project or phase. Uses select project investment choices, using one time and recurring costs and benefits. Various financial measures may be used such as net present value (NPV), return on investment (ROI), payback period and others.

Cost Budgeting: Allocating the cost estimates to individual project elements or tasks.

Cost Control: Controlling changes to the project budget.

Cost Effectiveness: Ensuring that there is a proper balance between the quality of service on the one side and expenditure on the other. Any investment that increases the costs of providing IT services should always result in enhancements to service quality or quantity.

Cost Estimate: An evaluation of all costs of the elements of a project or effort as defined by an agreed-upon scope.

Cost Estimating: Estimating the cost of the resources needed to complete project activities.

Cost Management: All the procedures, tasks and deliverables that are needed to fulfill an organization's costing and charging requirements.

Cost of Money: Capital cost of money (cost of capital) is an imputed cost determined by applying cost-of-money rate to capital employed in contract performance. Capital employed is determined without regard to whether its source is equity or borrowed capital.

Cost of Quality: The costs incurred to ensure quality. The cost of quality includes quality planning, quality control, quality assurance, and rework.

Cost Performance Index (CPI): The ratio of budgeted costs to actual costs (BCWP/ACWP). CPI is often used to predict the magnitude of a possible cost overrun or under-run. A relative percentage indicator of cost efficiency. Values greater than 1.0 indicate efficiency is better (e.g. CPI =1.3 indicates work has been accomplished 30% more efficiently than baseline). Values less than 1.0 indicate efficiency is worse (e.g. CPI = .80 indicates work has been accomplished 20% less efficiently than baseline).

Cost Plus Fixed Fee (CPFF) Contract: A type of contract where the buyer reimburses the seller for the allowable costs (allowable costs are defined by the contract) plus a fixed amount of profit (fee).

Cost Plus Incentive Fee (CPIF) Contract: A type of contract where the buyer reimburses the seller for the seller's allowable costs (allowable costs are defined by the contract), and the seller earns its profit if it meets defined performance criteria.

Cost Proposal: An all-inclusive statement of work effort and associated cost factors, which includes, but is not limited to equipment and human resources, software development, training, etc.

Cost Sharing: On a cost plus incentive fee (CPIF) type contract, a clause is included which defines a share ratio for cost over/underruns which normally is 80/20%. That is, the customer will reimburse the contractor 80% of the total overrun (100% of the overrun, less 20% of the overrun amount, from the fee); on underrun the contractor receives an additional 20% of the underrun amount as incentive fee.

Cost Variance (CV): (1) Any difference between the estimated cost of an activity and the actual cost of that activity. (2) In earned value, BCWP less ACWP.

Countermeasure: A check or restraint on the service designed to enhance security by reducing the risk of an attack (by reducing either the threat or the vulnerability), reducing the impact of an attack, detecting the occurrence of an attack and/or assisting in the recovery from an attack.

CPI: Cost Performance Index.

CPIF: Cost Plus Incentive Fee.

CPM: Critical Path Method.

Critical Activity (Task): Any activity (task) on a critical path. Most commonly determined by using the critical path method.

Critical Path: In a project network diagram, the series of activities (tasks) which determines the earliest completion of the project. The critical path will generally change from time to time as activities are completed ahead of, or behind schedule. Although normally calculated for the entire project, the critical path can also be determined for a milestone or a subproject. The critical path is usually defined as those activities with float equal to zero. See Critical Path Method.

Critical Path Method (CPM): A network analysis technique used to predict project duration by analyzing which sequence of activities or tasks (which path) has the least amount of scheduling flexibility (the least amount of float). Early dates are calculated by means of a forward pass using a specified start date. Late dates are calculated by means of a backward pass starting from a specified completion date (usually the forward pass's calculated project early finish date).

Critical Path Network: A plan for executing a project that consists of activities, their durations, and their logical relationships to one another.

CSF: Critical Success Factor

Critical versus Core: Many operations are critical to a business's operations but do not represent a differentiating competitive capability; that is, they are not core competencies. A classic example is payroll. Processing payroll accurately and timely is critical to the success of any organization, but is a core competence of very few organizations – mainly those that provide this service to other companies as their business.

Customer: The recipient and/or ultimate owner of the deliverable produced as a result of an agreement.

Customer Relationship Management (CRM): A system for managing a company's interactions with current and future customers. It often involves using technology to organize, automate and synchronize sales, marketing, customer service, and technical support.

Customer Reporting Level: The lowest level of the work breakdown structure at which performance data is reported to the customer.

CV: Cost Variance.

D:

Dashboard: A measurement tool for setting expectations for an organization at each level and continuous monitoring of the performance against set targets.

Database: Stores data generated by business apps, sensors, and transaction processing systems (TPS).

Data Classification Scheme: An enterprise-wide schema for classifying data on factors such as criticality, sensitivity and ownership.

Data Dictionary: A set of metadata that contains definitions and representations of data elements.

Data Marts: Small-scale data warehouses that support a single function or department.

Data Owners: Individuals, normally managers or directors, who have responsibility for the integrity, accurate reporting and use of computerized data.

Data Management: The function of organizing, cataloging, structuring, locating, storing, maintaining, retrieving, securing, and recovering data, including the processes of data modeling, data mining, data warehousing and database administration.

Data Virtualization: Any approach to data management that allows an application to retrieve and manipulate data without requiring technical details about the data, such as how it is formatted or where it is physically located.

Data Warehouses: Integrate data from multiple database and data silos and organize them for complex analysis, knowledge discovery, and to support decision making.

Deadline: A date by which a project, activity and/or task must be finished.

Decision Support System: Typically a computer-based system that supports business and organizational decision making. An increasing amount of data for DSS uses databases, big data and business intelligence tools and techniques.

Definitive Software Library (DSL): The library in which the definitive authorized versions of all software CIs are stored and protected. It is a physical library or storage repository where master copies of software versions are placed. They should be separate from development and test file store areas. The DSL may also include a physical store to hold master copies of bought-in software, e.g. fire-proof safe. Only authorized software should be accepted into the DSL, strictly controlled by change and release management. The DSL exists not directly because of the needs of the configuration management process, but as a common base for the release management and configuration management processes.

Deliverable: Any measurable, tangible, verifiable outcome, result, or item that must be produced to complete a project or part of a project.

Dependency: See Logical Relationship.

Depreciation: The loss in value of an asset due to its use and/or the passage of time. The annual depreciation charge in accounts represents the amount of capital assets used up in the accounting period. It is charged in the cost accounts to ensure that the cost of capital equipment is reflected in the unit costs of the services provided using the equipment. There are various methods of calculating depreciation.

Detail Schedule: Lowest-level method of scheduling and determining status of a work package that is contained in the cost account plan or budget.

Deviation: A departure from established requirements. A deviation in the work product may be classified as an imperfection, nonconformance, or defect, based on its severity in failing to meet or unnecessarily exceed the requirements.

Direct Costs: Any cost which can be identified specifically with a particular final cost objective. It consists of those costs (labor, material, etc.), that can be directly charged to the contract or product or service without distribution to an overhead unit.

Direct Labor: Any labor cost that can be specifically identified with a particular final contract objective. It consists of labor that can be directly charged to the contract or project without distribution to an overhead unit. It excludes materials, as well as overhead costs, and the cost of money.

Disaster Recovery: The process of executing a definitive plan for recovery from any act, natural or man-made, that caused the system, product or facility to fail.

Disaster Recovery Planning: A series of processes that focus only upon the recovery processes, principally in response to physical disasters that are contained within business continuity plan.

Discounted Cash Flow: An evaluation of the future net cash flows generated by a project by discounting them to their present-day value.

Division/Department: A group with a common operational orientation, such as technical, operations, quality assurance, finance or a strategic business unit.

Domain: Grouping of control objectives into logical stages in the IT investment lifecycle

Dummy Activity: An activity (task) of zero duration used to show a logical network relationship in the arrow diagramming method. Dummy activities are used when logical relationships cannot be completely or correctly described with regular activity arrows. Dummies are shown graphically as a dashed line headed by an arrow.

Duration (DU): The number of work periods (not including holidays or other nonworking periods) required to complete an activity or other project element. Usually expressed as workdays or workweeks. Sometimes incorrectly equated with elapsed time. See also Effort

Duration Compression: Shortening the project schedule without reducing the project scope. Duration compression is not always possible and often requires an increase in project cost.

E:

EAC: Estimate at Completion.

Early Finish Date (EF): In the critical path method, the earliest possible point in time at which the uncompleted portions of an activity (or the project) can finish based on the network logic and any schedule logical relationships. Early finish dates can change as the project progresses and changes are made to the project plan.

Early Start Date (ES): In the critical path method, the earliest possible point in time at which the unstarted portions of an activity (or the project) can start, based on the network logic and any schedule logical relationships. Early start dates can change as the project progresses and changes are made to the project plan.

Earned Value (EV): (1) A method for measuring project performance. It compares the amount of work that was planned with what was actually accomplished to determine if cost and schedule performance is as planned. See also Actual Cost of Work Performed (ACWP), Budgeted Cost of Work Scheduled (BCWS), Budgeted Cost of Work Performed (BCWP), Cost Variance (CV), Cost Performance Index (CPI), Schedule Variance (SV), and Schedule Performance Index (SPI). (2) The earned value cost at completion (EAC) = ACWP + work remaining/CPI.

Economies of Scale: Related to the production function, economies of scale occur when increases to inputs result in equivalent increases in outputs. Increasing economies of scale occur when increases to inputs result in disproportionately higher increases in outputs.

EF: Early Finish Date.

Effort: The number of labor units required to complete an activity or other project element. Usually expressed as staff hours, staff days, or staff weeks. Should not be confused with duration.

Eighty-Hour rule: All project work should be decomposed into 80-hour periods (two weeks) when deliverables should be produced and formal project status reviews should be held. There is no magic to the rule, it simply creates discipline, and incremental deliverables. It can be shorter, but should not be any longer.

EIS: An executive information system is a type of management information system that facilitates and supports senior executive information and decision-making needs. It provides access to internal and external information that is relevant to organizational goals. It is commonly considered a specialized form of decision support system. EIS emphasizes graphical displays and easy-to-use user interfaces.

End Item: The final product or service when completed and ready for release.

Engagement Model (EM): Used to develop better relationships between customers & IT that are built on trust, open communications, credibility, knowledge & understanding of each other's environments. The IT engagement manager is the interface between the customer and the IT origination.

Enterprise: A group of individuals working together for a common purpose, typically within the context of an organizational form such as corporation, public agency, charity or trust.

Enterprise Architecture: Business-oriented technology road map for the attainment of business goals and objectives.

Enterprise Architecture for IT: IT's delivery response, provided by clearly defined processes using its resources (applications, information, infrastructure and people).

Enterprise Data Dictionary: The name, type, range of values, source, system of record, and authorization for access for each data element used in the enterprise. It indicates which application programs use that data so that when a data structure is contemplated, a list of the affected programs can be generated.

Enterprise Governance: Represents the entire accountability and control framework of an organization, includes roles and responsibility of the board, the CEO and other managers, to ensure that the organization meets its objectives and plans in an ethical manner.

ES: Early Start Date.

eSCM®: The eSourcing capability models developed by the IT Services Qualification Center (ITSqc) at Carnegie Mellon University to improve sourcing relationships in the internet-enabled economy. ITSqc developed the eSourcing capability models for both service providers (eSCM-SP) and for client organizations (eSCM-CL).

E-Sourcing: Internet-based outsourcing that takes advantage of the application service provider (ASP) delivery model. See ASP

eSourcing Capability Model for Service Providers (eSCM-SP): A framework to help IT service providers develop their IT service management capabilities from a service sourcing perspective. eSCM-SP was developed by Carnegie Mellon University.

eSourcing Model for Client Organizations (eSCM-CL): A framework to help organizations guide their analysis and decisions on sourcing models and strategies. eSCML-CL was developed by Carnegie Mellon University.

Estimate: An assessment of the likely quantitative result. Usually applied to project costs and durations and should always include some indication of accuracy (e.g., ± x percent). Usually used with a modifier (e.g., preliminary, conceptual, feasibility). Some application areas have specific modifiers that imply particular accuracy ranges, e.g., order-of-magnitude estimate, budget estimate, and definitive estimate (in engineering and construction projects). Estimating should become more accurate with each project phase and with more experience.

Estimate At Completion (EAC): The expected total cost of an activity (task), a group of activities (tasks), or the project when the defined scope of work has been completed. Most techniques for forecasting EAC include some adjustment of the original cost estimate based on project performance to date. Also shown as 'estimated at completion'. Often shown as EAC=(Actuals-to-date)+ETC. See also Earned Value and Estimate to Complete.

Estimate To Complete (ETC): The expected additional cost needed to complete an activity, a group of activities, or the project. Most techniques for forecasting ETC include some adjustment to the original estimate based on project performance to date. Also called 'estimated to complete'. See also Earned Value and Estimate at Completion.

Estimated Work Remaining (EWR): The forecast of labor hours and costs (direct and indirect) required to complete the authorized work remaining. It is based on past performance plus knowledgeable projections of the scope of the work remaining to be accomplished.

ETC: Estimate (or Estimated) To Complete (or Completion).

EV: Earned Value.

Event-on-Node: A network diagramming technique in which events are presented by boxes (or nodes) connected by arrows to show the sequence in which the events are to occur. Used in the original Program Evaluation and Review Technique (PERT).

Exception Report: Document that includes only major variations from plan (rather than all variations).

F:

Family Tree: Hierarchical product, process or functional structure.

Fast Tracking: Compressing the project processes (schedule) by overlapping activities (tasks) that would normally be done in sequence, such as design and construction and using iterative lifecycle methodologies to frequently validate the results with the sponsor or customer.

Fee: The charge for the use of one's services to the extent specified in the contract.

FF: Free Float or Finish-to-Finish.

FFP: Firm Fixed Price.

Financial Management of IT Services: One of the ITIL processes that addresses the budgeting, costs, benefits and charging methods for IT services.

Finish Date: A point in time associated with an activity's completion. Usually qualified by one of the following: actual, planned, estimated, scheduled, early, late, baseline, target or current.

Finish-to-Finish (FF): See Logical Relationship.

Finish-to-Start (FS): See Logical Relationship.

Firm Fixed Price (FFP) Contract: A type of contract where the buyer pays the seller a set amount (as defined by the contract) regardless of the seller's costs.

Fiscal Year: The grouping of twelve accounting months.

Fixed Price Contract: See Firm Fixed Price Contract.

Fixed Price Incentive Fee (FPIF) Contract: A type of contract where the buyer pays the seller a set amount (as defined by the contract), and the seller can earn an additional amount if it meets defined performance criteria.

Forward Pass: The calculation of the early start and early finish dates for the unstarted portions of all network activities. See also Network Analysis and Backward Pass.

Forward Pricing: Use of progressively escalated rates to develop an escalated estimate. (Contrasted with 'constant dollar pricing' which uses a single unescalated set of rates to develop an unescalated estimate.)

Forward Pricing Rates: The progressively escalated rates used to develop an escalated estimate. See Forward Pricing.

FPIF: Fixed Price Incentive Fee.

Free Float (FF): The amount of time an activity (task) can be delayed without delaying the early start of any immediately following activities. See also Float.

FS: Finish-to-Start.

Full Cost: The total cost of all the resources used in supplying a service i.e. the sum of the direct costs of producing the output, a proportional share of overhead costs and any selling and distribution expenses. Both cash costs and non-cash costs should be included, including the cost of capital.

Full Risk Mitigation PM Process: Also known as classical or traditional program or project management, where the PM process is followed and no compression or short cuts are taken (see Fast Tracking).

Functional Manager: A manager responsible for activities in a specialized department or function (e.g., engineering, manufacturing, marketing). See Division/Department.

Functional Organization: An organization structure in which staff are grouped hierarchically by specialty (e.g., production, marketing, engineering, and accounting at the top level; with engineering, further divided into mechanical, electrical and others).

Functional Process Outsourcing: A company's business processes end at its true customers, the people paying the bills. There are, however, many internal processes that exist to support people within the company and are often performed within a single department. Human resources, finance and accounting, travel, and facilities services are examples. When these functional processes are outsourced, along with the supporting technologies and supply chains that feed into them, it is referred to as functional process outsourcing.

Funding: Represents the actual dollars available for expenditure in the accomplishment of contract effort. Funds are normally issued by the customer on a fiscal year or annual basis. Actual release of funds is frequently on an incremental basis within the year. The planning of work and the time-phasing of baselines for a given period must be consistent with the known available funding.

Funds: The sum of money authorized for a specific project or contract. Funds or funding refers to the transactions of real money, which is accounted for in expenditure and commitment reports.

G:

Gain-Sharing: A contract structure where both the customer and provider share financially in the value created through the relationship. One example is when a service provider receives a share of the savings it generates for its client.

Gantt Chart: See Bar Chart.

GERT: Graphical Evaluation and Review Technique.

Governance: The oversight and accountability of all aspects of a business, a function like IT or a project. It also defines the rules, responsibilities and decision authority of the board, executive management team and others in an organization. Areas of focus include: strategic management, investment management, project management, business/IT alignment, regulatory compliance, performance management, operational management, risk management, ethics and integrity and others.

Graphical Evaluation and Review Technique (GERT): A network analysis technique that allows for conditional and probabilistic treatment of logical relationships (i.e., some activities may not be performed).

Guideline: A description of a particular way of accomplishing something that is less prescriptive than a procedure or standard.

H:

Hardware/Software Evaluation: Assessment of compatibility between existing or required hardware and new application (or operating systems or database) software that will operate in the environment.

Hierarchy: An outline structure. Any group of tasks with indented levels of detail.

Histogram: A graphic representation of resource availability and utilization levels. A histogram represents these levels by means of a series of rectangular bars above a time scale, with different sizes representing different levels.

Hurdle rate: A rate typically set by corporate finance as a gate for capital investments. An investment with a projected return lower than the prescribed hurdle rate should not receive funding. A hurdle rate can be used as the discount rate in net present value (NPV) calculations to ensure that a project with a positive NPV is aligned with the company's overall investment policies.

Hybrid cloud: One of four cloud deployment models, a hybrid cloud is simply a combination of two or more cloud deployment models (public, private, or community). Typically, a management framework enables the environments to appear as a single cloud for the purposes of 'cloud peering' or 'bursting'.

Hybrid SDLC: Refers to a systems/software development lifecycle process that combines waterfall (sequential) and spiral (iterative) methodologies. See also Waterfall and Spiral.

I:

IFB: Invitation For Bid (similar to RFI and RFP).

Impact Analysis: The identification of critical business processes, and the potential damage or loss that may be caused to the organization resulting from a disruption to those processes.

Incident : Any event which is not part of the standard operation of a service and which causes, or may cause, an interruption to, or a reduction in, the quality of that service.

Incident Management: A process which aims to resolve the incident and restore the provision of services quickly. If an incident recurs, it is considered a problem.

Indirect Costs: Costs that because of their incurrence for common or joint objectives are not readily assignable to a particular contract or deliverable item. Therefore, indirect costs are allocated to the products/contracts involved on some consistent basis, which is in general accord with the extent to which each product/contract has benefited from the objective for which the costs were incurred.

Information Distribution: Making needed information available to project stakeholders in a timely manner.

Information Planning: Long and short-range goal setting and action planning with respect to a client firm's information technology activities, strategy formulation.

Infrastructure as a Service (IaaS): A cloud deployment model where the service provider delivers the necessary hardware resources (network, compute, storage) required to host and run a customer's applications. IaaS can be thought of as the inverse of Software as a Service (SaaS).

Initiation: Committing the organization to begin a project phase and should include such components as project charter, objectives, needs, deliverables, authorization, etc.

Intermediate Recovery: Previously called 'warm stand-by', typically involves the re-establishment of the critical systems and services within a 24 to 72 hour period, and is used by organizations that need to recover IT facilities within a predetermined time to prevent impacts to the business process.

Internal Rate of Return (IRR): IRR can be used in conjunction with net present value (NPV) analysis. A direct metric, IRR is essentially the rate required for NPV to equal zero.

International Organization for Standardization (ISO): The world's largest developer of standards. ISO is a non-governmental organization which is a network of the national standards institutes of 156 countries. Further information about ISO is available from http://www.iso.org/

Inventory: Raw materials, work in process, and finished products required for plant operation or the value of such material and other supplies.

Invitation for Bid (IFB): Generally, this term is equivalent to request for proposal (RRP). However, in some application areas, it may have a narrower or more specific meaning.

Ishikawa Diagram: A technique that helps a team to identify all the possible causes of a problem. Originally devised by Kaoru Ishikawa, the output of this technique is a diagram that looks like a fishbone.

ISO 17799: Information security standard.

ISO 20000: ISO Specification and Code of Practice for IT Service Management. ISO/IEC 20000 is aligned with ITIL best practice.

ISO 27001: ISO Specification for Information Security Management. The corresponding Code of Practice is ISO 17799.

ISO 9000: A generic term that refers to a number of international standards and guidelines for quality management systems. See http://www.iso.org/ for more information. See ISO.

ISO 9001: The internationally accepted set of standards concerning quality management systems.

Issue: A problem (or opportunity) that should be resolved to continue progress on a task, activity or project. The number of open issues on a project should be kept to a minimum.

IT Architecture: An integrated framework for evolving or maintaining existing IT resources and acquiring new IT to achieve the enterprise's strategic and business goals.

IT Governance: Is a sub-set of enterprise governance focused on IT value creation, business and IT alignment, risk management, and to better manage and control the performance of IT (e.g. project management, service management, etc.).

IT Investment Dashboard: Charting of costs and returns of IT-enabled investment projects in terms of business values for an enterprise.

IT Service Continuity Management: This process addresses the preparation and planning of disaster recovery measures for IT services in the event of a business interruption. It emphasizes the links with all the measures necessary to safeguard the continuity of the customer organization in the event of a disaster (business continuity management) as well as the measures to prevent such disasters. An ITIL process.

IT Service Management (ITSM): The implementation and management of quality IT services that meet the needs of the business. IT service management is performed by IT service providers through an appropriate mix of people, process and information technology.

IT Service Management Forum (itSMF): The IT Service Management Forum is an independent organization dedicated to promoting a professional approach to IT service management. The itSMF and its membership contribute to the development of ITIL and associated IT service management standards. See http://www.itsmf.com/ for more information.

IT Strategic Plan: A long-term plan, i.e., three- to five-year horizon, in which business and IT management co-operatively describe how IT resources will contribute to the enterprise's strategic objectives (goals).

IT Strategy Committee: Committee at the level of the board of directors to ensure the board is involved in major IT matters/decisions/plans.

IT Tactical Plan: A medium-term plan, i.e., six- to 18-month horizon that translates the IT strategic plan direction into required initiatives, resource requirements and ways in which resources and benefits will be monitored and managed.

Iterative SDLC: Refers to a systems/software lifecycle methodology that has frequent validations by the customer and other project constituencies as the system is built to ensure frequent corrections or adjustments to the scope, requirements and in-process system development efforts. See also Spiral SDLC.

ITIL (IT Infrastructure Library): A set of best practice guidance for IT service management. ITIL is owned by the AXELOS and consists of a series of publications giving guidance on the provision of quality IT services, and on the processes and facilities needed to support them. ITIL focuses on operational or infrastructure IT services. It consists of twelve IT service management and delivery processes. (Incident Management, Problem Management, Configuration Management, etc.). ITIL is being revised to a more IT service lifecycle process approach. See http://www.itil.co.uk/ for more information.

K:

Kano Model: A model developed by Noriaki Kano that is used to help understand customer preferences. The Kano model considers attributes of a product or IT service grouped into areas such as basic factors, excitement factors, performance factors, etc.

Key Performance Indicators (KPIs): The metrics used by management to assess the performance of an organization, function, process, individuals and/or teams.

L:

Lag: A modification of a logical relationship, which directs a delay in the successor, task. For example, in a finish-to-start dependency with a ten-day lag, the successor activity cannot start until ten days after the predecessor has finished. Depending on software capabilities, lag may be identified with a negative integer.

Late Finish Date (LF): In the critical path method, the latest possible point in time that an activity or task must be completed without delaying a specific milestone (usually the project finish date).

Late Start Date (LS): In the critical path method, the latest possible point in time that an activity or task may begin without delaying a specified milestone (usually the project finish date).

Latest Revised Estimate (LRE): The total end-point amount (forecast) which represents actual labor hours and costs (direct and indirect) to date, plus the estimate of labor hours and costs (direct and indirect) for authorized work remaining. The terms 'estimate at completion' and 'latest revised estimate' are synonymous.

Level of Detail: A policy or expression of the content of plans, schedules, and reports in accordance with the scale of the breakdown of information.

Level of Effort (LOE): Support-type activity (e.g., vendor or customer liaison) that does not readily lend itself to measurement of discreet accomplishment. It is generally characterized by a uniform rate of activity over a specific period of time.

Leveling: See Resource Leveling.

LF: Late Finish Date.

Lifecycle Costing: The concept of including acquisition, operating and disposal costs when evaluating various alternatives.

Lifecycle: A series of states, connected by allowable transitions. The lifecycle represents an approval process for systems or infrastructure phases with going to gates.

Line Manager: (1) The manager of any group that actually makes a product or performs a service. (2) A functional manager.

LOE: Level Of Effort.

Logical Relationship: A dependency between two project activities (tasks), or between a project activity and a milestone. See also Precedence Relationship. The four possible types of logical relationships are (1) Finish-to-finish: the 'from' activity must finish before the 'to' activity can finish. (2) Start-to start: the 'from' activity must start before the 'to' activity can start. (3) Start-to-finish: the 'from' activity must start before the 'to' activity can finish. (4) Finish-to-start: the predecessor activity must finish before the successor activity can start.

Loop: A network path that passes the same node twice. Loops cannot be analyzed using traditional network analysis techniques such as CPM and PERT. Loops are allowed in GERT.

LS: Late Start Date.

M:

Maintenance: Post-delivery modification of a software/hardware product to correct faults, to improve performance or other attributes, or to adapt the product to a changed environment.

Make versus Buy: Outsourcing is often referred to as a 'make versus buy' decision on the part of the customer. The question is, "Is it in the organization's best interests to continue to (or start to) perform the activity itself using its own people, process expertise, and technology or to 'buy' the activity from the service provider marketplace?"

Management Control Systems: The systems (e.g. planning, scheduling, budgeting, estimating, work authorization, cost accumulation, performance measurement, etc.) used by customers and contractors to plan and control the cost and scheduling of work.

Management Reserve: A separately planned quantity used to allow for future situations, which are impossible to predict (sometimes called 'unknown unknowns'). Management reserves may involve cost or schedule. Management reserves are intended to reduce the risk of missing cost or schedule objectives. Use of management reserve requires a change to the project's cost baseline.

Management Reserve Budget: An amount of the total allocated budget withheld for management control purposes, rather than designated for the accomplishment of a specific task or set of tasks.

Man-Month: The equivalent number of hours worked in a month by one person working standard time, taking into consideration the average labor loss factors.

Market-Driven Sourcing: A market-driven approach to sourcing means that the organization's sourcing decisions are in direct response to the capabilities of the marketplace of available providers. Where the organization's internal capabilities are superior to the marketplace of providers, the activity is performed internally; where they are not, the activity is performed externally.

Master Data Management (MDM): Is a set of processes to integrate data from various sources or enterprise applications to create and maintain a more unified view of a customer, product, or other core data entity that is shared across systems.

Master Reference File and Data Entities: MDM consolidates data from various data sources into a master reference file, which then feeds data back to the applications, thereby creating accurate and consistent data across the enterprise and developing a master reference file to obtain a more unified version of the data. A master data reference file is based on data entities.

Master Schedule: A summary-level schedule which identifies the major activities and key milestones. See also Milestone Schedule.

Material: All direct costs excluding labor and other direct costs (ODC). It consists of materials (including spares) and subcontract effort.

Material Requirements Planning (MRP): A system which uses bills of material, inventory and open order data, and master production schedule information to calculate requirements for materials. It makes recommendations to release replenishment orders for material. Further, since it is time-phased, it makes recommendations to reschedule open orders when due dates and need dates are not in phase.

Matrix Organization: Any organizational structure in which the project manager shares responsibility with the functional managers for assigning priorities and for directing the work of individuals assigned to the project.

Maturity Model: The degree to which an organization improves its level of effectiveness and efficiency based on an industry framework such as SEI's CMMI (Capability Maturity Model Integrated).

Measurement: The act or process of measuring to compare results to requirements. A quantitative estimate of performance. See Key Performance Indicators (KPIs).

Metadata: Describes other data and provides information about a specific item's content. As an example, a text document's metadata may contain information about how long a document is, who the author is, when it was created, and a short summary of the document.

Metrics: Specific quantitative measures that help in monitoring and controlling the progress of a program or project or initiative (e.g. CPI, SPI, budget/actual cost and schedule variances, number of open issues, status of tasks on critical path, etc.) or service (service level) or function.

Milestone Schedule: A summary-level schedule which identifies the major milestones. See also Master Schedule.

Mitigation: Taking steps to lessen risk by lowering the probability of a risk event's occurrence or reducing its effect should it occur.

Modern Project Management (MPM): A term used to distinguish the current broad range of project management (scope, cost, time, quality, risk, customer satisfaction, etc.) components.

Monitoring: The collection, analysis, and reporting of project performance, usually as compared to plan through the use of metrics.

Monte Carlo Analysis: A schedule risk assessment technique that performs a project simulation many times in order to calculate a distribution of likely results.

Moves, Adds, Changes (MAC): Fundamental functions required to provision IT services to clients, including the assignment of network addresses, disk storage, and so on.

MPM: Modern Project Management.

MPS: Master Program Schedule.

N:

Near-Critical Activity: An activity/task that has low total float.

Net present value (NPV): The NPV of an investment is the present value of all future benefits (cash flows, savings, offsets, deferrals, and so on) generated by that investment, discounted over set intervals of time, and net of any initial startup costs or investments. NPV analysis incorporates the principle of time value of money (TVM).

Network: See Project Network Diagram.

Network Analysis: The process of identifying early and late start and finish dates for the uncompleted portions of project activities. See also Critical Path Method, Program Evaluation and Review Technique, and Graphical Evaluation and Review Technique.

Network Diagram: A schematic display of activities and logical relationships of activities/tasks that comprise the project. Two popular drawing methods for scheduling are 'arrow' and 'precedence' diagramming methods.

Network Logic: The collection of activity/task dependencies that make up a project network diagram.

Network Planning: A broad generic term for techniques used to plan complex projects using logic diagrams (networks). Two of the most popular techniques are ADM (Arrow Diagramming Methods) and PDM (Precedence Diagramming Methods).

Node: One of the defining points of a network; a junction point joined to some or all of the other dependency lines. See also Arrow Diagramming Method and Precedence Diagramming Method.

O:

Objective: A predetermined result; the end towards which effort is directed.

OBS: Organization Breakdown Structure.

Offshore Outsourcing: The outsourcing of any operation, be it information technology, a business process, or manufacturing, to a firm whose principal base of operation is outside the country. Terms such as near-shore outsourcing or close-shore outsourcing are also used to indicate that while still outside the country, there is a closer proximity between the customer organization's primary operations and that of the provider. For example, for a U.S. company, Canada might be considered near-shore while India is offshore.

Offshoring: Performing or sourcing any part of an organization's activities at or from a location outside the company's home country. Companies create captive centers offshore, where the employees work for them, or outsource offshore, where the employees work for the outsourcing provider.

OLA (Operational Level Agreement): An internal agreement covering the delivery of services which support the IT organization in their delivery of services.

OLAP (Online Analytical Processing): A computer-based technique for analyzing data for business intelligence.

OPBOK: The Outsourcing Professional Body of Knowledge (OPBOK) was developed by the International Association of Outsourcing Professionals (IAOP) as a framework for understanding what outsourcing is and how it fits within contemporary business operations.

Operating Plan: The organized collection of short-range (one year or less) objectives and initiatives that provide direction for an organization.

Operational Costs: Those costs resulting from the day-to-day running of the IT services section, e.g. staff costs, hardware maintenance and electricity, and relating to repeating payments whose effects can be measured within a short timeframe, usually less than the 12-month financial year.

Operational Planning: Planning concerned with the development of control mechanisms to assure the effective implementation of actions in the strategic or tactical plans. Operational planning provides a basis for the measurement of actual performance relative to the plan and usually has a planning horizon of one year or less.

Opportunity Cost: The value of a benefit sacrificed in favor of an alternative course of action. That is the cost of using resources in a particular operation expressed in terms of foregoing the benefit that could be derived from the best alternative use of those resources.

Order of Magnitude Estimate: See Estimate.

Organizational Breakdown Structure (OBS): A depiction of the project organization that is arranged so as to relate work packages to organizational units, i.e. division/department.

Organizational Planning: Identifying, documenting, and assigning project roles, responsibilities, and reporting relationships.

Organizing: The process of defining certain parameters by which a project can be effectively administered.

Original Budget: The budget established at, or near, the time the contract or project authorization was signed and based on the negotiated contract cost.

Outline: The organization of tasks into related task groups or sub-projects. An outline illustrates a hierarchy by indenting successively lower levels of detail.

Outputs: Materials or information provided to others (internal or external customers).

Outsourcing: A long-term, results-oriented relationship with an external service provider for activities traditionally performed within the company. Outsourcing usually applies to a business or IT process or function. It assumes a degree of managerial control and risk on the part of the provider and buyer.

Outsourcing at the Customer Interface: Outsourcing where a provider assumes responsibility for direct interaction with an organization's customers. This interaction may be in person, over the telephone, via email, mail, or any other direct means.

Outsourcing Framework: A structure for mapping all of the activities of an organization in a way that allows consistent evaluation, planning, implementation, and management of sourcing decisions.

Outsourcing Process: A repeatable, multistage, management process for identifying outsourcing opportunities and moving those opportunities from concept through implementation and ongoing management.

Outsourcing Process Maturity: Use of an industry best practice framework (such as CMMI) to analyze current and target state maturity levels for outsourcing.

Outsourcing Teams: Multi-disciplinary working groups that form for specific purposes throughout the outsourcing process.

Overall Change Control: Coordinating changes across the entire project.

Overhead (OH): Costs, which because of their incurrence for common or joint objectives are not subject readily to treatment as direct costs (e.g. maintenance).

Overhead Costs: A specific category of indirect costs.

Overhead Pool: Grouping of incurred cost identified with two or more cost objectives but not identified specifically with a final cost objective. The cost within each pool has similar beneficial or causal relationships to cost objectives.

Overrun (Underrun): The value for the work performed to date minus the actual cost for that same work. When value exceeds actual cost, an underrun exists, When actual cost exceeds value, an overrun condition exists. See Earned Value.

P:

Parametric Estimating: An estimating technique that uses a statistical relationship between historical data and other variables (e.g., square footage in construction, lines of code in software development) to calculate an estimate.

Pareto Diagram: A histogram, ordered by frequency of occurrence, that shows how many results were generated by each identified cause.

Path: A set of sequentially connected activities or tasks in a project network diagram.

Path Convergence: In mathematical network analysis, the tendency of parallel paths of approximately equal duration to delay the completion of the milestone where they meet.

Path Float: See Float.

Payback Method: A direct metric that measures the length of time required to recoup the investment in a product or service. A product that allows the buyer to recoup his or her investment quickly is deemed a better investment than one that has a lengthy payback period.

PC: Percent Complete.

PCL: Project Control Log.

PCS: Project Control System.

PDM: Precedence Diagramming Method.

Percent Complete (PC): An estimate, expressed as a percent, of the amount of work which has been completed on an activity or group of activities (tasks).

Performance: The term performance is used as an attribute of the work product itself and as a general characteristic. The broad performance characteristics that are of interest to management are quality (effectiveness), cost (efficiency), and schedule. Performance is the highly effective common measurement that links the quality of the work product to efficiency and productivity.

Performance-Based Pricing: Contractual pricing mechanisms that link compensation to meeting specific performance objectives or outcomes.

Performance Management: The ability to manage any type of measurement including employee, team, process, operational or financial measurements. The term connotes closed-loop control and regular monitoring of the measurement.

Performance Measurement: The methods for measuring accomplishment on work package task(s), scheduled in accordance with achievement of higher level schedules.

Performance Measurement Baseline (PMB): The time-phased baseline plan against which contract or project performance is measured. It is formed by the baselines assigned to scheduled work and the applicable indirect baseline. For future effort, the performance measurement baseline also includes undistributed baselines. It equals the total contract baseline less authorized undefined work committed, but not incurred or used yet.

Performance Reporting: Collecting and disseminating information about project performance to help ensure project progress.

Performing Organization: The enterprise whose employees are most directly involved in doing the work of the project.

PERT: Program Evaluation and Review Technique.

PERT Chart: A specific type of project network diagram. See Program Evaluation and Review Technique.

PF: Planned Finish Date.

Phase: See Project Phase.

Plan: A predetermined course of action over a specified period of time which represents a projected response to an anticipated environment or condition in order to accomplish a specific set of objectives and actions.

Planned Finish Date (PF): See Scheduled Finish Date.

Planned Start Date (PS): See Scheduled Start Date.

Planning: The determination of an initiative's objectives, scope, requirements and deliverables with identification of the activities/tasks to be performed, processes and resources to be used for accomplishing the tasks, assignment of responsibility and accountability, and establishment of an integrated plan to achieve completion as required. It is also a process to produce a plan (e.g. business, project, etc...)

Platform as a Service (PaaS): One of three cloud service models, PaaS is best described as a development environment hosted on third-party infrastructure to facilitate rapid design and deployment of new applications. Google's App Engine, VMware's SpringSource, and Amazon's Amazon Web Services (AWS) are common examples of PaaS offerings.

PM: Project Manager or Product Manager.

PMB: Performance Measurement Baseline.

PMBOK (Guide): Project Management Body Of Knowledge - developed by PMI (Project Management Institute).

PMCS: Program or Project Management and Control System.

PMO: Project Management Office.

PMP: Project Management Professional who is certified through PMI (Project Management Institute). It is an individual certification.

Policy: A statement of principles and beliefs, or a settled course, adopted to guide the overall management of affairs in support of a stated aim or goal. It is mostly related to fundamental conduct and usually defines a general framework within which other business and management actions are carried out.

Portfolio Management: Process that ensures that IT investments are evaluated, prioritized, funded and approved in a consistent and optimized manner.

Precedence Diagramming Method (PDM): A network diagramming technique in which activities/tasks are represented by boxes (or nodes). Activities are linked by precedence relationships to show the sequence in which the activities are to be performed.

Precedence Relationship: The term used in the precedence diagramming method for a logical relationship. In current usage, however, precedence relationship, logical relationship, and dependency and constraint are widely used interchangeably regardless of the diagramming method in use.

Predecessor Activity: (1) In the arrow diagramming method, the activity which enters a node. (2) In the precedence diagramming method, any activity which is constrained to the activity in question by a logical relationship.

Price: The amount of money asked or given for a product or service (e.g. exchange value).

PRINCE2: The standard UK government method for project management.

Private Cloud: One of four cloud computing deployment models. Simply put, a computing environment dedicated to a single customer or tenant.

Problem: A question or situation proposed for solution. The result of not conforming to requirements or, in other words, a potential task resulting from the existence of defects. An unknown underlying cause of one or more incidents.

Problem Management: Attempts to identify the underlying cause. Once the causes have been identified (known errors), a business decision is taken on whether to make permanent improvements to the infrastructure in order to prevent new incidents.

Problem/Opportunity Analysis: Evaluation of problems and/or opportunities to determine the feasibility of developing a proposal or authorization for a project.

Procedure: A description of a particular way of accomplishing something; an established way of doing things; a series of steps followed in a definite regular order ensuring the consistent and repetitive approach to actions.

Process: Defined as the logical organization of people, materials, energy, equipment, systems, processes and procedures into work activities designed to produce a specified end result (work product). A process is continuous (e.g. processing a sales order).

Process Control: The set of activities employed to detect and remove special causes of variation in order to maintain or restore the stability of a process.

Process Enterprise: A process enterprise operates its business as a collection of end-to-end business processes where executive leadership, education, responsibilities, measurement, and reward systems are all oriented to this view of the business's operations. This process orientation is in direct contrast to the traditional hierarchical view of an organization.

Process Improvement: The set of activities employed to detect and remove common causes of variation in order to improve process capability. Process improvement leads to quality improvement.

Process Management: Management approach comprising quality management and process optimization.

Procurement Planning: Determining what to procure, when, how, how much and why.

Product Development Lifecycle: The phases of a product's lifecycle from concept through maturity and decline. Specific phases or stages include: idea generation and concept development; market research and validation; regulatory check (where appropriate); competitive analysis; develop product concept and prototype; test market; develop product/service; commercialize and launch product and post-launch product support.

Product Management: The dedicated management of a specific product or service to increase its profit contribution from current and potential markets accountable for all phases of the product development lifecycle (see Product Development Lifecycle)

Product Positioning: The relative positioning of a product in terms of its brand, functions, features, benefits and other criteria in comparison to competitor products.

Product Pricing: The price represents the cost of the product to the customer and revenues and profits to the supplier.

Production Environment: The hardware, software, communication links, and operating systems to be used when a system has been implemented, as determined during the business design phase and established during the implementation phase.

Production Planning: The function of setting the overall level of manufacturing or construction output. Its prime purpose is to establish production rates that will achieve management's objective, while usually attempting to keep the production force relatively stable.

Production Support: The process of operating, maintaining, and enhancing a computer or manufacturing system.

Program: A group of inter-related projects managed in a coordinated way. Programs usually are larger, more complex, higher risk and higher value than projects.

Program Evaluation and Review Technique (PERT): An event-oriented network analysis technique used to estimate project duration when there is a high degree of uncertainty with the individual activity duration estimates. PERT applies the critical path method to a weighted average duration estimate.

Program Management Office (PMO): Focal point for helping program and project managers to develop and/or administer the project management processes, tools and techniques. Can also be involved in project governance, reporting, training, project audits and related functions. May also be a center of excellence for project management competencies and skills.

Program Management: The management of a related series of projects (or one project) executed over a longer period of time, and which are designed to accomplish broad goals and objectives, to which the individual projects contribute.

Program Manager (PM): The individual who is assigned complete responsibility, authority, and control over all technical and administrative aspects of a program (project). The PM may delegate responsibilities to deputies who report to the PM.

Project: A structured set of activities concerned with delivering to the enterprise a defined capability (that is necessary but not sufficient to achieve a required business outcome) based on an agreed-upon schedule and budget.

Project Charter: A document authorized by senior management that provides the project manager with the scope, boundary and authority to apply organizational resources to project activities.

Project Communications Management: A subset of project management that includes the process required to ensure proper collection and dissemination of project status information.

It consists of communications planning, information distribution, performance reporting, and administrative closure.

Project Cost Management: A subset of project management that includes the processes required to ensure that the project is completed within the approved budget. It consists of resource planning, cost estimating, cost budgeting, and cost control.

Project Human Resource Management: A subset of project management that includes the processes required to ensure that the various people-related elements of the project are properly coordinated. It consists of project plan development, project plan execution, and overall change control.

Project Integration Management: A subset of project management that includes the processes required to ensure that the various elements of the project are properly coordinated. It consists of project plan development, project plan execution, and overall change control.

Project Lifecycle: A collection of generally sequential project phases whose name and number are determined by the control needs of the organization or organizations involved in the project (e.g. initiation, planning, executing and terminating).

Project Management (PM): The application of knowledge, skills, tools, and techniques to project activities in order to meet or exceed stakeholder needs and expectations from a project.

Project Management Body of Knowledge (PMBOK): An inclusive term that describes the sum of knowledge within the profession of project management. As with other professions such as law, medicine, and accounting, the body of knowledge rests with the practitioners and academics who apply and advance it. The PMBOK includes proven, traditional practices, which are widely applied, as well as innovative and advanced ones which have seen more limited use. Developed by PMI.

Project Management Professional (PMP): An individual certified as such by the Project Management Institute.

Project Management Software: A class of computer applications specifically designed to aid with planning, controlling, reporting project costs, schedules and resources.

Project Management Team: The members of the project team who are directly involved in project management activities. On some smaller projects, the project management team may include virtually all of the project team members.

Project Manager (PM): The individual responsible for managing a project.

Project Network Diagram: Any schematic display of the logical relationships of project activities. Always drawn from left to right to reflect project chronology (however, not scaled to reflect elapsed time). Often incorrectly referred to as a 'PERT chart'.

Project Phase: A collection of logically related project activities (tasks), usually culminating in the completion of a major deliverable.

Project Plan Development: Taking the results of other planning processes and putting them into a consistent, coherent document.

Project Plan: A formal, approved document used to guide both project execution and project control. The primary uses of the project plan are to document planning assumptions and decisions, to facilitate communication among stakeholders, and to document approved scope, cost, and schedule baselines. A project plan may be summary or detailed.

Project Plan Execution: Carrying out the project plan by performing the activities therein.

Project Planning: The development and maintenance of the project plan.

Project Procurement Management: A subset of project management that includes the processes required to acquire goods and services from outside the performing organization. It consists of procurement planning, solicitation planning, solicitation, end or selection, contract administration, and contract closeout.

Project Quality Management: A subset of project management that includes the processes required to ensure that the project would satisfy the need for which it was undertaken. It consists of quality planning, quality assurance, and quality control.

Project Risk Management: A subset of project management that includes the processes concerned with identifying, analyzing, and responding to project risk. It consists of risk identification, risk quantification, risk response development, risk response control, risk mitigation and contingency planning.

Project Schedule: The planned dates for performing activities and the planned dates for meeting milestones.

Project Scope Management: A subset of project management that includes the processes required to ensure that the project includes all of the work required, and only the work required, to complete the project successfully. It consists of initiation, scope planning, scope determination, scope verification, and scope change control.

Project Summary: A brief synopsis of the project that dearly states the project objectives, goals, constraints and deliverables.

Project Team Members: The people who report either directly or indirectly to the project manager.

Project Time Management: A subset of project management that includes the processes required to ensure timely completion of the project It consists of activity definition, activity sequencing, activity duration estimating, schedule development, and schedule control.

Projected Organization: Any organizational structure in which the project manager has full authority to assign priorities and to direct the work of individuals assigned to the project.

Projected Staffing Plan: A plan that describes the types of resources needed, how much of each type are needed, and when they are needed. Should include dates, resources needed to be hired, and when.

Proposal Development: The process of choosing the best alternative to meet a customer's need and developing a written requirements and scope document.

Prototype: A simulated view of a proposed system using actual data together with text and illustrations or models screens.

PS: Planned Start Date.

Public Cloud: One of four cloud computing deployment models. The public cloud deployment model is what is most often thought of as a cloud, in that it is multitenant-capable and is shared by a number of customers who likely have nothing in common. Amazon, Microsoft, Terremark, and Google, to name but a few, all offer public cloud services.

Q:

QA: Quality Assurance.

QC: Quality Control.

Quality Assurance (QA): (1) The process of evaluating overall project performance on a regular basis to provide confidence that the project will satisfy the relevant quality standards. (2) The organizational unit that is assigned responsibility for quality assurance.

Quality Control (QC): (1) The process of monitoring specific project results to determine if they comply with relevant quality standards and identifying ways to eliminate causes of unsatisfactory performance. (2) The organizational unit that is assigned responsibility for quality control.

Quality Planning: Identifying which quality standards are relevant to the project and determining how to satisfy them.

QMS: Quality management system. A system that outlines the policies and procedures necessary to improve and control the various processes that will ultimately lead to improved business performance.

R:

RACI: Authority matrix that identifies specific roles of individuals such as R = Responsible, A = Accountable, C = Consulted, and I = Informed.

RAM: Responsibility Assignment Matrix. Identifies rules and responsibilities for initiatives or tasks.

Release: A collection of new and/or changed CIs which are tested and introduced into a live environment together. Release management is the process of controlling releases.

Release Management: A release is a set configuration items (CIs) that are tested and introduced into the live environment together. The objective of release management is to ensure the successful rollout of releases, including integration, testing and storage. Release management is closely related to configuration management and change management activities.

Remaining Duration (RDU): The time needed to complete an activity/task once it has started.

Request for Change (RFC): Form, or screen, used to record details of a request for a change to any CI within an infrastructure, or to procedures and items associated with the infrastructure, or a change in project scope for deliverables.

Request for Information (RFI): Description of the products and/or services that a potential customer wishes to learn about from the vendors.

Request for Proposal (RFP): A document used to solicit proposals from prospective vendors of products or services, which typically requests solutions, pricing, payment terms, warranties, pre- and after-sales support, implementation assistance, etc.

Request for Quotation (RFQ): Generally, this term is equivalent to request for pricing only to help filter out select vendors.

Reserve: A provision in the project plan to mitigate cost and/or schedule risk. Often used with a modifier (e.g.: management reserve, contingency reserve) to provide further detail on what types of risk are meant to be mitigated.

Resource Leveling: Any form of network analysis in which scheduling decisions (start and finish dates) are driven by resource management concerns (e.g., limited resource availability or difficult-to-manage changes in resource levels). The process of manipulating network data to create the resource plan which most effectively utilizes project resources subject to project constraints.

Resource-Limited Schedule: A project schedule whose start and finish dates reflect expected resource availability. The final project schedule should always be resource limited.

Resource Plan: A list of the resources and quantities that will be required over time to perform the project work.

Resource Planning: Determining what resources (people, equipment, materials, systems) are needed, in what quantities, to perform project activities.

Responsibility: Originates when one accepts the assignment to perform assigned duties and activities, The acceptance creates a liability for which the assignee is held answerable for and to the assignor. It constitutes an obligation or accountability for performance.

Responsibility Assignment Matrix (RAM): A structure which relates the project organization structure to the work breakdown structure to help ensure that each element of the project's scope of work is assigned to a responsible individual.

Responsibility Center (RC): The number used for accumulating actual costs at the control account level.

Responsibility Chart: See Responsibility Assignment Matrix.

Responsibility Matrix: See Responsibility Assignment Matrix.

Responsible Organization: A defined unit within a company structure which is assigned the responsibility for accomplishing specific tasks and to which one or more control accounts are assigned.

Retainage: A portion of a contract payment that is held until contract completion in order to ensure full performance of the contract terms.

Return On Assets (ROA): A direct metric that measures net income after taxes against a company's asset base. ROA is a valuable measurement but is difficult to adapt for use with internal projects.

Return On Equity (ROE): A direct metric that measures returns against a company's shareholder equity. Given the use of shareholder equity, it is nearly impossible to adapt ROE for use with a single project or product.

Return On Investment (ROI): A direct metric used to determine the value of an investment. ROI = (gains from investment − costs of investment) / (costs of investment). ROI can be used with discounting to account for the time value of money (TVM). Unadjusted ROI assumes present value for all gains and costs.

Risk: A measure of the exposure to which an organization may be subjected. This is a combination of the likelihood of a business disruption occurring and the possible loss that may result from such a business disruption.

Risk Analysis: The identification and assessment of the level (measure) of the risks calculated from the assessed values of assets and the assessed levels of threats to, and vulnerabilities of, those assets.

Risk Identification: Determining which risk events are likely to affect the project, business or IT.

Risk Management: The process of identifying, evaluating, quantifying, mitigating and tracking risk items.

Risk Quantification: Evaluating the probability of risk event occurrence and effect.

Risk Reduction Measures: Measures taken to reduce the likelihood or consequences of disruption occurring (as opposed to planning to recover after a disruption).

Risk Response Control: Responding to changes in risk over the course of the project.

Risk Response Development: Defining enhancement steps for opportunities and mitigation steps for threats.

Root Cause: Original reason for nonconformance within a process. When the root cause is removed or corrected, the nonconformance will be eliminated.

S:

Schedule: See Project Schedule.

Schedule Analysis: See Network Analysis.

Schedule Compression: See Duration Compression.

Schedule Control: Controlling changes to the project schedule.

Schedule Development: Analyzing activity/task sequences, activity durations, and resource requirements to create the project schedule.

Schedule Performance Index (SPI): The ratio of work performed to work scheduled (BCWP/BCWS). See Earned Value.

Schedule Variance (SV): (1) Any difference between the scheduled completion of an activity and the actual completion of that activity. (2) In earned value, BCWP less BCWS.

Scheduled Finish Date (SF): The point in time that work is scheduled to finish on an activity. The scheduled finish date is normally within the range of dates delimited by the early finish date and the late finish date.

Scheduled Start Date (SS): The point in time that work is scheduled to start on an activity. The scheduled start date is normally within the range of dates delimited by the early start date and the late start date.

Scheduling: The assignment of desired start and finish times to each activity/task in the project within the overall time cycle required for completion according to plan.

Scope: The sum of the products and services to be provided as a project.

Scope Baseline: See Baseline.

Scope Change: Any change to the project scope. A scope change almost always requires an adjustment to the project cost or schedule.

Scope Change Control: Controlling changes to the project scope.

Scope Definition: Decomposing the major deliverables into smaller, more manageable components to provide better control.

Scope of Services: The services provided under an outsourcing agreement.

Scope Planning: Developing a written scope statement that includes the project justification, the major deliverables and the project objectives.

Scope Verification: Ensuring that all identified project deliverables have been completed satisfactorily.

SDLC: Systems Development Lifecycle. The phases deployed in the development or acquisition of a software system. Typical phases include the feasibility study, requirements study, requirements definition, detailed design, programming, testing, installation and post-implementation review.

Security: The protection of products, systems, facilities and people from accidental or malicious harm, access, use, modification, destruction, or disclosure. Security also pertains to personnel data, communications, and the physical protection of facilities, files, etc.

Security Management: The objective of security management is to protect the IT, organization and resources against unauthorized use or penetration.

Sequential SDLC: See Waterfall SDLC.

Service: One or more IT systems which enable a business or IT process.

Service Achievement: The actual service levels delivered by the IT organization to a customer within a defined life-span.

Service Catalogue: Written statement of IT services, pricing, descriptions and options. It is used to describe repetitive IT services that can be ordered by the customer.

Service Desk: The initial point of contact with the IT organization for users. The major task of the service desk is to record, resolve and monitor problems. A service desk can carry out activities belonging to several processes.

Service Improvement Program: A formal project undertaken within an organization to identify and introduce measurable improvements within a specified work area or work process.

Service Level Agreement (SLA): The service level agreement, or SLA, defines the intended or expected level of service. For example, how quickly a service will be performed, what availability, quality and cost targets will be met, what level of customer satisfaction will be achieved, etc.

Service Level Management: The process of defining, agreeing, documenting, measuring and managing the levels of customer IT service, that are required and cost justified.

Service Provider: A company that provides outsourcing services. Terms such as provider, vendor and partner are often used interchangeably, each carrying a slightly different connotation intended by the user.

Service Quality Plan: The written plan and specification of internal targets designed to guarantee the agreed service levels.

Service Request: Every incident not being a failure in the IT infrastructure or operation.

SF: Scheduled Finish Date or Start-to-Finish.

Shared Services (Shared Services Centers): Shared services are common activities that are used by more than one division or unit within the company. When these services are combined into a central operation they are often referred to as shared services centers.

Significant Variance: The differences between planned and actual cost and/or schedule performance which require further review, analysis or action by the CAM and are addressed in the monthly VAR. Appropriate thresholds are established as to the magnitude of variances which will be considered 'significant.

Six Sigma: A well-established quality initiative that includes the DMAIC methodology (define, measure, analyze, improve, control). The term *Six Sigma* comes from statistics: a process that shows a variation of six sigma—six standard deviations from the mean — allows no more than 3.4 defects per million.

Slack: Term used in PERT for float.

SMART: An acronym that helps to remember that plans should be Specific, Measurable, Achievable, Relevant and Timely.

Software as a Service (SaaS): One of three cloud service models, SaaS gives users the ability to consume a software package on a service provider's infrastructure. SaaS significantly reduces the CAPEX, OPEX and operating expenses typically associated with owning and implementing complex software packages.

Software Library: A controlled collection of SCIs designated to keep those with like status and type together and distinctly segregated, to aid in development, operation and maintenance.

Solicitation: Obtaining quotations, bids, offers, or proposals as appropriate.

Solicitation Planning: Documenting product requirements and identifying potential sources.

Sourcing: Sourcing is generally the broadest term used in the field. It reflects the simple but essential point that everything the organization does has to be 'sourced' in some way – internally, externally, or a mix of the two.

SOW: Statement of Work

Specification: A document containing a detailed description or enumeration of particulars. Formal description of a work product and the intended manner of providing it.

SPI: Scheduled Performance Index.

Spiral SDLC: See Iterative SDLC.

SS: Scheduled Start date or Start-to-Start.

Staff Acquisition: Getting the human resources needed assigned to and working on the project.

Stakeholder: Individuals and organizations that are involved in, or may be affected by, project activities.

Standard: A business practice or technology product that is an accepted practice endorsed by the enterprise or IT management team. Standards can be put in place to support a policy or a process, or as a response to an operational need. Like policies, standards must include a description of the manner in which noncompliance will be detected.

Standard Cost: A pre-determined calculation of how much costs should be under specified working conditions. Its main purposes are to provide bases for control through variance accounting, for the valuation of work in progress and for fixing selling prices.

Standard Costing: A technique which uses standards for costs and revenues for the purposes of control through variance analysis.

Start Date: A point in time associated with an activity's start, usually qualified by one of the following: actual, planned, estimated, scheduled, early, late, target, baseline, or current.

Start-to-Finish: See Logical Relationship.

Start-to-Start: See Logical Relationship.

Statement of Work (SOW): A narrative description of products or services to be supplied under contract.

Status: The condition or progress of the project at a specified point in time.

Status Date: The calendar date, which separates actual (historical) data from forecasted data.

Strategic Planning: The process of developing an organization's mission, vision, objectives, goals, strategies and long range initiatives.

Strawman: A preliminary concept or plan that is presented to a group as a basis for discussion. The word 'strawman' is used to emphasize the fact that the plan can be 'kicked around' without fear of damage to its authors; that is, the individuals who present the strawman should do so fully expecting, and welcoming, additions, deletions, and/or changes to the strawman.

Subcontract: A subcontract is procurement from another corporate plant or from a non-corporate subcontractor requiring a statement of work, specifications, and design and/or manufacturing engineering effort on the part of the supplier, as opposed to the procurement of 'off-the-shelf' items, or items made to a drawing/specification/formula not requiring design/manufacturing engineering by the supplier.

Successor Activity: (1) In the arrow diagramming method, the activity which departs a node. (2) In the precedence diagramming method, the 'to' activity.

Summary Level: Any level of the WBS higher than the bottom level. So named because each WBS level can be summarized into the next higher level.

Supply Chain Management (SCM): The interlinked chain of contractors and subcontractors that provide components, subcomponents, and services that become part of the company's deliverable to its customers. Typically used to refer to the chain of suppliers in a manufacturing company's operation, but is also used more generally in regard to any product or service.

SV: Schedule Variance.

System: An integrated composite that consists of one or more of the processes, hardware, software, network, facilities and people that provides a capability to satisfy a stated need or objective.

Systems Development Lifecycle: The use of any of several structured methodologies to plan, design, procure, test and implement a system (e.g. Waterfall (Sequential), Spiral (Iterative), Hybrid, etc.)

T:

Tactical Planning: Planning concerned with the effective deployment of an organization's resources in order to accomplish the objectives laid out in the strategic business plan. The planning horizon is typically shorter than a strategic plan.

Target Completion Date (TC): An imposed date which constrains or otherwise modifies the network analysis.

Target Finish Date (TF): The date work is planned (targeted) to finish on an activity.

Target Schedule: See Baseline.

Target Start Date (TS): The date work is planned (targeted) to start on an activity.

Task: See Activity.

Team Development: Developing individual and group skills to enhance project performance.

Team Members: See Project Team Members.

Technology Infrastructure Plan: A plan for the maintenance and development of the technology infrastructure

Template: A standardized document, developed to address redundant requirements. The document is developed once, saved in a library or repository, and used repeatedly within the system.

TF: Total Float or Target Finish Date.

Third-Party Supplier: An enterprise or group, external to the customer's enterprise, which provides services and/or products to that customer's enterprise.

Threshold: See Variance Threshold.

Time-Scaled CPM: A plotted or drawn representation of a CPM network where the length of the activities indicates the duration of the activity as drawn to a calendar scale.

Time-Scaled Network Diagram: Any project network diagram drawn in such a way that the positioning and length of the activity represents its duration. Essentially, it is a bar chart that includes network logic.

Time To Market (TTM): TTM measures the length of time required to implement a new application or go to market with a new service. TTM is a critical measure of a company's ability to execute. Bringing quality products to market quickly and efficiently is the simplest way to increase top-line revenue.

Time Value of Money (TVM): TVM is the principle that money has the potential to increase in value over time—the opportunity to invest means the potential to create value. Present value and future value are measures of TVM.

Total Contract Baseline: The negotiated contract cost.

Total Cost of Ownership (TCO): The sum total of all associated costs relating to the purchase, ownership, usage, and maintenance of a particular product or service.

Total Float (TF): See Float.

Total Quality Management (TQM)): A common approach to implementing a quality improvement program within an organization.

Tree Diagram: A graphical representation of an outline or WBS structure which shows work elements as boxes and subsequent levels of detail broken down in levels of boxes below it. An element or task can roll up into only one higher level box.

TS: Target Start Date.

U:

UB: Undistributed Baseline.

Unit Cost: Total costs for one unit of production (i.e., one part, one end item, etc.).

Update: To revise project activity data to reflect the most current information on the project.

V:

Value Chain: A concept outlined by Michael Porter in his classic book *Competitive Advantage: Creating and Sustaining Superior Performance.* Porter shows how firms can increase their competitive advantage in part by understanding the value of core operational and business support functions. Porter gives special attention to the concepts of economies and diseconomies of scale.

Value Proposition: What value is the organization looking to gain from a system, product or outsourcing arrangement.

VAR: Variance Analysis Report.

Variance: The difference by which cost and schedule vary from plan. Negative variances are unfavorable indicators (i.e. behind schedule or over cost) while positive variances are favorable indicators (i.e. ahead of schedule or under cost). See also specific items such as Cost Variance, Schedule Variance, etc.

Variance Analysis: Evaluation of variances and narrative description of the causes of the difference between BCWP and BCWS or ACWP, and between BAC and EAC in terms of cost and schedule at levels where the work is performed, or at various functional organization, WBS, or reporting summary levels, as required. Includes determination of the nature, scope, and potential impact of the problem, assignment of responsibility for corrective action, and the monitoring of results of the corrective action.

Variance Analysis Report (VAR): A report from control accounts or summary WBS levels that exceed the variance thresholds. The report/notice is completed by the responsible individual who must (1) explain the cause of the problem, (2) determine the impact on the immediate task and on the total program or project, and (3) describe any corrective actions to be taken.

Variance Threshold: Internal and external tolerances established by management direction or through negotiations with the customer. Variance conditions outside the threshold values must be addressed formally. See Variance Analysis Report.

Vendor: A supplier of products and/or services.

Version: An identified instance of a configuration item within a product breakdown structure or configuration structure for the purpose of tracking and auditing change history. Also used for software configuration items to define a specific identification released in development for drafting, review or modification, test or production.

Version Identifier: A version number, version date, or version date and time stamp.

Vulnerability: A weakness of the system and its assets, which could be exploited by threats.

W:

Waterfall SDLC: Refers to a systems/software lifecycle methodology that has frequent validations by the customer and other project constituencies as the system is built to ensure frequent corrections or adjustments to the scope, requirements and in-process system development efforts. See also Spiral SDLC.

WBS: Work Breakdown Structure.

WBS Dictionary: The Dictionary will describe the technical and cost content of every WBS element or task. It will describe what the element is and efforts associated with the WBS element (such as design, development, and manufacturing). For the WBS elements specified elsewhere for cost reporting, the WBS Dictionary definitions will also include the exact narrative of the directly associated work statement paragraphs, or a reference to the SOW paragraph or other document describing the work.

Work: Any and all obligations, duties, responsibilities, labor, materials, equipment, temporary facilities and incidentals, and the furnishing thereof necessary to complete the contract deliverable which are assigned to, or undertaken by the contractor, pursuant to the contract documents. Also, the entire completed contract deliverable or the various separately identifiable parts thereof required to be furnished under the contract documents. Work is the result of performing services, furnishing labor, and furnishing and incorporating materials and equipment into the contract deliverable, all as required by the contract documents.

Work Breakdown Structure (WBS): A deliverable-oriented grouping of project elements or tasks which organizes and defines the total scope of the project. Each descending level represents an increasingly detailed definition of a project component. Project components may be products, services processes or functions. Decomposes complex programs or projects into assignable work packages

Work Day: A unit expressing duration. Only those days when work is performed are counted. Holidays, weekends, and vacation days may or may not count.

Work Item: See Activity or Task

Workaround: A response to a negative risk event. Distinguished from contingency plan in that a workaround is not planned in advance of the occurrence of the risk event. Method of avoiding an incident or problem.

Work-In-Progress (WIP): Product in various stages of completion throughout the factory, including raw material that has been released for initial processing and completed processes and material awaiting final inspection and acceptance as finished product or shipment of a customer. Many accounting systems also include semi-finished stock and components in this category.

Workloads: The resources required to deliver a project or service deliverable and can be segmented by skills, functions and experience levels.

WP: Work Package.

Appendix B   References, alphabetical

Aasi, P., Rusu L. and Han S. (2014, January). *The Influence of Culture on IT Governance: A Literature Review.* In: 47th Hawaii International Conference on System Sciences (HICSS), 2014, pp. 4436-4445, IEEE.

Aazadnia, M. and Fasanghari, M. (2008). *Improving the Information Technology Service Management with Six Sigma.* In: International Journal of Computer Science and Network Security, 8(3), pp. 144-150.

Acharya, V. V., Gottschalg, O. F., Hahn, M. and Kehoe, C. (2013). *Corporate Governance and Value Creation: Evidence from Private Equity.* In: Review of Financial Studies, 26(2), pp. 368-402.

Adusumilli, S. (2011). *IT Strategy & Governance Explained.* In: IT Strategy.

Afuah, A. and Tucci, C. L. (2012). *Crowdsourcing as a Solution to Distant Search.* In: Academy of Management Review, 37(3), pp. 355-375.

Agrawal, A., Tripathi, M., Singh, S. and Maurya, L. S. (2013). *AGILE: Boon for Today's Software Industry - A Review.* In: International Journal of Scientific and Research Publications, p. 464.

Aguilera, R. V., Filatotchev, I., Gospel, H. and Jackson, G. (2008). *An Organizational Approach to Comparative Corporate Governance: Costs, Contingencies, and Complementarities.* In: Organization Science, 19(3), pp. 475-492.

Ahern, Dennise, Clouse, Aaron and Torner, Richard (2004). *CMMI™ Distiller - A Practical to Integrated Process Improvement*, Second Edition, Addison-Wesley.

Ahmad, N. and Shamsudin, Z. M. (2013). *Systematic Approach to Successful Implementation of ITIL.* In: Procedia Computer Science, pp. 17, 237-244.

Akker, Rolf (1992). *Generic Framework for Information Management, Program for Information Research*, University of Amsterdam.

Ali, S. and Green, P. (2012). *Effective Information Technology (IT) Governance Mechanisms: An IT Outsourcing Perspective.* In: Information Systems Frontiers, 14(2), pp. 179-193.

Alleman, G. B. (2013). *Agile Program Management: Moving from Principles to Practice.* In: Feedback, 4, p. 6.

Almeida, R., Pereira, R. and Da Silva, M.M. (2013). *IT Governance Mechanisms: A Literature Review.* In: Exploring Services Science, pp. 186-199, Springer, Berlin Heidelberg.

Almulla, S. A. and Yeun, C. Y. (2010). *Cloud Computing Security Management.* In: Second International Conference on Engineering Systems Management and It's Applications (ICESMA), pp. 1-7, March 2010, IEEE.

Alojail, M. (2013). *ITIL Usage, and Use of ITIL Recommended Practices and the IT Outsourcing Relationship Quality*, PhD Thesis, Business IT and Logistics, RMIT University.

Alojail, M., Rouse, A. C. and Corbitt, B. J. (2012). *The Impact of ITIL (Information Technology Infrastructure Library) Recommended Practices on the IT Outsourcing Relationship.* In: ACIS 2012: Location, location, location: Proceedings of the 23rd Australasian Conference on Information Systems 2012, pp. 1-10. ACIS.

AlShamy, M, E. Elfakharany, M. Abd ElAziem (2012). *Information Technology Service Management (ITSM) Implementation Methodology Based on Information Technology Infrastructure Library Ver. 3 (ITIL V3)* In: International Journal of Business Research and Management (IJBRM), Volume (3): Issue (3).Anand, S. (2006). *Sarbanes-Oxley Guide*, Second Edition, J. Wiley and Sons.

Andriole, S. J. (2013). *Today's Best Practices in Business Technology Management*. In: Feedback, 4, p. 6.

Anthony, Robert N. (1965). *Planning and Control Systems: A Framework for Analysis*, Harvard University Press, Cambridge, MA.

Apostolopoulos, C. (2008). *The Success of IT Projects Using the Agile Method*. In: Proceedings of the International Workshop on Requirements Analysis (IWRA 2008).

Arabalidousti, F. and Nasiri, R. (2013). *Improving IT Service Management Architecture in Cloud Environment on Top of Current Frameworks*. In: The International Conference on Digital Information Processing, E-Business and Cloud Computing (DIPECC2013), pp. 77-86. The Society of Digital Information and Wireless Communication.

Arabalidousti, F., Nasiri, R. and Razavi, Davoudi, M. (2014). *Developing a New Architecture to Improve ITSM on Cloud Computing Environment*. In: International Journal on Cloud Computing: Services and Architecture (IJCCSA), Vol. 4, No. 1, February 2014.

Artur, R. O. T. (2009). *IT Risk Management in the Context of IT Governance: Theory vs. Practice*. International Institute of Informatics and Systemics. July 2009, The 6th International Symposium on Risk Management and Cyber-Informatics: RMCI 2009, Poland.

Arun, H., Nilam, R., Namrata, R. and Purva, S. (2013). *Review on Techniques to Ensure Distributed Accountability for Data Sharing in the Cloud*, In: International Journal of Advanced Research in Computer and Communication Engineering, Vol. 2, Issue 10, October 2013.

Assuncao, M. D., Calheiros, R. N., Bianchi, S., Netto, M. A. and Buyya, R. (2013). *Big Data Computing and Clouds: Challenges, Solutions, and Future Directions*. arXiv preprint arXiv:1312.4722.

Avison, D., Jones, J., Powell, P. and Wilson, D. (2004). *Using and validating the strategic alignment model*. In: Journal of Strategic Information Systems, Volume 13.

AXELOS (2007). *Managing Successful Projects with PRINCE2*, TSO.

AXELOS (2011). *ITIL 2011 Edition - Life Cycle Publication Suite*, TSO.

AXELOS (2014). *The Importance of ITIL® - 2014 and Beyond*, In: Global Study.

Azeem, M., Hassan, M. and Kouser, R. (2013). *Impact of Quality Corporate Governance on Firm Performance: A Ten Year Perspective*. In: Pakistan Journal of Commerce and Social Sciences, 7(3), pp. 656-670.

Baggili, J., *Business-IT Alignment*, http://web.ics.purdue.edu/~baggili/Portal/B_IT_Alignment.html

Bahl, S. and Wali, O. P. (2014). *Perceived Significance of Information Security Governance to Predict the Information Security Service Quality in Software Service Industry: An Empirical Analysis*. In: Information Management & Computer Security, 22(1), pp. 2-23.

Bahli, B., and Rivard, S. (2013). *Cost Escalation in Information Technology Outsourcing: A Moderated Mediation Study*. In: Decision Support Systems, 56, pp. 37-47.

Bahsani, S., Himi, A., Moubtakir, H. and Semma, A. (2013). *Towards a pooling of ITIL V3 and COBIT*. In: International Journal of Computer Science, June 2013, pp. 8.

Bainbridge, S. (2008). *The New Corporate Governance in Theory and Practice*. Oxford University Press.

Baker, E. W. and Niederman, F. (2013). *Integrating the IS functions after Mergers and Acquisitions: Analyzing Business-IT Alignment*. In: The Journal of Strategic Information Systems.

Baker, M. and Bourne, M. (2014). *A Governance Framework for the Idea-to-Launch Process: Development and Application of a Governance Framework for New Product Development*. In: Research-Technology Management, 57(1), pp. 42-49.

Barafort, B., and Rousseau, A. (2009). *Sustainable Service Innovation Model: A Standardized IT Service Management Process Assessment Framework*. In: Software Process Improvement, pp. 69-80. Springer, Berlin Heidelberg.

Barafort, B., Jezek, D., Mäkinen, T., Stolfa, S., Varkoi, T. and Vondrak, I. (2008). *Modeling and Assessment in IT Service Process Improvement*. In: Software Process Improvement, pp. 117-128. Springer, Berlin Heidelberg.

Barkley, Brucet, Sr. (2006). *Integrated Project Management*, McGraw Hill, NY.

Barlow, M. (2013). *The Culture of Big Data*, O'Reilly Media.

Bartens, Y., Schulte, F. and Voss, S. (2014, January). *E-Business IT Governance Revisited: An Attempt towards Outlining a Novel Bi-directional Business/IT Alignment in COBIT5*. In: 47th Hawaii International Conference on System Sciences (HICSS), 2014, pp. 4356-4365. IEEE.

Baxter, R., Bedard, J. C., Hoitash, R. and Yezegel, A. (2013). *Enterprise Risk Management Program Quality: Determinants, Value Relevance, and the Financial Crisis*. In: Contemporary Accounting Research, 30(4), pp. 1264-1295.

Bayaga, A., Flowerday, S. and Cilliers, L. (2013). *Valuing Information Technology (IT) and Operational Risk Management, International Conference on ICT for Africa 2013*, Harare, Zimbabwe.

Beach, T., Rana, O., Rezgui, Y. and Parashar, M. (2013). *Governance Model for Cloud Computing in Building Information Management*. In: IEEE Transactions on Services Computing, 21 Nov. 2013. IEEE Computer Society.

Bebchuk, L. A. and Weisbach, M. S. (2010). *The State of Corporate Governance Research*. In: Review of Financial Studies, 23(3), pp. 939-961.

Beckman, Sara L. and Rosenfield, Donald B.(2008). *Operating Strategy*, McGraw-Hill, NY.

Beimborn, D., Schlosser, F. and Weitzel, T. (2009, January). *Proposing a Theoretical Model for IT Governance and IT Business Alignment*. In: 42nd Hawaii International Conference on System Sciences 2009. HICSS'09, pp. 1-11. IEEE.

Bensch, S., Andris, R. J., Gahm, C. and Tuma, A. (2014). *IT Outsourcing: An IS Perspective*. In: 47th Hawaii International Conference on System Sciences (HICSS), pp. 4210-4219, January 2014, IEEE.

Benson, R. J., Bugnitz, T.L. et al. (2004). *From Business Strategy to IT Action: Right Decisions for a Better Bottom Line*. Wiley, Hoboken, N.J.

Berggruen, N. and Gardels, N. (2013). *Intelligent Governance for the 21st Century: A Middle Way Between West and East*. John Wiley & Sons.

Bergvall-Kåreborn, B. and Howcroft, D. (2013, December). *The Apple Business Model: Crowdsourcing Mobile Applications*. In: Accounting Forum, Vol. 37, No. 4, pp. 280-289, Elsevier.

Bernard, P. (2011). Passing the ITIL V3 Intermediate Exams: The Study Guide. Van Haren Publishing.

Bernard, P. (2014). *IT service management Based on ITIL® 2011 Edition*, Van Haren Publishing.

Bernardo, D. and Hoang D. (2012). *Security Risk Assessment: Toward a Comprehensive Practical Risk Management*, In: Int. Journal of Information and Computer Security. Vol. 5, No. 2/2012, pp.77-104.

Bernardo, D. V. (2013). *Utilizing Security Risk Approach in Managing Cloud Computing Services*. In: 16th International Conference on Network-Based Information Systems (NBiS), pp. 119-125, September 2013, IEEE.

Bernroider, E. W. (2008). *IT Governance for Enterprise Resource Planning supported by the DeLone–McLean model of Information Systems Success*. In: Information & Management, 45(5), pp. 257-269.

Bernroider, E. W. and Ivanov, M. (2011). *IT Project Management Control and the Control Objectives for IT and Related Technology (COBIT) Framework*. In: International Journal of Project Management, 29(3), pp. 325-336.

Bertot, J. C., Jaeger, P. T. and Grimes, J. M. (2010, May). *Crowd-sourcing Transparency: ICTs, Social Media, and Government Transparency Initiatives*. In: Proceedings of the 11th Annual International Digital Government Research Conference on Public Administration Online: Challenges and Opportunities, pp. 51-58, Digital Government Society of North America.

Betz, Frederick (2003). *Managing Technological Innovation: Competitive Advantage from Change.* John Wiley, New York.

Bhadauria, R., Borgohain, R., Biswas, A. and Sanyal, S. (2013). *Secure Authentication of Cloud Data Mining API*. arXiv preprint arXiv:1308.0824.

Bhagat, S. and Bolton, B. (2008). *Corporate Governance and Firm Performance*. In: Journal of Corporate Finance, 14(3), pp. 257-273.

Bhatia, Mohan (2007). *IT Merger Due Diligence: A Blueprint*, In: Information Systems Control Journal, Volume 1, 2007.

Bin, S. (2010). *Agile Methods (Scrum, XP) Applying into Small (Micro) Enterprise Business*. In: Journal of Enterprise Information Management, 23(2).

Bisong, A. and Rahman, S. M. (2011). *An Overview of the Security Concerns in Enterprise Cloud Computing*. In: International Journal of Network Security & Its Applications, 3(1).

BMC Software (2004), Sarbanes-Oxley Section 404, White Paper, May 2004.

Board Effectiveness Partners (2004). *A Roadmap: Strengthening Corporate Governance*, In: Insights, Chapter 1, Version 2.0, January 2004.

Boardman, Bruce (2006). *Get Framed Compliance Policy Development (ISO, ITIL/ISMD & COBIT)*, Network Computing Conf., Sept. 28, 2006.

Boersma, D. (2012). *The Potential of Crowd Sourcing Applications in Organizational Context, A Railroad Case Study*.

Bonnet, Pierre (2013). *Enterprise Data Governance Reference and Master Data Management Semantic Model*, Wiley.

Bossidy, Larry and Ram, Charan (2002). *Execution - The Discipline of Getting things Done*, Crown Business.

Boston Consulting Group (1974). *Perspectives on Experience*.

Bott, M. and Young, G. (2012). *The Role of Crowdsourcing for Better Governance in International Development*. In: Praxis: The Fletcher Journal of Human Security, 27, pp. 47-70.

Boudreau, K. J. and Lakhani, K. R. (2013). *Using the Crowd as an Innovation Partner*. In: Harvard Business Review, 91(4), 60-9.

Brabham, D. C. (2013). *Crowdsourcing*. MIT Press.

Bragg, Steven M. (2006). *Outsourcing*, Second Edition, J. Wiley & Sons, NY.

Brammer, S. J., and Pavelin, S. (2013). *Corporate Governance and Corporate Social Responsibility*. In: The Oxford Handbook of Corporate Governance, pp.719-743.

Brandabur, R. E. (2013). *IT Outsourcing-A Management-Marketing Decision*. In: International Journal of Computers, Communications & Control, 8(2).

Breu, R., Kuntzmann-Combelles, A. and Felderer, M. (2014). *New Perspectives on Software Quality*. In: IEEE Software, 31(1).

Brewer, J. L. and Dittman, K. C. (2013). *Methods of IT Project Management*. Purdue University Press.

Breyfogle, F., Cupello, J. and Meadows, Becki (2001). *Managing Six Sigma*, Wiley.

Bridges, William (2005). *Managing Transitions*, 2nd Edition, Da Capo Press, Cambridge, Ma, 1991.

Britt, Darice (2012). *Crowdsourcing: The Debate Roars On*. www.instite.artinsitutes.edu, 12/4/2012.

Broadbent, Marianne and Kitzis, Ellen (2005). *The New CIO Leader*, In: HBR Press.

Brown, A. W., Ambler, S. and Royce, W. (2013, May). *Agility at Scale: Economic Governance, Measured Improvement, and Disciplined Delivery*. In: Proceedings of the 2013 International Conference on Software Engineering, pp. 873-881. IEEE Press.

Brown, Doug and Wilson, Scott (2005). *The Black Book of Outsourcing*, John Wiley & Sons.

Buckby, S., Best, P. and Stewart, J. (2009). *The Current State of Information Technology Governance Literature*. In: A. Cater-Steel (Ed.), Information Technology Governance and Service Management: Frameworks and Adaptations, pp. 1-43, Information Science Reference, Hershey, PA.

Budd, L. and Harris, L. (Eds.). (2013). *E-governance: Managing or Governing?* Routledge.

Budwig, M., Jeong, S. and Kelkar, K. (2009, April). *When User Experience Met Agile: A Case Study*. In: CHI'09 Extended Abstracts on Human Factors in Computing Systems. pp. 3075-3084, ACM.

Bullen, C., Lefave, R. and Selig, G. (2010). *Implementing Strategic Sourcing – A Manager's Guide to World Class Best Practices*, Van Haren Publishing.

Burkholder, Nicholas C. (2006). *Outsourcing*, J. Wiley & Sons, NY.

Burn, Jack and Moran, Linda (2000). *The New Self Directed Work Teams*, McGraw-Hill, New York.

Business Continuity Planning Guidelines, http://www.yourwindow.to/business-continuity/contents.htm

Business Continuity Planning Model, http://www.drj.com/new2dr/model/bcmodel.htm

Business Week (2006, January 30). Special Report on Outsourcing.

Byrne, A. (2014). *Governance, Strategic Risk, Internal Audit: What Auditors Need to Know*. In: EDPACS, 49(2), 6-14.

Cabral, A. Y., Ribeiro, M. B., Lemke, A. P., Silva, M. T., Cristal, M. and Franco, C. (2009). *A Case Study of Knowledge Management Usage in Agile Software Projects*. In: Enterprise Information Systems, pp. 627-638. Springer, Berlin Heidelberg.

Calder, A. (2009). *IT Governance: Implementing Frameworks and Standards for the Corporate Governance of IT*. IT Governance, UK.

Cao, L., Mohan, K., Ramesh, B. and Sarkar, S. (2013). *Evolution of Governance: Achieving Ambidexterity in IT Outsourcing*. In: Journal of Management Information Systems, 30(3), pp. 115-140.

Capgemini (2013). *World Quality Report 2013-14*, www.capgemini.com/thought-leadership/wprld-quality-quality-report-2013-14.

Cardozo, E., Neto, J. B. F. A., Barza, A., França, A. and Da Silva, F. (2010, April). *SCRUM and Productivity in Software Projects: A Systematic Literature Review*. In: 14th International Conference on Evaluation and Assessment in Software Engineering (EASE).

Carmel, Erran and Tjia, Paul (2005). *Offshoring Information Technology*, Cambridge University Press, UK.

Carr, N. (2003). *IT doesn't matter anymore*. In: Harvard Business Review (5), pp. 41-49.

Carter, Keith (2014). *Actionable Intelligence and Big Data*, Wiley.

Cater-Steel, A. (2009). *Information Technology Governance and Service Management: Frameworks and Adaptations*. Hershey, New York.

Catucci, Bill (2003). *Ten Lessons for Implementing the Balanced Scorecard*, In: Balanced Scorecard, January 15, 2003.

Catucci, Bill (2005). *A New Governance Model*, In: Balanced Scorecard, January 15, 2005.

Center for Technology Governance and Compliance (2006). *Raising the Bar for Governance and Compliance*, Sun Microsystems and Deloitte Consulting LLP, White Paper, February 2006.

Cervo, Dalton and Allan, Mark (2011). *Master Data Management in Practice*, Wiley.

Cervone, F. (2008). *ITIL: A Framework for Managing Digital Library Services*. In: OCLC Systems & Services, 24(2), pp. 87-90.

Cervone, H. F. (2011). *Understanding Agile Project Management Methods Using Scrum*. In: OCLC Systems & Services, 27(1), pp. 18-22.

Chambers, Don, (July, 2010). *Windows Azure: Using Windows Azure's Service Business to Solve Data Security Issues*, http://rebustechnologies.com/wpc.ntent/uploads/2011/12/windowsazure.pdf

Chan, P. C., Durant, S. R., Gall, V. M., and Raisinghani, M. S. (2010). *Aligning Six Sigma and ITIL to Improve IT Service Management*. In: International Journal of E-Services and Mobile Applications, 1, 2, pp. 62-82.

Chavan, P., Mendhekar, P., Varahan, S. and Nerur, S. (2012). *Impact of Agile Methodologies on Project Management*. In: Great Lakes Herald, Vol 6, No 2.

Chen, Y., Paxson, V. and Katz, R. H. (2010). *What's New About Cloud Computing Security?* University of California, Berkeley Report No. UCB/EECS-2010-5.

Chew, D. H. and Gillan, S. L. (Eds.) (2013). *Global Corporate Governance*, Columbia University Press.

Chew, E. K. and Gottschalk, P. (2013). *Knowledge Driven Service Innovation and Management: IT Strategies for Business Alignment and Value Creation*. Business Science Reference.

Chmieliauskas, A., Chappin, E. J., Davis, C. B., Nikolic, I. and Dijkema, G. P. (2012). *New Methods for Analysis of Systems-of-Systems and Policy: The Power of Systems Theory, Crowd Sourcing and Data Management*. In: System of Systems. InTech, pp. 77-98.

Choubey, R., Dubey, R. and Bhattacharjee, J. (2011). *A Survey on Cloud Computing Security, Challenges and Threats*. In: International Journal on Computer Science and Engineering (IJCSE), 3(3), pp. 1227-1231.

Chrissis, M., Konrad, M. and Shrum, S. (2003). *CMMI – Guidelines for Process Integration and Product Improvement*, Addison Wesley.

Ciborra, C. (1997). *De Profundis? Deconstructing the Concept of Strategic Alignment*. In: Scandinavian Journal of Information Systems, Volume 9, pp. 67-82.

Clark, G. L. and Wójcik, D. (2011). *The Geography of Finance: Corporate Governance in the Global Marketplace*. In: OUP Catalogue.

Clemons, E. K., Row. M.C., and Redi, S.P. (2002). *The Impact of IT on the Organization of Economic Activity*, In: Journal of Management Information Systems, Vol. 9, No. 2.

Click, Rick L. and Dvening, Thomas N. (2005). *Business Process Outsourcing*, J. Wiley & Sons, NY.

Cobb, C. G. (2011). *Agile Project Management*. In: Making Sense of Agile Project Management: Balancing Control and Agility, pp. 101-130, John Wiley & Sons.

Cochran, Mitchel. L. and Witman, P. D. (2011). *Governance and Service Level Agreement Issues in A Cloud Computing Environment*. In: Journal of Information Technology Management, 22(2), pp. 41-55.

Cohen, Beth, TACtical Research SmartTip. (2006, December). *Rethinking Internet Forum and Collaboration Tools*, In: The Advisory Council (TAC).

Colley, J., Doyle, J., Logan, G. and Stettinius, W. (2004). *What is Corporate Governance?*, McGraw-Hill.

Computing, C. (2011). *Cloud Computing Privacy Concerns on our Doorstep*. In: Communications of the ACM, 54(1).

Conger, S. and Probst, J. (2014). *Knowledge Management in ITSM: Applying the DIKW Model*. In: Engineering and Management of IT-based Service Systems, pp. 1-18. Springer, Berlin Heidelberg.

Cooke, J. L. (2013). *The Power of the Agile Business Analyst: 30 Surprising Ways a Business Analyst Can Add Value to Your Agile Development Team*. IT Governance Ltd.

Cooper, R.G., Edgett, S.J. and Kleinschmidt, E.J. (1998). *Portfolio Management for New Products*, Addison-Wesley, Reading, MA.

Corbett, Michael F. (2000, May 29). *Outsourcing 2000: Value-Driven Customer-Focused*, In: Fortune, pp. S36.

Corbett, Michael, (2004). *The Outsourcing Revolution*, In: Dearbon Trade Publication, Chicago, Il.

Cordite, James (1998). *Best Practices in Information Technology*, Prentice Hall.

Corporate Executive Board (2003). *IT Balanced Scorecards - End-to-End Performance Measurement for the Corporate IT Function*, Working Council for Chief Information Officers Report, 2003.

Cortina, S., Renault, A. and Picard, M. (2013). *TIPA Process Assessments: A Means to Improve Business Value of IT Services*. In: International Journal of Strategic Information Technology and Applications (IJSITA), 4(4), pp. 1-18.

COSO (Committee of Sponsoring Organizations of the Treadway Commission) (2013). *Integrated Control - Integrated Framework*.

Cots, S. and Casadesús, M. (2014). *Exploring the Service Management Standard ISO 20000*. In: Total Quality Management & Business Excellence, pp. 1-19.

Coughlan, J., Lycett, M. and Macredie, R.D. (2005). *Understanding the business-IT relationship. In: International Journal of Information Management*, Volume 25, pp. 303-319.

Covey, Stephen (1989). *The Seven Habits of Highly Effective People*, Simon and Schuster.

Cowan-Sahadath, K. (2010). *Business Transformation: Leadership, integration and Innovation–A Case Study*. In: International Journal of Project Management, 28(4), pp. 395-404.

Crawford, Ken (2014). *Project Management Maturity Model*, 3rd edition, CRC Press.

Cristal, M., Wildt, D. and Prikladnicki, R. (2008, August). *Usage of Scrum Practices within a Global Company.* In: Global Software Engineering, 2008. ICGSE 2008. IEEE International Conference on, pp. 222-226, IEEE.

Cronholm, S. and Salomonson, N. (2014). *Measures that Matters: Service Quality in IT Service Management.* In: International Journal of Quality and Service Sciences, 6(1), pp. 60-76.

Croteau, A. M. and Bergeron, F. (2009, January). *Interorganizational Governance of Information Technology.* In: 42nd Hawaii International Conference on System Sciences, 2009. HICSS'09, pp. 1-8. IEEE.

Crow, Ken (2002). *Customer Focused Development with QFD*, DRM Associates.

Crow, P. R. and Lockhart, J. (2013). *The Impact of Governance on the Performance of a High-Growth Company: An Exemplar Case Study.* In: Proceedings of the International Conference of Management, Leadership and Governance, pp. 41-47.

Curtis, D. B., Hefley, W. E. and Miller, S. A. (2007). *The People Capability Maturity Model: Guidelines for Improving the Workforce.* Addison-Wesley, Dorling Kindersley, India.

Cybercan Technology Solutions (2005). *ITIL (Information Technology Infrastructure Library) Foundation Workshop.*

Dahiya, D. and Mathew, S. K. (2013). *Review of Strategic Alignment, ICT Infrastructure Capability and E-Governance Impact.* In: ICT Innovations 2013 Web Proceedings, ISSN 1857-7288.

Dalal, Jagdish. (2002, October 23). *Off-shore Outsourcing*, In: The Outsourcing Research Council, Raleigh, NC, pp. 11, 13.

Dameri, R. P. (2013). *From IT Governance to IT Service Delivery. Implementing a Comprehensive Framework at Ansaldo STS.* In: Organizational Change and Information Systems. pp. 33-40, Springer, Berlin Heidelberg.

Data Management Association (2014). *DAMA – DMBOK2 Framework*, DAMA Int., March 6, 2014.

Davenport, T. (2014). *Big Data at Work: Dispelling the Myths, Uncovering the Opportunities.* Harvard Business Review Press.

Davenport, T. H. (2000). *Mission Critical: Realizing the Promise of the Enterprise Systems*, HBS Press, Boston, MA.

Davenport, T. H. and Dyche, J. (2013). *Big Data in Big Companies.* In: International Institute for Analytics, May 2013.

Davenport, T. H. and Kim, J. (2013). *Keeping Up with the Quants: Your Guide to Understanding and Using Analytics.* Harvard Business Review Press.

Davenport, T. H. and Manville, B. (2012). *Judgment Calls: Twelve Stories of Big Decisions and the Teams That Got Them Right.* Harvard Business Review Press.

De Haes, S. and Van Grembergen, W. (2008). *An Exploratory Study into the Design of an IT Governance Minimum Baseline through Delphi Research.* In: The Communications of the Association for Information Systems, 22, pp. 443-458.

De Haes, S. and Van Grembergen, W. (2008). *Practices in IT Governance and Business/IT Alignment.* In: Information Systems Control Journal, 2, pp. 1-6.

De Haes, S. and Van Grembergen, W. (2008, January). *Analyzing the Relationship between IT Governance and Business/IT Alignment Maturity.* In: Hawaii International Conference on System Sciences, Proceedings of the 41st Annual, pp. 428-428. IEEE.

De Haes, S. and Van Grembergen, W. (2009). *An Exploratory Study into IT Governance Implementations and its Impact on Business/IT Alignment.* In: Information Systems Management, 26(2), pp. 123-137.

De Haes, S. and Van Grembergen, W. (2009). *Exploring the Relationship Between IT Governance Practices and Business/IT Alignment through Extreme Case Analysis in Belgian Mid-to-Large Size Financial Enterprises.* In: Journal of Enterprise Information Management, 22(5), pp. 615-637.

De Haes, S. and Van Grembergen, W. van (2013). *Improving Enterprise Governance of IT in a Major Airline.* In: A Teaching Case. Journal of Information Technology Teaching Cases, 3(2), pp. 60-69.

De Haes, S., Van Grembergen, W. and Debreceny, R. S. (2013). *COBIT 5 and Enterprise Governance of Information Technology: Building Blocks and Research Opportunities*. In: Journal of Information Systems, 27(1), pp. 307-324.

De Vries, M. (2013). *A Method to Enhance Existing Business-IT Alignment Approaches*. In: South African Journal of Industrial Engineering, 24(2), pp. 111-126.

Debreceny, R. and Gray, G. L. (2009, January). *IT Governance and Process Maturity: A Field Study*. In: 42nd Hawaii International Conference on System Sciences, 2009. HICSS'09, pp. 1-10. IEEE.

Debreceny, R. S. (2013). *Research on IT Governance, Risk, and Value: Challenges and Opportunities*. In: Journal of Information Systems, 27(1), pp. 129-135.

DeCarlo, D. (2010). *Extreme Project Management: Using Leadership, Principles, and Tools to Deliver Value in the Face of Volatility*. Wiley.

Degraff, Jeff and Quinn, Shawn (2007). *Leading Innovation*, McGrawHill, NY.

Delmar, Yo (2014). *Leveraging Metrics for Business Innovation – Where Measurement meets Transformation in IT Governance*, In: ISACA Journal, Volume 4, 2014.

Deloitte Development, LLC (2004). *Eliminating Roadblocks to IT and Business Alignment*. In: CIO Magazine Supplement.

Deloitte, Consulting Report. (2005, December). *Calling a Change in the Outsourcing Model*. In: Deloitte Consulting.

Demirkan, H. and Nichols, J. (2008). *IT Services Project Management: Lessons Learned from a Case Study in Implementation*. In: International Journal of Project Organization and Management, 1(2), pp. 204-220.

Dillon, T., Wu, C. and Chang, E. (2010, April). *Cloud Computing: Issues and Challenges*. In: 24th IEEE International Conference on Advanced Information Networking and Applications (AINA), 2010, pp. 27-33). IEEE.

Dinsmore, P. C. and Rocha, L. (2013). *Enterprise Project Governance: A Guide to the Successful Management of Projects Across the Organization*. In: Project Management Journal, 44(1), p. 107.

Drnevich, P. L. and Croson, D. C. (2013). *Information Technology and Business-Level Strategy: Toward an Integrated Theoretical Perspective*. In: MIS Quarterly, 37(2).

Drucker, P. F. (2013). *Managing in a Time of Great Change*. Harvard Business Press.

Duarte, J. and Vasconcelos, A. (2010). *Evaluating Information Systems Constructing a Model Processing Framework*. In: International Journal of Enterprise Information Systems (IJEIS), 6(3), pp. 17-32.

Duffy, Jan. *Alignment: Delivering Results*, www.cio.com

Dunleavy, P., Margetts, H., Bastow, S. and Tinkler, J. (2011). *Digital Era Governance: IT Corporations, the State, and e-government*. In: OUP Catalogue.

Durrani, U., Richardson, J., Lenarcic, J. and Pita, Z. (2013). *Adaptable Management Systems Implementation for the Governance: A Case Study of Cloud Computing*. In: 26th Bled eConference, pp. 1-14, University of Maribor.

Dyba, T. and Dingsoyr, T. (2009). *What Do We Know About Agile Software Development?* In: Software, IEEE, 26(5), pp. 6-9.

Edwards, John. (2005, September). *Dream Catalogue*. In: CFO Magazine.

Edwards, P. and Bowen, P. (2013). *Risk Management in Project Organizations*. Routledge.

Egan, M. (1997). *Modes of Business Governance: European Management Styles and Corporate Cultures*. In: West European Politics, 20(2), pp. 1-21.

Elliott, S. (2008, March). *Agile Project management. In: Seminar on Current Trends in Software Industry*, University of Helsinki, Finland.

Elliott, T. (2013). *The Datafications of Daily Life*, In: Forbes, July 23, 2013. www.forbes.com/sites/sap/2013/07/24/The Datafiction-of-daily-life/

Elliott, T. E., Holmes, J. H., Davidson, A. J., Chance, L., Nelson, A. F. and Steiner, J. F. (2013). *Data Warehouse Governance Programs in Healthcare Settings: A Literature Review and a Call to Action*. In: eGEMs (Generating Evidence & Methods to Improve Patient Outcomes), 1(1), p. 15.

Ellis, James E., McDonnell Douglas. (1994 February 14). *Unfasten the Seat Belts*, In: BusinessWeek, pp. 36.

Emmanuel, William (2014). *Data Privacy and Big-Data-Compliance Issues and Considerations*, In: ISACA Journal, Volume 3, 2014.

Engardio, Pete et al. (2003, February 3). *The New Global Job Shift*, In: BusinessWeek.

Erek, K., Proehl, T. and Zarnekow, R. (2014). *Managing Cloud Services with IT Service Management Practices*. In: Engineering and Management of IT-based Service Systems, pp. 67-81. Springer, Berlin Heidelberg.

Erickson-Harris, Lisa (2006). *IT Governance: Round Em Up!* Intelligent Enterprise Conf., August 2006, p. 10-14.

Ernst and Young (2005). *48 Questions You Need to Answer for Sarbanes-Oxley Compliance*, Tech Republic, CNET Networks.

Esposito, A., and Rogers, T. (2013). *Ten Steps to ITSM Success: A Practitioner's Guide to Enterprise IT Transformation (Vol. 2)*. IT Governance Ltd.

Fabian, Robert (2007). *Interdependence of COBIT and ITIL*. In: Information Systems Control Journal, Volume 1.

Fairchild, A. (2013). *Governance in the Cloud: Role of Certification for SME Trust and Adoption*. In: CONF-IRM 2013 Proceedings, pp. 1-6.

Faisal, M. N. and Banwet, D. K. (2009). *Analyzing Alternatives for Information Technology Outsourcing Decision*: An Analytic Network Process Approach. In: International Journal of Business Information Systems, 4(1), pp. 47-62.

Farmand, M. (2013). *Proposing a Comprehensive Framework for ITSM Efficiency*, http://hdl. handle.net/2320/12479.

Farrar, J. H. (2008). *Corporate Governance: Theories, Principles and Practice*, Oxford University Press, Victoria, Australia.

Fasanghari, M., NasserEslami, F. and Naghavi, M. (2008, September). *IT Governance Standard Selection Based on Two Phase Clustering Method*. In: Networked Computing and Advanced Information Management, 2008. NCM'08. Fourth International Conference on Networked Computing and Advanced Information Management, Vol. 2, pp. 513-518. IEEE.

Federal Financial Institutions Examination Council (FFIEC) (2003). *Business Continuity Planning*, March 2003, http://www.ffiec.gov/ffiecinfobase/booklets/bcp/bus_continuity_plan.pdf

Fell, Greg (2013). *Decoding the IT Value Problem*, Wiley.

Feltus, C., Petit, M. and Dubois, E. (2009, November). *Strengthening Employee's Responsibility to Enhance Governance of IT: COBIT RACI chart Case Study*. In: Proceedings of the first ACM workshop on Information security governance, pp. 23-32. ACM.

Ferguson, C., Green, P., Vaswani, R., and Wu, G. H. (2013). *Determinants of Effective Information Technology Governance*. In: International Journal of Auditing, 17(1), pp. 75-99.

Fernandez, D. J. and Fernandez, J. D. (2008). *Agile Project Management–Agilism versus Traditional Approaches*. In: Journal of Computer Information Systems, 49(2), pp. 10-17.

Fernando, A. C. (2009). *Corporate Governance: Principles, Policies and Practices*. Pearson Education.

Fink, D. (2014). *Project Risk Governance: Managing Uncertainty and Creating Organizational Value*. Gower Publishing, Ltd.

Forrester Research (2004). *Sarbanes-Oxley Solutions- Invest or Pay Later: Hybrid Applications Emerge for Internal Controls Compliance*, Forrester Research Report, March 11, 2004.

Franke, U., Johnson, P., and König, J. (2013). *An Architecture Framework for Enterprise IT Service Availability Analysis*. In: Software & Systems Modeling, pp. 1-29.

Friedman, Debbie. (2006). *Demystifying Outsourcing*, J. Wiley & Sons.

Fullan, M. (2011). *The Six Secrets of Change: What the Best Leaders Do to Help Their Organizations Survive and Thrive*. John Wiley & Sons.

Gacenga, F. N. (2013). *A Performance Measurement Framework for IT Service Management*, In: Doctoral dissertation, University of Southern Queensland. Gacenga@usq.edu.au.

Galanis, M. M. and Dignam, M. A. (2013). *The Globalization of Corporate Governance*. Ashgate Publishing.

Galup, S. D., Dattero, R., Quan, J. J., and Conger, S. (2009). *An Overview of IT Service Management*. In: Communications of the ACM, 52(5), pp. 124-127.

Gama, N., Sousa, P., and Da Silva, M. M. (2013). *Integrating Enterprise Architecture and IT Service Management*. In: Building Sustainable Information Systems, pp. 153-165. Springer US.

Gandomani. T. J., Zulzalil, H., Ghani, A., Azim, A. and Sultan, A. B. (2013). *Important Considerations for Agile Software Development Methods Governance*. In: Journal of Theoretical & Applied Information Technology, 55(3).

Gartner (2001). *Building an IT Performance Management Program*, Gartner Measurement Presentation, July 24, 2001.

Gartner (2010). *Gartner Identifies Seven Major Projects CIOs Should Consider During the Next Three Years*, press release, 9 November 2010, www.granter.com/newsrooms/id/1465614.

Gayle, D. J., Tewarie, B., and White Jr, A. Q. (2011). *Governance in the Twenty-first-century university: Approaches to effective leadership and strategic management: ASHE-ERIC Higher Education Report (Vol. 14)*. John Wiley & Sons.

General Accounting Office (2004). *Information Technology Investment Management Model: A Framework for Assessing and Improving Process Maturity*, GAO Report 04-394G, Version 1.1.

General Electric Corp. (2005). *Six Sigma Training Workshop for Vendors*, GE.

Gido, J. and Clements, J. P. (2012). *Successful Project Management*. Cengage.

Gloger, B. (2010). *SCRUM*. In: Informatik-Spektrum, 33(2), pp. 195-200.

Goeken, M. and Alter, S. (2008). *IT Governance Frameworks as Methods*. In: Proceedings of the 10th International Conference on Enterprise Information Systems (ICEIS), June 2008, pp. 12-16.

Gokila, R. (2014). *Review of Security Services in Cloud Computing and Management*. In: Asian Journal of Research in Social Sciences and Humanities,4(2), pp. 189-198.

Gorla, N. and Somers, T. M. (2014). *The Impact of IT Outsourcing on Information Systems Success*. In: Information & Management, 51(3), pp. 320-335.

Gray, Clifford and Larson, Erik (2008). *Project Management - The Management Process*, Fourth Edition, McGraw Hill, NY.

Griffiths, M. (2011). *Crowd-sourcing Techniques: Participation, Transparency and the Factors Determining the Co-production of Policy*. In: The Proceedings of the 11th European Conference on EGovernment: Faculty of Administration, University of Ljubljana, Ljubljana, Slovenia, 16-17 June 2011, p. 288, Academic Conferences Limited.

Grobauer, B., Walloschek, T. and Stocker, E. (2011). *Understanding Cloud Computing Vulnerabilities*. In: Security & Privacy, IEEE, 9(2), pp. 50-57.

Guang-yong, H. (2011, May). *Study and Practice of import Scrum Agile Software Development*. In: Communication Software and Networks (ICCSN), 2011 IEEE 3rd International Conference, pp. 217-220, IEEE.

Gurjar, Y. S. and Rathore, V. S. (2013). *Cloud Business Intelligence – Is What Business Need Today*. In: International Journal of Recent Technology and Engineering, 1(6), pp. 81-86.

Haeckel, S. H. (1999). *Adaptive Enterprise: Creating and Leading Sense-and-Respond Organizations*. Harvard Business School Press, Boston, MA.

Hale, Judith. (2006). *Outsourcing Training and Development*, J. Wiley & Sons, NY.

Halvey, John K. and Melby, Barbara M. (2005). *Information Technology Outsourcing Transactions*, Second Edition, J. Wiley & Sons, NY.

Halvey, John K. and Melby, Barbara M. (2007). *Business Process Outsourcing*, J. Wiley & Sons, NY.

Hamaker, Stacey (2005). *Enterprise Governance & The Role of IT*, In: Information Systems Control Journal, Volume 6, 2005.

Hamel, Gary (2000). *Leading the Revolution*, Harvard Business School Press.

Hamm, Steve. (2007). *Bangalore Tiger,* McGraw-Hill, New York.

Hand, Anthony (2004). *Applying the Kano Model to User Experience Design*, UPA Boston mini-Conference, www.hadnweb.com/anthony/portfolio/kanoa-hand_kano-model_boston_may-12-2004.pdf

Haq, H., Howard, C. and Hargiss, K. M. (2013). *Looking at IT and Business Alignment from the Stone Age of Information Technology*. In: International Journal of Strategic Information Technology and Applications (IJSITA), 4(3), pp. 89-102.

Hardy, G. (2006). *Guidance on Aligning COBIT ITIL and ISO 17799*, In: Journal Online, ISACA.

Hardy, G., and Goldentops, E. (2005). *COBIT 4.0: The New Face of COBIT*, In: Information Systems Control Journal, Volume 6, 2005.

Hay, B. and Nance, K. et al. (2012). *Are Your Papers in Order? Developing and Enforcing Multi-Tenancy and Migration Policies in the Cloud*, 45th Hawaii International Conference on Systems Sciences, Vol.12, no., pp. 5473-5479.

Hayden, L. (2009). *Designing Common Control Frameworks: A Model for Evaluating Information Technology Governance, Risk, and Compliance Control Rationalization Strategies*. In: Information Security Journal: A Global Perspective, 18(6), pp. 297-305.

Heagney, J. (2011). *Fundamentals of Project Management*. AMACOM.

Hefley, William E. and Locsche, Ethel A. (2006). *The eSCM-CL v1.1: Model Overview, Part 1*, ITSqc, Carnegie Mellon University.

Hefley, William E. and Locsche, Ethel A. (2006). *The eSCM-CL v1.1: Model Overview, Part 2*, ITSqc, Carnegie Mellon University.

Heide, J. B., Kumar, A. and Wathne, K. H. (2013). *Concurrent Sourcing, Governance Mechanisms, and Performance Outcomes in Industrial Value Chains*. In: Strategic Management Journal.

Heier, H., Borgman, H. P. and Hofbauer, T. H. (2008, January). *Making the Most of IT Governance Software: Understanding Implementation Processes*. Hawaii International Conference on System Sciences, Proceedings of the 41st Annual, pp. 435-435. IEEE.

Heier, H., Borgman, H. P. and Mileos, C. (2009, January). *Examining the Relationship Between IT Governance Software, Processes, and Business Value: a Quantitative Research Approach*. In: 42nd Hawaii International Conference on System Sciences 2009. HICSS'09, pp. 1-11. IEEE.

Hemphill, T. (2013). *The ISO 26000 Guidance On Social Responsibility International Standard: What Are The Business Governance Implications?* In: Corporate Governance, 13(3), pp. 305-317.

Henderson, J., and Venkatraman, N. (1990). *Strategic Alignment: A Model for Organizational Transformation via Information Technology*. In: Working Paper 3223-90, Sloan School of Management, Massachusetts Institute of Technology, Cambridge, MA.

Henderson, J., and Venkatraman, N. (1999). *Strategic Alignment: Leveraging Information Technology for Transforming Organizations*. In: IBM Systems Journal, Vol. 38, Nos. 2 and 3.

Henderson, Tom and Allen, Brendan (2010). *Private Cloud: Not for the Faint of Health*, In: Network World, 12-20-2010.

Hendrikse, J. W. and Hendrikse, L. (2004). *Business Governance Handbook: Principles and Practices*. Juta Academic.

Herron, D., Andriole, S. J., and Moss, L. T. (2013). *Searching for Maturity*: In: The Impact of CMM on Outsourced Software Development. Feedback, 4, 6.

Hertis, M., and Juric, M. B. (2013). *Ideas on Improving the Business-IT Alignment in BPM Enabled by SOA*. In: Information and Communication Technology (ICoICT), 2013 International Conference of Information and Communication Technology, pp. 55-60, IEEE.

Highsmith, J. (2009). *Agile Project Management: Creating Innovative Products*. Pearson Education.

Highsmith, J. (2013). *Agile Project Management: Principles and Tools*. In: Feedback, 4, 6.

Highsmith, J., Wysocki, R. K. and Boyd, S. (2013). *How Agile Are Organizations Today?* In: Feedback, 4, 6.

Hilb, M. (2012). *New Corporate Governance: Successful Board Management Tools*. Springer.

Hinkle, Mark (9-6-2010), Three Cloud Lock-in Considerations, http://community.zenoss.org/blogs/zenossblog/2010/06/ThreeCloudLock-inConsiderations.

Hitt, M., et al.(2015). *Strategic Management – Competitiveness and Globalization, 11th Edition*, Thomson-South Western.

Hobbs, B., Aubry, M. and Thuillier, D. (2008). *The Project Management Office as an Organizational Innovation*. In: International Journal of Project Management, 26(5), pp. 547-555.

Hoffer, Jeffrey, Ramesh V. and Topi, Heikki. (2013). *Modern Data Management, 11th Ed.*, Pearson.

Hole, S. and Moe, N. B. (2008). *A Case Study of Coordination in Distributed Agile Software Development*. In: Software process improvement., pp. 189-200. Springer, Berlin Heidelberg.

Holub, E., Mingay, S., Brittain, K., Govekar, M. and Bittinger, S. (2007, June 5). *ITIL v3 Services Guidelines Expand Audience Through Update*, In: Gartner Research.

Hossain, E., Babar, M. A. and Paik, H. Y. (2009, July). *Using Scrum in Global Software Development: A systematic Literature Review*. In: Global Software Engineering, 2009. ICGSE 2009. Fourth IEEE International Conference on Global Software Engineering, pp. 175-184.

Howe, J. (2008). *Crowdsourcing: Why The Power of the Crowd is Driving the Future of Business*, In: The International Achievement Institute, 2008.

Howe, J.J. (2012). *The Sarbanes Oxley Act At 10*, Ernst & Young, LLP.

HP: *The Reference Model* (HP white papers) http://www.hp.com/large/itsm

Hsu, W. L. (2012). *Conceptual Framework of Cloud Computing Governance Model–An Education Perspective*. In: IEEE Technology and Engineering Education (ITEE), 7(2), p. 3.

Hsu, W.L. (2013). *Governance Model of Cloud Computing Service*, In: IEEE Technology and Engineering Education (ITEE), Vol. 7, No. 2, June 2012.

Huang, R., Zmud, R. W.and Price, R. L. (2010). *Influencing the Effectiveness of IT Governance Practices through Steering Committees and Communication Policies*. In: European Journal of Information Systems, 19(3), pp. 288-302.

Hughes, S. and Wilkinson, R. (2013). *Global Governance: Critical Perspectives*. Routledge.

Hyder, Elaine B., Heston, Keith M., and Mark, C.(2006). *The eSCM-SP v2.01: Model Overview, Part 1*, ITSqc, Carnegie Mellon University.

Hyder, Elaine B., Heston, Keith M., and Mark, C.(2006). *The eSCM-SP v2.01: Model Overview, Part 2*, ITSqc, Carnegie Mellon University.

IBM (1981). *Business Systems Planning, Planning Guide, GE20-0527*, White Plains, NY: IBM Corporation.

IBM, *IBM Process Reference Model for IT (PRM-IT), Version 3.0*, 2008.

Iden, J. and Eikebrokk, T. R. (2013). *Implementing IT Service Management: A Systematic Literature Review*. In: International Journal of Information Management, 33(3), pp. 512-523.

Institute of Internal Auditors (2005). Putting COSO's Theory into Practice, In: Tone at the Top, Issue 28, November 2005.

International Association of Outsourcing Professionals. (2006). *Outsourcing Professional Body of Knowledge, Version 6*, IAOP.

International Data Corporation (2012) *Data Management: A Unified Approach*, In: IDG Research Services White Paper, November 2012.

Ireland, R., West, B., Smith, N. and Shepherd, D. I. (2012). *Project Management for IT-related Projects*. BCS.

ISACA (2012). *COBIT°5 – Enabling Processes*, ISACA, Chicago, Il.

ISACA (2014). *Controls and Assurance in the Cloud: Using COBIT 5*.

IT Governance Institute (2003). *Board Briefing on IT Governance Report, Second Edition*, ITGI, Rolling Meadows, Il.

IT Governance Institute (2005). *Information Security Governance, 2nd Edition, Report on Guidance for Boards of Directors and Executive Management*. ITGI.

IT Governance Institute (2006). *The CEO's Guide to IT Value & Risk*. ITGI.

IT Governance Institute (2008), *Enterprise Value: Governance of IT Investments – The Val-IT Framework 2.0*.ITGI.

IT Governance Institute (2012). *COBIT 5.0*, ITGI.

IT Governance Institute and Office of Government Commerce (2005). *Aligning COBIT, ITIL, and ISO 17799, A Management Report*. ITGI.

Jain, R. (2010). *Investigation of Governance Mechanisms for Crowd Sourcing Initiatives*. In: AMCIS , p. 557.

Jamil, D. and Zaki, H. (2011). *Cloud Computing Security*. In: International Journal of Engineering Science and Technology, 3(4), pp. 3478-3483.

Jansen, W. and Grance, T. (2011). *Guidelines on Security and Privacy in Public Cloud Computing*. NIST Special Publication, 800-144.

Janszen, F. (2000). *The Age of Innovation: Making Business Creativity a Competence, not a Coincidence,* Prentice Hall, London.

Japan Users Association of Information Systems (2012). *The 19th Corporate IT Trend Survey.*

Jenkinson, T. and Mayer, C. (2012). *The Assessment: Corporate Governance and Corporate Control.* In: Oxford Review of Economic Policy, 8(3), pp. 1-10.

Jeston, J., and Nelis, J. (2014). *Business process management*. Routledge.

John, K., Litov, L. and Yeung, B. (2008). *Corporate Governance and Risk-Taking*. In: The Journal of Finance, 63(4), pp. 1679-1728.

Johnson, Carla (2002, June). *Creating Virtual Teams,* In: HR Magazine.

Johnston, E. W. and Hansen, D. L. (2011). *Design Lessons for Smart Governance Infrastructures.* In: American Governance, 3, pp. 197-212.

Jones, W. and Reddy, R. (2013). *Strategic Sourcing.* In: Feedback, 4, 6.

Jussi, S. (2013). *A Framework for IT Service Management Integration*, Lappeenranta University of Technology, School of Industrial Engineering and Management, Department of Software Engineering and Information Management.

Kabachinski, J. (2011). *Have you heard of ITIL? It's time you did*. In: Biomedical Instrumentation & Technology, 45(1), pp. 59-62.

Kaisler, S., Armour, F., Espinosa, J. A. and Money, W. (2013, January). *Big Data: Issues and Challenges Moving Forward*. In: 46th Hawaii International Conference on System Sciences (HICSS), 2013, pp. 995-1004, IEEE.

Kammermeier, M. (2010). *Agile Project Management in IT Development Projects with a Focus on Team Performance*. GRIN Verlag.

Kandukuri, B. R., Paturi, V. R. and Rakshit, A. (2009, September). *Cloud Security Issues.* In: International Conference on Services Computing, 2009. SCC'09, pp. 517-520, IEEE.

Kano Model, http://www.betterproductdesign.net/tools/definition/kano.htm

Kaplan, J. D. (2005). *Strategic IT Portfolio Management: Governing Enterprise Transformation*, Jeff Kaplan.

Kaplan, R. and Norton, D.(2001). *The Strategy Focused Company*, Harvard Business School Press.

Kaplan, R. and Norton, D. (1996). *Using the Balanced Scorecard as a Strategic Management System*, In: Harvard Business Review, Jan. – Feb. 1996, pp. 75-85.

Kaplan, Robert and Norton, David (1996). *The Balanced Scorecard*, HBR Press, Cambridge, MA.

Kaplan, Robert and Norton, David (2001). *The Strategy-Focused Organization: How Balanced Scorecard Companies Thrive in the New Business Environment*, Harvard Business School Press, Boston, MA.

Kaplan, Robert and Norton, David (2004). *Strategy Maps: Converting Intangible Assets into Tangible Outcomes*, Harvard Business School Press, Boston, MA.

Kapur, G. (2005). *Project Management for Information, Technology. Business and Certification*, Pearson Prentice Hall.

Katzenback, Jon and Smith, Doug. (2001). *The Discipline of Teams*, John Wiley, New York.

Kaufman, L. M. (2009). *Data Security in the World of Cloud Computing*. In: Security & Privacy, IEEE, 7(4), pp. 61-64.

Kavis, M. J. (2014). *Architecting the Cloud: Design Decisions for Cloud Computing Service Models (SaaS, PaaS, and IaaS)*. John Wiley & Sons.

Keen, J. and Digrius, B. (2003). *Making Technology Investments Profitable*, J. Wiley and Sons.

Keen, Jack (2006). *Solidifying Business-IT Alignment*, In: The Advisory Council Research Smart Tip, August 2006.

Kelly, Kevin (2010). *A Cloud Book For The Cloud*, www.kr.org/thetechniumarchives/2007/11/Cloudbook-for.PhP.retrived , 08-22-2010.

Kern, R., Mandelstein, D. J., Milman, I. M., Oberhofer, M. A. and Pandit, S. (2013). *Information Governance and Crowd Sourcing, U.S. Patent No. 20,130,275,803*. Washington, DC: U.S. Patent and Trademark Office.

Kerzner, H. R. (2013). *Project Management Metrics, KPIs, and Dashboards: A Guide to Measuring and Monitoring Project Performance*. John Wiley & Sons.

Kerzner, H. R. (2013). *Project Management: A Systems Approach to Planning, Scheduling, and Controlling. 11th Edition*, Wiley.

Kerzner, H. R. (2014). *Project Management-Best Practices: Achieving Global Excellence*. John Wiley & Sons.

Kim, Y. J., Lee, J. M., Koo, C. and Nam, K. (2013). *The Role of Governance Effectiveness in Explaining IT Outsourcing Performance*. In: International Journal of Information Management, 33(5), pp. 850-860.

Knahl, M. H. (2009). *A Conceptual Framework for the Integration of IT Infrastructure Management, IT Service Management and IT Governance*. In: Proceedings of the World Academy of Science, Engineering and Technology, p. 40.

Ko, D. and Fink, D. (2010). *Information Technology Governance: An Evaluation of the Theory-Practice Gap*. In: Corporate Governance, 10(5), pp. 662-674.

Kolk, A. (2008). *Sustainability, Accountability and Corporate Governance: Exploring Multinationals' Reporting Practices*. In: Business Strategy and the Environment, 17(1), pp. 1-15.

Korhonen, J. J., Melleri, I., Hiekkanen, K., and Helenius, M. (2013). *Designing Data Governance Structure: An Organizational Perspective*. In: GSTF Journal on Computing, 2(4).

Kotter, John P. (1996). *Leading Change*, In: HBR Press, Cambridge, MA.

Krag Brotby, W. (2009). *Information Security Management Metrics: A Definitive Guide to Effective Security Monitoring and Measurement*. CRC Press.

Kripalani, Manjeet and Engardio, Pete. (2003, December 8). *The Rise of India*, In: BusinessWeek, pp. 66-78.

Kroenke, David and Auer, David (2014). *Database Processing, 13th Ed.*, Pearson.

Krzanik, L., Rodriguez, P., Simila, J., Kuvaja, P. and Rohunen, A. (2010, January). *Exploring the Transient Nature of Agile Project Management Practices*. In: 43rd Hawaii International Conference on System Sciences (HICSS), 2010, pp. 1-8. IEEE.

Kshetri, N. (2012). *Privacy and Security Issues in Cloud Computing: The Role of Institutions and Institutional Evolution*. Telecommunications Policy.

Kuhn, Janet (2007). *Transitioning to ITIL v3*, In: DITY Weekly Newsletter, Vol. 3.29., 24 July 24 2007.

Lahtela, A., Hotti, V. and Salomaa, H. (2014). *Service Support in IT Governance, IT Management and Enterprise Architecture Context*. In: The Fourth International Conference on Digital Information Processing and Communications (ICDIPC2014), pp. 166-172, The Society of Digital Information and Wireless Communication.

Lam, J. (2014). *Enterprise Risk Management: From Incentives to Controls, 2nd Ed.*, John Wiley & Sons.

Lambeth, John (2007). *Using COBIT as a Tool to Lead Enterprise IT Organizations*, In: Information Systems Control Journal, Volume 1, 2007.

Larrocha, E. R., Minguet, J. M., Díaz, G., Castro, M., and Vara, A. (2010, April). *Filling the Gap of Information Security Management inside ITIL®: proposals for posgraduate students*. In: Education Engineering (EDUCON), 2010 IEEE, pp. 907-912. IEEE.

Lee, M. C. (2013). *IT Governance Implementation Framework in Small and Medium Enterprise*. In: International Journal of Management and Enterprise Development, 12(4), pp. 425-441.

Lee, S. and Yong, H. S. (2010). *Distributed Agile: Project Management in a Global Environment*. In: Empirical Software Engineering, 15(2), pp. 204-217.

Leganza, Gene (2003). *Overcoming Obstacles to the Alignment of IT and the Business*. In: Giga Research Paper, June 24, 2003.

Lemus, S. M., Pino, F. J. and Velthius, M. P. (2010, June). *Towards a Model for Information Technology Governance Applicable to the Banking Sector*. In: Information Systems and

Technologies (CISTI) 2010 5th Iberian Conference on Information Systems and Technologies, pp. 1-6. IEEE.

Li, Q., Wang, C., Wu, J., Li, J., and Wang, Z. Y. (2011). *Towards the Business–Information Technology Alignment in Cloud Computing Environment: An Approach Based on Collaboration Points and Agents.* In: International Journal of Computer Integrated Manufacturing, 24(11), pp. 1038-1057.

Linthicum, D. S. (2009). *Cloud Computing and SOA Convergence in your Enterprise: A Step-by-Step Guide.* Pearson Education.

Lohan, G., Lang, M. and Conboy, K. (2013). *A Performance Management Model for Agile Information Systems Development Teams.* In: Building Sustainable Information Systems, pp. 297-308. Springer US.

Lohr, Steve (2007). *IBM Showing That Giants Can Be Nimble,* In: New York Times, July 18, 2007.

Lonsdale, Derek, Clark, W. and Udvadia, B. (2006). *ITIL in a Complex World,* In: Journal Online, ISACA.

Loshin, D. (2013). *Big Data Analytics: From Strategic Planning to Enterprise Integration with Tools, Techniques, NoSQL, and Graph.* Elsevier.

Lucio-Nieto, T., and Colomo-Palacios, R. (2012, June). *ITIL and the Creation of a Service Management Office (SMO): A new challenge for IT professionals: An exploratory study of Latin American companies.* In: Information Systems and Technologies (CISTI), 2012 7th Iberian Conference on, pp. 1-6. IEEE.

Lucio-Nieto, T., Colomo-Palacios, R., Soto-Acosta, P., Popa, S., and Amescua-Seco, A. (2012). *Implementing an IT Service Information Management Framework: The Case of COTEMAR.* In: International Journal of Information Management.

Luftman, J., Ben-Zvi, T., Dwivedi, R. and Rigoni, E. H. (2010). *IT Governance: An Alignment Maturity Perspective.* In: International Journal of IT/Business Alignment and Governance (IJITBAG), 1(2), pp. 13-25.

Luftman, Jerry (2004). *Managing the Information Technology Resource,* Pearson - Prentice Hall

Luftman, Jerry, Papp, Raymond and Brier, Tom (1999). *Enablers and Inhibitors of Business-IT Alignment,* In: Communications of the Association for Information Systems, Volume 1, Article 11, March 1999.

Lukyanenko, R. and Parsons, J. (2012, November). *Conceptual modeling principles for crowdsourcing.* In: Proceedings of the 1st international workshop on Multimodal crowd sensing, pp. 3-6, ACM.

Lutchen, M. D. (2011). *Managing IT as a Business: A Survival Guide for CEOs.* John Wiley & Sons.

Lyngso, S. (2014). *Agile Strategy Management: Techniques for Continuous Alignment and Improvement.* CRC Press.

Mackaden, Frederick (2014). *Law and Best Practices for a Sarbanes-Oxley Systems Review,* In: ISACA Journal, Volume 4, 2014.

Mahnic, V. (2011). *A Case Study on Agile Estimating and Planning Using SCRUM.* In: Electronics and Electrical Engineering, 111(5), pp. 123-128.

Mahnic, V. (2012). *A Capstone course on Agile Software Development using SCRUM.* In: IEEE Transactions on Education, 55(1), pp. 99-106.

Maizlish, B., and Handler, R. (2010). *IT (Information Technology) Portfolio Management Step-by-Step: Unlocking the Business Value of Technology.* John Wiley & Sons.

Manoochehri, M. (2013). *Data Just Right: Introduction to Large-Scale Data and Analytics.* Pearson Education.

Marçal, A. S. C., de Freitas, B. C. C., Soares, F. S. F., Furtado, M. E. S., Maciel, T. M. and Belchior, A. D. (2008). *Blending SCRUM practices and CMMI project management process areas.* In: Innovations in Systems and Software Engineering, 4(1), pp. 17-29.

Marchand, D. A., Kettinger W.J. and Rollins, J.D. (2001). *Information orientation: the Link to Business Performance,* Oxford University Press, New York/Oxford.

Marjanovic, S., Fry, C. and Chataway, J. (2012). *Crowdsourcing Based Business Models: In Search of Evidence for Innovation 2.0.* In: Science and Public Policy, 39(3), pp. 318-332.

Marrone, M., Gacenga, F., Cater-Steel, A., and Kolbe, L. (2014). *IT Service Management: A Cross-National Study of ITIL Adoption.* In: Communications of the Association for Information Systems, 34(1), pp. 865-892.

Martens, B. and Teuteberg, F. (2011). *Risk and Compliance Management for Cloud Computing Services: Designing a Reference Model.* In: Americas' Conference on Information Systems (AMCIS).

Mayle, David. (2006). *Managing Innovation and Change*, Sage Publications.

McAvoy, J. and Butler, T. (2009). *The Role of Project Management in Ineffective Decision Making within Agile Software Development Projects.* In: European Journal of Information Systems, 18(4), pp. 372-383.

McCauley, C. and Van Velsor, Ellen, (Ed.) (2004). *Handbook of Leadership Development, 2nd Edition,* In: The Center for Creative Leadership, Jossey Bass.

McCelland, David (1995). *The Leadership Profile for Winning, Presentation on Leadership,* MIT Seminar.

McCreight & Company (2008). *Implementing Strategic Change. In: Strategy Implementation Insights, Chapter 13,* Version 1.0, January 2008.

McDermott, Lynda, Brawley, Nolan and Waite, William (1998). *World Class Teams,* John Wiley, New York.

McFarlan, W. and Cash. J. (1990). *Strategic Planning for Information Systems,* Wiley.

McIvor, Ronan. (2006). *The Outsourcing Process,* In: Cambridge University Press, NY.

McNulty, T., Zattoni, A. and Douglas, T. (2013). *Developing Corporate Governance Research Through Qualitative Methods: A Review of Previous Studies.* In: Corporate Governance: An International Review, 21(2), pp. 183-198.

McNurlin, Barbara and Sprague, Ralph (2006). *Information Systems in Practice, 7th Edition,* Pearson Education, Upper Saddle River, NJ.

Mel, Peter and Gronce, Timothy (2011):, *The NIST Definitions of Cloud Computing,* National Institute of Standards and Technology (NIST), SP 800-145. http://CSRC.NIST.GOV/Publications/nistpubs/800-145/SP800-145.pdf.

Melnicoff, Richard, Shearer, Sandy and Goyal, Deepak (2005).*Is There a Smarter Way to Approach IT Governance?,* In: Outlook, 2005, Number 1, Accenture.

Meredith, J. R. and Mantel Jr., S. J. (2012). *Project Management: A Managerial Approach. 8th Edition,* Wiley.

Mesquida, A. L., Mas, A., Amengual, E. and Calvo-Manzano, J. A. (2012). *IT Service Management Process Improvement based on ISO/IEC 15504: A systematic review.* In: Information and Software Technology, 54(3), pp. 239-247.

Miller, D. (2013). *Maximising the Business Impact of IT: Importance of Managing the Total Business Experience,* Doctoral dissertation, Middlesex University.

Mitchell, G. (2008). *Creating Sustainable Advantage Through IT Risk Management.* Internet paper.

Mithas, S., Lee, M. R., Earley, S., Murugesan, S. and Djavanshir, R. (2013). *Leveraging Big Data and Business Analytics.* In: IT Professional, 15(6), pp. 18-20.

Moeller, R. R. (2013). *Executive's Guide to IT Governance: Improving Systems Processes with Service Management, COBIT and ITIL.* John Wiley & Sons.

Mohanty, S., Jagadeesh, M. and Srivatsa, H. (2013). *Application Architectures for Big Data and Analytics.* In: Big Data Imperatives, pp. 107-154. Apress.

Monnoyer, Eric and Willmott, Paul (2005). *What IT Leaders Do,* In: The McKinsey Quarterly, August 2005.

Mora, M., Phillips-Wren, G., Cervantes-Pérez, F., Garrido, L. and Gelman, O. (2014). *Improving IT Service Management with Decision-Making Support Systems.* In: Engineering and Management of IT-based Service Systems, pp. 215-232. Springer, Berlin Heidelberg.

Morabito, V. (2013). *Strategic Information Governance Modeling and Assessment.* In: Business Technology Organization, pp. 143-163. Springer, Berlin Heidelberg.

Moreira, M. (2013). *Being Agile: Your Roadmap to Successful Adoption of Agile.* Apress.

Morris, P. and Pinto, J. K. (Eds.). (2010). *The Wiley Guide to Project Organization and Project Management Competencies, Vol. 8.* Wiley, NY.

Mosimann, Roland, Mosimann, Patrick and Dussault, Meg (2007). *The Performance Manager*, Cognos.

Moster, E. (2013). *Using hybrid scrum to meet waterfall process deliverables*, Thesis.

Nash, Kim (2012). *CIO 100 Award – Winners are Risk Busters*, July 27, 2012. http://www.cio.com/article/2394011/cio-role/cio-100-award-winners-are-risk-busters.html, July 27, 2012.

National Institute of Standards and Technology (2011). *The NIST Definitions of Cloud Computing, Special Publication Number 800-145*, US Department of Commerce, Sept. 2011.

Nee, N. (2010). *Successful Projects through Agile Project Management*. ESI International.

Neely, Matthew (2014). *Securing an Evolving Cloud Environment*, In: ISACA Journal, Volume 3, 2014.

Nimmer, R. T. and Feinberg, R. B. (1989). *Business Governance: Fiduciary Duties*, Business Judgment, Trustees and Exclusivity. In: Emory Bankruptcy Developments Journal, Chapter 11.

Nolan, R. and McFarlan, F. W. (2005). *Information Technology and the Board of Directors*, In: Harvard Business Review, October 2005.

Nolan, R. and Koot, W. (1992). *Nolan's Stage Theory Today*, In: Holland Management Review, Number 31.

Nourizadeh, Z., Nourizadeh, A. and Mahdavi, M. (2011, August). *Implementing Information Technology Governance using Val IT; Case study: Isfahan Municipality*. In: Artificial Intelligence, Management Science and Electronic Commerce (AIMSEC), 2011 2nd International Conference on Management Science and Electronic Commerce , pp. 4644-4647. IEEE.

Office of Government Commerce (2004). *Business Perspective: The IS View on Delivering Services to the Business*. In: OGC, ITIL© Managing IT Services (IT Infrastructure Library). TSO.

Olausson, M., Rossberg, J., Ehn, J. and Sköld, M. (2013). Introduction to Agile Planning, Development, and Testing. In: Pro Team Foundation Service, pp. 9-19. Apress.

Olson, D. L. and Rosacker, K. (2013). *Crowdsourcing and Open Source Software Participation*. In: Service Business, 7(4), pp. 499-511.

Oltsik, Jon (2003). *IT Governance: Is IT Governance the Answer?* In: Tech Republic, January 13, 2003.

Opelt, A., Gloger, B., Pfarl, W. and Mittermayr, R. (2013). *Agile Contracts: Creating and Managing Successful Projects with Scrum*. John Wiley & Sons.

O'Sheedy, D. G. (2012). *A Study of Agile Project Management Methods used for IT Implementation Projects in Small and Medium-sized Enterprises*. DBA thesis, Southern Cross University, Lismore, NSW.

Ougaard, M. and Leander, A. (Eds.) (2010). *Business and Global Governance*. Routledge.

Overby, Stephanie (2005). *The New IT Department*, www.cio.com, December 15, 2005 / January 1, 2005.

Overby, Stephanie (2005, October). *Simple Successful Outsourcing*, In: CIO Magazine - Business Technology Leadership, pp. 51-62.

Palvia, Shailendra (2003, July). *Off Shore Outsourcing – Creating a World of Difference*, Proceeding of the Second Annual International Outsourcing Conference, Center for Global Outsourcing, New York.

Papp, R. (1998). *Alignment of Business and Information Technology Strategy: How and Why?*, In: Information Management (11), 3/4, pp. 6-11.

Parent, M. and Reich, B. H. (2009). *Governing Information Technology Risk*. In: California Management Review, 51(3), pp. 134-152.

Parks, Hugh (2006). *Shifting Governance Roles & Responsibilities*, In: Information Systems Control Journal, Volume 5, 2006.

Paulk, Mark C. (2005, February). *Measurement & the eSourcing Capability Model for Service Providers v2*, ITSqc, Carnegie Mellon University, CMU-ISRI-04-128.

Pearson, S. and Benameur, A. (2010, November). *Privacy, Security and Trust Issues Arising from Cloud Computing.* In: Second International Conference on Cloud Computing Technology and Science (CloudCom), 2010, pp. 693-702, IEEE.

Pharro, Richard (2014). *Agile Project Management White Paper,* APMG International and DSDM Consortium.

Pichler, R. (2010). *Agile Product Management with Scrum: Creating Products that Customers Love.* Addison-Wesley Professional.

Poligadu, A. and Moloo, R. K. (2014). *An Innovative Measurement Programme for Agile Governance.* International Journal of Agile Systems and Management, 7(1), pp. 26-60.

Popper, Charles (2000). *Holistic Framework for IT Governance.* In:, Center for Information Policy Research, Harvard University, January 2000.

Porter, Michael (1985). *Competitive Advantage: Creating and Sustaining Superior Performance,* Free Press.

Posthumus, S., Von Solms, R. and King, M. (2010). *The Board and IT Governance: The What, Who and How.* In: South African Journal of Business Management, 41(3), pp. 23-32.

Prahaland, C. and Hamel, G. (1990). *The Core Competence of the Corporation,* In: Harvard Business Review, March/April 1990.

Prasad, A., Heales, J. and Green, P. (2009). *Towards a Deeper Understanding of Information Technology Governance Effectiveness: A Capabilities-Based Approach.* In: International Conference on Information Systems (ICIS) 2009, pp. 1-19. Association for Information Systems.

Prasad, A., Heales, J. and Green, P. (2010). *A Capabilities-based Approach to Obtaining a Deeper Understanding of Information Technology Governance Effectiveness: Evidence from IT Steering Committees.* In: International Journal of Accounting Information Systems, 11(3), pp. 214-232.

Praxiom Research Group, Ltd. ISO/IEC 27001 Overview. http://www.praxiom.com/iso-27001-intro.htm

Prentice, Robert (2005). *Sarbanes-Oxley Act- Student Guide,* Thomson Publishing.

Prewitt, Edward and Ware, Lorraine C. (2006). *The State of the CIO'06,* www.cio.com/archieve/010106/JAN1SOC.pdf .

Proctivity (2003). *Frequently Asked Questions, Guide to the Sarbanes-Oxley Act: IT Risks and Controls,* December 2003.

Proehl, T., Erek, K., Limbach, F. and Zarnekow, R. (2013, January). *Topics and Applied Theories in IT Service Management.* In: 46th Hawaii International Conference on System Sciences (HICSS), 2013. pp. 1367-1375. IEEE.

Project Management Institute (2004). *OPM3 – Organizational Project Management Maturity Model,* PMI.

Project Management Institute (2006). *The Standard for Portfolio Management,* PMI.

Project Management Institute (2013). *A Guide to the Project Management Body of Knowledge: PMBOK® Guide, 5th Edition.* PMI.

Prufer, J. (2013). *How to Govern the Cloud? Characterizing the Optimal Enforcement Institution that Supports Accountability.* In: Cloud Computing. TILEC Discussion Paper No. 2013-022. Available at SSRN: http://ssrn.com/abstract=2365713 or http://dx.doi.org/10.2139/ssrn.2365713.

Puccio, Gerard, Murdock, Mary and Mance, Marie (2007). *Creative Leadership,* Sage Publications.

Pultorak, David and Kerrigan, Jim (2005). *Conformance Performance and Rapport: A Framework for Corporate and IT Governance,* In: NACD – Directors Monthly, February 2005.

Qian, J., Ward, K., and Blaskovich, J. (2012). *Integrating IT Frameworks into the AIS Course.* In: AIS Educator Journal, 7(1), pp. 1-26.

Qian, R. and Palvia, P. (2013). *Towards An Understanding of Cloud Computing's Impact on Organizational IT Strategy.* In: Journal of Information Technology Case & Application Research, 15(4).

Quinn, James Brian (2000, Summer). *Outsourcing Innovation: The New Engine of Growth,* In: Sloan Management Review, pp. 13-27.

Racz, N., Weippl, E. and Seufert, A. (2010, July). *A Process Model for Integrated IT Governance, Risk, and Compliance Management.* In: Proceedings of the Ninth Baltic Conference on Databases and Information Systems (DB&IS'10), pp. 155-170.

Rafeq, A. (2005). *Using CobiT for IT Control Health Check Up,* In: Information Systems Control Journal Health, Volume 5, 2005.

Rahman, A. A., Doina, P. P. and Eugen, P. (2013). *A Survey in Information Systems: Integral Part and a Strategic Partner for Good Corporate Governance.* Ovidius University Annals, Series on Economic Sciences, 13(1).

Reiss, G. (2013). *Project Management Demystified: Today's Tools and Techniques.* Routledge.

Reynolds, P. and Yetton, P. (2013). *Aligning Business and IT Strategies in Multi-Business Organizations,* Thirty Fourth International Conference on Information Systems, Milan 2013.

Rezaeean, A. and Falaki, P. (2012). *Agile Project Management.* In: International Research Journal of Applied and Basic Sciences, 3(4), pp. 698-707.

Riffat, Muzamiz (2014). *Big Data – Not a Panacea,* In: ISACA Journal, Volume 3, 2014.

Rio-Belver, R., Cilleruelo, E., Garechana, G., Gavilanes, J. and Zabalza, J. (2012). *New Management Models based in Cloud-Computing.* International Scientific Conference "Business and Management 2012".

Ristola, T. (2011). *Risk Management in Information System Development.*

Robinson, Nick (2007). *The Many Faces of IT Governance,* In: Information Systems Control Journal, Volume 1, 2007.

Rockart, J., Earl, M. and Ross, J. (1996). *Eight Imperatives for the New IT Organization,* In: Sloan Management Review, Fall 1996, pp. 43-55.

Rockart, John (1979). *Chief Executives Define Their Own Data Needs,* In: Harvard Business Review, March-April, 1979.

Rosenberg, Jothy and Mateus, Arthur (2010). *The Cloud At Your Service,* Manning Publications.

Rothaermel, F. T. (2013). *Strategic Management: Concepts.* McGraw-Hill Irwin.

Rovers, M. (2013). *ISO/IEC 20000: 2011 – A Pocket Guide.* Van Haren Publishing.

Russom, Philip (May 6, 2010). *Introduction to Unified Data Management,* http://tdwi.org/articles/2010/05/06/ introduction-to-unified-data-management.aspx

Sabahi, F. (2011, May). *Cloud Computing Security Threats and Responses.* In: 3rd International Conference on Communication Software and Networks (ICCSN), 2011, pp. 245-249. IEEE.

Salo, O. and Abrahamsson, P. (2008). *Agile Methods in European Embedded Software Development Organizations: A Survey on the Actual Use and Usefulness of Extreme Programming and Scrum.* In: Software, IET, 2(1), pp. 58-64.

Sauer, C. and Burn, J.M. (1997). *The Pathology of Strategic Alignment,* In: C. Sauer, P.Y. Yetton and Associates, Steps to the Future - Fresh Thinking on the Management of IT-based Organizational Transformation, Jossey-Bass, San Francisco.

Schreiner, S. (2008, December). *A Survey of IT Governance through COBIT, ITIL, and ISO 17799.* In: Report, University of Illinois at Urbana-Champaign.

Schwaber, Ken and Sutherland, Jeff (2013). *The Scrum Guide,* Scrum.org.

Seiner, Robert (2004). *Simplified Approach to Stewartship,* In: The Data Administrator Newsletters, http://www.tdan.com/view-articles/5220/july1,2004.

Selig, Gad J. (1983). *Strategic Planning for Information Resource Management – A Multinational Perspective,* UMI Press.

Selig, Gad J. (2004). *Best Practices for IT Project Management in Fast Track Mode,* paper published in Proceedings of Project World, Fall 2004, Washington, DC.

Selig, Gad J. (2006). *Creating, Sustaining and Leading High Performance Co-Located and Virtual Teams and Team Leaders - Why, What and How?,* Proceedings of Southern New England Chapter of the Project Management Institute - First Annual Conference, Hartford Conference Center, Hartford, CT. May 23, 2006.

Selig, Gad J. (2006). *IT Governance - A Best Practice Roadmap,* ISACA - Greater Hartford Chapter Workshop, March 15, 2006.

Selig, Gad J. (2007). *Successful Business/IT Alignment, Execution & Governance Best Practices*, Society for Information Management Presentation, SIM Fairfield/Westchester Chapter Meeting, March 15, 2007, Doral Arrowwood Conf. Center, NY.

Selig, Gad J. (2007, February 18-21). *How to Win Deals in the Rapidly Changing World of Outsourcing - Critical Success Factors for Vendor/Customer Collaboration and Innovation to Grow Revenues*, The Outsourcing World Summit, Loews Hotel, Lake Las Vegas, Las Vegas, Nevada.

Selig, Gad J. and Waterhouse, Peter (2006). *IT Governance - An Integrated Framework and Roadmap: How to Plan, Deploy and Sustain for Competitive Advantage*, Computer Associates Sponsored White Paper, March 2006.

Senge, Peter M. (1990). *The Fifth Discipline: the Art and Practise of the Learning Organization*. New York: Currency/Doubleday.

Senthilkumar, T., Benruben, R., Sakthirajan, T. and Sivaram, N. M. (2012). *A Review on Some Agile Project Management Techniques*. In: Proceedings of the 2012 International Conference on Industrial Engineering and Operations Management, Istanbul, Turkey.

Shah, N., Dhanesha, A. and Seetharam, D. (2009, November). *Crowd Sourcing for e-Governance: Case study*. In: Proceedings of the 3rd international conference on Theory and practice of electronic governance, pp. 253-258, ACM.

Shanks, G., Bekmamedova, N. and Willcocks, L. (2013). *Using Business Analytics for Strategic Alignment and Organizational Transformation*, In: International Journal of Business Intelligence Research (IJBIR), 4(3), pp. 1-15.

Sharma, D., Stone, M. and Ekinci, Y. (2009). *IT Governance and Project Management: A Qualitative Study*. In: Journal of Database Marketing & Customer Strategy Management, 16(1), pp. 29-50.

Shaw, Melissa (2001). *Management Strategies*, In: Network Management Newsletter, 11/7/01.

Sheppard, J. A., Sarros, J. C., and Santora, J. C. (2013). *Twenty-First Century Leadership: International Imperatives*. Management Decision, 51(2), pp. 267-280.

Shivashankarappa, A. N., Smalov, L., Dharmalingam, R., and Anbazhagan, N. (2012, June). *Implementing IT Governance using COBIT: A Case Study Focusing on Critical Success Factors*. In: Internet Security (World CIS), 2012 World Congress on, pp. 144-149. IEEE.

Sia, S. K., Soh, C. and Weill, P. (2010). *Global IT Management: Structuring for Scale, Responsiveness, and Innovation*. In: Communications of the ACM, 53(3), pp. 59-64.

Sibbet, David (1997). *75 years of Management Ideas and Practice 1922-1997*, In: Harvard Business Review, Sep./Oct. 1997, Supplement Vol. 75, Issue 5.

Silva, E. and Chaix, Y. (2008, January). *Business and IT Governance Alignment Simulation Essay on a Business Process and IT Service Model*. In: Hawaii International Conference on System Sciences, Proceedings of the 41st Annual, pp. 434-434. IEEE.

Simonsson, M. and Johnson, P. (2008, January). *The IT Organization Modeling and Assessment tool: Correlating IT Governance Maturity with the Effect of IT*. In: Hawaii International Conference on System Sciences, Proceedings of the 41st Annual, pp. 431-431. IEEE.

Simonsson, M., Johnson, P. and Ekstedt, M. (2010). *The Effect of IT Governance Maturity on IT Governance Performance*. In: Information Systems Management, 27(1), pp. 10-24.

Singh, A. (2014). *Big Data in Cloud Computing Environments*. In: The International Journal of Big Data, 1(2).

Singh, R., Bhagat, A. and Kumar, N. (2012, September). *Generalization of Software Metrics on Software as a Service (SaaS)*. In: 2012 International Conference on Computing Sciences (ICCS), pp. 267-270. IEEE.

Singh-Latulipe, Rob (2007). *Val IT: From the Vantage Point of the COBIT 4.0 Pentagon Model for IT Governance*, In: Information Systems Control Journal, Volume 1, 2007.

Situation Leadership Model. (2006). http://www.chimaeraconsulting.com/sitleader.htm.

Smits, D. and Hillegersberg, J. van (2013, August). *The Continuing Mismatch Between IT Governance Theory and Practice*. In: Results From a Delphi Study with CIO's. AMCIS.

Snyder, Bill (2003, May). *Teams That Span Time Zones Face New Work Rules.*. http://gsb.stanford.edu/news/bmag/sbsm0305/feature_virtual_teams.shtml

So, K. (2011). *Cloud Computing Security Issues and Challenges.* In: International Journal of Computer Networks.

Software Engineering Institute (2002, 2005). *Capabilities Maturity Model Integrated – Staged and Continuous Model – Version 1.1,* Document Numbers CMU/SEI-2005-TR-011, CMU/SEI-2002-TR-028, CMU/SEI 2002-TR-029SEI, Carnegie Mellon University, 2002 and 2005.

Sosinsky, Barrie (2011). *Cloud Computing Bible,* Wiley.

Spanyi, A. (2010). *Business Process Management Governance.* In: Handbook on Business Process Management 2. pp. 223-238. Springer, Berlin Heidelberg.

Stare, A. (2013). *Agile Project Management. A Future Approach to the Management of Projects?* In: Dynamic Relationships Management Journal.

Stewart, W.E. (2001). *Balanced Scorecard for Projects,* In: Project Management Journal, Vol. 32, No. 1, March 2001, pp. 38-47.

Stouffer, D. and Rachlin, S. (2002). *A Summary of First Practices and Lessons Learned in Information Technology Portfolio Management.* In: Federal Chief Information Officer (CIO) Council Best Practices Committee, Washington, D.C., March 2002.

Sun Microsystems and Deloitte (2006). *Raising the Bar for Governance and Compliance,* White paper, February, 2006.

Symons, Craig (2005). *IT and Business Alignment, Are We There Yet?* In: CIO Magazine, April 13, 2005.

Tallon, P. P. (2013). *Corporate Governance of Big Data: Perspectives on Value, Risk, and Cost.* In: Computer, 46(6), pp. 32-38.

Tallon, P. P., Ramirez, R. V. and Short, J. E. (2013). *The Information Artifact in IT Governance: Toward a Theory of Information Governance.* In: Journal of Management Information Systems, 30(3), pp. 141-178.

Tech Republic (2005). *Forty Eight Questions You Need to Answer for Sarbanes-Oxley Compliance,* Ernst & Young, CNET Networks, Inc.

Thampi, S. M., Bhargava, B. and Atrey, P. K. (Eds.) (2013). *Managing Trust in Cyberspace.* CRC Press, Taylor & Francis Group, December 2013.

The Business Continuity Plan and Guide, http://www.bcpgenerator.com

Thompson, S., Ekman, P., Selby, D. and Whitaker, J. (2013). *A Model to Support IT Infrastructure Planning and the Allocation of IT Governance Authority.* Decision Support Systems.

Tignor, W. W. (2009, July). *Agile Project Management.* In: International Conference of the System Dynamics Society, Albuquerque, NM.

Topalov, Drago, (2013, May). *ITIL and ISO 20000: A Comparison* , www.2000Academy.com/Blog/March-2013/ITIL-and-ISO-20000-A Comparison.

Treacy, Michael (2003). *Double Digit Growth,* Penguin Group.

Treacy, Michael and Wiersema, Fred (1995). *The Discipline of Market Leaders,* Perseus Books.

Turban, Efraim, Volonino, Linda and Wood, Gregory (2013). *Information Technology for Management, 9th Edition,* Wiley.

Tzu, Sun (1971). *The Art of War,* Oxford University Press.

Vael, M. (2013). *Governance in the Cloud.* In: EDPACS, 48(2), pp. 7-12.

Valentine, E. L. and Stewart, G. (2013). *The Emerging Role of the Board of Directors in Enterprise Business Technology Governance.* In: International Journal of Disclosure and Governance, 10(4), pp. 346-362.

Van Grembergen W. (2004). *Strategies for Information Technology Governance,* IDEA Group Publishing.

Van Grembergen, W. and De Haes, S. (2008). *Strategies and Models for IT Governance.* In: Implementing Information Technology Governance: Models, Practices, and Cases, pp. 1-75, IGI Global.

Van Grembergen, W. and De Haes, S. (2009). *Enterprise Governance of Information Technology: Achieving Strategic Alignment and Value.* Springer.

Van Grembergen, W. and De Haes, S. (2010). *A Research Journey into Enterprise Governance of IT, Business/IT Alignment and Value Creation*. In: International Journal of IT/Business Alignment and Governance (IJITBAG), 1(1), 1-13.

Van Grembergen, W. and De Haes, S. (2012). *Business Strategy and Applications in Enterprise IT Governance*, IGI Global.

Van Haren Publishing (2014). *Global Standards and Publications – 2014/2015*, Van Haren Publishing.

Verheyen, G. (2013). *Scrum – A Pocket Guide*. Van Haren Publishing.

Violino, Bob (2006). *IT Directions*. In: CFO , January 2006.

Waguespack, L. J. and Schiano, W. T. (2012, January). *SCRUM Project Architecture and Thriving Systems Theory*. In: 2012 45th Hawaii International Conference on System Science (HICSS), pp. 4943-4951. IEEE.

Wailgum, Thomas (2005). *The Rules of IT*, In: CIO Magazine - Business Technology Leadership, October 1, 2005, pp. 90-100.

Wailgum, Thomas (2005). *Toyota's Big Fix: An IS Department Turnaround*, www.cio.com, April 15, 2005.

Wang, X., Zhou, X. and Jiang, L. (2008, October). *A Method of Business and IT Alignment Based on Enterprise Architecture*. In: IEEE International Conference on Service Operations and Logistics, and Informatics, 2008. IEEE/SOLI 2008. Vol. 1, pp. 740-745. IEEE.

Wang, Z. (2011, October). *Security and Privacy Issues within the Cloud Computing*. In: International Conference on Computational and Information Sciences (ICCIS), 2011, pp. 175-178, IEEE.

Watts, S. and Henderson, J.C. (2006). *Innovative IT Climates: CIO perspectives*. In: Journal of Strategic Information Systems Volume 15, pp. 125-151.

Weill, Peter and Broadbend, Marianne (1998). *Leveraging the New Infrastructure: How Market Leaders Capitalize on Information Technology*, Harvard Business School Press.

Weill, P. and Ross, J. W. (2004). *IT Governance: How Top Performers Manage IT Decision Rights Results*, Harvard Business Press, Cambridge, MA. 2004.

Wilcox, M. and Rush, S. (2004). *The CCL Guide to Leadership in Action, Center for Creative Leadership*, Jossey Bass.

Willcocks, L. and Cullen, S. (2013). *Intelligent IT Outsourcing*. Routledge.

Willcocks, L., Venters, W. and Whitley, E. (2013). *Moving to the Cloud Corporation: How to Face the Challenges and Harness the Potential of Cloud Computing*. Palgrave Macmillan.

Williams, B. (2012). *The economics of cloud computing*. Cisco Press.

Wind, S. (2011, September). *Open Source Cloud Computing Management Platforms: Introduction, Comparison, and Recommendations for Implementation*. In: Conference on Open Systems (ICOS), 2011, pp. 175-179. IEEE.

Womack, James P. and Jones, Daniel T. (2003). *Lean Thinking: Banish Waste and Create Wealth in Your Corporation, Revised and Updated*, Harper Business, 2003.

Wood, K. and Anderson, M. (2011). *Understanding the Complexity Surrounding Multitenancy in Cloud Computing*, In: 2011 Eighth IEEE International Conference on e-Business Engineering, Vol. 1, pp. 119-124.

Wright, J. N. and Basu, R. (2008). *Project Management and Six Sigma: Obtaining a Fit*. In: International Journal of Six Sigma and Competitive Advantage, 4(1), pp. 81-94.

Wright, M., Siegel, D. S., Keasey, K. and Filatotchev, I. (Eds.). (2013). *The Oxford Handbook of Corporate Governance*. Oxford University Press.

Wu, P. J. (2013). *The Role of Information Technology Governance Mechanisms in Achieving Organizational Goals*, Proceedings of the 21st European Conference on Information Systems (ECIS 2013).

Wysocki, Robert (2014). *Effective Project Management – Traditional, Agile and Extreme*, 7th Edition, Wiley.

Yamakawa, P., Noriega, C. O., Linares, A. N., and Ramírez, W. V. (2012). *Improving ITIL Compliance using Change Management Practices: A Finance Sector Case Study.* In: Business Process Management Journal, 18(6), pp. 1020-1035.

Yao, Z., and Wang, X. (2010, June). *An ITIL based ITSM practice: A case study of steel manufacturing enterprise.* In: Service Systems and Service Management (ICSSSM), 2010 7th International Conference on, pp. 1-5. IEEE.

Young, M. N., Peng, M. W., Ahlstrom, D., Bruton, G. D. and Jiang, Y. (2008). *Corporate Governance in Emerging Economies: A Review of the Principal Perspective.* In: Journal of Management Studies, 45(1), pp. 196-220.

Young, S. and Thyil, V. (2008). *A Holistic Model of Corporate Governance: a New Research Framework.* In: Corporate Governance, 8(1), pp. 94-108.

Yu, H., Rann, J. and Zhan, J. (2012, May). *SUCH: A Cloud Computing Management Tool.* In: 5th International Conference on New Technologies, Mobility and Security (NTMS), 2012, pp. 1-4. IEEE.

Zhang, Y., Zhang, J. and Chen, J. (2013, April). *Critical Success Factors in IT Service Management Implementation: People, Process, and Technology Perspectives.* In: International Conference on Service Sciences (ICSS), 2013, pp. 64-68, IEEE.

Zhi-gen, H., Quan, Y. and Xi, Z. (2009, July). *Research on Agile Project Management with Scrum Method.* In: IITA International Conference on Services Science, Management and Engineering, 2009. SSME'09, pp. 26-29. IEEE.

Internet sources

Corporate Governance: http://www.corpgov.net

European Corporate Governance Institute: http://www.ecgi.org

International Association of Outsourcing Professionals "COP Master Class Workshop", On-line Course Material, Syracuse University, May, 2007.

ITIL: http://www.itil.co.uk

National Association of Corporate Directors (USA): http://www.nacdonline.org

Summary of Sarbanes-Oxley Act of 2002 AICPA: http://www.aicpa.org/info/sarbanes_oxley_summary.htm

Appendix C References - Topic List

A. Strategic Planning, Business/IT Alignment and Portfolio Investment Management

Aasi, P., Rusu L. and Han S. (2014, January). *The Influence of Culture on IT Governance: A Literature Review.* In: *47th Hawaii International Conference on System Sciences (HICSS), 2014,* pp. 4436-4445, IEEE.

Akker, Rolf (1992). *Generic Framework for Information Management,* Program for Information Research, University of Amsterdam.

Almeida, R., Pereira, R. and Da Silva, M.M. (2013). *IT Governance Mechanisms: A Literature Review.* In: *Exploring Services Science,* pp. 186-199, Springer, Berlin Heidelberg.

Anthony, Robert N. (1965). *Planning and Control Systems: A Framework for Analysis,* Harvard University Press, Cambridge, MA.

Avison, D., Jones, J., Powell, P. and Wilson, D. (2004). *Using and validating the strategic alignment model.* In: *Journal of Strategic Information Systems,* Volume 13.

Baggili, J., *Business-IT Alignment,* http://web.ics.purdue.edu/~baggili/Portal/B_IT_Alignment.html

Baker, E. W. and Niederman, F. (2013). *Integrating the IS functions after Mergers and Acquisitions: Analyzing Business-IT Alignment.* In: *The Journal of Strategic Information Systems.*

Baker, M. and Bourne, M. (2014). *A Governance Framework for the Idea-to-Launch Process: Development and Application of a Governance Framework for New Product Development.* In: *Research-Technology Management,* 57(1), pp. 42-49.

Benson, R. J., Bugnitz, T.L. et al. (2004). *From Business Strategy to IT Action: Right Decisions for a Better Bottom Line.* Wiley, Hoboken, N.J.

Bossidy, Larry and Ram, Charan (2002). *Execution - The Discipline of Getting things Done,* Crown Business.

Boston Consulting Group (1974). *Perspectives on Experience.*

Byrne, A. (2014). *Governance, Strategic Risk, Internal Audit: What Auditors Need to Know.* In: *EDPACS,* 49(2), 6-14.

Carr, N. (2003). *IT doesn't matter anymore.* In: *Harvard Business Review* (5), pp. 41-49.

Ciborra, C. (1997). *De Profundis? Deconstructing the Concept of Strategic Alignment.* In: *Scandinavian Journal of Information Systems,* Volume 9, pp. 67-82.

Clemons, E. K., Row. M.C., and Redi, S.P. (2002). *The Impact of IT on the Organization of Economic Activity,* In: *Journal of Management Information Systems,* Vol. 9, No. 2.

Cooper, R.G., Edgett, S.J. and Kleinschmidt, E.J. (1998). *Portfolio Management for New Products,* Addison-Wesley, Reading, MA.

Cordite, James (1998). *Best Practices in Information Technology,* Prentice Hall.

Coughlan, J., Lycett, M. and Macredie, R.D. (2005). *Understanding the business-IT relationship.* In: *International Journal of Information Management,* Volume 25, pp. 303-319.

Covey, Stephen (1989). *The Seven Habits of Highly Effective People,* Simon and Schuster.

Crow, Ken (2002). *Customer Focused Development with QFD*, DRM Associates.

Dahiya, D. and Mathew, S. K. (2013). *Review of Strategic Alignment, ICT Infrastructure Capability and E-Governance Impact*. In: *ICT Innovations 2013 Web Proceedings*, ISSN 1857-7288.

Dameri, R. P. (2013). *From IT Governance to IT Service Delivery. Implementing a Comprehensive Framework at Ansaldo STS*. In: *Organizational Change and Information Systems*. pp. 33-40, Springer, Berlin Heidelberg.

Davenport, T. H. (2000). *Mission Critical: Realizing the Promise of the Enterprise Systems*, HBS Press, Boston, MA.

De Haes, S. and Van Grembergen, W. van (2013). *Improving Enterprise Governance of IT in a Major Airline*. In: *A Teaching Case. Journal of Information Technology Teaching Cases*, 3(2), pp. 60-69.

De Vries, M. (2013). *A Method to Enhance Existing Business-IT Alignment Approaches*. In: *South African Journal of Industrial Engineering*, 24(2), pp. 111-126.

Debreceny, R. S. (2013). *Research on IT Governance, Risk, and Value: Challenges and Opportunities*. In: *Journal of Information Systems*, 27(1), pp. 129-135.

Degraff, Jeff and Quinn, Shawn (2007). *Leading Innovation*, McGrawHill, NY.

Deloitte Development, LLC (2004). *Eliminating Roadblocks to IT and Business Alignment*. In: *CIO Magazine Supplement*.

Drnevich, P. L. and Croson, D. C. (2013). *Information Technology and Business-Level Strategy: Toward an Integrated Theoretical Perspective*. In: *MIS Quarterly*, 37(2).

Duffy, Jan. *Alignment: Delivering Results*, www.cio.com

Fell, Greg (2013). *Decoding the IT Value Problem*, Wiley.

Ferguson, C., Green, P., Vaswani, R., and Wu, G. H. (2013). *Determinants of Effective Information Technology Governance*. In: *International Journal of Auditing*, 17(1), pp. 75-99.

General Accounting Office (2004). *Information Technology Investment Management Model: A Framework for Assessing and Improving Process Maturity*, GAO Report 04-394G, Version 1.1.

Hamel, Gary (2000). *Leading the Revolution*, Harvard Business School Press.

Hand, Anthony (2004). *Applying the Kano Model to User Experience Design*, UPA Boston mini-Conference, www.hadnweb.com/anthony/portfolio/kanoa-hand_kano-model_boston_may-12-2004.pdf

Haq, H., Howard, C. and Hargiss, K. M. (2013). *Looking at IT and Business Alignment from the Stone Age of Information Technology* In: *International Journal of Strategic Information Technology and Applications (IJSITA)*, 4(3), pp. 89-102.

Henderson, J., and Venkatraman, N. (1999). *Strategic Alignment: Leveraging Information Technology for Transforming Organizations*. In: *IBM Systems Journal*, Vol. 38, Nos. 2 and 3.

Henderson, J., and Venkatraman, N. (1990). *Strategic Alignment: A Model for Organizational Transformation via Information Technology*. In: *Working Paper 3223-90*, Sloan School of Management, Massachusetts Institute of Technology, Cambridge, MA.

Hertis, M., and Juric, M. B. (2013). *Ideas on Improving the Business-IT Alignment in BPM Enabled by SOA*. In: *Information and Communication Technology (ICoICT), 2013 International Conference of Information and Communication Technology*, pp. 55-60, IEEE.

Hitt, M., et al.(2015). *Strategic Management – Competitiveness and Globalization*, 11th Edition, Thomson-South Western.

Hughes, S. and Wilkinson, R. (2013). *Global Governance: Critical Perspectives*. Routledge.

IBM (1981). *Business Systems Planning, Planning Guide*, GE20-0527, White Plains, NY: IBM Corporation.

Kano Model, http://www.betterproductdesign.net/tools/definition/kano.htm

Kaplan, J. D. (2005). *Strategic IT Portfolio Management: Governing Enterprise Transformation*, Jeff Kaplan.

Kaplan, R. and Norton, D. (2001). *The Strategy Focused Company*, Harvard Business School Press.

Keen, J. and Digrius, B. (2003). *Making Technology Investments Profitable*, J. Wiley and Sons.

Keen, Jack (2006). *Solidifying Business-IT Alignment*, In: *The Advisory Council Research Smart Tip*, August 2006.

Lahtela, A., Hotti, V. and Salomaa, H. (2014). *Service Support in IT Governance, IT Management and Enterprise Architecture Context*. In: *The Fourth International Conference on Digital Information Processing and Communications (ICDIPC2014)*, pp. 166-172, The Society of Digital Information and Wireless Communication.

Lee, M. C. (2013). *IT Governance Implementation Framework in Small and Medium Enterprise*. In: *International Journal of Management and Enterprise Development, 12*(4), pp. 425-441.

Leganza, Gene (2003). *Overcoming Obstacles to the Alignment of IT and the Business*. In: *Giga Research Paper*, June 24, 2003.

Li, Q., Wang, C., Wu, J., Li, J., and Wang, Z. Y. (2011). *Towards the Business–Information Technology Alignment in Cloud Computing Environment: An Approach Based on Collaboration Points and Agents*. In: *International Journal of Computer Integrated Manufacturing, 24*(11), pp. 1038-1057.

Lohr, Steve (2007). *IBM Showing That Giants Can Be Nimble*, In: *New York Times*, July 18, 2007.

Luftman, Jerry (2004). *Managing the Information Technology Resource*, Pearson - Prentice Hall, Upper Saddle River, NJ.

Luftman, Jerry, Papp, Raymond and Brier, Tom (1999). *Enablers and Inhibitors of Business-IT Alignment*, In: *Communications of the Association for Information Systems*, Volume 1, Article 11, March 1999.

Maizlish, B., and Handler, R. (2010). *IT (Information Technology) Portfolio Management Step-by-Step: Unlocking the Business Value of Technology*. John Wiley & Sons.

McCreight & Company (2008). *Implementing Strategic Change*. In: *Strategy Implementation Insights*, Chapter 13, Version 1.0, January 2008.

McFarlan, W. and Cash. J. (1990). *Strategic Planning for Information Systems*, Wiley.

Miller, D. (2013). *Maximizing the Business Impact of IT: Importance of Managing the Total Business Experience*, Doctoral dissertation, Middlesex University.

Morabito, V. (2013). *Strategic Information Governance Modeling and Assessment*. In: *Business Technology Organization*, pp. 143-163. Springer, Berlin Heidelberg.

Nash, Kim (2012). *CIO 100 Award – Winners are Risk Busters*, July 27, 2012. http://www.cio.com/article/2394011/cio-role/cio-100-award-winners-are-risk-busters.html, July 27, 2012.

Nolan, Richard and Koot, William (1992). *Nolan's Stage Theory Today*, In: *Holland Management Review*, Number 31.

Overby, Stephanie (2005). *The New IT Department*, www.cio.com, December 15, 2005 / January 1, 2005.

Papp, R. (1998). *Alignment of Business and Information Technology Strategy: How and Why?*, In: *Information Management* (11), 3/4, pp. 6-11.

Porter, Michael (1985). *Competitive Advantage: Creating and Sustaining Superior Performance*, Free Press.

Prahaland, C. and Hamel, G. (1990). *The Core Competence of the Corporation*, In: *Harvard Business Review*, March/April 1990.

Project Management Institute (2006). *The Standard for Portfolio Management*, PMI, Newtown Square, PA.

Reynolds, P. and Yetton, P. (2013). *Aligning Business and IT Strategies in Multi-Business Organizations*, Thirty Fourth International Conference on Information Systems, Milan 2013.

Rockart, J., Earl, M. and Ross, J. (1996). *Eight Imperatives for the New IT Organization*, In: *Sloan Management Review*, Fall 1996, pp. 43-55.

Rockart, John (1979). *Chief Executives Define Their Own Data Needs*, In: *Harvard Business Review*, March-April, 1979.

Rothaermel, F. T. (2013). *Strategic Management: Concepts*. McGraw-Hill Irwin.

Sauer, C. and Burn, J.M. (1997). *The Pathology of Strategic Alignment*, In: C. Sauer, P.Y. Yetton and Associates, *Steps to the Future - Fresh Thinking on the Management of IT-based Organizational Transformation*, Jossey-Bass, San Francisco.

Selig, Gad J. (1983). *Strategic Planning for Information Resource Management – A Multinational Perspective*, UMI Press.

Selig, Gad J. (2007). *Successful Business/IT Alignment, Execution & Governance Best Practices,* Society for Information Management Presentation, SIM Fairfield/Westchester Chapter Meeting, March 15, 2007, Doral Arrowwood Conf. Center, NY.

Shanks, G., Bekmamedova, N. and Willcocks, L. (2013). *Using Business Analytics for Strategic Alignment and Organizational Transformation,* In: *International Journal of Business Intelligence Research (IJBIR),* 4(3), pp. 1-15.

Sibbet, David (1997). *75 years of Management Ideas and Practice 1922-1997,* In: *Harvard Business Review,* Sep./Oct. 1997, Supplement Vol. 75, Issue 5.

Smits, D. and Hillegersberg, J. van (2013, August). *The Continuing Mismatch Between IT Governance Theory and Practice.* In: *Results From a Delphi Study with CIO's.* AMCIS.

Symons, Craig (2005). *IT and Business Alignment, Are We There Yet?* In: *CIO Magazine,* April 13, 2005.

Thompson, S., Ekman, P., Selby, D. and Whitaker, J. (2013). *A Model to Support IT Infrastructure Planning and the Allocation of IT Governance Authority.* Decision Support Systems.

Treacy, Michael and Wiersema, Fred (1995). *The Discipline of Market Leaders,* Perseus Books.

Treacy, Michael (2003). *Double Digit Growth,* Penguin Group.

Turban, Efraim, Volonino, Linda and Wood, Gregory (2013). *Information Technology for Management,* 9th edition, Wiley.

Valentine, E. L. and Stewart, G. (2013). *The Emerging Role of the Board of Directors in Enterprise Business Technology Governance.* In: *International Journal of Disclosure and Governance,* 10(4), pp. 346-362.

Wailgum, Thomas (2005). *Toyota's Big Fix: An IS Department Turnaround,* www.cio.com, April 15, 2005.

Watts, S. and Henderson, J.C. (2006). *Innovative IT Climates: CIO perspectives.* In: *Journal of Strategic Information Systems* Volume 15, pp. 125-151.

Weill, P. and Ross, J. W. (2004). *IT governance: How top performers manage IT decision rights for superior results.* Harvard Business Press.

Weill, Peter and Broadbend, Marianne (1998). *Leveraging the New Infrastructure: How Market Leaders Capitalize on Information Technology,* Harvard Business School Press.

Wu, P. J. (2013). *The Role of Information Technology Governance Mechanisms in Achieving Organizational Goals,* Proceedings of the 21st European Conference on Information Systems (ECIS 2013).

B. Program/Project Management, Agile Project Management and Scrum

Adusumilli, S. (2011). *IT Strategy & Governance Explained.* In: IT Strategy.

Agrawal, A., Tripathi, M., Singh, S. and Maurya, L. S. (2013). *AGILE: Boon for Today's Software Industry - A Review.* In: *International Journal of Scientific and Research Publications,* p. 464.

Alleman, G. B. (2013). *Agile Program Management: Moving from Principles to Practice.* In: *Feedback,* 4, p. 6.

Andriole, S. J. (2013). *Today's Best Practices in Business Technology Management.* In: *Feedback,* 4, p. 6.

Apostolopoulos, C. (2008). *The Success of IT Projects Using the Agile Method.* In: *Proceedings of the International Workshop on Requirements Analysis (IWRA 2008).*

AXELOS (2007). *Managing Successful Projects with PRINCE2,* TSO.

Barkley, Brucet, Sr. (2006). *Integrated Project Management,* McGraw Hill, NY.

Barlow, M. (2013). *The Culture of Big Data,* O'Reilly Media.

Bartens, Y., Schulte, F. and Voss, S. (2014, January). *E-Business IT Governance Revisited: An Attempt towards Outlining a Novel Bi-directional Business/IT Alignment in COBIT5.* In: *47th Hawaii International Conference on System Sciences (HICSS),* 2014, pp. 4356-4365. IEEE.

Beach, T., Rana, O., Rezgui, Y. and Parashar, M. (2013). *Governance Model for Cloud Computing in Building Information Management.* In: *IEEE Transactions on Services Computing,* 21 Nov. 2013. IEEE computer Society Digital Library. IEEE Computer Society.

Berggruen, N. and Gardels, N. (2013). *Intelligent Governance for the 21st Century: A Middle Way Between West and East.* John Wiley & Sons.

Bernroider, E. W. and Ivanov, M. (2011). *IT Project Management Control and the Control Objectives for IT and Related Technology (COBIT) Framework.* In: *International Journal of Project Management, 29*(3), pp. 325-336.

Bin, S. (2010). *Agile Methods (Scrum, XP) Applying into Small (Micro) Enterprise Business.* In: *Journal of Enterprise Information Management, 23*(2).

Breu, R., Kuntzmann-Combelles, A. and Felderer, M. (2014). *New Perspectives on Software Quality.* In: *IEEE Software, 31*(1).

Brewer, J. L. and Dittman, K. C. (2013). *Methods of IT Project Management.* Purdue University Press.

Budwig, M., Jeong, S. and Kelkar, K. (2009, April). *When User Experience Met Agile: A Case Study.* In: *CHI'09 Extended Abstracts on Human Factors in Computing Systems.* pp. 3075-3084, ACM.

Cabral, A. Y., Ribeiro, M. B., Lemke, A. P., Silva, M. T., Cristal, M. and Franco, C. (2009). *A Case Study of Knowledge Management Usage in Agile Software Projects.* In: *Enterprise Information Systems,* pp. 627-638. Springer, Berlin Heidelberg.

Cao, L., Mohan, K., Ramesh, B. and Sarkar, S. (2013). *Evolution of Governance: Achieving Ambidexterity in IT Outsourcing.* In: *Journal of Management Information Systems, 30*(3), pp. 115-140.

Cardozo, E., Neto, J. B. F. A., Barza, A., França, A. and Da Silva, F. (2010, April). *SCRUM and Productivity in Software Projects: A Systematic Literature Review.* In: *14th International Conference on Evaluation and Assessment in Software Engineering (EASE).*

Cervone, H. F. (2011). *Understanding Agile Project Management Methods Using Scrum.* In: *OCLC Systems & Services, 27*(1), pp. 18-22.

Chavan, P., Mendhekar, P., Varahan, S. and Nerur, S. (2012). *Impact of Agile Methodologies on Project Management.* In: *Great Lakes Herald,* Vol 6, No 2.

Chrissis, M., Konrad, M. and Shrum, S. (2003). *CMMI – Guidelines for Process Integration and Product Improvement,* Addison Wesley.

Cobb, C. G. (2011). *Agile Project Management.* In: *Making Sense of Agile Project Management: Balancing Control and Agility,* pp. 101-130, John Wiley & Sons.

Cooke, J. L. (2013). *The Power of the Agile Business Analyst: 30 Surprising Ways a Business Analyst Can Add Value to Your Agile Development Team.* In: IT Governance Ltd.

Crawford, Ken (2014). *Project Management Maturity Model,* 3rd edition, CRC Press.

Cristal, M., Wildt, D. and Prikladnicki, R. (2008, August). "Usage of Scrum Practices within a Global Company." In: Global Software Engineering, *2008. ICGSE 2008. IEEE International Conference on,* pp. 222-226, IEEE.

DeCarlo, D. (2010). *Extreme Project Management: Using Leadership, Principles, and Tools to Deliver Value in the Face of Volatility.* Wiley.

Demirkan, H. and Nichols, J. (2008). *IT Services Project Management: Lessons Learned from a Case Study in Implementation.* In: *International Journal of Project Organization and Management, 1*(2), pp. 204-220.

Dinsmore, P. C. and Rocha, L. (2013). *Enterprise Project Governance: A Guide to the Successful Management of Projects Across the Organization.* In: *Project Management Journal, 44*(1), p. 107.

Durrani, U., Richardson, J., Lenarcic, J. and Pita, Z. (2013). *Adaptable Management Systems Implementation for the Governance: A Case Study of Cloud Computing.* In: *26th Bled eConference,* pp. 1-14, University of Maribor.

Dyba, T. and Dingsoyr, T. (2009). *What Do We Know About Agile Software Development?* In: *Software,* IEEE, *26*(5), pp. 6-9.

Edwards, P. and Bowen, P. (2013). *Risk Management in Project Organizations.* Routledge.

Elliott, S. (2008, March). *Agile Project management.* In: *Seminar on Current Trends in Software Industry,* University of Helsinki, Finland.

Fairchild, A. (2013). *Governance in the Cloud: Role of Certification for SME Trust and Adoption.* In: *CONF-IRM 2013 Proceedings,* pp. 1-6.

Fernandez, D. J. and Fernandez, J. D. (2008). *Agile Project Management–Agilism versus Traditional Approaches.* In: *Journal of Computer Information Systems, 49*(2), pp. 10-17.

Fink, D. (2014). *Project Risk Governance: Managing Uncertainty and Creating Organizational Value.* Gower Publishing, Ltd.

Gandomani. T. J., Zulzalil, H., Ghani, A., Azim, A. and Sultan, A. B. (2013). *Important Considerations for Agile Software Development Methods Governance.* In: *Journal of Theoretical & Applied Information Technology*, 55(3).

Gido, J. and Clements, J. P. (2012). *Successful Project Management.* Cengage.

Gloger, B. (2010). SCRUM. In: *Informatik-Spektrum*, 33(2), pp. 195-200.

Gray, Clifford and Larson, Erik (2008). *Project Management - The Management Process*, Fourth Edition, McGraw Hill, NY.

Guang-yong, H. (2011, May). *Study and Practice of import Scrum Agile Software Development.* In: *Communication Software and Networks (ICCSN)*, 2011 IEEE 3rd International Conference, pp. 217-220, IEEE.

Heagney, J. (2011). *Fundamentals of Project Management.* AMACOM.

Highsmith, J. (2009). *Agile Project Management: Creating Innovative Products.* Pearson Education.

Highsmith, J. (2013). *Agile Project Management: Principles and Tools.* In: *Feedback*, 4, 6.

Highsmith, J., Wysocki, R. K. and Boyd, S. (2013). *How Agile Are Organizations Today?* In: *Feedback*, 4, 6.

Hobbs, B., Aubry, M. and Thuillier, D. (2008). *The Project Management Office as an Organizational Innovation.* In: *International Journal of Project Management*, 26(5), pp. 547-555.

Hole, S. and Moe, N. B. (2008). *A Case Study of Coordination in Distributed Agile Software Development.* In: *Software process improvement.*, pp. 189-200. Springer, Berlin Heidelberg.

Hossain, E., Babar, M. A. and Paik, H. Y. (2009, July). *Using Scrum in Global Software Development: A systematic Literature Review.* In: *Global Software Engineering, 2009. ICGSE 2009.* Fourth IEEE International Conference on Global Software Engineering, pp. 175-184.

Ireland, R., West, B., Smith, N. and Shepherd, D. I. (2012). *Project Management for IT-related Projects.* BCS.

Jones, W. and Reddy, R. (2013). *Strategic Sourcing.* In: *Feedback*, 4, 6.

Kammermeier, M. (2010). *Agile Project Management in IT Development Projects with a Focus on Team Performance.* GRIN Verlag.

Kapur, G. (2005). *Project Management for Information, Technology. Business and Certification*, Pearson Prentice Hall.

Kerzner, H. R. (2013). *Project Management Metrics, KPIs, and Dashboards: A Guide to Measuring and Monitoring Project Performance.* John Wiley & Sons.

Kerzner, H. R. (2013). *Project Management: A Systems Approach to Planning, Scheduling, and Controlling.* 11th Edition, Wiley.

Kerzner, H. R. (2013). *Project Management: A Systems Approach to Planning, Scheduling, and Controlling.* John Wiley & Sons.

Kerzner, H. R. (2014). *Project Management-Best Practices: Achieving Global Excellence.* John Wiley & Sons.

Korhonen, J. J., Melleri, I., Hiekkanen, K., and Helenius, M. (2013). *Designing Data Governance Structure: An Organizational Perspective.* In: *GSTF Journal on Computing*, 2(4).

Krzanik, L., Rodriguez, P., Simila, J., Kuvaja, P. and Rohunen, A. (2010, January). *Exploring the Transient Nature of Agile Project Management Practices.* In: *43rd Hawaii International Conference on System Sciences (HICSS), 2010*, pp. 1-8. IEEE.

Lee, S. and Yong, H. S. (2010). *Distributed Agile: Project Management in a Global Environment.* In: *Empirical Software Engineering*, 15(2), pp. 204-217.

Lohan, G., Lang, M. and Conboy, K. (2013). *A Performance Management Model for Agile Information Systems Development Teams.* In: *Building Sustainable Information Systems*, pp. 297-308. Springer US.

Lyngso, S. (2014). *Agile Strategy Management: Techniques for Continuous Alignment and Improvement.* CRC Press.

Mahnic, V. (2011). *A Case Study on Agile Estimating and Planning Using SCRUM.* In: *Electronics and Electrical Engineering*, 111(5), pp. 123-128.

Mahnic, V. (2012). *A Capstone course on Agile Software Development using SCRUM*. In: *IEEE Transactions on Education*, 55(1), pp. 99-106.

Marçal, A. S. C., de Freitas, B. C. C., Soares, F. S. F., Furtado, M. E. S., Maciel, T. M. and Belchior, A. D. (2008). *Blending SCRUM practices and CMMI project management process areas*. In: *Innovations in Systems and Software Engineering*, 4(1), pp. 17-29.

McAvoy, J. and Butler, T. (2009). *The Role of Project Management in Ineffective Decision Making within Agile Software Development Projects*. In: *European Journal of Information Systems*, 18(4), pp. 372-383.

Meredith, J. R. and Mantel Jr., S. J. (2012). *Project Management: A Managerial Approach*. 8th Edition, Wiley.

Miller, D. (2013). *Maximising the Business Impact of IT: Importance of Managing the Total Business Experience*, Doctoral dissertation, Middlesex University.

Moreira, M. (2013). *Being Agile: Your Roadmap to Successful Adoption of Agile*. Apress.

Morris, P. and Pinto, J. K. (Eds.). (2010). *The Wiley Guide to Project Organization and Project Management Competencies*, Vol. 8. Wiley, NY.

Moster, E. (2013). *Using hybrid scrum to meet waterfall process deliverables*, A Thesis.

Nee, N. (2010). *Successful Projects through Agile Project Management*. ESI International.

Olausson, M., Rossberg, J., Ehn, J. and Sköld, M. (2013). *Introduction to Agile Planning, Development, and Testing*. In: *Pro Team Foundation Service*, pp. 9-19. Apress.

Opelt, A., Gloger, B., Pfarl, W. and Mittermayr, R. (2013). *Agile Contracts: Creating and Managing Successful Projects with Scrum*. John Wiley & Sons.

O'Sheedy, D. G. (2012). *A Study of Agile Project Management Methods used for IT Implementation Projects in Small and Medium-sized Enterprises*. DBA thesis, Southern Cross University, Lismore, NSW.

Pharro, Richard (2014). *Agile Project Management White Paper*, APMG International and DSDM Consortium.

Pichler, R. (2010). *Agile Product Management with Scrum: Creating Products that Customers Love*. Addison-Wesley Professional.

Poligadu, A. and Moloo, R. K. (2014). An Innovative Measurement Programme for Agile Governance. *International Journal of Agile Systems and Management*, 7(1), pp. 26-60.

Project Management Institute (2013). *A Guide to the Project Management Body of Knowledge*, 5th Edition, PMI.

Project Management Institute (2004). *OPM3 – Organizational Project Management Maturity Model*, PMI.

Project Management Institute (2013). *A Guide to the Project Management Body of Knowledge: PMBOK® Guide*, 5th Edition. PMI.

Reiss, G. (2013). *Project Management Demystified: Today's Tools and Techniques*. Routledge.

Rezaeean, A. and Falaki, P. (2012). *Agile Project Management*. In: *International Research Journal of Applied and Basic Sciences*, 3(4), pp. 698-707.

Salo, O. and Abrahamsson, P. (2008). *Agile Methods in European Embedded Software Development Organizations: A Survey on the Actual Use and Usefulness of Extreme Programming and Scrum*. In: *Software, IET*, 2(1), pp. 58-64.

Schwaber, Ken and Sutherland, Jeff (2013). *The Scrum Guide*, Scrum.org.

Selig, Gad J. (2004). *Best Practices for IT Project Management in Fast Track Mode*, paper published in *Proceedings of Project World*, Fall 2004, Washington, DC.

Senthilkumar, T., Benruben, R., Sakthirajan, T. and Sivaram, N. M. (2012). *A Review on Some Agile Project Management Techniques*. In: *Proceedings of the 2012 International Conference on Industrial Engineering and Operations Management*, Istanbul, Turkey.

Shaw, Melissa (2001). *Management Strategies*, In: *Network Management Newsletter*, 11/7/01.

Software Engineering Institute (2002, 2005). *Capabilities Maturity Model Integrated – Staged and Continuous Model* – Version 1.l, Document Numbers CMU/SEI-2005-TR-011, CMU/SEI-2002-TR-028, CMU/SEI 2002-TR-029SEI, Carnegie Mellon University, 2002 and 2005.

Stare, A. (2013). *Agile Project Management. A Future Approach to the Management of Projects?* In: *Dynamic Relationships Management Journal*.

Tallon, P. P., Ramirez, R. V. and Short, J. E. (2013). *The Information Artifact in IT Governance: Toward a Theory of Information Governance.* In: *Journal of Management Information Systems, 30*(3), pp. 141-178.

Tignor, W. W. (2009, July). *Agile Project Management.* In: *International Conference of the System Dynamics Society,* Albuquerque, NM.

Vael, M. (2013). *Governance in the Cloud.* In: *EDPACS, 48*(2), pp. 7-12.

Verheyen, G. (2013). *Scrum – A Pocket Guide.* Van Haren Publishing.

Waguespack, L. J. and Schiano, W. T. (2012, January). *Scrum Project Architecture and Thriving Systems Theory.* In: *2012 45th Hawaii International Conference on System Science (HICSS),* pp. 4943-4951. IEEE.

Wright, J. N. and Basu, R. (2008). *Project Management and Six Sigma: Obtaining a Fit.* In: *International Journal of Six Sigma and Competitive Advantage, 4*(1), pp. 81-94.

Wysocki, Robert (2014). *Effective Project Management – Traditional, Agile and Extreme,* 7th Edition, Wiley.

Zhi-gen, H., Quan, Y. and Xi, Z. (2009, July). *Research on Agile Project Management with Scrum Method.* In: *IITA International Conference on Services Science, Management and Engineering, 2009. SSME'09,* pp. 26-29. IEEE.

C. Governance (Corporate, Business and IT), Performance Management, Management Controls, Quality & Risk

Acharya, V. V., Gottschalg, O. F., Hahn, M. and Kehoe, C. (2013). *Corporate Governance and Value Creation: Evidence from Private Equity.* In: *Review of Financial Studies, 26*(2), pp. 368-402.

Aguilera, R. V., Filatotchev, I., Gospel, H. and Jackson, G. (2008). *An Organizational Approach to Comparative Corporate Governance: Costs, Contingencies, and Complementarities.* In: *Organization Science, 19*(3), pp. 475-492.

Ahern, Dennise, Clouse, Aaron and Torner, Richard (2004). *CMMI™ Distiller - A Practical to Integrated Process Improvement,* Second Edition, Addison-Wesley.

Ali, S. and Green, P. (2012). *Effective Information Technology (IT) Governance Mechanisms: An IT Outsourcing Perspective.* In: *Information Systems Frontiers, 14*(2), pp. 179-193.

Anand, S. (2006). *Sarbanes-Oxley Guide,* Second Edition, J. Wiley and Sons.

Arabalidousti, F. and Nasiri, R. (2013). *Improving IT Service Management Architecture in Cloud Environment on Top of Current Frameworks.* In: *The International Conference on Digital Information Processing, E-Business and Cloud Computing (DIPECC2013).* pp. 77-86, The Society of Digital Information and Wireless Communication, United Arab Emirates.

Artur, R. O. T. (2009). *IT Risk Management in the Context of IT Governance: Theory vs. Practice.* International Institute of Informatics and Systemics. July 2009, The 6th International Symposium on Risk Management and Cyber-Informatics: RMCI 2009, Poland.

Azeem, M., Hassan, M. and Kouser, R. (2013). *Impact of Quality Corporate Governance on Firm Performance: A Ten Year Perspective.* In: *Pakistan Journal of Commerce and Social Sciences, 7*(3), pp. 656-670.

Bahl, S. and Wali, O. P. (2014). *Perceived Significance of Information Security Governance to Predict the Information Security Service Quality in Software Service Industry: An Empirical Analysis.* In: *Information Management & Computer Security, 22*(1), pp. 2-23.

Bainbridge, S. (2008). *The New Corporate Governance in Theory and Practice.* Oxford University Press.

Baxter, R., Bedard, J. C., Hoitash, R. and Yezegel, A. (2013). *Enterprise Risk Management Program Quality: Determinants, Value Relevance, and the Financial Crisis.* In: *Contemporary Accounting Research, 30*(4), pp. 1264-1295.

Bayaga, A., Flowerday, S. and Cilliers, L. (2013). *Valuing Information Technology (IT) and Operational Risk Management,* International Conference on ICT for Africa 2013, Harare, Zimbabwe.

Bebchuk, L. A. and Weisbach, M. S. (2010). *The State of Corporate Governance Research.* In: *Review of Financial Studies, 23*(3), pp. 939-961.

Beimborn, D., Schlosser, F. and Weitzel, T. (2009, January). *Proposing a Theoretical Model for IT Governance and IT Business Alignment*. In: *42nd Hawaii International Conference on* System Sciences *2009. HICSS'09*, pp. 1-11. IEEE.

Bernroider, E. W. (2008). *IT Governance for Enterprise Resource Planning supported by the DeLone–McLean model of Information Systems Success*. In: *Information & Management*, 45(5), pp. 257-269.

Bhagat, S. and Bolton, B. (2008). *Corporate Governance and Firm Performance*. In: *Journal of Corporate Finance*, 14(3), pp. 257-273.

Bhatia, Mohan (2007). *IT Merger Due Diligence: A Blueprint*, In: *Information Systems Control Journal*, Volume 1, 2007.

BMC Software (2004), *Sarbanes-Oxley Section 404*, White Paper, May 2004.

Board Effectiveness Partners (2004). *A Roadmap: Strengthening Corporate Governance*, In: *Insights*, Chapter 1, Version 2.0, January 2004.

Boardman, Bruce (2006). *Get Framed Compliance Policy Development (ISO, ITIL/ISMD & COBIT)*, Network Computing Conf., Sept. 28, 2006.

Bonnet, Pierre (2013). *Enterprise Data Governance Reference and Master Data Management Semantic Model*, Wiley.

Brammer, S. J., and Pavelin, S. (2013). *Corporate Governance and Corporate Social Responsibility*. In: *The Oxford Handbook of Corporate Governance*, pp. 719-743.

Brown, A. W., Ambler, S. and Royce, W. (2013, May). *Agility at Scale: Economic Governance, Measured Improvement, and Disciplined Delivery*. In: *Proceedings of the 2013 International Conference on Software Engineering*, pp. 873-881. IEEE Press.

Buckby, S., Best, P. and Stewart, J. (2009). *The Current State of Information Technology Governance Literature*. In: A. Cater-Steel (Ed.), *Information Technology Governance and Service Management: Frameworks and Adaptations*, pp. 1-43, Information Science Reference, Hershey, PA

Budd, L. and Harris, L. (Eds.). (2013). *E-governance: Managing or Governing?* Routledge.

Business Continuity Planning Guidelines, http://www.yourwindow.to/business-continuity/contents.htm

Business Continuity Planning Model, http://www.drj.com/new2dr/model/bcmodel.htm

Calder, A. (2009). *IT Governance: Implementing Frameworks and Standards for the Corporate Governance of IT*. IT Governance, UK.

Cater-Steel, A. (2009). *Information Technology Governance and Service Management: Frameworks and Adaptations*. Hershey, New York.

Catucci, Bill (2005). *A New Governance Model*, In: *Balanced Scorecard*, January 15, 2005.

Catucci, Bill (2003), *Ten Lessons for Implementing the Balanced Scorecard*, Balanced Scorecard, January 15, 2003.

Center for Technology Governance and Compliance (2006). *Raising the Bar for Governance and Compliance*, Sun Microsystems and Deloitte Consulting LLP, White Paper, February 2006.

Chew, D. H. and Gillan, S. L. (Eds.) (2013). *Global Corporate Governance*, Columbia University Press.

Chew, E. K. and Gottschalk, P. (2013). *Knowledge Driven Service Innovation and Management: IT Strategies for Business Alignment and Value Creation*. Business Science Reference.

Clark, G. L. and Wójcik, D. (2011). *The Geography of Finance: Corporate Governance in the Global Marketplace*. In: *OUP Catalogue*.

Colley, J., Doyle, J., Logan, G. and Stettinius, W. (2004). *What is Corporate Governance?*, McGraw-Hill, December 2004.

Corporate Executive Board (2003). *IT Balanced Scorecards - End-to-End Performance Measurement for the Corporate IT Function*, Working Council for Chief Information Officers Report, 2003.

COSO (Committee of Sponsoring Organizations of the Treadway Commission) (2013). *Integrated Control- Integrated Framework*.

Croteau, A. M. and Bergeron, F. (2009, January). *Interorganizational Governance of Information Technology*. In: *42nd Hawaii International Conference on System Sciences, 2009. HICSS'09*, pp. 1-8. IEEE.

Crow, P. R. and Lockhart, J. (2013). *The Impact of Governance on the Performance of a High-Growth Company: An Exemplar Case Study*. In: *Proceedings of the International Conference of Management, Leadership and Governance*, pp. 41-47.

Curtis, D. B., Hefley, W. E. and Miller, S. A. (2007). *The People Capability Maturity Model: Guidelines for Improving the Workforce*. Addison-Wesley, Dorling Kindersley, India.

De Haes, S. and Van Grembergen, W. (2008, January). *Analyzing the Relationship between IT Governance and Business/IT Alignment Maturity*. In: *Hawaii International Conference on System Sciences, Proceedings of the 41st Annual*, pp. 428-428. IEEE.

De Haes, S. and Van Grembergen, W. (2008). *An Exploratory Study into the Design of an IT Governance Minimum Baseline through Delphi Research*. In: *The Communications of the Association for Information Systems*, 22, pp. 443-458.

De Haes, S. and Van Grembergen, W. (2008). *Practices in IT Governance and Business/IT Alignment*. In: *Information Systems Control Journal*, 2, pp. 1-6.

De Haes, S. and Van Grembergen, W. (2009). *An Exploratory Study into IT Governance Implementations and its Impact on Business/IT Alignment*. In: *Information Systems Management*, 26(2), pp. 123-137.

De Haes, S. and Van Grembergen, W. (2009). *Exploring the Relationship Between IT Governance Practices and Business/IT Alignment through Extreme Case Analysis in Belgian Mid-to-Large Size Financial Enterprises*. In: *Journal of Enterprise Information Management*, 22(5), pp. 615-637.

De Haes, S., Van Grembergen, W. and Debreceny, R. S. (2013). *COBIT 5 and Enterprise Governance of Information Technology: Building Blocks and Research Opportunities*. In: *Journal of Information Systems*, 27(1), pp. 307-324.

Debreceny, R. and Gray, G. L. (2009, January). *IT Governance and Process Maturity: A Field Study*. In: *42nd Hawaii International Conference on System Sciences, 2009. HICSS'09*, pp. 1-10. IEEE.

Delmar, Yo (2014). *Leveraging Metrics for Business Innovation – Where Measurement meets Transformation in IT Governance*, In: *ISACA Journal*, Volume 4, 2014.

Duarte, J. and Vasconcelos, A. (2010). *Evaluating Information Systems Constructing a Model Processing Framework*. In: *International Journal of Enterprise Information Systems (IJEIS)*, 6(3), pp. 17-32.

Dunleavy, P. and Margetts, H. (2010). The Second Wave of Digital Era Governance. In: American Political Science Association Conference, 4 September 2010, Washington DC, USA.

Dunleavy, P., Margetts, H., Bastow, S. and Tinkler, J. (2011). *Digital Era Governance: IT Corporations, the State, and e-government*. In: *OUP Catalogue*.

Egan, M. (1997). *Modes of Business Governance: European Management Styles and Corporate Cultures*. In: *West European Politics*, 20(2), pp. 1-21.

Elliott, T. E., Holmes, J. H., Davidson, A. J., Chance, L., Nelson, A. F. and Steiner, J. F. (2013). *Data Warehouse Governance Programs in Healthcare Settings: A Literature Review and a Call to Action*. In: *eGEMs (Generating Evidence & Methods to Improve Patient Outcomes)*, 1(1), p. 15.

Erickson-Harris, Lisa (2006). *IT Governance: Round Em Up!* Intelligent Enterprise Conf., August 2006, p. 10-14.

Ernst and Young (2005). *48 Questions You Need to Answer for Sarbanes-Oxley Compliance*, Tech Republic, CNET Networks.

Fabian, Robert (2007). *Interdependence of COBIT and ITIL*. In: *Information Systems Control Journal*, Volume 1.

Faisal, M. N. and Banwet, D. K. (2009). *Analyzing Alternatives for Information Technology Outsourcing Decision: An Analytic Network Process Approach*. In: *International Journal of Business Information Systems*, 4(1), pp. 47-62.

Farrar, J. H. (2008). *Corporate Governance: Theories, Principles and Practice*, Oxford University Press, Victoria, Australia

Fasanghari, M., NasserEslami, F. and Naghavi, M. (2008, September). *IT Governance Standard Selection Based on Two Phase Clustering Method*. In: *Networked Computing and Advanced Information Management, 2008. NCM'08. Fourth International Conference on* Networked Computing and Advanced Information Management, Vol. 2, pp. 513-518. IEEE.

Federal Financial Institutions Examination Council (FFIEC) (2003). *Business Continuity Planning*, March 2003, http://www.ffiec.gov/ffiecinfobase/booklets/bcp/bus_continuity_plan.pdf

Feltus, C., Petit, M. and Dubois, E. (2009, November). *Strengthening Employee's Responsibility to Enhance Governance of IT: COBIT RACI chart Case Study.* In: *Proceedings of the first ACM workshop on Information security governance,* pp. 23-32. ACM.

Fernando, A. C. (2009). *Corporate Governance: Principles, Policies and Practices.* Pearson Education.

Forrester Research (2004). *Sarbanes-Oxley Solutions- Invest or Pay Later: Hybrid Applications Emerge for Internal Controls Compliance,* Forrester Research Report, March 11, 2004.

Galanis, M. M. and Dignam, M. A. (2013). *The Globalization of Corporate Governance.* Ashgate Publishing.

Gartner (2001). *Building an IT Performance Management Program*, Gartner Measurement Presentation, July 24, 2001.

Goeken, M. and Alter, S. (2008). *IT Governance Frameworks as Methods.* In: *Proceedings of the 10th International Conference on Enterprise Information Systems (ICEIS),* June 2008, pp. 12-16.

Hamaker, Stacey (2005). *Enterprise Governance & The Role of IT,* In: *Information Systems Control Journal,* Volume 6, 2005.

Hardy, G. (2006). *Guidance on Aligning COBIT ITIL and ISO 17799,* In: *Journal Online,* ISACA.

Hardy, G., and Goldentops, E. (2005). *COBIT 4.0: The New Face of COBIT,* In: *Information Systems Control Journal,* Volume 6, 2005.

Hayden, L. (2009). *Designing Common Control Frameworks: A Model for Evaluating Information Technology Governance, Risk, and Compliance Control Rationalization Strategies.* In: *Information Security Journal: A Global Perspective,* 18(6), pp. 297-305.

Heier, H., Borgman, H. P. and Hofbauer, T. H. (2008, January). *Making the Most of IT Governance Software: Understanding Implementation Processes.* Hawaii International Conference on System Sciences, Proceedings of the 41st Annual, pp. 435-435. IEEE.

Heier, H., Borgman, H. P. and Mileos, C. (2009, January). *Examining the Relationship Between IT Governance Software, Processes, and Business Value: a Quantitative Research Approach.* In: *42nd Hawaii International Conference on* System Sciences 2009. HICSS'09, pp. 1-11. IEEE.

Hemphill, T. (2013). *The ISO 26000 Guidance On Social Responsibility International Standard: What Are The Business Governance Implications?* In: *Corporate Governance,* 13(3), pp. 305-317.

Hendrikse, J. W. and Hendrikse, L. (2004). *Business Governance Handbook: Principles and Practices.* Juta Academic.

Howe, J.J. (2012). *The Sarbanes Oxley Act At 10*, Ernst & Young, LLP.

Huang, R., Zmud, R. W. and Price, R. L. (2010). *Influencing the Effectiveness of IT Governance Practices through Steering Committees and Communication Policies.* In: *European Journal of Information Systems,* 19(3), pp. 288-302.

IBM, *IBM Process Reference Model for IT (PRM-IT)*, Version 3.0, 2008.

ISACA (2012). COBIT®5 – *Enabling Processes,* ISACA, Chicago, Il.

Institute of Internal Auditors (2005). *Putting COSO's Theory into Practice,* In: *Tone at the Top,* Issue 28, November 2005.

IT Governance Institute and Office of Government Commerce (2005). *Aligning COBIT, ITIL, and ISO 17799*, A Management Report. ITGI.

IT Governance Institute (2003). *Board Briefing on IT Governance Report*, Second Edition, ITGI, Rolling Meadows, Il.

IT Governance Institute (2005). *Information Security Governance*, 2nd Edition, Report on Guidance for Boards of Directors and Executive Management. ITGI.

IT Governance Institute (2006). *The CEO's Guide to IT Value & Risk*. ITGI.

IT Governance Institute (2008), *Enterprise Value: Governance of IT Investments – The Val-IT Framework 2.0.*ITGI.

IT Governance Institute (2012). *COBIT 5.0*, ITGI.

Japan Users Association of Information Systems (2012). *The 19th Corporate IT Trend Survey.*

Jenkinson, T. and Mayer, C. (2012). *The Assessment: Corporate Governance and Corporate Control.* In: *Oxford Review of Economic Policy, 8*(3), pp. 1-10.

John, K., Litov, L. and Yeung, B. (2008). *Corporate Governance and Risk-Taking.* In: *The Journal of Finance, 63*(4), pp. 1679-1728.

Kaplan, R. S. and Norton, D. P. (1996). *Using the Balanced Scorecard as a Strategic Management System,* In: *Harvard Business Review,* Jan. – Feb. 1996, pp. 75-85.

Kaplan, Robert and Norton, David (2004). *Strategy Maps: Converting Intangible Assets into Tangible Outcomes,* Harvard Business School Press, Boston, MA.

Kaplan, Robert and Norton, David (2001). *The Strategy-Focused Organization: How Balanced Scorecard Companies Thrive in the New Business Environment,* Harvard Business School Press, Boston, MA.

Kaplan, Robert and Norton, David (1996). *The Balanced Scorecard,* HBR Press, Cambridge, MA.

Kim, Y. J., Lee, J. M., Koo, C. and Nam, K. (2013). *The Role of Governance Effectiveness in Explaining IT Outsourcing Performance.* In: *International Journal of Information Management, 33*(5), pp. 850-860.

Knahl, M. H. (2009). *A Conceptual Framework for the Integration of IT Infrastructure Management, IT Service Management and IT Governance.* In: *Proceedings of the World Academy of Science, Engineering and Technology,* p. 40.

Ko, D. and Fink, D. (2010). *Information Technology Governance: An Evaluation of the Theory-Practice Gap.* In: *Corporate Governance, 10*(5), pp. 662-674.

Kolk, A. (2008). *Sustainability, Accountability and Corporate Governance: Exploring Multinationals' Reporting Practices.* In: *Business Strategy and the Environment, 17*(1), pp. 1-15.

Krag Brotby, W. (2009). *Information Security Management Metrics: A Definitive Guide to Effective Security Monitoring and Measurement.* CRC Press.

Lam, J. (2014). *Enterprise Risk Management: From Incentives to Controls,* 2nd Ed., John Wiley & Sons.

Lambeth, John (2007). *Using COBIT as a Tool to Lead Enterprise IT Organizations,* In: *Information Systems Control Journal,* Volume 1, 2007.

Lemus, S. M., Pino, F. J. and Velthius, M. P. (2010, June). *Towards a Model for Information Technology Governance Applicable to the Banking Sector.* In: *Information Systems and Technologies (CISTI) 2010 5th Iberian Conference on Information Systems and Technologies,* pp. 1-6. IEEE.

Luftman, J., Ben-Zvi, T., Dwivedi, R. and Rigoni, E. H. (2010). *IT Governance: An Alignment Maturity Perspective.* In: *International Journal of IT/Business Alignment and Governance (IJITBAG), 1*(2), pp. 13-25.

Lutchen, M. (2004). *Managing IT as a Business: a Survival Guide for CEOs,* J. Wiley, Hoboken, N.J.

Mackaden, Frederick (2014). *Law and Best Practices for a Sarbanes-Oxley Systems Review,* In: *ISACA Journal,* Volume 4, 2014.

Marchand, D. A., Kettinger W.J. and Rollins, J.D. (2001). *Information orientation: the Link to Business Performance,* Oxford University Press, New York/Oxford.

McNulty, T., Zattoni, A. and Douglas, T. (2013). *Developing Corporate Governance Research Through Qualitative Methods: A Review of Previous Studies.* In: *Corporate Governance: An International Review, 21*(2), pp. 183-198.

McNurlin, Barbara and Sprague, Ralph (2006). *Information Systems in Practice,* 7th Edition, Pearson Education, Upper Saddle River, NJ.

Melnicoff, Richard, Shearer, Sandy and Goyal, Deepak (2005). *Is There a Smarter Way to Approach IT Governance?,* In: *Outlook,* 2005, Number 1, Accenture.

Mitchell, G. (2008). *Creating Sustainable Advantage Through IT Risk Management.* Internet, paper.

Monnoyer, Eric and Willmott, Paul (2005). *What IT Leaders Do,* In: *The McKinsey Quarterly,* August 2005.

Nimmer, R. T. and Feinberg, R. B. (1989). *Business Governance: Fiduciary Duties, Business Judgment, Trustees and Exclusivity.* In: Emory Bankruptcy Developments Journal, Chapter 11.

Nolan, R. and McFarlan, F. W. (2005). *Information Technology and the Board of Directors,* In: *Harvard Business Review,* October 2005.

Nourizadeh, Z., Nourizadeh, A. and Mahdavi, M. (2011, August). *Implementing Information Technology Governance using Val IT; Case study: Isfahan Municipality.* In: *Artificial Intelligence, Management Science and Electronic Commerce (AIMSEC), 2011 2nd International Conference on Management Science and Electronic Commerce,* pp. 4644-4647. IEEE.

Oltsik, Jon (2003). *IT Governance: Is IT Governance the Answer?* In: *Tech Republic,* January 13, 2003.

Ougaard, M. and Leander, A. (Eds.) (2010). *Business and Global Governance.* Routledge.

Parent, M. and Reich, B. H. (2009). *Governing Information Technology Risk.* In: *California Management Review, 51*(3), pp. 134-152.

Parks, Hugh (2006). *Shifting Governance Roles & Responsibilities,* In: *Information Systems Control Journal,* Volume 5, 2006.

Popper, Charles (2000). *Holistic Framework for IT Governance.* In:, *Center for Information Policy Research,* Harvard University, January 2000.

Posthumus, S., Von Solms, R. and King, M. (2010). *The Board and IT Governance: The What, Who and How.* In: *South African Journal of Business Management, 41*(3), pp. 23-32.

Prasad, A., Heales, J. and Green, P. (2009). *Towards a Deeper Understanding of Information Technology Governance Effectiveness: A Capabilities-Based Approach.* In: *International Conference on Information Systems (ICIS) 2009,* pp. 1-19. Association for Information Systems.

Prasad, A., Heales, J. and Green, P. (2010). *A Capabilities-based Approach to Obtaining a Deeper Understanding of Information Technology Governance Effectiveness: Evidence from IT Steering Committees.* In: *International Journal of Accounting Information Systems, 11*(3), pp. 214-232.

Prentice, Robert (2005). *Sarbanes-Oxley Act- Student Guide,* Thomson Publishing.

Proctivity (2003). *Frequently Asked Questions, Guide to the Sarbanes-Oxley Act: IT Risks and Controls,* December 2003.

Pultorak, David and Kerrigan, Jim (2005). *Conformance Performance and Rapport: A Framework for Corporate and IT Governance,* In: *NACD – Directors Monthly,* February 2005.

Racz, N., Weippl, E. and Seufert, A. (2010, July). *A Process Model for Integrated IT Governance, Risk, and Compliance Management.* In: *Proceedings of the Ninth Baltic Conference on Databases and Information Systems (DB&IS'10),* pp. 155-170.

Rafeq, A. (2005). *Using CobiT for IT Control Health Check Up,* In: *Information Systems Control Journal Health,* Volume 5, 2005.

Ristola, T. (2011). *Risk Management in Information System Development.*

Robinson, Nick (2007). *The Many Faces of IT Governance,* In: *Information Systems Control Journal,* Volume 1, 2007.

Selig, Gad J. and Waterhouse, Peter (2006). *IT Governance - An Integrated Framework and Roadmap: How to Plan, Deploy and Sustain for Competitive Advantage,* Computer Associates Sponsored White Paper, March 2006.

Selig, Gad J. (2006). *IT Governance - A Best Practice Roadmap,* ISACA - Greater Hartford Chapter Workshop, March 15, 2006.

Sharma, D., Stone, M. and Ekinci, Y. (2009). *IT Governance and Project Management: A Qualitative Study.* In: *Journal of Database Marketing & Customer Strategy Management, 16*(1), pp. 29-50.

Sia, S. K., Soh, C. and Weill, P. (2010). *Global IT Management: Structuring for Scale, Responsiveness, and Innovation.* In: *Communications of the ACM, 53*(3), pp. 59-64.

Silva, E. and Chaix, Y. (2008, January). *Business and IT Governance Alignment Simulation Essay on a Business Process and IT Service Model*. In: *Hawaii International Conference on System Sciences, Proceedings of the 41st Annual*, pp. 434-434. IEEE.

Simonsson, M. and Johnson, P. (2008, January). *The IT Organization Modeling and Assessment tool: Correlating IT Governance Maturity with the Effect of IT*. In: *Hawaii International Conference on System Sciences, Proceedings of the 41st Annual*, pp. 431-431. IEEE.

Simonsson, M., Johnson, P. and Ekstedt, M. (2010). *The Effect of IT Governance Maturity on IT Governance Performance*. In: *Information Systems Management*, 27(1), pp. 10-24.

Singh, R., Bhagat, A. and Kumar, N. (2012, September). *Generalization of Software Metrics on Software as a Service (SaaS)*. In: *2012 International Conference on Computing Sciences (ICCS)*, pp. 267-270. IEEE.

Singh-Latulipe, Rob (2007). *Val IT: From the Vantage Point of the COBIT 4.0 Pentagon Model for IT Governance*, In: *Information Systems Control Journal*, Volume 1, 2007.

Stewart, W.E. (2001). *Balanced Scorecard for Projects*, In: *Project Management Journal*, Vol. 32, No. 1, March 2001, pp. 38-47.

Stouffer, D. and Rachlin, S. (2002). *A Summary of First Practices and Lessons Learned in Information Technology Portfolio Management*. In: *Federal Chief Information Officer (CIO) Council Best Practices Committee*, Washington, D.C., March 2002.

Sun Microsystems and Deloitte (2006). *Raising the Bar for Governance and Compliance*, White paper, February, 2006.

Tallon, P. P. (2013). *Corporate Governance of Big Data: Perspectives on Value, Risk, and Cost*. In: *Computer*, 46(6), pp. 32-38.

Tech Republic (2005). *Forty Eight Questions You Need to Answer for Sarbanes-Oxley Compliance*, Ernst & Young, CNET Networks, Inc.

The Business Continuity Plan and Guide, http://www.bcpgenerator.com

Van Grembergen W. (2004). *Strategies for Information Technology Governance*, IDEA Group Publishing.

Van Grembergen, W. and De Haes, S. (2008). *Strategies and Models for IT Governance*. In: *Implementing Information Technology Governance: Models, Practices, and Cases*, pp. 1-75, IGI Global.

Van Grembergen, W. and De Haes, S. (2009). *Enterprise Governance of Information Technology: Achieving Strategic Alignment and Value*. Springer.

Van Grembergen, W. and De Haes, S. (2010). "A Research Journey into Enterprise Governance of IT, Business/IT Alignment and Value Creation." International Journal of IT/Business Alignment and Governance (IJITBAG), 1(1), 1-13.

Van Grembergen, W. and De Haes, S. (2012). "*Business Strategy and Applications in Enterprise IT Governance*", IGI Global.

Van Haren Publishing (2014). *Global Standards and Publications – 2014/2015*, Van Haren Publishing.

Violino, Bob (2006). *IT Directions* In: *CFO*, January 2006.

Wang, X., Zhou, X. and Jiang, L. (2008, October). *A Method of Business and IT Alignment Based on Enterprise Architecture*. In: *IEEE International Conference on Service Operations and Logistics, and Informatics, 2008. IEEE/SOLI 2008*. Vol. 1, pp. 740-745. IEEE.

Weill, Peter and Ross, Jeanne (2004). *IT Governance: How Top Performers Manage IT Decision Rights Results*, Harvard Business Press, Cambridge, MA. 2004.

Womack, James P. and Jones, Daniel T. (2003). *Lean Thinking: Banish Waste and Create Wealth in Your Corporation*, Revised and Updated, Harper Business, 2003.

Wright, M., Siegel, D. S., Keasey, K. and Filatotchev, I. (Eds.). (2013). *The Oxford Handbook of Corporate Governance*. Oxford University Press.

Young, M. N., Peng, M. W., Ahlstrom, D., Bruton, G. D. and Jiang, Y. (2008). *Corporate Governance in Emerging Economies: A Review of the Principal Perspective*. In: *Journal of Management Studies*, 45(1), pp. 196-220.

Young, S. and Thyil, V. (2008). *A Holistic Model of Corporate Governance: a New Research Framework.*" In: *Corporate Governance*, 8(1), pp. 94-108.

D. IT Service Management and IT Infrastructure Library (ITIL)

Aazadnia, M. and Fasanghari, M. (2008). *Improving the Information Technology Service Management with Six Sigma*. In: *International Journal of Computer Science and Network Security, 8*(3), pp. 144-150.

Ahmad, N. and Shamsudin, Z. M. (2013). *Systematic Approach to Successful Implementation of ITIL*. In: *Procedia Computer Science*, pp. 17, 237-244.

Alojail, M. (2013). *ITIL Usage, and Use of ITIL Recommended Practices and the IT Outsourcing Relationship Quality*, PhD Thesis, Business IT and Logistics, RMIT University.

Alojail, M., Rouse, A. C. and Corbitt, B. J. (2012). *The Impact of ITIL (Information Technology Infrastructure Library) Recommended Practices on the IT Outsourcing Relationship*. In: *ACIS 2012: Location, location, location: Proceedings of the 23rd Australasian Conference on Information Systems 2012*, pp. 1-10. ACIS.

Author, B. (2012). *Information Technology Service Management (ITSM) Implementation Methodology Based on Information Technology Infrastructure Library Ver. 3 (ITIL V3)* In: *International Journal of Business Research and Management (IJBRM)*, Volume (3): Issue (3).

AXELOS, (2011). *ITIL 2011 Edition - Life Cycle Publication Suite*, TSO.

AXELOS. (2014). *The Importance of ITIL® - 2014 and Beyond*, In: *Global Study*.

Bahsani, S., Himi, A., Moubtakir, H. and Semma, A. (2013). *Towards a pooling of ITIL V3 and COBIT*. In: *International Journal of Computer Science*, June 2013, pp. 8.

Barafort, B., and Rousseau, A. (2009). *Sustainable Service Innovation Model: A Standardized IT Service Management Process Assessment Framework*. In: *Software Process Improvement*, pp. 69-80. Springer, Berlin Heidelberg.

Barafort, B., Jezek, D., Mäkinen, T., Stolfa, S., Varkoi, T. and Vondrak, I. (2008). *Modeling and Assessment in IT Service Process Improvement*. In: *Software Process Improvement*, pp. 117-128. Springer, Berlin Heidelberg.

Bernard, P. (2011). *Passing the ITIL V3 Intermediate Exams: The Study Guide*. Van Haren Publishing.

Bernard, P. (2014). *IT service management Based on ITIL® 2011 Edition*, Van Haren Publishing.

Breyfogle, F., Cupello, J. and Meadows, Becki (2001). *Managing Six Sigma*, Wiley.

Cervone, F. (2008). *ITIL: A Framework for Managing Digital Library Services*. In: *OCLC Systems & Services, 24*(2), pp. 87-90.

Chan, P. C., Durant, S. R., Gall, V. M., and Raisinghani, M. S. (2010). *Aligning Six Sigma and ITIL to Improve IT Service Management*. In: *International Journal of E-Services and Mobile Applications, 1, 2*, pp. 62-82.

Conger, S. and Probst, J. (2014). *Knowledge Management in ITSM: Applying the DIKW Model*. In: *Engineering and Management of IT-based Service Systems*, pp. 1-18. Springer, Berlin Heidelberg.

Cortina, S., Renault, A. and Picard, M. (2013). *TIPA Process Assessments: A Means to Improve Business Value of IT Services*. In: *International Journal of Strategic Information Technology and Applications (IJSITA), 4*(4), pp. 1-18.

Cots, S. and Casadesús, M. (2014). *Exploring the Service Management Standard ISO 20000*. In: *Total Quality Management & Business Excellence*, pp. 1-19.

Cronholm, S. and Salomonson, N. (2014). *Measures that Matters: Service Quality in IT Service Management*. In: *International Journal of Quality and Service Sciences, 6*(1), pp. 60-76.

Cybercan Technology Solutions (2005). *ITIL (Information Technology Infrastructure Library) Foundation Workshop*.

De Jong, A., Kolthof, A., and Pieper, M. (2008). *Continual Service Improvement Based on ITIL V3 - A Management Guide*. Van Haren Publishing.

Edwards, John. (2005, September). *Dream Catalogue*. In: *CFO Magazine*.

Erek, K., Proehl, T. and Zarnekow, R. (2014). *Managing Cloud Services with IT Service Management Practices*. In: *Engineering and Management of IT-based Service Systems*, pp. 67-81. Springer, Berlin Heidelberg.

Esposito, A., and Rogers, T. (2013). *Ten Steps to ITSM Success: A Practitioner's Guide to Enterprise IT Transformation* (Vol. 2). IT Governance Ltd.

Farmand, M. (2013). *Proposing a Comprehensive Framework for ITSM Efficiency*, http://hdl. handle.net/2320/12479.

Franke, U., Johnson, P., and König, J. (2013). *An Architecture Framework for Enterprise IT Service Availability Analysis*. In: *Software & Systems Modeling*, pp. 1-29.

Gacenga, F. N. (2013). *A Performance Measurement Framework for IT Service Management*, In: Doctoral dissertation, University of Southern Queensland. Gacenga@usq.edu.au.

Galup, S. D., Dattero, R., Quan, J. J., and Conger, S. (2009). *An Overview of IT Service Management*. In: *Communications of the ACM, 52*(5), pp. 124-127.

Gama, N., Sousa, P., and Da Silva, M. M. (2013). *Integrating Enterprise Architecture and IT Service Management*. In: *Building Sustainable Information Systems*, pp. 153-165. Springer US.

Gartner (2005). *ITSM and ITIL Study.*

General Electric Corp. (2005). *Six Sigma Training Workshop for Vendors*, GE.

Hamm, Steve. (2007). *Bangalore Tiger*, McGraw-Hill, New York.

Holub, E., Mingay, S., Brittain, K., Govekar, M. and Bittinger, S. (2007, June 5). *ITIL v3 Services Guidelines Expand Audience Through Update*, In: *Gartner Research.*

HP: *The Reference Model (HP white papers)* http://www.hp.com/large/itsm

Iden, J. and Eikebrokk, T. R. (2013). *Implementing IT Service Management: A Systematic Literature Review*. In: *International Journal of Information Management, 33*(3), pp. 512-523.

Jussi, S. (2013). *A Framework for IT Service Management Integration*, Lappeenranta University of Technology, School of Industrial Engineering and Management, Department of Software Engineering and Information Management.

Kabachinski, J. (2011). *Have you heard of ITIL? It's time you did*. In: Biomedical Instrumentation & Technology, *45*(1), pp. 59-62.

Kuhn, Janet (2007). *Transitioning to ITIL v3*, In: DITY Weekly Newsletter, Vol. 3.29., 24 July 24 2007.

Lahtela, A., Hotti, V., and Salomaa, H. (2014). *Service Support in IT Governance, IT Management and Enterprise Architecture Context*. In: *The Fourth International Conference on Digital Information Processing and Communications (ICDIPC2014)*. pp. 166-172. The Society of Digital Information and Wireless Communication.

Larrocha, E. R., Minguet, J. M., Díaz, G., Castro, M., and Vara, A. (2010, April). *Filling the Gap of Information Security Management inside ITIL®: proposals for posgraduate students*. In: *Education Engineering (EDUCON), 2010 IEEE*, pp. 907-912. IEEE.

Lonsdale, Derek, Clark, W. and Udvadia, B. (2006). *ITIL in a Complex World*, In: *Journal Online*, ISACA.

Lucio-Nieto, T., and Colomo-Palacios, R. (2012, June). *ITIL and the Creation of a Service Management Office (SMO): A new challenge for IT professionals: An exploratory study of Latin American companies*. In: *Information Systems and Technologies (CISTI), 2012 7th Iberian Conference on*, pp. 1-6. IEEE.

Lucio-Nieto, T., Colomo-Palacios, R., Soto-Acosta, P., Popa, S., and Amescua-Seco, A. (2012). *Implementing an IT Service Information Management Framework: The Case of COTEMAR*. In: *International Journal of Information Management.*

Marrone, M., Gacenga, F., Cater-Steel, A., and Kolbe, L. (2014). *IT Service Management: A Cross-National Study of ITIL Adoption*. In: *Communications of the Association for Information Systems, 34*(1), pp. 865-892.

Mesquida, A. L., Mas, A., Amengual, E. and Calvo-Manzano, J. A. (2012). *IT Service Management Process Improvement based on ISO/IEC 15504: A systematic review*. In: Information and Software Technology, *54*(3), pp. 239-247.

Moeller, R. R. (2013). *Executive's Guide to IT Governance: Improving Systems Processes with Service Management, COBIT and ITIL*. John Wiley & Sons.

Mora, M., Phillips-Wren, G., Cervantes-Pérez, F., Garrido, L. and Gelman, O. (2014). *Improving IT Service Management with Decision-Making Support Systems*. In: *Engineering and Management of IT-based Service Systems*, pp. 215-232. Springer, Berlin Heidelberg.

Office of Government Commerce (2004). Business Perspective: *The IS View on Delivering Services to the Business*. In: *OGC, ITIL© Managing IT Services (IT Infrastructure Library)*. TSO.

Praxiom Research Group, Ltd. *ISO/IEC 27001 Overview.* http://www.praxiom.com/
  iso-27001-intro.htm

Proehl, T., Erek, K., Limbach, F. and Zarnekow, R. (2013, January). *Topics and Applied Theories
  in IT Service Management.* In: *46th Hawaii International Conference on System Sciences
  (HICSS), 2013.* pp. 1367-1375. IEEE.

Qian, J., Ward, K., and Blaskovich, J. (2012). *Integrating IT Frameworks into the AIS Course.* In:
  AIS Educator Journal, 7(1), pp. 1-26.

Rovers, M. (2013). *ISO/IEC 20000: 2011 – A Pocket Guide.* Van Haren Publishing.

Schreiner, S. (2008, December). *A Survey of IT Governance through COBIT, ITIL, and ISO 17799*
  In: *Report, University of Illinois at Urbana-Champaign.*

Shivashankarappa, A. N., Smalov, L., Dharmalingam, R., and Anbazhagan, N. (2012, June).
  *Implementing IT Governance using COBIT: A Case Study Focusing on Critical Success
  Factors.* In: Internet Security (World CIS*), 2012 World Congress on,* pp. 144-149. IEEE.

Topalov, Drago, (2013, May). *ITIL and ISO 20000: A Comparison* www.2000Academy.com/
  Blog/March-2013/ITIL-and-ISO-20000-A Comparison.

Yamakawa, P., Noriega, C. O., Linares, A. N., and Ramírez, W. V. (2012). *Improving ITIL
  Compliance using Change Management Practices: A Finance Sector Case Study.* In: *Business
  Process Management Journal, 18(6),* pp. 1020-1035.

Yao, Z., and Wang, X. (2010, June). *An ITIL based ITSM practice: A case study of steel
  manufacturing enterprise.* In: *Service Systems and Service Management (ICSSSM), 2010 7th
  International Conference on,* pp. 1-5. IEEE.

Zhang, Y., Zhang, J., and Chen, J. (2013, April). *Critical Success Factors in IT Service
  Management Implementation: People, Process, and Technology Perspectives.* In: *International
  Conference on Service Sciences (ICSS), 2013,* pp. 64-68. IEEE.

E. Strategic Sourcing, Outsourcing and Vendor Management

Bahli, B., and Rivard, S. (2013). *Cost Escalation in Information Technology Outsourcing: A
  Moderated Mediation Study.* In: *Decision Support Systems, 56,* pp. 37-47.

Beckman, Sara L. and Rosenfield, Donald B. (2008) *Operating Strategy,* McGraw-Hill, NY.

Bragg, Steven M. (2006). *Outsourcing,* Second Edition, J. Wiley & Sons, NY.

Brown, Doug and Wilson, Scott (2005). *The Black Book of Outsourcing,* John Wiley & Sons.

Burkholder, Nicholas C. (2006). *Outsourcing,* J. Wiley & Sons, NY.

Bullen, C., Lefave, R. and Selig, G. (2010). *Implementing Strategic Sourcing – A Manager's Guide
  to World Class Best Practices,* Van Haren Publishing.

Business Week (2006, January 30). *Special Report on Outsourcing.*

Carmel, Erran and Tjia, Paul (2005). *Offshoring Information Technology,* Cambridge University
  Press, UK.

Chew, E. K., and Gottschalk, P. (2013). *Knowledge Driven Service Innovation and Management:
  IT Strategies for Business Alignment and Value Creation.* In: *Business Science Reference.*

Click, Rick L. and Dvening, Thomas N. (2005). *Business Process Outsourcing,* J. Wiley & Sons,
  NY.

Corbett, Michael F. (2000, May 29). *Outsourcing 2000: Value-Driven Customer-Focused,* In:
  Fortune, pp. S36.

Corbett, Michael, (2004). *The Outsourcing Revolution,* In: *Dearbon Trade Publication, Chicago,
  Il.*

Dalal, Jagdish. (2002, October 23). *Off-shore Outsourcing,* In: *The Outsourcing Research Council,
  Raleigh, NC,* pp. 11, 13.

Deloitte, Consulting Report. (2005, December). *Calling a Change in the Outsourcing Model.* In:
  Deloitte Consulting.

Ellis, James E., McDonnell Douglas. (1994 February 14). *Unfasten the Seat Belts,* In:
  BusinessWeek, pp. 36.

Engardio, Pete et al. (2003, February 3). *The New Global Job Shift,* In: *BusinessWeek.*

Friedman, Debbie. (2006). *Demystifying Outsourcing,* J. Wiley & Sons.

Hale, Judith. (2006). *Outsourcing Training and Development,* J. Wiley & Sons, NY.

Halvey, John K. and Melby, Barbara M. (2007). *Business Process Outsourcing,* J. Wiley & Sons, NY.

Halvey, John K. and Melby, Barbara M. (2005). *Informatiom Technology Outsourcing Transactions,* Second Edition, J. Wiley & Sons, NY.

Hefley, William E. and Locsche, Ethel A. (2006). *The eSCM-CL v1.1: Model Overview,* Part 1, ITSqc, Carnegie Mellon University.

Hefley, William E. and Locsche, Ethel A. (2006). *The eSCM-CL v1.1: Model Overview,* Part 2, ITSqc, Carnegie Mellon University.

Herron, D., Andriole, S. J., and Moss, L. T. (2013). *Searching for Maturity*: In: *The Impact of CMM on Outsourced Software Development.* Feedback, 4, 6.

Hyder, Elaine B., Heston, Keith M., and Mark, C.(2006). *The eSCM-SP v2.01: Model Overview,* Part 1, ITSqc, Carnegie Mellon University.

Hyder, Elaine B., Heston, Keith M., and Mark, C.(2006). *The eSCM-SP v2.01: Model Overview,* Part 2, ITSqc, Carnegie Mellon University.

International Association of Outsourcing Professionals. (2006). *Outsourcing Professional Body of Knowledge,* Version 6, IAOP.

Kim, Y. J., Lee, J. M., Koo, C., and Nam, K. (2013*). The Role of Governance Effectiveness in Explaining IT Outsourcing Performance.* In: *International Journal of Information Management, 33*(5), pp. 850-860.

Kripalani, Manjeet and Engardio, Pete. (2003, December 8). *The Rise of India,* In: *BusinessWeek,* pp. 66-78.

McIvor, Ronan. (2006). *The Outsourcing Process,* In: *Cambridge University Press,* NY.

Overby, Stephanie (2005, October). Simple Successful Outsourcing, In: CIO Magazine - Business Technology Leadership, pp. 51-62.

Palvia, Shailendra (2003, July). *Off Shore Outsourcing – Creating a World of Difference,* Proceeding of the Second Annual International Outsourcing Conference, Center for Global Outsourcing, New York.

Paulk, Mark C. (2005, February). *Measurement & the eSourcing Capability Model for Service Providers v2,* ITSqc, Carnegie Mellon University, CMU-ISRI-04-128.

Quinn, James Brian (2000, Summer). *Outsourcing Innovation: The New Engine of Growth,* In: Sloan Management Review, pp. 13-27.

Selig, Gad J. (2007, February 18-21). *How to Win Deals in the Rapidly Changing World of Outsourcing - Critical Success Factors for Vendor/Customer Collaboration and Innovation to Grow Revenues,* The Outsourcing World Summit, Loews Hotel, Lake Las Vegas, Las Vegas, Nevada.

F. Leadership, Teams, Managing Change & Innovation

Baker, M., and Bourne, M. (2014). *A Governance Framework for the Idea-to-Launch Process: Development and Application of a Governance Framework for New Product* Development. *Research-Technology Management, 57*(1), pp. 42-49.

Betz, Frederick (2003). *Managing Technological Innovation: Competitive Advantage from Change.* John Wiley, New York.

Bridges, William (2005). *Managing Transitions,* 2nd Edition, Da Capo Press, Cambridge, Ma, 1991.

Broadbent, Marianne and Kitzis, Ellen (2005). *The New CIO Leader,* In: *HBR Press.*

Burn, Jack and Moran, Linda (2000). *The New Self Directed Work Teams,* McGraw-Hill, New York.

Cohen, Beth, TACtical Research SmartTip. (2006, December). *Rethinking Internet Forum and Collaboration Tools,* In: *The Advisory Council (TAC).*

Cowan-Sahadath, K. (2010). *Business Transformation: Leadership, integration and Innovation–A Case Study.* In: *International Journal of Project Management, 28*(4), pp. 395-404.

Drucker, P. F. (2013). *Managing in a Time of Great Change.* Harvard Business Press.

Drucker, Peter (1997). *Managing in a Time of Great Change,* Butterworth-Heinemann.

Fullan, M. (2011). *The Six Secrets of Change: What the Best Leaders Do to Help Their Organizations Survive and Thrive.* John Wiley & Sons.

Gayle, D. J., Tewarie, B., and White Jr, A. Q. (2011). *Governance in the Twenty-first-century university: Approaches to effective leadership and strategic management: ASHE-ERIC Higher Education Report* (Vol. 14). John Wiley & Sons.

Haeckel, S. H. (1999). *Adaptive Enterprise: Creating and Leading Sense-and-Respond Organizations.* Harvard Business School Press, Boston, MA

Hilb, M. (2012). *New Corporate Governance: Successful Board Management Tools.* Springer.

Janszen, F. (2000). *The Age of Innovation: Making Business Creativity a Competence, not a Coincidence,* Prentice Hall, London.

Jeston, J., and Nelis, J. (2014). *Business process management.* Routledge.

Johnson, Carla (2002, June). *Creating Virtual Teams,* In: *HR Magazine.*

Katzenback, Jon and Smith, Doug. (2001). *The Discipline of Teams,* John Wiley, New York.

Kotter, John P. (1996). *Leading Change,* In: *HBR Press,* Cambridge, MA.

Lutchen, M. D. (2011). *Managing IT as a Business: A Survival Guide for CEOs.* John Wiley & Sons.

Mayle, David. (2006). *Managing Innovation and Change,* Sage Publications.

McCauley, C. and Van Velsor, Ellen, (Ed.) (2004). *Handbook of Leadership Development,* 2nd Edition, In: *The Center for Creative Leadership,* Jossey Bass.

McCelland, David (1995). *The Leadership Profile for Winning,* Presentation on Leadership, MIT Seminar.

McDermott, Lynda, Brawley, Nolan and Waite, William (1998). *World Class Teams,* John Wiley, New York.

Mosimann, Roland, Mosimann, Patrick and Dussault, Meg (2007). *The Performance Manager,* Cognos.

Prewitt, Edward and Ware, Lorraine C. (2006). *The State of the CIO'06,* www.cio.com/archieve/010106/JAN1SOC.pdf.

Puccio, Gerard, Murdock, Mary and Mance, Marie (2007). *Creative Leadership,* Sage Publications.

Selig, Gad J. (2006). *Creating, Sustaining and Leading High Performance Co-Located and Virtual Teams and Team Leaders - Why, What and How?,* Proceedings of Southern New England Chapter of the Project Management Institute - First Annual Conference, Hartford Conference Center, Hartford, CT. May 23, 2006.

Senge, Peter M. (1990). *The Fifth Discipline: the Art and Practise of the Learning Organization.* New York: Currency/Doubleday.

Sheppard, J. A., Sarros, J. C., and Santora, J. C. (2013). *Twenty-First Century Leadership: International Imperatives.* Management Decision, 51(2), pp. 267-280.

Situation Leadership Model. (2006). http://www.chimaeraconsulting.com/sitleader.htm.

Snyder, Bill, Teams That Span Time Zones Face New Work Rules. (2003, May). http://gsb.stanford.edu/news/bmag/sbsm0305/feature_virtual_teams.shtml

Spanyi, A. (2010). *Business Process Management Governance.* In: *Handbook on Business Process Management 2.* pp. 223-238. Springer, Berlin Heidelberg.

Tzu, Sun (1971). *The Art of War,* Oxford University Press.

Wailgum, Thomas (2005). *The Rules of IT,* In: *CIO Magazine - Business Technology Leadership,* October 1, 2005, pp. 90-100.

Wilcox, M. and Rush, S. (2004). *The CCL Guide to Leadership in Action,* Center for Creative Leadership, Jossey Bass.

G. Cloud Computing and Data Management

Almulla, S. A. and Yeun, C. Y. (2010). Cloud Computing Security Management. In: *Second International Conference on Engineering Systems Management and Its Applications (ICESMA),* pp. 1-7, March 2010, IEEE.

Arabalidousti, F. and Nasiri, R. (2013). *Improving IT Service Management Architecture in Cloud Environment on Top of Current Frameworks.* In: *The International Conference on Digital Information Processing, E-Business and Cloud Computing (DIPECC2013),* pp. 77-86. The Society of Digital Information and Wireless Communication.

Arabalidousti, F., Nasiri, R. and Razavi, Davoudi, M. (2014). *Developing a New Architecture to Improve ITSM on Cloud Computing Environment.* In: *International Journal on Cloud Computing: Services and Architecture (IJCCSA)*, Vol. 4, No. 1, February 2014.

Arun, H., Nilam, R., Namrata, R. and Purva, S. (2013). *Review on Techniques to Ensure Distributed Accountability for Data Sharing in the Cloud*, In: *International Journal of Advanced Research* in *Computer and Communication Engineering*, Vol. 2, Issue 10, October 2013.

Assuncao, M. D., Calheiros, R. N., Bianchi, S., Netto, M. A. and Buyya, R. (2013). *Big Data Computing and Clouds: Challenges, Solutions, and Future Directions.* arXiv preprint arXiv:1312.4722.

Barlow, M. (2013). *The Culture of Big Data*, O'Reilly Media.

Bensch, S., Andris, R. J., Gahm, C. and Tuma, A. (2014). *IT Outsourcing: An IS Perspective.* In: *47th Hawaii International Conference on System Sciences (HICSS)*, pp. 4210-4219, January 2014, IEEE.

Bernardo, D. V. (2013). *Utilizing Security Risk Approach in Managing Cloud Computing Services.* In: *16th International Conference on Network-Based Information Systems (NBiS)*, pp. 119-125, September 2013, IEEE.

Bernardo, D. and Hoang D. (2012). *Security Risk Assessment: Toward a Comprehensive Practical Risk Management*, In: *Int. Journal of Information and Computer Security.* Vol. 5, No. 2/2012, pp. 77-104.

Bhadauria, R., Borgohain, R., Biswas, A. and Sanyal, S. (2013). *Secure Authentication of Cloud Data Mining API.* arXiv preprint arXiv:1308.0824.

Bisong, A. and Rahman, S. M. (2011). *An Overview of the Security Concerns in Enterprise Cloud Computing.* In: *International Journal of Network Security & Its Applications*, 3(1).

Bonnet, Pierre (2013). *Enterprise Data Governance Reference and Master Data Management Semantic Model*, Wiley.

Brandabur, R. E. (2013). *IT Outsourcing-A Management-Marketing Decision.* In: *International Journal of Computers, Communications & Control*, 8(2).

Britt, Darice (2012). *Crowdsourcing: The Debate Roars On.* www.instite.artinsitutes.edu, 12/4/2012.

Capgemini (2013). *World Quality Report 2013-14*, www.capgemini.com/thought-leadership/wprld-quality-quality-report-2013-14.

Carter, Keith (2014). *Actionable Intelligence and Big Data*, Wiley.

Chen, Y., Paxson, V. and Katz, R. H. (2010). *What's New About Cloud Computing Security?* University of California, Berkeley Report No. UCB/EECS-2010-5.

Cervo, Dalton and Allan, Mark (2011). *Master Data Management in Practice*, Wiley.

Chambers, Don, (July, 2010). *Windows Azure: Using Windows Azure's Service Business to Solve Data Security Issues*, http://rebustechnologies.com/wpc.ntent/uploads/2011/12/windowsazure.pdf

Choubey, R., Dubey, R. and Bhattacharjee, J. (2011). *A Survey on Cloud Computing Security, Challenges and Threats.* In: *International Journal on Computer Science and Engineering (IJCSE)*, 3(3), pp. 1227-1231.

Cochran, Mitchel. L. and Witman, P. D. (2011). *Governance and Service Level Agreement Issues in A Cloud Computing Environment.* In: *Journal of Information Technology Management*, 22(2), pp. 41-55.

Computing, C. (2011). *Cloud Computing Privacy Concerns on our Doorstep.* In: *Communications of the ACM*, 54(1).

Data Management Association (2014). *DAMA – DMBOK2 Framework*, DAMA Int., March 6, 2014.

Davenport, T. (2014). *Big Data at Work: Dispelling the Myths, Uncovering the Opportunities.* Harvard Business Review Press.

Davenport, T. H. and Dyche, J. (2013). *Big Data in Big Companies.* In: *International Institute for Analytics*, May 2013.

Davenport, T. H. and Kim, J. (2013). *Keeping Up with the Quants: Your Guide to Understanding and Using Analytics.* Harvard Business Review Press.

Davenport, T. H. and Manville, B. (2012). *Judgment Calls: Twelve Stories of Big Decisions and the Teams That Got Them Right.* Harvard Business Review Press.

Dillon, T., Wu, C. and Chang, E. (2010, April). *Cloud Computing: Issues and Challenges.* In: *24th IEEE International Conference on Advanced Information Networking and Applications (AINA), 2010,* pp. 27-33). IEEE.

Elliott, T. (2013). *The Datafications of Daily Life,* In: *Forbes,* July 23, 2013. www.forbes.com/sites/sap/2013/07/24/The Datafiction-of-daily-life/

Emmanuel, William (2014). *Data Privacy and Big-Data-Compliance Issues and Considerations,* In: *ISACA Journal,* Volume 3, 2014.

Gartner (2010). *Gartner Identifies Seven Major Projects CIOs Should Consider During the Next Three Years,* press release, 9 November 2010, *www.granter.com/newsrooms/id/1465614*

Gokila, R. (2014). *Review of Security Services in Cloud Computing and Management.* In: *Asian Journal of Research in Social Sciences and Humanities,* 4(2), pp. 189-198.

Gorla, N. and Somers, T. M. (2014). *The Impact of IT Outsourcing on Information Systems Success.* In: *Information & Management,* 51(3), pp. 320-335.

Grobauer, B., Walloschek, T. and Stocker, E. (2011). *Understanding Cloud Computing Vulnerabilities.* In: *Security & Privacy,* IEEE, 9(2), pp. 50-57.

Gurjar, Y. S. and Rathore, V. S. (2013). *Cloud Business Intelligence – Is What Business Need Today.* In: *International Journal of Recent Technology and Engineering,* 1(6), pp. 81-86.

Hay, B. and Nance, K. et al. (2012). *Are Your Papers in Order? Developing and Enforcing Multi-Tenancy and Migration Policies in the Cloud,* 2012 45th Hawaii International Conference on Systems Sciences, Vol.12, no., pp. 5473-5479.

Henderson, Tom and Allen, Brendan (2010). *Private Cloud: Not for the Faint of Health,* In: *Network World,* 12-20-2010.

Hinkle, Mark (9-6-2010), *Three Cloud Lock-in Considerations, HTTP://community.zenoss.org/blogs/zenossblog/2010/06/ThreeCloudLock-inConsiderations.*

Howe, J. (2008). *Crowdsourcing: Why The Power of the Crowd is Driving the Future of Business,* In: *The International Achievement Institute,* 2008.

Hoffer, Jeffrey, Ramesh V. and Topi, Heikki. (2013). *Modern Data Management,* 11th Ed., Pearson.

Hsu, W. H. L. (2012). *Conceptual Framework of Cloud Computing Governance Model–An Education Perspective.* In: *IEEE Technology and Engineering Education (ITEE),* 7(2), p. 3.

Hsu, L. W. H. (2013). *Governance Model of Cloud Computing Service,* In: *IEEE Technology and Engineering Education (ITEE),* Vol. 7, No. 2, June 2012.

International Data Corporation (2012) *Data Management: A Unified Approach,* In: *IDG Research Services White Paper,* November 2012.

ISACA (2014). *Controls and Assurance in the Cloud: Using COBIT 5.*

Jamil, D. and Zaki, H. (2011). *Cloud Computing Security.* In: *International Journal of Engineering Science and Technology,* 3(4), pp. 3478-3483.

Jansen, W. and Grance, T. (2011). *Guidelines on Security and Privacy in Public Cloud Computing.* NIST Special Publication, 800-144.

Kaisler, S., Armour, F., Espinosa, J. A. and Money, W. (2013, January). *Big Data: Issues and Challenges Moving Forward.* In: *46th Hawaii International Conference on System Sciences (HICSS), 2013,* pp. 995-1004, IEEE.

Kandukuri, B. R., Paturi, V. R. and Rakshit, A. (2009, September). *Cloud Security Issues.* In: *International Conference on Services Computing, 2009. SCC'09,* pp. 517-520, IEEE.

Kaufman, L. M. (2009). *Data Security in the World of Cloud Computing.* In: *Security & Privacy,* IEEE, 7(4), pp. 61-64.

Kavis, M. J. (2014). *Architecting the Cloud: Design Decisions for Cloud Computing Service Models (SaaS, PaaS, and IaaS).* John Wiley & Sons.

Kelly, Kevin (2010). *A Cloud Book For The Cloud,* www.kr.org/thetechniumarchives/ 2007/11/Cloudbook-for.PhP.retrived, 08-22-2010.

Kroenke, David and Auer, David (2014). *Database Processing,* 13th Ed., Pearson.

Kshetri, N. (2012). *Privacy and Security Issues in Cloud Computing: The Role of Institutions and Institutional Evolution. Telecommunications Policy.*

Linthicum, D. S. (2009). *Cloud Computing and SOA Convergence in your Enterprise: A Step-by-Step Guide.* Pearson Education.

Loshin, D. (2013). *Big Data Analytics: From Strategic Planning to Enterprise Integration with Tools, Techniques, NoSQL, and Graph.* Elsevier.

Manoochehri, M. (2013). *Data Just Right: Introduction to Large-Scale Data and Analytics.* Pearson Education.

Martens, B. and Teuteberg, F. (2011). *Risk and Compliance Management for Cloud Computing Services: Designing a Reference Model.* In: *Americas' Conference on Information Systems (AMCIS).*

Mel, Peter and Gronce, Timothy (2011):, *The NIST Definitions of Cloud Computing,* National Institute of Standards and Technology (NIST), SP 800-145. http://CSRC.NIST.GOV/Publications/nistpubs/800-145/SP800-145.pdf

Mithas, S., Lee, M. R., Earley, S., Murugesan, S. and Djavanshir, R. (2013). *Leveraging Big Data and Business Analytics.* In: *IT Professional, 15*(6), pp. 18-20.

Mohanty, S., Jagadeesh, M. and Srivatsa, H. (2013). *Application Architectures for Big Data and Analytics.* In: *Big Data Imperatives,* pp. 107-154. Apress.

National Institute of Standards and Technology (2011). *The NIST Definitions of Cloud Computing,* Special Publication Number 800-145, US Department of Commerce, Sept. 2011.

Neely, Matthew (2014). *Securing an Evolving Cloud Environment,* In: *ISACA Journal,* Volume 3, 2014.

Pearson, S. and Benameur, A. (2010, November). *Privacy, Security and Trust Issues Arising from Cloud Computing.* In: *Second International Conference on Cloud Computing Technology and Science (CloudCom),* 2010, pp. 693-702, IEEE.

Prufer, J. (2013). *How to Govern the Cloud? Characterizing the Optimal Enforcement Institution that Supports Accountability in Cloud Computing.* TILEC Discussion Paper No. 2013-022. Available at SSRN: http://ssrn.com/abstract=2365713 or http://dx.doi.org/10.2139/ssrn.2365713

Qian, R. and Palvia, P. (2013). *Towards An Understanding of Cloud Computing's Impact on Organizational IT Strategy.* In: *Journal of Information Technology Case & Application Research, 15*(4).

Rahman, A. A., Doina, P. P. and Eugen, P. (2013). *A Survey in Information Systems: Integral Part and a Strategic Partner for Good Corporate Governance.* Ovidius University Annals, Series on Economic Sciences, 13(1).

Riffat, Muzamiz (2014). *Big Data – Not a Panacea,* In: *ISACA Journal,* Volume 3, 2014.

Rio-Belver, R., Cilleruelo, E., Garechana, G., Gavilanes, J. and Zabalza, J. (2012). *New Management Models based in Cloud-Computing.* International Scientific Conference "Business and Management 2012".

Rosenberg, Jothy and Mateus, Arthur (2010). *The Cloud At Your Service,* Manning Publications.

Russom, Philip (May 6, 2010). *Introduction to Unified Data Management,* http://tdwi.org/articles/2010/05/06/ introduction-to-unified-data-management.aspx

Sabahi, F. (2011, May). Cloud Computing Security Threats and Responses. In: *3rd International Conference on Communication Software and Networks (ICCSN),* 2011, pp. 245-249. IEEE.

Seiner, Robert (2004). *Simplified Approach to Stewartship,* In: *The Data Administrator Newsletters,* http://www.tdan.com/view-articles/5220/july1,2004

Singh, A. (2014). *Big Data in Cloud Computing Environments.* In: *The International Journal of Big Data, 1*(2).

So, K. (2011). *Cloud Computing Security Issues and Challenges.* In: *International Journal of Computer Networks.*

Sosinsky, Barrie (2011). *Cloud Computing Bible,* Wiley.

Thampi, S. M., Bhargava, B. and Atrey, P. K. (Eds.) (2013). *Managing Trust in Cyberspace.* CRC Press, Taylor & Francis Group, December 2013.

Wang, Z. (2011, October). *Security and Privacy Issues within the Cloud Computing.* In: *International Conference on Computational and Information Sciences (ICCIS), 2011,* pp. 175-178, IEEE.

Willcocks, L. P., Venters, W. and Whitley, E. A. (2013). *Moving to the Cloud Corporation: How to Face the Challenges and Harness the Potential of Cloud Computing.* Palgrave Macmillan.

Willcocks, L. and Cullen, S. (2013). *Intelligent IT Outsourcing.* Routledge.

Williams, B. (2012). *The economics of cloud computing.* Cisco Press.

Wind, S. (2011, September). *Open Source Cloud Computing Management Platforms: Introduction, Comparison, and Recommendations for Implementation.* In: *Conference on Open Systems (ICOS), 2011,* pp. 175-179. IEEE.

Wood, K. and Anderson, M. (2011). *Understanding the Complexity Surrounding Multitenancy in Cloud Computing,* In: 2011 Eighth IEEE International Conference on e-Business Engineering, Vol. 1, pp. 119-124.

Yu, H., Rann, J. and Zhan, J. (2012, May). *SUCH: A Cloud Computing Management Tool.* In: *5th International Conference on New Technologies, Mobility and Security (NTMS), 2012,* pp. 1-4. IEEE.

Zhang, Y., Zhang, J. and Chen, J. (2013, April). *Critical Success Factors in IT Service Management Implementation: People, Process, and Technology Perspectives.* In: *International Conference on Service Sciences (ICSS), 2013,* pp. 64-68, IEEE.

H. Crowd Sourcing

Afuah, A. and Tucci, C. L. (2012). *Crowdsourcing as a Solution to Distant Search.* In: *Academy of Management Review, 37*(3), pp. 355-375.

Bergvall-Kåreborn, B. and Howcroft, D. (2013, December). *The Apple Business Model: Crowdsourcing Mobile Applications.* In: *Accounting Forum,* Vol. 37, No. 4, pp. 280-289, Elsevier.

Bertot, J. C., Jaeger, P. T. and Grimes, J. M. (2010, May). *Crowd-sourcing Transparency: ICTs, Social Media, and Government Transparency Initiatives.* In: *Proceedings of the 11th Annual International Digital Government Research Conference on Public Administration Online: Challenges and Opportunities,* pp. 51-58, Digital Government Society of North America.

Boersma, D. (2012). *The Potential of Crowd Sourcing Applications in Organizational Context,* A Railroad Case Study.

Bott, M. and Young, G. (2012). *The Role of Crowdsourcing for Better Governance in International Development.* In: *Praxis: The Fletcher Journal of Human Security, 27,* pp. 47-70.

Boudreau, K. J. and Lakhani, K. R. (2013). *Using the Crowd as an Innovation Partner.* In: *Harvard Business Review, 91*(4), 60-9.

Brabham, D. C. (2013). *Crowdsourcing.* MIT Press.

Chmieliauskas, A., Chappin, E. J., Davis, C. B., Nikolic, I. and Dijkema, G. P. (2012). *New Methods for Analysis of Systems-of-Systems and Policy: The Power of Systems Theory, Crowd Sourcing and Data Management.* In: *System of Systems.* InTech, pp. 77-98.

Griffiths, M. (2011). *Crowd-sourcing Techniques: Participation, Transparency and the Factors Determining the Co-production of Policy.* In: *The Proceedings of the 11th European Conference on EGovernment: Faculty of Administration,* University of Ljubljana, Ljubljana, Slovenia, 16-17 June 2011, p. 288, Academic Conferences Limited.

Heide, J. B., Kumar, A. and Wathne, K. H. (2013). *Concurrent Sourcing, Governance Mechanisms, and Performance Outcomes in Industrial Value Chains.* In: *Strategic Management Journal.*

Jain, R. (2010). *Investigation of Governance Mechanisms for Crowd Sourcing Initiatives.* In *AMCIS,* p. 557.

Johnston, E. W. and Hansen, D. L. (2011). *Design Lessons for Smart Governance Infrastructures.* In: *American Governance, 3,* pp. 197-212.

Kern, R., Mandelstein, D. J., Milman, I. M., Oberhofer, M. A. and Pandit, S. (2013). *Information Governance and Crowd Sourcing,* U.S. Patent No. 20,130,275,803. Washington, DC: U.S. Patent and Trademark Office.

Lukyanenko, R. and Parsons, J. (2012, November). *Conceptual modeling principles for crowdsourcing.* In: *Proceedings of the 1st international workshop on Multimodal crowd sensing*, pp. 3-6, ACM.

Marjanovic, S., Fry, C. and Chataway, J. (2012). *Crowdsourcing Based Business Models: In Search of Evidence for Innovation 2.0.* In *Science and Public Policy, 39*(3), pp. 318-332.

Olson, D. L. and Rosacker, K. (2013). *Crowdsourcing and Open Source Software Participation.* In: *Service Business, 7*(4), pp. 499-511.

Shah, N., Dhanesha, A. and Seetharam, D. (2009, November). *Crowd Sourcing for e-Governance: Case study.* In: *Proceedings of the 3rd international conference on Theory and practice of electronic governance*, pp. 253-258, ACM.

I. Internet sources

Corporate Governance: http://www.corpgov.net

European Corporate Governance Institute: http://www.ecgi.org

International Association of Outsourcing Professionals "COP Master Class Workshop", On-line Course Material, Syracuse University, May, 2007.

IT Infrastructure Library: http://www.itil.co.uk

National Association of Corporate Directors (USA): http://www.nacdonline.org

Summary of Sarbanes-Oxley Act of 2002 AICPA: http://www.aicpa.org/info/sarbanes_oxley_summary.htm

Appendix D Managing Accelerating Change and Transformation Framework

---

Critical Success Enablers for Managing Change, Accelerating Change and Cultural Transformation

Change Acceleration Framework – overall prerequisites for effecting accelerating change and transformation.
- People, Organization Architecture and Leadership
- Scalable and Flexible Processes
- Enabling Technology

Most organizations grossly underestimate the amount of, and strength of, resistance to change – it comes in many forms: overt, covert, conscious and unconscious.

- **Creating a shared need** – the reason for change is instilled within the organization – widely understood, motivational, pragmatic, achievable and embraced. The felt need (and benefits of the change) for the change must exceed the (natural) resistances.
- **Shaping a vision** – the desired outcomes of the change are clear, widely understood and shared. Individuals can envision the impacts and opportunities of the change for themselves (demonstrate and sell the benefits of the vision as it evolves and materializes, linking goals, objectives and strategies to vision).
- **Mobilizing commitment** – there is a strong commitment for the change from key constituents. They are committed to make it happen, make it work and invest their attention and energy.
- **Making change last** – change is reinforced, supported and refreshed so that it endures and flourishes throughout the organization.
- **Monitoring progress and learning** - progress is real (needs a baseline). Measurement systems are established, benchmarks are set and realized. **Learnings** are shared throughout the organization. **Current and evolving best practices** (both internal and external) are used as a basis for continuous improvement.
- **Changing systems, structures, capabilities and attitudes** – develop policies, practices and processes which facilitate, support and sustain change.

People/Organization Architecture & Leadership
- Obtain **executive sponsorship** and champion(s) – need "leadership" at the highest levels
- **Get the right people** involved at the right time (phases):
  - Know the skills and competencies of your people
  - Develop and maintain a current database
  - Define roles and responsibilities
  - Co-location

- **Create peer pressure** that forces behavior change based on:
  - Value propositions
  - Speed
  - Acceptable attitude about taking prudent risks and making mistakes (learn from them)
  - Balance risk with appropriate rewards
  - Define optimum individual performance objectives and measure progress:
      Energy – how much energy you demonstrate on your job?
      Energize – how effective are you in influencing others?
      Edge – do you know and take advantage of your core competencies?
      Execution – how effectively do you implement?
      Ethics – honesty and integrity
      Excellence – "be all that you can be"
- Set **bold cycle time** reduction objectives:
  - Establish current state baseline
  - Establish desired state baseline
  - Define transitional approach
  - Time-sensitive performance metrics and vital signs
- Embrace **speed and excellence**
  - Establish "speed" incentives and rewards (balance with quality, risk and customer involvement)
  - Incentivize employees to challenge the norms **(think and do out-of-the box; dare to be different)**
  - Recognize people and teams for a superior job
  - Continuous reinforcement of a job well done
  - Make decisions locally and in real time
- Create **"speed" teams**
  - Fast teams have strong leaders (well trained)
  - Keep team focused
  - Knock obstacles out of the way or neutralize them
  - Best-in-class talent
  - Establish ultra-clear priorities, roles and responsibilities
  - Reduce/eliminate job fragmentation **(do what you do best – do not sub-optimize)**
  - Fast electronic communications (24/7) – cell, teleconferencing, videoconferencing
  - Make fast adjustments
  - Leapfrog and compete on speed
  - Act within the spirit of the process (not strictly by the process)
  - Rotate "high potential team members" (at end of project) as change agents (to other initiatives) and incentivize them
  - Leverage the same project manager across similar type projects
- Conduct **fast team meetings:**
  - Do your homework
  - Don't mind your manners
  - Stand up meetings make meetings short (no coffee or doughnuts) - Focus fast and keep focused
  - Encourage fast follow-up
  - Make fast work out of peripheral issues
  - Bump up, not down (for meeting attendees)
  - Turn off cell phones
  - No side conversation – listen when someone else is talking
- **Create flatter, smaller and nimbler organizations based on effective teams:**
  - Increase span of control – virtual organization with access to **global brains**
  - Change fast
  - Multifunctional and team-based
  - Work on **building effective teams** – Forming, Storming, Norming and Performing
  - Real-time communication amongst team members

- **70/30% Decision Process** – it is an attitude about how sure you have to be to make a decision that provides permission to speed things up by not working harder, but smarter:
  - Complete consensus not required
  - **Time box scope and deliverables**
  - Use your judgment and previous experience – **odds are you are right**

– Set time constraints on decisions
– Make decisions and then move on - no rehash
– Mistakes are acceptable – **but fix them fast**
– Frequent customer validations
– Take informed risks – **no pain, no gain**
– Encourage continuous improvement
– Learn how much you need to engage others to be 70% certain of your decision
– Learn how much information is required to be 70% certain of your decision
– Champion the 70% solution
– Less stress
– Encourage all to support and commit – it's an attitude that affects behavior change

> A good decision today is better than a perfect decision tomorrow

- Create and sustain a **continuous learning** environment:
  – Know the skills-sets of employees **(skills database)**
  – Establish minimum competencies for various positions
  – Know the gaps
  – Encourage personal development, education and training programs and subsidize
  – Invest in continuous education and training (set minimum requirements per Employee per year)
  – Design training and education offerings to fit "speed" criteria (e.g. webcasts, video conferencing, three hour focused modules, etc.)
  – Encourage regular (senior to junior) and reverse (junior to senior) mentoring programs
  – Establish **knowledge management** processes to capture and access **lessons learned**

- **Best practice benchmarking:**
  – Form peer (external) group to share best practices
  – Continuously monitor, improve and adopt
  – Ensure that the organization develops as a learning system

Scalable and Flexible Processes

- Develop **scalable, flexible and tailored business, project and innovation processes (e.g. ideation process)**
- Define **Mandatory (minimum) and Discretionary** phases, components, templates, procedures, etc.
  – Accommodate **multiple program/project/process types** (e.g. new, enhancements, operational software, infrastructure, product, etc.) & **complexity - size/value/reach/integration/funding/etc.**
  – Accommodate **outsourcing, in-sourcing and hybrid models**
  – Accommodate **fast track and full risk mitigation initiatives**
- Define business process models (how the business should operate), streamline and then automate

- Establish and enforce a well defined **governance process** with simple clear metrics, reporting guidelines and escalation processes:
  – **Clear roles and responsibilities**
  – **Issues management**
  – **Change management**
  – Employ **multiple communications techniques and frequencies** (especially prior to due dates for deliverables, milestones, meetings, etc. - 60 days, 30 days, 15 days, 7 days, 2 days, 1 day reminder notices)
  – Use **meaningful dashboards, metrics and graphs** (color coded) to convey successes and show laggards
  – **Escalate sooner** than later
- Institute a **Portfolio Investment Management process** –formalize the selection, evaluation prioritization and funding of initiatives based on business criteria:
  – Reprioritize active projects on an on-going basis
  – Do not classify each project as a priority

- **Time Box Scope:**
  - Smallest and clearest scope possible
  - Decompose large initiatives into programs and/or interrelated projects with time boxing
  - Chunk scope into time slots (no individual initiative exceeds three months, but interrelated projects can be longer as a group)
- **Time Box Deliverables:**
  - Short term incremental deliverables (80 hour rule)
  - Frequent iterations with constituencies, customer(s), team, etc.
  - Acceptance criteria
- **Outsource** (non-core initiatives or tasks, domestically or internationally) with a limited number of qualified (and certified) vendors:
  - Have a vendor selection and RFP process in place
  - Have a vendor management, escalation and metrics process in place
- Create **knowledge management cafes and repositories (capture intellectual capital for reuse)**:
  - Lessons learned, best of breed processes, training for junior and senior folks
  - Leverage process experience to create templates, etc. for reuse

Enabling Technology

- Streamline the workflow before automation
- Encourage collaborative tools (share documents, central repository for projects, groupware, etc.)
- Automate, automate, automate – web and sub-webs, tools, templates, PM software, lessons learned repository, knowledge management
- Easy to use, easy to locate
- Use expert systems and knowledge management to capture and re-use best practices and change poor practices
- Fast electronic communications (24/7)

About the Author

 Dr. Selig is the Associate Dean for Business Development and Director of the Technology Management Graduate Degree Programs in the Graduate Studies and Research Division and the School of Engineering at the University of Bridgeport. He also manages the CTech IncUBator at UB in partnership with Connecticut Innovations. He earned degrees from City, Columbia, and Pace Universities in Economics, Engineering, and Business. He has authored five books and over 70 articles, chapters in books, conference proceedings and presentations. He is a dynamic and popular in demand speaker at industry conferences and corporate events in the U.S. and abroad.

Dr. Gad J. Selig is Managing Partner and founder of GPS Group, Inc., a consulting, research and education firm that focuses on strategic marketing and growth, business and technology transformation, new product development, product management and innovation, IT strategy and governance, program/project management, strategic sourcing issues and opportunities and entrepreneurship and new corporate venturing.

Dr. Selig has thirty+ years of diversified domestic/international executive, management and consulting experience with both Fortune 500 and smaller organizations in multiple industries. His experience includes: marketing, sales, planning, operations, business development, mergers and acquisitions, general management (with full P & L responsibility), systems/network integration, strategic sourcing and outsourcing, MIS/CIO, product development, project management, business process transformation, governance and entrepreneurship.

Dr. Selig is Co-Chairman of the Board of the CTech IncUBator and has been a board member of Telco Research, BIS Group, Ltd. and AGS. He is a member of: the Academy of Management, Society for Information Management (SIM), Project Management Institute (PMI), ASEE, IAOP and ISACA. He holds a Top Secret Clearance with the Federal Government.

Dr. Gad J. Selig, PMP, COP
Associate Dean, Business Development & Director, Technology Management Degree Programs, University of Bridgeport & Founder and Managing Partner, GPS Group, Inc.
E-mail: gadselig@bridgeport.edu; gjselig@optonline.net

Made in the USA
Coppell, TX
03 March 2023

13706208R00247